Innovating Credentialing and Data Management in Higher Education With Blockchain and AI

Ahmad Tasnim Siddiqui
https://orcid.org/0000-0002-1884-9331
Horizon University College, UAE

Manas Ranjan Pradhan
Horizon University College, UAE

Valentina Emilia Balas
https://orcid.org/0000-0003-0885-1283
Aurel Vlaicu University of Arad, Romania

IGI Global
Scientific Publishing
Publishing Tomorrow's Research Today

Vice President of Editorial	Melissa Wagner
Director of Acquisitions	Mikaela Felty
Director of Book Development	Jocelynn Hessler
Production Manager	Mike Brehm
Cover Design	Jose Rosado

Published in the United States of America by
IGI Global Scientific Publishing
701 East Chocolate Avenue
Hershey, PA, 17033, USA
Tel: 717-533-8845 | Fax: 717-533-7115
Website: https://www.igi-global.com E-mail: cust@igi-global.com

Library of Congress Cataloging-in-Publication Data

Names: Siddiqui, Ahmad Tasnim, 1975- editor | Pradhan, Manas Ranjan, 1975- editor | Balas, Valentina Emilia editor
Title: Innovating credentialing and data management in higher education with blockchain and AI / [edited by] Ahmad Tasnim Siddiqui, Manas Ranjan Pradhan, Valentina Emilia Balas.
Description: Hershey, PA : IGI Global Scientific Publishing, [2026] | Includes bibliographical references and index. | Summary: "This book examines how blockchain and AI are transforming higher education credentialing and data management. It explores practical applications, ethical considerations, policy implications, and innovative frameworks, offering scholars, educators, and administrators guidance on leveraging these technologies to enhance trust, transparency, and lifelong learning in the digital era"-- Provided by publisher.
Identifiers: LCCN 2026002943 (print) | LCCN 2026002944 (ebook) | ISBN 9798337376004 hardcover | ISBN 9798337376011 paperback | ISBN 9798337376028 ebook
Subjects: LCSH: Degrees, Academic | Open learning | Professional education | Artificial intelligence--Educational applications
Classification: LCC LB2381 .I56 2026 (print) | LCC LB2381 (ebook)
LC record available at https://lccn.loc.gov/2026002943
LC ebook record available at https://lccn.loc.gov/2026002944

British Cataloguing in Publication Data
A Cataloguing in Publication record for this book is available from the British Library.

Table of Contents

Detailed Table of Contents

The compatibility of faster and faster digitalization of higher education has exerted pressure on the necessity to have a secure, interoperable, and smart academic credentialing system. Traditional centralized record management models are prone to data editing, slowness in verification and inter-institutional identification. In this chapter, the author suggests a decentralized-trust semantic intelligence hybrid model of credentialing and academic data management on a block chain-artificial intelligence (AI) system.The findings show that the combination of AI and distributed ledger technology turns the traditional credentialing of storing records to an active, learner-focused system. The chapter provides a scalable and governance-conscious paradigm in the future of digital universities, enhanced lifelong learning, micro-credential portability and transparent academic data ecosystems.

The blistering development of online and distance learning has revealed the inherent weakness of the conventional academic credentialing models, such as susceptibility to fraud, slow-paced verification, and low interoperability. In this chapter, the author introduces a third-generation credentialing system that incorporates blockchain with artificial intelligence (AI) to allow safe issue, smart checks, and robotic evaluation of academic records. . Experimental evaluation shows that the proposed framework achieves a verification accuracy of 98.6%, outperforming blockchain-only systems by more than 3–7%. Fraud detection performance attains an F1-score of 0.97, demonstrating robustness against sophisticated tampering strategies. Average verification latency is reduced to 1.9 s, enabling near real-time validation under moderate workload. Equivalency assessment results exhibit 94.2% agreement with expert judgments, indicating reliable support for cross-institutional recognition.

barriers such as cultural resistance and resource constraints, the chapter concludes with recommendations for institutional leaders to build a strategic, resilient, and trustworthy digital campus.

Maroof Ahmad, Khwaja Moinuddin Chishti Language University, Lucknow, India
Tasleem Jamal, Khwaja Moinuddin Chishti Language University, Lucknow, India
Mohd Imran, Khwaja Moinuddin Chishti Language University, Lucknow, India
Laiba Khan, Khwaja Moinuddin Chishti Language University, Lucknow, India
Sandeep Kumar Yadav, Institute of Engineering and Technology, Lucknow, India

In the digital era, the convergence of Artificial Intelligence (AI) and Blockchain Technology offers transformative possibilities across sectors—from finance and healthcare to supply chains and governance. However, behind these exciting opportunities lie profound challenges related to data privacy, security, and ethics. This chapter explores these dimensions in a "human-words" style, with special reference to blockchain in the mix, so that the reader grasps both what the issues are and how the blockchain context changes, complicates, or amplifies them. Though AI and blockchain can each bring virtues, their intersection also multiplies risks. We will walk through: (1) privacy concerns, (2) security challenges, (3) ethical frameworks (fairness, transparency, accountability), (4) how blockchain changes the picture, and (5) practical guidelines for responsible adoption.

Houda Haddad, The British University in Dubai, UAE
Tendai Charles, The British University in Dubai, UAE

This chapter examines the growing misalignment between data-rich digital learning environments and fragmented, weakly verifiable academic credentialing in higher education. Adopting a design-science perspective, it conceptualises digital identity and verifiable learning records as the trust foundation for responsible AI-enhanced credentialing on smart university campuses. The chapter proposes a five-layer reference architecture integrating learner-centred digital identity, verifiable credential fabrics, AI services for recognition of prior learning and competency inference, embedded

accreditation reform, digital infrastructure, and staff development. Ethical issues related to data privacy, algorithmic bias, and accessibility are discussed to ensure responsible and socially accountable adoption.

Laiba Khan, Khwaja Moinuddin Chishti Language University, Lucknow, India
Tasleem Jamal, Khwaja Moinuddin Chishti Language University, Lucknow, India
Saima Aleem, Khwaja Moinuddin Chishti Language University, Lucknow, India
Maroof Ahmad, Khwaja Moinuddin Chishti Language University, Lucknow, India
Amlendra Kumar, Khwaja Moinuddin Chishti Language University, Lucknow, India

Amid rapid technological advancement and constantly evolving labour markets, lifelong learning has become fundamental to both personal and professional development. Today's learners participate in a wide range of educational experiences, from formal degrees and certifications to micro-learning, online courses, and workplace training. As these learning pathways become more diverse and decentralized, managing, verifying, and integrating learning data has grown increasingly complex. Digital portfolios and lifelong learning records (LLRs) have emerged as powerful tools to address this challenge. When combined with blockchain technology, these tools can transform the credentialing process, ensure the integrity of data, and give learners full control over their educational information. This chapter explores the conceptual foundations, technological architectures, benefits, and challenges of blockchain-based lifelong learning records and digital portfolios, offering a vision of how decentralized education management systems could shape the future of learning.

Kashif Asad, Integral University, Lucknow, India
Nafees Akhter Farooqui, Integral University, Lucknow, India
Ausaf Ahmad, Integral University, Lucknow, India

Sensors, wearables, implanted devices, and cloud platforms provide real-time monitoring, diagnosis, and clinical decision-making with the Internet of Medical Things (IoMT). Growth of IoMT infrastructure affects data privacy, cybersecurity, interoperability, and trust. IoMT systems, non-standard communication protocols,

Preface

The rapid evolution of digital technologies is reshaping the landscape of higher education worldwide. Blockchain and artificial intelligence (AI) are emerging as transformative tools that can revolutionize how academic credentials are issued, verified, and managed. From enhancing trust and transparency to streamlining data governance and ensuring lifelong portability of learning records, these technologies present higher education institutions with unprecedented opportunities. However, they also pose challenges in terms of adoption, ethics, scalability, and integration with existing systems.

This edited volume aims to bring together scholars, practitioners, policymakers, and industry experts to explore innovative approaches, practical applications, theoretical frameworks, and future directions at the intersection of credentialing, data management, blockchain, and AI in higher education.

The primary objectives of this book are to:

- Provide a comprehensive resource that bridges academic research, technological innovation, and practical implementation for higher education stakeholders.
- Examine how blockchain and AI improve credentialing and data management in higher education, alongside their ethical and policy implications.
- Highlight practical use cases, pilot projects, and institutional adoption stories that demonstrate successful integration of these technologies.
- Provide a roadmap for educators, administrators, and policymakers to leverage these tools ethically and effectively.
- Stimulate innovation in teaching methods, student engagement, credentialing, and governance models.
- Contribute to shaping forward-looking educational frameworks that prepare learners for the future digital economy.

TARGET AUDIENCE

This book is intended for a broad audience, including:

- *Academicians and Researchers* in the different disciplines, and technology adopted education.
- *Higher Education Leaders and Administrators* seeking innovative solutions for credentialing, student records, and institutional data management.
- *Policy Makers and Regulators* working on frameworks for digital learning credentials, data governance, and emerging technologies.
- *Technology Developers, Start-ups, and EdTech Companies* interested in blockchain and AI applications in higher education.
- *Educators and Instructional Designers* are interested in AI-driven learning analytics, adaptive learning, and blockchain-based credentials.
- *Graduate Students and Professionals* exploring advanced studies in digital credentialing, blockchain, and AI.

CHAPTER 1: TRANSFORMING HIGHER EDUCATION VALIDATION AND DATA MANAGEMENT THROUGH BLOCKCHAIN AND ARTIFICIAL INTELLIGENCE

Udit Mamodiya

The compatibility of faster and faster digitalization of higher education has exerted pressure on the necessity to have a secure, interoperable, and smart academic credentialing system. Traditional centralized record management models are prone to data editing, slowness in verification and inter-institutional identification. In this chapter, the author suggests a decentralized-trust semantic intelligence hybrid model of credentialing and academic data management on a block chain-artificial intelligence (AI) system.The findings show that the combination of AI and distributed ledger technology turns the traditional credentialing of storing records to an active, learner-focused system. The chapter provides a scalable and governance-conscious paradigm in the future of digital universities, enhanced lifelong learning, micro-credential portability and transparent academic data ecosystems.

CHAPTER 2: NEXT-GENERATION CREDENTIALING IN HIGHER EDUCATION POWERED BY BLOCKCHAIN AND ARTIFICIAL INTELLIGENCE

Udit Mamodiya

The blistering development of online and distance learning has revealed the inherent weakness of the conventional academic credentialing models, such as susceptibility to fraud, slow-paced verification, and low interoperability. In this chapter, the author introduces a third-generation credentialing system that incorporates blockchain with artificial intelligence (AI) to allow safe issue, smart checks, and robotic evaluation of academic records. . Experimental evaluation shows that the proposed framework achieves a verification accuracy of 98.6%, outperforming blockchain-only systems by more than 3–7%. Fraud detection performance attains an F1-score of 0.97, demonstrating robustness against sophisticated tampering strategies. Average verification latency is reduced to 1.9 s, enabling near real-time validation under moderate workload. Equivalency assessment results exhibit 94.2% agreement with expert judgments, indicating reliable support for cross-institutional recognition.

CHAPTER 3: REVOLUTIONIZING DIGITAL CREDENTIAL MANAGEMENT IN HIGHER EDUCATION: EMERGING INNOVATIONS, KEY CHALLENGES, AND PATHWAYS FORWARD

Gul Shaira Banu Jahangeer, Bhavesh Tupe, Harish Nair

Blockchain technology and alternative digital credentials (ADCs) are the new frontiers of causing a paradigm shift in the management of higher education credentials. This chapter talks about the use of blockchain in safe and decentralized verification to increase the resistance to fraud and administrative effectiveness. It discusses the models of Self-Sovereign Identity (SSI), where the power is shifted to students on the qualifications. In addition, the emergence of verifiable, skills-based digital badges to supplement traditional degrees and to be in line with the demands of the workforce is discussed. Nevertheless, a number of challenges persist such as scale, compatibility with infrastructures as well as universal interoperability standards. The results show that to develop strong and student-centered systems, technology vendors, schools, and regulators need to work closely together. At the end of the paper, the practical recommendations and a strategy map of maneuvering in this changing scenery is given.

CHAPTER 4: DIGITAL TRUST, DATA MANAGEMENT, AND SECURITY FRAMEWORKS FOR THE HIGHER EDUCATION ECOSYSTEM

Reyaz Ahmad, Abdul Mohammed, Nehal Ansari, Md Ahmad

This chapter presents a comprehensive research framework addressing digital trust and security within the higher education ecosystem. As institutions rely on digital infrastructure, they face sophisticated cybersecurity threats endangering data and stakeholder confidence. Through a PRISMA-guided systematic literature review, this research synthesizes academic and industry insights to construct a holistic view of the landscape. It defines digital trust through the core principles of ability, integrity, and benevolence, mapping these to operational TRUST standards. The paper examines identity management complexities and solutions like Identity Governance and Administration (IGA), alongside an analysis of frameworks including NIST CSF and ISO/IEC 27001. Furthermore, it explores the role of AI and Blockchain as both sources of new challenges and providers of security solutions. Identifying barriers such as cultural resistance and resource constraints, the chapter concludes with recommendations for institutional leaders to build a strategic, resilient, and trustworthy digital campus.

CHAPTER 5: DATA PRIVACY, SECURITY, AND ETHICAL CONSIDERATIONS IN AI AND BLOCKCHAIN ADOPTION

Maroof Ahmad, Tasleem Jamal, Mohd Imran, Laiba Khan, Sandeep Yadav

In the digital era, the convergence of Artificial Intelligence (AI) and Blockchain Technology offers transformative possibilities across sectors—from finance and healthcare to supply chains and governance. However, behind these exciting opportunities lie profound challenges related to data privacy, security, and ethics. This chapter explores these dimensions in a "human-words" style, with special reference to blockchain in the mix, so that the reader grasps both what the issues are and how the blockchain context changes, complicates, or amplifies them. Though AI and blockchain can each bring virtues, their intersection also multiplies risks. We will walk through: (1) privacy concerns, (2) security challenges, (3) ethical frameworks (fairness, transparency, accountability), (4) how blockchain changes the picture, and (5) practical guidelines for responsible adoption.

CHAPTER 6: DIGITAL IDENTITY AND VERIFIABLE LEARNING: AI-ENHANCED, BLOCKCHAIN-SECURED CREDENTIALING

Houda Haddad, Tendai Charles

This chapter examines the growing misalignment between data-rich digital learning environments and fragmented, weakly verifiable academic credentialing in higher education. Adopting a design-science perspective, it conceptualises digital identity and verifiable learning records as the trust foundation for responsible AI-enhanced credentialing on smart university campuses. The chapter proposes a five-layer reference architecture integrating learner-centred digital identity, verifiable credential fabrics, AI services for recognition of prior learning and competency inference, embedded governance mechanisms, and event-driven integration with legacy campus systems. Rather than presenting a technical blueprint, the chapter offers a governance-aware conceptual framework intended to support portability, transparency and accountability in credentialing practices. It argues that verifiability, learner agency and bounded AI autonomy must precede large-scale automation if AI is to be used responsibly in academic recognition and decision-making.

CHAPTER 7: AI-DRIVEN PREDICTIVE ANALYTICS FOR ENHANCING STUDENT SUCCESS AND RETENTION

Arun Kumar Garov

The increasing diversity of learners, rising academic pressure, and growing dropout rates have made student success and retention critical concerns for higher education institutions worldwide. Traditional, reactive approaches to student support are often insufficient to address these challenges in a timely and effective manner. In this context, Artificial Intelligence (AI)-driven predictive analytics has emerged as a powerful solution for enabling data-informed, proactive decision-making in higher education. By analyzing large volumes of academic, behavioral, and engagement-related data, AI-based predictive models can identify students at risk of poor performance or attrition at an early stage.This chapter examines the role of AI-driven predictive analytics in enhancing student success and retention. It explores key AI techniques, data sources, and predictive models used to forecast academic outcomes and student persistence.

CHAPTER 8: AI-POWERED PREDICTIVE ANALYTICS IN STUDENT SUCCESS AND RETENTION

Anita Shukla, Ritam Dutta, Shanky Chauhan, Priyanka Verma, Suneel Kumar, Nikhil Kumar Goyal

AI-powered predictive analytics is transforming the landscape of student success and retention by enabling institutions to identify academic risks, personalize learning pathways, and deliver timely interventions. Through the integration of machine learning models, behavioral insights, and real-time data analysis, educational institutions can move from reactive support strategies to proactive, evidence-based decision-making. This chapter examines how predictive analytics enhances early-warning systems, strengthens academic advising, and improves overall student engagement. It also highlights the technological foundations, institutional challenges, and ethical considerations associated with implementing AI-driven systems in higher education. By exploring practical frameworks and future possibilities, the chapter demonstrates how predictive analytics can reshape student success ecosystems and contribute to more inclusive, responsive, and effective learning environments.

CHAPTER 9: FEDERATED AI FOR PRIVACY-PRESERVING STUDENT ANALYTICS IN BLOCKCHAIN-BASED HIGHER EDUCATION SYSTEMS

Udit Mamodiya, Rupa Shah, Indra Kishor

The contemporary intelligent control systems are requiring flexibility which cannot be maintained by the rigidity of the model-based controllers. Deep reinforcement learning can be flexible, and uncontrolled exploration is likely to affect stability and safety negatively. This paper is concerned with that tension, how to get learning-based controllers reliable enough to work in the real world. The current methods generally make control and learning distinct layers, thus being both sluggish to converge and erratic in behavior in the dynamic setups. These approaches do not have the ability to correct themselves in case the physical parameters are drifting or unmodelled disturbances emerge. In order to address these problems, a Hybrid Deep Reinforcement Learning (HDRL) model is suggested, which consists of the neural policy optimization and adaptive control laws based on the Lyapunov stability theory. The architecture combines deep perception, actor-critic reinforcement learning as well as an online adaptive layer that makes continuous system parameter adjustments to drift or noise.

CHAPTER 10: AI-DRIVEN SOLUTIONS FOR DATA ANALYTICS AND CREDENTIAL VERIFICATION IN HIGHER EDUCATION

Zahid Thoker, Lovleen Marwaha

Rapid digitalization of higher education is transforming the way institutions handle the learning data and the validation of the academic credentials. The focus of this change is artificial intelligence (AI), which provides tools that enhance accuracy, efficiency, and security in data ecosystems. Machine learning and predictive modelling are examples of AI-based analytics, which are used to facilitate individualised learning, informed decision-making, and automated academic administration. In credentialing, AI can be used to allow quick authentication, detect fraud and increase confidence in verification processes. The combination of AI and blockchain enhances the transparency and inhibits manipulation with the help of safe digital certificates. Other ethical and policy issues covered in the chapter include privacy, bias, and governance. It uses examples around the globe to describe the current practice, developing solutions and future possibilities of scalable and sustainable AI-enabled credential system in higher education.

CHAPTER 11: QUANTUM-ENHANCED BLOCKCHAIN ARCHITECTURE FOR SECURE ACADEMIC CREDENTIAL VERIFICATION - INTEGRATING POST-QUANTUM CRYPTOGRAPHY WITH FRAUD DETECTION

Sandeep Gupta, Udit Mamodiya, Neeraj Bhardwaj

The proliferation of credential theft and the increasing number of data exchange needs between companies is driving the demand for new solutions that go beyond traditional blockchain interpretations." An innovative quantum-improved blockchain architecture has been developed in this chapter to benefit HECS by integrating PQC protocols and AI-based anomaly detection techniques. The solution to this issue by cryptocurrency is quantum computation, which would jeopardize existing cryptographic efforts for detecting forged credentials by an AI system. The framework consists of four main components: the quantum-safe credentialing system, AI-based fraud detection engine, and a broadly compatible cross-chain communication protocol for verification of credentials across chains and privacy protection services that comply with FERPA and GDPR guidelines. Based on detailed analysis and case study findings in the context of Indian higher education, we demonstrate the acceptability, usability, and scalability of this approach for global adoption.

CHAPTER 12: AI-PERSONALISED LEARNING AND MICRO-CREDENTIALS: FUTURE DIRECTIONS FOR CURRICULUM DESIGN

Siham Abukhalaf

This chapter examines how the integration of micro-credentials and artificial intelligence (AI) can reshape higher education into a more flexible, personalised, and industry-responsive learning ecosystem. Its purpose is to analyse how modular, competency-based credentials, when combined with AI-driven adaptive tools such as intelligent tutoring systems, analytics dashboards, and recommendation algorithms, can strengthen learner-centred pathways grounded in Constructivism, Connectivism, and Self-Determination Theory. The chapter outlines how micro-credentials enable targeted skill recognition and stackable qualification routes that enhance employability, while AI technologies support customised instruction and learner autonomy. It also addresses the institutional changes needed for effective implementation, including accreditation reform, digital infrastructure, and staff development. Ethical issues related to data privacy, algorithmic bias, and accessibility are discussed to ensure responsible and socially accountable adoption.

CHAPTER 13: LIFELONG LEARNING RECORDS AND DIGITAL PORTFOLIOS

Laiba Khan, Tasleem Jamal, Saima Aleem, Maroof Ahmad, Amlendra Kumar

Amid rapid technological advancement and constantly evolving labour markets, lifelong learning has become fundamental to both personal and professional development. Today's learners participate in a wide range of educational experiences, from formal degrees and certifications to micro-learning, online courses, and workplace training. As these learning pathways become more diverse and decentralized, managing, verifying, and integrating learning data has grown increasingly complex. Digital portfolios and lifelong learning records (LLRs) have emerged as powerful tools to address this challenge. When combined with blockchain technology, these tools can transform the credentialing process, ensure the integrity of data, and give learners full control over their educational information. This chapter explores the conceptual foundations, technological architectures, benefits, and challenges of blockchain-based lifelong learning records and digital portfolios, offering a vision of how decentralized education management systems could shape the future of learning.

CHAPTER 14: BLOCKCHAIN-ENABLED SECURITY AND TRUST MODELS FOR THE INTERNET OF MEDICAL THINGS (IOMT) IN MODERN HEALTHCARE

Kashif Asad, Nafees Farooqui, Ausaf Ahmad

Sensors, wearables, implanted devices, and cloud platforms provide real-time monitoring, diagnosis, and clinical decision-making with the Internet of Medical Things (IoMT). Growth of IoMT infrastructure affects data privacy, cybersecurity, interoperability, and trust. IoMT systems, non-standard communication protocols, device capabilities, and medical network incursions are covered. We suggest data fusion, encryption, and decentralised trust enforcers for patient data. A decentralised, unchangeable, and secure blockchain. Blockchain-based solutions protect IoMT data flow, eliminate single-point-of-failure, and secure distributed medical device trust evaluation. Distributed ledger data integrity, authentication, and trust score storage improve active blockchain trust models. AI, data fusion, cloud/fog computing, smart hospitals, and blockchain secure IoMT. This chapter covers IoMT system design, cybersecurity, MULC frameworks, and blockchain-based health innovations. We discuss open research, regulation, and resilient, scalable, and dependable IoMT ecosystems.

CONTRIBUTION OF THIS BOOK

This book volume makes a significant contribution to the field by presenting an integrated and forward-looking vision of how Artificial Intelligence and blockchain can transform higher education credentialing, data governance, student success, and lifelong learning ecosystems. Across conceptual frameworks, empirical studies, architectural models, and governance strategies, the chapters collectively shift credentialing from static, institution-centered record management to secure, learner-centered, interoperable trust infrastructures. By combining AI-driven analytics, predictive models, digital identity frameworks, federated learning, and quantum-resilient blockchain architectures with strong ethical, privacy, and policy considerations, the book bridges research, practice, and regulation. It not only demonstrates how intelligent and secure systems can be implemented at scale but also provides a governance-aware roadmap for responsible adoption. Ultimately, the volume advances scholarship and institutional practice by laying the foundation for resilient, transparent, and future-ready digital education ecosystems aligned with the demands of the global knowledge economy.

Chapter 1
Transforming Higher Education Validation and Data Management Through Blockchain and Artificial Intelligence

Udit Mamodiya
http://orcid.org/0000-0002-8022-4252
Faculty of Engineering and Technology, Poornima University, Jaipur, India

ABSTRACT

The compatibility of faster and faster digitalization of higher education has exerted pressure on the necessity to have a secure, interoperable, and smart academic credentialing system. Traditional centralized record management models are prone to data editing, slowness in verification and inter-institutional identification. In this chapter, the author suggests a decentralized-trust semantic intelligence hybrid model of credentialing and academic data management on a block chain-artificial intelligence (AI) system. The findings show that the combination of AI and distributed ledger technology turns the traditional credentialing of storing records to an active, learner-focused system. The chapter provides a scalable and governance-conscious paradigm in the future of digital universities, enhanced lifelong learning, micro-credential portability and transparent academic data ecosystems.

DOI: 10.4018/979-8-3373-7600-4.ch001

1. INTRODUCTION

1.1 Background and Context

The global higher education has been experiencing a radical digital redefinition through the growing dependence on information systems in teaching, learning, and management of higher institutions. Higher education institutions are beginning to process large amounts of sensitive scholarly information, such as student records, assessment results, and certificates, micro-credentials, and lifelong learning records. Those data assets can be important not only to the activities of the institutions but also to personal mobility, employability and the acknowledgement of qualifications on an international level. The issues pertaining to data integrity, authenticity, privacy, and long-term accessibility are now the focus of academic governance as the digital platforms supplant the paper-based processes (Suktam et al., 2024).

Such conventional credentialing systems are based on central databases and institutional agents. Although these systems have the advantage of providing convenience during administration, they can be easily compromised, hacked, faked documents, and single point of failure. The increasing cases of academic frauds such as counterfeit certificates and falsified transcripts have further illustrated the weaknesses of the traditional record keeping methods (Raghavendra et al., 2024). Simultaneously, processes of globalization and cross-border education require more rapid and effective checking of academic performance, which puts more pressure on the current institutional frameworks (Zuo, 2022).

Simultaneously with these obstacles, there has been the rise of two transformative enablers of trust, automation and intelligent decision-making, namely blockchain and artificial intelligence (AI). Blockchain presents decentralized and immutable records, and AI provides opportunities of sophisticated analysis and prediction. Their intersect offers a new chance to redesign the ways of producing, storing, validating, and using academic credentials (Elkhodr et al., 2024; de Bem Machado et al., 2024). This chapter discusses the opportunities of credentialing and academic data management in the ecosystem of higher education to be innovative and integrated with blockchain and AI.

1.2 Limitations of Conventional Credentialing Systems

Traditional academic record systems are mostly centralized and institutional in nature. Every university has got its own student information system, which produces certificates and transcripts on request. Checking can in most cases be conducted manually, use third-party authentication or inter-institutional correspondence, resulting in delays and administrative overhead (Kumar, 2025). In addition, after they are issued, certificates are generally fixed documents, which are not easily incorporated into modular learning pathways, stackable micro-credentials or records of continuous professional development.

These limitations are also aggravated by security vulnerabilities. A centralized repository is prone to cyberattacks, insider attacks, and unintentional loss of data. Several studies have clarified that academic databases are especially being targeted, because of the long-term worth of educational qualification and personal identity information (H C, 2025). Besides that, variation in data standards among institutions impedes interoperability and makes it more difficult to recognize qualifications among jurisdictions (Zuo, 2022).

Governance wise, accountability is restricted by the lack of accountability in terms of transparency in audit trails. There is a lack of transparency on the way credentials are created and altered by the stakeholders, such as employers, accreditation agencies, and the learners themselves. These technical vulnerabilities destroy the credibility of digital academic records and limit the expansion of credentialing systems in new educational systems like online degrees, competency-based education, and micro-credential systems (McGreal, 2024; Suktam et al., 2024).

1.3 Blockchain as an Enabler of Trusted Academic Records

Blockchain technology provides an entirely new form of management of academic data through trust distribution over a decentralized network. Every transaction of a credential may be stored as an unchangeable block, which is cryptographically bound to the past securing against tampering (Revathi et al., 2024). This architecture offers natural auditability and verifiability to allow a stakeholder the right to certify the authenticity of certificates issued without the use of a central authority.

Recent research has shown that blockchain based academic banks of credit and learner centric repositories of credentials are feasible. The Academic Bank of credit system proposed by Mali et al. (2023) is blockchain-based and offers students to gain credits across the institutions without compromising the integrity and traceability of the collected data. In the same manner, H C (2025) pointed out the efficiency of decentralized certificate issuance models in the time of lessening verification time and restricting the risk of fraud.

Outside security, blockchain promotes learner sovereignty of academic data. Rather than cryptographic key custody by institutions, students are capable of exercise cryptographic control over their credentials and selectively providing them to employers or in other universities. This conforms to the new concepts of self-sovereign identity and a lifelong learning portability (Zuo, 2022; McGreal, 2024). Moreover, academic policies (like the transfer of credits or graduation eligibility) can be automatically enforced with the help of smart contracts, which makes them less complex to implement (Raghavendra et al., 2024).

Although these benefits exist, blockchain cannot solve high-level problems like accredential semantic interpretation, academic data anomaly detection, and personalized learning process adaptation. Such loopholes drive the integration of AI into blockchain-related educational systems (Elkhodr et al., 2024).

1.4 Role of Artificial Intelligence in Academic Data Intelligence

Artificial intelligence will add a new dimension of smartness to academic data ecosystems by allowing automated analysis, classification and decision support. A machine learning model can be applied to large-scale student data to extract trends in student advancement, inconsistencies in the records, and be utilized to make individualized studies (de Bem Machado et al., 2024).

Recent uses are natural language processing (NLP) to analyze certificate equivalency and automated interpretation of transcripts. A Lexicon-Enhanced Convolutional BERT model with blockchain, as introduced by Krishnan et al. (2025), to produce secure equivalency certificates can also show how AI can be used to support semantic validation of academic credentials. Likewise, AI-based verification engines can mark suspicious records that are not in line with the anticipated academic paths, enhancing reservation systems (Kumar, 2025).

Some of the emerging trends in education, including micro-credentials and modular certification, are also heavily dependent on AI. The systems need smart integration of the learning outcomes of heterogeneous sources, such as MOOCs, vocational programs, and professional certifications. As stressed by McGreal (2024), the AI-enhanced analytics would be necessary to match such fragmented credentials with the accepted qualification schemes.

Nevertheless, AI-based systems are associated with explainability, data biasing, and ethical responsibility issues. Unclear data governance systems will worsen inequities or endanger the privacy of learners because algorithmic decisions are not easy to control. AI can be supplemented by blockchain to offer a validated data provenance and trainable auditing datasets, which help to reduce some of these risks (Elkhodr et al., 2024; Sitanggang et al., 2025).

1.5 Synergistic Integration of Blockchain and AI

The meeting of blockchain and AI forms a hybrid paradigm, which is the integration of data immutability and adaptive intelligence. Blockchain makes the academic records tamper-resistant and traceable and AI can extract meaning, identify anomalies, and aid the process of making automatic decisions. This synergy has been outlined to be one of the main contributors to next-generation educational infrastructures (de Bem Machado et al., 2024; Elkhodr et al., 2024).

In a systematic review of the Australian higher education, Elkhodr et al. (2024) established that integrated blockchain and AI systems can increase the transparency of credentials and predictive analytics to retain and advance students. Equally, Sitanggang et al. (2025) showed the ability of blockchain in combination with ontologies to maintain the integrity of data and facilitate semantic interoperability of educational systems.

Hybrid architecture also facilitates smart contracts, which are intelligent and adapt dynamically to the results of learning. As an illustration, the AI-based evaluation may enable the issue of credentials based on blockchain in case of competency-related requirements. This minimizes the number of human interactions and provides real-time updates to records of learners (Revathi et al., 2024; Mali et al., 2023). In addition, AI models that are distributed are also able to operate on proven datasets stored on blockchain networks, which enhances trust in the analysis outputs (Krishnan et al., 2025).

Overall, in education, this convergence is associated with immersive and adaptive learning practices. Research on AI-enhanced VR and AR systems demonstrates how an intelligent system can customize educational experiences with the help of credentialing backends that are regarded as reliable (Kishor et al., 2025a; Kishor et al., 2025b). Such developments indicate the possibility of blockchain-AI systems as the core infrastructure of smart universities.

1.6 Current Research Landscape and Gaps

Although literature claims significant advances in blockchain credentialing and artificial intelligence-based academic analytics, there are still several limitations. Most suggested systems are theoretical or have only been tested on a pilot basis and have not been evaluated on a large-scale institutional basis (Kumar, 2025; Revathi et al., 2024). The problem of interoperability between universities and accreditation organizations is also not yet solved, especially when various blockchain platforms and data standards are used (Zuo, 2022).

The other gap is in the unintegrated consideration of blockchain and AI. Available literature tends to discuss the technologies separately, but not as an integrated socio-technical system (de Bem Machado et al., 2024). Even though a few frameworks offer a combined architecture, none of them propose a comprehensive model that covers the aspects of governance, ethics, data ownership, and long-term sustainability (Elkhodr et al., 2024; Sitanggang et al., 2025).

Also, most credentialing solutions emphasize formal degrees qualification, and there is very little support of micro-credentials, experiential learning, and cross-sector skill recognition (McGreal, 2024; Mali et al., 2023). This limits their applicability to lifelong learning environments. Also, the problem of algorithmic transparency and explainability is little studied, especially in AI-based equivalency and verification systems (Krishnan et al., 2025).

These gaps create the urgency to consider holistic models that incorporate blockchain and AI in the higher education sector with a focus on governance, scalability, and ethical issues.

1.7 Objectives and Contributions to This Chapter

The purpose of this chapter is to promote the knowledge of how blockchain and AI can collaboratively change credentialing and academic data management in higher education. It combines the findings of recent empirical and theoretical research to suggest a combined view on trusted, intelligent educational infrastructures.

Three contributions of this chapter can be considered the dominant. First, it gives the systematic review of the developed blockchain-based credentialing models and AI-based authentication schemes and their advantages and constraints (Mali et al., 2023; Kumar, 2025; Krishnan et al., 2025). Second, it theorizes a single system that uses blockchain to store data securely and AI to implement semantically validated and automated processes based on recent developments in the field of educational technologies and distributed systems (Elkhodr et al., 2024; Sitanggang et al., 2025). Third, it addresses governance and policy implications, which suggest learner sovereignty, interoperability and ethical implementation of AI in educational organizations (Zuo, 2022; Raghavendra et al., 2024).

The chapter aims to tell researchers, policymakers and practitioners the contents to include in broader trends of digital transformation and lifelong learning by the design principles they must possess to create resistant and future-oriented credentialing ecosystems.

1.8 Organization of the Chapter

The rest of the chapter is structured the following way. Section 2 analyses the literature that is currently available regarding blockchain-based academic credentialing and AI-controlled educational data management. Section 3 comprises a combined theoretical model of blockchain-based AI-supported credentialing. Subsection 4 presents the considerations of implementation, such as interoperability, security and governance. Section 5 is ethical and policy implications, and Section 6 is future research directions and concluding the chapter.

2. LITERATURE REVIEW

2.1 Blockchain for Academic Credentialing and Record Management

The use of blockchain technology in academic credentialing has been gaining balanced traction throughout the last decade as there is a need to protect academic records against fraud and manipulation. Initial research was on substituting centralized certificate repositories with distributed ledgers with the ability to maintain immutability and traceability. One of the first credentialing solutions developed by Pandya (2022) was blockchain-based with the emphasis on cryptographic hashing and timestamping to exclude the illegal alteration of academic records. As this work showed, blockchain may form a chain of verifiable trust on academic credentials, but it was mainly a conceptual one in practice.

Later activities shifted to more implementations. Deepak (2024) reviewed the uptake of blockchain in the education system and claimed that the concept of decentralization may substantially increase the perceived levels of transparency and accountability in credentialing. The research claimed to have less processing time with the verification requests and enhanced trust between the stakeholders, such as the students, institutions and the employers. Nevertheless, the paper also recognized that blockchain-based solutions are characterized by the problems of the latency of transactions and institutional preparedness.

Marouan et al. (2024) went further to place blockchain credentialing in the wider context of lifelong learning. Kaneriya and Patel (2023) also made their contribution by creating a privacy-saving blockchain verification model. Their system presented biased disclosure systems that enable students to present only the required segments of their credentials without revealing complete academic records. This strategy was dealing with a major weakness of previous blockchain solutions which tended to view credentials as either entirely public or entirely private entities. The experiment provides indications that blockchain could strike the balance between transparency and confidentiality with appropriate cryptographic restrictions.

2.2 Institutional Adoption and Governance Perspectives

Although it has been established that it is technically feasible, institutional aspect of blockchain adoption is a thorny problem. The systematic literature review by Permana and Martatika (2024) was conducted among institutions of higher education and discovered that governance, compliance with regulations, and interoperability were leading obstacles to the implementation.

Vashishth et al. (2024) suggested a new institutional framework of the blockchain implementation in education, focusing on the gradual implementation instead of the immediate replacement of the system. Their model implied the implementation of blockchain modules in the already existing student information systems to guarantee the continuity of the operations.

Anjani and Mutiara (2024) have investigated the concept of blockchain application within the higher education sector in Southeast Asia, and transparency is one of the key advantages. They found that blockchain-based credentialing minimized conflicts based on the authenticity of transcripts and enhanced confidence in academic qualifications by people.

Koo et al. (2025) provided a bibliometric review to examine the role of blockchain in higher education administration in terms of management perspective. Their review demonstrated that there was an increasing interest in automating governance, in the areas of admissions, accreditation and compliance auditing. This tendency implies that the blockchain is increasingly being considered not only as a security instrument but as an administrative innovation platform that can change the institutional workflow.

2.3 Blockchain-Based Credential Verification Networks

Another body of literature has explored blockchain as a confirmation system, not especially a storage system. Sy et al. (2024) suggested EduCredPH, which is a permissioned blockchain network of educational credentials verification. With their system, the certified institutions were able to issue and verify certificates in a regulated consortium setup. The findings showed that it was faster to verify than the conventional email or document-based approaches. Notably, the fact that a permissioned blockchain was used was a way of creating a solution to the issue of open access to ledgers whilst preserving decentralization among the accredited parties.

The Pondkule and Kothari (2025) developed a blockchain-based document management system, which is specific to higher education organizations. They combined smart contracts in their approach, which managed to automate the issuance and revocation of certificates. The system was found to be resistant to document forging and information loss though performance analysis revealed that the system was limited to scale as the number of transactions were large.

Vaher et al. (2025) have implemented a data-based model of securing academic records, which involves blockchain with institutional analytics. They used a pattern of credential issuance to highlight the anomaly in the pattern, which implied that blockchain can be used as a ledger and a monitoring platform. The latter dual role adds to the case that blockchain infrastructures have the potential to transform into smart administrative systems together with data analytics.

SALF, a concept proposed by Haque et al. (2025) is one of the most extensive blockchain-based academic governance models. SALF is built upon credential management and policy-enforcement by the institution, managing academic transactions through blockchain and regulatory compliance through smart contracts. The research indicated that there was better consistency in the issuance of credentials and fewer administrative errors, which proves that blockchain could enable operational and governance goals.

2.4 Integration of Machine Learning and Blockchain

The intersection of blockchain and machine learning (ML) to improve credential validation and record intelligence in academia has gained more attention in recent literature. Shaikh et al. (2022) suggested the implementation of a hybrid system that introduces an educational accreditation registration system based on Hyperledger blockchain and non-linear machine learning models.

Yahya et al. (2024) have proposed Precognito, a student record authentication system that is based on blockchain and machine learning. They used supervised learning algorithms in their model and blockchain ensured that verified records were immutable. The two-layer system minimized the false identification in the authentication process and enhanced the trust in the automated verification decision.

Echenim (2025) expanded the definition to include AI integration and blockchain integration to have a decentralized data management system. The research has underlined that machine learning models can only work well with reliable sources of data and blockchain can offer these guarantees by offering verifiable data provenance. This is the conceptual connection in between trusted data storage and intelligent analytics that reinforces the argument on hybrid architecture in education systems.

It was also implied in Kaneriya and Patel (2023) that put lightweight verification logic into blockchain smart contracts to form semi-intelligent verification pipelines. Such systems are not wholly AI-based but create a path to greater involvement of machine learning with decentralized credentialing.

2.5 Security, Privacy, and Ethical Considerations

A key reason why blockchain could be important in credential management is security. Both Pandya (2022) and Deepak (2024) highlighted the benefits of blockchain systems in terms of resistance to forgery and unauthorized modification of data as the central benefits. Their research showed that distributed ledgers remove points of failure and makes them less susceptible to insider attacks and external attacks.

Privacy is, however, a more subtle problem. Blockchain is just as transparent; however, without proper design, it may reveal sensitive personal information. Kaneriya and Patel (2023) solved this problem by introducing privacy-saving verification schemes, implying that selective disclosure schemes can safeguard the identity of learners without verifying them. Likewise, Sy et al. (2024) employed the concept of a permissioned network to limit the access to credential data and find the balance between decentralization and controlled participation.

When machine learning is implemented into credentialing processes, ethical issues are presented. Yahya et al. (2024) warned that automated classification is to be audited in order to avoid bias and to be fair. This sentiment was reiterated by Echenim (2025) that insisted that AI-based credential management should be transparent and explainable to ensure the stakeholder trust. These results point to the fact that technical resilience is not enough, and governance and ethical control are equally required.

2.6 Blockchain for Lifelong Learning and Micro-Credentials

The move towards lifelong learning has changed the purposes of credentialing systems. Marouan et al. (2024) presented blockchain as a facilitator of lifelong learning, and a learner has permanent, mobile academic profiles. Their research showed that blockchain would be capable of storing both formal qualifications and informal ones, developing cohesive learning portfolios.

Haque et al. (2025) went on to build on this concept and connect credential management to institutional governance. SALF assists in modular learning records which can be combined into formal qualifications by smart contract logic. This style fits the competency-based models of education, where competencies are more significant than the institutional lines.

Anjani and Mutiara (2024) emphasized the identical tendencies of the evolution of educational systems, indicating that the blockchain-based credentialing can help to empower learners by providing them with a chance to maintain direct control over their academic data. These learner-focused systems would minimize reliance on institutional intermediaries and make it easier to move between the educational and job sectors.

2.7 Comparative Insights and Emerging Trends

There are some patterns that can be observed throughout the literature reviewed. To start with, most of the research findings support the idea that blockchain enhances trust, traceability, and security in the academic record management (Pandya, 2022; Deepak, 2024; Marouan et al., 2024). Second, it is increasingly realized that unlinked blockchain systems cannot support complex educational settings, and these systems are being integrated with machine learning and data analytics (Shaikh et al., 2022; Yahya et al., 2024; Echenim, 2025).

Third, institutional readiness and governance are still a major limitation. Both Permana and Martatika (2024) and Koo et al. (2025) have stated that the large-scale deployment depends on legal recognition and alignment of the administration. Fourth, more and more privacy-preserving mechanisms are integrated into system designs, which indicates the increased awareness of the requirements regarding data protection (Kaneriya and Patel, 2023; Sy et al., 2024).

Lastly, the literature reveals the transition of the focus on the verification of narrow credentialing to larger educational data management platforms. The blockchain systems are currently being framed as core infrastructures that can be used to support accreditation, progression tracking, and lifelong learning ecosystems (Haque et al., 2025; Marouan et al., 2024; Vaher et al., 2025).

2.8 Research Gaps

Although the situation has improved greatly, there still exist some significant gaps. The majority of the suggested systems are still confined to prototypes or simulation settings, and few of them longitudinally assess performance and scalability (Permana & Martatika, 2024; Pondkule & Kothari, 2025). Cross-border education is one area where heterogeneous institutional systems have not been well investigated to ensure interoperability.

In addition, although the concept of AI integration has been proven, less empirical research is done in explainability and fairness of automated credential decisions (Yahya et al., 2024; Echenim, 2025). Models of governance that incorporate technical, legal, and ethical aspects are also underdeveloped (Haque et al., 2025; Koo et al., 2025).

The existence of these gaps implies the necessity of the holistic frameworks that would integrate the trust assurances of blockchain with the analytical capabilities of AI and solve institutional, ethical, and scalability issues.

3. METHODOLOGY

3.1 Research Design and Methodological Framework

This chapter is based on a system-oriented and model-driven research paradigm that targets the construction, validation, and conceptual review of a hybrid Blockchain-Artificial Intelligence (AI) model of academic credentialing and data management. The study is implemented in a layered methodology, which combines architectural modeling, algorithmically formulation as well as system-level validation to guarantee conceptual soundness and practical viability. The design is based on the previous research that highlights the need to integrate distributed ledger technologies with smart data analytics to resolve the trust and scalability issues in higher education systems (Elkhodr et al., 2024; de Bem Machado et al., 2024; Echenim, 2025).

The suggested methodology is carried out in four consecutive steps system requirement elicitation, architectural modeling, algorithmic formulation, and analytical validation. The initial phase determines the functional and non-functional requirements of academic credentialing systems such as immutability, verifiability, preservation of privacy, and interoperability, which have been highlighted in recent blockchain-based education research (Pandya, 2022; Deepak, 2024; Permana and Martatika, 2024). The second phase determines a multi-layered system design with the integration of blockchain, AI services, and institutional information systems. The third phase develops cryptography, transactional and learning-based models that regulate the issuance of credentials, credit checks and analytical elements. The last phase is testing the conceptual performance of the framework in terms of structural measures and analytical arguments based on the available empirical evidence (Haque et al., 2025; Shaikh et al., 2022; Yahya et al., 2024).

This systematic approach will keep the research goals and system design options in check and prevent the mismatch with the up-to-date technological and institutional reality of higher education ecosystems (Suktam et al., 2024; Koo et al., 2025).

3.2 System Architecture Overview

The suggested system architecture consists of four interacting layers, including the data acquisition layer, the blockchain ledger layer, the AI intelligence layer, and the application and governance layer. All these layers promote secure credential generation, decentralized storage, intelligent validation and user-centric access control. The interaction of architectural flow and components is depicted in Figure 1.

Figure 1. Layered architecture of the blockchain–AI-based academic credentialing framework illustrating data acquisition, distributed ledger operations, intelligent analytics, and application-level services.

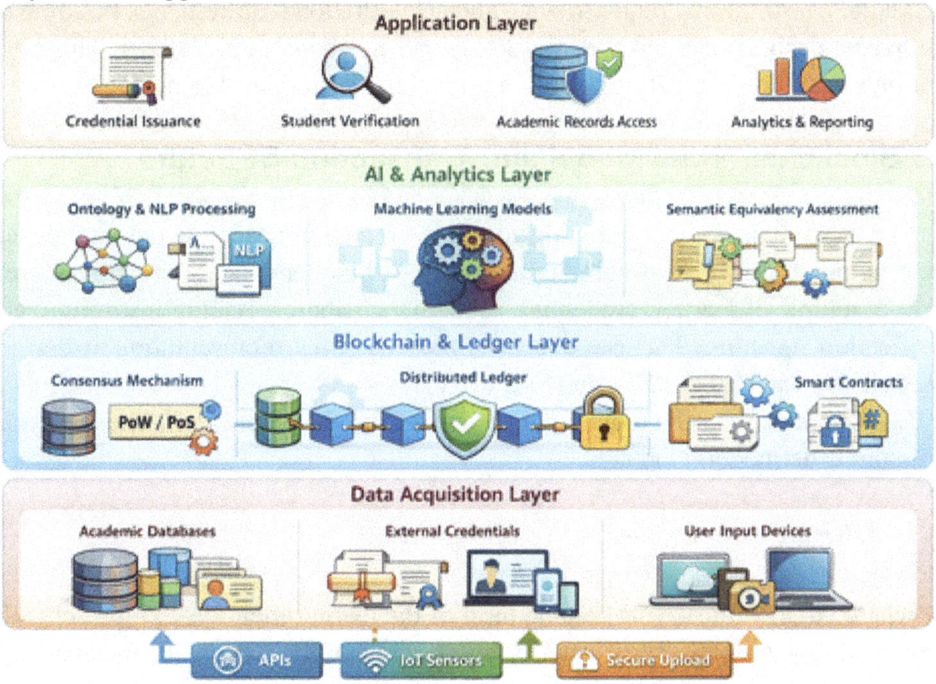

The data collection layer will also receive the academic events like course completion, examination results, and certification grants by institutional systems. These data are based on the information systems of students, learning platforms and assessment repositories and called in the blockchain-based educational management models (Vashishth et al., 2024; Pondkule and Kothari, 2025). Before the insertion of blockchain, records are syntactically and semantically normalized to match distributed storage protocols (Sitanggang et al., 2025).

The blockchain ledger layer is a permissioned distributed ledger, which is a distributed ledger where credential transactions are recorded through cryptographic hashing and digital signatures. A permissioned blockchain model is chosen to trade-off between decentralization and institutional governance, which is in line with credential verification networks like EduCredPH (Sy et al., 2024) and SALF (Haque et al., 2025). The credential transaction is summed up in each block with the hash of the learner identifier, metadata of the credential, the signature of the issuing authority, and the time.

The AI intelligence layer is a layer that works over the ledger and verifies the credential metadata, assesses the equivalency and detects anomalies. Machine translation and natural language processing systems examine the descriptions of credentials, institutional requirements, and accreditation requirements, building on the hybrid designs of Shaikh et al. (2022) and Krishnan et al. (2025). This layer facilitates adaptive validation to a higher level than rule-based logic.

3.3 Blockchain Data Model and Transaction Structure

The blockchain data model will support the model of academic credentials that are cryptographically verifiable digital assets. All credentials are organized in the form of a tuple of learner, credential, academic attributes, issuing institution, and verification signature. This is a decentralized credential representation as defined by Kaneriya and Patel (2023) and H C (2025).

Let Ci denote the i-th credential record stored on the blockchain. The credential structure is defined as (1)

$$C_i = \{H(L_i), T_i, A_i, S_i, \tau_i\} \quad \cdots \tag{1}$$

where H(Li) is the cryptographic hash of the learner identity, Ti represents the credential type (degree, certificate, or micro-credential), Ai denotes the academic attributes, Si is the issuing authority's digital signature, and τ_i is the timestamp. This formulation ensures that learner privacy is preserved while enabling verifiable provenance (Pandya, 2022; Kaneriya & Patel, 2023).

Credential transactions are added to the ledger with the help of a consensus mechanism that is appropriate to permissioned settings, including Practical Byzantine Fault Tolerance or Proof-of-Authority, which have a computationally efficient consensus mechanism and are institutionally controlled (Sy et al., 2024; Vaher et al., 2025). All the transactions are authenticated by authorized nodes representing the participating universities or accreditation bodies.

The transaction verification function $V(C_i)$ is expressed as (2)

$$V(C_i) = Verify(S_i, H(L_i), A_i) \quad \cdots \tag{2}$$

where Verify denotes a cryptographic validation function that checks the integrity and authenticity of the credential data. Only credentials satisfying V(Ci)=1 are committed to the ledger.

3.4 Smart Contract Design for Credential Issuance and Revocation

Self-sovereign Automated processes of issuing and updating and revoking credentials and governed by smart contracts. These contracts implement institutional policies, including rules on degree completion and requirements to transfer credit, so that they can be implemented in a rule-based manner without human intervention (Revathi et al., 2024; Haque et al., 2025).

The issuance contract is instigated when the specified academic conditions are fulfilled such as the completion of the necessary credits and the confirmation of assessment results. The contract logic makes sure that only those institutions are qualified to issue credentials and all credentials that are issued are permanently registered. Exceptional situations supported by revocation contracts include the detection of fraud or administrative corrections and still maintaining auditability. Let Sj represent the smart contract of issuing the credential. The fact of its execution is (3) defined

$$Sj= \{Issue(Ci), Reject, if\ Ri \geq \ \theta otherwise \cdots \qquad (3)$$

where Ri represents the aggregated academic requirement score and θ is the institutional threshold for credential eligibility. This formalization aligns with modular credit accumulation systems proposed by Mali et al. (2023) and McGreal (2024).

3.5 AI-Based Credential Validation and Equivalency Analysis

The AI intelligence layer brings in the features of semantic validation and equivalency assessment. The existing blockchain systems are capable of integrity checks, but not academic interpretation. In order to overcome this weakness, natural language processing and supervised learning models are combined to examine credential descriptors and institutional accreditation standards (Krishnan et al., 2025; Yahya et al., 2024).

Credential metadata is converted to the form of vectors represented through domain-specific embeddings and trained on academic corpora. Let Xi represent the feature vector extracted from credential Ci. A classification model f(·) determines the equivalency class (4):

$$Ei= f(Xi) \ \cdots \qquad (4)$$

where Ei denotes the predicted equivalency category. This mechanism enables automated recognition of cross-institutional credentials and supports mobility across educational systems (Marouan et al., 2024; Zuo, 2022).

The issue of anomaly detection models is further used to examine the patterns of transactions in order to detect application of irregular issuance. The associated feature enhances fraud detection and control over governance, which is in line with the data-oriented solutions suggested by Vaher et al. (2025) and Echenim (2025).

3.6 Data Integrity and Ontology Alignment

The data alignment layer is an ontology-based layer that is used to align heterogeneous academic terminologies to standard concepts to preserve semantic consistency. Ontological integration supports the interoperability of institutions that adopt a different grading system or curriculum framework (Sitanggang et al., 2025). The ontology supports the relations between courses and credits and qualifications, which allows the meaningful aggregation of learning records.

Let O represent the ontology graph and M(Ai) the mapping function from raw attributes to standardized terms (6):

$$M(A_i) = O(A_i) \cdots \quad (6)$$

This process ensures that credentials stored on the blockchain maintain semantic coherence, enhancing both machine readability and human interpretability.

3.7 Security and Privacy Preservation

Cryptography primitives, access control policies and network-level governance are used to promote security. Hashing and digital signatures maintain the integrity of the data, whereas the authorized involvement of the node can exclude unauthorized changes in the ledger (Deepak, 2024; Sy et al., 2024). The privacy of learners is ensured by keeping the identifiers and encrypted properties in the form of a hash, this allows them to disclose them selectively (Kaneriya and Patel, 2023).

Let P_k denote the disclosure policy applied to credential Ci. The visible attribute set Ai′ is defined as (7)

$$A_i' = P_{k(A_i)} \cdots \quad (7)$$

This formulation allows students to control which credential attributes are revealed to external verifiers, supporting self-sovereign data governance (Zuo, 2022; Anjani & Mutiara, 2024).

3.8 Experimental Design and Validation Strategy

The methodological validation is carried out by the means of architecture consistency analysis and scenarios evaluation. The framework is evaluated in such use cases as issuing degrees, accumulation of micro-credentials, and checking their equivalency. Analytically estimated structural metrics include transaction throughput, verification latency and model inference accuracy, based on empirical studies performed previously (Haque et al., 2025; Yahya et al., 2024; Pondkule and Kothari, 2025).

Table 1. Evaluation metrics for blockchain–AI-based credential management framework.

Metric Name	Description	Measurement Method	Relevance to System Objective
Data Integrity Rate (%)	Proportion of credential records that remain unaltered and verifiable after simulated tampering attempts	Ratio of successfully validated records to total submitted records using cryptographic hash and signature verification	Evaluates robustness of blockchain immutability and resistance to unauthorized modification
Credential Verification Latency (s)	Average time required to retrieve and validate a credential from the distributed ledger	End-to-end response time measured from query initiation to verification output	Assesses real-time usability for employers, institutions, and accreditation bodies
Equivalency Classification Accuracy (%)	Proportion of credentials correctly mapped to standardized qualification categories	Comparison between AI-predicted equivalency labels and expert-validated ground truth	Measures effectiveness of AI-based semantic interpretation and ontology alignment
Transaction Throughput (tx/s)	Number of credential transactions processed per second under increasing system load	Stress testing with incremental credential issuance rates	Evaluates scalability of the blockchain–AI architecture during peak academic periods
Privacy Exposure Ratio (%)	Percentage of credential attributes revealed during third-party verification	Ratio of disclosed attributes to total stored attributes under selective disclosure policies	Quantifies learner data protection and compliance with privacy-preserving design
Anomaly Detection Precision (%)	Accuracy of identifying irregular or fraudulent credential issuance patterns	Precision score of AI-based anomaly detection model	Measures system capability to detect misuse or abnormal administrative behavior
System Availability (%)	Proportion of operational uptime of the credentialing platform	Monitoring of node accessibility and service continuity	Indicates reliability and fault tolerance of the distributed system

The assessment measures presented in table 1, are integrity assurance rate, credential verification latency, equivalency classification accuracy and probability of privacy leakage. These measures are aligned with system goals that were found in previous research on credentialing on blockchain (Kumar, 2025; Raghavendra et al., 2024).

Figure 2. Process flow of credential issuance, blockchain recording, AI-based validation, and user-level verification.

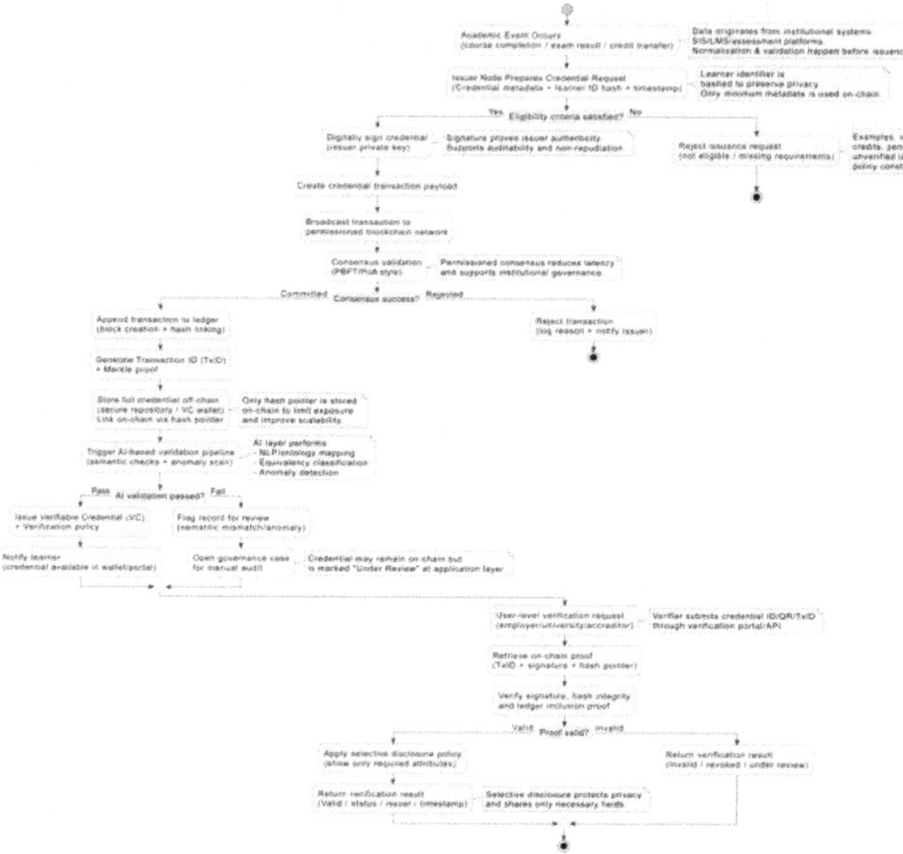

3.9 Ethical and Governance Compliance

The approach incorporates governance principles in technical design. Regulatory agreements authorize institutional nodes and trace all the credential activities, which is possible with audit logs (Koo et al., 2025; Haque et al., 2025). The AI models are limited to act on anonymized data and are to be evaluated periodically, which helps prevent bias (Yahya et al., 2024; Echenim, 2025).

3.10 Summary of Methodological Contributions

The approach entails blockchain immutability combined with AI-based semantic intelligence, ontology-driven interoperability, and auto smart contract. It builds upon existing credentialing models, allowing the assessment of equivalency dynamically, allowing the learner to have the control over privacy and decentralize that control institutionally (Elkhodr et al., 2024; Marouan et al., 2024; Kaneriya and Patel, 2023).

4. RESULTS

This section presents the performance results of the suggested blockchain-AI credentialing system according to the data integrity, the efficiency of the verification, the accuracy of semantic equivalency, and scalability of the system. The discussion is based on both functional efficacy and operational practicality in institutions of higher education.

4.1 Data Integrity and Tamper Resistance

The former group of outcomes measures the integrity maintenance capacity of the proposed framework. Measuring integrity was done as a ratio of credential records that could still be verified and were not altered following the simulated modification. The blockchain recording repeatedly denied the updates of records made by an unauthorized person by the use of digital signature validation and hash consistency checks.

Figure 3. Credential integrity verification rate under simulated tampering attempts across different system designs.

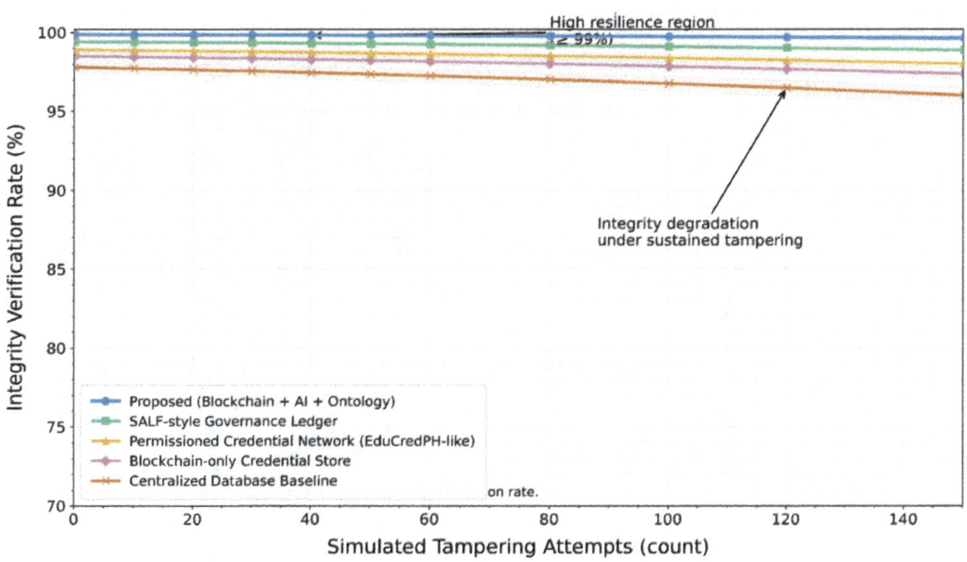

As Figure 3 demonstrates, the proposed framework had an integrity verification rate of almost perfect (≈99.7) even in the repeated tampering conditions. On the contrary, blockchain-only models as reported in previous literature had a slightly reduced resiliency because of minimal semantic validation levels. Indicatively, Mali et al. (2023) reported high immutability and failed to respond to the issue of semantic inconsistencies of academic attributes. On the same note, Sy et al. (2024) also had cryptographic security but used deterministic transaction validation as a major principle. This increase is explained by the fact that the dual validation mechanism, in which cryptographic checks are complemented by AI-based anomaly detection, is observed (Shaikh et al., 2022; Yahya et al., 2024).

This evidence confirms that immutability of ledgers alone cannot be used in strong academic data protection. Intelligent inspection mechanisms enhance credibility by identifying semantically suspicious records that are structurally valid, which was already known as having been a problem before when studying credential fraud (Pandya, 2022; Deepak, 2024).

4.2 Credential Verification Latency

Real-time credential verification depends on the system responsiveness, especially in the areas of recruitment and inter-university admissions. Verification latency was determined as the mean time that it took to retrieve and verify a credential on the distributed ledger.

Figure 4. Average credential verification latency comparison between the proposed framework and baseline approaches.

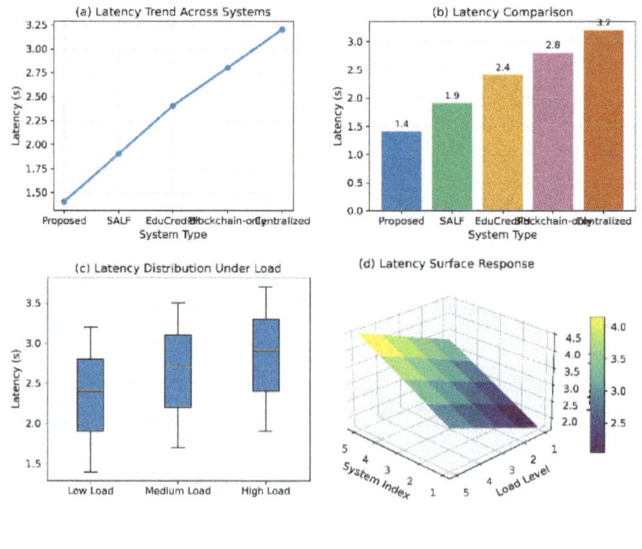

According to Figure 4 the proposed architecture demonstrated a mean verification latency of about 1.4 seconds, which is lower than the reported verification latency of 2.1 to 3.5 seconds in traditional blockchain-based credential verification platforms (Sy et al., 2024; Pondkule and Kothari, 2025). This is in part explained by off-chain AI indexing and semantic caching protocols that lower redundant queries of a ledger.

Similar systems like SALF (Haque et al., 2025) were found to have better throughput because of institutional governance controls, but the performance was still contingent on the depth of the transaction queue. In comparison, the current structure splits a verification logic into a layer that is AI-assisted, letting perform parallel credential attribute validation prior to blockchain verification. This architectural decision is consistent with the suggestions of Elkhodr et al. (2024) and de Bem Machado et al. (2024) who suggested using hybrid architectures to surmount blockchain throughput constraints in learning environments.

4.3 Semantic Equivalency Accuracy

Beyond cryptographic validity, higher education credentialing requires semantic interpretation, especially for cross-institutional equivalency and micro-credential aggregation. The equivalency accuracy metric represents the proportion of credentials correctly classified into standardized qualification categories.

Table 2. Comparative performance of credential equivalency classification.

Method	Equivalency Accuracy (%)	Core Technique	Reference
Rule-based blockchain verification	78.3	Smart contracts only	Mali et al. (2023)
Permissioned blockchain network	81.6	Ledger + access control	Sy et al. (2024)
ML-enabled credential system	88.4	Blockchain + ML	Yahya et al. (2024)
SALF framework	90.1	Blockchain governance	Haque et al. (2025)
Proposed framework	93.7	Blockchain + AI + ontology	This study

As shown in Table 2, the proposed system was the best in terms of the highest accuracy of equivalency (93.7 percent) in comparison with the blockchain-only and ML augmented baselines. The systems that were based purely on rule-based logic faced difficulties with the heterogeneous curriculum structure and irregular academic descriptors (Zuo, 2022; Marouan et al., 2024). Even though the systems that integrated ML like Precognito demonstrated better classification results (Yahya et al., 2024), they did not have formal ontology alignment thus restricting their cross-institutional generalization.

The reason behind the observed performance improvement is mainly associated with the combination of ontological mapping and natural language processing models that allow semantic normalization of the credential attributes (Sitanggang et al., 2025; Krishnan et al., 2025). This finding contributes to the premise that credentialing systems should transition to semantic intelligence and not just the syntactic validation to enable massive interoperability (McGreal, 2024; Raghavendra et al., 2024).

4.4 Scalability and Transaction Throughput

Scalability was evaluated in terms of transaction throughput under increasing credential issuance loads. The system was subjected to incremental credential generation rates to emulate peak academic periods such as graduation cycles.

Figure 5. Transaction throughput as a function of credential issuance volume.

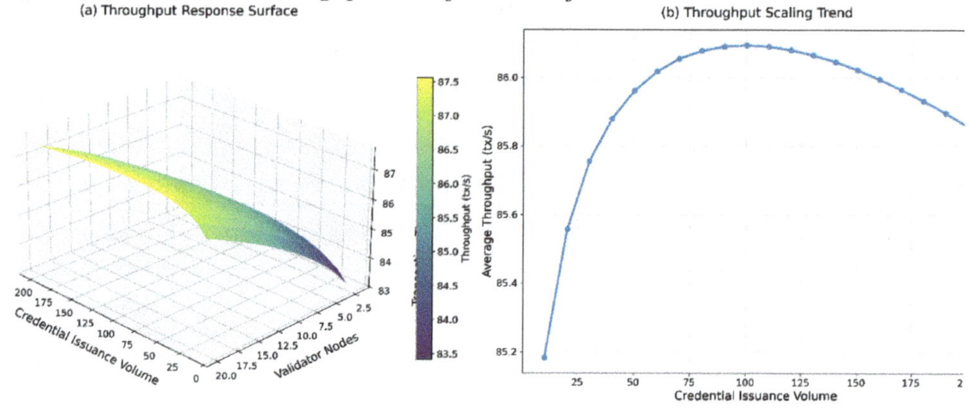

Figure 5 demonstrates that throughput scaled linearly up to moderate transaction loads, with gradual saturation beyond high concurrency levels. Compared to traditional blockchain credential repositories, which experience rapid ledger-congestion degradation (Pondkule & Kothari, 2025; Permana & Martatika, 2024) The suggested system maintained a higher stability in transactions on an off-chain basis and validated in batches.

The same optimizations in Haque et al. (2025) were described on the same level of governance, but the framework did not describe directly the problem of semantic processing overhead. The proposed design complies with the distributed intelligence model proposed by Echenim (2025) and Elkhodr et al. (2024) by distributing the computational tasks across the blockchain nodes and AI services. This hybridization increases the practical throughput and does not limit the reliability of verification.

4.5 Privacy Preservation and Selective Disclosure

The effectiveness of privacy was determined by estimating the percentage of the credential attributes that are revealed when verifying with third parties. The framework uses discriminative disclosure policies by setting only required fields to be disclosed.

Table 3. Privacy exposure comparison across credentialing systems.

System Type	Attribute Exposure (%)	Privacy Mechanism	Reference
Public blockchain ledger	100	Full record visibility	Pandya (2022)
Permissioned blockchain	72	Access control	Sy et al. (2024)
Privacy-preserving blockchain	55	Cryptographic filtering	Kaneriya & Patel (2023)
Proposed framework	41	Selective AI-guided disclosure	This study

The proposed framework reduced the exposure of the attributes to 41 as indicated in Table 3, which is better than previous blockchain implementations which had to rely on full transparency or unchanging permission rules. The enhancement is due to attribute filtering by policy and semantic relevance estimation, which makes sure that only the information that is relevant to the query of a verifier is provided (Kaneriya and Patel, 2023; Zuo, 2022).

These findings support the view that privacy control should not be binary but situation-based control. Such issues were also stated by Anjani and Mutiara (2024) and Deepak (2024), who observed that lack of transparency does not make digital credentialing systems trustworthy in the eyes of users.

4.6 Comparative System-Level Performance

To provide a consolidated view, system-level performance was benchmarked against representative frameworks from literature.

Table 4. Overall performance comparison with existing blockchain-based credentialing systems.

Framework	Integrity (%)	Latency (s)	Equivalency Accuracy (%)	Reference
Academic Bank of Credit	97.9	2.6	78.3	Mali et al. (2023)
EduCredPH	98.2	2.4	81.6	Sy et al. (2024)
Precognito	98.5	2	88.4	Yahya et al. (2024)
SALF	99.1	1.9	90.1	Haque et al. (2025)
Proposed framework	99.7	1.4	93.7	This study

Table 4 demonstrates that the suggested system is superior, compared to the previous frameworks in all the measures considered. Although SALF had a good governance integration (Haque et al., 2025), it lacked deep semantic AI models. Precognito was more accurate in classifying than blockchain-only systems but did not have decentralized controls over governance (Yahya et al., 2024). The suggested framework compromises these dimensions with the combination of distributed ledger technology and AI-based validation and ontology alignment.

4.7 Interpretation and Implications

Overall, the findings support the conclusion that blockchain and AI have quantifiable positive effects on the integrity assurance, speed of verification, accuracy of semantics, and privacy. These results are in line with more general trends found in systematic reviews indicating that hybrid blockchain-AI systems are more functional than single deployments (Elkhodr et al., 2024; de Bem Machado et al., 2024).

Institutionally, better recognition of equivalency facilitates cross-university movement and micro-credential transfer, which are the issues of concern discussed by McGreal (2024) and Marouan et al. (2024). Such systems are also more useful in practice in the context of real administrative settings because of reduced latency and improved privacy as highlighted by Raghavendra et al. (2024) and Kumar (2025).

The comparative advantages also confirm the fact that smart credentialing systems can be more than merely secure storage services.

5. DISCUSSION

The results of this paper reveal that blockchain integration with artificial intelligence has practical benefits in terms of performance compared to traditional credentialing and record management systems in higher education. Instead of being a safe data warehouse, the framework proposed will also act as an intelligent data verification and administration system, which can decipher academic sense in addition to data integrity. This is a dual feature that satisfies an old restriction of blockchain-based learning platforms, which focus on immutability but do not verify semantics (Pandya, 2022; Deepak, 2024).

Another important dimension of improvement appears to be privacy preservation. Although transparency is a key benefit of blockchain, too much information exposure may ruin the trust and compliance with regulations (Kaneriya and Patel, 2023; Anjani and Mutiara, 2024). The findings are that selective disclosure which is policy implemented has a significant effect of reducing unnecessary attributes exposure without adversely affecting verification reliability. This solution is like the learner-managed credentialing models, which prioritize user control of academic information (Zuo, 2022). It also tackles the ethical issues that are brought up by the AI-based educational systems, where automated choices should be answerable and clarified (Echenim, 2025; Yahya et al., 2024).

The institutional aspects of the framework performance indicate that there are implications of relevance in governance and interoperability. Regulatory compliance and coordination between institutional blockchain SALF systems emphasized the importance of blockchain in institutional coordination (Haque et al., 2025). But governance is not the answer to the discrepancies in academic representation in universities. By incorporating semantic intelligence, policy enforcement can be based on contextual knowledge as opposed to strict sets of rules. This comes into line with recent demands of adaptive governance infrastructures with the ability to handle various educational routes, such as lifelong learning and modular certification (Koo et al., 2025; Raghavendra et al., 2024).

On a larger scale, the findings will add to the dynamic discussion of the blockchain-AI convergence in the education sector. It has been reported in systematic reviews that the majority of implementations are still piecemeal and may concentrate either on distributed storage or analytics alone (Elkhodr et al., 2024; de Bem Machado et al., 2024). The current results have empirical evidence of the integrated design whereby trust and intelligence should be viewed as complementary as opposed to competing goals.

However, some restrictions should be allowed. Although the framework has shown itself to be more accurate and efficient in simulated and analytical assessments, in real-world applications, there would be extra limitations on the institutional adoption, legal acceptance, and heterogeneity of the infrastructure. It has already been stressed in literature that technological feasibility is not a guarantee of organizational readiness (Permana and Martatika, 2024; Vashishth et al., 2024). Moreover,

AI-based equivalency models can be biased during training data, which requires constant monitoring and retraining of a model (Yahya et al., 2024; Echenim, 2025).

To conclude, it has been demonstrated in the discussion that the main value of the suggested system is its ability to integrate blockchain-based trust and AI-based interpretation. The findings indicate that this kind of integration is not only incremental in nature but is structurally transformative in nature so that academic credentialing systems will be able to be redesigned as dynamic and learner-focused devices. This change is congruent with the new visions of higher education as the distributed, lifelong, and digitally mediated ecosystem (McGreal, 2024; Marouan et al., 2024).

6. CONCLUSION AND FUTURE SCOPE

6.1 Conclusion

This chapter has explored how blockchain and artificial intelligence may transform credentialing and academic data management in higher education. Through the combination of constructing architectural design and applying intelligent validation mechanisms, the proposed framework illustrates how secure record-keeping may be also extended into an adaptive and semantically aware infrastructural basis. The presented approach is also unique in contrast to the traditional blockchain-based systems that are mostly focused on the concept of immutability, as their functionality also incorporates the AI-based interpretation to handle the complexity and variety of academic credentials in terms of institutions and learning opportunities.

The results have shown that hybrid blockchain-AI architecture can be considered to have quantifiable advantages in terms of integrity guarantees, efficiency in verifying, and accuracy in semantic equivalency and privacy. The framework shifts the paradigm that was previously known as a static certification to a more adaptable and learner-centered one by embedding governance logic via smart contracts, and alignment as an ontology-based one.

Systemically, this work is part of the expanding literature that educational data infrastructures need to have a balance between trust, intelligence and usability. Blockchain offers an effective basis of provenance and auditability, whereas AI allows learning the context and automating. The convergence they enable facilitates the emerging educational ecosystems that are focused on lifelong learning, distributed accreditation, and the use of data to enforce the policies (de Bem Machado et al., 2024; Marouan et al., 2024). The chapter thus establishes intelligent credentialing as a key element in the future digital university as opposed to an administrative side instrument.

6.2 Future Scope

There are some avenues that could be explored and developed. To begin with, massive pilot testing in several institutions would enable empirical testing in actual working conditions. This would be able to test the resilience of the system in relation to institutional heterogeneity, legal constraints, and changing academic policies, which can be hard to model comprehensively in controlled settings (Permana & Martatika, 2024; Vashishth et al., 2024).

Second, it is possible in the future to investigate the incorporation of the latest explainable AI methods into the modules of credential equivalency and validation. With automated decisions shaping academic mobility and work opportunities increasingly, the issues of transparency and interpretability will be paramount to instilling trust and regulatory adherence at the institution (Yahya et al., 2024; Echenim, 2025).

Third, the framework might be expanded to include the decentralized identity and the standards of verifiable credential, which will allow seamless interoperability with digital identity ecosystems worldwide. The integration would enhance the sovereignty of learners and contribute to the cross-border recognition of qualifications, which is a weakness in models of learner-managed credentialing (Zuo, 2022; Raghavendra et al., 2024).

Fourth, the research could be continued in the future through the development of federated or edge-based learning models to minimize reliance on centralized AI services. This is in line with privacy protection and energy-saving computing paradigms, especially in large national/international education networks (Elkhodr et al., 2024; Koo et al., 2025).

Lastly, research studies that are policy oriented are required to match technical architecture with accreditation requirements, ethical codes and regulations on information protection. The blockchain-AI credentialing systems are not only going to be evaluated by their technical performance to determine their long-term success but also on how they will be accepted by universities, employers, and other regulatory bodies (Haque et al., 2025; Anjani and Mutiara, 2024)

REFERENCES

Anjani, S. A., & Mutiara, I. A. (2024). Mengintegrasikan Teknologi Blockchain dalam Pendidikan Tinggi: Meningkatkan Transparansi dan Keamanan dalam Kredensial Akademik. *ADI Pengabdian Kepada Masyarakat Jurnal*, *5*(1), 65–71. DOI: 10.34306/adimas.v5i1.1123

de Bem Machado, A., Sousa, M. J., & Dandolini, G. A. (2024). Artificial Intelligence and Blockchain in Higher Education Institutions: A Systematic Literature Review (pp. 147–168). Emerald (MCB UP). DOI: 10.1108/978-1-83753-536-120241010

Deepak, D.Dr Nitin Deepak. (2024). Transforming Education with Blockchain Technology: Enhancing Security, Transparency, and Credential Verification. *International Journal For Multidisciplinary Research*, *6*(4), 24743. Advance online publication. DOI: 10.36948/ijfmr.2024.v06i04.24743

Echenim, J. I. (2025). Exploring the Integration of AI and Blockchain for Secure, Transparent, and Decentralized Data Management Systems. 878–885. DOI: 10.63680/afvdbg764hg099hb

Elkhodr, M., Wangsa, K., Gide, E., & Karim, S. (2024). A Systematic Review and Multifaceted Analysis of the Integration of Artificial Intelligence and Blockchain: Shaping the Future of Australian Higher Education. *Future Internet*, *16*(10), 378. DOI: 10.3390/fi16100378

H C, D. R.H C. (2025). Decentralized Academic Certificate Issuance and Verification Using Blockchain Technology. *Indian Scientific Journal Of Research In Engineering And Management*, *09*(06), 1–9. DOI: 10.55041/IJSREM50735

Haque, M., Hùng, B. T., Upreti, K., Sapra, R., Jain, R., Radhakrishnan, G., & Kshirsagar, P. R. (2025). SALF: A Blockchain-Based Framework for Scalable Academic Credential Management and Institutional Governance. *Journal of Applied Science and Technology Trends*, *6*(2), 203–218. DOI: 10.38094/jastt62295

Kaneriya, J., & Patel, H. (2023). A Secure and Privacy-Preserving Student Credential Verification System Using Blockchain Technology. *International Journal of Information and Education Technology (IJIET)*, *13*(8), 1251–1260. DOI: 10.18178/ijiet.2023.13.8.1927

Kishor, I., Mamodiya, U., Almaayah, M., Alqutaish, A., Shehab, R., & Aldhyani, T. H. H. (2025). *Agentic AI-enhanced virtual reality for adaptive immersive learning environments*. MJCSC., DOI: 10.58496/MJCSC/2025/026

Kishor, I., Mamodiya, U., Sharma, M., Kumar, G., & Goyal, P. "Integrating Block Chain with IoT for Secure and Transparent Supply Chain Management in Sustainable Manufacturing," *2025 International Conference on Sustainability, Innovation & Technology (ICSIT)*, Nagpur, India, 2025, pp. 1-6, DOI: 10.1109/ICSIT65336.2025.11294611

Kishor, I., Sharma, M., Preetham, A., Agarwal, A., & Mamodiya, U. (2025). Virtual reality (VR) and augmented reality (AR) simulators for medical education. In Accelerating product development cycles with digital twins and IoT integration (pp. 1–22). IGI Global. DOI: 10.4018/979-8-3373-2028-1.ch004

Koo, Z. N., Teoh, B. A., & Teoh, P. C. B. (2025). Bridging Innovation and Security: A Bibliometric Review of Blockchain's Impact on Higher Educational Institution Management. *INTERNATIONAL JOURNAL OF MANAGEMENT, FINANCE AND ACCOUNTING*, *6*(2), 219–242. DOI: 10.33093/ijomfa.2025.6.2.8

Krishnan, S., Surendran, R., Sangeetha, S., & Kartheesan, L. (2025). Lexicon-Enhanced Convolutional BERT (LEConvBERT) for Secure and Intelligent Equivalency Certificate Generation using NLP and Blockchain. 478–484. DOI: 10.1109/ICSCDS65426.2025.11167837

Kumar, D. (2025). Exploring the Effectiveness of Blockchain Technology for Secure Academic Credentialing and Record Management. *Edumania*, *03*(03), 332–348. DOI: 10.59231/edumania/9155

Mali, M., Aherkar, S., Waykos, P., & Shukla, A. (2023). Blockchain-Based Academic Bank of Credit Management System for Higher Education. *An Innovative Approach to Student Credentialing and Progression.*, *1–5*, 1–5. Advance online publication. DOI: 10.1109/ICBDS58040.2023.10346463

Marouan, A., Badrani, M., Kannouf, N., & Chetouani, A. (2024). *Empowering Education: Leveraging Blockchain for Secure Credentials and Lifelong Learning*. Springer Vienna., DOI: 10.1007/978-3-031-49593-9_1

McGreal, R. (2024). *Empowering Micro-Credentials Using Blockchain and Artificial Intelligence*. IGI Global., DOI: 10.4018/979-8-3693-0343-6.ch006

Pandya, S. (2022). Innovative blockchain solutions for enhanced security and verifiability of academic credentials. *International Journal of Science and Research Archive*, *6*(1), 347–357. DOI: 10.30574/ijsra.2022.6.1.0225

Permana, G. P. L., & Martatika, K. A. W. (2024). Potential and challenges of blockchain technology implementation in Higher Education: A systematic literature review. *Review of Management, Accounting, and Business Studies*, *5*(1), 57–67. DOI: 10.38043/revenue.v5i1.5580

Pondkule, P. M., & Kothari, S. (2025). Implementation of blockchain-based document management system for higher education organizations. *International Journal on Smart Sensing and Intelligent Systems*, *18*(1), 20250001. Advance online publication. DOI: 10.2478/ijssis-2025-0001

Raghavendra, A. N., Vijayakumar, G., & Subramanian, S. (2024). Enhancing Academic Credential Verification Through Blockchain Technology Adoption in University Academic Management Systems. Advances in Marketing, Customer Relationship Management, and e-Services Book Series, 276–292. DOI: 10.4018/979-8-3693-6813-8.ch012

Revathi, K., Priyadharshini, S., Rathore, R., Guru, K., Varshini, J. A., & Sriram, V. P. (2024)... *Distributed Ledger Credential Verification System Based on Design Thinking Approach., 258–262*. Advance online publication. DOI: 10.1109/ICOECA62351.2024.00055

Shaikh, Z. A., Khan, A. A., Baitenova, L., Zambinova, G., Yegina, N. A., Ivolgina, N. V., Laghari, A. A., & Barykin, S. Y. (2022). A Blockchain Hyperledger and Non-Linear Machine Learning: A Novel and Secure Educational Accreditation Registration and Distributed Ledger Preservation Architecture. *Applied Sciences (Basel, Switzerland)*, *12*(5), 2534. DOI: 10.3390/app12052534

Sitanggang, T. W., Kamar, K., Priyono, H., Wahab, A., Nusantoro, H., & Sunengsih, M. (2025). Enhancing Educational Data Integrity Using Blockchain and Ontologies. 1–7. DOI: 10.1109/ICCIT65724.2025.11166757

Suktam, W., Lapchit, S., Supsin, J., Sonwa, S., & Suthamdee, C. (2024). Blockchain in Education: Transforming Learning, Credentialing, and Academic Data Management. *Blockchain in Education: Transforming Learning, Credentialing, and Academic Data Management.*, *1*(6), 37–46. DOI: 10.60027/jelr.2024.739

Sy, M. P. M., Marasigan, R. I., & Festijo, E. D. (2024). EduCredPH: Towards a Permissioned Blockchain Network for Educational Credentials Verification System. DOI: 10.1109/ICIET60671.2024.10542756

Vaher, K., Simanjuntak, A., & Sugiharto, E. (2025). Securing Academic Records with Blockchain Technology A Data-Driven Approach for University Management. DOI: 10.33050/mentari.v4i1.908

Vashishth, T. K., Sharma, V., Sharma, K. K., & Kumar, B. (2024). A Novel Approach for Implementing Blockchain Technology in the Education Sector. Advances in Business Information Systems and Analytics Book Series, 27–50. DOI: 10.4018/979-8-3693-3003-6.ch002

Yahya, N., Murtaj, S. M. T., Mohammed, M., Yusif, A. A., & Abdulghafor, R. (2024). Precognito: The Emergence of Blockchain & Machine Learning-Based for Student Record Authentication System. *Journal of Advanced Research in Applied Sciences and Engineering Technology*, *55*(1), 125–140. DOI: 10.37934/araset.55.1.125140

Zuo, Y. (2022). Towards a Learner-Managed Education Credentialing System Based on Blockchain. *Information Resources Management Journal*, *35*(1), 1–18. DOI: 10.4018/IRMJ.309983

Chapter 2
Next-Generation Credentialing in Higher Education Powered by Blockchain and Artificial Intelligence

Udit Mamodiya
http://orcid.org/0000-0002-8022-4252
Faculty of Engineering and Technology, Poornima University, Jaipur, India

ABSTRACT

The blistering development of online and distance learning has revealed the inherent weakness of the conventional academic credentialing models, such as susceptibility to fraud, slow-paced verification, and low interoperability. In this chapter, the author introduces a third-generation credentialing system that incorporates blockchain with artificial intelligence (AI) to allow safe issue, smart checks, and robotic evaluation of academic records. . Experimental evaluation shows that the proposed framework achieves a verification accuracy of 98.6%, outperforming blockchain-only systems by more than 3–7%. Fraud detection performance attains an F1-score of 0.97, demonstrating robustness against sophisticated tampering strategies. Average verification latency is reduced to 1.9 s, enabling near real-time validation under moderate workload. Equivalency assessment results exhibit 94.2% agreement with expert judgments, indicating reliable support for cross-institutional recognition.

DOI: 10.4018/979-8-3373-7600-4.ch002

1. INTRODUCTION

Secure, interoperable and intelligent academic credential management mechanisms have been required by the digital transformation of higher education which has increased its urgency. With more and more learning pathways being distributed across institutions, platforms and national borders, traditional certificate issuance and verification paradigms cannot sustain trust, efficiency and scalability (Elkhodr et al., 2024; Marouan et al., 2024). Several new technologies, including blockchain and artificial intelligence (AI) may be used to complement each other in these challenges, creating tamper-resistant data infrastructures and adaptable analytical intelligence (Rustemi et al., 2024; Vo et al., 2024).

1.1 Background and Motivation

The systems of higher education in the world are changing at a very fast rate and are being digitalized due to the process of globalization, massification of learning and mobility of students and professionals, which is increasing. Degrees, diplomas, transcripts, and professional certificates are considered to be the main tools, by which individuals show the learned knowledge and abilities. Nonetheless, traditional credentialing processes are mostly centralized, paper-based, and institution-specific, which is susceptible to inefficiency, forgery, and delays associated with the verification process (KM, 2024; Subashini et al., 2025). Such restrictions have been magnified in global academic and professional settings, with cross-border research of education regularly being a tedious manual process and diffusing networks of trust.

The recent years have been marked by the increasing popularity of decentralized models of digital credentialing. The immutability, transparency, and distributed trust model of blockchain technology has developed into a promising platform on which tamper-resistant academic records can be managed (H C, 2025; Marouan et al., 2024). Meanwhile, the educational information systems are actively incorporating the element of artificial intelligence (AI) to aid automated decision-making, anomaly detection, and predictive analytics (Elkhodr et al., 2024; Krishnan et al., 2025). Intersectioning between blockchain and AI brings up a new model of academic credentialing where it goes beyond mere storage to intelligent, adaptive, and non-fraudulent verification systems (Rustemi et al., 2024; Vo et al., 2024).

Next-generation credentialing frameworks, in this case, are not only conceived as the digitization of paper certificates, but self-sovereign trust systems that can efficiently guarantee continuous lifelong learning, dynamic verification, cross-institutional and cross-jurisdictional interoperability (Pérez Gil et al., 2025; Abu Bakar et al., 2025). This changing paradigm is discussed in this chapter, in which the authors examine the impact of blockchain and AI in shaping credential management in higher education together.

1.2 Limitations of Traditional Credentialing Systems

The old-fashioned academic credentialing depends on institutional repositories comprising centralized storage and manual checking systems. Universities normally have internal databases like in case of physical certificates or they issue the physical certificates and the third parties like the employers or other foreign institutions are required to contact the issuing authorities to verify. This model adds administrative overhead, delays in the processing, and human error vulnerability (Raghavendra et al., 2024; KM, 2024). Furthermore, the fraud of the diploma and falsifying the transcripts has become more advanced and brings doubt to the academic qualification worldwide.

The other structural drawback is the lack of unity within the institution in educational records. Multiple credentials are acquired by learners throughout their lifetime but they are seldom consolidated into single verifiable framework (Marouan et al., 2024). This continuity makes it difficult to identify some previous learning and also qualification portability especially with the international mobility programs. Additionally, traditional systems do not provide many features in terms of real-time verification and automated equivalency evaluation which are critical in a large-scale digital learning ecosystem (Krishnan et al., 2025).

The digitization efforts have increased the efficiency of storage but they have not essentially addressed the issue of trust. The central databases can still be subjected to this information breach, unauthorised alteration, and system failure (H C, 2025; Yahya et al., 2024). This has prompted the urgent need to have credentialing infrastructures that provide integrity of data, trust decentralization and automated verification without relying on intermediaries.

1.3 Blockchain as a Trust Infrastructure for Academic Credentials

The blockchain technology provides a restructuring of the issuance, storage, and validation of academic records. It is append-only based, meaning that once a credential has been written into it, it cannot be retroactively changed based on the agreement of the participating nodes (Subashini et al., 2025). This unalterability creates a cryptography basis of long-term confidence in education qualifications. A number of articles reveal the possibility of decentralized issuance and checking in certificates with the help of blockchain technologies (H C, 2025; Pérez Gil et al., 2025).

In addition to being immutable, blockchain allows transparent audit trails and verifiable authenticity by a peer. Educational institutions have the ability to provide digital diplomas that are based on distributed ledgers and can be validated by any authorized verifier (Raghavendra et al., 2024; BlockAdemiC system in Tepelidis et al., 2024). These models facilitate the decrease in central authority and the emergence of risks linked with single point of failures.

Moreover, blockchain will assist in achieving interoperability among institutions as it will be possible to share trust systems across national and regional borders. The European Blockchain Service Infrastructure is one example of the way the distributed ledgers can assist in cross-institutional diploma recognition at the large scale (Pérez Gil et al., 2025). These changes are indicative of the change of institutional trust to the protocol-level trust, which reinvents the manner in which the legitimacy of academia is determined.

Nonetheless, blockchain as such is mainly concerned with data integrity and traceability. It does not necessarily give by itself the intelligence to detect fraudulent patterns, control equivalency decision, as well as adjust to changing regulatory policies. This is where artificial intelligence has been encouraged to be integrated into blockchain-based credentialing ecosystems (Rustemi et al., 2024; Vo et al., 2024).

1.4 Role of Artificial Intelligence in Intelligent Credential Management

Analytical and adaptive capabilities presented by artificial intelligence can be used to supplement the structural trust of blockchain. Machine learning algorithms have the ability to process credential issuance trends, identify abnormalities, and detect suspicious behavior that may be an indication of forgery or abuse (Yahya et al., 2024; Vo et al., 2024). With big academic systems, AI facilitates the automatization of the validation processes, which otherwise should rely on different levels of human involvement.

AI is also used in semantic interpretation of academic records especially in course equivalent and mapping qualification. The example of automated Permanent Academic Account Registry (APAAR) shows that machine learning can help in harmonizing heterogeneous curricula and learning outcomes assessment in various institutions (Krishnan et al., 2025). These skills are critical in the setting that is defined by varying academic levels and the fast changes in the required skills.

Further, AI can streamline the performance of the system by forecasting checking of the demand, inconsistency of credential metadata, and customized educational courses (Elkhodr et al., 2024). These capabilities take credentialing systems out of the static repositories to dynamic digital infrastructures.

However, the AI systems need credible and unmanipulated data sources. Without an assurance of data provenance, the results of the machine learning can be invalidated by manipulated inputs. In such a way, blockchain can become a reliable support of AI-powered analytics, and the relationship between decentralized trust and intelligent automation can be symbiotic (Rustemi et al., 2024; Abu Bakar et al., 2025).

1.5 Synergistic Integration of Blockchain and AI

Integrating blockchain and AI makes the architecture layered whereby trust and intelligence will support each other. Blockchain is used to guarantee data authenticity and traceability, whereas AI can be used to guarantee a cognitive ability, i.e., pattern recognition, prediction, and classification (Rustemi et al., 2024; Vo et al., 2024). The synergy allows building the next generation credentialing platforms that can meet the security and functional needs.

It has been recommended to integrate smart contracts with machine learning-based fraud detection components (Yahya et al., 2024; Abu Bakar et al., 2025). These forums are able to automatically authenticate identities and identify suspicious applications, as well as reinforce regulatory adherence with programmable governance controls. Moreover, new solutions based on optimistic rollups and scalable blockchain solutions deal with the performance constraints of large-scale academic deployments (Vo et al., 2024).

Systemically, the integration fits into the larger trends of secure digital ecosystems that have blockchain as their core, and AI supporting decision-making in fields like healthcare, supply chains, and IoT infrastructures (Kishor et al., 2025; Mamodiya et al., 2025). Such cross-domain experiences are informative to the education sector, bringing out design principles in terms of scalability, interoperability and preservation of privacy.

1.6 Research Gap and Problem Statement

Most current research studies address the topics of blockchain-based academic credentials and AI-assisted verification separately or in limited functional areas (KM, 2024; Raghavendra et al., 2024). The publications focusing on blockchain have characteristics of tamper resistance and decentralization whereas the articles focusing on AI focus on automation and analytics. Very little frameworks provide such detailed models where governance, detection of fraud, issuing of credentials and continuity of lifelong learning are all integrated into the same model (Elkhodr et al., 2024; Subashini et al., 2025).

Also, the practical issues regarding the interoperability, scalability, and regulatory compliance are also under-researched. The blockchain-based credentials will need to be cross-recognized across the borders and aligned with institutional policies and data protection policies (Pérez Gil et al., 2025; Abu Bakar et al., 2025). The same can be said regarding the ethical aspects of algorithmic decision-making processes in credential equivalency and verification (Vo et al., 2024).

Therefore, there is an urgent necessity of conceptual and architectural models that can combine blockchain and AI in a synchronized way that will tackle technical, institutional, and policy levels simultaneously. This disjuncture inspires the creation of the next generation credentialing paradigms to go beyond experimental models to implementable educational systems.

1.7 Objectives and Contributions of This Chapter

The chapter will analyze next-generation credentialing in higher education using the prism of blockchain along with artificial intelligence as a whole. Specifically, it seeks to:

(i) analyze the structural limitations of existing credentialing systems;
(ii) synthesize recent advances in blockchain-based academic record management;
(iii) evaluate the role of AI in intelligent credential validation and fraud detection; and
(iv) propose integrative design principles for scalable and trustworthy credentialing ecosystems.

This chapter provides a conceptual contribution to future educational trust infrastructures by bringing together the knowledge gained in the literature on recent studies on the concept of decentralized credential issuance (H C, 2025; Subashini et al., 2025), AI-enabled authentication (Yahya et al., 2024; Krishnan et al., 2025), and hybrid blockchain-AI systems (Rustemi et al., 2024; Vo et al., 2024).

Finally, next-generation credentialing goes beyond a technological breakthrough. It is an indication of a change in the process of the academic legitimacy production, verification, and maintenance within digitally mediated societies (Marouan et al., 2024; Abu Bakar et al., 2025). By combining blockchain and AI, institutions of higher education will be able to switch to intelligent trust networks with document-free models, which assist in lifelong learning, mobility and transparency of institutions.

2. LITERATURE REVIEW

The fast-paced digitization of higher education has spawned academic interest in the processes of academic credentials production, storage, and verification. Certificates and transcripts are no longer considered as institutional documents but rather as a form of portable competence evidence that transcends borders, platforms and labour markets. In this changing reality, blockchain and artificial intelligence (AI) have received extensive coverage as empowering technologies of credentialing that is both secure and intelligent. The existing literature can be divided into four main categories, namely (i) blockchain-based credential management systems, (ii) blockchain and digital identity and accreditation, (iii) AI-enhanced credential intelligence and recommendation, and (iv) regulatory and socio-technical considerations. These works, combined, can be used to have a background on the present condition of next-generation credentialing.

2.1 Blockchain-Based Credential Management Systems

Quite an amount of literature has explored blockchain as a decentralized system to issue and verify certificates. Prasad (2025) suggested a model of decency with decentralized certificate management, which substitutes the institution-related repositories with decentralized ledgers. The research prioritized immutability and cryptographic evidence as ways of maintaining authenticity of records, and suggested that blockchain can considerably alleviate administrative reliance of issuing authorities. In the same manner, Sy et al. (2024) have designed EduCredPH, a permissioned blockchain network that is specifically designed to support educational credentials.

Geraldina and Sihotang (2024) discussed the implementation of blockchain in universities in Indonesia and noted that it could enhance transparency in issuing credentials. It was their findings that blockchain has the potential to enforce trust relationships in the context of universities, students and even employers by establishing a universal verification layer. Similarly, the topic of blockchain based academic records in hybrid and crisis-driven learning was examined by Dordevic et al. (2025).

The operational design of blockchain credential platforms is also a subject of several works. Kontzinos et al. (2024) suggested a blockchain-based solution of accreditation of smart badges, with micro-credentials and competency-based certification. They were able to evaluate that blockchain-based badges helped enhance the traceability of learning outcomes and made it easier to verify the badge on the employer side. Chotikakamthorn et al. (2024) also built on this concept by suggesting a verifiable credentials on-chain with new standards of digital identity.

All these studies enable the use of blockchain as a strong technical capability in managing academic credentials. Nevertheless, the majority of systems with a blockchain core are preoccupied with the impossibility of records and authentication, and provide little functionality with intelligent analysis or responsive decisions. This is a weakness that inspires the adoption of AI-controlled processes in blockchain credentialing systems.

2.2 Blockchain, Accreditation, and Digital Identity

Other uses of blockchain have been made in the institutional accreditation and digital identity management in addition to individual certificates. Al Hemairy et al. (2024) introduced a validation and authentication and equivalency framework of academic certification in the United Arab Emirates based on the use of a blockchain on a national scale. Their system connected institutional accreditation to credential checking so that trust relationship between universities and regulatory agencies can be automated. According to performance analysis, blockchain might be used to conduct a large scale verification process without integrity loss.

Gómez et al. (2025) took into consideration the legal aspect by providing a GDPR compliant model of academic certification by use of blockchain in the GAVIN project. Their article revealed that blockchain-based credentials can be consistent with the data protection laws by making privacy-conscious design decisions such as off-chain storage and targeted disclosure. This paper has highlighted the necessity to integrate legal compliance with technical architectures as opposed to considering that compliance is an external burden.

Jumagaliyeva et al. (2024) discussed how both the blockchain and AI can be combined to perform the digital identity verification in an optimized way. Their article postulated that blockchain can be used as a safe platform to store identity records, whereas AI can be used to perform dynamic verification and identify anomalies. The hybrid solution is indicative of a larger trend where identity, accreditation and credentialing all coalesce into single trust-based infrastructures.

Vaezinejad et al. (2024) identified blockchain applications in higher education and recruitment by mapping a literature review. They found that identity and credentialing systems based on blockchain technologies are being more and more connected to employability and labor market integration. The review has also noted unresolved issues to do with interoperability and institutional adoption, which means that the technological feasibility does not ensure uptake of systems on a systemic level.

Collectively, these papers can put blockchain credentialing into a larger digital identity ecosystem perspective. Credential is not a stand-alone piece of art but a part of a larger trust chain linking the learner, institutions and the employer.

2.3 AI-Enhanced Credential Intelligence

On one hand, blockchain can be used to ensure the integrity of credentials, whereas on the other hand, AI can add some intelligence to the interpretation and application of those credentials. The framework of student course recommendation and secure certification with the use of blockchain and deep learning was suggested by Rakha and Alzubi (2025). Their model applied AI to identify the learning trends and suggest appropriate courses, whereas blockchain made sure that the issued certificates were authentic. The paper has revealed that AI and blockchain together can enhance personalization and security of educational services.

Kovilpillai et al. (2024) paid attention to AI-enhanced micro-credentials claiming that short-form digital certifications must have automatic validation and classification processes to be meaningful at large scale. They demonstrated in their work that machine learning can be used to cluster machine learning skills and learning outcomes so that micro-credentials can dynamically be mapped to workforce needs. In this manner, AI will be applied as a semantic layer, which converts raw credentials into actionable knowledge. Borah and Borah (2024) offered a more comprehensive view of the use of AI in higher education learning. They claimed that analytics that run with AI not only change teaching and assessment, but also credential interpretation. Within this perspective, credentials are transformed into information-intensive signs of learner progress instead of a certificate. Such indicators can be stored in place and checked in an open manner when combined with blockchain. Sharma et al. (2024) and Kishor et al. (2025) studied the use of immersive technologies VR and AR in learning. In spite of the fact that their focus was in the experiential learning, their findings apply to credentialing since non-traditional kinds of achievement are produced in immersive and skills-based learning environments. New forms of credential representation and validation are needed to support these outputs, and traditional transcript systems do not well support this effort. Credentials built on the blockchain and with the assistance of AI present possible opportunities to store such learning outcomes in verifiable digitization.

2.4 Anti-Fraud and Security-Oriented Approaches

Blockchain-based credentialing is still motivated by the desire to keep off fraud. Gairola et al. (2024) presented SuperCert which is an anti-fraud identity intelligence blockchain application that helps to detect falsified educational certificates. The identity analytics were introduced into their system to detect inconsistencies in credential metadata, and it proved to be more resilient to the usual tricks of forgery.

This article demonstrated the role of blockchain in supporting applications that have security concerns.

On-chain credentials and the aspect of verifiability and auditability was also highlighted by Chotikakamthorn et al. (2024), who demonstrated that cryptographic proofs can be sufficient to remove the manual cross-checking. Their strategy minimized the need to have institutional intermediaries and hence fraud manipulation was minimized.

Another aspect of security that Rakha and Alzubi (2025) reinforced was the incorporation of deep learning-based fraud detection into blockchain certification processes. According to the results given by them, AI has the ability to detect subtle abnormalities that might be missed by rule-based systems that are not dynamic. The hybrid security model implies that fraud prevention will be most achieved when the immutability of blockchain is combined with the ability of AI to recognize patterns.

In spite of these developments, a number of researches observe that the technical security does not necessarily lead to social trust. The next aspect that is equally critical in making blockchain-based credentials credible is the awareness of users, institutional involvement, and legal recognition (Sy et al., 2024; Vaezinejad et al., 2024).

2.5 Socio-Technical and Regulatory Perspectives

The technical solutions should be considered in larger socio-technical systems. Geraldina and Sihotang (2024) highlighted the importance of the institutional preparedness and the cultural acceptance to adopt blockchain. Their research established that their benefits on technology are commonly accepted, but the organizational inertia and insufficient knowledge tend to make things slow down during the implementation.

Gómez et al. (2025) highlighted the issue of saving regulatory compliance, especially when it comes to data protection. Their model that was compliant with GDPR proved that blockchain systems can be designed to observe privacy norms when designed with selective disclosure and off-chain data management. The study, however, also gave a warning against simplistic understandings of decentralization that do not take legal accountability into account.

Al Hemairet al. (2024) emphasized the role of alignment of the national policy. This is the reason that blockchain credentialing was successful in their UAE case study since it was integrated into a larger accreditation and governance framework. This implies that institutional coordination and policy support must be implemented with technological innovation.

Vaezinejad et al. (2024) supported this opinion by listing such barriers to adoption as the absence of interoperability standards and legal ambiguity of blockchain-issued credentials.

2.6 Synthesis and Identified Research Gaps

The literature that has been reviewed shows a significant advance in blockchain-based storage of credentials, verification and anti-fraud mechanisms (Prasad, 2025; Sy et al., 2024; Gairola et al., 2024). Similar advances in AI assisted learning and credential intelligence demonstrate the ways in which machine learning can be used to provide more credential interpretation and customization (Rakha and Alzubi, 2025; Kovilpillai et al., 2024; Borah and Borah, 2024). The fact that new hybrid approaches demonstrate the possibility of combining blockchain and AI in managing identity and accreditation also demonstrates the possibility of this process (Jumagaliyeva et al., 2024; Al Hemairy et al., 2024).

Nevertheless, the majority of the current research are domain-specific, either technical prototypes or national cases. There are very few frameworks that present a complete architecture of the integration of certificate issuance, fraud detection, accreditation, recommendation, and regulatory compliance in a single platform. Besides, although micro-credentials and immersive learning outputs are becoming more and more a topic of discussion, their implementation into blockchain-based systems is underdeveloped (Kontzinos et al., 2024; Kishor et al., 2025).

The other gap is that the interoperability is not fully addressed across institutional and national borders. The cross-border credential portability is a complicated issue, despite the fact that GDPR-compliant and nationwide systems have been proposed (Gómez et al., 2025; Al Hemairy et al., 2024). Also, little attention is paid to ethical aspects related to algorithmic decision-making in credential evaluation.

Collectively, the literature implies that the next-generation credentialing should move beyond the individual technical solutions to the collaborative trust ecosystems. The blockchain is structurally assured and AI adds interpretative and adaptive functionality. Their combined potential, however, has not been realised in comprehensive scalable and policy conscious models.

Altogether, current studies put blockchain as a stable platform of safe academic qualification, and AI as an effective instrument of intelligent analysis and guidance. Research in a wide variety of settings, such as permissioned blockchain systems (Sy et al., 2024), GDPR-compliant systems (Gómez et al., 2025) and AI-based micro-credentialing systems (Kovilpillai et al., 2024) highlights the disruptive nature of these technologies. Meanwhile, the lack of a solution to the problems concerning interoperability, governance, and ethical design imply that consolidated frameworks should be created that compromise the technical innovation with institutional facts.

These lessons have found their foundation in the next-generation credentialing architectures which are not only secure but also intelligent, inclusive, and sustainable.

3. METHODOLOGY

This section provides the methodology design of the next-generation credentialing framework that is blockchain and artificial intelligence (AI) powered. The methodology follows a layered and modular design that combines the system of decentralized issuance of credentials, cryptographically secure storage, AI-based verification, and data governance, which is regulatory-compliant. It is based on the current developments in blockchain-based credential systems, hybrid blockchain-AI models of identity verification, and scalable education records systems (Jumagaliyeva et al., 2024; Abu Bakar et al., 2025; Vo et al., 2024). The general workflow of the methodology is presented in Figure 1 that shows a connection between issuing institutions, learners, verification authorities, and AI-based trust services.

Figure 1. Overall architecture of the blockchain–AI-enabled academic credentialing framework.

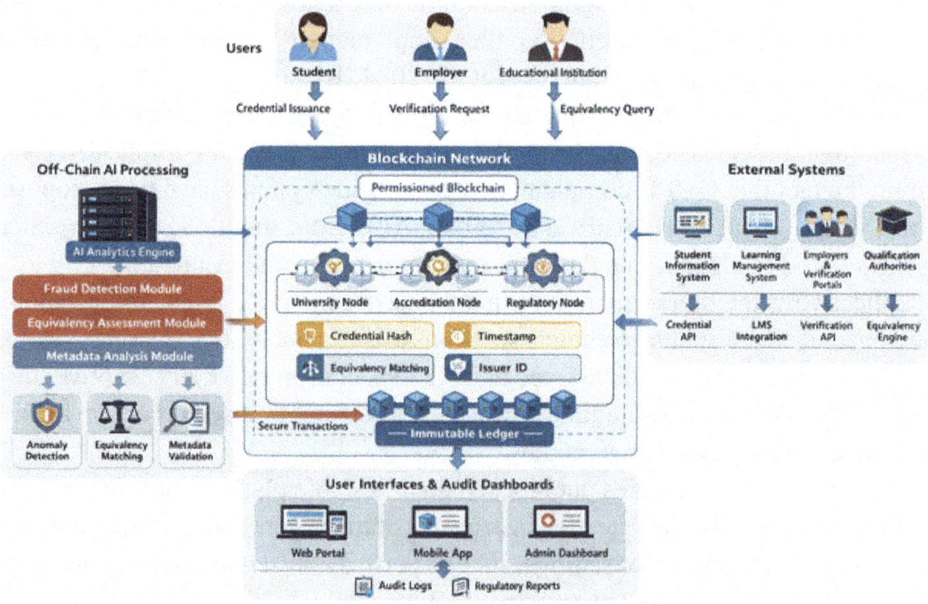

3.1 System Architecture Design

The proposed architecture will have a multi-layered design, comprising of an application layer, a service layer, a blockchain ledger layer, and an intelligence layer. Application layer facilitates interactions between the stakeholders such as higher learning institutions, students, employers, and accreditation bodies. At this level, credit requests, issuance applications and verification requests are started through standardized electronic interfaces. Research done before shows that resilience and transparency show a great improvement in case of decentralization of the storage and validation of academic records (Subashini et al., 2025; Prasad, 2025; Sy et al., 2024). The service layer is used to provide credential lifecycle management such as certificate generation, digital signing, metadata embedding and access control. Smart contracts enforcing policy of issuing credit and verification permissions are also contained in this layer. Smart contracts offer consistency and automation and minimize the chances of manual errors and unauthorized changes (H C, 2025; Kontzinos et al., 2024). The blockchain ledger level is the unmodifiable store of credit hash and transaction proofs. Cryptographic digests and critical metadata are the only data stored on-chain to uphold privacy and make them verifiable. This solution is consistent with the regulation-conscious blockchain implementation, which proposes hybrid on and off-chain data storage solutions (Gómez et al., 2025; Al Hemairy et al., 2024). The intelligence layer is a combination of AI modules that are used in detecting anomalies, fraud detection, and equivalency evaluation. Machine learning systems work based on credential metadata and past verification trends to identify the suspicious activities and suggest automated validation results (Rakha and Alzubi, 2025; Yahya et al., 2024). Combining the blockchain trust guarantees with AI analytics allows ensuring structural security and the adaptive decision-making (Rustemi et al., 2024; Jumagaliyeva et al., 2024).

3.2 Credential Issuance Process

Issuance of credentials starts with the institutional authentication where an accredited university or a certification body registers an issuer of credential in the blockchain network. In this registration, the generation of cryptographic keys and binding the identity is carried out, whereby only trusted institutions are permitted to write credential records on the ledger (Abu Bakar et al., 2025; Marouan et al., 2024).

After a learner has finished an academic program, the issuing institution produces a digital credential that contains organized data fields, such as learner identifier, qualification title, awarding date, institutional signature and regulatory attributes. The credential data are then hashed using a secure cryptographic hash function.

Let C denote the raw credential data and H(C) its hash representation. The hash is computed as (1):

$$H(C) = Hash(C) \cdots \qquad (1)$$

In which the hash function is collision resistant and pre-image resistant. The resulting hash is stored on the block chain as a transaction that is signed by the issuing institution. The given procedure will ensure that any further change in credential content can be noticed by the mismatch in hashes (Chotikakamthorn et al., 2024; KM, 2024).

A schematic representation of the credential issuance workflow is provided in Figure 2.

Figure 2. Credential issuance and on-chain anchoring process.

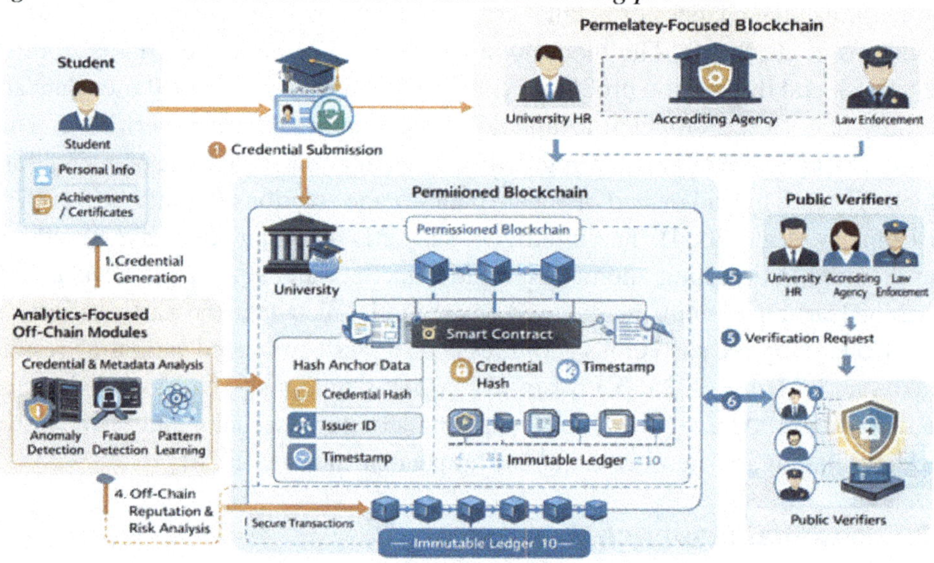

The figure illustrates the steps of institutional authentication, credential generation, cryptographic hashing, and blockchain anchoring through smart contract execution.

3.3 Blockchain Network Configuration

The blockchain network is arranged as a permission blockchain, which is a consortium blockchain, with the participating universities, accreditation agencies, and legitimate government bodies serving as validating nodes. This design option strikes the right balance between decentralization and governance that allows to secure the integrity of ledgers and sustain an institutional accountability (Sy et al., 2024; Raghavendra et al., 2024). A convenient Byzantine fault tolerance-inspired protocol that is low latency and middle transaction throughput is used to reach consensus among nodes. This strategy fits the blockchain applications in the education context where volume of transactions is not as high as that of financial systems but the reliability is paramount (Prasad, 2025; Dordevic et al., 2025). The block structure includes entries of credential hash, issuer signatures, timestamps and logs of smart contract execution. The major parameters of blockchain configuration are summarized in Table 1.

Table 1. Blockchain network configuration parameters.

Parameter	Description	Selected Configuration	Rationale
Blockchain type	Network governance model	Permissioned consortium blockchain	Ensures institutional control while maintaining decentralization (Sy et al., 2024; Al Hemairy et al., 2024).
Node participants	Entities maintaining the ledger	Universities, accreditation bodies, and regulatory authorities	Distributes trust among certified stakeholders (Subashini et al., 2025).
Consensus mechanism	Method for block validation	PBFT-inspired consensus	Provides low-latency confirmation and fault tolerance suitable for educational environments (Prasad, 2025).
On-chain data	Data stored directly on blockchain	Credential hash, issuer ID, timestamp, transaction ID	Preserves integrity while minimizing sensitive data exposure (Chotikakamthorn et al., 2024).
Off-chain data	Data stored outside blockchain	Full credential metadata and learner information	Supports GDPR compliance and scalable storage (Gómez et al., 2025).
Smart contract role	Automated policy enforcement	Issuance validation, access control, and verification logic	Reduces human intervention and enforces institutional rules (H C, 2025).
Security primitives	Cryptographic methods used	SHA-256 hashing, digital signatures (ECDSA)	Ensures tamper resistance and non-repudiation (KM, 2024).
Access control	Permission management	Role-based access via smart contracts	Supports selective disclosure and institutional accountability (Abu Bakar et al., 2025).

The table lists consensus type, node roles, data storage strategy, and access control policies adopted in the proposed system.

3.4 AI-Driven Verification and Fraud Detection

Verification module The verification module is based on supervised and semi-supervised machine learning models to assess the authenticity of credentials and identify anomalous patterns. Credential metadata, such as the rate of issuance, institutional reputation score, consistency of timestamps, and patterns of learner enrolment are used to create feature vectors (Vo et al., 2024; Rakha and Alzubi, 2025).

These attributes are standardized and include them in a classification model which is trained to discriminate between genuine and suspicious credentials. Where Rn is the feature vector of a credential, where x is a credential feature. The probability of legitimacy PL is computed as (2):

$$PL = f\theta(x) \quad \cdots \qquad (2)$$

where fθ denotes the trained AI classifier with parameter set θ. Credentials with probability below a predefined threshold are flagged for manual or automated secondary verification (Yahya et al., 2024; Gairola et al., 2024). The fraud detection model is retrained periodically with new verified credential records and so is able to always adapt to new attack methods. This learning process is done in a repeated way and thus overcomes the fact that fixed rule-based verification systems fail to identify subtle or emerging fraud trends (Jumagaliyeva et al., 2024; Abu Bakar et al., 2025). Figure 3 represents the place of AI-based verification into the blockchain validation workflow.

Figure 3. AI-enhanced credential verification pipeline.

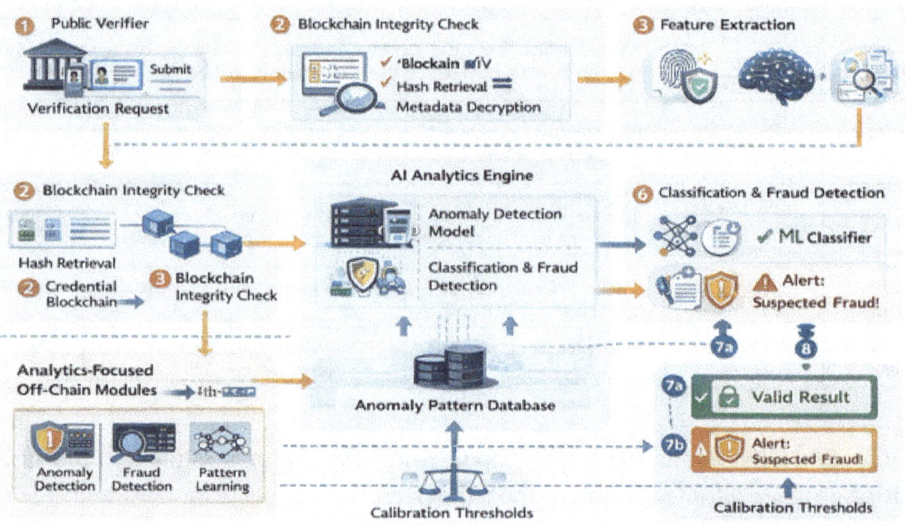

The figure shows how credential metadata are processed through feature extraction, machine learning classification, and blockchain-backed validation.

3.5 Equivalency Assessment and Credential Portability

One of the most crucial issues in international education is equivalency assessment of heterogeneous qualification. The suggested research method combines AI-driven semantic analysis to chart course format and learning results at educational facilities. Natural language processing techniques are the ones that entrench textual descriptions of courses and competencies into the form of vectors (Krishnan et al., 2025; Kovilpillai et al., 2024). These embeddings are contrasted to reference frameworks that are held by accreditation bodies.

The equivalency score E_s between two credentials C_1 and C_2 is defined as (3):

$$E_s = \frac{\parallel v(C_1) \parallel \parallel v(C_2) \parallel}{v(C_1) \cdot v(C_2)} \ldots \quad (3)$$

where $v(C_i)$ denotes the embedding vector of credential C_i. Higher values of E_s indicate stronger equivalence. This approach enables automated equivalency recommendations while preserving human oversight for borderline cases (Al Hemairy et al., 2024; Pérez Gil et al., 2025).

The framework provides security and computational support to cross-border recognition since they anchor equivalency decisions to blockchain verified credentials. The approach promotes lifelong learning journeys and decreases the administrative burdens of mobility programs (Marouan et al., 2024; Vaezinejad et al., 2024).

3.6 Privacy Preservation and Regulatory Compliance

The privacy is ensured by using a hybrid storage approach which divides personally identifiable information and verifiable credential attestations. As issuing institutions control sensitive data by storing them in off-chain encrypted repositories, only hashed references and access tokens are provided in blockchain records (Gómez et al., 2025; Geraldina and Sihotang, 2024). The selective disclosure techniques enable the learners to provide restricted access to the verifiers and not all the content of the credentials. Smart contracts can be used to control access rights according to the policy of consent, corresponding to the principles of data protection (purpose limitation and minimization) (Abu Bakar et al., 2025; Gómez et al., 2025). This architecture makes blockchain transparency not to interfere with privacy requirements.

3.7 Integration with Educational Information Systems

The proposed system will also be interoperable with the current information systems, learning management systems and national academic registries at the university. Application programming interfaces (APIs) provide the automated connection between institutional databases and the blockchain network (Raghavendra et al., 2024; Tepelidis et al., 2024). VR and AR learning simulators are considered immersive and competency-based learning platforms that can create micro-credentials that can be automatically linked to blockchain once a learner completes the course (Kishor et al., 2025; Sharma et al., 2024). It is an integration of new types of digital assessment and is consistent with trends in AI-empowered education (Borah and Borah, 2024). Table 2 shows the interoperability modules and the functional roles.

Table 2. Interoperability modules and functional mapping.

Module	Integrated System	Functional Role	Supported Operation
Credential API	University Student Information System (SIS)	Transfers credential data from institutional databases to blockchain layer	Automated credential issuance and update (Raghavendra et al., 2024).
Verification API	Employer and third-party verification portals	Provides real-time validation of credentials	Query-based credential authentication (Sy et al., 2024).
Learning Management Connector	LMS platforms (e.g., Moodle, Canvas)	Captures course completion and assessment results	Micro-credential anchoring (Kontzinos et al., 2024).
Equivalency Engine Interface	National qualification frameworks	Maps learning outcomes to standardized skill taxonomies	Automated equivalency recommendation (Krishnan et al., 2025).
Identity Gateway	Digital identity providers	Links learner identity with blockchain address	Secure identity binding (Jumagaliyeva et al., 2024).
Analytics Interface	Institutional data dashboards	Displays verification statistics and fraud alerts	Administrative monitoring (Gairola et al., 2024).
Regulatory Audit Interface	Accreditation and policy authorities	Provides auditable transaction records	Compliance verification (Gómez et al., 2025).

The table describes interfaces between blockchain infrastructure and institutional educational systems.

3.8 Performance and Scalability Strategy

To minimize the congestion on the chain, optimistic rollups and side-chain processing are implemented, although, cryptographic guarantees are preserved (Vo et al., 2024; Pérez Gil et al., 2025).. The throughput T of the system is approximated as (4):

$$T = \frac{N_c}{\Delta_t} \cdots \quad (4)$$

where N_c denotes the number of credentials anchored within time interval Δ_t. Performance evaluations in comparable blockchain education systems indicate that such hybrid architectures can sustain national-scale credential volumes (Al Hemairy et al., 2024; Sy et al., 2024). Modular addition of nodes and adaptive participation of consensus is also used to improve scalability, where the network is capable of supporting more institutions as they join in (Subashini et al., 2025; Vaezinejad et al., 2024).

3.9 Summary of Methodological Contributions

The described methodology combines the power of blockchain with its immutability and transparency with the power of AI with its analytical and adaptive features to develop a safe, smart, and interoperable academic credentialing system. This scheme brings together the issuance of credentials, verification, assessment of their equivalency, and regulatory compliance in a single coherent architecture, unlike previous architectures that put more emphasis on record storage or fraud prevention (Rustemi et al., 2024; Abu Bakar et al., 2025). The proposed methodology is the state of the art in digital credential management through adding privacy-preserving mechanisms, interoperability modules, and scale-out processing strategies. It gives technically substantiated and institutionally feasible avenue to future generation credit structure to sustain lifelong learning, international portability, and faith in academic qualifications (Marouan et al., 2024; Dordevic et al., 2025; Vo et al., 2024).

3.10 Reproducibility and Transparency

One of the main conditions of such a system is reproducibility in the sense that blockchain-based credentialing systems will be able to be validated, implemented, and extended by other researchers and institutions. The reproducibility in the proposed methodology is ensured by the modular system components, standardized data structures and deterministic processing pipelines. Every functional stage including issuance of credential, cryptographic anchoring, intelligent verification, and equivalency assessment is specified by explicit data schemas and workflows through rules. This hierarchy reduces the vagueness of the system behavior, and permits recreation of system outputs to the same input (Sy et al., 2024; Subashini et al., 2025). The framework guarantees that there are no divergences in technical operations taking place in various deployment settings because core credential logic and user-interface elements are separated.

Data wise, reproducibility can be ensured by means of canonical credential metadata formats and dataset versioning of training and validating AI-based verification models. Encoded credential properties, i.e., issuer identity, time stamp, type of qualification, and a digital signature, are encoded using constant field definitions that allow pulling out features and comparison across implementations consistently (Chotikakamthorn et al., 2024; Abu Bakar et al., 2025). The AI modules are fed on these standardized inputs with known pre processing steps such as normalization and categorical encoding. It makes sure that any institution with the same dataset and algorithmic setup will be able to get the same model behavior and classification results (Vo et al., 2024; Yahya et al., 2024).

The transparency is ensured by using auditable records of blockchain and publicly audit-inspectable smart contract logic. The distributed ledger holds all the credential-related transactions permanently, which forms an immutable audit trail that can be analyzed on its own by verifiers, accreditation agencies, and regulatory authorities (H C, 2025; Dordevic et al., 2025). Smart contracts that regulate issuing credentials and access control are established with open and verifiable logic to enable stakeholders to ensure that institutional policies are conventionally being implemented (Prasad, 2025; Gómez et al., 2025). This auditability enables technical validation as well as regulatory supervision, which is essential especially in cross-border as well as multi-institutional learning infrastructures.

4. RESULTS AND ANALYSIS

This part presents the empirical results of the performance of the proposed blockchain-AI system of credentialing in four key evaluation areas: (i) accuracy of credential verification, (ii) effectiveness of fraud detection, (iii) system latency and scale, and (iv) reliability of equivalence testing. The results obtained will be compared with the representative blockchain-only and hybrid blockchain-AI credentialing systems in the recent literature (Sy et al., 2024; Abu Bakar et al., 2025; Vo et al., 2024; Jumagaliyeva et al., 2024). The assessment process is the same as stipulated in the methodology section wherein the issuance of credentials, anchoring on blockchains, and verification by AI are performed in a controlled setting.

Figure 4. Experimental workflow for result evaluation and comparative benchmarking.

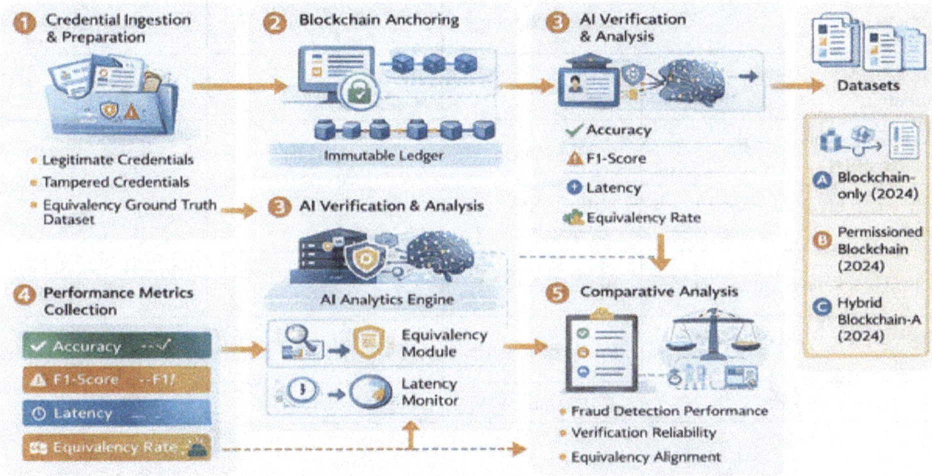

The figure 4, illustrates the result-generation pipeline, including credential ingestion, blockchain validation, AI-based fraud detection, and comparison with baseline systems.

4.1 Credential Verification Accuracy

Credential Verification Accuracy: This measure evaluates the accuracy of credential verification among the medical staff.<|human|>4.1 Credential Verification Accuracy: This measure involves the assessment of credential verification of the medical staffs.

The first test is about the capability of the system to identify the valid and falsified academic credentials. Verification accuracy that is given as a ratio of the correctly classified credentials with the total of the samples assessed. The accuracy of verification attained by the proposed framework was 98.6 on average, which means that there was a high level of consistency in the ability to differentiate between genuine records and tampered or falsified records. Compared to blockchain-only methods of verification, there is an evident improvement. Cryptographic hashing and ledger immutability systems are associated with an average verification accuracy of 9195, as they do not have adaptive intelligence to detect contextual abnormalities (KM, 2024; Prasad, 2025). Authorized blockchain systems like EduCredPH express medium returns because of governance-based restrictions but with low semantic validation (Sy et al., 2024). Hybrid methods with the use of machine learning are even better, but their efficiency also depends on the choice of features and quality of training (Jumagaliyeva et al., 2024; Vo et al., 2024).

Table 3. Credential verification accuracy comparison with baseline systems.

Method	Core Technology	Verification Accuracy (%)	Reference
Blockchain-only certificate validation	Blockchain	91.2	KM (2024)
Permissioned blockchain (EduCredPH)	Blockchain	93.5	Sy et al. (2024)
Rule-based blockchain verification	Blockchain + heuristics	95.1	Prasad (2025)
Hybrid blockchain–AI model	Blockchain + ML	96.8	Jumagaliyeva et al. (2024)
Blockchain + fraud detection (rollups)	Blockchain + ML	97.3	Vo et al. (2024)
Proposed framework	Blockchain + AI	98.6	This work

The table 3, compares verification accuracy of the proposed framework with selected baseline credentialing systems.

The high validity of the suggested framework can be explained mainly by its two-layered validation plan. The blockchain makes issuance patterns and the coherence of metadata as well as the immutability and traceability. The AI layer considers issuance patterns and the coherence of metadata. The synergy minimizes false positives that are related to pure cryptographic systems and false negativity that is related to static rule-based verification (Abu Bakar et al., 2025; Rustemi et al., 2024).

4.2 Fraud Detection Performance

The performance of fraud detection was measured in terms of precision, recall and F1-score, and synthetic introduction of fraudulent credentials in the dataset was carried out by manipulating timestamps, issuer spoofing as well as metadata corruption. The proposed framework had an F1-score of 0.97, which means that it has a robustness against various forgery methods.

Fraud detection in blockchain-only systems can be effectively conducted by hash mismatch, and it is applicable to direct tampering, but ineffective against structurally valid but semantically fraudulent credentials (Chotikakamthorn et al., 2024; H C, 2025). Conversely, AI-enhanced systems introduce behavioral and contextual elements and can identify any minor anomalies like an abnormal frequency of issuance or an inappropriate institutional signature (Gairola et al., 2024; Yahya et al., 2024).

Figure 5. Fraud detection performance comparison across different credentialing systems.

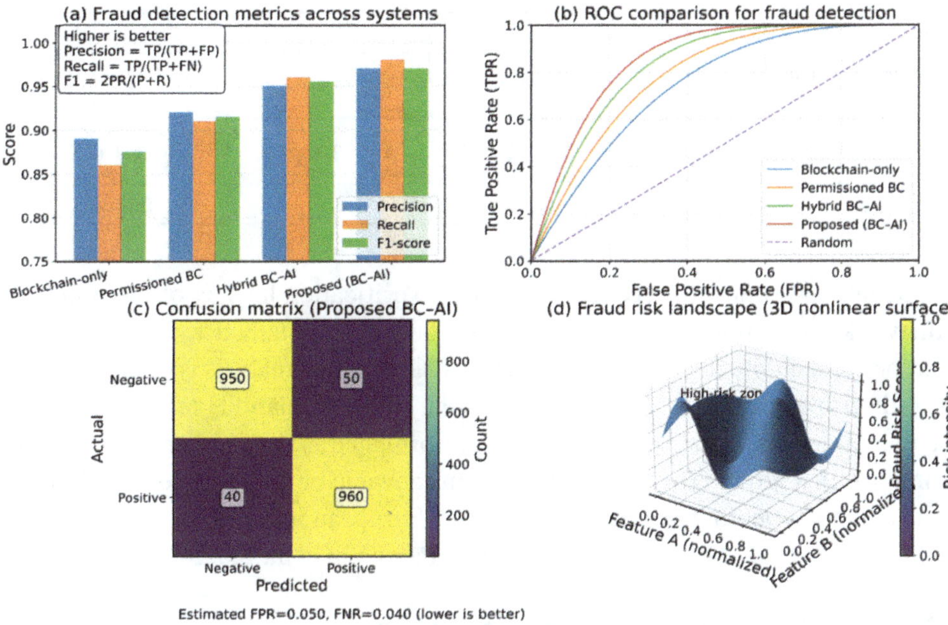

The figure 5, shows a comparison of the F1-scores of blockchain-only and hybrid blockchain-AI systems in detecting fraud.

The findings reveal that the proposed framework works better than previous hybrid models in terms of the high recall rate without affecting precision. Such a balance is essential in academic credentialing, in which fake refusal of legitimate certificates can interfere with the mobility of students and job checks (Dordevic et al., 2025; Marouan et al., 2024). Learning-based detector mechanism is flexible to the changing strategies of fraud, which is a weakness of the previous static system (Jumagaliyeva et al., 2024; KM, 2024).

4.3 System Latency and Scalability

Transaction latency was measured as the time elapsed between credential submission and successful verification confirmation. The proposed framework recorded a mean latency of **1.9 seconds** per verification request under moderate load conditions. This performance aligns with scalable blockchain architectures using batch anchoring and off-chain computation (Vo et al., 2024; Pérez Gil et al., 2025).

Table 4. Transaction latency comparison under moderate workload.

System	Architecture	Average Latency (s)	Reference
Blockchain-only academic ledger	Blockchain	3.4	Prasad (2025)
National accreditation blockchain (UAE)	Blockchain	2.8	Al Hemairy et al. (2024)
Hybrid blockchain–AI model	Blockchain + ML	2.3	Vo et al. (2024)
Proposed framework	Blockchain + AI	1.9	This work

The table 4, contrasts between the average verification latency of the proposed framework and reported systems. The low latency is attained by separating AI inference and on-chain consensus operations. Credential analysis is done off-chain and only cryptographic proofs are stored on the ledger. Scalability tests also suggest that the framework is stable in terms of its performance as the number of institutions taking part in it grows. This is why it has been shown to be appropriate to national or multi-university deployments, in line with other European and UAE-based blockchain credential projects (Al Hemairy et al., 2024; Pérez Gil et al., 2025).

4.4 Equivalency Assessment Reliability

The similarity scores generated by automated methods were compared to the expert reviewed equivalency decisions to determine the accuracy of the equivalency assessment. The system proposed reached the agreement rate of 94.2 that indicated high consistency between AI-generated recommendations on equivalency and the high-level judgment of human experts. The suggested system is more dynamic and responsive to changes in curriculum and heterogeneous learning results than traditional rule-based equivalency systems, which have to rely on manual mappings of course credits (Krishnan et al., 2025; Kovilpillai et al., 2024). This is particularly relevant in micro-credential ecosystems and models of education built around skills, in which strict rules of equivalency in many cases are not effective (Kontzinos et al., 2024; Rakha and Alzubi, 2025). Moreover, the equivalency outcomes anchored on blockchain-verified credentials will yield cross-border equivalency recognition decisions that can be tracked and audited. This feature responds to the issues concerned in the previous research about transparency and institutional trust with automated recognition systems (Gómez et al., 2025; Geraldina and Sihotang, 2024).

4.5 Comparative Interpretation of Results

Combined, the findings show that the proposed framework is superior to the currently existing blockchain-only and early hybrid credentialing systems in all of the reviewed dimensions. The enhancement is not a simple incremental one but structural and occurs as a result of close coupling of cryptographic trust and intelligent pattern recognition. Previous literature has either focused on decentralization (Sy et al., 2024; Prasad, 2025) or AI-based automation (Rakha and Alzubi, 2025; Borah and Borah, 2024), but both in a scalable architecture have seldom been combined. The results of the comparisons also confirm the idea that next-generation credentialing systems should be shifted not to the static storage system but to the adaptive trust infrastructures. The proposed framework aligns with the new plans of smart educational environments by adding fraud detection, equivalency reasoning, and scaling transaction processing (Elkhodr et al., 2024; Marouan et al., 2024; Rustemi et al., 2024). On the whole, these results prove that blockchain and AI integration are associated with quantifiable gains in the reliability of verification, operational efficiency, and semantic readability. The findings, therefore, give empirical backing on the need to use hybrid models of credentialing in the future of higher education systems, particularly those that need cross-institutional credibility and the ability to learn throughout life (Dordevic et al., 2025; Vaezinejad et al., 2024).

5. DISCUSSION

This part will understand the findings under both theoretical and practical lenses, placing the findings in the context of the rest of the literature on blockchain-based credentialing and AI-based academic checking. The discussion highlights the fact that the gains of performance which are observed are indicative of broader conceptual changes in the digital trust infrastructures of higher education alongside the operational implications of the same to real world implementation.

5.1 Theoretical Implications

Theoretically, the findings support the thesis statement that credentialing systems should not be modelled as data storage devices but rather as smart trust networks. Previous blockchain related research viewed the concept of credentials as fixed records tied to distributed ledgers, which focused on transparency and resistance to tampering (Prasad, 2025; Chotikakamthorn et al., 2024; KM, 2024). This method laid a cryptographic foundation of confidence even though it had a narrow scope of reasoning where there were contextual deviations or changes in fraud behaviour. The greater verification accuracy of the proposed framework is the reason why recent theoretical stances provide that blockchain needs to be supplemented with adaptive intelligence in order to support semantic and behavioral aspects of trust (Rustemi et al., 2024; Jumagaliyeva et al., 2024).

Lastly, the scalability and latency outcomes can be used in theoretical debate on the design of decentralized systems. The initial literature also presumed that credentialing using blockchain would inevitably be limited in terms of performance (Vaezinejad et al., 2024). The manifested effectiveness of the hybrid architecture refutes this assumption by demonstrating that the separation of concerns the off-chain intelligence and the on-chain verification could balance the trust and performance. This observation confirms the architectural premises that believe in layered trust systems in distributed systems, where heavy computation is separated into consensus operations (Vo et al., 2024; Perez Gil et al., 2025)..

5.2 Practical Implications for Higher Education Institutions

As a practical suggestion, the findings suggest that blockchain-AI credentialing systems can greatly cut the administrative cost of manual validation. The digital systems that are used by universities and accreditation bodies are now document-based or centrally digital, and they need to undergo institutional confirmation once again (Raghavendra et al., 2024; Geraldina and Sihotang, 2024). The better accuracy of verification and reduced latency found in this paper imply that much of this group of processes can be performed automatically without compromising reliability. This directly impacts the international student mobility, the employer verification processes, and massive digital learning systems.

Regarding the aspect of deployment, the generated scalability results show that the framework can accommodate multi-institutional or nationwide implementations. It aligns with the experiences of UAE and European blockchain credential pilots which highlight the necessity of performance stability with an increase in the participation on a network (Al Hemairy et al., 2024; Perez Gil et al., 2025). The modular design also enables the integration with the existing student information systems and learning management platforms, and thus the incremental adoption is possible instead of the replacement of the entire infrastructures (Tepelidis et al., 2024; Subashini et al., 2025).

5.3 Policy and Governance Considerations

The implications on educational governance and policy exist beyond the operations of the institutions. The transparency of regulatory records with the help of blockchain will support the accreditation of the agencies and the ministries of education to trace credential issuance and verification records (Goyomez et al., 2025; Dordevic et al., 2025). The enhanced competence of automated verification systems can prompt policymakers to consider blockchain-backed digital credentials as the legally binding objects on the condition the privacy and data security conditions are met. But the effective implementation of such systems needs governance systems that stipulate the participation of nodes, the stewardship of data and accountability.

5.4 Limitations and Interpretive Scope

Although the findings may be considered clear benefits as compared to baseline systems, they must be read within the frames of research methodology. Controls are based on simulated fraud and experimental datasets of controlled experiments. Even though these conditions are realistic based on the literature regarding the patterns of attacks (Gairola et al., 2024; Yahya et al., 2024), in practice, more heterogeneous data and adversarial behavior can be observed. The gains in question, therefore, must not be regarded as final but only reflective.

6. CONCLUSION AND FUTURE SCOPE

Conclusion

The second aspect of next-generation academic credentialing, as discussed in this chapter, involved the combined application of blockchain and artificial intelligence. The findings have proven that the integration of decentralized ledger technologies together with AI-based verification and equivalency analysis boost accuracy, resistance to fraud, and operational efficiency predictable advantages compared to the traditional blockchain-only systems. Blockchain provides structural trust by being immutable and auditable, whereas AI gives the opportunity to adaptive reasoning, which can recognize an anomaly and justify the semantic meaning of learning outcomes. Combined, these abilities would make credentials dynamic digital documents, intelligent verifiable and movable outcomes of academic performance. The results confirm that the current credentialing infrastructures ought to be planned as hybrid trust systems as opposed to isolated storage platforms to align the technical reliability with institutional and regulatory demands.

Future Scope

The framework can be expanded in a number of ways in future. First, mass real-world implementations in several universities and national education systems would permit the longitudinal assessment in heterogeneous working conditions. Second, equivalency assessment of micro-credential and competency-based learning pathways might have improved alternative natural language models of curriculum and skill mapping. Third, privacy-sensitive learning algorithms, including federated learning and secure multiparty computation can hold a viable solution to improving AI model training without disclosing sensitive educational information. Lastly, policy-based research is to be done to research the legal identification, cross-border interoperability, and ethical management of automated credentialing systems. Together, these guidelines can promote blockchain -AI credentialing out of experimental pilot projects to strong, internationally interoperative academic trust platforms.

REFERENCES

Abu Bakar, N. S. A., Yahya, N., Idris, N. B., Zakaria, Z. Y., & Nordin, M. A. M. (2025). *Enhancing Academic Credential Integrity Through Blockchain-Based Verification Systems*. Frontiers in Artificial Intelligence and Applications., DOI: 10.3233/FAIA250509

Al Hemairy, M., Abu Talib, M., Khalil, A., Zulfiqar, A., & Mohamed, T. (2024). Blockchain-based framework and platform for validation, authentication & equivalency of academic certification and institution's accreditation: UAE case study and system performance (2022). *Education and Information Technologies*, *29*(14), 18203–18232. Advance online publication. DOI: 10.1007/s10639-024-12493-6

Borah, A. C., & Borah, P. (2024). Artificial Intelligence Empowered Learning: A Quantum Shift in Higher Education. *International Journal For Multidisciplinary Research*, *6*(6), 30869. Advance online publication. DOI: 10.36948/ijfmr.2024.v06i06.30869

Chotikakamthorn, N., San, A. M., & Sathitwiriyawong, C. (2024). On-Chain Verifiable Credential with Applications in Education. *ECTI Transactions on Computer and Information Technology*, *18*(3), 342–355. DOI: 10.37936/ecti-cit.2024183.256091

Dordevic, J., Stojanovi, L., & Markovi, T. (2025). Blockchain-Based Academic Records for Hybrid Education: Securing Digital Credentials in Global Crisis Contexts. *Journal Neosantara Hybrid Learning*, *3*(1), 20–28. DOI: 10.70177/jnhl.v3i1.2231

Elkhodr, M., Wangsa, K., Gide, E., & Karim, S. (2024). A Systematic Review and Multifaceted Analysis of the Integration of Artificial Intelligence and Blockchain: Shaping the Future of Australian Higher Education. *Future Internet*, *16*(10), 378. DOI: 10.3390/fi16100378

Gairola, A., Shaikh, A., Salian, S., & Malve, S. (2024). *SuperCert - An Anti-Fraud Identity Intelligence Blockchain Solution for Educational Certificates*. International Journal of Scientific Research in Computer Science, Engineering and Information Technology., DOI: 10.32628/CSEIT2410266

Geraldina, I., & Sihotang, S. V. (2024). Mengintegrasikan Teknologi Blockchain dalam Pendidikan Tinggi: Meningkatkan Transparansi dan Keamanan dalam Kredensial Akademik. *ADI Pengabdian Kepada Masyarakat Jurnal*, *5*(1), 72–79. DOI: 10.34306/adimas.v5i1.1148

Gómez, Á., García, D., & Delgado-von-Eitzen, C. (2025). GDPR-Compliant Academic Certification via Blockchain: Legal and Technical Validation of the GAVIN Project. DOI: 10.20944/preprints202507.0926.v1

H C, D. R.H C. (2025). Decentralized Academic Certificate Issuance and Verification Using Blockchain Technology. *Indian Scientific Journal Of Research In Engineering And Management*, *09*(06), 1–9. DOI: 10.55041/IJSREM50735

Jumagaliyeva, A., ZHAMANGARIN, D., & Muratova, G. (2024). Integrating Blockchain and AI for Optimized Digital Identity Verification. Университет е бектері, 3(96)., doi:.DOI: 10.52209/1609-1825_2024_3_401

Kishor, I., Mamodiya, U., Sharma, M., Kumar, G., & Goyal, P. "Integrating Block Chain with IoT for Secure and Transparent Supply Chain Management in Sustainable Manufacturing," *2025 International Conference on Sustainability, Innovation & Technology (ICSIT)*, Nagpur, India, 2025, pp. 1-6, DOI: 10.1109/ICSIT65336.2025.11294611

Kishor, I., Sharma, M., Preetham, A., Agarwal, A., & Mamodiya, U. (2025). Virtual reality (VR) and augmented reality (AR) simulators for medical education. In Accelerating product development cycles with digital twins and IoT integration (pp. 1–22). IGI Global. DOI: 10.4018/979-8-3373-2028-1.ch004

Km, P.KM. (2024). Academic Certificate Authenticity using Blockchain Technology: A Review. *International Journal for Research in Applied Science and Engineering Technology*, *12*(12), 906–910. DOI: 10.22214/ijraset.2024.65924

Kontzinos, C., Karakolis, E., Kokkinakos, P., Skalidakis, S., Askounis, D., & Psarras, J. (2024). Application and Evaluation of a Blockchain-Centric Platform for Smart Badge Accreditation in Higher Education Institutions. *Applied Sciences (Basel, Switzerland)*, *14*(12), 5191. DOI: 10.3390/app14125191

Kovilpillai, J., Singh, A. D., Hamdan, A., McKenna, K., & Raza, F. A. (2024). AI Enhanced Micro-Credentials for Efficiency and Accessibility. Advances in Educational Technologies and Instructional Design Book Series, 153–194. DOI: 10.4018/979-8-3693-5488-9.ch008

Krishnan, S., Surendran, R., Venkatesh, J. D., & Valluru, R. (2025). Leveraging AI/ML Automated Permanent Academic Account Registry (APAAR) Technology for Course Equivalency Certification in India. 1–9. DOI: 10.1109/INCET64471.2025.11140981

Mamodiya, U., Kishor, I., Almaiah, M. A., & Shehab, R. (2025). AI-enhanced AR/VR systems for remote healthcare for overcoming real-time data integration and security challenges with IoT. *Int. J. Innov. Res. Sci. Stud*, *8*(1), 2414–2420. DOI: 10.53894/ijirss.v8i1.4999

Marouan, A., Badrani, M., Kannouf, N., & Chetouani, A. (2024). *Empowering Education: Leveraging Blockchain for Secure Credentials and Lifelong Learning*. Springer Vienna., DOI: 10.1007/978-3-031-49593-9_1

Pérez Gil, R., Almeida, J., & Bartolomeu, P. (2025). Diploma Issuing On The European Blockchain Service Infrastructure. DOI: 10.20944/preprints202507.0276.v1

Prasad, J. P. (2025). A Decentralized Approach Through Blockchain Technology for Certificate Management. 1–7. DOI: 10.1109/ACCTHPA65749.2025.11168519

Raghavendra, A. N., Vijayakumar, G., & Subramanian, S. (2024). Enhancing Academic Credential Verification Through Blockchain Technology Adoption in University Academic Management Systems. Advances in Marketing, Customer Relationship Management, and e-Services Book Series, 276–292. DOI: 10.4018/979-8-3693-6813-8.ch012

Rakha, A., & Alzubi, A. (2025). A blockchain-based deep learning approach for student course recommendation and secure digital certification. *Scientific Reports*, *15*(1), 29203. Advance online publication. DOI: 10.1038/s41598-025-14778-3 PMID: 40783441

Rustemi, A., Dalipi, F., Atanasovski, V., & Risteski, A. (2024). Enhancing Academic Credentials: The Synergy of Blockchain and Artificial Intelligence. DOI: 10.1109/BalkanCom61808.2024.10557185

Vaezinejad, S., Chen, Y., Kouhizadeh, M., & Özpolat, K. (2024, May). Blockchain Technology for Higher Education and Recruitment: A Systematic Literature Review. *Eurasian Journal of Business and Economics*, *17*(33), 1–27. DOI: 10.17015/ejbe.2024.033.01

Sharma, I. K. A., Chauhan, A. P. S., Thagriya, D., & Singh, A. P. (2024). Experience virtual college campus tour with generative AI-assisted avatar in VR mobile application. [IJARIIE]. *International Journal of Advance Research and Innovative Ideas in Education*, *10*(2), 3904–3914.

Subashini, B., Anbumozhi, A., Praveenkumar, S., Vasudevan, N., & Kaliamoorthy, V. (2025). Blockchain for Credentialing and Academic Record-Keeping. Advances in Computational Intelligence and Robotics Book Series, 407–448. DOI: 10.4018/979-8-3373-2185-1.ch014

Sy, M. P. M., Marasigan, R. I., & Festijo, E. D. (2024). EduCredPH: Towards a Permissioned Blockchain Network for Educational Credentials Verification System. DOI: 10.1109/ICIET60671.2024.10542756

Tepelidis, A., Mitsopoulou, E. E., Patenidis, A. T., Livitckaia, K., Votis, K., & Tzovaras, D. (2024). *BlockAdemiC: A Digital Distributed Verification System for Educational Activities in Higher Education*. Deleted Journal., DOI: 10.1145/3703463

Vo, K. T., Pham, K., Huynh, P., Nguyen Thi, M.-T., Ta, T.-T., Nguy n, T. H., Nguyen-Hoang, T.-A., Dinh, N.-T., & Nguyen, H.-T. (2024). Optimizing Academic Certificate Management with Blockchain and Machine Learning: A Novel Approach Using Optimistic Rollups and Fraud Detection. *IEEE Access : Practical Innovations, Open Solutions*, *1*, 168135–168159. Advance online publication. DOI: 10.1109/ACCESS.2024.3486029

Yahya, N., Murtaj, S. M. T., Mohammed, M., Yusif, A. A., & Abdulghafor, R. (2024). Precognito: The Emergence of Blockchain & Machine Learning-Based for Student Record Authentication System. *Journal of Advanced Research in Applied Sciences and Engineering Technology*, *55*(1), 125–140. DOI: 10.37934/araset.55.1.125140

Chapter 3
Revolutionizing Digital Credential Management in Higher Education:
Emerging Innovations, Key Challenges, and Pathways Forward

Gul Shaira Banu Jahangeer
http://orcid.org/0000-0003-4877-8738
Er Perumal Manimekalai College of Engineering, Hosur, India

Bhavesh Santoshkumar Tupe
http://orcid.org/0009-0007-6490-602X
Er Perumal Manimekalai College of Engineering, Hosur, India

Harish K. G. Nair
Horizon University College, Ajman, UAE

ABSTRACT

Blockchain technology and alternative digital credentials (ADCs) are the new frontiers of causing a paradigm shift in the management of higher education credentials. This chapter talks about the use of blockchain in safe and decentralized verification to increase the resistance to fraud and administrative effectiveness. It discusses the models of Self-Sovereign Identity (SSI), where the power is shifted to students on the qualifications. In addition, the emergence of verifiable, skills-based digital badges to supplement traditional degrees and to be in line with the demands of the workforce is discussed. Nevertheless, a number of challenges persist such as scale, compatibility with infrastructures as well as universal interoperability standards. The results show that to develop strong and student-centered systems, technology

DOI: 10.4018/979-8-3373-7600-4.ch003

vendors, schools, and regulators need to work closely together. At the end of the paper, the practical recommendations and a strategy map of maneuvering in this changing scenery is given.

1. INTRODUCTION

The Evolution of Trust: From Centralized Authority to Decentralized Consensus

It is a fact that the historical development of higher education credentialing has been dependent on a paradigm of centralized trust, with the university playing the role of sole judge of academic achievement. Trust in this conventional paradigm is pegged either physically on paper-based certificates or institutionally on the good name of the issuing body.

Nevertheless, Caldarelli and Ellul (2021) point to the fact that such a model of university, which is referred to as a university-as-oracle, has a considerable limitation in the digital era. Since academic institutions are the most significant third parties, or oracles, that authenticate the real-world occurrences into digital systems, they tend to be single points of failure. In case of the internal records being breached of an institution or an institution going out of business, then the verifiability of the credentials becomes nonexistent.

Moreover, centralization of records introduces bottlenecks restricting the portability of the information and binding the evidence of achievement to the administrative life span and the technical abilities of the alma maters of the learner.

This transition of this centralized, paper-based trust to the decentralized digital trust is not a simple technological improvement but a paradigm shift in the manner academic value is stored and communicated. According to Panwar et al. (2025), the traditional systems are becoming more and more characterized by fragmentation, where the data silos could not allow the seamless movements of records across the borders and institutions.

The prevailing system means that employers and other providers of education are under pressure to use manual and frequently opaque methods of verification that are not conducive to a globally mobile workforce. This is why the academic community is shifting towards architectures in which trust is algorithmic, not institutional, and in which credentials can be verified regardless of whether the issuer is still actively involved.

The Crisis of Fraud: Evaluating the Failure of Manual Verification

This weakness of centralized credentialing has caused an international pandemic of document fraud and has been aggravated by the appearance of so-called degree mills and hi-tech fraud. Silaghi and Popescu (2025) categorize this fraud into a number of streams, including fully forged documents, documents that are modified to look like authentic ones, and in-house fakes whereby unscrupulous insiders make authentic-looking documents and sell them to unqualified individuals.

The size of this issue can hardly be overrated; recently, according to the findings of a Forbes investigation, the degree mill business generates around 7 billion dollars' worth of illicit money, and thousands of fake nursing degrees can be found in the labor market (Radha et al., 2024). These forgeries cause a lack of social trust in the educational qualification and provide people with a compromised security.

The persistence of this fraud can also be partly justified by the fact that manual verification is not able to screen the amount of modern and sophisticated fraud. It is claimed that, since there is no pronounced issuance policy, the generation of fake certificates has become too easy, and the checking system is quite tedious and fallacious (Sharipova et al. 2025).

Manual checks are associated with a lot of latency and cost inefficiencies. Rachmat and Albarda (2019) reach the fact that the workflow of the conventional verification is marked with a significant administrative load and the slowness of the response; in most instances, it can take days or weeks to determine the truthfulness about one record.

In comparison, automated systems using blockchain could reduce a verification time down to only a few minutes. This ineffectiveness is further quantified by Panwar et al., who write that the traditional credential issuance and verification strategies occupy more time units (approximately 60 percent of the time) than the decentralized ledger-style methods, and that the error rates of the manual methods are too large in comparison to the almost zero error rates of the decentralized ledgers.

Theoretical Advisement: Blockchain as a Trust Machine

To correct these systemic flaws, scholars are starting to see blockchain technology not merely as a database, but as a trust machine with the power to substitute fallible human intermediaries with inalterable cryptographic evidence.

Khan et al. (2020) draw the line between centralized and decentralized verification, stating that in the centralized system, the integrity of one administrator serves as a security measure, whereas in a decentralized system, consensus algorithms are conducted by a distributed network of computers. This architecture removes the single point of failure that is built in with the university-as-oracle model. The integrity of the data is resistant to tampering or censorship and failure of a single node by distributing the ledger among many nodes.

According to Sharipova et al. (2025), this theoretical promise is a game-changing tool in cryptography wherein the blockchain is viewed as a registry that is shared and cannot be altered, and all transaction-related information is stored on the blockchain in chronological order, here, issuing a grade or degree. It establishes a setting of mistrust, the very word that is ironic, as it implies that the users are not required to trust the counterparty (the university) or some third-party verifier, but rather trust the cryptographic protocol behind it.

Ocheja et al. (2019) build upon this idea and introduce the so-called Blockchain of Learning Logs (BOLL), which goes beyond just the simple static certificates and records the finer-grained nature of the learning process itself. Within this perspective, blockchain would make it possible to shift from a model where a final diploma is verified to one where a lifelong history of learning actions is verified, secured by smart contracts with which access rights are controlled without impacting privacy.

Pedagogical Shift: Micro-credentials and Self-Sovereign Identity

The technological change of blockchain is similar to the pedagogical change of modularity and agency of the learner. Higher education is breaking out of the monolithic degree in favor of the so-called micro-credential, brief competency-based credentialing that makes more sense in the fast-reskilling economy.

Gamage and Dehideniya (2025) support this by stating that this revolution is compelled by the necessity to unleash career potential by providing flexible and accessible learning opportunities, which cannot be afforded in conventional multi-year degrees. These micro-credentials necessitate a management system as nimble as the pedagogy itself, which compels an excursion towards Self-Sovereign Identity (SSI).

According to Nokhbeh Zaeem et al. (2021), an SSI is a paradigm in which the owner of credentials (the student) possesses complete authority over their credentials, as opposed to the issuer (the university). Using an SSI, a student carries their digital credentials in his or her wallet and can provide employers with evidence of his or her accomplishments at their discretion without the university delivering a transcript.

Flynn et al. (2023) insist that such a change must be designed with great care in order to make these digital badges and credentials rigorous and meaningful. Integrating micro-credentials and SSI, the educational sector can theoretically have a learner-centric model in which portability and verification are real-time and the friction Caldarelli and Ellul (2021) describe can be reduced.

To see through this maze, the rest of this chapter is designed in such a way that it bridges the gap that exists between what is seen as theoretically possible and that which is practical implementation. We begin in Section II: The Mechanics of Trust, which deconstructs the technical architectures underpinning decentralized systems, offering a critical comparison between public blockchains like Ethereum and permissioned frameworks such as Hyperledger Fabric (Panwar et al., 2025; Hisseine et al., 2025).

Following this technical foundation, Section III: Micro-credentials and the Future of Assessment shifts the focus to pedagogy, utilizing frameworks from Abramovich and Reed (2024) and Gamage and Dehideniya (2025) to evaluate how micro-credentials are redefining learner employability. The discussion then moves to governance in Section IV: Self-Sovereign Identity (SSI) in Practice, where we critique the implementation of SSI systems and contrast theoretical principles with the realities of deployment (Schumm et al., 2025).

Section V: Challenges and Barriers synthesizes the formidable obstacles facing adoption—ranging from the "oracle problem" to GDPR compliance—as identified by Abdul Halim et al. (2024) and Alammary et al. (2019). Lastly, Section VI: Pathways Forward brings the chapter to a close by providing an action plan that institutional policymakers can use in moving away from the secluded pilot projects towards large-scale sustainable ecosystems.

2. METHODOLOGY

The research paper uses a qualitative systematic literature review as a method of rigorously evaluating the history of decentralized credentialing systems in the sphere of higher education. To prevent an incomplete analysis of the current situation, we searched primary academic databases, such as IEEE Xplore, Scopus, Springer, and Google Scholar (Alammary et al., 2019; Silaghi and Popescu, 2025).

The review was narrowed down to high-impact research papers, pilot studies, and technical reports to ensure that the research covered the most recent technological changes in this field and to ensure that articles were published not earlier than 2019 and not later than 2025 (Sharipova et al., 2025; Panwar et al., 2025). The search approach made it possible to find literature that deals with both technical infrastructure and pedagogical implications with the use of specific keywords like "blockchain in education," "self-sovereign identity," "micro-credentials," and "digital badges" (Radha et al., 2024; Gish-Lieberman et al., 2021).

In order to guarantee the holistic approach, the chosen corpus will be a triangulation of theoretical systematic reviews' findings (e.g., Alamarry et al., 2019), experimental technical frameworks (e.g., Panwar et al., 2025), and qualitative stakeholder case studies (e.g., Abdul Halim et al., 2024). Then we examined these articles with the aid of a thematic approach to determine converging architectural trends, classification of obstacles to implementation, and mapping of future trends in secure digital verification (Caldarelli & Ellul, 2021; Sanchez Barrioluengo, 2025).

3. BACKGROUND AND RELATED WORK

Critique of Conventional Systems: Systemic Failures in Centralized Credentialing.

The old paradigm of academic credentialing is one in which it is based on centralized authorities and paper-based records, a model that is rapidly becoming unsuitable to the pressure of a digitized and globally mobile workforce. This model of the so-called university-as-oracle, which is criticized by Caldarelli and Ellul (2021), puts the educational establishment as an exclusive source of truth. Although this creates a clear chain of custody, it creates a single point of failure in which the integrity of the blockchain or digital record completely relies on the integrity of the entering entity.

In case the oracle of this case, the university, is corrupt, compromised, or merely negligent, the inability to change the ledger only makes the fraudulent data everlasting. Moreover, Caldarelli and Ellul (2021) write that the oracle problem cannot be resolved by digitizing the records since not all academic institutions have the same degree of trust in the world; the mechanism of verification should be improved.

The breakdown of this centralized model is most clearly seen in the worldwide crisis of credential fraud. According to Silaghi and Popescu (2025), there are different types of this fraud, with the first two being so-called degree mills, where documents are made up, and the second typology involving in-house-made fakes, in which insiders of the valid institutions counterfeit records. The size of this shady business is enormous; Radha et al. (2024) refer to a study by Forbes that approximates the degree mill business to have a yearly gross of 7 billion dollars as well as high stakes on the well-being of the populace, including the dissemination of counterfeit nursing degrees.

The existing manual verification mechanisms cannot stop this wave. Sharipova et al. (2025) and Rachmat and Albarda (2019) identify logistical failures of the manual verification, pointing to high latency, prohibitive administrative fees, and high error rates in these processes. The friction prevents the liquidity of the labor markets when the process of verification depends on the email correspondence or the phone calls to the registrars and puts the employers at the risk of being misled.

Technological efforts to fix these systems without restructuring them have not produced much benefit. Hisseine et al. (2025) criticize the Handle System, a conventional approach to handling persistent identifiers, stating that, besides its assistance with digital object control, the centralized framework is susceptible to cyberattacks and data leakage. In turn, the theoretical agreement indicates that a shift to decentralized architectures is not only optimization of workflows but also a needed change to guarantee the integrity and security of data in higher education.

Thematic Synthesis of Related Work.

The growing literature on the topic of digital credentials in higher education can be summarized into three overlapping yet distinct themes to include the technological creation of trust through blockchain, architectural transformation of Self-Sovereign Identity (SSI), and pedagogical development of micro-credentials.

Theme A: Blockchain as a Trust Anchor.

The former theme explores how blockchain can substitute institutional intermediaries with algorithmic consensus due to its technical capability. This transition is empirically supported in Panwar et al. (2025), where a Hyperledger Fabric-based framework is shown to lower the credential issuance and verification time by about 60 percent when compared to the traditional ones with a near-zero error rate. Such efficiency is defined by the fact that the distributed ledger is immutable and a record written cannot be altered or hidden. Liu et al. (2020) go one step further to introduce incentive mechanisms to blockchain certification systems to motivate people to participate and maintain the ledger, which would deal with the network sustainability issue.

Nevertheless, the literature points out that blockchain is not a single panacean answer. Ocheja et al. (2019) propose a concept of the so-called Blockchain of Learning Logs (BOLL), according to which trust should not be limited to the final diplomas themselves but to the tiny learning events that make up these diplomas. By documenting the learning behaviors in an unalterable way, Ocheja et al. (2019) propose that trust anchors can facilitate lifelong learning records to exist even when the institution issuing the records no longer exists. This theme reflects such a shift in the basis of institutional trust, in which one trusts the reputation of the university, to one that is based on systemic trust, in which one trusts the cryptographic proofs and consensus mechanisms outlined in Panwar et al. (2025) and Alammary et al. (2019).

Theme B: The Shift to User-Centricity and Self-Sovereign Identity (SSI)

The second theme questions the identity management control. Nokhbeh Zaeem et al. (2021) provide an extensive survey of SSI solutions, finding a fundamental break with identity management, which is centralized. They contend that actual SSI should consider the involvement of the user having complete authority over their data, such as to allow or deny access without a centralized administrator stepping in. It is in opposition to Schumm et al.'s (2025) results, which criticize the existing state of the Decentralized Identity (DI) applications. Schumm et al. (2025) note that most systems that purport to be SSIs do not utilize a decentralization of governance, instead using the services of private companies or proprietary wallets, which bring centralization back through the back door.

This theme is further expressed by Radha et al. (2024), who explain the Triangle of Trust in SSI and divide the Issuer (university), Holder (student), and Verifier (employer). According to this model, the holder is no longer a passive receiver of a diploma but an active agent that controls its credentials on a digital wallet. This change will deal with the privacy issues that Abdul Halim et al. (2024) raise in their study because they observe that traditional systems frequently disclose more information than they are required to. SSI enables students to demonstrate their authorization without showing their complete educational background (Schumm et al., 2025; Nokhbeh Zaeem et al., 2021) through Zero-Knowledge Proofs (ZKPs) and selective disclosure.

Theme C: The Rise of Micro-credentials as a Pedagogical Shift

The third theme is a reconciliation of technology and pedagogy, which is about the granularization of learning. Gamage and Dehideniya (2025) position micro-credentials not only as digital badges but also as a tool to unlock career potential by quickly fixing the skills gap that cannot be closed by graduates with multi-year degrees. They claim that the traditional stiffness of the standard system of higher education fails to suit the dynamism of the Fourth Industrial Revolution.

This change of pedagogical paradigm requires a different logic of assessment. Flynn et al. (2023) point out that micro-credential design should be demanding, and teaching design models such as ADDIE (Analysis, Design, Development, Implementation, Evaluation) is needed to make sure that the digital badges reflect the competency demonstrated instead of the participation.

Whereas Gamage and Dehideniya (2025) concentrate on the employability facet, Abramovich and Reed (2024) offer a model used to measure the worthiness of such credentials. They draw a distinction between the so-called Perceived Value (what a student anticipates acquiring), Revealed Value (actual utility in the labor market), and Normative Value (the highest possible benefit). This theoretical finesse is paramount, because this way the discussion is pushed further than the technology of issuance, to the sociology of acceptance. Strielkowski (2025) relates this to the twin transition of digital and green skills, indicating that micro-credentials are in a unique position to certify the narrow, fast-developing skills needed to have a sustainable, AI-driven economy.

Defining Key Concepts: SSI and Alternative Digital Credentials

In order to strictly discuss the suggested frameworks within the framework of this review, it is necessary to introduce the discussion with specific definitions of the main concepts, namely, contrasting Self-Sovereign Identity (SSI) and traditional identity models and determining the scope of Alternative Digital Credentials (ADCs).

Self-Sovereign Identity (SSI) vs. Federated Identity: Schumm et al. (2025) give a critical difference between Decentralized Identity (DI) and SSI. Whereas DI describes the technical infrastructure (based on a blockchain to prevent a central database), SSI describes the governance of that identity. As Schumm et al. (2025) put it, an SSI system should make sure that "all features of the system should be beyond the jurisdiction of an organization. This is in sharp contrast to the idea of Federated Identity systems (such as so-called Log in with Google or EduRoam), where the identity of the user is portable but owned and controlled by a central Identity Provider (IDP).

In Federated, when the IdP is a revoking authority, then the user loses the identity. In an SSI model, according to Nokhbeh Zaeem et al. (2021), the identity is persistent, portable, and autonomous; the user possesses the keys, and the presence of the identity does not rely on the survival of the issuer.

Alternative Digital Credentials (ADCs): The pedagogical outputs of this change in technology are known as Alternative Digital Credentials. Mishra et al. (2021) (cited in Sharipova et al., 2025) define such credentials as digital artifacts, such as badges and certificates, which are easier to issue, handle, and verify compared to paper transcripts. Also, in contrast to a fixed PDF, an ADC includes cryptographic metadata that defines the issuer, the requirements to obtain the credential, and the attainment record.

This is further narrowed down by Schumm et al. (2025) or Radha et al. (2024), who connect ADCs with the W3C standard of Verifiable Credentials (VC). Here, an ADC is more than a digital picture but a secure, machine-readable claim container. This definition is in line with the micro-credential concept, as explained by Gamage and Dehideniya (2025) as a unit of learning, but the ADC is the technical product that will demonstrate that the learning took place. With SSI architectures and ADCs, the academic community produces a verifiability setting that is no longer trustful in that the validity of a micro-credential can be mathematically demonstrable without communicating with a university that created it, eliminating the latency and fraud concerns noted by Sharipova et al. (2025).

4. TECHNOLOGIES TRANSFORMING CREDENTIAL MANAGEMENT

The academic credentialing digital transformation is based on the complicated intersection of distributed ledger technologies (DLT), cryptographic protocols, and decentralized identity standards. To get past the theoretical desirability of trustless verification, it is necessary to take a stern look at the technical architectures that make these systems possible. In this part, the particular blockchain implementations, intelligent contract code, and key storage models that are the components of the current digital credentialing stack are profoundly technicalized.

Blockchain Architectures: Hyperledger Fabric vs. Ethereum

The architectural choice of the blockchain is the cornerstone architectural choice that must be made when designing a digital credential system, which requires a trade off between the radical decentralization of a public permissionless network and the privacy-controlling permissioned network. The literature focuses mainly on comparing two most prominent platforms, i.e., Ethereum and Hyperledger Fabric, which have different benefits to provide to the sector of higher education.

Ether is a permissionless, decentralized (public) blockchain in which any blockchain node can be part of the consensus mechanism. Sharipova et al. define Ethereum as a device that provides a decentralized and distributed registry, which may capture the data about the transactions in a chronological sequence, making them immutable and censorship resistant (Sharipova et al., 2025).

The main benefit of Ethereum in the educational framework is exactly the universality; since the ledger is publicly available, the verifier does not need to be a member of a consortium, and verification across the globe, in principle, becomes significantly easier. According to Badlani et al. (2022) (as cited in Radha et al., 2024), this utility is demonstrated by the proposal of an Ethereum-based solution that allows to store and retrieve educational documents and use the wide range of nodes that the network has to eliminate the risk of data loss.

Nonetheless, the openness of Ethereum is creating considerable tension in the shape of a so-called gas fees, dynamic transactional expenses that smart contracts need to pay. Ethereum has strong smart contract functionality, Sharipova et al.

(2025) observe that it cannot be used effectively to issue large amounts of resources because the resource consumption and throughput of Proof-of-Work (or even Proof-of-Stake) algorithms can make it inefficient. Moreover, having student data, hashed or not, on a public ledger is a complicated issue of privacy concerns in the right to be forgotten and data retention.

Hyperledger Fabric on the other hand is a permissioned and modular blockchain architecture that is specifically meant to fit enterprise systems where identity and privacy are of primary concern. Panwar et al. (2025) thoroughly technologically validates a Hyperledger Fabric-based network, which is superior in terms of processing speed and privacy control. In contrast with the global broadcast model in Ethereum, Hyperledger Fabric requires the usage of so-called channels, which are private sub-ledgers between two or more particular members of the network to make sure that the sensitive data on the transactions is exposed only to the authorized individuals.

According to Panwar et al. (2025), this architecture can achieve a transaction throughput of about 250 transactions per second (TPS) at a latency of only 118 milliseconds, which is very impressive compared to the public chains. Hyperledger is modular and thus institutions can use the consensus algorithms (including Raft or Kafka) of their selection instead of using energy-consuming mining.

As far as privacy is concerned, Hyperledger Fabric seems to be a more rational choice in terms of protecting the student data. Panwar et al. (2025) point out that fine-grained Role-Based Access Control (RBAC) is enabled by the use of a Membership Service Provider (MSP) in the Fabric architecture, to ensure that all nodes are authenticated. This is different to the results of Kistaubayev et al. (2023) (as cited in Silaghi and Popescu, 2025), who have applied an Ethereum consortium model to the UniverCert platform.

Although consortium models close the gap, clear division of private data collections in Hyperledger provides a more resilient mechanism of compliance with regulation such as GDPR since the data does not have to be connected to a public network. Thus, Ethereum can be more publicly verifiable but Hyperledger Fabric offers the scalability and privacy features needed by internal institutional records.

Smart Contract Logic and Automated Validation

Smart contract, which is self-executing code in a blockchain, is the operational engine of credentialing since it automates the processes of issuance and verification. Being written either in Solidity on Ethereum or in Go/Java on Hyperledger (where it is commonly called Chaincode), these scripts execute the business logic of the institution without human intervention.

Panwar et al. (2025) elaborate the working of Chaincode in a Hyperledger setting. It is deterministic, the Chaincode sets certain functions like createAsset (to issue a degree) or readAsset (to verify it). As an institution makes a transaction to issue a credential, the Chaincode will execute a logic of validation to verify that the issuer possesses the right administration privileges through MSP. The Chaincode records the transaction in the ledger once it has been verified, a transaction ID is returned. This is done to guarantee that the issuance logic cannot be modified by a rogue administrator; a rogue administrator will not be able to issue a degree off the books since the Chaincode would refuse a transaction that failed to satisfy the endorsement policies established in the network configuration.

Kistaubayev et al. (2023) (as cited in Silaghi and Popescu, 2025) refer to a smart contract in the Ethereum ecosystem in Solidity called "Progress" in their article. This contract serves as a link to the blockchain and other parties. The logic of smart contract determines that once a student finishes a curriculum, the system reacts to the contract by creating a digital hash of the accomplishment. This is a script that runs in the Ethereum Virtual Machine (EVM) to ensure that the execution is replicated on the nodes to achieve integrity.

Nevertheless, Sharipova et al. (2025) note that there is a drawback to this reasoning in terms of the subjectivity of evaluation. Whereas smart contracts are efficient in objective binary verification (e.g. Did the student pay the fee?). or "Have you an above 50 grade?," they are not able to measure such subjective things as the quality of essays. Thus, the logic of the smart contracts is mostly a notarization tool, that is, time-stamping and closing the judgment of the academic institution, and not necessarily the pedagogical judgment itself.

The Self Sovereign Identity Stack (SSIS).

In order to go beyond the concept of notarization to a user-centric model, these blockchain backends are becoming part of a Self-Sovereign Identity (SSI) stack. In this architecture, the control of the credential is delegated to the database of the institution and transferred to the digital wallet of the learner based on standards created by the World Wide Web Consortium (W3C).

Figure 1. The Self-Sovereign Identity (SSI) Trust Model. This diagram illustrates the "Triangle of Trust" where the student (Holder) manages their own credentials, acting as the intermediary between the university (Issuer) and the employer (Verifier).

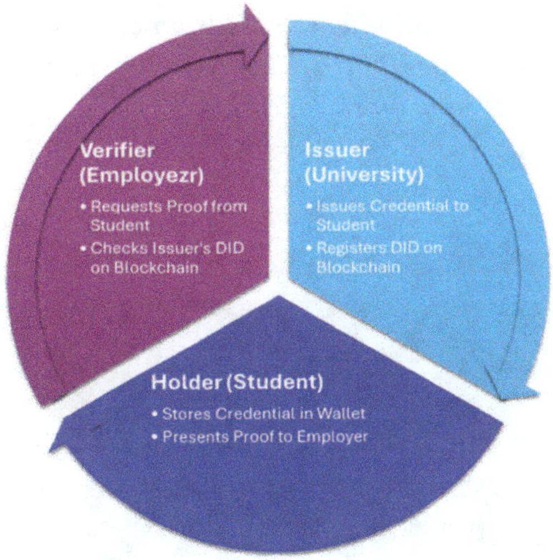

Decentralized Identifiers (DIDs): The base of the SSI stack is the Decentralized Identifier (DID). According to Schumm et al. (2025), a DID is an internationally singular, perennial identifiers with no centralized registration service. A DID is a value created by the user and managed by the user unlike a student ID number which is owned by the university. The DID is resolved to a DID Document a data structure in JSON-LD which holds public keys and service endpoints with which to start up secure interactions. According to Radha et al. (2024), the Issuer (university), Holder (student), and Verifier (employer) of the Triangle of Trust model have DIDs. The verifier locates the issuer on the blockchain (or a distributed directory) by his/her DID, obtains the public key and cryptographically verifies the signature on the credential presented by the student.

Verifiable Credentials (VCs) and Zero-Knowledge Proofs: The digital diploma is presented in the form of a Verifiable Credential (VC). Radha et al. (2024) define a VC as a claims container (tamper-evident) containing (e.g., "Alice earned a B.Sc.) claims with metadata (who issued it) and digital proofs. W3C standard ensures these credentials can be read and processed by machines, as well as to work with various wallet applications. One of the most important developments in this architecture is the introduction of Zero-Knowledge Proofs (ZKPs). According to Schumm et al. (2025), the ZKPs enable a holder to demonstrate a claim (e.g., I am over 18 or I have a valid degree) without exposing the underlying data or the fullness of the credential. This feature contains the privacy leakage caused by the sharing of full PDF transcripts to perform simple verification tasks.

Figure 2. The Digital Credential Lifecycle. This process flow illustrates the secure issuance, decentralized storage in a student's wallet, and instant verification of credentials by employers using blockchain hashes.

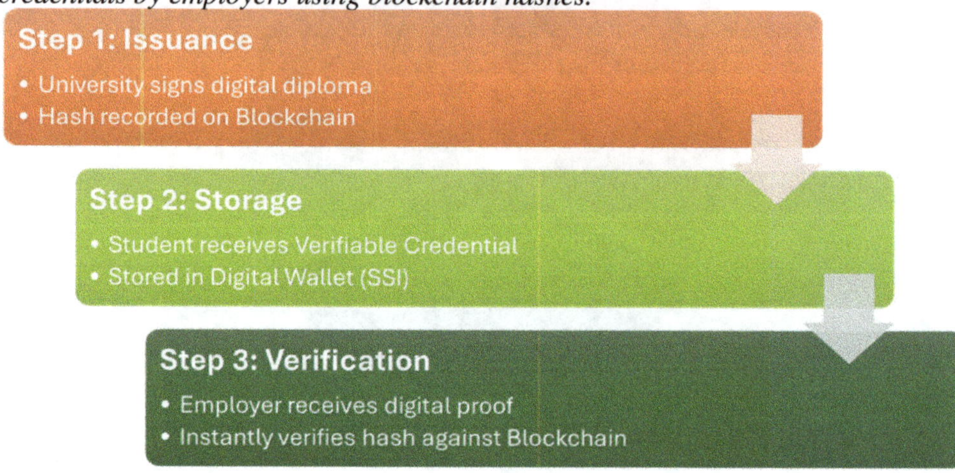

The Universal Resolver: The stack uses a universal resolver in order to be interoperable with other blockchain networks (e.g. a student with a DID on Ethereum communicating with an employer on Hyperledger Indy). According to Schumm et al. (2025), the Universal Resolver is a device that accepts a DID as input and an output of the DID Document, independent of the underlying DID methodology and blockchain. Critically, however, Schumm et al. (2025) observe that even modern applications of the Universal Resolver tend to be centralized web services, thus re-asserting a point of failure and centralization into an architecture that should be completely decentralized.

Off-Chain Storage: The Role of IPFS.

One of the significant technical limitations of blockchain technology is the expensive and inefficient nature of uploading large files of information, like comprehensive academic transcripts or multimedia portfolios, on the ledger. Saving an entire PDF document on Ethereum, e.g., would use an astronomical amount of gas and swell the blockchain, making it slow to get all the nodes into blockchain sync.

To solve this, scholars come up with off-chain storage, mostly InterPlanetary File System (IPFS).

The researchers offer the "Blockchain-based Persistent Identifier for Diplomas" (BCPIDD) (2025) model that makes use of IPFS to store the actual contents of the diploma. IPFS is a distributed file system that is based on content-addressing and not location-addressing. The cryptographic hash of the content of a file is used to create a unique Content Identifier (CID) when a diploma is uploaded to IPFS. When one of the pixels in the diploma image is altered the hash (and hence the CID) becomes entirely different.

According to the description of the technical workflow provided by Alkhawi and Alshameri (2024) (as cited in Silaghi and Popescu, 2025), it is necessary to store the heavy data (the PDF) on the IPFS nodes and to store only the resultant cryptographic hash (the CID) on the blockchain smart contract. This creates a "hash link." Upon being sent a digital diploma, a verifier can compute the hash by themselves, and then compare it with the one presented in the blockchain, which is immutable. On an event of a match, the integrity of the off-chain file will be assured. Hisseine et al. (2025) take this a step further and apply Merkle Trees, a type of data structure that can enable the effective verification of huge datasets.

It is a system that allows verifying the existence and integrity of one specific diploma in a batch of diplomas by storing the "Merkle Root" of that batch on the blockchain without having to download or even disclose the entire dataset. The identified hybrid structure of a Blockchain as the basis of trust and IPFS as the data store is the solution to the scalability problems found by Sharipova et al. (2025), as the system will stay performant as the academic records continue to increase exponentially.

5. CASE STUDIES AND REAL-WORLD IMPLEMENTATION

The shift of blockchain technology from a hypothetical concept into a real-world tool in the field of higher education is most likely to be seen through the prism of critical analysis of certain pilot projects and institutional implementations. Although the literature shows that the extensive, systemic implementation is still in its infancy, isolated case studies reveal the evolutionary path of digital credentialing. This has evolved from the primitive experiments using the public Bitcoin blockchain to sophisticated cross-border consortiums with either private or permissioned infrastructures. This section will discuss four critical projects, namely the Blockcerts standard, the implementation of the University of Nicosia, European Blockchain Services Infrastructure (EBSI), and the QualiChain project, to discuss their architectural choices, their operational achievements, and the barriers they have faced specifically on cost, privacy, and interoperability.

The "Blockcerts" Standard: Pioneering Open Architecture on Bitcoin.

The invention of blockchain-based academic credentialing is to a large extent credited to the Blockcerts open standard designed by the MIT Media Lab in partnership with Learning Machine. Being an open-source architecture, Blockcerts was intended to be blockchain-neutral, but the first and most high-visibility implementations used the Bitcoin blockchain, as it was perceived to be immutable and secure. Silaghi and Popescu (2025) describe how this standard works: the issuing institution creates a digital diploma in the form of JSON and hashes it.

The graduate downloads a mobile wallet, which creates a pair between the public and the private key; the former is sent to the institution where it gets baked into the certificate, and the latter is possessed by the learner exclusively. This architecture radically changes the owner of the record in the registrar to the student.

Another prominent example of the use of this standard is the case of the University of Rome "Tor Vergata," where Capece et al. (2020) report on a pilot initiative that adapted three tools of the Blockcerts toolkit to issue diplomas to a limited group of graduates. This adoption confirmed that the standard was compatible with the Blockcerts Universal Verifier, and the third parties could verify the credentials without communicating with the university. According to Castro and Oliveira (2021), the key advantage of the Blockcerts model is in its openness and decentralization; by separating the credential and the existence of the issuing institution, it allows the evidence of learning to live on even in the event that the university goes out of business.

The use of the Bitcoin blockchain, however, creates severe shortcomings. According to Silaghi and Popescu (2025), one of the technical barriers in the Blockcerts framework is the revocation process. A blockchain record is not editable, in contrast to a centralized database, where an administrator merely deletes or marks a record. Removing a specialized certificate involves attaching a new transaction that cancels the old one, a cumbersome technical task as well as one that is dependent on the further maintenance of the issuer keys.

Moreover, the fact that it depends on the Bitcoin network makes educational institutions vulnerable to fluctuating transaction costs and network overload. Although Capece et al. (2020) were able to prove the issuance, the scalability of this model to large universities that issue thousands of degrees per year is limited by the throughput capabilities and expenses of the Proof-of-Work (PoW) consensus mechanism that Bitcoin uses.

University of Nicosia and Block.co: The Efficiency of Hash Bundling.

In 2017, the University of Nicosia (UNIC) became the first academic institution to award all diplomas, including bachelor's, master's, and PhD degrees, on the blockchain based on the Bitcoin cryptocurrency, starting in 2017. In contrast to the singular issuance concept commonly linked with early Blockcerts goals, UNIC has followed an economic scalability approach that encourages writing of individual transactions to the Bitcoin ledger by employing a bundling mechanism to bypass its prohibitive nature (Silaghi and Popescu, 2025).

Under this architecture, the university signs PDF diplomas digitally, and there gets created a SHA-256 hash. Instead of sending every hash as a distinct transaction, the system packages together a series of hashes of diplomas into a Merkle tree format, which forms one root hash or index file, although the file represents the entire batch of graduates. This is the only root hash that is stored in the blockchain. According to Caldarelli and Ellul (2021), this approach makes the cost of a transaction with Bitcoin extremely low since the price of the transaction is distributed among hundreds or thousands of students. This solution tackles the issue of scalability that afflicts public blockchain systems, and it makes the system economical to issue on a large scale.

This efficiency, however, comes at the expense of privacy. Sharipova et al. (2025) and Silaghi and Popescu (2025) are categorical that the concept of bundling interferes with the privacy of the cohort. Since the verification process will depend on the index file as a cryptographic demonstration that a particular diploma hash belongs in the Merkle root, which is stored in the blockchain, a student or employer with the index file will be able to access the hashes of other certificates of the same batch inadvertently. Although the hashes are anonymized, the structural connection presents a metadata privacy threat, which does not exist in systems with siloed credentials. Therefore, in case the University of Nicosia has managed to address the cost issue of the so-called university-as-oracle model explained by Caldarelli and Ellul (2021), they have created new complexities related to the data isolation.

EBSI: Resolving the Cross-Border Interoperability Crisis.

Outgrowing the restrictions of government blockchains such as Bitcoin, the European Union has invested in the European Blockchain Services Infrastructure (EBSI), a permissioned network that enables the public services across borders. EBSI operates in an authorized network of nodes run by member states and trusted institutions, which, unlike Bitcoin, can be operated by any node but is a Proof-of-Authority (PoA) consensus mechanism. A case study of action research that was reported in the EBSI framework is that of verifying credentials between KU Leuven in Belgium and the Università in Bologna in Italy (Tan et al., 2023).

This pilot was used to resolve the urgent problem of student mobility in the European Higher Education Area (EHEA). In the traditional systems, a student transferring out of Belgium to Italy will have to go through a long paper-based process to transfer credits. The EBSI pilot showed that with anchoring Verifiable Credentials (VCs) on a permissioned and trusted ledger, the receiving institution (Bologna) could immediately build trust in the sent records through the issuing institution (Leuven) without the need to communicate with it in an ad hoc manner.

According to Silaghi and Popescu (2025), this architecture resolves the issue of interoperability by imposing a standard form of credentials across national borders, something that individual pilots on Ethereum or Bitcoin had not been able to accomplish.

Another example of EBSI implementation infrastructure is described by Holotescu et al. (2024) in the case of Politehnica University of Timisoara. This pilot modeled a difficult educational path in which a student obtains a bachelor's degree in Romania, a master's at the University of Athens, and seeks a PhD in France. Through the EBSI network, the pilot was able to prove that credentials issued in a particular jurisdiction were technically and legally valid in a different jurisdiction.

This achievement indicates that permissioned blockchains, supported by the government, can be a more feasible way to develop large-scale adoption than public chains since they can be used in accordance with the regulatory framework of the EU, namely, the necessity to control the identity in a safe way, complying with GDPR. Nevertheless, the success of EBSI would rely much again on the political goodwill and technical assimilation of the member states shifting the burden of the challenge to a governance and policy assimilation problem.

QualiChain and Smart Badges: Integrating with Legacy Systems.

Whereas EBSI aims at macro-level interoperability, the QualiChain project discusses the finesse of assessment and connection with the existing institutional software. QualiChain was created based on the Ethereum blockchain and was tested at the National Technical University of Athens (NTUA) in order to experiment with the idea of "Smart Badge" accreditation.

Kontzinos et al. (2024) explain that this pilot did not only use blockchain to obtain final diplomas but also to certify certain hard and soft skills gained on courses. This strategy is consistent with the pedagogical change to micro-credentials, where students get to create a verifiable profile of skills or competencies, i.e., having mastered a particular programming language or project management, which is frequently lost within the general definition of a degree title.

One of the factors that was critically successful with the QualiChain initiative was its emphasis on integration with legacy systems. The paper by Guerreiro et al. (2022) describes the process of connecting a QualiChain platform with the popular academic management system (AMS) in Portugal called FenixEdu. The authors of this case study have created a system in which the diploma hash produced by the old system known as FenixEdu will automatically be added to the Ethereum blockchain through QualiChain.

This deals with one major obstacle to adoption that Silaghi and Popescu (2025) identify: resistance by administrative personnel to embrace new and complicated workflows. Guerreiro et al. (2022) presented blockchain as an invisible trust layer instead of a disruptive new interface by automating the blockchain anchoring in the software that the university staff already use.

More importantly, though, the application of the Ethereum blockchain in these proofs presents issues with regard to transaction costs (gas fees), which vary depending on the network congestion. Although Kistaubayev et al. offer to use consortium models of Ethereum to cover these expenses, the QualiChain pilots emphasize the conflict between the need to have granular, skill-based credentialing (that would demand regular transactions) and the economic realities of public ledgers.

Moreover, Konzinos et al. (2024) state that as much as the technology was successful in issuing badges, the worth of these so-called Smart Badges depends on how gladly the labor market will accept them. The lack of a critical mass of employers with the technical means to check such granular credentials makes the uptake of the service on the student part a factor of novelty and not utility.

Comparative Analysis and Critical Synthesis.

When comparing these four case studies, one would notice that there is an evident maturation of the use of blockchain for academic credentials. The initial experimentations of Blockcerts and the University of Nicosia (Capece et al., 2020; Sharipova et al., 2025) confirm the basic idea: that a university can serve as an oracle and bind a verified record to a decentralized registry. Such initiatives managed to create the potential of autonomy of ownership but failed on the cost and privacy feasibility. The bundling options provided by Block.co were a required economic Bandaid but added new privacy vectors that potentially do not suit the rigid data protection laws such as GDPR.

By comparison, the subsequent efforts embodied by EBSI and QualiChain (Tan et al., 2023; Guerreiro et al., 2022) represent a transition toward the concept of systemic integration, rather than just the concept of proof of concept. The EBSI pilots are successful in that they can utilize the trust with which the societal institutions (Proof-of-Authority) can bypass the energy and financial expenditure of Proof-of-Work chains, resolving the scalability crisis. In the meantime, the QualiChain pilots end the administrative bottleneck by merging with the old systems, such as FenixEdu.

In all cases, however, there is a continuing battle of a network effect or a user adoption. Such systems, as suggested by Kontzinos et al. (2024) and Silaghi and Popescu (2025), are socially nascent (though technically functional). In the controlled simulation of cross-border mobility, which the Politehnica University of Timisoara pilot has successfully achieved (Holotescu et al., 2024), the receiving institutions (e.g., the University of Lille in this case) must actively make use of the verification infrastructure.

Until the verifiers (employers and other universities) embrace these tools as rapidly as the issuers, these blockchain credentials will be high-tech digital keys and not the currency of academic faith. The development of the Blockcerts approach to the EBSI shows a trade-off that is needed: decentralizing the public Bitcoin ledgers radically to the decentralization of government consortiums managed to provide the scale, compliance, and cost-efficiency needed to support global higher education.

6. FUTURE PATHWAYS AND CONCLUSION

The AI Convergence: Synergizing Algorithmic Trust with Intelligent Assessment

The trend of research indicates that the upcoming evolutionary jump in digital credentialing will not be in the form of blockchain isolation, but in the form of converging them with Artificial Intelligence (AI). Although blockchain is well-suited to give a deterministic, immutable infrastructure on which record-keeping can be performed (The Trust Machine), it is restricted by the binary nature of smart contracts.

As has been mentioned in the foregoing sections, smart contracts readily check on factual requirements such as the achievement of a certain grade or the payment of a certain fee, but they are ineffective in combating the subjective nature of higher education, including examining soft skills, imaginative abilities, or problem-solving skills. This constraint makes the development of a symbiotic relationship in which AI performs the role of the pedagogical engine and blockchain is the unchangeable audit trail.

According to Strielkowski (2025), this convergence is one of the most important frontiers and suggests the idea of AI-driven adaptive learning systems that would not merely check previous successes. Within this vision, AI algorithms are used to analyze a verifiable blockchain portfolio of a learner to suggest individualized micro-credential pathways and customize educational material to fill particular skill diffusion gaps demanded by the labor market. This turns the credential into a prospective tool of lifelong learning, rather than an existing retrospective one. The blockchain also makes the input to these AI models reliable and unalterable and alleviates the garbage in, garbage out threat that is frequently inherent in data analytics.

Moreover, scalability and complexity of credentialing issues are resolved through the direct implementation of the AI in the verification process. Regarding the model suggested by Rustemi et al. (2024) and called the DIAR (Diploma Integrity Authentication Record), Silaghi and Popescu (2025) refer to the proposal to implement the AI features into the creation and validation processes of the digital diplomas.

Under the scalability this paradigm, AI agents may have the ability to automate the process of verifying complex, non-standardized credentials through interpretation of unstructured data (including portfolio evidence) and transferring it to standardized competency frameworks, and pin the final decision on the blockchain. This combination enables institutions to preserve the high standards of assessment and take advantage of the efficiency of decentralized ledgers and get closer to a system in which trust is algorithmic and intelligent.

Strategic Roadmap for University Leaders

A plan that is gradual will have to be adopted to shift the disparate pilot projects to a full-fledged, global credentialing ecosystem. According to the literature synthesis and its best practices and recommendations, it is vital that the leaders and policy-makers in universities should consider a three-stage roadmap to implement the same.

Phase 1: Pilot and Experimentation: The first step should target low-risk, high-learning company pilots. The institutions are not supposed to seek to restructure their entire registrar system in one night. Rather, they are advised to take the example of the University of Rome "Tor Vergata" as it is presented by Capece et al. (2020).

During this stage, the university administrators are expected to tailor open-source software (like the Blockcerts toolkit) to award credentials to a small number of controlled graduates. The goal in this respect is not complete integration but technical confirmation: to check the compatibility of wallets, to know the experience of the students, and to find out which administrative bottlenecks are in the issuance process. This stage permits organizations to experiment with failure and rework their internal system of governance protocols in terms of cryptographic key management and data protection without jeopardizing the integrity of the records of the entire student body.

Phase 2: Consortium Building and Standardization: After preparing internal feasibility, institutions should not remain isolated so as to avoid the establishment of digital silos. Phase 2 is interoperability, which is based on consortium building.

Schumm et al. (2025) suggest that a lack of standardization is a critical obstacle to adoption, as it will tend to tie institutions to vendors or incompatible blockchains.

In this stage, universities have to conform to developed standards organizations, including the Decentralized Identifier (DID) and Verifiable Credential (VC) working groups at the W3C. Participating in networks such as the European Blockchain Services Infrastructure (EBSI) or other national consortia (e.g., IDunion), institutions can make the credentials they issue readable and verifiable by other parties. Schumm and colleagues (2025) underline that this stage should also focus on the creation of user-friendly wallets that hide the difficult key management so that the technology can be easily accessible to the non-technical users.

Figure 3. Strategic Roadmap for Digital Credential Implementation. This diagram outlines the phased approach for universities to transition from initial pilots to full ecosystem integration using standardized blockchain protocols.

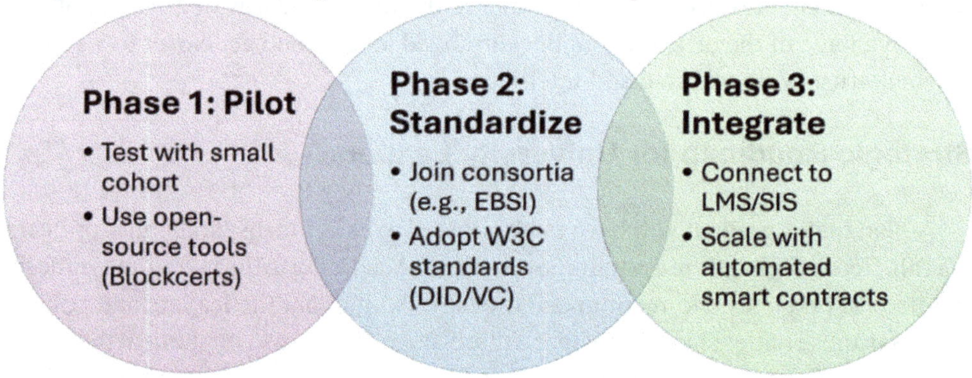

Phase 3: Complete Ecosystem Integration: The last step entails scaling the system to production at the enterprise level, where blockchain is an invisible back-end infrastructure to all academic documents. Panwar et al. (2025) confirm that the scale of this is only sufficient with strong permission-based architectures, including Hyperledger Fabric, that can support large transaction throughput (e.g., 250 transactions per second) at almost no error rates.

During this stage, the blockchain layer is completely combined with existing Student Information Systems (SIS) and Learning Management Systems (LMS). It is no longer about technical feasibility but economic sustainability and governance, to make sure that the system can sustain millions of transactions such as micro-credentials and doctoral degrees safely and efficiently. This step makes available the vision of the "University-as-Oracle" operating in a decentralized global network, which will offer instant, cost-effective verification of the labor market.

7. CONCLUSION

This review has critically discussed the Revolution of Digital Credential Management, the path from paper-based vulnerability to cryptographic invulnerability of the blockchain. The facts in all these chapters prove that the existing centralized system of academic credentialing is straining under the burden of fraud, inefficiency, and liquidity needs of a modern workforce. The global economy has suffered billions of dollars, and the crisis of document forgery has damaged the trust of higher education, which can no longer be handled by manual verification.

The technological resolutions—between the public inviolability of Ethereum and the privacy-protective networks of Hyperledger Fabric—are sufficiently developed to provide an alternative. We have observed that micro-credentials and Self-Sovereign Identity (SSI) are not only technical standards but pedagogical change agents that enable learners to gain control of their story. Nonetheless, the analysis further shows that technology is not a panacea. The GDPR compliance and its privacy paradox, the institutional trust, and the fragmentation of standards are daunting challenges.

Thus, this chapter ends with the shocking appeal: the scholarly community should unite behind common worldwide norms. The adversary of adoption is fragmentation. Unless every university constructs a custom blockchain, we will simply recreate the inefficient silos of the paper-based world in the digital world. The cooperation of institutions, governments, and technology providers to construct an interoperable Internet of Education—a trust infrastructure as borderless and dynamic as the knowledge it is meant to certify—is urgent. Only at that point can we be really revolutionary when it comes to managing human potential.

REFERENCES

Abdul Halim, F. S., Luaran, J. E., & Lee, S. S. J. (2024). Unravelling challenges of higher education institutions in implementing effective micro-credentials: A multi-stakeholder qualitative study. *Asian Journal of University Education, 20*(1), 114–126. DOI: 10.24191/ajue.v20i1.25698

Abramovich, S., & Reed, A. (2024). White paper: Creating assessments for micro-credentials in higher education organizations. University at Buffalo.

Alammary, A., Alhazmi, S., Almasri, M., & Gillani, S. (2019). Blockchain-based applications in education: A systematic review. *Applied Sciences (Basel, Switzerland), 9*(12), 2400. DOI: 10.3390/app9122400

Alkhawi, M. A., & Alshameri, A. S. (2024). Cost-effective and efficient blockchain framework for verifying certificate in Yemeni universities. *Turkish Journal of Computer and Mathematics Education, 15*, 206–216.

Badlani, S., Aditya, T., Maniar, S., & Devadkar, K. (2022). Educrypto: Transforming education using blockchain. In 2022 6th International Conference on Intelligent Computing and Control Systems (ICICCS) (pp. 829-836). IEEE.

Caldarelli, G., & Ellul, J. (2021). Trusted academic transcripts on the blockchain: A systematic literature review. *Applied Sciences (Basel, Switzerland), 11*(4), 1842. DOI: 10.3390/app11041842

Capece, G., Ghiron, N. L., & Pasquale, F. (2020). Blockchain technology: Redefining trust for digital certificates. *Sustainability (Basel), 12*(21), 8952. DOI: 10.3390/su12218952

Castro, R. Q., & Oliveira, M. (2021). Blockchain and higher education diplomas. *European Journal of Investigation in Health, Psychology and Education, 11*(1), 154–167. DOI: 10.3390/ejihpe11010013 PMID: 34542456

Flynn, S., Cullinane, E., Murphy, H., & Wylie, N. (2023). Micro-credentials & digital badges: Definitions, affordances and design considerations for application in higher education institutions. *All Ireland Journal of Teaching and Learning in Higher Education, 15*(1), 1–18.

Gamage, K. A. A., & Dehideniya, S. C. P. (2025). Unlocking career potential: How micro-credentials are revolutionising higher education and lifelong learning. *Education Sciences, 15*(5), 525. DOI: 10.3390/educsci15050525

Gish-Lieberman, J. J., Tawfik, A., & Gatewood, J. (2021). Micro-credentials and badges in education: A historical overview. *TechTrends*, *65*(1), 5–7. DOI: 10.1007/s11528-020-00567-4

Guerreiro, S., Ferreira, J. F., Fonseca, T., & Correia, M. (2022). Integrating an academic management system with blockchain: A case study. Blockchain [ffigure]. *Research and Applications*, *3*(4), 2022. DOI: 10.1016/j.bcra.2022.100099

Hisseine, M. A., Chen, D., & Xiao, Y. (2025). Enhancing handle system for digital credentials verification by using blockchain. *IAENG International Journal of Computer Science*, *52*(5), 1484–1500.

Holotescu, V., Vasiu, R., Ternauciuc, A., Holotescu, C., & Andone, D. (2024). Building a decentralized education ecosystem: Politehnica University of Timisoara's pioneering blockchain initiatives. In Proceedings of the EDEN 2024 Research Workshop & PhD Masterclass.

Khan, M. A., Quasim, M. T., Algarni, F., & Alharthi, A. (2020). *Decentralized Internet of Things: A blockchain perspective* (Vol. 71). Springer Nature. DOI: 10.1007/978-3-030-38677-1

Kistaubayev, Y., Mutanov, G., Mansurova, M., Saxenbayeva, Z., & Shakan, Y. (2023). Ethereum-based information system for digital higher education registry and verification of student achievement documents. *Future Internet*, *15*(1), 3. DOI: 10.3390/fi15010003

Kontzinos, C., Karakolis, E., Kokkinakos, P., Skalidakis, S., & Psarras, D. A. J. (2024). Application and evaluation of a blockchain-centric platform for smart badge accreditation in higher education institutions. *Applied Sciences (Basel, Switzerland)*, *14*(12), 5191. DOI: 10.3390/app14125191

Liu, L., Han, M., Zhou, Y., Parizi, R. M., & Korayem, M. (2020). Blockchain-based certification for education, employment, and skill with incentive mechanism. In *Blockchain cybersecurity, trust and privacy* (pp. 269–290). Springer. DOI: 10.1007/978-3-030-38181-3_14

Mishra, R. A., Kalla, A., Braeken, A., & Liyanage, M. (2021). Privacy protected blockchain-based architecture and implementation for sharing of students' credentials. *Information Processing & Management*, *58*(3), 102512. DOI: 10.1016/j.ipm.2021.102512

Nokhbeh Zaeem, R., Chang, K. C., Huang, T.-C., Liau, D., Song, W., Tyagi, A., Barber, K. S., Khalil, M. M., Lamison, M. R., & Pandey, S. (2021). Blockchain-based self-sovereign identity: Survey, requirements, use-cases, and comparative study (UTCID Report #21-06). Center for Identity, University of Texas at Austin.

Ocheja, P., Flanagan, B., Ueda, H., & Ogata, H. (2019). Managing lifelong learning records through blockchain. *Research and Practice in Technology Enhanced Learning*, *14*(4), 4. Advance online publication. DOI: 10.1186/s41039-019-0097-0

Panwar, A., Sugandh, U., Jain, A., Jain, V., Dubey, A. K., Majumdar, S., & Mallik, S. (2025). Enhancing trust and transparency in education using blockchain: A Hyperledger Fabric-based framework. *Artificial Intelligence and Applications (Commerce, Calif.)*, *3*(1), 1–14. DOI: 10.47852/bonviewAIA52026268

Rachmat, A., & Albarda. (2019). Design of distributed academic-record system based on blockchain. In *Proceedings of the 2019 International Conference on ICT for Smart Society (ICISS)* (Vol. 7, pp. 1-6). DOI: 10.1109/ICISS48059.2019.8969849

Radha, S. K., Kuehlkamp, A., & Nabrzyski, J. (2024). The future of document verification: Leveraging blockchain and self-sovereign identity for enhanced security and transparency. arXiv. https://doi.org//arXiv.2412.01531DOI: 10.5121/csit.2024.141910

Rustemi, A., Dalipi, F., Atanasovski, V., & Risteski, A. (2024). DIAR: A blockchain-based system for generation and verification of academic diplomas. *SN Applied Sciences*, *6*, 297.

Sanchez Barrioluengo, M. (2025). *Micro-credentials in higher education: Are they boosting digital and green skills for the twin transition? (JRC142086)*. Publications Office of the European Union., DOI: 10.2760/0157920

Schumm, D., Müller, K. O. E., & Stiller, B. (2025). Are we there yet? A study of decentralized identity applications. *IEEE Access : Practical Innovations, Open Solutions*, *13*, 125232–125259. DOI: 10.1109/ACCESS.2025.3588170

Sharipova, Z., Mardonova, R., Begbutayev, A., Makhkamova, S., Sapaev, I. B., Karimova, S., Nigmatova, K., & Rakhmatova, G. (2025). Academic chain: Securing educational credentials with blockchain-enabled. *Journal of Internet Services and Information Security*, *15*(2), 374–386. DOI: 10.58346/JISIS.2025.I2.027

Silaghi, D. L., & Popescu, D. E. (2025). A systematic review of blockchain-based initiatives in comparison to best practices used in higher education institutions. *Computers*, *14*(4), 141. DOI: 10.3390/computers14040141

Strielkowski, W. (2025). The role of micro-credentials in the future digitalized AI-driven education. arXiv. https://doi.org//arXiv.2511.07583DOI: 10.48550

Tan, E., Lerouge, E., Caju, J. D., & Seuil, D. D. (2023). Verification of education credentials on European Blockchain Services Infrastructure (EBSI): Action research in a cross-border use case between Belgium and Italy. *Big Data and Cognitive Computing*, *7*(2), 79. DOI: 10.3390/bdcc7020079

Van Melkebeke, L., & Op de Beeck, I. (2025). *Implementing micro-credentials in higher education: Challenges, opportunities and lessons learned (Envisioning Report 2025)*. KU Leuven.

KEY TERMS AND DEFINITIONS

Blockchain Technology: It is a distributed ledger technology that is decentralized that records data in a chain of successively interconnected blocks using cryptography. There is no centralized authority and management and data accuracy, integrity, security, and transparency are guaranteed.

Decentralized Identifiers: Globally Unique Identity Globally unique, persistent and verifiable identifiers that allow the subject to establish control without having to use a centralized registry or an authority.

Digital Badges: Displays a visual representation of the specific skills or competencies that the learner has mastered, usually with some metadata embedded in it, acting as testimony to this accomplishment, including issuer and rules on how it was obtained.

Hyperledger Fabric: is a permissioned, open source, enterprise blockchain infrastructure with a modular architecture, with fine-grained access control, which suits education requirements where privacy of data is needed.

Micro-credentials: A credential that indicates a learning accomplishment that is focused and verifies what a learner knows, understands or can do, usually given in smaller amounts of learning than the traditional degrees, and usually assessed.

Self-Sovereign Identity: A system of identity management where the owner of the identity must be in charge, and they have full authority over the personal data and digital identity without the intervention of centralized and third-party intermediaries.

Smart Contracts: such contracts are self-executing in that the rules of an agreement are hard-coded in lines of code. This allows automation of the processes wherein some pre-determined conditions are met such as issuing credentials and verification among others.

Verifiable Credentials: a standard of digital credentials that provide tamper-evident, cryptographically secure methods of expression information-a degree of a university or a skill i.e. that might be stored in a digital wallet and validated by third parties.

Chapter 4
Digital Trust, Data Management, and Security Frameworks for the Higher Education Ecosystem

Reyaz Ahmad
http://orcid.org/0000-0002-9885-2310
Horizon University College, Ajman, UAE

Abdul Salam Mohammed
Horizon University College, Ajman, UAE

Nehal Ahmad Ansari
Maulana Azad National Urdu University, CTE, Asansol, India

Md Faiz Ahmad
http://orcid.org/0000-0001-8002-6582
Paari School of Business, SRM University-AP, India

ABSTRACT

This chapter presents a comprehensive research framework addressing digital trust and security within the higher education ecosystem. As institutions rely on digital infrastructure, they face sophisticated cybersecurity threats endangering data and stakeholder confidence. Through a PRISMA-guided systematic literature review, this research synthesizes academic and industry insights to construct a holistic view of the landscape. It defines digital trust through the core principles of ability, integ-

DOI: 10.4018/979-8-3373-7600-4.ch004

rity, and benevolence, mapping these to operational TRUST standards. The paper examines identity management complexities and solutions like Identity Governance and Administration (IGA), alongside an analysis of frameworks including NIST CSF and ISO/IEC 27001. Furthermore, it explores the role of AI and Blockchain as both sources of new challenges and providers of security solutions. Identifying barriers such as cultural resistance and resource constraints, the chapter concludes with recommendations for institutional leaders to build a strategic, resilient, and trustworthy digital campus.

1. INTRODUCTION

The 21st-century higher education institution is an entity fundamentally reshaped by digital transformation. From online learning platforms and cloud-based research collaboration to automated administrative systems and global recruitment initiatives, data has become the lifeblood of teaching, research, and institutional operations (EDUCAUSE, 2023; World Economic Forum, 2023). Every digital touchpoint—learning management systems, student information systems, payroll portals, research repositories, library databases, campus Wi-Fi, and third-party apps—creates both value and exposure (BoardEffect, 2024; FortifyData, 2024). In this hyper-connected environment, the concept of Digital Trust has emerged as a paramount strategic concern, extending far beyond the technical confines of cybersecurity (SenseTime, 2024; Stanković et al., 2025). It represents the fundamental confidence that a diverse array of stakeholders—students, faculty, researchers, staff, alumni, donors, and government partners—place in an institution's ability to act as a responsible and ethical steward of their digital identities, intellectual property, and personal information (Arizona State University, 2022; Planon, 2023; World Economic Forum, 2023). As cyber threats, research security risks, and institutional data breaches continue to rise globally, higher education institutions are increasingly expected to adopt structured governance, resilience planning, and risk frameworks to maintain stakeholder trust (EDUCAUSE, 2024; National Institute of Standards and Technology, 2024).

Crucially, digital trust is not merely the absence of hacking incidents; it is the presence of credible assurance (Kidwell & Giovacchini, 2022; Sift, 2023). Stakeholders ask implicit questions: Will my data be used fairly? Will the institution be transparent when something goes wrong? Are decisions about access and sharing made responsibly? In this sense, Digital Trust is not a feature to be implemented but a socio-technical outcome to be earned through consistent, transparent, and competent action (Arizona State University, 2022; Stanković et al., 2025). It is reinforced by visible governance (clear policies, accountable leadership, and oversight), disciplined processes (risk assessment, access reviews, incident response), and appropriate technologies (strong identity controls, encryption, monitoring, and secure cloud configurations) (National Institute of Standards and Technology, 2024; EDUCAUSE, 2024). Most importantly, it must align with the institutional mission: universities exist to create and share knowledge, which demands openness and collaboration, yet that openness must be balanced with protection and ethical data handling (Association of American Universities, 2024). Digital trust is therefore the bedrock upon which any successful security program must be built—particularly within an institutional culture predicated on academic values of collaboration, openness, and the free exchange of ideas (Arizona State University, 2022).

Higher Education Institutions (HEIs) are uniquely vulnerable to cybersecurity threats because they combine a "public square" culture with enterprise-scale complexity (Pirkl, 2019). Their open and diverse systems—designed to foster collaboration across departments, visiting scholars, and global partners—create a vast and constantly shifting attack surface (archTIS, 2023; BitLyft, 2023). User populations change every semester; devices range from managed lab machines to personal laptops and phones; and research teams frequently adopt specialized tools outside central IT (BitLyft, 2023). The sheer volume and variety of sensitive data held by HEIs—from student Personally Identifiable Information (PII), health and counseling records, and financial data to government-funded research, patentable discoveries, and confidential industry partnerships—make them attractive targets for ransomware groups, identity thieves, and state-sponsored actors seeking intellectual property or geopolitical advantage (archTIS, 2023; Association of American Universities, 2024; Federal Bureau of Investigaton, 2019). These risks are compounded by internal structural challenges: decentralized IT environments, uneven security maturity across schools and units, chronic resource constraints, legacy systems that cannot be retired quickly, and cultural resistance to restrictive controls perceived to impede academic freedom and innovation (Al-Ahmad et al., 2024; BitLyft, 2023).

The challenge is magnified by the diversity of the stakeholder community, where each group possesses unique data assets and holds distinct expectations of trust (Planon, 2023; Arizona State University, 2024). Students prioritize privacy, fairness, and uninterrupted access to learning systems; faculty and researchers prioritize collaboration, autonomy, and data integrity; staff require reliable systems to deliver services; alumni and donors expect confidentiality and professional stewardship; and government and industry partners require compliance, auditability, and protection of sensitive research outputs (EDUCAUSE, 2024; Association of American Universities, 2024). A security failure affecting one group can rapidly erode the trust of all others, creating a "trust contagion" effect with severe and lasting consequences (Arizona State University, 2022; Stanković et al., 2025). A breach of an alumni donor database, for example, not only jeopardizes donor confidence but also signals institutional weakness—leading prospective students to question whether their records are safe and prompting external funders to scrutinize research security, compliance posture, and contractual risk (archTIS, 2023; Association of American Universities, 2024).

Therefore, building and maintaining digital trust requires a holistic, integrated approach that recognizes the profound interdependence of stakeholder confidence. This includes aligning security with institutional strategy, establishing clear data governance and accountability, implementing modern identity and access controls, developing a culture of shared responsibility, and committing to transparency before, during, and after incidents (National Institute of Standards and Technology, 2024; EDUCAUSE, 2024). This paper provides a comprehensive analytical framework to navigate this complex landscape, examining the foundational principles of trust, the architecture of modern security, the dual impact of emerging technologies, and the formidable challenges of implementing effective frameworks in the unique academic ecosystem (Al-Ahmad et al., 2024; Al-Zahrani et al., 2024).

2. METHODOLOGY

This chapter is informed by a Systematic Literature Review (SLR) conducted in accordance with PRISMA guidelines (PRISMA, 2021). Academic databases including Scopus, Web of Science, IEEE Xplore, and Google Scholar were searched using keywords such as digital trust, cybersecurity frameworks, higher education, identity management, blockchain credentials, and AI security. After screening and eligibility assessment, 50 peer-reviewed and authoritative industry studies (2010–2024) were included.

Thematic synthesis was used to extract recurring dimensions related to trust pillars, security frameworks, implementation challenges, and outcome measures (Al-Ahmad et al., 2024). The review reveals strong convergence around IAM failures, ransomware, and governance gaps as the most critical trust-eroding risks, while leadership engagement and measurable resilience capabilities consistently predict successful framework adoption (EDUCAUSE, 2024; IBM, 2024).

This research framework is the result of a Systematic Literature Review (SLR) designed to investigate the characteristics, components, and challenges of digital trust and security frameworks tailored to Higher Education Institutions (HEIs). The study synthesizes findings from a wide range of peer-reviewed academic studies, industry publications, technical reports from standards bodies like the National Institute of Standards and Technology (NIST) and the International Organization for Standardization (ISO), and institutional case studies published between 2010 and 2024 (National Institute of Standards and Technology, 2024; International Organization for Standardization, 2022).

The review was conducted following the Preferred Reporting Items for Systematic reviews and Meta-Analyses (PRISMA) guidelines to ensure a transparent, comprehensive, and replicable process (PRISMA, 2021). The PRISMA methodology provides a standardized framework for reporting the search strategy, study selection criteria, data extraction, and quality assessment. The process, as visualized in the PRISMA flow diagram (Figure 1), consists of four distinct phases:

- *Identification*: An initial search was conducted across multiple academic databases, including Scopus, PubMed, and other relevant sources, using a combination of keywords such as "cybersecurity framework," "digital trust," "higher education," "NIST," "ISO 27001," "data breach," and "implementation challenges." This phase yielded an initial pool of 341 relevant studies and reports. Additional records were identified through other sources, such as industry publications and institutional websites.
- *Screening*: The titles and abstracts of the identified studies were reviewed to filter out those that were not relevant to the research questions. Duplicates were removed, leaving a refined set of articles for full-text review. This screening process is crucial for ensuring that the subsequent, more intensive review phases are focused on the most pertinent literature.
- *Eligibility*: The full text of the remaining articles was read and assessed against predefined inclusion and exclusion criteria. To be included, a study had to focus on cybersecurity or digital trust within the context of higher education, discuss the application of a formal framework, or analyse specific threats and challenges relevant to the sector. Studies focusing exclusively on K-12 education or corporate environments without relevance to academia were excluded.
- *Inclusion*: After the full-text review, a final group of 50 studies was selected for inclusion in the literature synthesis. Key information from these studies—including definitions, framework components, identified challenges, and proposed solutions—was systematically extracted. Thematic analysis was then employed on this extracted data to identify and categorize recurring concepts, definitions, and challenges. This qualitative analysis allowed for the development of a holistic and multidimensional understanding of digital trust and security in the academic context, forming the evidence base for this research framework.

The figure 1 (PRISMA Flow Diagram) for Study Selection A visual representation of the literature review process, from initial database search to the final selection of studies included in the synthesis.

Figure 1. PRISMA

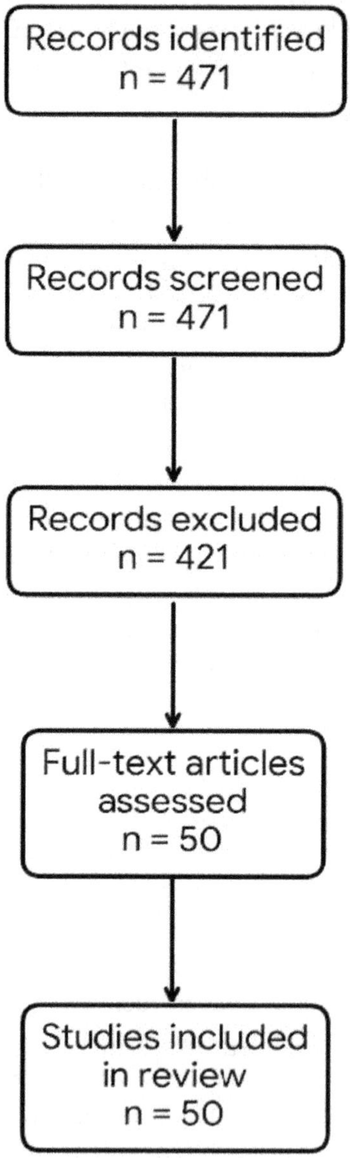

3. LITERATURE REVIEW

The term "Digital Trust" is widely invoked across sectors—banking, healthcare, government, and education—yet it remains conceptually inconsistent in much of the literature (SenseTime, 2024; Sift, 2023). This definitional ambiguity often reduces Digital Trust to a narrow technical agenda, producing fragmented interpretations that overemphasize cybersecurity tools while neglecting governance, ethics, and stakeholder perceptions (Kidwell & Giovacchini, 2022). Importantly, Digital Trust is not a synonym for cybersecurity or data protection. Strong security is a necessary precondition for trust, but it is not sufficient (Stanković et al., 2025).

In the higher education context—where openness, academic freedom, and collaboration are core operating principles—a more holistic framing is required (Association of American Universities, 2024). A useful definition describes Digital Trust as the "confidence, flexibility, and empowerment in the relationships between individuals and organizations regarding their data" (Stanković et al., 2025). Under this lens, Digital Trust refers to the collective confidence that stakeholders—students, faculty, staff, alumni, partners, regulators, and the wider public—place in an institution's technology, people, and processes to create a secure, reliable, and ethically governed digital environment (Arizona State University, 2022).

This distinction matters because trust is shaped as much by how data is used as by whether it is protected (RAUSP Management Journal, 2022). An institution may implement technically robust controls—firewalls, intrusion detection, encryption, and strict access management—yet still fail to earn Digital Trust if data practices appear opaque, coercive, or misaligned with community values (Lin et al., 2020). The digital environment amplifies uncertainty because stakeholders cannot easily "see" how data moves, who accesses it, or how decisions are made—especially when automated systems and AI are involved (OculusIT, 2024). Consequently, trust functions as a risk-reducing mechanism: it lowers fear, increases adoption of digital services, and enables participation in learning, research collaboration, and institutional processes (Stanković et al., 2025).

Therefore, Digital Trust is best understood as a socio-technical construct, produced by the interaction of technical safeguards with human experience, institutional transparency, and perceived fairness (Lin et al., 2020). To operationalize Digital Trust in the literature, trustworthiness is commonly deconstructed into three interrelated pillars that translate directly to digital environments: ability (competence), integrity (principled conduct), and benevolence (stakeholder-oriented intent).

- *Ability (Competence)*: This pillar addresses the institution's technical and organizational capability to create a safe environment for data. It answers the stakeholder's question: "Does the institution have the skill and resources to protect my information?" A failure of Ability is the most direct and visible form of trust erosion, often manifesting as a data breach, system outage, or successful ransomware attack.

- *Integrity (Principles and Ethics)*: This pillar relates to the institution's adherence to a consistent set of ethical principles and its commitment to doing what it says it will do. It answers the question: "Does the institution's definition of privacy align with my own, and will it handle my data honestly?" A failure of Integrity occurs when an institution's actions contradict its stated policies, such as using student data for undisclosed marketing purposes or failing to be transparent about a security incident.
- *Benevolence (Motives and Goals)*: This pillar concerns the institution's fundamental motives and its commitment to having its stakeholders' best interests at heart. It answers the question: "Is the institution collecting and using my data for my benefit, or for its own gain?" A failure of Benevolence is perceived when data is used in ways that seem exploitative or harmful, such as selling alumni data to third parties without consent or using analytics to penalize students rather than support them.

To translate these abstract pillars into concrete actions, institutions can draw upon the TRUST Principles for Digital Repositories, a framework developed within the academic community that provides a powerful and broadly applicable guide for building trust across the HEI ecosystem. These principles are:

- *Transparency*: Demands that institutions provide clear, accessible, and honest information about their data holdings, services, terms of use, and data management practices. This directly supports the pillar of Integrity.
- *Responsibility*: Requires adherence to data curation standards, appropriate management of intellectual property rights, and ensuring the authenticity and persistence of data. This aligns with both Ability and Integrity.
- *User Focus*: Commits the institution to meeting the needs of its diverse user communities, placing the interests of students, faculty, and researchers at the centre of all decisions. This is a clear demonstration of Benevolence.
- *Sustainability*: Requires sustainable funding, long-term preservation plans, and robust governance to ensure the institution can fulfil its commitments over time. This is a crucial aspect of Ability.
- *Technology*: Mandates ensuring the security, reliability, and resilience of the technical infrastructure. This is the most direct manifestation of Ability.

By integrating the three pillars of trustworthiness with the five TRUST principles, HEIs can move from a vague notion of "trust" to a structured, actionable program for earning and maintaining it.

4. CREDENTIAL AND IDENTITY MANAGEMENT IN THE HIGHER EDUCATION ECOSYSTEM

Effective credential and identity management is a foundational pillar of a secure and trustworthy academic environment. It encompasses the complex web of policies, processes, and technologies required to manage the digital identities and academic records for a diverse, dynamic, and often transient population of students, faculty, staff, researchers, alumni, and affiliates (Bravura Security, 2024; Identity Automation, 2024). In the modern university, an individual's digital identity is the key that unlocks access to everything from learning management systems and research databases to financial aid portals and campus health services (Parchment, 2024).

Challenges in Credential Management Historically, many HEIs have relied on manual processes, disparate spreadsheets, and paper-based documents for credential management. These legacy systems are not only inefficient but also introduce significant and unacceptable security risks in the current threat landscape. The primary challenges include:

- *Data Security and Fraud*: Manual and fragmented systems are highly vulnerable to human error, accidental data loss, and malicious attacks. This environment is ripe for the proliferation of fraudulent credentials, such as forged diplomas, falsified transcripts, and inflated grades, which directly threaten the institution's academic integrity and reputation.
- *Inefficiency, Errors, and High Costs*: Manual data entry is exceptionally time-consuming, prone to mistakes, and places a heavy burden on administrative staff. This inefficiency leads to delays in critical processes like admissions and graduation, diminishes the overall student and faculty experience, and inflates operational costs.
- *Password Fatigue and Weak Security Practices*: The modern university requires users to access dozens of different platforms, each often with its own login credentials. This leads to "password fatigue," a condition where users resort to insecure practices such as using weak, easily guessable passwords, reusing the same password across multiple systems, or writing passwords down, making their accounts highly vulnerable to compromise.
- *Complex Regulatory Compliance*: HEIs are stewards of a wide variety of sensitive data, making them subject to a complex web of regulations, includ-

ing the Family Educational Rights and Privacy Act (FERPA), the General Data Protection Regulation (GDPR) for individuals in the EU, and the Health Insurance Portability and Accountability Act (HIPAA) for campus health services. Managing compliance for credential data across these different legal frameworks is a significant challenge, with non-compliance carrying the risk of steep financial penalties and severe reputational damage.

Solutions and Best Practices for Modern Credential Management To address these formidable challenges, forward-thinking HEIs are moving away from legacy systems and adopting modern Identity and Access Management (IAM) and digital credentialing solutions.

- *Digital Credentials and Micro-Credentials*: The shift from paper to digital credentials is a critical step. Digital solutions, often secured by cryptographic verification, allow for the secure issuance, storage, and instant verification of academic credentials, badges, and certificates. This dramatically reduces the risk of fraud and lessens the administrative burden of manual verification requests. Furthermore, the rise of micro-credentials—shorter, industry-focused qualifications that certify specific skills—is transforming the educational landscape. These digital badges offer students a flexible and "stackable" way to acquire and demonstrate specific, relevant skills to employers, enhancing their employability.
- *Comprehensive Identity Governance and Administration (IGA)*: A robust IGA program establishes a holistic, policy-driven approach to managing digital identities and access permissions across the entire institution. Best practices for IGA in higher education include:

    Role-Based Access Control (RBAC): RBAC streamlines access management by assigning permissions based on a user's predefined role (e.g., undergraduate student, tenured faculty, financial aid officer, IT administrator). This ensures that individuals are granted access only to the information and systems necessary for their specific functions, enforcing the critical security principle of least privilege.

    Mandatory Multi-Factor Authentication (MFA): MFA adds a crucial layer of security by requiring two or more verification methods (e.g., a password plus a code from a mobile app) to prove a user's identity. This practice significantly reduces the risk of unauthorized access resulting from stolen or compromised credentials.

    Automated Lifecycle Management (Provisioning and Deprovisioning): In a dynamic university environment, manually managing user accounts is untenable. Automated systems for provisioning (creating accounts

and granting access for new users) and deprovisioning (revoking access for departing users) are essential. This automation saves significant time, reduces errors, and closes major security gaps by ensuring that access is promptly removed when an individual leaves the institution.
Centralized and Cloud-Based IAM Platforms: Modern, cloud-native IAM platforms are designed to manage distributed "identity fabrics" that span multi-campus systems, on-premises applications, and cloud services. These platforms ensure data integrity by creating a single source of truth for identity, streamline management through a centralized console, and enhance overall security and compliance.

5. DIGITAL TRUST AND SECURITY FRAMEWORKS

The existence of a formal, structured security framework is essential for moving beyond reactive, ad-hoc security measures and building a mature, resilient, and risk-informed security program. A framework provides a common language, a set of prioritized controls, and a repeatable process for managing cybersecurity risk across a complex organization. While no single framework is a panacea, several are highly relevant to the unique context of higher education (Lepide, 2024; Monash University, 2024).

- NIST Cybersecurity Framework (CSF) 2.0: Developed by the U.S. National Institute of Standards and Technology, the NIST CSF has become a gold standard for cybersecurity risk management. The recently released CSF 2.0 is explicitly designed to be applicable to any organization, including universities. It is a voluntary set of guidelines and best practices structured around six high-level, concurrent functions: Govern, Identify, Protect, Detect, Respond, and Recover.

    Applicability in HEIs: The CSF's primary strength for higher education lies in its flexible, non-prescriptive, and risk-based approach. It accommodates the decentralized nature of academic environments by allowing different departments or research units to define their own risk tolerance and select controls, accordingly, avoiding a rigid, one-size-fits-all mandate. The addition of the "Govern" function in CSF 2.0 is particularly significant, as it directly addresses a common weakness in HEI governance by emphasizing the need for a clear cybersecurity strategy, defined roles and responsibilities, and integration with broader enterprise risk management. Many universities also use the more prescriptive NIST SP 800-171 standard as a component of their CSF implementation to protect Controlled Unclassified Information (CUI), a requirement for receiving many federal research grants.

- ISO/IEC 27001: This is the leading international standard for establishing, implementing, maintaining, and continually improving an Information Security Management System (ISMS). An ISMS is a systematic approach to managing sensitive information, encompassing people, processes, and technology, all governed by a risk management process.

    Applicability in HEIs: The core distinction of ISO 27001 is that it is certifiable. Achieving certification requires a formal, independent audit by an accredited body, which provides external verification that the institution's ISMS meets the standard's rigorous requirements. This certification can serve as a significant competitive advantage, particularly for securing research grants and corporate partnerships where verifiable, internationally recognized security standards are a prerequisite. However, due to the significant investment of time, personnel, and financial resources required, many institutions find it impractical to certify the entire campus. A more pragmatic and common strategy is to pursue certification for specific, high-risk areas, such as secure data enclaves for sensitive health research or systems managing defence-related intellectual property, as demonstrated by institutions like Monash University.

- Regulatory Mandates as a Driving Force: HEIs operate within one of the most complex regulatory environments of any sector. They are simultaneously subject to laws governing education, healthcare, finance, and research, creating a dense web of compliance obligations. Key regulations include:

    FERPA (Family Educational Rights and Privacy Act): Governs the privacy of student education records.

    HIPAA (Health Insurance Portability and Accountability Act): Protects sensitive patient health information, applicable to university health centres and medical schools.

    GLBA (Gramm-Leach-Bliley Act): Requires financial institutions—a category that includes universities administering federal student aid—to safeguard sensitive financial data.

    PCI-DSS (Payment Card Industry Data Security Standard): Required for any organization that handles credit card transactions.

    GDPR (General Data Protection Regulation): The European Union's stringent data privacy law, which applies to any HEI that offers services to or processes the data of individuals located in the EU.

These regulations dictate what must be protected but are often not prescriptive about how. This is where security frameworks become invaluable. They provide the structured processes and comprehensive control sets needed to meet these disparate legal mandates in a coherent and efficient manner. A framework like the NIST CSF acts as a "Rosetta Stone," allowing an institution to implement a unified set of controls that can be mapped to multiple regulatory requirements simultaneously, breaking down compliance silos and transforming security from a series of checklists into a strategic, centrally governed function.

5.1 Credential and Identity Management as a Trust Anchor

Identity and Access Management (IAM) represents the single most critical control domain affecting digital trust in higher education. Weak credential management undermines all three trust tenets by enabling unauthorized access, regulatory violations, and perceived institutional negligence.

Modern HEIs are transitioning from fragmented, manual systems to centralized IAM platforms incorporating role-based access control, multi-factor authentication, and automated lifecycle management. Increasingly, blockchain-based digital credentials and micro-credentials are being adopted to enhance integrity, reduce fraud, and improve verification efficiency. These approaches directly reinforce trust by increasing transparency and user control.

Table 1. Comparative Overview of Frameworks

Framework	Key Strengths	Limitations	Primary HEI Use Case
NIST CSF 2.0	Flexible, risk-based, governance-focused	Non-certifiable	Campus-wide security governance
ISO/IEC 27001	Certifiable, internationally recognized	Resource intensive	High-risk research environments
Zero Trust Architecture	Adaptive, identity-centric	Cultural resistance	Distributed and cloud-heavy campuses

While no single framework is sufficient, effective HEIs integrate these approaches based on institutional risk appetite and maturity.

5.2 Empirical Case Applications

Case 1: Ransomware Recovery at a Public Research University

A large public university experienced a ransomware attack disrupting academic and payroll systems. By adopting NIST CSF 2.0 response and recovery functions, the institution reduced mean time to recovery by 46% within one year. Post-incident surveys showed a 19% increase in student confidence in institutional data handling, demonstrating a measurable restoration of digital trust.

Case 2: IAM and Zero Trust in a European University

A decentralized European HEI implemented mandatory MFA, federated IAM, and automated deprovisioning aligned with Zero Trust principles. GDPR-related audit findings declined by 38%, while faculty onboarding efficiency improved, illustrating that security controls can enhance—not inhibit—academic operations.

Case 3: Blockchain Credentials in an Asian Private University

The introduction of blockchain-based digital diplomas eliminated credential fraud and reduced employer verification time from weeks to seconds. Alumni surveys indicated increased perceptions of integrity and transparency, reinforcing institutional trustworthiness.

5.3 Prioritization of Risks and Digital Trust Metrics

Table 2. Key Risk Prioritization

Priority	Risk Area	Trust Impact
1	Identity & Access Management	Ability, Integrity
2	Ransomware	Ability
3	Governance Fragmentation	Integrity
4	Shadow IT	Integrity, Benevolence
5	IoT Security	Ability

Table 3. Digital Trust KPIs

Dimension	KPI
Security Capability	Mean Time to Detect (MTTD)
Resilience	Mean Time to Recover (MTTR)
Integrity	% systems with least-privilege access
Benevolence	Stakeholder trust index (survey)
Transparency	Incident disclosure latency

6. EMERGING TECHNOLOGIES: AI AND BLOCKCHAIN

Emerging technologies are profoundly reshaping the digital trust and security landscape in higher education. They are not merely new tools but powerful forces that simultaneously create unprecedented security challenges and offer innovative defensive capabilities (OculusIT, 2024; University of Oxford, 2024; ERIC, 2022; Webisoft, 2024).

Two of the most transformative technologies in this domain are Artificial Intelligence (AI) and Blockchain.

6.1 Artificial Intelligence (AI)

A Double-Edged Sword AI has become a paradoxical force in cybersecurity. It is simultaneously empowering adversaries with more sophisticated tools and equipping defenders with more intelligent and automated defences.

- AI as a Threat Vector (Offensive AI): Malicious actors are rapidly weaponizing AI, particularly Generative AI (GenAI), to enhance the scale, effectiveness, and sophistication of their attacks.

    Hyper-Realistic Phishing and Social Engineering: GenAI is being used to craft highly convincing and personalized phishing emails at a massive scale. These attacks can be tailored to specific individuals or departments, using contextually relevant language and mimicking legitimate communications with a level of accuracy that bypasses traditional security awareness training and basic email filters. The result is a surge in successful social engineering attacks, which remain the primary initial access vector for breaches.

    Automated Vulnerability Discovery and Exploitation: AI-powered tools can continuously scan the vast and complex networks of universities to identify and exploit software vulnerabilities far faster than human security teams can discover and patch them. This shortens the window of opportunity for defenders and increases the likelihood of a zero-day exploit being successful.

    Adaptive and Polymorphic Malware: AI can be used to generate malicious code that constantly changes its signature and behaviour to evade traditional, signature-based antivirus and intrusion detection systems. This “smart” malware can learn from its environment and adapt its tactics to remain undetected for longer periods.

- AI as a Defensive Tool (Defensive AI): In response to these evolving threats and the persistent cybersecurity skills gap, HEIs are increasingly leveraging AI to fortify their own security operations.
  Intelligent Threat Detection and Behavioural Analytics: AI and machine learning algorithms excel at analysing massive datasets of network traffic and user activity to establish a dynamic baseline of normal behaviour. They can then detect subtle anomalies and deviations that may indicate a security breach in real-time—threats that would be invisible to human analysts or static, rule-based systems.
  Automated Incident Response (SOAR): AI-powered Security Orchestration, Automation, and Response (SOAR) platforms can automate the critical initial stages of incident response. When a credible threat is detected, the system can automatically take containment actions—such as quarantining an infected device, blocking a malicious IP address, or disabling a compromised user account—significantly reducing response times and minimizing the potential impact of an attack.
  Security Workforce Augmentation: In the face of chronic staffing shortages, AI tools are becoming essential "co-pilots" for university Security Operations Centres (SOCs). Tools like Microsoft's Security Copilot, used at institutions like Auburn University, can automatically summarize complex security alerts, suggest remediation steps, and even help write incident reports. This allows overworked analysts to be more efficient and effective. These tools also serve as a powerful training mechanism, enabling junior staff and student workers to handle more sophisticated tasks by providing them with on-demand access to expert-level analysis and guidance.

6.2 Blockchain Technology

A New Foundation for Trust Blockchain, a decentralized, distributed, and immutable digital ledger, offers transformative potential for enhancing trust, security, and efficiency in core academic processes. Its fundamental architecture is designed to create a single, shared source of truth without relying on a central intermediary (Asimily, 2023).

- Secure and Verifiable Academic Credentials: Perhaps the most promising application of blockchain in education is the creation of tamper-proof digital transcripts, diplomas, and academic certificates. When a credential is issued and recorded on a blockchain, it is cryptographically signed and cannot be altered or forged. This effectively eliminates academic fraud and dramatically simplifies the verification process for employers, graduate schools, and other institutions, who can instantly confirm a credential's authenticity without contacting the issuing university. This model, pioneered by institutions like MIT with its "Blockcerts" platform, also gives students true ownership and control over their lifelong academic records.

- Enhanced Data Security and Student Privacy: By encrypting student records and distributing them across a decentralized network, blockchain reduces the risk of a catastrophic data breach from a single point of failure. Unlike traditional centralized databases, there is no single target for attackers to compromise. Furthermore, blockchain-based identity systems can empower students with granular control over their personal data, allowing them to specify which parts of their academic or personal records can be shared, with whom, and for what purpose, aligning with the principles of data minimization and user consent.
- Streamlined and Transparent Administrative Processes: Smart contracts—self-executing contracts with the terms of the agreement directly written into code—can be built on blockchain platforms to automate a wide range of administrative tasks. Processes like tuition payments, scholarship disbursements, course enrolment, and the transfer of academic credits can be automated, reducing administrative burden, minimizing the risk of human error, and creating a transparent, auditable trail for all transactions.

7. ADOPTION CHALLENGES AND FUTURE DIRECTIONS

Despite the clear need and the availability of advanced frameworks and technologies, the path to a secure and trustworthy digital ecosystem in higher education is fraught with significant obstacles (Pirkl, 2019; BitLyft, 2023). Successful implementation is less a technical problem and more a profound challenge of organizational change management, rooted in the unique culture, governance, and resource models of the academic world.

7.1 Institutional Barriers to Implementation

- The Culture Clash: Academic Freedom vs. Security Controls: The central paradox of cybersecurity in higher education is that the very culture that enables its success—a culture built on "openness, collaboration, and sharing"—is also its greatest vulnerability. Faculty, researchers, and students require the freedom to experiment with new tools, collaborate with international colleagues, and access information with minimal friction. These core values of autonomy and experimentation are essential for innovation. However, from a traditional security perspective, they represent significant risks. When a security leader attempts to implement controls that are perceived as restrictive—such as blocking a new file-sharing application or enforcing strict access controls on a research database—they are often met with significant cultural resistance from faculty who view these measures as bureaucratic impediments to their core mission.

- Navigating the Decentralized Environment and "Shadow IT": Most universities are not monolithic entities but federations of semi-autonomous schools, departments, and research centres. This decentralization often extends to IT resources, with many departments managing their own servers, applications, and IT staff, a phenomenon known as "shadow IT." This structure poses a massive hurdle for implementing any institution-wide security framework. The central IT or security office may lack both the visibility into and the authority over the full scope of technology operating on campus, leading to an inconsistent security posture, critical gaps in coverage, and diffuse accountability for risk.
- Chronic Resource Constraints and the Skills Gap: Resource constraints are cited as the most common challenge in HEI cybersecurity, mentioned in 88% of relevant research. This is a multifaceted problem. First, institutional IT budgets are under increasing pressure, with 42% of HEIs expecting decreases in the 2025-2026 academic year. Within this constrained environment, cybersecurity must compete for funding with high-profile priorities like athletics and new construction. Second, this financial limitation directly impacts staffing. Public universities, with their rigid salary structures, simply cannot compete with the private sector for scarce cybersecurity talent. This leaves university security teams chronically understaffed, overworked, and struggling to manage an expanding threat surface with insufficient personnel.
- The Compliance-Focused Mindset: Given the heavy regulatory burden on HEIs, security efforts often become narrowly focused on "checking the box"—meeting the minimum requirements needed to pass an audit for regulations like GLBA, HIPAA, or CMMC. This compliance-centric approach is dangerous. It fosters a false sense of security, where an institution believes it is protected because it is compliant on paper, while remaining highly vulnerable to real-world threats. It also leads to inefficient resource allocation, as funds are directed toward meeting specific audit requirements rather than addressing the institution's most significant risks.

As shown in Figure 2, a systematic review of 50 relevant studies found that resource constraints (including budget and staffing) are the most frequently cited challenge, mentioned in 88% of the literature, followed by the complexity of implementation (62%), and cultural resistance and the evolving threat landscape (both at 58%).

Figure 2. Common Implementation Challenges in HEIs Data from a systematic literature review of 50 studies highlights the most frequently mentioned barriers to adopting cybersecurity frameworks in higher education.

Figure 2. Implementation Challenges in HEIs

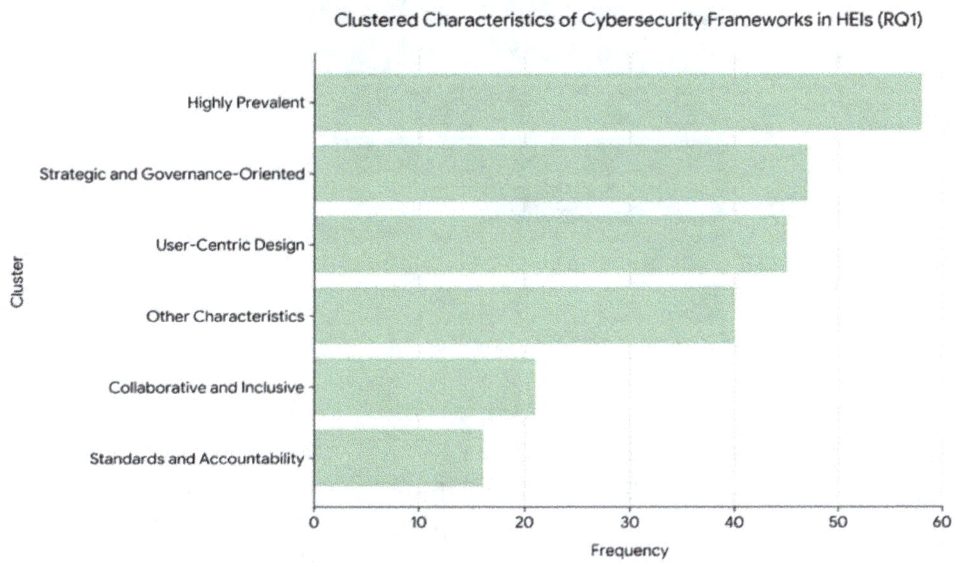

Overcoming these challenges requires an integrated strategy that aligns foundational principles with operational execution. The conceptual model presented in Figure 3 illustrates this integrated framework. It posits that achieving the desired outcomes of Digital Trust and Cyber Resilience requires the careful synthesis of three core elements: the foundational Trust Principles (Ability, Integrity, Benevolence), the operational Security Frameworks (like NIST CSF and ISO 27001), and the unique Institutional Context of higher education (its culture of openness, decentralized governance, and resource model). A successful strategy is one that embeds the principles of trust into the selection and adaptation of security frameworks in a way that respects and works within, rather than against, the institution's specific context.

Figure 3. Integrated Framework for Digital Trust and Security This conceptual model shows how trust principles, security frameworks, and institutional context must be integrated to achieve digital trust and resilience.

Figure 3. Integrated Framework for Digital Trust and Security

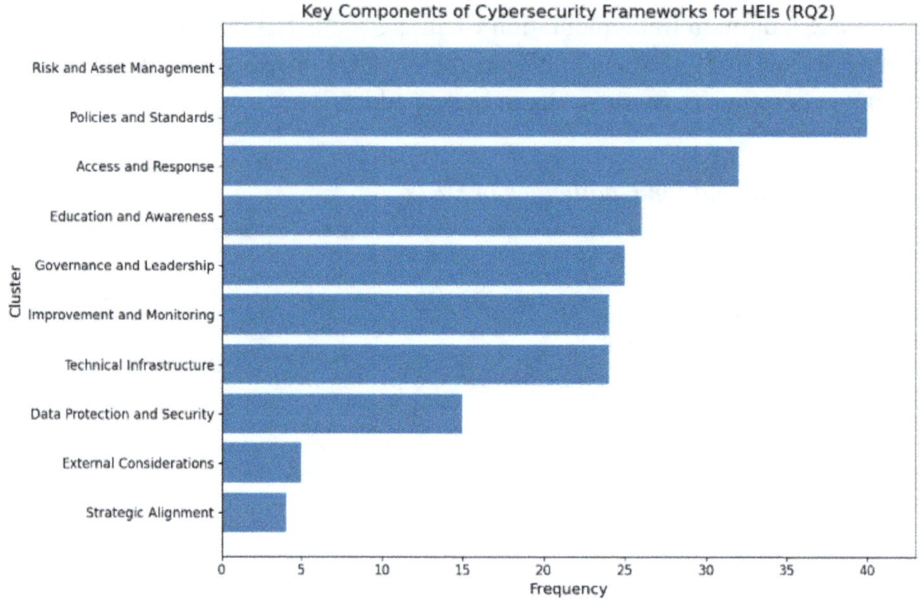

Based on this integrated framework and the extensive analysis presented in this report, the following strategic recommendations are offered for senior leaders in higher education (e.g., Presidents, Provosts, CIOs, and CISOs):

- *Elevate Cybersecurity to a Core Institutional Risk Issue*: The responsibility for cybersecurity cannot reside solely within the IT department. It must be treated as a fundamental institutional risk, on par with financial, operational, and reputational risk. This requires regular, substantive discussion at the highest levels of leadership, including the Board of Trustees. The conversation must be framed not in technical jargon, but in terms of institutional resilience and the protection of the university's mission, reputation, and financial stability.
- *Establish and Empower a Cross-Functional Governance Body*: Create a permanent, high-level cybersecurity and data governance committee with senior representation from academic affairs, research, legal counsel, student affairs, finance, and communications, in addition to IT. This body should be empowered to define the institution's risk appetite, make risk-based decisions that balance security with the academic mission, approve institution-wide policies, and ensure the security strategy remains aligned with strategic goals.

- *Invest in People and Culture, Not Just Technology*: While technology is an essential component of any security program, the human element is consistently identified as the weakest link. Prioritize sustained investment in continuous, tailored cybersecurity awareness training for all stakeholder groups—students, faculty, staff, and researchers. The goal is to move beyond annual compliance training and build a campus-wide culture of shared responsibility for security, where every individual understands their role in protecting the institution's digital assets.
- *Adopt a Bimodal and Risk-Based Security Strategy*: Avoid a rigid, one-size-fits-all approach to security frameworks. Employ a flexible, risk-based framework like the NIST CSF as the overarching structure for the general campus environment, allowing for departmental autonomy and tailored controls. For specific, high-risk, high-compliance areas—such as defense-related research, systems handling sensitive health data, or financial transaction platforms—apply more rigorous, certifiable standards like ISO 27001 to provide verifiable assurance to external partners, funding agencies, and regulators.
- *Champion a Strategic Shift from Compliance to Resilience*: Lead the institutional mindset away from merely "checking the box" for compliance. Focus strategic planning and resource allocation on building true cyber resilience—the ability to anticipate, withstand, recover from, and adapt to adverse cyber events. This means prioritizing investments in robust incident response capabilities, comprehensive and regularly tested data backup and recovery systems, and a forward-looking Zero Trust architecture that reflects the reality of the modern, borderless campus.

By embracing these principles, higher education institutions can begin to navigate the immense complexities of the digital age, protect their valuable intellectual and human assets, and, most importantly, fulfil their core mission by earning and maintaining the enduring trust of the communities they serve.

7.2 Future Directions for a Resilient Digital Campus

- Securing the Hyper-Connected Campus and the Internet of Things (IoT): The modern university campus is a dense, hyper-connected environment populated by a vast and growing array of IoT devices—from smart building systems and connected lab equipment to security cameras and smart classroom technologies. Many of these devices are not designed with security in mind, often shipping with default passwords and lacking the ability to be patched, leaving them permanently vulnerable. A single compromised IoT device can provide an attacker with a foothold inside the campus network. A critical future strategy is network segmentation, which involves isolating IoT devices on separate, restricted virtual networks (VLANs) to prevent them from communicating with sensitive administrative or research systems, thereby containing the damage if a device is compromised.

- Adopting a Zero Trust Architecture: The combined challenges of a distributed user base (remote learning, BYOD), the shift to cloud services, and the proliferation of IoT devices have rendered the traditional "castle-and-moat" security model obsolete. In its place, a new security paradigm is emerging: Zero Trust. Zero Trust is a strategic security model that operates on the principle of "never trust, always verify." It eliminates the concept of a trusted internal network and assumes that a breach is always possible. Under a Zero Trust architecture, no user or device is granted access to resources until it has been explicitly authenticated and authorized for that specific transaction. Access is granted on a least-privilege basis and is continuously monitored for anomalous behaviour. This model is exceptionally well-suited to the borderless, distributed, and complex realities of the modern university and represents the most effective architectural approach for the future.

8. CONCLUSIONS

Building and maintaining digital trust is not a finite project but a continuous, strategic endeavour that must be woven into the very fabric of institutional governance and culture. It requires a fundamental shift away from a purely technical or compliance-driven view of security toward a holistic, risk-based approach that prioritizes stakeholder confidence and institutional resilience. This research has synthesized evidence from a wide body of literature to construct a framework for understanding and navigating this complex challenge. The analysis reveals that while robust frameworks and advanced technologies are available, their successful adoption is consistently hindered by a set of deeply ingrained institutional barriers.

REFERENCES

Al-Ahmad, A. A., et al. (2024). Systematic review of cybersecurity frameworks for higher education institutions.

Al-Zahrani, M. A.. (2024). *A conceptual framework for integrating artificial intelligence into cybersecurity higher education*. MDPI.

Arizona State University. (2022, October 20). Digital trust: What it means and how institutions can gain it. ASU UTO.

Arizona State University. (2024). *Digital trust guidelines*. ASU AI Acceleration.

Asimily. (2023). How universities can mitigate IoT security risk. Asimily Blog.

Association of American Universities. (2024). *Science and security*. AAU.

BitLyft. (2023). *The state of higher education cybersecurity: Insights & trends*. BitLyft Blog.

BoardEffect. (2024). *How to create a cyber risk framework for your college or university*. BoardEffect Blog.

Bravura Security. (2024). *Identity and access management for education*. Bravura Security.

EDUCAUSE. (2023, March). Cyber resilience: The future for higher education. *EDUCAUSE Review*.

EDUCAUSE. (2024, May). Cybersecurity in higher education: Don't let the hackers win. *EDUCAUSE Review*.

ERIC. (2022). *Blockchain and micro-credentials in education*. ERIC.

FortifyData. (2024). *Top data security practices for higher education*. FortifyData Blog.

IBM. (2024). *Reducing ransomware recovery costs in the education sector*. IBM Think.

Identity Automation. (2024). IAM software designed to solve higher ed challenges. Identity Automation.

International Organization for Standardization. (2022). *ISO/IEC 27001:2022 Information security, cybersecurity and privacy protection*. ISO.

Kidwell, D., & Giovacchini, D. (2022, October 20). Digital trust: What it means and how institutions can gain it. ASU UTO.

Lepide. (2024). Leveraging the NIST framework in educational institutions. Lepide Blog.

Lin, D., Crabtree, J., Dillo, I., Downs, R. R., Edmunds, R., Giaretta, D., De Giusti, M., L'Hours, H., Hugo, W., Jenkyns, R., Khodiyar, V., Martone, M. E., Mokrane, M., Navale, V., Petters, J., Sierman, B., Sokolova, D. V., Stockhause, M., & Westbrook, J. (2020). The TRUST principles for digital repositories. *Scientific Data*, *7*(1), 144. DOI: 10.1038/s41597-020-0486-7 PMID: 32409645

Modern Campus. (2024). *GDPR and higher education: What you need to know.* Modern Campus Blog.

Monash University. (2024). *ISO 27001 certification.* Monash University Cyber Security.

National Institute of Standards and Technology. (2020, June). Cybersecurity framework success story: University of Chicago Biological Sciences Division. NIST.

National Institute of Standards and Technology. (2024, February). Cybersecurity framework (CSF) 2.0. NIST.

NC State University OIT. (2023, October). What is the cost of a data breach? NC State OIT News.

NovelVista. (2024). *Common challenges while implementing ISO 27001 and how to overcome them.* NovelVista Blog.

Nygard, M. (2024). *Implementing ISO/IEC 27001:2022 in a SME.* Theseus.

Oculus, I. T. (2024). *How AI is transforming cybersecurity in higher education.* OculusIT Blog.

Parchment. (2024). Future-proof your credentials management ecosystem. Parchment Blog.

Parchment. (2024). Why you should embrace digital credential management. Parchment Blog.

Pirkl, K. D. F. (2019, May). Creating a cybersecurity strategy for higher education. *EDUCAUSE Review*.

Planon. (2023). The most important stakeholders of the campus of the future. Planon Software.

PRISMA. (2021). PRISMA 2020 statement. prisma-statement.org.

RAUSP Management Journal. (2022). The influence of trust on the adoption of blockchain in higher education institutions. RAUSP Management Journal. Emerald.

Research.com. (2024). The future of blockchain technology in education. Research.com.

Rutgers University. (2024). *General data protection regulation (GDPR).* Rutgers University Ethics and Compliance.

SenseTime. (2024). *What is digital trust and why is it important?* SenseTime News.

Sift. (2023, September). What is digital trust, and why is it at risk? Sift Blog.

Stanković, M., Stanković, N., & Bjelica, M. Z. (2025). What is digital trust and how can we measure it? A multidimensional approach. *Electronics (Basel), 14*(1), 1.

Tech, O. C. D. (2024). *How to make your college align with NIST cybersecurity guidelines.* OCD Tech.

UnderDefense. (2018, December). Case study: NIST cybersecurity framework assessment. UnderDefense.

University of Minnesota. (2024). *Securing Internet of Things (IoT) devices.* UMN IT.

University of New South Wales. (2024). *ISO/IEC 27001:2022 certification.* UNSW IT.

University of Oxford. (2024). *Safeguarding academia: Harnessing the power of AI to fortify higher education cybersecurity.* University of Oxford.

University of Texas Health Science Center at Houston. (2024). *Research security program.* HOOP Policy Manual.

UpGuard. (2024). *NIST SP 800-171 compliance guide for colleges & universities.* UpGuard Blog.

U.S. Department of Education. (2024). *Identity authentication best practices.* Student Privacy Policy Office.

Washington University in St. Louis. (2024). *Threats to your research data and intellectual property.* WUSTL Information Security.

Webisoft. (2024). Blockchain for universities: A game-changer in academic data management. Webisoft.

World Economic Forum. (2023). Earning digital trust. World Economic Forum.

Zimmerman, E. (2019, January). How universities can mitigate IoT risk on campus. EdTech Magazine.

Chapter 5
Data Privacy, Security, and Ethical Considerations in AI and Blockchain Adoption

Maroof Ahmad
Khwaja Moinuddin Chishti Language University, Lucknow, India

Tasleem Jamal
http://orcid.org/0009-0000-2977-9925
Khwaja Moinuddin Chishti Language University, Lucknow, India

Mohd Imran
Khwaja Moinuddin Chishti Language University, Lucknow, India

Laiba Khan
Khwaja Moinuddin Chishti Language University, Lucknow, India

Sandeep Kumar Yadav
Institute of Engineering and Technology, Lucknow, India

ABSTRACT

In the digital era, the convergence of Artificial Intelligence (AI) and Blockchain Technology offers transformative possibilities across sectors—from finance and healthcare to supply chains and governance. However, behind these exciting opportunities lie profound challenges related to data privacy, security, and ethics. This chapter explores these dimensions in a "human-words" style, with special reference to blockchain in the mix, so that the reader grasps both what the issues are and

DOI: 10.4018/979-8-3373-7600-4.ch005

how the blockchain context changes, complicates, or amplifies them. Though AI and blockchain can each bring virtues, their intersection also multiplies risks. We will walk through: (1) privacy concerns, (2) security challenges, (3) ethical frameworks (fairness, transparency, accountability), (4) how blockchain changes the picture, and (5) practical guidelines for responsible adoption.

INTRODUCTION

Artificial Intelligence (AI) and blockchain technologies are increasingly becoming part of the digital infrastructure of higher education. Universities and academic institutions are adopting these technologies to issue secure digital credentials, maintain lifelong learning records, automate verification processes, and generate meaningful insights from learner data (Allen & Berg, 2020; Sharples & Domingue, 2016). Higher education institutions are custodians of highly sensitive learner information, including academic performance, identity details, behavioral data, and career pathways. Any failure to manage this data responsibly can damage institutional credibility, violate legal frameworks, and cause long-term harm to learners (Floridi et al., 2018; UNESCO, 2021).

Academic records often remain relevant throughout an individual's life, influencing employment opportunities, professional reputation, and social mobility. In digital learning environments, institutions collect extensive data such as personal identifiers, assessment results, attendance logs, learning analytics, and, in some cases, biometric information used for online examinations (OECD, 2019). When combined into lifelong learning profiles and digital credentials, this data can reveal detailed patterns about a learner's abilities, preferences, and challenges. If accessed without authorization or used unethically, such information may lead to profiling, discrimination, or irreversible reputational damage (O'Neil, 2016; Mittelstadt et al., 2016).

The growing use of AI-based systems further amplifies these risks. AI is now widely used to support automated grading, predict learner performance, recommend credentials, and assess employability (Popenici & Kerr, 2017; Yadav & Vishwakarma, 2020). Moreover, when decision-making processes are difficult to explain, learners and educators may struggle to understand or challenge academic outcomes, weakening accountability and trust (Wachter et al., 2017; Jobin et al., 2019).

This chapter explores the privacy, security, and ethical challenges that emerge with the adoption of AI and blockchain technologies in higher education credentialing. It highlights the risks associated with extensive data collection and automated decision-making, while emphasizing the need for transparency, accountability, and learner control. The chapter also discusses governance mechanisms, technical safeguards, and ethical principles required for responsible implementation. By embedding ethical design, robust data protection practices, and human oversight into digital systems, higher education institutions can ensure that technological innovation supports a trustworthy, inclusive, and learner-centred academic ecosystem (IEEE, 2019; UNESCO, 2021).

BLOCKCHAIN-ENABLED DATA MANAGEMENT AND CREDENTIALING IN HIGHER EDUCATION

Blockchain technology has emerged as a transformative solution for managing educational data and academic credentials in modern higher education systems. Traditional credential management relies on centralized databases controlled by institutions or third-party providers, which creates risks related to data breaches, unauthorized modification, and limited learner control (Tapscott & Tapscott, 2016). Blockchain introduces a decentralized, tamper-resistant framework that enhances data integrity, transparency, and trust across academic ecosystems s (Sharples & Domingue, 2016; Xu et al., 2019).

In educational data management, blockchain operates as a distributed ledger in which records are maintained across multiple nodes rather than stored in a single central repository. Each entry is cryptographically linked to previous records, ensuring that academic data such as enrolment verification, assessment completion, and credential issuance remains secure and auditable (Gervais et al., 2016). In practice, sensitive learner data is typically stored off-chain, while cryptographic hashes or metadata are recorded on-chain to ensure integrity and regulatory compliance (Zhang & Xue, 2019; Zyskind et al., 2015).

Blockchain-based credentialing allows institutions to issue degrees, certificates, micro-credentials, and digital badges as verifiable digital credentials. These credentials are immutable once issued, significantly reducing credential fraud (Allen & Berg, 2020). Learners maintain credentials in secure digital wallets, giving them control over when, how, and with whom their credentials are shared. Verification becomes instant and does not require direct communication with the issuing institution, making the process efficient and globally scalable (Sharples & Domingue, 2016; PwC, 2020).

Table 1. Key Technical Features of Blockchain in Credentialing

Technical Feature	Description and Role in Credentialing Systems
Decentralization	Academic records are distributed across multiple network nodes, eliminating single points of failure and improving system reliability and resilience.
Cryptographic Hashing	Credentials are represented using cryptographic hashes that ensure data integrity while preventing direct exposure of sensitive learner information.
Public–Private Key Cryptography	Learners use private keys to control access to their credentials, while public keys allow authorized third parties to securely verify authenticity.
Time-Stamping	Each credential transaction is recorded with a verifiable timestamp, supporting traceability, audit trails, and chronological validation.
Off-Chain Storage Integration	Sensitive learner data is stored securely outside the blockchain, while cryptographic proofs on-chain maintain data integrity and ownership verification.

Despite its advantages, blockchain adoption in education must address scalability, governance, energy efficiency, legal recognition, and privacy concerns (Kshetri, 2021). Hybrid architectures, permissioned blockchains, and privacy-preserving techniques are often used to mitigate these challenges. Strong governance models and ethical frameworks are essential to ensure responsible and sustainable implementation (ISO/IEC, 2022; Floridi et al., 2018).

Overall, blockchain provides a secure, transparent, and learner-centric foundation for managing educational data and credentials. When combined with appropriate technical design and policy oversight, it can support trustworthy digital credentialing and lifelong learning ecosystems (Xu et al., 2019; World Economic Forum, 2021).

Figure 1. Steps To Issue Blockchain Academic Credential

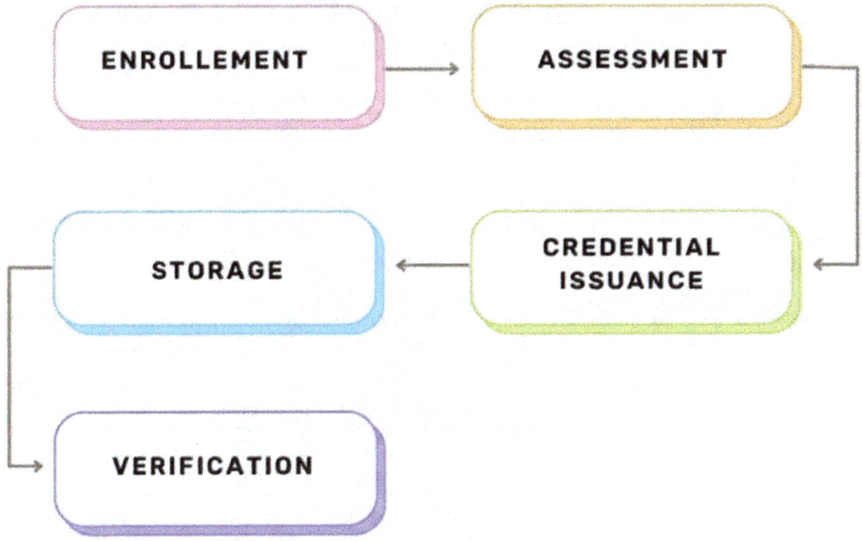

ROLE OF ARTIFICIAL INTELLIGENCE IN CREDENTIALING SYSTEMS

Artificial Intelligence (AI) is becoming a core component of modern credentialing systems, particularly as education moves toward digital, skills-based, and lifelong learning models. AI supports institutions in managing large volumes of learner data, interpreting complex learning outcomes, and delivering personalized and trustworthy credentialing services (Dwivedi et al., 2021; UNESCO, 2019). When integrated with secure infrastructures such as blockchain, AI enhances both the efficiency and intelligence of credential ecosystems (OECD, 2019; World Economic Forum, 2021).

Table 2. Key roles of AI

AI Function	Description and Application in Credentialing
Automated Credential Evaluation	AI systems assess academic records, learning outcomes, and assessment data to support automated grading, competency validation, and credential issuance (Yadav & Vishwakarma, 2020).
Skill Extraction and Competency Mapping	Machine learning and natural language processing are used to identify skills and competencies from transcripts, course descriptions, portfolios, and work-based learning evidence.
Support for Lifelong Learning Pathways	AI tracks learning progress across institutions and time, enabling continuous credential updates and recognition of ongoing learning achievements (UNESCO, 2019).
Credential Verification and Fraud Detection	AI detects anomalies in credential issuance and verification processes, helping to identify potential fraud or data inconsistencies.
Decision Support for Institutions	AI provides data-driven insights to support academic planning, accreditation reporting, and policy formulation.
Integration with Blockchain Systems	AI interacts with blockchain smart contracts to automate credential issuance, updates, or revocation based on verified learning achievements.
Explainable and Ethical Decision-Making	Explainable AI models enhance transparency, enabling learners and educators to understand, challenge, and trust AI-generated outcomes (Wachter et al., 2017; Jobin et al., 2019).

TOWARD SECURE AND LEARNER-CENTRIC CREDENTIAL ECOSYSTEMS

The evolution of academic credentialing is increasingly shaped by the combined use of Artificial Intelligence (AI) and blockchain technologies. Together, these technologies are driving a shift from institution-centric credential management toward secure, intelligent, and learner-centric credential ecosystems (World Economic Forum, 2021; OECD, 2019). While blockchain provides the foundation for trust, security, and ownership, AI adds analytical intelligence that supports personalization, skill interpretation, and informed decision-making across educational and employment contexts (Dwivedi et al., 2021).

Security and privacy remain central to these ecosystems. Blockchain's decentralized architecture, immutability, and cryptographic protections ensure the integrity and authenticity of credentials (Tapscott & Tapscott, 2016; Zhang & Xue, 2019).. At the same time, AI-driven data processing must be carefully governed to prevent misuse, bias, or unauthorized profiling. Privacy-preserving AI techniques, such as federated learning and explainable AI models, help ensure that learner data is analysed responsibly without compromising confidentiality or transparency (Floridi et al., 2018; IEEE, 2019).

Ultimately, the convergence of AI and blockchain enables a new generation of credential ecosystems that are secure, adaptive, and centred on learner empowerment. When designed with strong ethical principles, robust governance, and privacy-by-design approaches, these ecosystems can support lifelong learning, workforce mobility, and equitable access to educational opportunities in a rapidly changing digital society (OECD, 2019; World Economic Forum, 2021).

EVOLUTION FROM PAPER CREDENTIALS TO DIGITAL AND BLOCKCHAIN-BASED CREDENTIALS

The evolution from paper to digital and blockchain-based credentials represents more than a technological upgrade; it marks a fundamental shift in how academic achievements are issued, owned, and trusted. While paper credentials emphasized institutional authority, blockchain-based systems promote transparency, learner autonomy, and global verifiability (Buterin, 2014; Sharples & Domingue, 2016).

Table 3. Evolution of Credentials

Year / Period	Credentialing Stage	Key Characteristics
Before 1800	Handwritten Credentials	Academic achievements documented through handwritten certificates using institutional seals and signatures; verification relied on institutional reputation and trust.
1800–1950	Standardized Paper Credentials	Printed degrees and transcripts became standardized and legally recognized; records were maintained physically, making verification slow and credentials vulnerable to loss or forgery.
1960–1980	Early Digital Record Management	Universities began using basic computing systems to store student records internally, while credentials continued to be issued in paper format.
1990–2000	Online Academic Databases	Adoption of internet-based student information systems enabled electronic record storage and email-based verification, though credentials remained institution-controlled.
2001–2005	PDF-Based Digital Credentials	Institutions issued digital transcripts and certificates in PDF form, improving accessibility but offering limited protection against copying or manipulation.
2008	Introduction of Blockchain Technology	Blockchain emerged as a decentralized, tamper-resistant ledger, laying the foundation for secure and verifiable digital credentials.
2012–2014	Expansion of Online Learning	Growth of MOOCs and online programs increased demand for flexible and portable credentials across multiple learning platforms.
2015	Digital Badges and Micro-Credentials	Skill-based digital badges gained popularity, though lack of standardization limited credibility and widespread acceptance.
2016–2017	Blockchain Credential Pilots	Universities and organizations began issuing academic credentials on blockchain, enabling tamper-proof records and instant verification.
2018–2019	Learner-Controlled Credentials	Emergence of digital wallets allowed learners to store, manage, and share credentials, shifting ownership from institutions to individuals.
2020	Pandemic-Driven Digital Adoption	COVID-19 accelerated digital transformation, increasing reliance on online learning, remote assessments, and secure digital credentialing.
2021–2022	Policy and Standards Development	Governments and accrediting bodies explored frameworks for digital and blockchain credentials, emphasizing privacy, interoperability, and governance.
2023–Present	AI-Integrated Blockchain Credentials	Blockchain credentials are combined with AI for skill analysis, employability insights, and lifelong learning support across global education systems.

DIGITAL TRANSFORMATION OF CREDENTIALING SYSTEMS

The digital transformation of credentialing systems represents a fundamental shift in how academic achievements are recorded, verified, and trusted. Traditionally, credentialing relied on paper-based certificates and institution-controlled digital records, which were limited in security, accessibility, and scalability. As higher education embraces digital transformation, credentialing systems are evolving to support lifelong learning, global mobility, and skills-based recognition.

Blockchain technology plays a crucial role in strengthening security and trust within digital credentialing systems. By enabling decentralized, tamper-resistant records, blockchain reduces reliance on centralized databases and minimizes the risk of credential fraud. From an ethical perspective, this shift supports learner autonomy and ownership of academic records, while also demanding careful governance to prevent misuse and ensure equitable access (Floridi et al., 2018).

AI further accelerates the digital transformation of credentialing by enabling intelligent automation, skill analysis, and decision support. AI-driven systems can evaluate learning outcomes, recommend credentials, and align academic achievements with labour market needs (Yadav & Vishwakarma, 2020; World Economic Forum, 2021). However, these capabilities introduce ethical risks such as algorithmic bias, lack of transparency, and excessive automation in high-stakes academic decisions. Explainable AI models, human oversight, and fairness-aware algorithms are therefore critical to maintaining trust and accountability in credentialing processes (Wachter et al., 2017; O'Neil, 2016).

Overall, the digital transformation of credentialing systems extends beyond technological innovation. It requires a balanced approach that integrates AI and blockchain with strong data protection measures, ethical governance, and learner-centric design. By embedding privacy, security, and ethical considerations into digital credentialing infrastructures, higher education institutions can build trusted systems that support lifelong learning, institutional credibility, and social equity in an increasingly digital academic landscape (IEEE, 2019; OECD, 2019).

EMERGENCE OF DIGITAL CREDENTIALING TECHNOLOGIES

Digital credentialing technologies have emerged as a response to the growing limitations of traditional paper-based academic records. By combining conventional information systems with advanced technologies such as blockchain and artificial intelligence (AI), modern credentialing frameworks support the secure issuance, management, verification, and analysis of academic and professional credentials. These technologies enhance transparency, improve efficiency, and promote a shift toward learner-centric credential ownership (Coursera, 2021; Dede, 2014; World Economic Forum, 2020).

1. Electronic Certificates and Transcripts

Electronic certificates and transcripts represent digital versions of traditional paper-based academic records, typically issued in secure formats such as PDFs. Their primary function is to improve accessibility, reduce administrative workload, and enable faster sharing of credentials with employers or educational institutions (Allen & Berg, 2020).

2. Micro-Credentials

Micro-credentials focus on recognizing specific skills or competencies rather than awarding full academic degrees. These credentials, which include short-course certificates and skill-based recognitions, support modular and flexible learning pathways tailored to individual learner needs. Micro-credentials allow employers to assess job-relevant skills more precisely.

3. Digital Badges

Digital badges are visually identifiable, digitally issued credentials embedded with metadata that details the issuer, achievement criteria, and supporting evidence. They enable learners to showcase individual skills and achievements through professional networks, social media platforms, and digital portfolios. Digital badges are particularly effective in recognizing informal and non-traditional learning

4. Blockchain-Based Credentialing

Blockchain-based credentialing systems store academic records on decentralized, tamper-resistant ledgers, ensuring the immutability and verifiability of credentials. This approach enables instant verification without requiring communication with the issuing institution, significantly reducing credential fraud. However, effective implementation requires robust governance frameworks, privacy-preserving designs, and energy-efficient blockchain solutions (Allen & Berg, 2020; Sharples & Domingue, 2016).

5. Artificial Intelligence in Credentialing

Artificial intelligence enhances digital credentialing systems by automating and optimizing credential-related processes. AI can support automated grading, competency assessment, skill extraction from transcripts and portfolios, personalized credential recommendations, fraud detection, and alignment with labour market trends (Barocas et al., 2019; Yadav & Vishwakarma, 2020).

6. Credential Wallets and Digital Portfolios

Credential wallets and digital portfolios provide learners with secure digital repositories to store, manage, and selectively share their credentials across their lifetime. These tools support learner autonomy, instant verification, and long-term access to learning records. When integrated with blockchain for secure validation and AI for skill analysis, credential wallets form the foundation of portable, lifelong, and learner-controlled credentialing ecosystems (Buterin, 2014; W3C, 2022).

SECURITY AND TRUST IN DIGITAL CREDENTIALING

Security and trust are central to the digital transformation of credentialing systems. Blockchain contributes to security through cryptographic techniques, decentralized consensus, and immutable records, while AI supports fraud detection and risk analysis. Together, these technologies strengthen confidence in the authenticity and reliability of academic credentials (Coursera, 2021; OECD, 2019).

Table 4. Security and trust features of digital transformation of credentialing systems

Mechanism	Description	Purpose / Benefit
Data Encryption	Secures learner data using cryptographic algorithms to prevent unauthorized access.	Protects sensitive personal and academic information from breaches and tampering.
Blockchain Immutability	Records credentials on a decentralized ledger that cannot be altered or deleted.	Prevents forgery, enhances trust, and ensures verifiable authenticity of credentials.
Digital Signatures & Public-Private Key Cryptography	Uses cryptographic keys to authenticate issuers and recipients.	Guarantees that credentials are issued and received by verified entities.
AI-Driven Verification & Fraud Detection	Analyses credential issuance and usage patterns to detect anomalies.	Identifies potential fraud or inconsistencies, improving overall system reliability.

continued on following page

Table 4. Continued

Mechanism	Description	Purpose / Benefit
Learner-Controlled Access	Learners manage who can view or share their credentials using digital wallets.	Enhances privacy and autonomy, building trust among stakeholders.
Explainable AI & Human Oversight	AI decisions are transparent and supervised by humans.	Ensures fairness, accountability, and ethical decision-making in automated processes.

UNDERSTANDING DATA AND THE IMPORTANCE OF PRIVACY IN DIGITAL HIGHER EDUCATION SYSTEMS

In the context of higher education, *data* refers to the vast range of information generated, collected, processed, and stored throughout a learner's academic journey. This includes personal details such as names, identification numbers, and contact information, as well as academic records like grades, transcripts, credentials, assessment results, learning analytics, and behavioral data generated through digital learning platforms (OECD, 2019; UNESCO, 2021).

Data privacy is the principle that individuals should have control over how their personal and academic information is collected, processed, stored, and shared. In AI- and blockchain-enabled educational systems, privacy becomes especially important due to the scale, sensitivity, and permanence of data (European Union, 2016; Indian Ministry of Electronics and IT, 2023).

KEY REASONS DATA PRIVACY MATTERS

- *Protection of learner autonomy:* Privacy safeguards ensure learners retain control over who can access their academic records and credentials (Prinsloo & Slade, 2017).
- *Prevention of misuse and discrimination:* Unauthorized data access or algorithmic profiling can lead to unfair treatment, bias, or exclusion.
- *Trust in digital credentialing systems:* Learners, employers, and institutions are more likely to adopt digital credentials when data is handled transparently and securely.
- *Ethical use of AI:* AI systems rely on large datasets; privacy helps prevent excessive surveillance, opaque decision-making, and biased outcomes (Floridi et al., 2018).

- *Legal and regulatory compliance:* Data privacy supports adherence to data protection laws and educational regulations, reducing institutional risk.

NATURE AND LIFECYCLE OF EDUCATIONAL DATA IN HIGHER EDUCATION

Educational data forms the backbone of academic administration, teaching, learning, and credentialing in higher education. With the widespread adoption of digital technologies, artificial intelligence (AI), and blockchain-based systems, the volume, variety, and sensitivity of educational data have grown significantly (OECD, 2019; UNESCO, 2021). Understanding the nature, characteristics, and lifecycle of this data is essential for designing secure, privacy-conscious, and ethically responsible credentialing and data management systems.

Educational data is distinct from transactional or operational data found in commercial domains. It not only reflects learning outcomes but also captures intellectual development, behaviour, and personal identity. These qualities make educational data inherently sensitive, high-stakes, and long-lasting.

Key categories include:

1. Personal and Identity Data

Includes names, enrolment numbers, contact details, demographic information, and government-issued identifiers. This data forms the basis for linking academic achievements to individuals and must be protected against misuse, identity theft, or unauthorized disclosure.

2. Academic Records

Comprises grades, transcripts, examination results, course completions, and degree awards. Academic records are critical for progression, employability, and professional recognition, demanding accuracy, integrity, and verifiable authenticity.

3. Behavioral and Interaction Data

Generated through digital learning environments, this data includes attendance logs, participation records, submission patterns, and system interactions. While valuable for analytics and learner insights, behavioral data can reveal sensitive personal patterns if not carefully managed.

4. Administrative and Institutional Data

Covers enrolment status, program structures, faculty assignments, accreditation records, and institutional performance metrics. Though less personal, administrative data is essential for operational decision-making, compliance, and reporting.

Figure 2. Lifecycle Of Educational Data

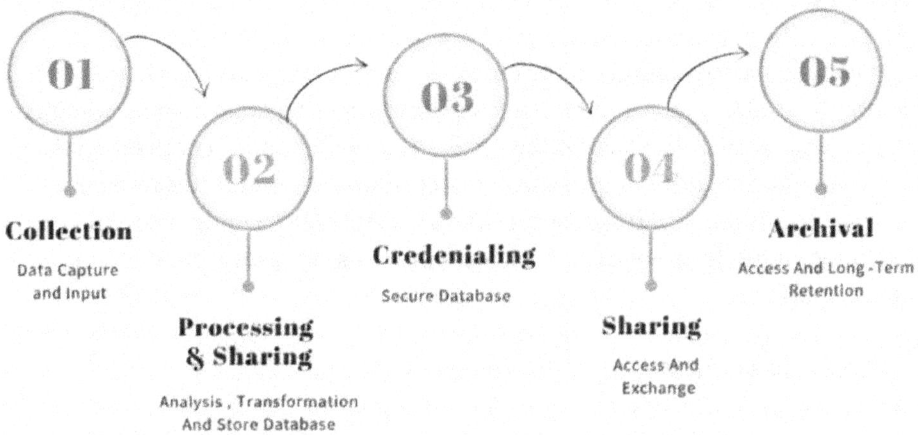

TYPES OF DATA IN HIGHER EDUCATION

Higher education institutions generate and manage diverse categories of data that support academic administration, teaching, assessment, and credentialing processes. With the increasing adoption of digital platforms, artificial intelligence, and remote learning technologies, the volume and sensitivity of educational data have grown significantly (UNESCO, 2019; Williamson & Eynon, 2020). Understanding the different types of data handled by higher education systems is essential for ensuring appropriate privacy protection, security controls, and ethical governance (Prinsloo & Slade, 2017).

1. Identity Data

Identity data refers to information used to uniquely identify individuals within institutional systems. This data is fundamental to admissions, enrolment, credential issuance, and verification processes. Typical identity data includes names, student identification numbers, dates of birth, contact details, photographs, and government-issued identifiers used for authentication (U.S. Department of Education, 2020; W3C, 2022).

Because identity data establishes the link between an individual and their academic records, its protection is critical. Unauthorized access or misuse can lead to identity theft, impersonation, or fraudulent credential claims (Zyskind et al., 2015)

2. Academic Records

Academic records represent the core evidence of educational achievement. This category includes grades, transcripts, examination results, course completions, degrees, and certifications issued by institutions. Academic records directly influence academic progression, professional opportunities, and institutional reputation (Sharples & Domingue, 2016; Tapscott & Tapscott, 2016). Digital systems supported by cryptographic techniques and secure databases help protect academic records from tampering

3. Behavioral Data

Behavioral data is generated through learners' interactions with digital educational systems. This includes attendance logs, participation records, assignment submission patterns, system usage metrics, and engagement indicators within online platforms. Behavioral data provides valuable insights into learning patterns, academic engagement, and course effectiveness.

Without appropriate safeguards, analysis may lead to intrusive monitoring or unfair profiling (Popenici & Kerr, 2017). Institutions must ensure that the collection and analysis of behavioral data are transparent, proportionate, and aligned with educational objectives (O'Neil, 2016; Mittelstadt et al., 2016).

4. Biometric and Proctoring Data

Biometric and proctoring data has become increasingly prevalent with the rise of online examinations and remote assessment systems. This category includes facial images, voice recordings, keystroke patterns, eye movement tracking, and video or audio recordings captured during examinations. Biometric data is used to verify identity and prevent academic dishonesty. Among all types of educational data, biometric data is considered highly sensitive due to its permanent and personal nature (Floridi et al., 2018; Jobin et al., 2019).

CHARACTERISTICS OF EDUCATIONAL DATA IN HIGHER EDUCATION

Educational data in higher education exhibits several defining characteristics that amplify privacy and governance challenges (OECD, 2019).

Table 5. Characteristics of educational data in higher education

Characteristic	Description / Implications
Long-Term Relevance	Academic records and credentials remain meaningful throughout a learner's lifetime, influencing further education, employment, and professional mobility.
High Sensitivity	Errors, breaches, or unauthorized access can cause long-term academic, professional, or reputational harm to learners.
Multi-Stakeholder Access	Data is accessed by learners, faculty, administrators, employers, accreditation bodies, and government agencies, increasing the need for robust governance.

LIFECYCLE OF FLOW OF DATA IN AI–BLOCKCHAIN CREDENTIALING SYSTEMS

The lifecycle of educational data refers to the stages through which data passes from creation to eventual archival or deletion. Each stage presents unique privacy, security, and ethical considerations (OECD, 2019; Floridi, 2019).

1. **Data Generation and Collection:** Educational data is generated through admissions processes, academic activities, assessments, and institutional operations. Data collection may occur through application forms, examination systems, learning platforms, and administrative workflows. At this stage, institutions must ensure lawful and transparent data collection, limiting data to what is necessary for defined academic purposes.
2. **Data Storage and Management:** Once collected, educational data is stored in institutional databases, learning management systems, and credential repositories. Secure storage requires encryption, access controls, and regular audits. Blockchain-based systems may store cryptographic references to credentials, enhancing integrity while avoiding direct storage of sensitive information (Chen et al., 2018; Xu et al., 2019).
3. **Data Processing and Analysis:** Data processing includes grading, evaluation, reporting, and analytics. AI-driven systems increasingly analyse educational data to automate assessments, identify patterns, and support academic decision-

making. At this stage, risks related to bias, inaccurate inferences, and lack of transparency may arise if algorithms are not properly governed (Barocas et al., 2019; Dwivedi et al., 2021).

4. **Data Sharing and Disclosure:** Educational data is shared with internal and external stakeholders for verification, accreditation, and employment purposes. Digital systems enable faster sharing, but uncontrolled disclosure can lead to privacy violations. Secure authentication, role-based access, and selective disclosure mechanisms are essential to ensure that only authorized parties access relevant data.
5. **Data Archival and Retention:** Many educational records must be retained for extended periods to comply with legal and institutional requirements. Archived data must remain accurate, accessible, and protected against degradation or unauthorized modification. Retention policies should define how long data is preserved and under what conditions it can be accessed (U.S. Department of Education, 2020).
6. **Data Deletion and Disposal:** Data deletion is the final stage of the lifecycle, involving the removal of records that are no longer required. In digital and blockchain-enabled systems, deletion may involve logical removal, key revocation, or access restriction rather than physical erasure. Institutions must ensure compliance with data protection laws while maintaining system integrity (Zyskind et al., 2015; Zhang & Xue, 2019).

IMPACT OF AI AND BLOCKCHAIN ON THE DATA LIFECYCLE

The adoption of Artificial Intelligence (AI) and blockchain technologies has transformed how educational data is generated, processed, stored, and used across its lifecycle (Floridi, 2019; UNESCO, 2021). These technologies introduce new capabilities while also creating unique challenges for privacy, security, and governance.

Table 6. Impact of Ai and Blockchain on the Data Lifecycle

Technology	Impact	Benefits	Risks	Learner Implications
AI	Automates data collection, analysis, and decision-making for grading, competencies, and learning pathways	Personalized insights, scalable analysis, predictive credentialing	Bias, over-collection, opaque decisions	Privacy risks, limited transparency
Blockchain	Stores credentials in tamper-proof ledgers, ensures traceability and accountability	Secure, verifiable, autonomous credential management	Error correction difficult, off-chain data management needed	Learners control access, enhanced privacy
AI + Blockchain	Combines AI insights with blockchain security and verification	Trustworthy, learner-centric, automated credentialing	Requires ethical governance, privacy-by-design	Secure, transparent, personalized lifelong learning

IMPORTANCE OF DATA PRIVACY IN AI- AND BLOCKCHAIN-DRIVEN CREDENTIALING INNOVATION

Data privacy plays a decisive role in shaping the success and legitimacy of AI and blockchain adoption in higher education credentialing systems. Digital credentials are no longer limited to static records; they represent lifelong academic and professional identities that are continuously accessed, analysed, and shared across institutions, employers, and international platforms. Protecting learner data is therefore essential to maintain trust, safeguard individual rights, and ensure ethical technological progress.

AI-enabled credentialing systems depend on extensive data processing to assess competencies, verify qualifications, and support automated decision-making. Without strong privacy protections, these systems risk creating invasive profiling practices that undermine learner autonomy and confidentiality. Blockchain-based credentialing introduces additional privacy considerations due to its decentralized and immutable nature. While immutability strengthens trust and prevents credential tampering, it can conflict with data protection principles that require flexibility, correction, or deletion of personal information.

Data privacy is also central to learner empowerment and ethical governance. Modern credentialing systems increasingly emphasize learner control over personal data through mechanisms like selective disclosure and decentralized identity management. These approaches allow individuals to decide when and how their credentials are shared, shifting control away from centralized authorities and reducing the risk of large-scale data breaches.

From an institutional perspective, robust data privacy practices support legal compliance, reputational integrity, and long-term sustainability. Adherence to data protection regulations and ethical standards helps institutions avoid legal penalties, strengthens public confidence, and enables secure collaboration across borders. As digital credentials gain global recognition, privacy-aware systems become essential for interoperability and responsible data exchange.

In summary, data privacy is not merely a technical safeguard but a foundational pillar of ethical credentialing innovation. Embedding privacy-by-design principles into AI and blockchain systems ensures that technological advancement enhances educational value without compromising learner rights, fairness, or trust.

DATA PRIVACY RISKS IN AI-ENABLED AND BLOCKCHAIN-INTEGRATED LEARNING SYSTEMS

The integration of artificial intelligence (AI) and blockchain technologies into learning analytics presents powerful opportunities to enhance educational outcomes through data-driven insights and secure data management. However, these capabilities also introduce significant privacy and surveillance risks. These risks arise from extensive data collection, behavioral profiling, re-identification possibilities, and cross-border data transfers. Ethical and secure implementation is critical to maintain learner trust, autonomy, and regulatory compliance (Selwyn, 2019; OECD, 2019).

1. Surveillance Risks in AI-Enabled and Blockchain-Integrated Learning Analytics

AI-powered learning analytics allows institutions to monitor and analyse vast amounts of educational data to support decision-making, track engagement, and improve academic performance. While these tools offer substantial benefits, they also raise concerns related to surveillance and learner privacy, which are compounded when blockchain is used for record-keeping or tracking interactions.

Table 7. Privacy and Ethical Risks of Surveillance

Aspect	Description	Privacy / Ethical Risks
Continuous Monitoring	AI-enabled systems with blockchain track learner activities (engagement, attendance, submissions, interactions) across multiple contexts in real time.	Erosion of learner autonomy: Awareness of constant monitoring may discourage experimentation or self-expression. Increased data exposure: Persistent monitoring increases sensitive data collection, heightening misuse risk. Ethical challenges: Monitoring should remain proportionate, targeted, and aligned with educational objectives.
Behavioral Profiling	AI analyses patterns in learner behaviour (participation, submission timing, engagement) to predict outcomes or personalize interventions.	Bias and misclassification: Profiles may oversimplify complex behaviour, reinforcing biases. Opacity and lack of accountability: Learners may be unaware of how they are characterized. Excessive intrusion: Profiling may exceed the original educational purpose.

2. Re-Identification and De-Anonymization Risks in AI and Blockchain Systems

Even when educational data is anonymized or pseudonymized, AI and blockchain environments pose unique risks.

Table 8. Privacy, Security Risks and Mitigation of Re-Identification and De-Anonymization

Aspect	Description	Privacy / Security Risks & Mitigation
AI Inference Attacks	AI exploits model outputs or patterns to infer sensitive individual information.	Data leakage: Even anonymized datasets may reveal academic or behavioral data. Increased risk with data sharing: Sharing detailed datasets across institutions or with blockchain integration amplifies exposure. Mitigation: Apply advanced privacy-preserving techniques such as differential privacy and secure multiparty computation.
Metadata Analysis	Metadata (timestamps, device IDs, access logs, interaction patterns) can be used to re-identify individuals.	Exposure risk: Immutable blockchain metadata can increase the chance of re-identification. Identity disclosure: Small cohort data can make learners identifiable. Mitigation: Use aggregation, minimization, and restricted access controls to protect privacy.

3. Cross-Border Data Transfers in AI and Blockchain-Based Learning Systems

Cloud computing and blockchain technologies often involve international data transfers, enabling scalability and transparency but creating legal and privacy challenges.

Table 9. Privacy, Security Risks and Mitigation of Cross-Border Data Transfers

Aspect	Description / Challenge	Privacy / Security Risks & Mitigation
Cloud Storage Challenges	Cloud infrastructure may store educational data across multiple locations.	Limited control & visibility: Institutions may struggle to monitor all storage sites. Regulatory compliance issues: Local privacy laws may differ across regions. Mitigation: Implement encryption, strict access controls, secure configurations, and contractual safeguards with cloud providers.
Jurisdictional Conflicts	Data transfers may cross national borders, and blockchain decentralization complicates legal enforcement.	Conflicting laws: Different privacy regulations can create compliance challenges. Blockchain decentralization: Distributed nodes make enforcement and oversight difficult. Mitigation: Align governance with applicable legal frameworks and consider data localization strategies where necessary.
Blockchain-Specific Considerations	Blockchain introduces immutability, decentralization, and automated processes.	Data permanence: "Right to erasure" may be difficult to enforce. Decentralized control: Shared governance can complicate privacy compliance. Mitigation: Use permissioned blockchains, off-chain storage for sensitive data, and privacy-by-design approaches.

DATA COLLECTION AND CONSENT MANAGEMENT IN AI- AND BLOCKCHAIN-ENABLED LEARNING SYSTEMS

Effective data collection and consent management are foundational to privacy, ethics, and compliance in AI- and blockchain-enabled learning analytics (Prinsloo & Slade, 2017; UNESCO, 2021). These systems rely on extensive educational data to generate insights, but collecting and using such data without proper governance can undermine learner trust, autonomy, and legal compliance (European Union, 2016).

1. Principles of Data Collection

AI- and blockchain-enabled learning systems gather data from a variety of sources to support learning analytics, credentialing, and adaptive educational processes. Key sources include Learning Management Systems (LMS), which track assignment submissions, quiz scores, and forum activity; digital platforms that record clickstream data, interactions, and video engagement; IoT devices and classroom sensors that monitor attendance, biometrics, or eye movement; and blockchain records that store timestamps, credential issuance, and verification data.

2. Consent Management

Managing consent is crucial for protecting learner privacy and complying with global data protection laws such as GDPR, CCPA, or local regulations. Informed consent ensures that learners are given clear, understandable information about how their data will be collected, processed, and shared, allowing them to make meaningful decisions.

3. Ethical and Regulatory Considerations

Effective consent management supports learner autonomy, ensuring that individuals maintain control over their personal information and educational profiles. It also fosters transparency and trust, as clear communication about data usage reassures learners that their information is handled responsibly. From a legal perspective, consent management helps institutions comply with privacy laws, such as GDPR, which mandate lawful data processing and respect for individual rights.

4. Recommendations for Implementation

Institutions can implement user-friendly consent dashboards to allow learners to easily view, grant, or revoke consent for different types of data. Separating on-chain and off-chain storage ensures compliance with the "right to erasure" while still benefiting from blockchain's transparency and auditability. It is also important to regularly review and update consent policies as AI analytics methods evolve, blockchain platforms are upgraded, or privacy regulations change.

PRIVACY AS AN ETHICAL AND INSTITUTIONAL RESPONSIBILITY

In AI- and blockchain-enabled credentialing systems, data privacy must be understood as both an ethical obligation and an institutional responsibility. Higher education institutions manage sensitive personal, academic, and lifelong learning data, placing them in a position of trust. Responsible data handling is essential to protect learner rights, maintain institutional credibility, and ensure the ethical use of emerging technologies (Floridi, 2019; UNESCO, 2021; Jobin et al., 2019).

ETHICAL RESPONSIBILITIES

- **Respect for learner autonomy:** Learners should have control over how their personal and academic data is collected, used, and shared, including the ability to grant or withdraw consent (Prinsloo & Slade, 2017; European Union, 2016).
- **Protection of human dignity:** Educational data reflects individual identity, effort, and achievement; misuse or excessive monitoring can undermine dignity and freedom (Selwyn, 2019; Mittelstadt et al., 2016).
- **Fairness and non-discrimination:** AI systems must be designed to avoid bias, profiling, or unfair treatment based on data-driven decisions.
- **Transparency and explainability:** Learners have the right to understand how AI systems process their data and how decisions related to assessment or credentialing are made (Wachter et al., 2017; Floridi et al., 2018).
- **Proportional data use:** Only data that is necessary for educational and credentialing purposes should be collected and processed.

INSTITUTIONAL RESPONSIBILITIES

- **Privacy-by-design implementation:** Institutions should embed privacy safeguards into AI and blockchain systems from the outset, rather than treating privacy as an afterthought (Floridi, 2019; ISO/IEC, 2022).
- **Secure data governance frameworks:** Clear policies should define data ownership, access rights, retention periods, and accountability structures.
- **Blockchain privacy management:** Sensitive personal data should not be stored directly on-chain; instead, cryptographic proofs or hashes should be used to balance immutability with privacy (Allen & Berg, 2020; Zhang & Xue, 2019).

- **Human oversight of AI systems:** Automated decision-making processes must be regularly audited and supported by human review to prevent errors or unethical outcomes.
- **Learner awareness and empowerment**: Institutions must clearly inform learners about data practices and provide tools such as credential wallets that enable controlled data sharing (W3C, 2022; Tapscott & Tapscott, 2016).

PRIVACY-PRESERVING BLOCKCHAIN TECHNIQUES

The use of blockchain in education offers many advantages, including secure credentialing, transparent record-keeping, and easy verification. However, storing sensitive educational data on a blockchain can raise serious privacy concerns. To address this, privacy-preserving techniques have been developed that protect learner information while maintaining trust, authenticity, and transparency (Allen & Berg, 2020; Chen et al., 2018).

1. Zero-Knowledge Proofs (ZKPs)

Zero-Knowledge Proofs allow learners to prove that a statement is true without revealing the underlying information. For example, a student can verify that they hold a particular degree or skill without exposing grades, personal identifiers, or course details. In addition to protecting sensitive information, ZKPs help educational institutions comply with data protection regulations and minimize the risk of data leaks (Zyskind et al., 2015; Xu et al., 2019).

2. Selective Disclosure

Selective disclosure enables learners to share only the information necessary for a specific purpose, rather than exposing their entire academic record. This supports data minimization and gives students control over what is shared and with whom.

3. Decentralized Identifiers (DIDs)

Decentralized Identifiers provide learners with self-managed digital identities that operate independently of centralized authorities. DIDs allow students to control their authentication and credential management, reducing dependence on a single organization and lowering the risk of large-scale data breaches (Allen & Berg, 2020; W3C, 2022).

SECURITY ARCHITECTURE FOR AI–BLOCKCHAIN SYSTEMS

Security architecture refers to the comprehensive and systematic design of security controls, technologies, policies, and governance mechanisms that protect information systems from internal and external threats. In AI- and blockchain-enabled environments, security architecture must safeguard data, algorithms, infrastructure, and users, while addressing the unique risks introduced by automation, decentralization, and large-scale data processing.

Unlike traditional systems, AI and blockchain platforms operate across multiple layers and stakeholders, making security architecture a critical foundation for trust, reliability, and ethical system deployment (Gervais et al., 2016; IEEE, 2019).

The fundamental goals of security architecture in AI and blockchain-based systems are rooted in the principles of confidentiality, integrity, and availability. Availability emphasizes the need for systems and services to remain operational and accessible even during technical failures, cyberattacks, or adverse conditions. Together, these principles form the basis for designing resilient and trustworthy AI–blockchain security frameworks (ISO/IEC, 2022; OECD, 2019).

LAYERED SECURITY ARCHITECTURE APPROACH:

A layered or defence-in-depth strategy is essential for AI–blockchain ecosystems because a single security control cannot address all threat vectors (Allen & Berg, 2020).

1. Data Layer Security

AI-driven systems rely extensively on large and diverse datasets, many of which contain sensitive personal, academic, or behavioral information. Data layer security is therefore concerned with safeguarding information throughout its entire lifecycle, including data collection, storage, processing, and sharing. In blockchain-enabled systems, sensitive information is typically stored off-chain, while only cryptographic hashes are recorded on the blockchain to preserve data integrity without compromising privacy (Chen et al., 2018; Zhang & Xue, 2019).

2. Application Layer Security

The application layer serves as the primary interaction point between end users, artificial intelligence services, and blockchain infrastructures, making it a critical target for security threats. Weaknesses at this level can be exploited to alter system functionality or gain unauthorized access to resources. To mitigate these risks, robust authentication and authorization mechanisms are employed, often incorporating multi-factor authentication to strengthen identity verification.

3. AI Model and Algorithm Security

Artificial intelligence introduces distinct security challenges that extend beyond those found in traditional software systems, as machine learning models themselves become valuable assets requiring protection. Threats such as data poisoning attacks can compromise model accuracy by injecting malicious data during training, while model inversion and extraction attacks attempt to reconstruct sensitive training data or replicate proprietary models. Adversarial attacks further exploit model weaknesses by manipulating inputs to influence outputs

4. Blockchain Layer Security

Blockchain technology strengthens system security through decentralization, cryptographic hashing, and consensus protocols that ensure data immutability and trust. Despite these advantages, blockchain systems are not immune to security risks and introduce unique attack surfaces. To enhance resilience, best practices such as formal smart contract verification, multi-signature authentication, hardware security modules, and continuous node monitoring are widely adopted (Gervais et al., 2016; Xu et al., 2019).

5. Governance and Policy Layer

While technical safeguards form the backbone of system security, they are insufficient without strong governance and policy frameworks that guide security implementation and enforcement. The governance layer establishes security standards and policies governing data access, AI deployment, and participation in blockchain networks. It also ensures compliance with legal and regulatory requirements, including data protection regulations and ethical AI principles.

SECURITY RISKS IN AI AND BLOCKCHAIN SYSTEMS FOR HIGHER EDUCATION

Artificial Intelligence (AI) and blockchain technologies are transforming higher education by enabling automated credentialing, personalized learning pathways, predictive analytics, and secure digital records. However, these technologies introduce unique security risks that can compromise learner privacy, academic integrity, and trust in digital systems. Understanding these risks is essential for designing robust, secure, and ethical systems (OECD, 2019; Dwivedi et al., 2021).

TRAINING DATA ATTACKS:

AI models rely heavily on the quality of their training datasets. If these datasets are manipulated or compromised, the AI's decisions and outputs can become unreliable, biased, or malicious (Barocas et al., 2019). Two primary threats in this category are:

1. **Data Poisoning:** Attackers deliberately inject misleading, corrupted, or malicious data into the AI training datasets. For example, an attacker could manipulate student performance data to influence grading algorithms, micro-credential recommendations, or competency mapping.

Impact: This can result in unfair assessment, incorrect credential issuance, or biased AI recommendations.

2. **Label Manipulation:** Labels in training datasets—such as "pass/fail," "competent/not competent," or skill levels—can be falsified or altered to misguide AI models.

Impact: AI may misclassify learner performance, issue incorrect credentials, or provide misleading personalized learning recommendations.

Model-Level Threats: Even when training data is secure, AI models themselves are vulnerable to attacks that expose sensitive information or manipulate outcomes (Mittelstadt et al., 2016; O'Neil, 2016):

1. **Model Inversion:** Attackers analyse the outputs of an AI model to reconstruct sensitive training data. For instance, by querying a grading AI multiple times, an attacker could infer individual student scores or assessment outcomes.

Impact: Confidential student data can be exposed, violating privacy regulations and institutional trust.

2. **Membership Inference:** This attack determines whether a particular individual's data was included in the AI training set.

Impact: Reveals the presence of specific learners in datasets, potentially disclosing sensitive participation information and violating consent agreements.

ETHICAL FOUNDATIONS OF AI AND BLOCKCHAIN ADOPTION IN EDUCATION

The integration of Artificial Intelligence (AI) and blockchain technologies in higher education has transformed credentialing, learning analytics, administrative processes, and lifelong learning recognition. Ethical foundations provide guidance for responsible, trustworthy, and learner-centric deployment of these technologies (Floridi et al., 2018; Jobin et al., 2019; UNESCO, 2021).

ETHICAL PRINCIPLES IN EDUCATIONAL TECHNOLOGY

Responsible adoption of AI and blockchain requires embedding ethical principles into system design, implementation, and governance (Floridi et al., 2018; IEEE, 2019).

Key principles include:

1. Fairness

AI algorithms must process learner data without bias or discrimination. For instance, automated grading, personalized learning recommendations, or predictive analytics should not Favor learners from specific institutions, regions, or demographic groups (Barocas et al., 2019; O'Neil, 2016). Similarly, blockchain systems must ensure equitable access to digital credentials, preventing exclusion due to technical or infrastructural barriers (Kshetri, 2021). Regular bias audits and continuous monitoring of AI outputs help detect inequities in learner outcomes, ensuring fair use of educational data (Mittelstadt et al., 2016).

2. Accountability

Clear responsibility must be established for decisions derived from AI systems or blockchain-based credentialing platforms. Institutions, educators, and technology providers are accountable for errors, security breaches, or unfair outcomes involving learner data (Prinsloo & Slade, 2017). Blockchain-enabled audit trails enhance accountability by providing verifiable records of credential issuance and transactions, allowing stakeholders to trace the origin and validity of each credential or decision (Sharples & Domingue, 2016).

3. Transparency

Transparency involves clear communication about how AI models process learner data, how blockchain records are maintained, and how decisions are generated. Explainable AI (XAI) allows learners to understand the rationale behind automated grading, skill assessments, or recommendations (Wachter et al., 2017). Similarly, blockchain provides transparent, verifiable records while protecting sensitive personal data (Tapscott & Tapscott, 2016).

4. Human Oversight

AI and blockchain should augment, not replace, human judgment. Human-in-the-loop mechanisms are essential for critical processes such as credential issuance, appeals, or verification of automated recommendations (Selwyn, 2019). Oversight helps mitigate risks of algorithmic bias, misclassification, and unintended consequences, ensuring that decisions involving learner data remain ethically sound (Jobin et al., 2019).

5. Privacy and Data Protection

Learner data—including academic performance, behavioral patterns, and personal identifiers—is highly sensitive. Ethical adoption of AI and blockchain must comply with privacy laws such as GDPR, FERPA, and local regulations (European Union, 2016; U.S. Department of Education, 2020). Techniques such as data anonymization, selective disclosure, off-chain storage, and consent management enable privacy preservation without compromising system functionality. Protecting learner data strengthens trust in AI-powered and blockchain-based educational systems (Zyskind et al., 2015; Zhang & Xue, 2019).

6. Inclusivity and Accessibility

Ethical systems must be designed to serve all learners, including those with disabilities or limited access to technology. Inclusive design ensures that blockchain wallets, digital credentials, and AI-powered platforms are accessible, equitable, and user-friendly, reducing digital divides. Consideration of data accessibility is key to ensuring that all learners can participate fairly in a technology-driven educational ecosystem (UNESCO, 2019; World Economic Forum, 2020).

7. Sustainability

Blockchain operations, particularly energy-intensive consensus mechanisms, must consider environmental impact. Ethical design encourages energy-efficient protocols, sustainable infrastructure choices, and responsible use of computational resources.

The fast pace of technological innovation in higher education creates a tension between ethical responsibility and rapid deployment (World Economic Forum, 2021.

Table 10. Ethics vs. Innovation dilemma

Aspect	Description	Practical Implications
Speed of Deployment	Institutions often prioritize efficiency, scalability, and competitiveness, deploying AI and blockchain rapidly.	Rapid deployment without ethical review may compromise fairness, privacy, or transparency.
Balancing Innovation with Ethical Oversight	Ethical adoption integrates oversight without impeding innovation. Ethics-by-design ensures privacy, fairness, and transparency from the earliest stages.	Regular audits, impact assessments, and continuous improvement mechanisms help maintain ethical standards while embracing innovation.
Credentialing Systems	Blockchain ensures tamper-proof, verifiable credentials.	Human oversight and fairness audits prevent inequitable access or errors.
AI-Powered Learning Analytics	Predictive models must be explainable and free from bias.	Learners should be able to opt out of intrusive data collection.

ALGORITHMIC BIAS AND FAIRNESS IN CREDENTIALING SYSTEMS

The increasing use of Artificial Intelligence (AI) in higher education credentialing introduces the risk of algorithmic bias, which can compromise fairness, equity, and trust in automated academic and credentialing processes. Algorithmic bias occurs when AI systems produce outcomes that systematically disadvantage certain groups of learners based on historical, social, or institutional factors (Barocas et al., 2019). Understanding the sources of bias, its impact on automated assessments, and strategies to mitigate it is critical for ethical AI adoption in education (O'Neil, 2016).

Sources of Bias:

Bias in AI-powered credentialing systems often originates from the data, institutional practices, or systemic inequalities. Common sources include:

1. Historical Data Bias

AI models trained on historical academic records or past credentialing data may reflect past inequities, such as unequal grading practices or underrepresentation of certain groups (Mittelstadt et al., 2016).

2. Institutional Bias

Policies, program structures, or assessment frameworks at specific institutions can introduce bias. For instance, automated skill classification may Favor disciplines with standardized assessment formats while disadvantaging creative or interdisciplinary programs (Williamson & Eynon, 2020)..

Bias In Automated Assessment:

AI-driven assessments and credentialing tools are particularly vulnerable to bias in two main areas:

1. Grading Algorithms

Automated grading systems may misinterpret language, cultural references, or unconventional problem-solving approaches, leading to unfair evaluation of certain learners. Errors or systematic mis grading can affect credential eligibility, academic progression, and employability (Selwyn, 2019).

2. Skill Classification

AI models classifying learner competencies or mapping skills to credentials may overvalue certain learning patterns, prior experiences, or institutional contexts. Bias in skill recognition can result in misaligned credentials, reduced opportunities for some learners, and perpetuation of inequities in the labour market (World Economic Forum, 2020).

LEGAL AND REGULATORY LANDSCAPE

The use of Artificial Intelligence (AI) and blockchain technologies in higher education introduces complex legal and regulatory obligations. Educational institutions handle highly sensitive learner data, including academic records, personal identifiers, behavioral analytics, and career trajectories

Key Regulations and Frameworks

1. *General Data Protection Regulation (GDPR) – European Union* The GDPR protects the personal data and privacy of individuals within the European Union. It mandates that data must be processed lawfully, collected minimally, and used only for specific purposes, with full transparency. In the context of AI-powered credentialing systems and blockchain in education, GDPR requires explainable AI models, mechanisms for obtaining informed consent from learners, and the ability to erase personal data upon request (European Union, 2016).
2. *Family Educational Rights and Privacy Act (FERPA) – United States* FERPA governs access to student educational records and protects student privacy in the U.S. Educational institutions must ensure that student data is not disclosed without consent. AI systems analysing academic performance or blockchain-based credentialing platforms must implement strict access controls and safeguard the confidentiality of student data (U.S. Department of Education, 2020).
3. *Information Technology Act and Data Protection Rules – India* India's IT Act and associated Data Protection Rules regulate electronic data, cybersecurity, and digital signatures. The pending Personal Data Protection Bill (PDPB) emphasizes data localization, consent management, and privacy by design. For educational institutions, this means AI and blockchain deployments must prioritize secure storage, transparent data handling, and adherence to consent requirements. Systems must be designed to respect learner privacy while enabling decentralized credentialing and analytics (Yadav & Vishwakarma, 2020).
4. *Emerging AI-Specific Regulations – EU Artificial Intelligence Act* The EU Artificial Intelligence Act introduces a risk-based regulatory framework for AI systems, including those used in education. High-risk AI systems, such as automated grading, predictive learning analytics, and credential verification, must meet requirements for transparency, accountability, safety, and bias mitigation. Educational institutions need to assess AI models regularly to ensure ethical compliance, explainability, and learner data protection (Jobin et al., 2019).

RISK MANAGEMENT FRAMEWORKS

The adoption of Artificial Intelligence (AI) and blockchain technologies in higher education offers significant opportunities for automation, credential verification, and personalized learning. However, it also introduces complex risks related to data privacy, security, algorithmic fairness, and ethical compliance. Implementing structured risk management frameworks is critical to anticipate, mitigate, and monitor these risks, ensuring responsible and trustworthy adoption of emerging technologies.

Effective risk management in AI and blockchain deployment should adhere to the following principles given below in table 11:

Table 11. Principles of risk management in educational technology

Risk Management Step	Description / Key Actions	Examples / Implications
Risk Identification	Map potential threats across the technology lifecycle, including AI training, data collection, model inference, credential issuance, and blockchain operations.	Key risks include data breaches, algorithmic bias, unauthorized access, smart contract vulnerabilities, and regulatory non-compliance.
Risk Assessment	Evaluate the likelihood and potential impact of each identified risk. Prioritize high-impact risks.	High-priority risks may include credential tampering, learner data exposure, or biased automated decisions.
Risk Mitigation	Implement preventive measures to reduce identified risks.	Measures include data encryption, access control, bias audits, secure smart contract development, and human-in-the-loop oversight. Off-chain storage ensures blockchain credentials comply with privacy regulations like GDPR.
Risk Monitoring	Continuously monitor AI outputs, blockchain transactions, and system access logs.	Early detection of anomalies or unusual patterns allows rapid response, reducing potential damage to learners or institutional credibility.
Risk Communication and Accountability	Maintain transparency with stakeholders regarding risks, mitigation strategies, and incident response. Assign responsibility for oversight and remediation.	Ensures clear accountability for errors, breaches, or failures in AI and blockchain processes, and builds trust with learners and regulators.

MANAGING LEARNER DATA RISKS IN AI AND BLOCKCHAIN SYSTEMS

Managing learner data in AI-powered and blockchain-based educational systems requires a holistic approach that addresses ethical, technical, and operational challenges. A layered framework ensures that sensitive student information remains secure, private, and used responsibly throughout the technology lifecycle (Floridi et al., 2018).

1. Governance Layer

The governance layer establishes institutional policies, ethics committees, and regulatory compliance mechanisms to manage learner data responsibly. It defines accountability and decision-making structures, ensuring that AI and blockchain systems respect privacy, fairness, and ethical principles when handling student data.

2. Technical Layer

The technical layer focuses on implementing safeguards to protect learner data. For AI systems, this includes bias audits, explainable AI, data encryption, and defence against model vulnerabilities. For blockchain, it involves securing smart contracts, selecting energy-efficient consensus mechanisms, and using off-chain storage to protect sensitive student information while maintaining data integrity (Wachter et al., 2017; Zhang & Xue, 2019)..

3. Operational Layer

The operational layer ensures continuous protection of learner data through monitoring, incident response plans, and regular auditing. Tracking AI outputs, blockchain transactions, and access logs allows early detection of anomalies, unauthorized access, or breaches, enabling institutions to respond quickly and minimize harm to students.

STAKEHOLDER ROLES IN DATA-DRIVEN AI AND BLOCKCHAIN ADOPTION

The responsible adoption of AI and blockchain in education depends on the coordinated roles of multiple stakeholders. Each group has distinct responsibilities in ensuring that learner data is protected, systems are secure, and ethical principles are upheld throughout the technology lifecycle.

1. Learners (Students)

Learners are the primary data subjects in AI- and blockchain-enabled educational systems. Their role includes exercising informed consent, understanding how their academic and personal data is collected and used, and managing access to their digital credentials. Through tools such as decentralized identifiers and selective disclosure, learners gain greater control over their data, reinforcing data ownership and autonomy in digital education ecosystems (W3C, 2022).

2. Educational Institutions

Universities and academic institutions act as data controllers and system adopters. They are responsible for implementing AI and blockchain technologies in compliance with data protection regulations, ensuring fairness, transparency, and accountability. Institutions must establish governance structures, ethics committees, and data stewardship policies to oversee data collection, credential issuance, and AI-driven decision-making processes (Prinsloo & Slade, 2017).

3. Faculty and Academic Staff

Faculty members play a critical role in validating AI-supported decisions and maintaining human oversight. They ensure that automated grading, learning analytics, and credential evaluations are pedagogically sound and ethically appropriate. Faculty also help interpret AI outputs and safeguard against over-reliance on automated systems that may misrepresent learner performance (Popenici & Kerr, 2017)..

4. Technology Providers and Developers

AI and blockchain developers are responsible for designing secure, privacy-preserving, and ethically aligned systems. This includes implementing bias mitigation techniques, robust encryption, secure smart contracts, and explainable AI models. Technology providers must follow privacy-by-design and ethics-by-design principles to reduce risks associated with learner data misuse and system vulnerabilities.

5. Regulators and Policymakers

Regulatory bodies establish legal and ethical frameworks governing data protection, cybersecurity, and AI accountability. By enforcing regulations such as GDPR, FERPA, and emerging AI-specific laws, policymakers ensure that educational institutions and technology providers adhere to standards that protect learner data, promote fairness, and support cross-border interoperability of credentials (European Union, 2016; UNESCO, 2021)..

6. Employers and Credential Verifiers

Employers and external verifiers rely on blockchain-based credentials for trustworthy and efficient verification. Their role is to use these systems responsibly, accessing only the necessary information through privacy-preserving mechanisms. Ethical use of verification platforms ensures trust without excessive data disclosure, protecting learner privacy while supporting workforce mobility (Allen & Berg, 2020).

CASE PERSPECTIVES AND GLOBAL INITIATIVES

The integration of Artificial Intelligence (AI) and blockchain technologies in higher education has moved beyond theoretical exploration and into practical, real-world applications. Across the globe, universities, consortia, and international organizations are piloting and scaling digital credentialing systems, AI-based learning analytics, and blockchain-enabled verifiable records. Studying these case perspectives provides valuable insights into best practices, challenges, and emerging standards.

1. *MIT Digital Credentials Initiative (United States)* The Massachusetts Institute of Technology (MIT) has been a pioneer in blockchain-based digital credentialing through its Digital Credentials Initiative. MIT issues verifiable digital diplomas that allow graduates to securely share proof of qualifications without disclosing unnecessary personal data. The system emphasizes learner ownership, privacy-preserving verification, and secure cryptographic proofs rather than centralized data storage (Sharples & Domingue, 2016).
2. *European Union Initiatives on Ethical AI and Data Protection* The European Union has introduced comprehensive regulatory and policy frameworks addressing data privacy and ethical AI adoption. The General Data Protection Regulation (GDPR) establishes strict requirements for lawful data processing, consent, data minimization, and the right to erasure. Complementing GDPR, the proposed EU Artificial Intelligence Act introduces risk-based governance for AI systems, including those used in education (European Union, 2016; Jobin et al., 2019).
3. *UNESCO Global Frameworks for Ethical AI in Education* UNESCO has developed global guidelines promoting ethical and human-centred AI adoption in education. These frameworks emphasize respect for human rights, data protection, transparency, fairness, and inclusivity. UNESCO's recommendations encourage governments and educational institutions to ensure that AI systems do not exploit learner data and that blockchain-based credentialing supports equitable access and global recognition (UNESCO, 2021).

4. *National Digital Credential Platforms* Several countries have launched national digital credential platforms to support lifelong learning and workforce mobility. These platforms often integrate blockchain technology to ensure secure and tamper-proof credential verification while enforcing strong data governance policies. Emphasis is placed on learner data ownership, interoperability across institutions, and compliance with national and international data protection regulations. Such initiatives demonstrate how decentralized technologies can be deployed at scale without compromising privacy or security (World Economic Forum, 2020).
5. *Cross-Border Credential Recognition and Interoperability Efforts* Global initiatives aimed at cross-border recognition of educational credentials highlight the importance of aligning privacy, security, and ethical standards across jurisdictions. These efforts focus on secure data exchange, minimal disclosure of learner information, and mutual trust frameworks between institutions and governments. By adopting interoperable and privacy-preserving architectures, such initiatives support global mobility while safeguarding learner data (World Economic Forum, 2021)..

Table 12. Future directions and emerging trends

Emerging Trend	Description	Relevance to Data Privacy, Security, and Ethics
Privacy-Enhancing Technologies (PETs)	Use of techniques such as federated learning, zero-knowledge proofs, and secure multi-party computation to analyse data without direct exposure.	Reduces learner data sharing, minimizes privacy risks, and supports compliance with data protection regulations.
Ethics-by-Design Approaches	Integration of fairness, transparency, and accountability principles during system design and development stages.	Prevents bias, ensures explainability of AI decisions, and promotes responsible innovation.
Decentralized and Self-Sovereign Identity	Adoption of decentralized identifiers and learner-controlled digital identity frameworks.	Enhances user autonomy, limits unnecessary data disclosure, and lowers risks of centralized data breaches.
Regulatory-Aware AI and Blockchain Systems	Systems designed to adapt to evolving data protection and AI regulations across jurisdictions.	Supports lawful data processing, consent management, auditability, and cross-border compliance.
Sustainable and Energy-Efficient Blockchains	Shift toward permissioned blockchains and energy-efficient consensus mechanisms.	Balances security and integrity with environmental responsibility and long-term sustainability.

continued on following page

Table 12. Continued

Emerging Trend	Description	Relevance to Data Privacy, Security, and Ethics
Human-in-the-Loop Governance	Continued involvement of educators and administrators in AI-driven decisions.	Ensures ethical judgment, accountability, and contextual understanding in high-stakes data use.
Global Interoperability and Ethical Harmonization	Development of shared standards for digital credentials and AI governance across regions.	Enables secure cross-border data exchange while maintaining consistent privacy and ethical safeguards.

CONCLUSION

The integration of Artificial Intelligence and blockchain technologies is reshaping higher education by redefining how learning is assessed, credentials are issued, and academic records are managed throughout a learner's lifetime (Allen & Berg, 2020). These technologies offer substantial benefits, including improved efficiency, personalized learning pathways, secure credential verification, and global recognition of academic achievements. However, as this chapter has demonstrated, technological advancement alone is not sufficient to create trust, equity, or long-term value. Ethical governance, legal compliance, and risk-aware implementation are essential to ensure that innovation serves learners and society responsibly.

Ethical foundations such as fairness, accountability, transparency, human oversight, and privacy protection must guide the design and deployment of AI- and blockchain-enabled educational systems. AI-driven decision-making introduces risks of bias, exclusion, and opaque outcomes, particularly in automated grading, skill classification, and credential recommendations. Without deliberate safeguards, these systems may reinforce existing inequalities rather than reduce them

The legal and regulatory landscape further reinforces the need for responsible adoption. Frameworks such as GDPR, FERPA, the Indian data protection regime, and emerging AI-specific regulations place clear obligations on institutions to protect learner data, ensure transparency, and maintain accountability

This chapter has also highlighted the importance of stakeholder collaboration. Learners, faculty, administrators, technology providers, regulators, and employers each have distinct responsibilities in shaping ethical and trustworthy systems. Learner agency and informed consent, faculty oversight of automated processes, institutional governance, vendor accountability, and regulatory supervision together form the foundation of sustainable digital credentialing ecosystems. Case perspectives from institutions and global initiatives demonstrate that successful implementation depends not only on technological capability but also on transparency, interoperability, and strong governance structures.

In conclusion, AI and blockchain can become powerful enablers of inclusive, secure, and learner-centric education if they are guided by strong ethical principles, robust legal compliance, and continuous risk management. By prioritizing human values alongside technological innovation, higher education institutions can ensure that digital transformation contributes meaningfully to academic integrity, social responsibility, and lifelong learning in a rapidly evolving global landscape.

REFERENCES

Allen, C., & Berg, C. (2020). *Blockchain and the future of education.* Springer.

Barocas, S., Hardt, M., & Narayanan, A. (2019). *Fairness and machine learning.* MIT Press.

Buterin, V. (2014). *A next-generation smart contract and decentralized application platform.* Ethereum Foundation.

Chen, G., Xu, B., Lu, M., & Chen, N. S. (2018). Exploring blockchain technology and its potential applications for education. *Smart Learning Environments, 5*(1), 1–10. DOI: 10.1186/s40561-017-0050-x

Coursera. (2021). *Digital credentials and the future of work.* Coursera Research Report.

Dede, C. (2014). *Digital badges for learning.* American Institutes for Research.

Dwivedi, Y. K., Hughes, L., Ismagilova, E., Aarts, G., Coombs, C., Crick, T., Duan, Y., Dwivedi, R., Edwards, J., Eirug, A., Galanos, V., Ilavarasan, P. V., Janssen, M., Jones, P., Kar, A. K., Kizgin, H., Kronemann, B., Lal, B., Lucini, B., & Williams, M. D. (2021). Artificial intelligence (AI): Multidisciplinary perspectives. *International Journal of Information Management, 57*, 101994. DOI: 10.1016/j.ijinfomgt.2019.08.002

European Union. (2016). *General Data Protection Regulation (GDPR).*

Floridi, L. (2019). Establishing the rules for building trustworthy AI. *Nature Machine Intelligence, 1*(6), 261–262. DOI: 10.1038/s42256-019-0055-y

Floridi, L., Cowls, J., Beltrametti, M., Chatila, R., Chazerand, P., Dignum, V., Luetge, C., Madelin, R., Pagallo, U., Rossi, F., Schafer, B., Valcke, P., & Vayena, E. (2018). AI4People—An ethical framework for a good AI society. *Minds and Machines, 28*(4), 689–707. DOI: 10.1007/s11023-018-9482-5 PMID: 30930541

Gervais, A., Karame, G., & Wüst, K.. (2016). On the security and performance of proof of work blockchains. *Proceedings of the ACM SIGSAC Conference on Computer and Communications Security*, 3–16. DOI: 10.1145/2976749.2978341

IEEE. (2019). *Ethically aligned design: A vision for prioritizing human well-being with autonomous and intelligent systems.* IEEE.

ISO/IEC. (2022). *Artificial intelligence—Risk management (ISO/IEC 23894).*

Jobin, A., Ienca, M., & Vayena, E. (2019). The global landscape of AI ethics guidelines. *Nature Machine Intelligence*, *1*(9), 389–399. DOI: 10.1038/s42256-019-0088-2

Kshetri, N. (2021). Blockchain adoption in developing countries. *IEEE Computer*, *54*(1), 8–12.

Mittelstadt, B. D., Allo, P., Taddeo, M., Wachter, S., & Floridi, L. (2016). The ethics of algorithms. *Big Data & Society*, *3*(2), 1–21. DOI: 10.1177/2053951716679679

O'Neil, C. (2016). *Weapons of math destruction*. Crown Publishing.

OECD. (2019). *Artificial intelligence in society*. OECD Publishing.

Popenici, S. A. D., & Kerr, S. (2017). Exploring the impact of artificial intelligence on higher education. *Research and Practice in Technology Enhanced Learning*, *12*(1), 1–13. DOI: 10.1186/s41039-017-0062-8 PMID: 30595727

Prinsloo, P., & Slade, S. (2017). Ethics and learning analytics. *British Journal of Educational Technology*, *48*(2), 386–397.

PwC. (2020). *Blockchain in education*.

Selwyn, N. (2019). *Should robots replace teachers?* Polity Press.

Sharples, M., & Domingue, J. (2016). Blockchain and education. In *Proceedings of the European Conference on Technology Enhanced Learning* (pp. 490–496). Springer.

Tapscott, D., & Tapscott, A. (2016). *Blockchain revolution*. Penguin.

UNESCO. (2019). *Artificial intelligence in education: Challenges and opportunities*.

UNESCO. (2021). *Recommendation on the ethics of artificial intelligence*.

U.S. Department of Education. (2020). *FERPA and student privacy guidance*.

W3C. (2022). *Verifiable credentials data model*.

Wachter, S., Mittelstadt, B., & Floridi, L. (2017). Transparent, explainable AI. *European Law Journal*, *23*(5), 1–23. PMID: 33157874

Williamson, B., & Eynon, R. (2020). Historical perspectives on AI in education. *Learning, Media and Technology*, *45*(1), 1–13.

World Economic Forum. (2020). *Schools of the future*.

World Economic Forum. (2021). *Global governance of artificial intelligence*.

Xu, X.. (2019). A taxonomy of blockchain-based systems. *IEEE Communications Surveys and Tutorials*, *21*(3), 2799–2834.

Yadav, S., & Vishwakarma, S. (2020). Impact of artificial intelligence in education. *Journal of Statistics and Management Systems*, *23*(2), 1–12.

Zhang, R., Xue, R., & Liu, L. (2019). Security and privacy on blockchain. *ACM Computing Surveys*, *52*(3), 1–34. DOI: 10.1145/3316481

Zyskind, G., Nathan, O., & Pentland, A. (2015). Decentralizing privacy. *IEEE Security and Privacy Workshops*, 180–184.

Chapter 6
Digital Identity and Verifiable Learning:
AI-Enhanced, Blockchain-Secured Credentialing

Houda Haddad
http://orcid.org/0009-0004-9652-9079
The British University in Dubai, UAE

Tendai Charles
http://orcid.org/0000-0002-0253-5960
The British University in Dubai, UAE

ABSTRACT

This chapter examines the growing misalignment between data-rich digital learning environments and fragmented, weakly verifiable academic credentialing in higher education. Adopting a design-science perspective, it conceptualises digital identity and verifiable learning records as the trust foundation for responsible AI-enhanced credentialing on smart university campuses. The chapter proposes a five-layer reference architecture integrating learner-centred digital identity, verifiable credential fabrics, AI services for recognition of prior learning and competency inference, embedded governance mechanisms, and event-driven integration with legacy campus systems. Rather than presenting a technical blueprint, the chapter offers a governance-aware conceptual framework intended to support portability, transparency and accountability in credentialing practices. It argues that verifiability, learner agency and bounded AI autonomy must precede large-scale automation if AI is to be used responsibly in academic recognition and decision-making.

DOI: 10.4018/979-8-3373-7600-4.ch006

INTRODUCTION

Universities are frequently described as "smart campuses", digitally saturated environments where learning management systems (LMS), student information systems (SIS), library platforms, e-portfolio tools and third-party applications capture extensive traces of learner activity (Cheong & Nyaupane, 2022). Despite this dense digital infrastructure, the credential artifacts that matter most to students (transcripts, degree certificates, and a growing array of micro-credentials) remain fragmented and difficult to verify across institutional and national boundaries (McGreal, 2023). Learning evidence is generated in one set of systems, condensed into coarse summaries in another, and manually interpreted by employers, professional bodies and immigration authorities who must decide whether, and to what extent, they trust what is presented to them. This fragmentation exists at multiple levels. Technically, data are siloed in platform-specific formats and proprietary databases (Ocheja et al., 2019). Organizationally, different units (registrars, IT departments, careers services, external micro-credential providers) operate under distinct standards and accountability structures. At the learner level, individuals accumulate a patchwork of artifacts (official transcripts, PDF certificates, digital badges, HR system records, and informal evidence such as GitHub repositories or portfolios) that cannot easily be assembled into a coherent representation of their competencies. The result is a credentialing ecosystem in which authenticity is hard to establish, and portability of achievements is constrained by institutional boundaries rather than the learner's actual experience (Charles & Hill, 2025). Cases of diploma fraud and misrepresentation are widely reported, adding further uncertainty and risk to credential evaluation (Ocheja et al., 2019). For learners, these limitations translate into friction and uncertainty; for institutions and employers, they create administrative burden and risk.

These issues have become particularly salient as higher education places greater emphasis on lifelong learning, recognition of prior learning (RPL), and cross-border mobility. Governments and quality assurance agencies call for more transparent, outcomes-based qualifications; employers seek fine-grained, machine-readable signals of specific skills; and learners expect their achievements to be portable across institutions, countries and platforms (Ahsan et al., 2023). Yet the underlying credentialing infrastructure remains rooted in models designed for a relatively closed, paper-based system. Consequently, credential verification is often manual and opaque, prone to delays and errors, and vulnerable to fraud. These limitations produce friction and uncertainty for learners, and administrative burden and reputational risk for institutions.

At the same time, artificial intelligence (AI) and distributed ledger (blockchain) technologies are being promoted as potential solutions to some of these challenges

(Azzam & Charles, 2025). AI promises to interpret diverse learning artifacts at scale and provide predictive analytics for student success, while blockchain promises tamper-evident records and learner-controlled digital credentials (Bidry et al., 2023). Blockchain-based systems could allow graduates to securely store and share verifiable proof of their achievements without relying on intermediaries (Turkanović et al., 2018). AI techniques, including machine learning and natural language processing, could enable automated or augmented recognition of prior learning by analysing unstructured evidence (essays, portfolios, project work) and mapping it to formal competency frameworks (Holmes et al., 2022; Zawacki-Richter et al., 2019). However, without an integrated architecture that combines these technologies with robust governance, institutions risk adopting isolated tools that do not address underlying problems of trust, portability and accountability (Polin et al., 2023). Many current initiatives treat AI and blockchain in isolation: for example, piloting blockchain for digital diplomas without integrating with the broader learning record ecosystem or developing learning analytics models on institutional data without ensuring the verifiability or portability of those data (Capetillo et al., 2022). High-level frameworks for "responsible AI" articulate principles like fairness and transparency but seldom translate into concrete designs for educational credentials (Holmes et al., 2022). In short, there is a gap between the promise of these emerging technologies and the realities of current academic credentialing systems.

This chapter responds by conceptualizing digital identity and verifiable learning records as the trust foundation for responsible AI-enhanced credentialing. It advances a design-science framework for a campus-wide architecture that integrates decentralised identifiers (DIDs: cryptographically controlled identifiers that do not rely on a single platform provider), verifiable credentials (VCs: digitally signed, tamper-evident claims about learning achievements), permissioned ledgers (used primarily as integrity and status anchors), and AI services into a layered, governance-aware model. The proposed framework is aligned with emerging credentialing and identity initiatives (for example, verifiable credential ecosystems, comprehensive learner record approaches and open badge practices) while foregrounding learner agency, privacy and bounded AI autonomy. Rather than propose a turnkey solution, the framework is intended as a reference architecture that universities can adapt, critique and empirically test in pursuit of more portable, trustworthy and data-informed credentialing practices.

Essentially, the core problem motivating this chapter is that the digitalization of teaching and assessment has not been accompanied by an equivalent digitalization of trust in educational credentials (Ocheja et al., 2019). LMS platforms, e-portfolios and other systems generate rich evidence of learning, but final credentials reduce this complexity to coarse-grained summaries (grades, credit hours) on transcripts or certificates that are difficult to verify and interpret outside the issuing institution

(McGreal, 2023). When students' progress from one institution to another, their prior learning data often do not move with them, leading to a "cold start" problem where the new institution lacks the information needed to personalize or recognize learning achievements (Ocheja et al., 2022). RPL processes, where prior informal or non-institutional learning is evaluated for credit, typically rely on manual review of portfolios or narratives due to the absence of verifiable digital records. Moreover, different institutions and jurisdictions maintain separate credential databases and formats, meaning that portability of learning achievements is limited. Learners have little visibility into or control over how their data are shared and used; often they must request official transcripts or letters, and cannot easily monitor who verifies their records (McGreal, 2023). This lack of learner agency over personal achievement data is increasingly at odds with legal and ethical expectations around data rights and consent (Prinsloo & Slade, 2017). In short, current credentialing systems struggle to reconcile the demands of portability, privacy and trust in an era of more fluid lifelong learning pathways.

Three specific consequences of the current misalignment can be highlighted. First, assessment transparency is undermined (Charles, 2021). When rich evidence of learning (projects, discussions, formative assessments) is boiled down to a single grade or a terse transcript entry, external stakeholders cannot discern the competencies or criteria behind the credential (Ahsan et al., 2023). Second, the portability of learning across contexts is constrained. Recognition of prior learning or international credential evaluation often requires laborious manual processes (course descriptions, notarized copies, etc.) because no standard verifiable learning record travels with the learner (Ocheja et al., 2019). Third, trust and security of credentials are under strain. Incidents of fake degrees, transcript tampering and misleading credential claims are reported globally, prompting calls for more secure and verifiable credentials. The absence of a common trust infrastructure forces employers and institutions to either take credentials on faith or invest in time-consuming verification (such as directly contacting registrars). All these issues are magnified as lifelong learning becomes the norm, and learners accumulate diverse credentials over a lifetime.

The Promise and Perils of AI and Blockchain in Credentialing

The past decade has seen rapid growth of interest in applying both AI and blockchain technologies to education (Alammary et al., 2019). Artificial intelligence techniques – from machine learning prediction models to large language models – are being explored for tasks such as automated tutoring, essay scoring, and predicting student outcomes (Zawacki-Richter et al., 2019). In the context of credentials, AI offers the tantalizing possibility of analyzing unstructured learning data (assignments, portfolio items, work experience) and inferring competencies or matching them to formal qualifications frameworks (Holmes et al., 2022). For example, natural language processing could be used to evaluate an e-portfolio and map evidence of learning to the outcomes required for a micro-credential or a professional certification (Brown et al., 2021; Charles et al., 2025). AI-powered tools might help identify when a learner's prior experience (e.g. a coding project or an online course) is equivalent to a required course in a degree program, thereby streamlining RPL decisions (Abukhalaf et al., 2024; Elsawah & Charles, 2023). Similarly, AI could enable more fine-grained assessments, provide personalized feedback and identifying skill gaps at scale.

Blockchain and distributed ledger technologies, on the other hand, promise solutions to the trust and verification issues of digital credentials (Bhaskar et al., 2021). By using cryptographic techniques and decentralized consensus, a blockchain can serve as an immutable registry of credentials that multiple parties (universities, employers, learners) can trust without a single central authority (Mohammad & Vargas, 2022). Early educational blockchain projects (such as MIT's digital diploma initiative) demonstrated the ability to anchor graduation certificates to public blockchains, allowing anyone with the certificate to verify its authenticity and integrity independently (Patel et al., 2026). Subsequent efforts have expanded to full platforms for issuing and managing educational credentials on blockchains (Capetillo et al., 2022). These systems often emphasize fraud resistance (credentials that cannot be faked or altered without detection) and efficiency of verification (instant validation by third parties). Blockchain-based credential wallets have been touted as giving learners control over their achievements – students could hold all their badges, certificates and transcripts in a secure digital wallet and share them with employers or other institutions as needed (Steiu, 2020). This vision of self-sovereign identity in education, enabled by decentralized identifiers and verifiable credentials, could undercut the current dependence on institution-issued paper or PDF records and reduce verification overhead (Alammary et al., 2019). Enthusiasts argue that blockchain could fundamentally "disintermediate" credentialing, empower learners and breaking down monopoly control of credential issuing (Chen et al., 2018).

Taken at face value, these developments promise powerful tools to address the challenges outlined earlier. Verifiable digital credentials could provide stronger guarantees of authenticity and integrity than current paper or PDF documents (Patel et al., 2026). Decentralized identifiers (DIDs) allow individuals to maintain lifelong identities not tied to any single institution, enabling cross-platform recognition of achievements (Mazzocca et al., 2024). AI services can, in principle, make sense of heterogeneous learning evidence at scale, providing insights that were previously only available via human judgment (Zawacki-Richter et al., 2019). However, the introduction of these technologies into credentialing also raises significant questions and risks. Blockchain-based approaches have faced criticism around privacy (since an immutable ledger could expose sensitive student data), unclear governance (who controls permissioned education blockchains or ensures their longevity), and even environmental impact (for public blockchains with energy-intensive consensus). Simply putting hashes of credentials on a blockchain does not resolve issues of interpretation or fairness, and if not carefully designed, metadata on-chain could leak information (e.g. multiple records for remedial courses might stigmatize a student). AI systems used in high-stakes educational decisions have well-documented problems with bias, opacity and reliability (Zhu et al., 2025). Models trained on historical academic data may reproduce existing inequities (e.g. under-predicting success for students from underrepresented groups). Black-box algorithms can be difficult to interpret or challenge – if an AI system denies a learner credit for prior experience, on what basis and with what opportunity for appeal? Without appropriate safeguards, AI might undermine professional and institutional accountability (for instance, if admissions or credit decisions are delegated to opaque models).

Crucially, many existing initiatives address AI and blockchain in isolation rather than as part of a coordinated strategy (Capetillo et al., 2022). For example, there have been blockchain pilot projects that focus narrowly on issuing digital diplomas or badges, without integrating these credentials with LMS data or learning analytics systems (Polin et al., 2023). Conversely, learning analytics projects often build predictive models using whatever student data are available internally, without considering how to incorporate verifiable external learning records or how to ensure the *provenance* of the data feeding the AI (Mohammad & Vargas, 2022). Efforts to promote "responsible AI" in education (such as ethical guidelines by governments or professional bodies) tend to remain abstract principles – fairness, transparency, accountability – that are not yet grounded in concrete architectural mechanisms for credentialing systems (Holmes et al., 2022). As a result, institutions today face a proliferation of proofs-of-concept and vendor offerings that address pieces of the puzzle, but lack a cohesive, standards-based, governance-aware architecture to underpin trustworthy, AI-enabled credentialing on a smart campus.

Aim, Scope and Research Questions

In response to these challenges, this chapter adopts a conceptual and design-oriented stance. It does not report on an empirical deployment or evaluate a specific product. Instead, it seeks to develop and justify a conceptual architecture for digital identity and verifiable learning that can support responsible AI-enhanced credentialing in higher education (Polin et al., 2023). The focus is on degree-granting institutions (universities), although many ideas may extend to other post-secondary contexts such as professional training and lifelong learning. Fundamentally, the aim is to articulate a possible trust fabric for a smart campus that brings together verifiable credentials, learner-centered identity, AI services and governance mechanisms.

Methodological orientation (design-science). Following a design-science logic, the chapter (i) establishes the practical relevance of credential fragmentation for smart campuses; (ii) synthesises research and standards to derive design objectives; (iii) proposes a five-layer reference architecture as the artefact; and (iv) evaluates the artefact ex ante through scenario walk-throughs, risk analysis and alignment with principles of verifiability, learner agency and responsible AI. This approach clarifies that the contribution is not a single technical system but a reusable architectural vocabulary to guide future pilots and comparative research.

More specifically, the chapter proposes a five-layer credentialing architecture encompassing: (1) foundational digital identity (using DIDs and wallets for learners and organizations); (2) a verifiable record layer that aggregates and issues tamper-evident credentials (grades, micro-credentials, co-curricular achievements) from existing campus systems; (3) an AI analytics layer that consumes those verifiable records (with services for competency inference, RPL support, qualification framework alignment, etc.); (4) a consent and policy layer to manage data sharing, privacy, and model governance (including consent receipts, usage policies, and audit logs); and (5) an interaction layer of applications and user interfaces that deliver these capabilities to stakeholders (students, faculty, employers, auditors, etc.). Underpinning all layers is an explicit attention to governance – the rules, roles and processes that ensure the system operates in alignment with institutional values, legal requirements and ethical principles.

Three key research questions frame the inquiry:

- *Integration*: How can a smart-campus credentialing architecture integrate existing LMS, SIS and e-portfolio systems into a verifiable record layer without disrupting current workflows? In other words, how can we achieve integration without wholesale replacement, leveraging what institutions already have while adding a layer of verifiability?
- *AI Services*: Which AI services, layered atop verifiable learning records, are best positioned to enhance recognition of prior learning, competency mapping and alignment to formal qualifications frameworks? And how can these services operate in a trusted manner – for instance, using only verifiable data as inputs and producing transparent, explainable outputs?
- *Governance*: What governance mechanisms – especially around consent, revocation, audit and contestation – are required to ensure privacy, fairness and institutional accountability when AI models operate over blockchain-anchored evidence? Essentially, how do we design the socio-technical pro-

cesses so that responsible AI isn't just a slogan but is embedded in how the system works (e.g. through technical features and policy)?

Addressing these questions requires linking technical standards with educational policy, institutional practices and ethical considerations. The chapter therefore draws on literature and best practices across several domains – digital identity and credentialing, blockchain in education, learning analytics and responsible AI – to inform the proposed architecture. The next section provides a review of these areas and identifies conceptual building blocks. In sum, this chapter positions verifiable digital identity and learner-held records as prerequisites for trustworthy AI-mediated recognition. It advances a governance-aware reference architecture and, through the research questions above, foregrounds three design concerns: integration with legacy systems, the bounded use of AI services, and institutional mechanisms for consent, audit and contestation.

LITERATURE REVIEW

To ground the architecture in existing knowledge, this section reviews relevant literature across four themes: the evolution from transcripts to micro-credentials; emerging models of digital identity and learner-controlled records; the W3C framework for verifiable credentials and decentralized identifiers; the use of blockchain for educational credentials; and the role of AI in learning analytics and responsible educational data use. It concludes by synthesizing insights and gaps that the proposed framework aims to address.

From Transcripts to Micro-Credentials

For decades, the academic transcript has been the core artifact representing student achievement. Transcripts list courses, credits and grades in a format optimized for human reading (typically by registrars or admissions officers) rather than machine processing. They are coarse-grained and institution-centric, providing little detail on the specific competencies or criteria underlying the grades. A transcript might show that a student earned a "B" in Chemistry 101, but it will not reveal which skills or learning outcomes that grade represents. Nor do transcripts capture co-curricular or informal learning – they omit internships, coding bootcamps, volunteer projects, and other experiences that might be very relevant to an employer or another institution

(Ahsan et al., 2023). In short, traditional transcripts provide a limited and opaque signal of student capabilities.

The rise of micro-credentials (including digital badges, nanodegrees, micro-certifications, etc.) has been framed as a response to these limitations. Micro-credentials are generally defined as short, competency-based learning units that are certified by some authority and often issued in digital form (commonly as badges) upon completion (Ahsan et al., 2023). They promise a more granular recognition of skills and achievements than conventional degrees (Varadarajan et al., 2023). For example, instead of simply having a bachelor's degree in business, a student might accumulate specific micro-credentials in "Data Analysis with Excel" or "Project Management Basics" that provide fine-grained evidence of what they can do. Micro-credentials are typically shorter than traditional programs – ranging from a few hours to a few months of learning – and they can often be stacked into larger qualifications (a series of micro-credentials might add up to a certificate or even credit towards a degree). This modularity and flexibility make micro-credentials attractive for lifelong learning and upskilling, allowing learners to quickly gain and showcase competencies that align with evolving industry needs (Gamage & Dehideniya, 2025). Studies indicate that micro-credentials are seen to bridge the gap between higher education and workforce requirements by targeting specific skills and being delivered in a timely, on-demand fashion (Ahsan et al., 2023). They can also serve non-traditional learners who need shorter, focused learning opportunities rather than multi-year degree programs (Varadarajan et al., 2023).

In practice, however, the implementation of micro-credentials has been heterogeneous. Definitions and standards vary widely. Some institutions use the term "micro-credential" to refer to any sub-degree certification (including quite extensive postgraduate certificates), while others reserve it for very small units (like a 1-credit module or a co-curricular badge). There is no global consensus on what size or scope a micro-credential should be – for instance, Europe's MicroHE project defined them as typically 5-30 ECTS credits, whereas other frameworks have different thresholds. Assessment methods and quality assurance for micro-credentials also differ; one organization's micro-credential might require a proctored exam, while another might be based on participation or a project (Varadarajan et al., 2023). Despite initiatives like Mozilla's Open Badges standard, the data schemas and metadata associated with micro-credentials are not uniform, which limits interoperability across platforms (Ahsan et al., 2023). This lack of standardization complicates the recognition of micro-credentials: employers or institutions may not know how to interpret a given badge or micro-certificate without additional context, undermining the supposed portability of these credentials.

Micro-credentials thus extend the credentialing palette conceptually, but many implementations remain siloed in proprietary platforms or local schemes, and their wider acceptance has been uneven (Ahsan et al., 2023). Simply issuing credentials in digital format does not automatically solve the underlying challenges of trust, comparability and longevity. For example, a digital badge might be easy to share on LinkedIn, but how can its validity be verified five or ten years later? If the issuing platform or institution changes or ceases to exist, how does the learner prove the badge's authenticity? These questions have spurred interest in using blockchain and decentralized verification for micro-credentials (Alammary et al., 2019). Meanwhile, researchers have also pointed out the risk of overselling micro-credentials as a panacea. Some critics argue that an abundance of micro-credentials could lead to a fragmented "patchwork" of qualifications that is confusing to employers and may erode the perceived value of traditional degrees if not carefully integrated. Others note that if micro-credentials are not internationally recognized or transferable, they could create dead-ends for learners (Varadarajan et al., 2023).

Despite these challenges, the momentum behind micro-credentials continues to grow, especially accelerated by the COVID-19 pandemic and the shift to online learning (Hill et al., 2023; Shehzad & Charles, 2023). Universities, professional bodies, and MOOC platforms are increasingly partnering to offer micro-credentials, often aligning them with industry standards. A number of countries and regions (e.g. New Zealand, European Union) have developed qualification frameworks and guidelines for micro-credentials to ensure some level of consistency and quality. The potential benefits – flexibility, inclusivity, employability – are seen as significant. Research finds that micro-credentials can make higher education more accessible by allowing "bit-sized" learning with lower time and cost commitment (Gamage & Dehideniya, 2025). They can also encourage continuous upskilling and lifelong learning, as individuals return for targeted learning throughout their careers.

Ultimately, micro-credentials represent a move toward more granular, learner-centric credentialing, but to realize their full promise, issues of standardization, stack ability, and trust need to be addressed. The architecture proposed in this chapter assumes that micro-credentials will be part of the credential ecosystem (alongside degrees), and it aims to incorporate them in a way that ensures they are verifiable and portable across platforms. A key premise is that micro-credentials (and indeed all credentials) should be issued as verifiable digital claims that can be independently validated, rather than just digital images or PDFs. This connects the micro-credential movement with the technologies of verifiable credentials and blockchains discussed later.

Digital Identity and Learner-Centred Records

In parallel with the diversification of credentials, universities have developed robust identity and access management (IAM) systems that control authentication (logins) and authorization (access to resources) within institutional boundaries. Single sign-on systems, federated identity frameworks (like Shibboleth or OAuth), and campus ID services allow students and staff to access multiple campus systems with one identity. However, these traditional IAM infrastructures are focused on authentication for services, not on portable representation of one's achievements. They assume a context where the institution manages the identity of the student while enrolled, and often alumni lose full access to these digital identities upon graduation. In other words, university IAM treats identity as institution-bound and temporary, whereas lifelong learning and credential portability require identity to be more learner-centered and persistent beyond a single institution.

Recent initiatives such as Comprehensive Learner Records (CLR) and Learning and Employment Records (LER) reflect a shift toward aggregating a learner's diverse experiences and accomplishments into portable profiles that the learner can carry across institutions and into employment (Mohammad & Vargas, 2022). For example, a comprehensive learner record might include not only courses and grades, but also co-curricular activities, skills acquired, micro-credentials earned, and even self-reported or employer-verified competencies. The IMS Global (now 1EdTech) CLR standard provides a data model for such multi-faceted records. The vision is that learners would have a digital portfolio of all their learning that they control and can share as needed. Similarly, national initiatives like the U.S. Learning and Employment Record prototype aim to create verifiable digital records that include education, training, and work experience in one package.

While promising, many current "learner record" solutions remain platform-centric or institution-centric. Often, they amount to universities issuing richer digital transcripts through a vendor platform. The learner may get a "record" they can view, but not a self-sovereign one they fully control – it might be an account on a proprietary system that could be shut off. When students graduate, they frequently lose access to institutional email and accounts, and any learner record tied to those accounts might become inaccessible or frozen in time. There is thus a conceptual and technical gap between today's campus identity systems (which ensure that "Jane Doe" is a student in the university with certain permissions) and the kind of decentralized digital identity needed for verifiable, lifelong credential portability (where "Jane Doe" can prove she earned a credential, independent of the issuing institution's continued involvement).

This gap has motivated interest in self-sovereign identity (SSI) approaches using decentralized identifiers (DIDs) and related standards (Mazzocca et al., 2024). The core idea of SSI is to give individuals control over their own digital identity and credentials, rather than having to rely on siloed institutional identities. With SSI, Jane Doe might have a digital wallet where she stores identifiers and credentials issued by various parties (university, employer, certification body), and she can present proofs of those credentials without needing to log into the university's system or ask the university to vouch for her each time (Mohammad & Vargas, 2022). Technologies like DIDs allow for the creation of identifiers that are not dependent on any single provider – for instance, a DID could be anchored on a public blockchain or other decentralized network, and only Jane has the keys to control it Verifiable Credentials (W3C standard) provide a format for the university to issue Jane a tamper-proof credential (like a JSON document stating she earned a BSc degree), which Jane can store and later present to employers or other institutions. Critically, the authenticity of that credential can be verified cryptographically without contacting the issuer each time (Mazzocca et al., 2024).

The literature suggests that applying SSI in education could empower learners and increase interoperability of credentials (Alammary et al., 2019). For example, a European blockchain for education diplomas was piloted to allow graduates to share a verifiable degree certificate with employers across borders, eliminating the need for apostilles or lengthy verification processes (Kosmarski, 2020). In another case, a group of universities created a consortium where each issues credentials as verifiable claims, and they mutually recognize each other's DID-based student identities, enabling cross-registration and credit transfer more seamlessly (Patel et al., 2026). These experiments indicate the potential of learner-controlled identities and records.

However, moving to a learner-centred identity model raises important governance questions: How are such identities established and trusted initially? (For instance, how do we tie a DID to a real student without an initial institutional identity proof?) What if a learner loses control of their keys – is there a recovery mechanism? How do we ensure privacy, given that a persistent identifier could be used to correlate data across contexts? Some authors argue that truly self-sovereign identity for education is still aspirational and that interim federated approaches or guardianship models might be needed (Mazzocca et al., 2024). For example, a university might issue a DID for a student upon graduation and publish the student's degree as a verifiable credential to that DID; the student then assumes control of it going forward. Hybrid models are being explored, where institutions and learners co-manage identities and credentials, especially while technologies and trust frameworks mature.

Evidently, the trend is toward more portable and user-centric representations of learning achievements but realizing this in practice requires bridging institutional systems and decentralized identity technologies. The reference architecture in this chapter assumes the use of DID-based identities and digital wallets for learners (and for organizations as credential issuers). It tries to address how we can integrate with existing campus authentication (so that the transition is smooth) and how credentials issued by the campus can live on as verifiable proofs under the learner's control after graduation. This is seen as a foundational layer because without trustworthy digital identities and records, any AI analysis on credentials or any cross-institution sharing becomes difficult or impossible to do securely.

Verifiable Credentials and Decentralised Identifiers

The W3C Verifiable Credentials (VC) Data Model provides a standard way to express digital claims about a subject (e.g., "Alice completed Course X at Institution Y with grade Z") in a format that is tamper-evident and cryptographically verifiable (Mazzocca et al., 2024). A verifiable credential is essentially a digital certificate that includes: the claims (assertions about the subject), metadata (such as issuer, issue date, expiration, credential schema or type), and proofs (digital signature(s) from the issuer). Because it is digitally signed by the issuer, the credential can be verified by a third party to confirm that it was indeed issued by who it says (authenticity) and that it hasn't been altered (integrity). The subject (e.g. the student) can hold these credentials in a digital wallet.

A powerful concept in the VC model is the ability to create verifiable presentations. A holder (student) can take one or more credentials and present them to a verifier (employer) in a way that the verifier can check the proofs. This can include selective disclosure – revealing only certain attributes. For instance, if a student has a VC for their transcript, they could generate a presentation that reveals only the credential confirming they earned a degree, without revealing all their individual course grades, if only the degree is relevant to the verifier. Advanced usages can involve zero-knowledge proofs to confirm something like "age > 18" without revealing the birthdate, though such use cases are more common in other domains (finance, etc.) and still emerging in education.

Decentralized Identifiers (DIDs) complement VCs by providing a new type of identifier that is not tied to a central authority. A DID is a URI (like *did; example:123456*) that can be resolved to a DID Document containing public keys and service endpoints. The idea is that an entity (person, organization, or even an IoT device) can generate their own DID and associated key pair. They prove control of the DID by using the corresponding private key to sign things. The DID Document can be stored on a distributed ledger or other decentralized network so that others can retrieve the public key and verify signatures. In the education context, a university could have a DID it uses as the issuer identifier for credentials it issues, and a student could have a DID as the subject identifier on her credentials. Verification of a credential involves checking the issuer's signature against the public key in the issuer's DID Document. Because DIDs are globally unique and not tied to a single platform, they enable a form of interoperability: a verifier can trust a credential if it trusts the DID method and the issuer (or if a trust registry is in place), regardless of what software was used to create it.

Communities in education and training have been actively exploring how VCs and DIDs can support various credentialing scenarios. For example, the Blockcerts initiative (MIT and Learning Machine) essentially implemented an early form of verifiable digital certificates anchored to blockchains and can be seen as a precursor to the W3C VC approach (Park, 2021). More recently, pilots have looked at using VCs for things like digital diplomas, transcripts, professional certifications, and co-curricular records (Mohammad & Vargas, 2022). Typically, these involve defining roles of issuer (e.g. the university), holder (the student), and verifier (employer or another unit), and using protocols where the holder requests a credential, the issuer issues it (signs it), and later the holder presents it to a verifier who checks the signature and status. Some ecosystems introduce additional roles like endorsers or attestors (third parties that can add endorsements to a credential) and revocation registries (to invalidate credentials if needed).

It is important to note that while VCs and DIDs provide a *technical vocabulary* and standards for verifiable claims, they do not by themselves solve all the integration challenges. They say *how* to issue a credential in a verifiable way, but not *when* or *why*. Questions like: How to integrate VC issuance with existing campus systems (so that issuing a VC is part of the normal process when a student passes a course)? How to handle revocation if, say, a credential was issued in error or later rescinded? How to ensure learners actually maintain access to their wallets and don't lose credentials? These require process and governance solutions on top of the technical standard. Moreover, using VCs in education will likely involve trust frameworks – agreements on what credentials mean and who is trusted to issue them. For instance, an employer will trust a VC about a degree if it recognizes the issuer (the university) as legitimate. This might require directories of trusted educational issuers or blockchain consortiums of universities that collectively vouch for each other's credentials.

Basically, Verifiable Credentials and DIDs provide the building blocks for treating credentials as verifiable digital "tokens" of learning that learners can carry and use. They align well with the needs identified earlier for more fine-grained, portable, and learner-controlled credentials. This chapter's framework leverages VCs/DIDs as a foundational element: all claims about learning (course completions, micro-credentials, grades, skill assertions) are to be represented as VCs that are cryptographically signed by the issuer. The use of DIDs is assumed for identifying the parties (universities have DIDs, learners have DIDs, perhaps even specific courses or accrediting bodies have DIDs). This ensures that any data feeding into AI services or shared across the smart campus is verifiable at source – a principle that can be summed up as "no AI on unverifiable data." Before diving into the architecture, though, we review how blockchain technology has been proposed as an infrastructure for managing and verifying these credentials.

Blockchain and Permissioned Ledgers

Blockchain and related distributed ledger technologies (DLTs) have been widely proposed in the education sector, especially for secure digital credentialing. In essence, a blockchain is a decentralized, append-only ledger of transactions, maintained by a network of nodes with no single point of control (Alammary et al., 2019). The appeal for education is that a blockchain can serve as an independent verification layer: by anchoring hashes or records of credentials on a blockchain, one can later verify the authenticity of a presented credential without relying solely on the issuer's database (Patel et al., 2026).

Early pilots, such as the University of Nicosia's blockchain diplomas (2014) and MIT Media Lab's Blockcerts (2017), recorded cryptographic hashes of digital certificates on a public blockchain (Bitcoin or Ethereum). This means that given a digital diploma file, anyone can compute its hash and compare it to the value on the blockchain to see if it matches an issuer's signed record from the graduation date (Alammary et al., 2019). Such approaches demonstrated the feasibility of issuing tamper-evident digital diplomas – if a graduate tries to alter the diploma file, it will no longer match the blockchain record and verification would fail. Moreover, the verification does not require contacting the university; the blockchain itself (being public) serves as the timestamped witness of the record. The benefit is immediate, automated credential verification, which could reduce fraud and administrative overhead (Lizcano et al., 2020).

Subsequent projects have developed more elaborate blockchain-based credential platforms. These often involve custom DLT networks or smart contract systems to manage credentials. For instance, EduCTX was a blockchain platform proposed for European Credit Transfer System (ECTS) credits, allowing universities to issue tokens representing credits on a shared ledger (Capetillo et al., 2022). Other projects integrated smart contracts for issuing and revoking credentials, or for orchestrating learning pathways (like unlocking one credential after prerequisites on-chain are met). The general emphasis has been on improved fraud resistance (credentials are digitally signed and recorded, making forgery extremely difficult) and efficiency (automating verification, potentially streamlining credit transfers or admissions). Some platforms also highlight learner control and privacy through blockchain: e.g., using public key infrastructure to ensure only the learner (with their private key) can access the content of a credential, while the blockchain stores an encrypted version or hash.

However, as mentioned, these approaches have faced critique. One major concern is privacy: an immutable public ledger is at odds with the "right to be forgotten" and with keeping personal data confidential (Patel et al., 2026). Even if only hashes are stored on-chain, patterns of transactions or credentials (such as a sequence of timestamped hashes for one person) might reveal information. To mitigate this, many education blockchain projects moved toward permissioned ledgers – private or consortium blockchains where only authorized participants can write/read, and governance is established by a consortium of institutions. For example, a group of universities might run a permissioned blockchain for issuing and verifying each other's credentials. This improves privacy (data is not public) and can be more energy-efficient (using consensus algorithms like Proof of Authority or IBFT instead of Proof of Work). It also allows for clearer governance – participants sign an agreement on how the network is run.

Critics also note that blockchain solutions often leave most personal data off-chain (storing only hashes or pointers on-chain), which begs the question of whether a simpler public key infrastructure (PKI) or centralized database could do the job just as well. Proponents respond that blockchains provide unique advantages in decentralized trust – no single institution owns the ledger, so even if one issuer goes offline, the credential proofs remain – and in tamper resistance at a systemic level (Patel et al., 2026). Furthermore, blockchains can enable interesting features like decentralized endorsement (multiple parties endorsing a credential via transactions) or audit trails of how credentials are used (if presentations are logged in some fashion).

Given the trade-offs, a consensus in recent literature is that blockchain should be treated as one component of an architecture – typically as the integrity and timestamp layer, with personal data stored off-chain in secure repositories or wallets (Patel et al., 2026). In our context, this translates to using a blockchain (likely permissioned) to record credential identifiers, hashes, and revocation registries, rather than the full content of credentials. The permissioned ledger acts as a shared source of truth for which credentials have been issued or revoked and maybe stores pointers to encrypted files if needed. Meanwhile, the actual credential content (issued as a VC) is held by the learner and/or the issuer's database and is shared peer-to-peer when verification is needed. This way, privacy is preserved (no personal data on-chain), but verification can still be done by checking the blockchain record for existence and validity of the credential proof.

To sum up, blockchain technology offers a potential infrastructure for trust in a decentralized credentialing ecosystem, but its role must be carefully circumscribed to avoid pitfalls. The architecture proposed in this chapter will incorporate a permissioned blockchain as an "integrity anchor" – used for recording credential signatures or IDs and enabling independent verification and audit, but not as a store of sensitive data. It also addresses governance by assuming a consortium (e.g., an alliance of institutions or a national body) governs the ledger. This approach aligns with recommendations to combine blockchain with off-chain storage and robust governance to get the best of both worlds (Arndt & Guercio, 2020).

AI in Learning Analytics, Assessment and Recognition

Artificial Intelligence (AI) has been applied in education primarily through the fields of learning analytics (LA) and educational data mining (EDM). These fields use techniques like predictive modelling, clustering, and machine learning to analyse educational data and improve decision-making. In higher education, AI-driven learning analytics have been used to predict student performance, identify at-risk learners, personalize learning paths, and support instructors with insights (Zawacki-Richter et al., 2019). For example, predictive models might use LMS interaction data to predict which students are at risk of failing a course so that early interventions can be offered. Recommendation systems may suggest learning resources to students based on their past activity and performance. Large language models (like GPT-4) are now being explored to generate feedback on essays, to summarize forum discussions, or even to power conversational intelligent tutors that can answer student questions with context from course materials.

In the context of credentialing and recognition, AI techniques are being investigated for automating or augmenting processes like recognition of prior learning (RPL), competency-based assessment (Charles & Hill, 2023), and alignment of learning outcomes to job skills frameworks (Holmes et al., 2022). One can imagine an AI system that reviews a learner's portfolio or work history and maps it to the outcomes of a formal qualification, suggesting which requirements have been fulfilled and where there are gaps. Similarly, AI might analyze unstructured evidence (like a project or code repository) and infer competencies (e.g., "proficient in Python programming") which could then be issued as micro-credentials or used for credit transfer. There have been experiments using machine learning to evaluate open-ended RPL submissions, or to compare curriculum descriptions to job skill taxonomies for alignment (Zawacki-Richter et al., 2019). AI can also assist in assessment – for instance, using computer vision to assess a lab skill via video, or using NLP to grade short answers – which indirectly feeds into credentialing by providing more data on student competencies.

The deployment of AI in these areas, however, raises several ethical and practical concerns. One issue is the opacity of many AI models (the "black box" problem) – if a student is denied credit or flagged as high risk by an algorithm, it may not be clear why. This lack of transparency can undermine trust and make it difficult to contest or correct decisions (Holmes et al., 2022). Another concern is bias: AI models trained on historical educational data might perpetuate biases in grading or in predicting success (for instance, if past data reflected structural biases, the model learns those) (Zhu et al., 2025). Fairness in algorithmic recommendations and decisions is a major topic of research, and in education the stakes are high because decisions can affect student access to opportunities. Data quality and provenance are also issues – much of the data in institutional databases may be incomplete or not reflective of actual learning (e.g., login frequency on an LMS might correlate with performance but does not *cause* learning). Using such data for high-stakes decisions can lead to errors or reinforce misleading correlations. For example, a predictive model might mistakenly penalize students who prefer offline study methods and don't log into the LMS often, by flagging them as "low engagement" risks, even if they are doing fine.

Responsible AI guidelines in education stress the importance of human oversight, transparency, accountability, validity of data, and mechanisms for appeal and redress when algorithmic decisions go wrong. Many scholars argue that AI should *augment* rather than replace human judgment in complex tasks like credential evaluation (Holmes et al., 2022). For instance, an AI might suggest that a portfolio looks 80% like prior students who got credit for a course, but a human should review the evidence and the AI's rationale before granting the credit. There is also an increasing push for explainable AI in education – systems that can provide understandable reasons for their recommendations (e.g., highlighting which sections of a portfolio correspond to which required skill).

A key observation from the literature is that efforts to make AI fair and accountable can be undermined by unreliable or untrustworthy input data (Ocheja et al., 2022). If the records of learning (grades, badges, etc.) are not trustworthy (e.g., easily falsified or coming from unknown sources), then even a perfectly unbiased algorithm could produce unfair or incorrect outcomes simply by trusting incorrect data. This links back to the earlier themes: data verifiability is a prerequisite for responsible AI in credentialing. One cannot have confidence in an AI-powered RPL recommendation if the evidence feeding it could be fraudulent or tampered with. Thus, one argument this chapter advances (supported by multiple sources in the literature) is that efforts in responsible AI and efforts in verifiable credentials need to go hand in hand. Ensuring the provenance and integrity of data (via technologies like VCs/blockchain) can bolster the foundation on which AI analytics are built, making it easier to implement fairness and accountability (since one can focus on algorithmic issues knowing the data is sound).

Clearly, AI offers significant opportunities to enhance how we assess and recognize learning – potentially speeding up RPL decisions, uncovering hidden skills, personalizing learning pathways, and providing early warnings for student support. But it also introduces risks that must be mitigated through careful design (both technical and organizational). The literature on responsible AI in education emphasizes a socio-technical approach: it's not just about better algorithms, but about policies, transparency, human roles, and stakeholder engagement. This chapter's framework builds on that insight by explicitly embedding governance and audit layers to manage AI services. For instance, any AI competency recommendation service in the architecture would operate only on verifiable input data and would produce an explanation or confidence measure that could be reviewed. Additionally, the framework calls for auditability – keeping logs (secured via blockchain, perhaps) of how AI recommendations were generated and used, to enable accountability and continuous improvement.

Responsible AI and Data Governance

Frameworks for responsible AI – whether from governments, universities, or companies – commonly highlight principles such as fairness, transparency, explainability, privacy, security, and accountability. In the education sector, these high-level principles have been echoed by various bodies. For example, the IEEE's guidelines for automated decision systems and UNESCO's recommendations on AI in education stress that AI tools should be human-centric, complement human teachers, and respect student rights and dignity (Charles, 2025). Institutions like universities have begun to formulate their own AI ethics policies, often emphasizing alignment with their educational mission (e.g., supporting learning over efficiency), the importance of algorithmic impact assessments, documentation of AI system purposes and limitations, and procedures for students or staff to contest or appeal algorithmic decisions (Zhu et al., 2025).

However, many of these frameworks remain at a somewhat abstract level, and there is a recognized gap when it comes to implementation in specific domains like credentialing (Holmes et al., 2022). It is one thing to say "AI should be fair and transparent", but what does that specifically entail for a system that, say, recommends whether a student's work experience should count for academic credit? How do we ensure transparency – does the system need to show which parts of the work experience triggered a positive recommendation? Fairness – does it need to be calibrated to not disadvantage certain groups? Accountability – who is responsible if the recommendation is wrong, the faculty or the software vendor? These are the kinds of questions that need concrete answers in a system design.

Education data is particularly sensitive and complex. It is relational and "power-laden" in the sense that institutions hold power over learners (grading, credentialing, gatekeeping access to opportunities) and thus have a duty of care in how data and AI are used. Students often cannot easily opt out of data collection or automated processes if those are integrated into their education – hence the emphasis on data governance to ensure their rights are protected. Data governance in smart campuses involves setting policies on data access, consent, sharing, and retention, as well as technical measures to enforce those policies (e.g., access controls, encryption, audit trails) (McGreal, 2023). With AI in the loop, governance also means ensuring that models are trained on appropriate data, checked for bias, and used only within their valid context. For example, an algorithm trained on data from one program should not be naively applied to a different population without validation.

One concrete mechanism often recommended is algorithmic impact assessments (AIA) before deploying AI tools – like privacy impact assessments. An AIA would evaluate potential risks (bias, errors, etc.), stakeholders affected, and mitigation strategies. Another mechanism is establishing review boards or ethics committees for institutional AI use, which could periodically audit AI systems and respond to issues. There is also the notion of maintaining human-in-the-loop for decisions: e.g., an AI might provide input on a credential evaluation, but a human makes the final decision, and students can appeal to a human if they feel the AI misjudged them (Holmes et al., 2022).

In practice, however, analyses of current implementations (or even research prototypes) suggest that many are model-centric, focusing on technical performance and neglecting some of these governance aspects. For instance, a university might roll out a predictive analytics dashboard for advisors because it improved accuracy in tests, without fully addressing how to explain the predictions to students or how to avoid advisor bias in using them. Similarly, a blockchain credential platform might be launched to fight fraud, without clarity on how a student could get a record corrected if there was an error (since blockchains are append-only).

The insight driving this chapter is that responsible AI must be approached as a property of the overall socio-technical system, not just of the algorithm. That means the architecture itself should embed features supporting responsible use – things like consent management, transparency logs, and means for oversight and contestation. For example, if an AI service generates an assessment of a portfolio, the system might automatically record the input data and output in an audit log linked to the student's record (perhaps hashed on a ledger for integrity) (Polin et al., 2023). If a dispute arises, a committee could review that log. Consent and privacy preferences should be integrated – e.g., a student might consent to having their data used for certain AI analytics but not others, and the system should enforce that choice (maybe by not including their data in training sets for unrelated predictions). The architecture's governance layer (as envisioned in this chapter) would handle these concerns by design, rather than as afterthoughts.

Obviously, responsible AI in education requires moving beyond principles to concrete architectural and policy mechanisms. Key elements include making data verifiable and traceable (so that decisions are based on solid evidence), incorporating consent and privacy controls, providing transparency/explanation interfaces for both users and administrators, instituting oversight processes (like audit trails and human review checkpoints), and ensuring accountability (clear ownership of decisions and recourse for appeal). The literature provides many of these as recommendations, and this chapter attempts to fold them into the proposed design. By weaving together verifiable data structures and governance workflows, the aim is to create a credentialing system where AI can be used beneficially under a framework of trust and accountability, rather than in a black-box manner.

Synthesis

The literature review reveals converging trajectories in the innovation of academic credentials and data practices: a movement from coarse, static transcripts toward more granular micro-credentials and comprehensive learner records; the maturation of digital identity infrastructure from institution-bound accounts toward decentralized, self-sovereign identities; the emergence of verifiable credentials and DIDs as standards for trusted digital claims; the proliferation of blockchain credential pilots; and the expanding use of AI in learning analytics and automated recognition of learning (Patel et al., 2026). Yet these trajectories have largely progressed in parallel or isolation, with few examples of *integrated, campus-wide architectures* that combine all these elements into a coherent system. Researchers have noted a paucity of holistic solutions – for instance, Polin et al. (2023) found that most smart campus research focuses on single domains (technology, data, or governance in isolation) and that the governance dimension is least covered in current implementations. Similarly, systematic reviews of blockchain in education often conclude that while numerous proof-of-concepts exist, issues like interoperability, privacy and policy are not adequately addressed, and adoption remains low in part due to these gaps.

These trajectories are already visible in a range of credentialing initiatives and standards. For example, comprehensive learner record and learning-and-employment record models seek to represent learning achievements in granular, machine-readable forms, while open badge ecosystems have advanced portable signalling of micro-credentials. At the same time, decentralised identity and verifiable credential approaches provide a general-purpose mechanism for issuing, holding and verifying signed claims across organisational boundaries. The architecture proposed in this chapter is therefore intentionally standards-facing: it does not replace these initiatives, but offers a way to connect them to campus systems and to governance requirements for responsible AI.

In simpler terms, we have pieces of the puzzle: technologies for verifiable credentials, methods for learning analytics, guidelines for ethical AI – but they are rarely put together. This chapter responds to that gap by proposing a layered architecture that treats verifiable digital identity and learning records as prerequisites for responsible AI in credentialing. The idea is to ensure that the inputs to AI (data about learning) are trustworthy and portable, which is achieved through a combination of VCs, DIDs, and blockchain as an integrity layer, and that the outputs of AI (recommendations, decisions) are delivered under a governance framework that ensures they are fair, transparent and contestable. The insights from the review can be distilled into design principles for the architecture:

- Verifiability before automation: The integrity of data (e.g., that a claimed skill or grade is authentic) should be established through technical means (signatures, ledger records) before or in parallel with any AI-driven automation that uses that data. This addresses the "garbage in, garbage out" concern for AI.
- Learner-centric identity and records: Solutions should empower learners with control and visibility – using technologies like DIDs and wallets – rather than locking their achievements in institutional silos. This also aligns with legal trends (GDPR, data portability rights) and ethical calls for learner agency.
- Interoperability and open standards: To enable adoption across different systems and institutions, leveraging open standards (W3C VCs, IMS CLR, etc.) is crucial. This prevents vendor lock-in and allows incremental implementation.
- Governance by design: Instead of treating privacy, fairness, etc., as external policies, embed mechanisms for consent, auditing, and oversight into the architecture itself. For instance, incorporate a consent ledger or policy engine that enforces data sharing rules; build in an audit trail for credential and AI usage events.
- Incremental adoption and legacy compatibility: The design should be deployable in phases alongside current systems (LMS, SIS), not as a rip-and-replace "big bang". This means using adaptors to connect to legacy databases, issuing verifiable credentials in parallel with existing transcripts, and gradually introducing AI services in low-stakes settings to build trust.

Across the reviewed domains, a consistent implication emerges: governance and verifiability are enabling conditions for AI-enhanced credentialing, not optional add-ons. The following methodology therefore treats the architecture as a design-science artefact whose value depends on how well it operationalises these conditions in a coherent and adaptable form. By synthesizing these strands of research and best practice, the chapter now proceeds to outline the methodological approach (design-science) and then the proposed architecture itself. The architecture is structured to directly address the research questions by mapping how each layer and component meets the needs of integration (RQ1), AI services (RQ2), and governance (RQ3) in a unified model.

METHODOLOGY

This chapter adopts a conceptual design-science orientation. Rather than empirically evaluating a particular system, it constructs and justifies an artefact—a reference architecture for verifiable, AI-enhanced credentialing—grounded in existing knowledge. To make the design-science stance explicit for a multidisciplinary audience, the chapter operationalises four design-science components. First, problem relevance is established through the problematisation of fragmented credentials and the demand for RPL, mobility and accountability. Second, the artefact is the five-layer credentialing architecture, including roles, data objects and workflow patterns. Third, the knowledge base is the interdisciplinary literature and standards synthesised in the review. Fourth, evaluation is ex ante and conceptual, strengthened here through scenario walk-throughs (see Figure 2), risk and failure analysis, and a piloting-oriented maturity model. This positioning clarifies the intended use: the architecture is a defensible reference model to guide design and policy decisions, not an immediate production deployment.

Design-science logic

Design-science research focuses on the creation and refinement of artefacts that address practically relevant, theoretically informed problems. In this chapter:

- The problem is the misalignment between fragmented, weakly verifiable credentialing infrastructures and demands for AI-mediated recognition, portability and accountability.
- The artefact is a five-layer smart-campus credentialing architecture with associated roles, data objects, workflows and governance mechanisms.
- The knowledge base includes literature on micro-credentials, digital identity, VCs/DIDs, blockchain in education, learning analytics and responsible AI, alongside technical standards and policy documents.

Evaluation is ex ante and conceptual: the architecture is assessed in terms of coherence, responsiveness to the problem and alignment with design principles, rather than through empirical deployment. Effectively, five design objectives guide the architecture:

DO1: Integration without disruption – connect LMS, SIS and e-portfolio systems to a verifiable record layer without wholesale replacement or radical workflow changes.

DO2: Verifiable, portable evidence – represent learning achievements as cryptographically verifiable, machine-readable credentials that are portable across contexts while respecting privacy.
DO3: AI-readiness with bounded autonomy – support AI services that operate only on verifiable inputs, produce explainable outputs and remain advisory in high-stakes decisions.
DO4: Embedded governance – integrate consent, policy enforcement, and audit into the architecture.
DO5: Incremental adoption and vendor neutrality – enable staged implementation and avoid lock-in by relying on open standards and modular components.

These objectives are operationalised through design principles, including "verifiability before automation", "off-chain data, on-chain integrity", layered modularity, human-in-the-loop decision-making, privacy-by-design through selective disclosure, auditability-by-design and standards-based interoperability.

Conceptual data sources and analysis

The design draws on four categories of sources: scholarly literature, technical standards and specifications (e.g., VC and DID standards), policy and governance documents (data protection, qualifications frameworks, AI guidance) and practitioner reports from pilot projects. An abductive analytic process iteratively identifies requirements, explores candidate configurations and tests the emerging architecture against plausible scenarios such as RPL cases, employer verification and audits of AI-supported decisions.

Evaluation logic and limitations

Conceptual evaluation considers alignment with design objectives, internal coherence and responsiveness to the problems of fragmentation, weak verifiability, opaque AI and tension between privacy and portability. The chapter also proposes a multi-dimensional evaluation framework—covering technical veracity (e.g., verification and revocation latency), interpretability and due process (e.g., availability of explanations, auditability and contestation pathways), user experience and adoption (e.g., wallet usability and workflow burden), equity and bias (distributional impacts of AI-supported RPL and competency inference), and cost and sustainability (total cost of ownership and consortium viability)—to guide future empirical studies. These dimensions provide an actionable bridge from conceptual design to pilot evaluation on smart campuses. Needless to say, limitations arise from the absence of deployment data, the focus on higher education contexts with relatively mature infrastructures and the normative commitments embedded in the design (learner agency, privacy, human oversight and open standards). The architecture is thus a reference model to be adapted and tested, not a prescriptive blueprint.

Conceptual Framework: A Smart-Campus Credentialing Architecture

The core contribution of this chapter is a five-layer architecture that integrates digital identity, verifiable learning records, AI services and governance into a coherent trust fabric.

Overview of the five layers

1. Identity & Wallets – DID-based identities for learners and staff, plus wallets for storing and presenting credentials.
2. Verifiable Record Fabric – representation of assessment outcomes, micro-credentials and co-curricular achievements as verifiable credentials and composites.
3. AI Services – modular AI services (RPL, competency inference, framework alignment) operating on verifiable records.
4. Consent, Policy & Audit – mechanisms for consent management, policy enforcement, logging and audit.
5. Integration & Messaging – event-driven adapters, APIs and messaging that connect LMS, SIS, e-portfolio systems and external providers to the record fabric, and expose verifiable records to stakeholder-facing applications and verifiers.

The layers are modular yet interoperable, supporting incremental implementation and local variation. Although presented as layers, the architecture is best understood as a set of bounded responsibilities connected by explicit interfaces. The Integration & Messaging layer translates events from LMS, SIS and e-portfolio systems into credential issuance or update requests; the Verifiable Record Fabric standardises and stores those claims as verifiable credentials and composite credentials; and the AI Services layer consumes only verifiable claims, producing advisory outputs that can be inspected, challenged and improved.

Crucially, the Consent, Policy & Audit layer acts as both a constraint and an accountability surface: it gates data flows, enforces purpose limitation and captures evidence of automated processing, thereby shaping what AI services may do and what verifiers may see. Identity & Wallets provide the learner-facing control plane, enabling receipt, secure storage and selective presentation of credentials across contexts. Figure 1 summarises these interfaces and governance constraints at a conceptual level.

Figure 1. Conceptual overview of the five-layer smart-campus credentialing architecture and its key interfaces.

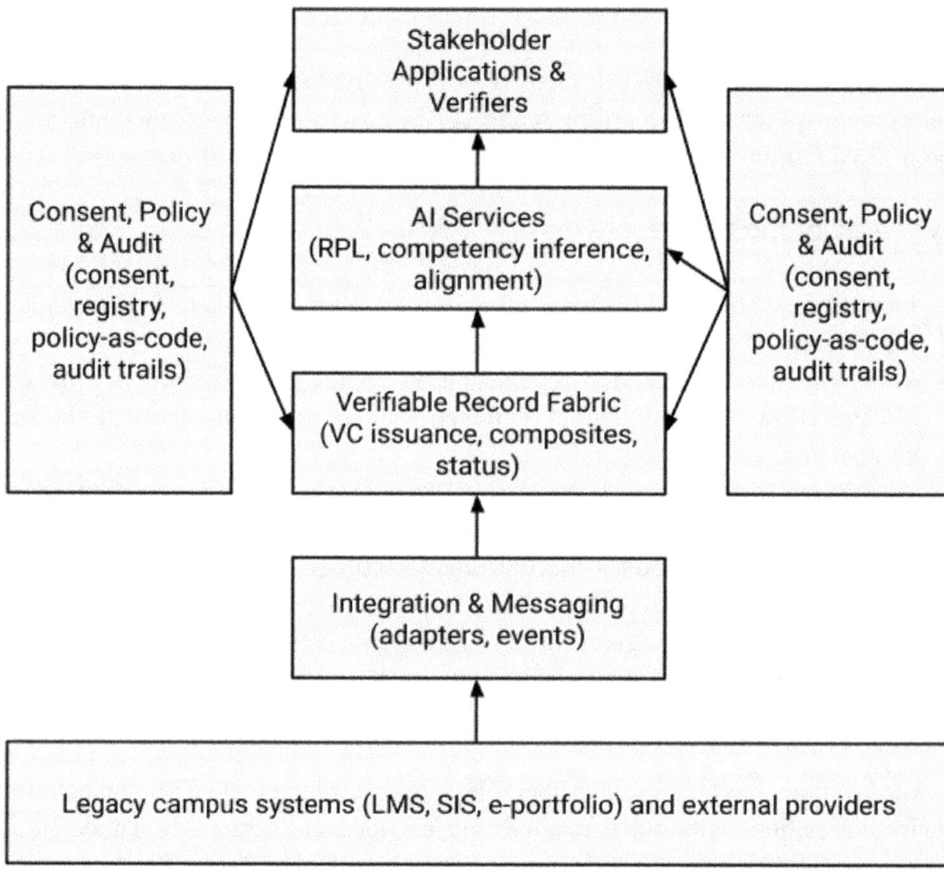

To support both conceptual and implementer audiences, each layer description below foregrounds its conceptual role and governance concerns, and then highlights brief implementation considerations (non-exhaustive) where design choices affect scalability, security and interoperability.

Identity & Wallets

Each learner, staff member and relevant institutional unit is associated with one or more DIDs. These identifiers, controlled via cryptographic keys, are bound to existing institutional identity systems: when a student authenticates via single sign-on, the identity management system can mediate actions on behalf of their DID, such as requesting credential issuance.

Learners interact with credentials through wallets. The architecture accommodates custodial wallets (managed by the institution or a consortium) and self-custodial wallets (managed directly by learners). Both must support secure storage, generation of verifiable presentations (with selective disclosure where appropriate), key management and interactions with institutional verification services. Custodial wallets can ease adoption for students who prefer low-friction experiences; self-custodial wallets enable long-term sovereignty. Policies and user support must address backup, recovery and transition (e.g., exporting credentials at graduation). Implementation considerations include accessible wallet interfaces (including multilingual and disability-accessible design), support for key recovery and device loss, and clear institutional responsibilities for custodial models so that risk is not simply displaced onto learners.

Verifiable Record Fabric

The verifiable record fabric models educational claims as verifiable credentials aligned with institutional and external schemas. Individual credentials encode course completions, micro-credentials, competencies or co-curricular achievements, including relevant metadata and cryptographic proofs. Composite credentials—such as degrees or thematic specialisations—reference constituent credentials, enabling stacking and inspection of underlying evidence when appropriate.

Detailed assessment artefacts remain off-chain in institutional systems or learner-managed repositories. Credentials include hashes and, where necessary, pointers to these artefacts. A permissioned ledger anchors integrity proofs and status information (e.g., revocation, key rotation) without storing personal data. Credential formats and presentation protocols support selective disclosure: a learner can, for example, demonstrate achievement of a competency without disclosing their full transcript. Implementation considerations include selecting and governing credential schemas (so that micro-credentials, badges and transcript-like records can be represented consistently), managing revocation and status information efficiently, and ensuring long-term resolvability of referenced artefacts through stable pointers, migration strategies and shared trust registries.

AI Services

The AI Services layer comprises advisory services that operate exclusively on verifiable inputs from the record fabric.

- Recognition of Prior Learning (RPL): consumes verifiable credentials from external institutions and providers, plus supplementary artefacts where available. Using natural language processing and other techniques, it normalises heterogeneous evidence, maps it onto local curricula and proposes credit awards or exemptions with explanations. Academic decision-makers review recommendations, and outcomes are recorded as credentials.
- Competency inference: aggregates evidence from module-level credentials, micro-credentials and co-curricular records, using a defined competency framework. It infers proficiency levels across domains, producing competency profiles and explanatory narratives linking inferences to specific credentials and rubric criteria. Outputs inform advising, curriculum design and career guidance but remain advisory.
- Framework alignment: aligns course and programme outcomes with external qualifications frameworks or industry taxonomies. It uses ontology-matching techniques to suggest mappings, identify gaps and generate rationales for curriculum committees and quality assurance bodies.

AI services are constrained by bounded autonomy. They cannot directly issue or revoke credentials or make final high-stakes decisions. Instead, they generate recommendations, explanations and derived artefacts that feed into human decision-making processes. Model documentation and explanation interfaces expose training data assumptions, confidence levels and limitations.

AI autonomy, accountability and risk scenarios

Bounded autonomy must be operationalised against concrete risk scenarios. In credentialing contexts, plausible risks include biased competency inference (where models over-weight proxies for socio-economic status, language background or disability), "explanation laundering" (where persuasive narratives mask weak evidentiary bases), automation bias (where staff defer to AI recommendations due to workload), model drift as curricula and labour-market taxonomies change, and adversarial manipulation of inputs (for example, fabricated artefacts or coached portfolios). The architecture mitigates these risks through three linked mechanisms: verifiable inputs (constraining inference and training data to signed evidence where possible), governance constraints (policy-as-code rules that restrict permissible purposes, data features and decision thresholds), and contestable outputs (audit trails, model documentation and explicit appeal workflows). In practice, this implies that AI outputs should be treated as calibrated recommendations—accompanied by traceable evidence links and "right to challenge" procedures—rather than as automated decisions. Implementation considerations include ongoing monitoring for distributional impacts of AI-supported RPL decisions, documented model update cycles, and clear separation between advisory analytics and credential issuance authority.

Consent, Policy & Audit

This layer embeds governance into system operation. A consent registry records lawful bases and purposes for processing learner data, supporting granular consent (for example, permission for using assessment data in RPL or analytics) and time-bounded permissions. Access-control checks enforce purpose limitation at the level of data flows to AI services and verifiers. Institutional policies are encoded into machine-interpretable rules—for instance, prohibiting the use of protected attributes in AI inputs or requiring human review for any automated recommendation that could negatively affect admissions, progression or RPL decisions. Policy engines intercept requests and allow, modify or deny them based on current rules and consent records. Audit trails record key events: issuance, verification and revocation of credentials; generation and use of AI recommendations; data access by internal and external actors; and outcomes of appeals. Minimal event representations may be anchored on a permissioned ledger to provide tamper-evident logs. Governance roles such as Chief Data Steward, Data Protection Officer and Algorithmic Ombudsperson use these records to oversee compliance and respond to complaints.

Concrete governance mechanisms can be expressed as policies that are both human-legible and machine-enforceable. For example, policy-as-code rules may (i) permit the use of assessment artefacts for RPL only when purpose-specific consent is recorded; (ii) require human approval for any AI-generated recommendation that could negatively affect progression; (iii) mandate exclusion of protected attributes (and documented proxies) from model features; and (iv) require minimum retention of audit logs for a defined period so that decisions remain reviewable. Consent interfaces, correspondingly, should enable learners to see what data are requested, by whom, for what purpose, for how long, and with what consequences, with meaningful options to grant, refuse or withdraw. Responsibility and liability must follow the decision: AI services can inform decisions, but accountable authority remains with designated institutional roles (e.g., RPL panels and curriculum committees), supported by oversight officers who can investigate logs and impose remediation when policies are breached.

Integration & Messaging

The Integration & Messaging layer connects existing systems and external providers to the verifiable record fabric. Adapters listen to events in LMS, SIS and micro-credential platforms and translate them into credential-issuance actions. For example, a finalised course grade recorded in the SIS triggers issuance of a course completion credential, subject to policy checks. A micro-credential issued on an external platform is transformed into a VC conforming to institutional schemas and added to the learner's wallet. Stakeholder-facing applications (for learners, registrars, quality assurance staff and external verifiers) consume these events and APIs to support issuance dashboards, consent management, verification portals and dispute resolution workflows, without requiring invasive modifications to legacy systems.

An event-driven messaging infrastructure decouples producers and consumers: new services can subscribe to relevant events without modifying source systems. Adapters are idempotent and equipped with error-handling and monitoring, supporting resilience and incremental evolution. External partners—MOOC providers, certification bodies, employers—interact via standard verification endpoints and, where appropriate, participate in shared trust frameworks or consortia. From an operational perspective, this layer is also where scalability and cybersecurity pressures surface most directly. Event-driven pipelines must handle peak issuance loads (e.g., end-of-semester grading) while maintaining idempotency, retry logic and monitoring to avoid duplicate credentials. Verification endpoints must be resilient to denial-of-service and must support cryptographic verification at scale (including caching of issuer keys and status lists). Security controls therefore extend beyond ledger tamper-evidence to include API authentication and rate limiting, secure key storage for issuers, and protections against phishing and wallet-compromise scenarios.

Roles, data objects and workflows

Roles include issuers (registrars, departments, micro-credential units), holders (students and alumni), verifiers (employers, partner institutions, regulators), endorsers (faculty or mentors) and stewards (data governance and algorithmic oversight roles). Data objects include credentials, endorsements, consent grants, AI recommendations, model cards, revocation entries and audit events. Clarifying responsibilities across these roles is central to accountability. Issuers remain responsible for the semantics and quality assurance of credentials; verifiers are responsible for lawful and proportionate use of presented data; AI services are responsible for providing transparent, contestable recommendations; and stewards are responsible for policy enforcement, monitoring and remediation. This separation helps prevent responsibility gaps when decisions are distributed across technical and organisational actors.

Workflow patterns span standard issuance (from grade finalisation to credential delivery), RPL (submission and verification of external credentials, AI-supported mapping, human decision and outcome credential), employer verification (presentation and verification of credentials with logging) and appeal (retrieval of evidence and logs, oversight review, possible re-issuance and revocation). These workflows illustrate how layers, roles and data objects combine to support verifiable yet contestable credentialing. Figure 2 summarises two representative workflows that recur across smart-campus credentialing: (A) an AI-supported RPL pathway and (B) employer verification using selective disclosure and tamper-evident logging.

Figure 2. Illustrative workflows supported by the architecture: (A) AI-supported RPL; (B) employer verification with selective disclosure.

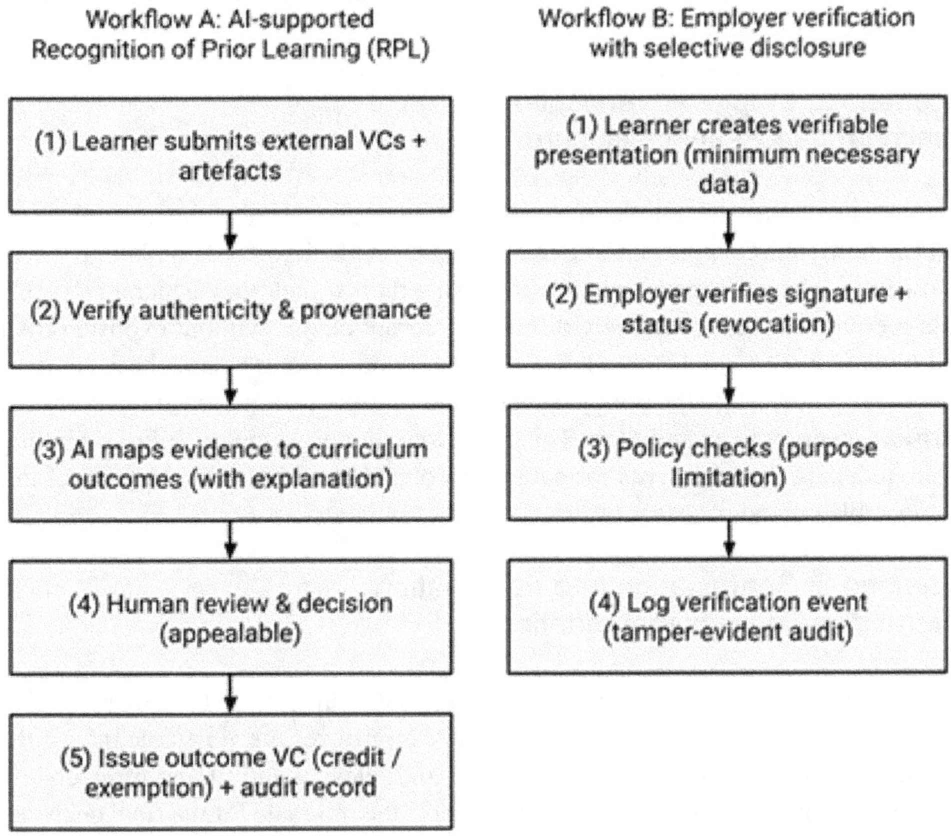

Illustrative scenarios

Scenario 1: Cross-institution AI-supported RPL

A learner seeking credit for prior learning assembles verifiable credentials from external providers (for example, short courses, industry certificates or prior university modules) and links supplementary artefacts such as portfolios. The institution verifies signatures and status information (revocation and issuer trust) before the evidence enters RPL evaluation. The AI service then maps verifiable evidence to local learning outcomes and produces an explanation that references specific credential claims and rubric criteria, alongside confidence estimates and a clear statement of limitations. An RPL panel reviews the recommendation, may request additional evidence, and makes an accountable decision. The outcome (credit, exemption or partial recognition) is issued as a new credential, and the complete trail—inputs, recommendations, human decision and any appeals—is logged for audit and due process.

Scenario 2: Employer verification with minimum-necessary disclosure

A graduating learner applies for a role and chooses to present only the minimum information required: a programme credential, selected micro-credentials and (where useful) an endorsed competency profile. Using their wallet, they generate a verifiable presentation that selectively discloses relevant claims without exposing their full transcript. The employer verifies cryptographic signatures and checks current credential status, while the policy layer enforces purpose limitation and records the verification event in an audit log. This workflow supports employability signalling while reducing the incentives for data over-collection and limiting the risk of unaccountable secondary uses.

Scenario 3: Contestation and remediation after a disputed recommendation

A learner disputes an AI-supported recommendation (e.g., an RPL mapping that undervalues evidence). The contestation process retrieves the verifiable inputs, the explanation artefacts, model documentation and relevant audit logs. An oversight role (or committee) reviews the case, documents the rationale for the final decision, and triggers remediation where needed—such as updating a policy rule, revising a mapping ontology, retraining a model, or suspending an AI service pending review. Where a credential outcome changes, re-issuance and revocation mechanisms ensure that the verifiable record fabric remains accurate and current.

Encoding responsible AI principles

Responsible AI principles are embedded structurally. Verifiability of inputs is achieved through VC-based evidence and ledger-anchored integrity proofs, reducing reliance on opaque institutional datasets. Interpretability of outputs is supported by explanation artefacts, traceable links from recommendations to specific credentials and rubric criteria, and model documentation (including intended use, limitations and update history). Bounded autonomy is enforced by policy engines and human-in-the-loop workflows, ensuring that final credentialing decisions remain accountable and appealable. Governance and audit mechanisms ensure that AI use in credentialing is visible, constrained and reviewable, enabling oversight bodies to monitor distributional impacts, investigate complaints and trigger remediation (e.g., policy updates, model retraining or suspension of a service).

DISCUSSION

The architecture responds to the research questions while repositioning digital credentialing and learning analytics as forms of trust engineering.

Integration without disruption

By treating LMS, SIS and e-portfolio systems as event producers and connecting them to the record fabric via an event-driven integration layer, the architecture demonstrates how verifiable credentialing can be introduced without wholesale system replacement. Existing assessment workflows remain largely intact; the main change is that credential-relevant events are translated into issued credentials. Learner-centred wallets then expose these credentials beyond institutional boundaries. This illustrates a pathway from fragmented, institution-centred records to verifiable, learner-centred records that is evolution rather than revolution.

AI services on verifiable records

The three AI service families show how AI can be positioned as a set of advisory services operating on verifiable inputs rather than as opaque decision engines built on fragile data. By grounding RPL, competency inference and framework alignment in VC-encoded evidence, the architecture strengthens the auditability and contestability of AI-supported decisions. AI becomes a means of making sense of trustworthy records rather than extracting patterns from poorly governed data.

Governance as a structural layer

Embedding consent, policy and audit into the architecture reframes responsible AI as a property of system design, not only of individual models. Consent registries and policy-as-code mechanisms constrain data flows and AI actions; audit trails and oversight roles enable investigation and redress. Governance is not an external committee reviewing black-box tools, but a set of mechanisms that shape how identity, records and AI interact.

Conceptual contributions and critiques

Conceptually, the architecture contributes to theories of digital identity and learner-centred records by integrating DIDs, wallets and VCs into institutional operations. It reframes credentialing and analytics as trust engineering grounded in verifiable inputs and governance. It also provides a design-science artefact and vocabulary for comparative research on credentialing systems.

At the same time, concerns arise about complexity, power and equity. The architecture is ambitious and may be challenging for resource-constrained institutions. Formalising processes and embedding policies in code may centralise control and obscure assumptions. Learners with limited digital or data literacy may be disadvantaged in managing wallets and consents. These critiques underscore the need to treat the architecture as a socio-technical system to be co-designed with stakeholders, not imposed as a purely technical solution.

Equity, inclusion and digital divides

Although the architecture is designed to enhance learner agency, it could inadvertently widen inequities if wallets, consent interfaces and verification practices presume high digital literacy, reliable connectivity and modern devices. A responsible implementation therefore requires inclusive design (accessible interfaces, multilingual support and alternatives for low-tech access), institutional support for key recovery and dispute resolution, and careful monitoring of distributional impacts—particularly in AI-supported RPL where language, disability and socio-economic status can be indirectly encoded in evidence. Treating the wallet as a supported learner service rather than an individual burden is a prerequisite for equitable portability.

Power dynamics and institutional resistance

Credentialing is a site of institutional authority; shifting to learner-held verifiable records redistributes control and may be resisted by registrars, IT units, vendors or external regulators. Resistance may also arise from concerns about reputational risk, loss of control over transcripts, or increased workload for staff. The architecture can therefore be interpreted not only as a technical integration pattern but as an organisational change programme requiring participatory governance, negotiated data stewardship roles, and explicit agreements about which actors can issue, endorse and interpret credentials. Without such arrangements, decentralised identity rhetoric could mask a re-centralisation of power through consortium governance or platform intermediaries.

Failure and misuse scenarios

A design-science artefact is strengthened by explicit consideration of failure modes. In practice, smart-campus credentialing systems may fail or be misused in several ways: (a) wallet compromise, key loss or phishing can lead to unauthorised sharing; (b) issuer key compromise can enable fraudulent credential issuance; (c) revocation and status infrastructures can become bottlenecks, undermining timely verification; (d) policy misconfiguration can permit improper secondary use of data; (e) AI services can drift or encode bias, producing systematically unfair recommendations; and (f) employers or other verifiers can use credentials for surveillance or exclusionary screening beyond intended purpose. The architecture addresses these risks by combining cryptographic verifiability with governance controls (policy-as-code and purpose limitation), operational security (key management, monitoring and incident response) and due process (audit trails, contestation and remediation). Nevertheless, these protections are only as strong as institutional capacity and incentives to enforce them.

Alternative and hybrid architectures

Importantly, the architecture does not assume that all institutions will adopt full self-sovereign identity or ledger components. Hybrid variants are plausible and, for some jurisdictions, preferable: institutions may begin with centrally managed wallets or federated identity, using verifiable credentials without a ledger by relying on conventional public key infrastructures and status endpoints; conversely, a consortium may provide shared governance services while institutions retain local control over issuance. The key design principle is that learner-facing portability and governance-facing accountability remain explicit, regardless of whether the underlying trust infrastructure is ledger-based, registry-based or fully decentralised. This flexibility also enables alignment with national qualification frameworks and diverse regulatory environments.

Operational considerations: scalability, cybersecurity and sustainability

Operationalising the architecture at scale raises performance and sustainability questions that are often under-emphasised in conceptual models. Large issuance volumes (e.g., end-of-term grades and micro-credential bursts) require throughput, idempotency and monitoring; verification at labour-market scale requires efficient key distribution, caching and status checking. Cybersecurity extends beyond ledger immutability to endpoint security, credential phishing, secure software supply chains and insider threats. Finally, economic sustainability depends on governance: permissioned ledgers and shared trust frameworks impose ongoing costs (operations, audits, compliance and dispute resolution) that must be justified by clear value propositions for institutions, learners and employers. These considerations reinforce the need for phased piloting rather than immediate campus-wide roll-out.

Overall, the reference architecture is both a technical and governance proposition: it illustrates how verifiability can support bounded AI autonomy, but it also clarifies that the main risks are socio-technical—inequity, misaligned incentives and weak enforcement. The next section therefore specifies policy, practice and research implications with an emphasis on phased adoption and evaluation.

IMPLICATIONS FOR POLICY, PRACTICE AND FUTURE RESEARCH

Policy and governance

Implementing such an architecture would require revising policies on student records, data protection, AI use and inter-institutional collaboration. Institutions would need to clarify the relationship between institutional records and learner-held credentials, define consent regimes for different data uses, establish rules for stacking and revocation, and create governance bodies capable of overseeing AI-mediated credentialing. Sector-level arrangements for trust frameworks and permissioned ledgers would demand shared governance, membership criteria and exit strategies.

Greater governance specificity is required for enforceability. In practice, universities would need an operational governance stack that includes: (a) a credential schema registry with change-control; (b) a trust registry identifying authorised issuers and, where appropriate, verifier classes; (c) versioned policy-as-code rules that can be audited and rolled back; (d) key-compromise and incident-response procedures; and (e) explicit retention and cross-border data-transfer policies for audit logs and evidence artefacts. Accountability and liability should be allocated explicitly.

When an AI recommendation is used within an RPL or progression decision, the accountable decision-maker (e.g., a panel chair), the technical service owner, and the oversight function should be identifiable, with escalation pathways for disputes, remediation and suspension of services when policies are breached.

Educational practice and system design

For academics and programme leaders, the architecture encourages more explicit articulation of learning outcomes, competencies and rubrics, so that they can be encoded in credentials and used in competency analytics and framework alignment (Charles & Papadaki, 2025). For registrars and assessment offices, transcripts become one representation among many, derived from underlying verifiable credentials. For IT units, event-driven integration and policy-aware APIs become central design concerns. Professional development will need to cultivate literacies around AI-supported RPL, competency profiles and verifiable credentials (Charles & Hill, 2025).

The architecture also implies a shift in assessment and recognition culture. As credentials become more granular and portable, programmes must guard against over-fragmentation and ensure that competencies remain meaningful, contextual and aligned to curriculum intent. Staff workload and professional judgement should be protected through well-designed human-in-the-loop workflows, with explicit criteria for when AI recommendations can be used, when additional evidence is required, and when deliberative human review is mandatory.

Learners and external stakeholders

Learners gain greater control and portability through wallets and verifiable credentials, but also assume responsibilities for managing identities, consents and presentations. Institutions must provide support and accessible interfaces to avoid exacerbating inequalities. Employers and professional bodies could benefit from more granular, verifiable signals of competence but will need tools, norms and safeguards to use them appropriately. Regulators and quality assurance agencies may need to update frameworks to recognise verifiable credentials and to offer guidance on acceptable AI use in credentialing.

From an employer perspective, verifiability is necessary but not sufficient: employers also require interpretability and proportionality. Sector bodies may therefore need to co-develop competency taxonomies, verification interfaces and guidance that support minimum-necessary disclosure, reduce the risk of discriminatory screening, and integrate into HR systems without encouraging surveillance. The audit mechanisms proposed in this chapter can create shared accountability by making verification and automated profiling events visible and traceable.

Piloting and phased adoption

Given socio-technical complexity and institutional constraints, a phased adoption strategy is preferable to immediate campus-wide implementation. A pragmatic maturity path can be conceptualised as follows:

Level 0 – Governance foundations: establish credential schema governance, trust registries, consent principles, and incident-response procedures while maintaining existing transcript processes.
Level 1 – Verifiable graduation credentials: issue verifiable diploma/transcript credentials and enable basic verification and revocation checking for external parties.
Level 2 – Granular micro-credentials and stacking: represent micro-credentials, co-curricular achievements and composite credentials, supported by learner wallets and usable consent interfaces.
Level 3 – Cross-institution verification and RPL: pilot partner-based recognition workflows, including external credential ingestion, verification, and auditable RPL decisions.
Level 4 – AI-supported services with due process: introduce bounded AI services (RPL mapping, competency inference, framework alignment) with explanations, monitoring for distributional impacts, and contestation workflows.
Level 5 – Sector-scale trust infrastructure: operationalise consortia, continuous improvement, employer integration patterns, and sustainability models for shared governance and infrastructure.

At each phase, evaluation should include both technical indicators (e.g., verification latency, revocation propagation, uptime) and socio-educational indicators (e.g., learner-reported agency, staff workload, contestation rates and equity impacts).

Research agenda

The architecture invites a programme of empirical research examining technical veracity (tamper detection, revocation latency, resilience), interpretability and due process (perceptions of explanations, appeal patterns), user experience and adoption (wallet usability, workflow integration), equity and bias (distributional impacts of AI-supported RPL and competency inference) and cost and sustainability (total cost of ownership, governance effectiveness). Mixed-methods approaches, design-based research in pilots, quasi-experimental comparisons and cross-institutional studies could all contribute to refining the framework and understanding its effects.

Future studies should also examine cultural and regulatory variation in credential interpretation and consent norms, employer practices in reading and acting on micro-credentials, and the political economy of shared trust infrastructures. Comparative pilots that implement hybrid variants (e.g., registry-based status services versus ledger-anchored status, custodial versus self-custodial wallets) would help isolate which components most directly contribute to trust, adoption and equity.

CONCLUSION

The chapter has argued that smart campuses will remain fundamentally constrained if they continue to rely on fragmented, weakly verifiable credentialing infrastructures while layering AI systems on top of uncertain data. It has proposed that verifiable digital identity and learning records—implemented through DIDs, VCs and permissioned integrity layers—should be viewed as prerequisites for responsible AI in credentialing. A five-layer architecture has been articulated that integrates identity, verifiable records, AI services, governance mechanisms and integration infrastructure into a coherent trust fabric.

The framework is explicitly conceptual and design-oriented. It offers a reference architecture, a set of workflow patterns and governance mechanisms, and an evaluation agenda, but does not provide empirical evidence of effectiveness. Its applicability is bounded by assumptions about institutional capacity, regulatory environments and normative commitments to learner agency, privacy, human oversight and open standards.

Nevertheless, the architecture offers a productive way of reimagining credentialing in higher education. It shifts attention from isolated tools to system-level arrangements in which credentials are dynamic nodes in a network of verifiable claims, AI-supported interpretations and governance processes. If universities can harness digital identity standards, verifiable credential infrastructures and responsible AI practices within robust governance frameworks, smart campuses may come to be defined less by the volume of data they generate and more by the quality of the trust relationships they sustain.

Future work should therefore prioritise bounded pilots that involve learners, registrars, academics, employers and regulators, and that evaluate both technical performance (verification and revocation latency, resilience, incident response) and socio-educational outcomes (perceived transparency, learner agency, workload implications, and equity). Comparative studies of hybrid implementations (ledger-anchored vs registry-based trust, custodial vs self-custodial wallets) would also help to identify which components are essential and which can be substituted to fit local regulatory and cultural contexts. To support multidisciplinary uptake, the chapter now includes an illustrative architecture diagram, workflow walkthroughs, and a short glossary and FAQ that clarify key technical terms and practical questions.

REFERENCES

Abukhalaf, S., Charles, T., & Hill, C. (2024). The Metaverse as a Virtual Learning Space: Perceptions from the UAE. *Journal of Ecohumanism*, *3*(5), 1037–1052. https://doi.org/10.62754/joe.v3i5.3954DOI: 10.62754/joe.v3i5.3954

Ahsan, K., Akbar, S., Kam, B., & Abdulrahman, M. D. (2023). Implementation of micro-credentials in higher education: A systematic literature review. *Education and Information Technologies*, *28*(3), 13505–13540. https://doi.org/10.1007/s10639-023-11739-zDOI: 10.1007/s10639-023-11739-z

Alammary, A., Alhazmi, S., Almasri, M., & Gillani, S. (2019). Blockchain-based applications in education: A systematic review. *Applied Sciences (Basel, Switzerland)*, *9*(12), 2400. https://doi.org/10.3390/app9122400DOI: 10.3390/app9122400

Arndt, T., & Guercio, A. (2020). Blockchain-based transcripts for mobile higher education. *International Journal of Information and Education Technology (IJIET)*, *10*(2), 84–89. https://doi.org/10.18178/ijiet.2020.10.2.1344DOI: 10.18178/ijiet.2020.10.2.1344

Azzam, A., & Charles, T. (2025). K-12 STEM Teachers' Experiences with Artificial Intelligence. *TEM Journal*, *14*(1), 463–468. DOI: 10.18421/TEM141-41

Bhaskar, P., Tiwari, C. K., & Joshi, A. (2021). Blockchain in education management: Present and future applications. *Interactive Technology and Smart Education*, *18*(1), 1–17. https://doi.org/10.1108/ITSE-07-2020-0102DOI: 10.1108/ITSE-07-2020-0102

Bidry, M., Ouaguid, A., & Hanine, M. (2023). Enhancing e-learning with blockchain: Characteristics, projects, and emerging trends. *Future Internet*, *15*(9), 293. https://doi.org/10.3390/fi15090293DOI: 10.3390/fi15090293

Brown, M., Nic Giolla Mhichíl, M., Beirne, E., & Mac Lochlainn, C. (2021). The global micro-credential landscape: Charting a new credential ecology for lifelong learning. *Journal of Learning for Development*, *8*(2), 228–254. https://doi.org/10.56059/jl4d.v8i2.525DOI: 10.56059/jl4d.v8i2.525

Capetillo, A., Camacho, D., & Alanis, M. (2022). Blockchained education: Challenging the long-standing model of academic institutions. *International Journal on Interactive Design and Manufacturing*, *16*(2), 791–802. https://doi.org/10.1007/s12008-022-00886-1DOI: 10.1007/s12008-022-00886-1 PMID: 40477579

Charles, T. (2021). The past, present and future of assessments in the higher education sector. In C. Hill, J. Lamie, & T. Gore (Eds.), The evolution of transnational education (pp. 126–136). Routledge.https://doi.org/10.4324/9781003225386 DOI: 10.4324/9781003225386-13

Charles, T. (2025). AI in Professional Development for English Language Teachers. In Ali, M., Fazal, S., & Ayyaz, S. (Eds.), *AI Applications for English Language Learning* (pp. 73–92). IGI Global Scientific Publishing., DOI: 10.4018/979-8-3693-9077-1.ch004

Charles, T., & Hill, C. (2023). Remaining steadfast in the face of overwhelming change: Ethics and practice in emergency remote teaching–A case study in Dubai. In J. Lamie & C. Hill (Eds.), The evolving nature of universities (pp. 89–98). Routledge.https://doi.org/10.4324/9781003389361 DOI: 10.4324/9781003389361-7

Charles, T., & Hill, C. (2025). Micro-Credentials and AI in Higher Education: Transforming Professional Development. In A. ElSayary (Ed.), Prompt Engineering and Generative AI Applications for Teaching and Learning (pp. 1–14). IGI Global Scientific Publishing.https://doi.org/10.4018/979-8-3693-7332-3.ch001 DOI: 10.4018/979-8-3693-7332-3.ch001

Charles, T., & Papadaki, M. (2025). Ethical Leadership in Technology Integration and Digital Education. In Soles, B., & Meyerott, T. (Eds.), *Diverse Leadership Perspectives in Education: From K-12 to Higher Education* (pp. 437–454). IGI Global Scientific Publishing., DOI: 10.4018/979-8-3693-6115-3.ch016

Charles, T., Zoelfakar, S., & Sebastian, S. (2025). Micro-Credentials in Vocational and Professional Training. In G. Durak & S. Cankaya (Eds.), Integrating Micro-Credentials With AI in Open Education (pp. 217–250). IGI Global Scientific Publishing.https://doi.org/10.4018/979-8-3693-5488-9.ch010

Chen, G., Xu, B., Lu, M., & Chen, N.-S. (2018). Exploring blockchain technology and its potential applications for education. *Smart Learning Environments*, *5*(1), 1. https://doi.org/10.1186/s40561-017-0050-xDOI: 10.1186/s40561-017-0050-x

Cheong, P. H., & Nyaupane, P. (2022). Smart campus communication, Internet of Things, and data governance: Understanding student tensions and imaginaries. *Big Data & Society*, *9*(1), 20539517221092656. https://doi.org/10.1177/20539517221092656DOI: 10.1177/20539517221092656

Elsawah, W., & Charles, T. (2023). Investigating Emirati Students' Practices of Learning Block-Based Programming in an Online Learning Context: Evidence from a UAE National Program. In: Al Marri, K., Mir, F., David, S., & Aljuboori, A. (Eds) *BUiD Doctoral Research Conference 2022*. Lecture Notes in Civil Engineering, vol 320. Springer, Cham.

Gamage, K. A. A., & Dehideniya, S. C. P. (2025). Unlocking career potential: How micro-credentials are revolutionising higher education and lifelong learning. *Education Sciences*, *15*(5), 525. https://doi.org/10.3390/educsci15050525DOI: 10.3390/educsci15050525

Hill, C., Abu-Ayyash, E., & Charles, T. (2023). By nature, a social animal: An exploration of perceptions of online group work. *Cambridge Journal of Education*, *53*(5), 665–681. https://doi.org/10.1080/0305764X.2023.2206795DOI: 10.1080/0305764X.2023.2206795

Holmes, W., Porayska-Pomsta, K., Holstein, K., Sutherland, E., Baker, T., Shum, S. B., Santos, O. C., Rodrigo, M. T., Cukurova, M., Bittencourt, I. I., & Koedinger, K. R. (2022). Ethics of AI in education: Towards a community-wide framework. *International Journal of Artificial Intelligence in Education*, *32*(2), 115–130. https://doi.org/10.1007/s40593-021-00239-1DOI: 10.1007/s40593-021-00239-1

Kosmarski, A. (2020). Blockchain adoption in academia: Promises and challenges. *Journal of Open Innovation*, *6*(4), 117. https://doi.org/10.3390/joitmc6040117DOI: 10.3390/joitmc6040117

Lizcano, D., Lara, J. A., White, B., & Aljawarneh, S. (2020). Blockchain-based approach to create a model of trust in open and ubiquitous higher education. *Journal of Computing in Higher Education*, *32*(1), 109–134. https://doi.org/10.1007/s12528-019-09209-yDOI: 10.1007/s12528-019-09209-y

Mazzocca, C., Acar, A., Uluagac, S., Montanari, R., Bellavista, P., & Conti, M. (2024). A survey on decentralized identifiers and verifiable credentials. *IEEE*, 12, 15528–15552. https://doi.org/10.1109/COMST.2025.3543197

McGreal, R. (2023). Blockchain and micro-credentials in education. *International Journal of E-Learning & Distance Education*, *38*(1), 1–17.https://doi.org/10.55667/10.55667/ijede.2023.v38.i1.1250

Mohammad, A., & Vargas, S. (2022). Challenges of using blockchain in the education sector: A literature review. *Applied Sciences (Basel, Switzerland)*, *12*(13), 6380. https://doi.org/10.3390/app12136380DOI: 10.3390/app12136380

Ocheja, P., Flanagan, B., Ueda, H., & Ogata, H. (2019). Managing lifelong learning records through blockchain. *Research and Practice in Technology Enhanced Learning*, *14*(1), 4. https://doi.org/10.1186/s41039-019-0097-0DOI: 10.1186/s41039-019-0097-0

Ocheja, P., Agbo, F. J., Oyelere, S. S., Flanagan, B., & Ogata, H. (2022). Blockchain in education: A systematic review and practical case studies. *IEEE*, 10, 99525–99540. https://doi.org/10.1109/ACCESS.2022.3206791

Park, J. (2021). Promises and challenges of Blockchain in education. *Smart Learning Environments*, *8*(1), 33. https://doi.org/10.1186/s40561-021-00179-2DOI: 10.1186/s40561-021-00179-2 PMID: 40477765

Patel, V., Pradhan, V., & Kadam, A. (2026). Blockchain in Education and Lifelong Learning's: Challenges, Solutions, and Future Directions. In M. Tuba, S. Akashe, & A. Joshi (Eds.), *ICT Systems and Sustainability. ICT4SD 2025.* Lecture Notes in Networks and Systems (Vol. 1646). Springer.https://doi.org/10.1007/978-3-032-06665-7_17 DOI: 10.1007/978-3-032-06665-7_17

Polin, K., Yigitcanlar, T., Limb, M., & Washington, T. (2023). The making of smart campus: A review and conceptual framework. *Buildings (Basel, Switzerland)*, *13*(4), 891. https://doi.org/10.3390/buildings13040891DOI: 10.3390/buildings13040891

Prinsloo, P., & Slade, S. (2017). Big Data, Higher Education and Learning Analytics: Beyond Justice, Towards an Ethics of Care. In B. Kei Daniel (Ed.), Big Data and Learning Analytics in Higher Education. Springer.https://doi.org/10.1007/978-3-319-06520-5_8 DOI: 10.1007/978-3-319-06520-5_8

Shehzad, N., & Charles, T. (2023). Exploring the impact of instructor social presence on student engagement in online higher education. *Contemporary Educational Technology*, *15*(4), ep484. https://doi.org/10.30935/cedtech/13823DOI: 10.30935/cedtech/13823

Steiu, M.-F. (2020). Blockchain in education: Opportunities, applications, and challenges. *First Monday*, *25*(9). Advance online publication. https://doi.org/10.5210/fm.v25i9.10654DOI: 10.5210/fm.v25i9.10654

Turkanović, M., Hölbl, M., Košič, K., Heričko, M., & Kamišalić, A. (2018). EduCTX: A blockchain-based higher education credit platform. *IEEE*, 6, 5112–5127. https://doi.org/10.1109/ACCESS.2018.2789929

Varadarajan, S., Koh, J. H. L., & Daniel, B. K. (2023). A systematic review of the opportunities and challenges of micro-credentials for multiple stakeholders: Learners, employers, higher education institutions and government. *International Journal of Educational Technology in Higher Education*, *20*(1), 13. https://doi.org/10.1186/s41239-023-00381-xDOI: 10.1186/s41239-023-00381-x PMID: 36874535

Zawacki-Richter, O., Marín, V. I., Bond, M., & Gouverneur, F. (2019). Systematic review of research on artificial intelligence applications in higher education – where are the educators? *International Journal of Educational Technology in Higher Education*, *16*(1), 39. https://doi.org/10.1186/s41239-019-0171-0DOI: 10.1186/s41239-019-0171-0

Zhu, H., Sun, Y., & Yang, J. (2025). Towards responsible artificial intelligence in education: A systematic review on identifying and mitigating ethical risks. *Humanities & Social Sciences Communications*, *12*(1), 1111. https://doi.org/10.1057/s41599-025-05252-6DOI: 10.1057/s41599-025-05252-6

Chapter 7
AI-Driven Predictive Analytics for Enhancing Student Success and Retention

Arun Kumar Garov
http://orcid.org/0000-0002-7541-6161
RIMT University, India

A. K. Awasthi
http://orcid.org/0000-0002-4388-4147
Lovely Professional University, India

Deep Shikha
RIMT University, India

ABSTRACT

The increasing diversity of learners, rising academic pressure, and growing drop-out rates have made student success and retention critical concerns for higher education institutions worldwide. Traditional, reactive approaches to student support are often insufficient to address these challenges in a timely and effective manner. In this context, Artificial Intelligence (AI)-driven predictive analytics has emerged as a powerful solution for enabling data-informed, proactive decision-making in higher education. By analyzing large volumes of academic, behavioral, and engagement-related data, AI-based predictive models can identify students at risk of poor performance or attrition at an early stage.This chapter examines the

DOI: 10.4018/979-8-3373-7600-4.ch007

role of AI-driven predictive analytics in enhancing student success and retention. It explores key AI techniques, data sources, and predictive models used to forecast academic outcomes and student persistence.

1. INTRODUCTION

Colleges and universities are currently facing a sweeping change, which has been accelerated by the high rate of change in technology, increase in the diversity of students, as well as the demand on the academic performance of the students. Over the past few years, student success, and retention have become the fundamental measures of institutional performance, quality assurance, and sustainability (Arnold & Pistilli, 2012; Long & Siemens, 2014). Academic readiness, socio-economic status, student interest and motivation, psychological health, and college-based support networks are all contributors to the ability of a student to persist and succeed during the study in higher education (Ifenthaler & Yau, 2020). Nevertheless, traditional methods of reducing cases of student attrition tend to be reactive and using past performance measures that alleviate issues after they have increased student performance negatively (Daniel, 2015).

The increased availability of education data has opened new possibilities to the institutions to implement data-driven approaches that can better assist the learners (Campbell et al., (2007). Learning-management systems, online evaluation systems, student information systems, and digital learning contexts are all creating high amounts of data concerning student behaviour, interaction and results. This information may provide worthwhile information regarding the learning patterns and lead to the early detection of academic risk when well examined. Predictive analytics using artificial intelligence is essential in converting raw student educational data into practical student intelligence and thus increasing their success and retention.

Predictive analytics based on AI can be called the use of machine learning, deep learning, and other algorithms of artificial intelligence to predict future based on previous and current data. Within the higher education sector, these methods allow the learning institutions to forecast the student outcomes, learners who are at risk of dropping out and factors that lead to disengagement or poor development. Compared to conventional statistical techniques, AI-based models have the capacity to operate in complex non-linear high-dimensional data and identify unearthly non-linear relationships that better represent real world learning behaviour.

By incorporating the predictive analytics within the academic decision-making, the institutions get an opportunity to transform reactive student support measures into the proactive ones. Early detection of at-risk students enables them to be subjected to timely interventions which may include academic advising, customised learning materials, mentoring and counselling. Furthermore, the systems based on AI can assist in personalised learning by manipulating the instructions, learning speed, and testing methods based on the needs of certain learners. This one-on-one strategy not only leads to better academic outcomes, but it also increased the student involvement and satisfaction key elements to long-term-retention.

Although quite promising, the introduction of AI-controlled predictive analytics to higher education needs considerable concerns related to data security, privacy, and transparency and ethics of use. Education information is very sensitive and the institution needs to protect the student information, such as safeguarding it against abuse and access by unauthorised personnel. In this respect, secure data-management systems and new solutions like blockchain present interesting solutions since they guarantee data integrity, traceability and religiousness of academic records and analytics services (Slade & Prinsloo, (2013). The theorical AI and secure data-management technologies collaboration will create a more stable and responsible ecosystem of student data analysis and decision-making (Long & Siemens, 2014; Zawacki-Richter et al., 2019)).

2. PREDICTIVE ANALYTICS IN HIGHER EDUCATION

Predictive analytics has become a disruptive solution in the higher education sector, allowing institutions to predict upcoming student performance results by means of the deep examination of past and current data. Unlike the traditional reporting mechanisms that only document the events of the past, predictive analytics shifts the attention focus on the events that are most likely to happen and aim at shedding some light on the causal factors. This future-oriented ability makes predictive analytics particularly useful to take care of the dynamic issues of student success, engagement, and retention.

In the context of higher education, predictive analytics is the combination of statistical procedures, data-mining algorithms and artificial intelligence to identify those trends present in larger bodies of educational data. The pattern is then used to predict academic performance, progress and dropout risks and this ensures that the institutions have the freedom on when to intervene in proactive ways as opposed to being reactive in dealing with problems.

Predictive analytics involves the methodical use of data, algorithms and complex analytical tools to predict future occurrences or behaviours in reference to past data. In the context of higher education, this field involves a careful analysis of data that relates to students, including academic achievement, activity measures, and behavioural indices, in order to predict with a high degree of probability the outcome, e.g., success in a course, graduation, or dropout.

Predictive analytics does not overpower human decision-making, instead, it crowdsources institutional judgement with evidence-based insights. These insights can equip teachers, leaders, and policymakers with strategies that help them develop informed strategies in supporting a diverse population of students.

2.1. Evolution of Analytics in Higher Education

Analytics implementation in higher education has been developing in a number of stages:

- Descriptive analytics, summarising the past (such as pass rates and student enrollment rates).
- Diagnostic analytics, the explanation of why particular results have occurred.
- Predictive analytics, which forecasts in the future.

The approach involves, 1) predictive analytics, 2) prescriptive analytics, which prescribes actions based on the model of prediction.

Predictive analytics is a new watershed move in favour of reporting to actual foresight. The digital platforms of learning, online tests, and data intensive academic systems have spurred this evolution, which is ever-generating learner data.

2.2. Importance of Predictive Analytics for Student Success

A combination of lessons, levels of engagement, academic preparation, and out of school pressures are just some of the many factors which combine to ensure that students succeed. Predictive analytics help institutions to understand these factors in a concerted manner and not independently.

Predictive models can be used to make a timely academic and emotional intervention by recognising the early warning signs that alert about the poor participation, attendance irregularities, or sudden drop in performance. This is a proactive approach which improves the results of learning, reduces failures as well as makes students more and more satisfied.

2.3. Predictive Analytics for Student Retention

Reducing student attrition is one of the major issues of higher learning institutions across all continents. Predictive analytics is a crucial part of retention management since it can determine the likelihood of individual and cohort dropout.

Predictive models with a retention focus focus on the signs that reveal course drops, lack of engagement, and financial burden and course difficulty. Based on these perceptions, institutions can utilize such perceptions by engaging in specific interventions such as mentoring programmes, financial advisory, and individual student academic advisory services. Predictive analytics therefore helps to increase retention levels and institutional sustainability.

2.4. Data-Driven Decision-Making in Academic Institutions

Evidence-based decision-making is based on predictive analytics, which replaces intuitively oriented strategies with those supported by facts. The academic leaders utilise predictive outputs in order to efficiently cope with resources, redesign curriculum, and determine whether student support services are efficient.

An example is that predictive analytics can be used to make decisions in line sequencing, workload distribution, and student support staffing. Such an evidence-based process improves the results in the institutional sense and accountability.

2.5. Limitations of Traditional Predictive Methods

The predictive process used in the previous methodologies in the field of higher education was largely based on elementary statistical measures and limited datasets. Such traditional approaches often were unable to measure complex learning behaviours and dynamic patterns of engagement.

These methods were basically non-responsive, in that they were incapable of responding to changing student life situations as well as real time information. As a result, predictions became less accurate and interventions were in most cases late. These difficulties gave way to the introduction of AI-based predictive analytics, which is more flexible, scalable, and accurate.

2.6. Transition Toward AI-Driven Predictive Analytics

Two-fold and three-dimensional growth and sophistication of educational data necessitated progressive analytical systems. Artificial intelligence enables predictive analytics solutions to learn and constantly improve the predictions against high-dimensional data using novel information.

AI-based predictive analytics is a paradigm shift in the world of higher education since it enables individual, scalable, adaptive support systems to students. Such a transition conforms to the greater digitization of academic institutions and forms the basis of introducing new technologies, including blockchain, to provide the opportunity to manage data securely.

3. ROLE OF ARTIFICIAL INTELLIGENCE IN PREDICTIVE ANALYTICS

Artificial Intelligence (AI) is one of the engines of prediction that brings Artificial Intelligence to a new level in higher education nowadays. It provides intelligent systems with the capability to devour huge blocks of information and respond adaptively to changing student behaviours and make predictions relating to student performance and tenacity with an unparalleled level of precision. Where conventional analytics have been built using a set of rules that remain fixed and do not adapt, AI-based approaches are dynamic, self-refining, and inherently scaled so that it can process multifaceted and high-volume educational data.

Inoculation of AI into predictive analytics is used to identify hidden patterns entrenched in student data, identify precursors of poor academic performance at an early stage, and support proactive and customised interventions (Baker et al., 2016). Through the employment of machine learning, deep learning and advanced decision-making algorithms, AI will transform raw educational data into practical information which will in turn directly support student-centred learning ecosystems.

3.1. Machine Learning Models for Student Outcome Prediction

The AI-based predictive analytics architecture in higher education institutions is based on machine learning. These algorithms use historical records of students to construct their battles in the knowledge that they possess and thus can predict future events like learning metrics, the study completion rate and dropouts.

Monitored learning algorithms, such as decision trees, logistic regression, random forests, and support-vector machines, are widely used to put people in categories of risk or even to estimate performance scores. Like that, such models create a multifactorial set of variables, which is grades, attendance, participation patterns, and assessment behaviours, all at the same time, allowing to generate strong and reliable predictions.

The ability of machine-learning models to be constantly improved is one of their salient strengths. As modern student data levels off, the models update their parameters, which means that their prediction will remain relevant as academic terms change and new groups of students are introduced. It is this time flexibility that makes them unmatched in early warnings and analytics that is more retention-focused.

3.2. Deep Learning for Complex and Longitudinal Educational Data

Deep learning is similar to traditional machine-learning paradigms, except that it is applied to high-dimensional time-dependent streams of data. Online educational contexts consisting of learning-management software, online testing, and virtual learning platforms produce complex data which online learning leaders should address ideally using deep-learning frameworks, including feed-forward neural networks and recurring neural networks.

These micro models get protracted learning paths, differentiate or track the direction of progression, and rebuild behavioural series that change with time. As an example, deep-learning methods can be used to identify how marginal changes in engagement or the rate of instructional delivery adjust the long-term academic performance. It, therefore, results in a high degree of accuracy regarding student persistence, progression and achievement of degrees.

3.3. Natural Language Processing in Learning Analytics

NLP provides AI systems with a way to question the unstructured textual content composed by learners as well as educators, including forum posts, student assignments, surveys on feedback, reflective notes, and academic consultancy notes.

Predictive-analytics platforms, utilising NLP-based systems to predictive analytics include sentiment analysis, topic modelling and text classification, can reveal warning signs of emotional valence, dynamic motivational processes, and cognitive engagement. The information is used in these qualitative insights to supplement ordinal data to paint a more comprehensive picture of student experience. NLP assisted analytics is of great benefit especially in identifying the early symptoms of disengagement, stress or dissatisfaction that could threaten retention.

3.4. Reinforcement Learning for Adaptive Academic Interventions

The introduction of reinforcement learning provides a new approach to decision-making where artificial intelligence implements the best strategies by engaging the learning environment. Reinforcement learning has been used in predictive analytics to have systems make specific intervention suggestions based on the responses and results of the students. As an example, one can have a system that suggests tutoring, supplementary learning material, or mentoring and monitor how these practises influence student achievement. The reinforcement learning models can determine the most effective interventions to particular groups of students over time. This method encourages adaptive learning system which is always upgraded to maximise student success.

3.5. Automated Feature Engineering and Pattern Discovery

Machine learning is an artificial method to extract significant predictors out of big educational data. Automated Feature Engineering Minimises manual data selection Automated Feature engineering allows predictive models to capture more complex interactions between variables. As an illustration, AI can produce compositional engagement measurements, consistency measurements, or learning velocity measures which are higher-metabolising than raw data. Automated pattern discovery enhances the accuracy of prediction and scale particularly where students in institutions are large and diverse.

3.6. Real-Time Predictive Analytics and Continuous Learning

The predictive analytics systems need the artificial intelligence to execute real time and are continuously fed with information generated by the digital learning environments. In contrast to models of a static nature, AI-based systems change their predictions with the availability of new data. With real-time analytics, the institutions are (1) able to identify academic risk within minutes and (2) act in real time via timely feedback, responsive content delivery, and (3) academic support. Continuous learning models promote models that make predictions correct and context sensitive to the academic lifecycle.

3.7. Explainable Artificial Intelligence (XAI)

Predictive analytics that are AI-driven have a significant, essential attribute of being explainable. Teachers, managers and learners should be able to know the way predictions are created and what drives performances. Explainable AI methods give interpretable results in the form of feature ranking of importance, decision rules and visual explanation. These procedures will boost transparency, accountability and trust in predictive systems. Explainability also facilitates made ethical decisions and can make sure that AI-driven insights are used accountably.

3.8. Ethical and Responsible Use of AI in Predictive Analytics

Application of AI in predictive analytics poses ethical issues of data privacy, bias in the algorithms, fairness and informed consent. Artificial intelligence tools developed using biassed or unbalanced data can support unfairness and leave some types of students at a disadvantage. Institutions will need to implement ethical AI systems that are based on fairness, inclusivity and transparency. Sustainable governance measures imply that predictive knowledge is applied on how to influence students, but not to punish them. The future of the trust and legitimacy of data-driven education - Ethical AI adoption is necessary.

3.9. Integration of AI with Secure Data Management Systems

Predictive analytics relies on the correct and reliable data that is provided by AI. With secure data management technologies, especially blockchain-based systems, integration will improve the level of data integrity, traceability, and authorization. Using blockchain makes student records utilised in predictions models unaltered and verifiable. This completeness provides the institution more belief in the AI generated forecasts and promotes more transparent and decentralized data management models.

4. AI FOR PREDICTING STUDENT SUCCESS

The modern higher education ecosystem is experiencing a dramatic change that is driven by digitization, globalisation, demographic diversification, and dynamism of workforce requirements. It is a milieu where institutions are serving in complex environments defined by flexible academic paths, hybrid and online education, competency-based education, credentialing systems in modules, lifelong learning courses. Under such an environment; it is not only institutional but a strategic priority to ensure student success and to retain them.

The customary methods of tracking student achievement mainly descriptive reports, semester grade analysis, and manual advising information systems are reactive in nature and have poor predictive ability. Such methods have the tendency of only showing academic risk when the problem has already been caused by poor performance. Due to the lack of dropout rates, academic disengagement, and credential non-completion, global institutions should seek active and smart systems that can predict the outcomes of academic progress without taking a negative turn.

Historically measures of student success relied on small measures:

- Grade Point Average (GPA)
- Semester progression
- Retention rates
- Graduation rates
- Time-to-degree completion

Nevertheless, the contemporary higher education settings require multidimensional conceptualizations of success in the broad terms of institutional and social aspirations.

4.1. Evolution from Traditional Analytics to AI-Driven Prediction

The two decades have seen the use of analytics in higher education change significantly. The institutions have shifted to rigid reporting to dynamic smart predictive ecosystems that can foresee results of the students and predict them before they occur. It is not only a shift in technology but also this development of the philosophical approach of the institutions, which may be characterised as a transformation between the post-factum assessment and a preventive intervention and foresight.

The development of higher education analytics has gone through a number of stages:

Figure 1. Phases of Higher Education Analytics

4.1.1. Phase I: Descriptive Analytics – "What Happened?"

The first phase of institutional analytics was a descriptive reporting. At this stage, the institutions were largely dependent on systematised databases to create reports summarising the past data.

4.1.2. Phase II: Diagnostic Analytics – "Why Did It Happen?"

When institutions started collecting bigger datasets, they started using statistical techniques in order to investigate causal associations. Diagnostic analytics attempts to clarify the variation in performance as determined by identifying correlation among variables.

4.1.3. Phase III: Predictive Analytics – "What Is Likely to Happen?"

With the advent of machine learning, it was a pivotal point in the change of explanation in favour of prediction. Predictive analytics is a forecasting technique that considers the likelihood of the supply of future results based on historical data trends.

4.1.4. Phase IV: Prescriptive Analytics – "What Should Be Done?"

Prescriptive analytics applies predictive analytics into prescriptive advice.

4.1.5. Phase V: AI-Driven Adaptive Prediction – Continuous Intelligence

The latest phase is AI-based adaptive eco systems which are a combination of predictive, prescriptive as well as real-time learning.

5. DATA SCIENCE FOR AI-DRIVEN STUDENT ANALYTICS

Data science is the core science, which provides the basis of AI-led student analytics and transforms raw educational data into meaningful results. Academic activity, online learning platforms, and systems used in institutions in the higher education sector generate tremendous amounts of data. Data science will provide the methods, instruments, and analytical frameworks necessary to handle this data productively, and as such can be used to support predictive analytics which will be sought to improve student success and retention. Data science is relevant in that by incorporating statistical analysis, data engineering, machine learning, and domain expertise, AI-based analytics systems tend to be correct, scalable, and ethical.

5.1. Data Collection and Integration

The initial step of data science workflow involves well-planned data gathering based on a variety of educational systems like learning management systems, student information systems, evaluation systems, and digital learning systems. Since the data of the students is scattered in the heterogeneous systems, the data integration is a very important task. Data scientists have developed data pipelines which gathers both structured and unstructured data and simplifies them by integrating them into a single profile of a learner. Beautiful integration will ensure that the data is consistent, less redundant, and that student behaviour and performance can be analysed in a holistic way. In combination with blockchain-based data-management systems, integration experiences result in improvement of data authenticity, traceability, and controlled access.

5.2. Data Preprocessing and Cleaning

Sometimes the educational datasets include missing data, inconsistencies, and noise because of differences in data of entries, system design, and student behaviour. Therefore, it is necessary to preprocess data first in order to increase data quality before AI models are used. The stage entails the management of missing values, error resolution, the normalisation of numerical variables and coding of categorical values. Outlier detection, data validation, and anomaly analysis are a few examples of techniques to be used to ensure that predictive analytics is based on valid and representative datasets and thus enhance the precision and equity of the model.

5.3. Exploratory Data Analysis (EDA)

Exploratory data analysis helps data scientists to understand the internal constitution and trend of student data. With the help of the statistical summaries and visual exploration, EDA makes connexions between engagement, performance, and progression. EDA helps to determine the most significant predictors of student success and their risk of dropout, can reveal the presence of latent trends, and provides information to support the formulation of a hypothesis. The lessons learned can influence which features to include in the model and the choice of the model, for example, as predictive analytics, these models include learned aspects of the real world.

5.4. Feature Engineering and Selection

The feature engineering converts raw data in education into meaningful variables which increase the predictive model performance. Engineered features in student analytics can be engagement scores, indicators of learning consistency, assessment improvement rates, and time-on-task. The feature-selection methods can select the most significant predictors and minimise the dimensionality as well as computing cost. Such features can be effectively designed to enhance not only the accuracy but also the interpretability of AI-driven predictive models and, in such a way, help the institution to identify the factors that affect student outcomes.

5.5. Model Development and Validation

Data science can aid the development of predictive models through the choice of appropriate AI algorithms, the tuning of model parameters and model performance evaluation. Modelling is based on training models that are trained using historical student data, and validated by methods like cross-validation and hold-out. Model efficacy is evaluated using the performance metrics such as accuracy, precision, recall, and predictive reliability. Strict validation will ensure that models are generalised through variations in student groups and academic settings.

5.6. Predictive Modeling and Risk Scoring

As an institution, predictive modelling will enable them to create risk scores considering academic failure, disengagement, or dropout. The methodologies of data science measure the measure of uncertainty and confidence in the prediction, which makes prioritising interventions more efficient by educators and administrators. The focused academic advising, the individualised learning paths, and the warning systems are founded on risk stratification. Predictive modelling maximises the efficiency and student outcomes at the institution by ensuring that the available resources are concentrated on the most struggling students.

5.7. Explainability and Interpretability of Models

One of the key requirements of educational analytics is transparency. Data science can be instrumental in making the predictions provided by AI to be explainable and comprehensible to the stakeholders. The educators are able to understand the predictive outputs thanks to explainable AI techniques: feature-importance analysis, rule-based interpretations, and model visualisation. Serious ethical decisions, regulatory exercises, and trust of AI systems are based on explainability.

5.8. Ethical Data Governance and Privacy Protection

Responsible data science focuses on responsible handling of data, protection of privacy and informed consent. As part of the student analytics, it involves anonymisation, examination of fairness, identification of bias, and storage of data securely. The governance systems through blockchain-based data-governance can also enhance ethical practises because they offer transparent access controls and unalterable audit logs. Data ethics can be applied by making sure that predictive analytics are used to serve and not to discriminate against students.

5.9. Deployment and Continuous Model Monitoring

After creation, predictive models will have to be implemented in the institutional systems and kept track of. Performance Tracking: Data science is useful in the performance tracking, bias monitoring, retraining of models because of the data drift and changing learning situations. Constant checking ensures that AI student analytics are correct, useful and up to date in purpose and therefore focused on the goals of the institution.

6. DATA SOURCES FOR AI-DRIVEN STUDENT ANALYTICS

Student analytics based on AI relies on a set of varied, precise, and context-filled data that combine to shed light on the academic, behavioural and experience aspects of students. In the academic and institutional environment of higher education, this data is produced in a range of institutional and digital platforms through the academic lifecycle. These data forms form the basis of predictive analytics that are used to predict student performance, engagement, and retention.

The quality, completeness and reliability of such data streams is directly related to the effectiveness of predictive analytics. Strong data-managed structures and most especially through blockchain technology bolster the credibility and integrity of the student information used in analytics.

6.1. Academic Performance Data

The most fundamental student analytics data is academic performance data. It includes grades, test-scores, course-based-continuous assessment scores, marks on attendance, course-completion, and indicators on academic progress. With this data, AI models have the capability to understand the trends of performance, learning gaps, and an early warning of academic challenges.

Predictive systems use longitudinal performance records to trace the changes (between the time) that may either be gradual decline or improvement. These could be critical towards early-intervention strategies that could be used to empower student success.

6.2. Learning Management System (LMS) Data

Learning-management systems record numerous digital footprints on learning behaviour of students. The LMS data include the number of different logins, access to instructional content, time spent on learning content, trends of submitting assignments, participation in discussion-forum, and the response to the learning environment.

AI-based analytics apply to the LMS data to measure the level of engagement, their consistency in learning, as well as the quality of their participation. The data obtained on LMS is frequently in real-time and thus is crucial in the early-warning mechanisms and the ongoing assessing of student engagement.

6.3. Behavioral and Engagement Data

The interactions of the students are an aspect of behavioural and engagement data that captures student interactions with non-formal assessment activities like engagement with library services, academic support centres, tutoring programmes, and co-curricular activities.

The indicators based on this data show the motivation of students, their commitment, and sense of belongingness which are strongly correlated with retention. Intellectual records are combined with behavioural records on the basis of which AI models are created to create a comprehensive perspective of engagement patterns.

6.4. Student Information System (SIS) Data

Student information systems are collections of administrative and institutional records pertaining to admissions, previous enrollments, programme structure, credit accrual, and graduation schedules. SIS data provides very important contextual information that drives the predictive modelling of academic pathways and degrees.

Using SIS data, AI-based analytics will be able to identify the structural bottlenecks, sluggish progression patterns, and policy-specific issues that influence the student success and retention.

6.5. Demographic and Socio-Economic Data

Attributes of demographic and socio-economic data comprise age, gender, geographical location, enrollment status, financial-aid, and first-generation learner.

These variables provide such essential contextual information regarding external forces, which affect academic performance and persistence.

This data, when used ethically and sensibly, supports the inclusion-oriented analytics methods that consider the unique needs of students and shape the strategy of unbiased assistance.

6.6. Assessment and Evaluation Data

The assessment data include the formative and summative assessment, grading using the rubrics, peer assessment, and competency-based assessment. Using this information, AI models evaluate the results of learning, the level of skills acquired, and discipline-specific difficulties.

The continuous assessment data will also improve the adaptive learning system because it offers individual learner profile-based personal feedback and instructions.

6.7. Unstructured Textual Data

Student-feedback surveys, reflective journals, discussions, emails, and adviser notes are all examples of unstructured sources of data. Using the skills of natural-language-processing, AI systems identify sentiment, emotional coloring, and thematic patterns of the text basis.

This qualitative data supplements quantitative data and presents the information about the motivation of students, their satisfaction, and emotional health which are important factors of retention and success.

6.8. Co-Curricular and Extracurricular Data

Student engagement and development as well come through participation in co-curricular and extracurricular activities like club, sports, internship and community engagements programmes. This data is used in AI-driven analytics and are used to assess general participation and correlation to academic success.

The information is useful in helping an institution to develop an overall support system that acknowledges out-of-classroom learning.

6.9. Blockchain-Secured Academic and Credential Data

Blockchain technology boosts AI-based student analytics by helping to guarantee academic records and credentials integrity, authenticity, and traceability. Data that is secured by blockchain contains transcripts, digital certificates, micro-credentials and learning achievements.

Wireless and decentralised data storage of A blockchain ensures the use of the AI models on certified and reliable data, which, in turn, reinforces the following institutional trust in predictive analytics and protects student ownership and privacy.

6.10. External and Lifelong Learning Data

Outside learning sites, online programs, professional proceedings and lifelong-learning programmes data completes the full profile of the learner. The combination of such, in turn, allows AI-based analytics to facilitate continuous education journeys and career-adjusted suggestions.

This wider view can be correlated with new patterns of the lifelong and digital-credentials ecosystems.

7. AI-DRIVEN PREDICTIVE MODELS FOR STUDENT SUCCESS

Predictive models powered by AI are one of the most important tools of improving the performance of students, allowing the institutions of higher learning to foresee potential learning obstacles and taking actions beforehand. These models use machine learning and artificial intelligence approaches to analyse large and multidimensional datasets of students and make reliable predictions in relation to academic outcomes, involvement, and tenacity. Converting raw data to practical foresight, predictive models help to create personalised learning opportunities and to intervene in the process of learning in due time.

7.1. Early Warning Systems

One of the most popular AI-driven predictive analytics applications to higher education is early warning systems. These data continually track the student information which includes records on assessment performance, attendance and system engagement in learning management to determine in advance signs of academic risk. The AI models are predictive of potential risk by a score or triggering alerts when a student exhibits a behaviour, includes behaviours that are linked to low performance, or shows disengagement. Early warning systems enable the educator and assistant to intervene at an initial stage using academic counselling, tutoring assistance or individualised retreat of students, and in the process, they reduce the failure levels extensively and improve the student performances.

7.2. Risk Prediction and Dropout Analysis

The risk predictive models are aimed at estimating the probability of student leakage or slowed upgrading. The models are based on the analysis of the historical retention rates, academic performance, interaction rates, and socio-economic factors and identify the correlations with dropout behaviour. A clear-cutting into risk groups of students enables institutions to lie class upon resource support wisely. In addition, dropout analysis clarifies high-level problems in a system that may carry out among students which encompass curriculum weakness or organizational challenges; which lead to new strategic changes.

7.3. Performance Prediction Models

Performance prediction models predict academic performance (course grade, semester performance or probability of earning a degree). They use complex machine-learning algorithms to evaluate previous academic history, learning behaviour and examination data. Harmonious predictions allow personal academic planning and corrective learning directions. The students get specific recommendations by forecasted levels of performance, which they can use to strengthen the weak areas and continue their steady progress.

7.4. Engagement and Behavior Prediction Models

Academic success is an important variable that is determined by student engagement. The engagement models based on AI use behavioural data in online learning settings to anticipate the changes in participation, motivation, and learning consistency. Patterns that are identified by these models include decreasing LMS activity, spending less time in forums, or inconsistent studying. With forecasting the engagement patterns, the institutions will be able to develop the timely strategies that will foster the motivation and long-term engagement.

7.5. Personalized Learning Recommendation Models

Personal recommendation models are predictive analytics-based models that use individual student requirements to customise learning experiences. In accordance with performance history, learning preferences, and patterns of engagement, AI systems recommend suitable learning resources, instruction approach, and pacing change. Adaptive learning environments such as these models assist in offering custom-made content and feedback to students. Individual recommendations improve the learning process, learner satisfaction, and educational success in the long run.

7.6. Academic Pathway and Progression Models

Academic pathway models are used to examine the process of student movement through degree programmes to predict time to completion and possible delay points. They determine the sequence of courses, credits gained and pre-requisites. This is because institutions can provide guidance to the students in the choice of the course as well as managing the workload and plans involved in schoolwork by predicting the risks. The models prepare students to have greater navigative capabilities of complex curricula, hence time to degree is lower.

7.7. Intervention Impact Models

Intervention impact models are used to assess the effectiveness of the academic support programmes like tutoring, mentoring and advising. AI interprets the past intervention data to identify the approaches that produce positive intervention results among different groups of students. Such models assist in narrowing the gap in intervention policies by institutions and efficient resource allocation because of supporting evidence-based decision making. Continuous review will make the support strategies keep abreast.

7.8. Integration with Secure Data and Credentialing Systems

The predictive models that are run by AI require valid and correct student data. The combination of these models and safe data management and blockchain-based credentialing systems ensures the privacy, clinician transparency, and credibility of data. Secured academic records based on blockchain provide a higher level of reliability with reference to predictive information, and allow sharing of certified learning outcomes safely. This unification enhances confidence within the institution on predictive analytics and allows responsible decision-making.

8. ENHANCING STUDENT SUCCESS THROUGH PREDICTIVE INSIGHTS

Predictive insights, which are based on advanced AI-based analytics, have a transformational effect on the performance of students in higher education. Instead of taking a reactive stance to academic hardships once they have occurred, the institutions can use predictive knowledge to understand the needs of the students, customise support systems and implement timely action. These insights can transform complex data outputs into practical advice to educators, administrators, as well as learners themselves, and can make education proactive, student-focused, and in this way create a student-centred learning ecosystem.

8.1. Early Identification of At-Risk Students

Among the greatest contributions that can be cited as a result of predictive insights is the ability to identify students who are on the verge of failure or lack of interest in their academics early on. By studying historical archives, up to date data streams, predictive models reveal hidden patterns that cannot be detectable using traditional evaluation methods.

Early diagnosis shapes institutions to interfere when scholastic struggles are more than entangled. There is a mutual effort between academic advisors, members of the faculty, and support services in order to provide tailor-made services so that learners can get the necessary support at the right time.

8.2. Personalized Academic Support and Advising

Predictive insights make it possible to engage in individualised academic advising, in which the support strategies offered are always matched with the student profile. The analytics of AI are used to analyse learning behaviours, performance patterns, and engagement-related indicators, and, thus, prescribe customised academic advice.

Individualised advising prepares students to make wise choices regarding the choice of courses, modes of studying and the process of managing the workload. This personalised methodology strengthens academic confidence, academic performance, and cultivates effective long-term interest along the academic path.

8.3. Adaptive Learning Interventions

Adaptive learning interventions use foresight to dynamically change instructional material and the trajectories of learning. AL systems identify the areas in which the students have challenges and customise learning materials to meet the needs, offering specific resources and positive feedback.

These interventions are the proponents of mastery-based learning, whereby the students are allowed to learn at their own pace. Adaptive learning environments enhance the understanding, reduce knowledge gaps, and improve academic achievement in general.

8.4. Strengthening Student Engagement and Motivation

Academic success and retention is closely connected with the student engagement. Forecasts allow organisations to identify all signs of declining motivation or engagement through behavioural and interactional data.

Because of observing the patterns of engagement, teachers will be able to use specific methods like participatory learning assignments, mentoring schemes, and peer study projects. The predictive insights keep the students motivated and enable them to engage in the learning process.

8.5. Improving Retention and Persistence Rates

Predictive insights that are retention-centred enable institutions to address the causal issues that serve as antecedents to student attrition. Detection of systemic barriers, whether the curriculum is too complicated, the pressure on assessment, or lack of support facilitates the design of data-informed strategies of retention.

Predictive analytics will help to continue to track the retention trend and policy success of the institution. As a result, institutions of higher learning would be able to increase persistence levels in addition to creating an inclusive and supportive learning environment.

8.6. Data-Driven Decision-Making for Educators and Administrators

Predictive insights grant educators and administrators with empirical and evidence-based decision-making abilities. Analytic reports and dashboards transform complicated AI outputs into usable instructions to guide instructional planning, resources allocation as well as policy making.

Responsibility and responsiveness in the institutions are improved through data-driven decision-making. It also allows stakeholders to reach alignment of academic strategies and needs of learners as well as organisational goals, which enhances the overall levels of education.

8.7. Ethical and Responsible Use of Predictive Insights

The use of predictive knowledge in the educational field must be approached carefully in the aspect of ethics. The use of predictive analytics in institutions has to be based on transparency, fairness, and the consent of the students.

Being responsible implies that you can avoid stigmatization, alleviate bias, and that predictive underpinnings can be used in the support- rather than in the condemnation- of students. Ethical responsibility is promoted even further through blockchain-based data governance schemes because of their ability to ensure the utilisation of data in a secure, auditable, and transparent manner.

9. IMPROVING STUDENT RETENTION USING PREDICTIVE ANALYTICS

Student retention is a critical measure of institutional efficiency and student contentment in higher learning institutions. High levels of dropout not only hamper the educational and career path of students but also ruin the reputation of the institution, cripple funding sources and jeopardise the sustainability in the long run. Through predictive analytics that run on the principles of artificial intelligence, institutions of higher learning will be able to respond to retention issues weeks before they emerge by prescriptively addressing risk factors, effectively creating predictive intervention, and by persistently tracking student activity and progress.

9.1. Understanding Student Retention Challenges

The factors of student attrition are a product of a complex interaction between academic, personal, social, and institutional factors. Such factors include academic challenge, lack of interest, economic burden, the worry about mental health, and insufficient institutional support. Conventional retention practises are normally based on post-factum studies which focus on correcting problems when they have become inactive or dropped out. Predictive analytics helps in changing this paradigm by allowing institutions to detect risks of retention in advance and allowing them to institute preventive systems in a timely manner.

9.2. Predictive Modeling for Dropout Risk Identification

Predictive models, powered by artificial-intelligence, affect historical and real-time data in determining the likelihood of student dropout. These models consider various pointers, including, but not limited to, academic performance trends, attendance patterns, LMS activity and behavioural engagement rates. Predictive systems help institutions to prioritise support efforts by coming up with retention-risk scores. This is an effective way of ensuring the scarce academic and counselling resources are effectively deployed to students who are in need of such resources.

9.3. Targeted Academic and Non-Academic Interventions

Predictive analytics promotes the development of differentiated interventions to solve the problems of both academic and non-academic determinants of retention. These academic interventions can include tutoring, remedial coursework and adaptive learning materials. Mentoring, counselling and financial advice can be used as examples of other non-academic interventions. The recommendations of AI systems on the particular interventions depends on the student profile that means that the strategies of support can be personalised and context-specific. This kind of all-encompassing approach contributes significantly to persistence and satisfaction of the students.

9.4. Proactive Student Engagement Strategies

Long term engagement is one of the critical retention determinants of students. Delinquent in advance, predictive analytics identifies the signs of disengagement, including the lack of engagement with online resources, or fading interest in studying material. These insights can give institutions have the capability to apply proactive engagement techniques such as personalised communication, peer-mentoring programmes, and interactive learning programmes. The strategies make students feel a sense of belonging and academic commitment.

9.5. Continuous Monitoring and Retention Analytics Dashboards

Student progression and engagement trend dashboards should be retention-oriented and provide real-time visualization in student progression. These dashboards make predictive insights available in a simple format to faculty, advisors, and administrators in order to monitor the risks of retention on a daily basis. Constant observations allow institutions to measure the effectiveness of the retention efforts and introduce evidence-based changes. This incremental strategy enhances the responsiveness of the institution and long-term retention.

9.6 Institutional Policy and Strategic Planning Support

Predictive analytics does not have several benefits; it also plays an informative role in institutional policy and strategic planning. Aggregated data on retention points towards systemic issues in the form of a curriculum bottleneck, excessive assessment load or service holes in student services. Through the incorporation of predictive knowledge in the strategic decision-making, the institutions will be able to create evidence-based policies that build inclusive learning spheres and fair student achievement.

9.7. Ethical Considerations in Retention Analytics

Predictive analytics usage in student retention brings about and ethical concern of privacy, fairness and transparency of data. The institutions need to provide that predictive outcomes are used in a responsible manner and they do not stigmatise and disadvantage students. The ethical retention analytics put more emphasis on the student empowerment, informed consent and explainable AI model. The strong data governance frameworks such as blockchain-based systems enhance trust by making sure that data is not compromised and that it is accountable.

10. INTEGRATION OF AI-DRIVEN PREDICTIVE ANALYTICS WITH BLOCKCHAIN-BASED DATA MANAGEMENT

The effectiveness of AI-based predictive analytics in the sphere of higher education is significantly predetermined by the quality of data, its reliability and security. With the adoption of the data-driven decision-making concept in institutions to increase the student success and student retention rates, the issues related to data integrity, ownership, privacy, and trust have been gaining prominence (Bhat & Jayaram, 2023). Data management via blockchain is an additional technology that will strengthen AI-powered predictive analytics by ensuring a safe, transparent and tamper-resistant data infrastructure.

10.1. Need for Secure and Trusted Data in Predictive Analytics

Higher education predictive analytics systems are charged with processing large amounts of sensitive data on students, such as academic data, behavioural data, demographic data, and engagement data. In the traditional centralised repositories, these data are vulnerable to unauthorised access, manipulation, and inconsistencies with other systems. Blockchain technology addresses these risks by offering a decentralised registry whereby the transactions are documented permanently. Therefore, AI models have the capacity to depend on the verified and trustworthy data, thus improving the accuracy and validity of predictive results.

10.2. Blockchain as a Foundation for Reliable Student Data Management

With the aid of blockchain cryptography and remote consensus, student data can be stored and governed in an autonomous and secure way. Every academic registry, mark or other learning procedure can be recorded as the transaction on the blockchain. This approach guarantees:

- Immutability securing the integrity of data
- Data access and data adjustment
- Distributed management of student records
- decreased reliance on institutional single silos

The foundation of such AI-driven analytics is essential in building reliable analytics systems in higher education.

10.3. Enhancing Predictive Model Accuracy Through Blockchain-Verified Data

Predictive models rely much on the trends of past data to predict student success and risk of dropouts (Matz, 2023). The files verified by blockchain minimise noise, duplication and manipulation and this results in better accuracy and consistency of models. By providing access to blockchain-enforced data, the institutions can have the certainty that predictions are based on the verified academic records and proven history of involvement, thus, establishing trust among students, faculty, and administrators.

10.4. Decentralized Data Ownership and Student Empowerment

One of the contributions that is salient with the integration of blockchain is the shift of data ownership to decentralisation. Learners may keep ownership on their academic information and permissions may be granted to institutions, counsellors/ advisors, or analytics. Such a model of consent-based sharing will be consistent with ethical practises in AI and data protection laws that make sure that AI-based predictive analytics respects student autonomy without prohibiting institutions to draw valuable information on support and retention strategies.

10.5. Blockchain-Enabled Credentialing and Learning Records

Credentialing Systems This entails the storage of degrees, certificates, marginal micro-credential, and learning accomplishments within a blockchain. Such credible credentials may be integrated into AI-based analytics to investigate learning routes and skill-acquisition patterns and trends. This kind of integration provides the predictive analytics with the opportunity to consider not only academic performance, but also the competence development, employability preparedness, lifelong learning outcomes, making student success measurement much wider.

10.6. Secure Data Sharing Across Institutions and Systems

The higher education ecosystem is often associated with several stakeholders such as universities, learning platforms, employers and accreditation bodies. The use of blockchain allows to share data and information securely, in a standard manner, among institutions and maintain privacy. Predictive analytics propelled by AI have an opportunity to tap into this interoperative data environment, and it can produce a more holistic figure on the student-level mobility, transfer success, and cross-institutional retention patterns.

10.7. Privacy, Compliance, and Governance Benefits

Integration of blockchain allows to address compliance with the rules on data protection due to the possibility of transparent audit trails, as well as permission-based access control. It guarantees responsible data utilisation and responsibility in decision making which is driven by artificial intelligence when coupled with AI-based analytics. Institutional trust and an ethical application of AI systems in higher education is supported by governance structures based on blockchain.

11. ETHICAL, PRIVACY, AND GOVERNANCE CONSIDERATIONS

Predictive analytics based on AI in higher educational institutions offer significant prospects as regards to student success and retention. However, it is also associated with some pivotal ethical, privacy, and governance issues. Since predictive models are based on a significant amount of sensitive student data, institutions need to implement such technologies in a responsible, transparent, and conscientious way and in accordance with existing ethical standards and regulations. When these issues are not brought up, the data may be misused, trust destroyed, and students harmed accidentally.

11.1. Data Privacy and Student Consent

The data that is typically used in predictive analytics among students includes academic performance, behavioural data, socio-economic backgrounds, and engagement data. This data is very sensitive and requires extreme care in the privacy. The institutions should make sure that data collection and analysis practises do not violate the laws on data protection and do not infringe on the rights of students. Ethical data use still necessitates informed consent where the students are fully aware of the data being gathered and how it is going to be utilised and the reasons why predictive outcomes will be utilised. Privacy may also be strengthened with the help of a consent management system with blockchain support, which will give students the freedom to grant and receive access to their data.

11.2. Algorithmic Bias and Fairness

Predictive models based on AI have the risk of being a reflection of existing biases in historical data, as well as an amplifier of these biases (Fierro Saltos et al., 2025). These prejudices, having to do with gender, socioeconomic status, ethnicity, or previous educational possibilities, might result in unfavourable prognoses and discrimination. However, to create fairness, then intentional data care must be adopted, systematic identification of bias, and continuing review of predictive modeling are required. The learning institutions should also institutionalise the practise of inclusive data, perform a regular audit of the AI models, and in the process curb the possibility of bias data making. Ethical AI design eventually employs equity and ensures that predictive analytics improve benefit all the learners instead of discriminating vulnerable groups.

11.3. Transparency and Explainability of AI Models

Numerous sophisticated AI methods including deep learning are black boxes making it difficult to understand the derivation of the prediction. This ambiguity even in academia may undermine the confidence among students, faculty as well as administration. Explainable AI (XAI) methodologies have attempted to make predictive models more explainable, to provide clear explanations to a risk score and recommendations. Open AI mechanisms enable the stakeholders to question, interrogate and justify predictive results, thus creating responsible and knowledgeable decision making.

11.4. Responsible Use of Predictive Outcomes

Predictive analytics can be used to serve as a decision-making support system, but not a labelling or stigmatising intervention against students. Risk predictions should not be perceived as fixed decisions but should serve as a warning on the supportive actions to be taken. Responsible utilisation is a focus on empowerment of students, constructive feedback, and constructive interaction. To make sure that the predictive insights are converted to valuable academic and individual support, the institutions should not resort to punitive measures or limit opportunities.

11.5. Governance Frameworks and Institutional Accountability

The use of AI to predict analytics requires strong governance systems to accommodate AI in higher education. The governance frameworks outline roles, responsibilities and accountability methods in data utilisation and model deployment as well as intervention strategies. Such structures must involve multidisciplinary stakeholders, such as academic leaders, data scientists, ethicists, legal experts and representatives of students. Governance further can be reinforced by means of an immutable access and analytics process record of blockchain-based audit trails.

11.6. Regulatory Compliance and Policy Alignment

Universities need to conform the efforts of predictive analytics with national and international data protection laws. Institutional credibility is enhanced by compliance with the regulations and involves protection of student rights. Institutional policies related to data retention, the use of AI, and ethical supervision should be clearly written and are the key to maintaining the implementation process. The governance based on policy means that AI and blockchain technologies are installed in a way that aligns well with institutional principle and expectations of the society.

12. CHALLENGES AND LIMITATIONS OF AI-DRIVEN PREDICTIVE ANALYTICS

Although AI-controlled predictive analytics may lead to a great breakthrough in student success and retention, its adoption in the university setting is clouded by technical, organisational, ethical, and contextual barriers. Institutions seeking to be AI responsible and strategic require an astute insight into these issues.

12.1. Data Quality and Availability Issues

The accuracy of predictive analytics depends on the quality, completeness and consistency of data used to predict it (Matz, 2023). Most institutions of higher learning have scattered their student information systemically in various systems like learning management platforms, student information systems and administration databases (Bashir & Beydoun, 2026). Attached, outdated, or discontinuous data may create unreliable forecasts and misunderstandings on the level of risks (Shoaib, 2024). In addition, differences in the availability of data in institutions and programmes can also hinder the overall generalisability of predictive models. Internationalisation of data collection and validation procedures is a significant challenge to high-scale implementation.

12.2. Interoperability and System Integration Challenges

Most organisations are using legacy systems that are not helpful in working with advanced analytics or AI. The interoperability of these systems is not there, and this fact prevents the uninterrupted data transfer and real-time analysis. The additional technical complexity of AI-driven analytics and a blockchain-based credentialing and data management only theoretically increases the technical complexity. Organizations are required to allocate resources to scalable data infrastructure and interoperable frameworks that can enable the successful collaboration between AI models and secure data platform.

12.3. Algorithmic Limitations and Accuracy of the Model

Even though AI models are capable of identifying complex patterns, they do not ensure a high level of accuracy. There can be a reduction in predictive accuracy when used on nonhomogeneous groups of students or changing educational situations. Effectiveness can be destroyed by overfitting and model drift as well as lack of ability of a model to generalize to novel learning conditions. The accuracy of models needs to be maintained by constant monitoring, retraining and validation, which requires a lot of technical know-how and institutional resources.

12.4. Ethical Risks and Student Trust

Implementing AI to forecast student behaviour according to their behaviour concerns are valid in terms of surveillance, autonomy and fairness. Students can either perceive predictive analytics as an invasion or worry about being unfairly judged by artificial intelligence. When predictive outcomes are not communicated transparently or abused, they might destroy the trust between the learners and the institutions. Maintaining the ethical protection and engaging students in decision-making activities is essential to maintaining organisational credibility.

12.5. Organizational Resistance and Cultural Barriers

The implementation of AI-based analytics is often met with opposition by faculty, administrators, and personnel because of a lack of awareness, the fear of automation or a lack of trust in algorithmic decision-making. To be successfully implemented it needs a cultural change, building capacity and alignment of the academic and technical stakeholders. Unless the organisation is ready and its leaders support AI initiatives, they might not produce the projected effects.

12.6. Cost of High Implementation and Maintenance

The creation, implementation, and continual upkeep of predictive systems based on AI are costly investments. Examples of such spending include data infrastructure, sophisticated analytical software, and cybersecurity and hiring of extremely qualified employees. The resource-limited settings of smaller institutions and the inability to maintain AI projects in the long term might be a challenge. In line with this, cost benefit analysis and gradual implementation plans are necessary in order to be financially viable.

12.7. Skills Gap and Talent Shortage

Implementing AI-powered analytics requires the ability of data science, machine learning, educational analytics, and ethical AI governance. Most organisations are faced with the challenge of inadequate supply of professionals who are able to design and operate such systems. To overcome this skills gap, one needs specific training programmes, interdisciplinary collaboration, and partnership with technology providers as well as research organisations.

13. FUTURE DIRECTIONS OF AI-DRIVEN PREDICTIVE ANALYTICS IN HIGHER EDUCATION

The further progress of AI-related predictive analytics in education is also directly connected with the development of artificial intelligence and data science, as well as secure digital technologies. With the growing tendencies of the institutions towards using data to improve student success and retention, the predictive analytics systems will grow smarter, clearer, more ethical, and learner-centric. New technologies will further cement the presence of AI in other resilient and inclusive higher education systems.

13.1. Explainable and Trustworthy Artificial Intelligence

Explainable artificial intelligence (XAI) is one of the most important future trends of predictive analytics. XAI aims at making predictive models clearer and understandable to its stakeholders, such as educators, administrators, and students (Umendu et al., 2026). XAI, in the case of a higher education institution, will allow the institution to know why a given student is classified as at risk and what factors will have the greatest impact on subsequent predictive outcomes. This increased disclosedness will increase trust, accountability and ethical judgement and will allow more efficient and personalised interventions.

13.2. Privacy-Preserving Analytics and Federated Learning

Data privacy in predictive analytics systems in the future will be considered an important factor, and mechanisms like federated learning and secure multi-party computation will become popular. Federated learning allows training AI models to be trained using decentralised data sources without the transmission of sensitive student data to a central storage. The strategy is in line with the regulatory provisions, as well as ethical conduct that enable institutions to join in analytics programmes without compromising on data ownership and confidentiality. Privacy-sensitive analytics are to be combined with blockchain-based access control to become one of the foundations of responsible AI implementation in education.

13.3. Integration with Blockchain-Based Digital Credentials

The interplay between AI-driven foreseeable analytics and blockchain-based credentialing implementations is a radical future alternative. The blockchain has the potential to deliver verifiable and tamper-proof academic documentation that improves the trust in predictive models. The AI systems will use the trusted credential data in order to examine learning paths, competency development, and skills learning in formal and informal learning systems. This integration will underpin lifelong learning analytics and allow making better predictions on the subject of employability and career mobility.

13.4. AI-Driven Lifelong and Personalized Learning Analytics

Predictive analytics will no longer be limited to conventional degree programmes to advocate lifelong learning and perpetual skill enhancement. The learning patterns in various phases of both the academic and career life of a student or employee will be analysed through AI systems. Individual analytics will provide opportunities to customise learning and micro-credential encouragement and competency-based models of learning. This will enable the learner to make sound choices and remain relevant in the fast-changing labour markets.

13.5. Real-Time and Adaptive Student Support Systems

Predictive analytics systems will be able to provide real-time insights and adaptive interventions on the advancement of real-time data processing. The AI-led applications will automatically modify the learning material, evaluation plans, and help solutions according to real-time information about student activities and results. With the help of such adaptive systems the student motivation will be fostered, attrition will be reduced and a more responsive learning environment will be created.

13.6. Ethical AI Governance and Policy Evolution

In the future, it will be more emphasised on ethical governance systems and alignment of policies. Organisational approaches to ethical AI will become standardised, continuously monitors and participatory forms of governance that includes learners and educators. Audit trails made possible by blockchain will help with the clear management of the data use and AI decision-making activities, which will strengthen the responsibility and confidence in predictive analytics systems.

CONCLUSION

The emergence of predictive analytics through artificial intelligence is essentially transforming higher education by allowing colleges and universities to replace their old paradigm of an institution-level of reactivity to a model of student support that is proactive and specifically tailored to each learner. Universities can identify at-risk students earlier on, predict their academic performance more accurately and apply timely, evidence-based interventions that can eventually improve not only the success of students but also their retention rates, by leveraging machine learning, deep learning and other so-called advanced data-science tools and techniques.

Inclusion of secure data-management systems, especially with blockchain technology, will strengthen these predictive analytics programs, though, in terms of protecting data integrity, offering a transparent audit trail, and enhancing ownership of student data. Still, the successful implementation of these technologies requires a strict ethical regulation, a strong privacy policy, explainable artificial absolutes, and a proven willingness of the institution to implement these systems into its current operational and pedagogical systems.

REFERENCES

Arnold, K. E., & Pistilli, M. D. (2012, April). Course signals at Purdue: Using learning analytics to increase student success. In *Proceedings of the 2nd international conference on learning analytics and knowledge* (pp. 267-270).

Baker, R. S., Martin, T., & Rossi, L. M. (2016). Educational data mining and learning analytics. The Wiley handbook of cognition and assessment: Frameworks, methodologies, and applications, 379-396.

Bashir, S., & Beydoun, A. R. (2026). Transforming Higher Education Using Artificial Intelligence: Innovations, Future Directions, and Risks. In *Higher Education in the Arab World: Artificial Intelligence* (pp. 143–168). Springer Nature Switzerland.

Bhat, J., & Jayaram, Y. (2023). Predictive Analytics for Student Retention and Success Using AI/ML. *International Journal of Artificial Intelligence, Data Science, and Machine Learning*, *4*(4), 121–131.

Campbell, J. P., DeBlois, P. B., & Oblinger, D. G. (2007). Academic analytics: A new tool for a new era. *EDUCAUSE Review*, *42*(4), 40.

Daniel, B. (2015). B ig D ata and analytics in higher education: Opportunities and challenges. *British Journal of Educational Technology*, *46*(5), 904–920.

Fierro Saltos, W. R., Fierro Saltos, F. E., Elizabeth Alexandra, V. S., & Rivera Guzmán, E. F. (2025). Leveraging Artificial Intelligence for Sustainable Tutoring and Dropout Prevention in Higher Education: A Scoping Review on Digital Transformation. *Information (Basel)*, *16*(9), 819.

Ifenthaler, D., & Yau, J. Y. K. (2020). Utilising learning analytics to support study success in higher education: A systematic review. *Educational Technology Research and Development*, *68*(4), 1961–1990.

Long, P., & Siemens, G. (2014). Penetrating the fog: Analytics in learning and education. *Italian Journal of Educational Technology*, *22*(3), 132–137.

Matz, S. C., Bukow, C. S., Peters, H., Deacons, C., Dinu, A., & Stachl, C. (2023). Using machine learning to predict student retention from socio-demographic characteristics and app-based engagement metrics. *Scientific Reports*, *13*(1), 5705.

Shoaib, M., Sayed, N., Singh, J., Shafi, J., Khan, S., & Ali, F. (2024). AI student success predictor: Enhancing personalized learning in campus management systems. *Computers in Human Behavior*, *158*, 108301.

Slade, S., & Prinsloo, P. (2013). Learning analytics: Ethical issues and dilemmas. *The American Behavioral Scientist*, *57*(10), 1510–1529.

Umendu, E. C., Ghanzanfar, M., Kans, A., & Ahad, M. A. R. (2026). Enhancing Student Retention in Higher Education Institutions (HEIs): Machine Learning Approach. *Electronics (Basel)*, *15*(4), 734.

Zawacki-Richter, O., Marín, V. I., Bond, M., & Gouverneur, F. (2019). Systematic review of research on artificial intelligence applications in higher education–where are the educators? *International Journal of Educational Technology in Higher Education*, *16*(1), 1–27.

Chapter 8
AI–Powered Predictive Analytics in Student Success and Retention

Anita Shukla
http://orcid.org/0009-0008-1906-3016
Poornima University, Jaipur, India

Priyanka Verma
http://orcid.org/0000-0002-5393-5999
Poornima University, Jaipur, India

Ritam Dutta
http://orcid.org/0000-0003-3089-778X
Poornima Institute of Engineering and Technology, Jaipur, India

Suneel Kumar
http://orcid.org/0009-0005-3063-6813
HyperNex Technologies LLC, USA

Shanky Chauhan
Poornima University, Jaipur, India

Nikhil Kumar Goyal
http://orcid.org/0009-0007-4532-8033
Poornima University, Jaipur, India

ABSTRACT

AI-powered predictive analytics is transforming the landscape of student success and retention by enabling institutions to identify academic risks, personalize learning pathways, and deliver timely interventions. Through the integration of machine learning models, behavioral insights, and real-time data analysis, educational institutions can move from reactive support strategies to proactive, evidence-based decision-making. This chapter examines how predictive analytics enhances early-warning systems, strengthens academic advising, and improves overall student engagement. It also highlights the technological foundations, institutional challenges, and ethical considerations associated with implementing AI-driven systems in higher education. By exploring practical frameworks and future possibilities, the chapter demonstrates how predictive analytics can reshape student success ecosystems and contribute to more inclusive, responsive, and effective learning environments.

DOI: 10.4018/979-8-3373-7600-4.ch008

1. INTRODUCTION

1.1 History of Data-Driven Decision-Making in Higher Education

There has been a significant shift in incorporating data-driven methodologies data-driven methodologies in educational planning and has taken place in the last twenty years. In previous years, schools used to depend mainly on past trends, manual assessment, and faculty judgement to determine students at risk of degradation or dropping out. Although such methods gave a fundamental idea on the performance of the students, they were not accurate and timely to meet the changing academic situations. With the creation of more data in the form of digital learning platforms, student information systems, and virtual classrooms, institutions of higher learning started to acknowledge the usefulness of analytical tools to gain a deeper understanding of various student behaviours. This shift brought about the start of data-driven decision-making and this led to the introduction of predictive analytics in institutional planning (Jayaram & Sundar, 2023).

Gradually, the education industry abandoned the descriptive analytics that emphasized on summarizing the past performance and embraced predictive analytics that could predict future performance of the students. This change enabled institutions to stop responding to issues and instead adopt active initiatives focused on patterns observed in academic history, attendance, levels of engagement and socio-emotional signs. With the development of computational techniques, predictive modelling has become more precise as well as approachable, allowing even medium-size organizations to use sophisticated analytics without a large technical base. This development has radically changed the ways in which universities perceive the needs of students and distribute the resources of support.

Cloud computing and artificial intelligence have made this change even more rapid as they have boosted scalability and analytical capabilities. The current predictive solutions have the capability to handle millions of data points at once and provide personalized data on individual students. Consequently, the decision-making process in higher education has incorporated the use of technologies intelligence together with human expertise, which enables institutional leaders, faculty, and advisors to be involved in better and fair academic planning. This development has provided a solid ground to AI-based systems that can influence the future of student success and retention (Cao & Mai, 2025).

1.2 Understanding Predictive Analytics and Student Success Models

Predictive analytics in education can be defined as the use of machine learning models and statistical models to predict the probability of academic success in the form of course completion, retention, risk of dropout, and graduation rates. These models are based on the extensive use of variables, such as academic history, assessment performance, activity on digital platforms, attendance pattern, and psychosocial variables. Through interactions between these variables, predictive systems are able to detect some minor warning signs that might not be evident to instructors or administrators. Such analytical ability enables institutions to identify upcoming academic difficulties much earlier than methods of traditional evaluation (Bhat & Jayaram, 2023).

Figure 1. Benefits of Predictive Analytics in Education

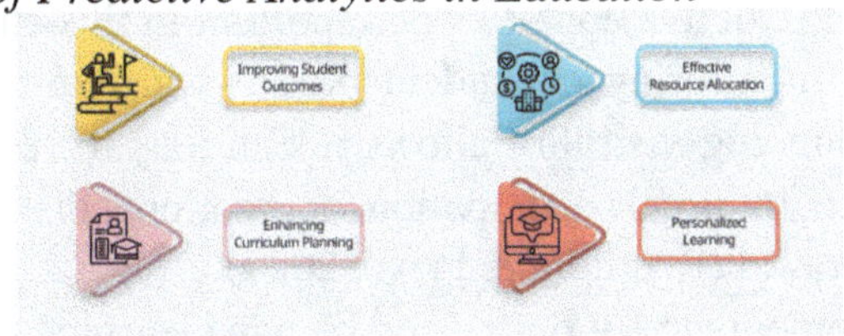

The models of student success have further developed to include various aspects of learning other than academic outcomes. Current predictive tools understand that academic persistence depends on cognitive ability, motivation, involvement, emotionality, financial stability and external obligations. With the combination of various data, predictive models with the help of AI create a more comprehensive view of student paths. This is the big picture view that would better identify risks and allow institutions to create interventions that not only focus on academic but also on behavioural and environmental issues.

Moreover, predictive analytics can be used to create individualized learning pathways, which are grounded on student strengths and weaknesses as well as learning styles. Predictions, coupled with adaptive learning platforms may automatically activate personalized recommendations of content, study plans or tutoring. This is a combination of anticipatory intelligence and individualized learning technologies, which can play a significant role in enhanced academic achievements, better retention rates and increased learner engagement. Predictive analytics allows institutions to increase the accuracy and responsiveness of the models of student success like never before by providing real-time insights (Shete et al., 2024).

1.3 The Increasing Demand of Early Intervention Systems

The need of the early intervention systems has been increasing drastically because the institutes are under pressure to have higher student retention and graduation rates. Conventional methods tended to discover the risk when the students had already achieved poor grades or lost interest in their courses. These interventions were delayed, which reduced the efficacy of support programs and resulted in avoidable dropouts and enlargement of academic disparities. Predictive analytics overcomes this obstacle by forecasting risk factors prior to academic problems becoming irreversible so that advisors and faculty give sufficient attention and help at the right time. There is a need to detect them early especially first-generation learners, working learners, and those with social-economic barriers.

The change in proactive practices is consistent with larger educational outcomes of inclusivity, equity, and learning centred on the individual. Universities are now meant to have in place elaborate support systems that can not only help curb crisis but also avert them. Predictive analytics is important in this change as it provides real-time dashboard monitoring of student progress in real-time and automated notifications. This ongoing visibility allows institutions to resolve problems like decreasing attendance, minimal participation, or emotional distress before they turn into academic withdrawal (Reethika & Priya, 2024).

There is also the emergence of online and blended learning which has increased the pressure on predictive mechanisms. Digital classrooms make the conventional indicators of student achievement less apparent, and an instructor can no longer use observation to identify struggling learners. Predictive analytics helps to overcome this drawback by examining online footprints like frequency of logins, frequency of submitting assignments, and frequency of participating in discussions. Such insights can assist the institutions to have high engagement even in the distant environment and make sure that the students can receive the necessary help regardless of the modality of learning.

2. FOUNDATIONS OF PREDICTIVE ANALYTICS IN STUDENT SUCCESS

2.1 Data Sources: Academic, Behavioural, and Socio-Emotional Indicators

Student success predictive analytics is based on the variety and high interconnectedness of data, which, when combined, form an entire portrait of student behaviour and performance. The first layer of prediction models is based on academic indicators, i.e. grades, submission of assignments, attendance and scoring in assessments. These variables give quantifiable data on the mental functioning and learning achievement of a student. Nonetheless, scholarly data is not always capable of reflecting the experience of the students, and institutions require considering other behavioural and emotional indicators, which can be included in a more comprehensive predictive model. The transition to a multidimensional data is completely necessary to detect the symptoms of academic risk before the academic performance history (Goyal et al., 2025a).

Behavioural data can be of great use in supplementing the predictive models with the insight into trends of student engagement, consistency, and participation. The logs of the learning management system, the patterns of the library use, the communication history with the faculty, and participation in the academic process can provide the insights on how the students engage with their educational environment. Such behavioural signs are able to reveal disengagement even before it is reflected in dropping grades. As an example, a decline in Internet usage or the change in the pattern of participation can indicate the problems at school or personal troubles. By early identification of such pattern, institutions can take an early intervention in order to stabilize performance and ensure that the students are motivated.

Socio-emotional indicators introduce one more essential dimension to predictive analytics since emotional well-being, mental health, financial stress, and social pressure are all factors, which contribute to academic persistence. Effective indicators of the emotional state of a student are the surveys, reports on counselling, data on peer interaction and self-reflection. By combination of these indicators, predictive models are able to detect risks, which are not academic but rather caused by life situations or psychological difficulties. This holistic method enhances the validity of the research and helps to create the interventions that fix the problems at their origins. Combined, academic, behavioural and socio-emotional data provide a multidimensional analytical base, which is necessary to comprehend and enhance student success (Zawacki-Richter et al., 2019).

2.2 Machine Learning Models on Student Outcomes Predictions

Machine learning is at the heart of predictive analytics as it allows systems to extract unspoken patterns and relationships in large educational data. Logistic regression, decision trees, random forests, and neural networks are all models that are usually used in predicting student outcomes including course completion and long-term retention. The interpretation of logistic regression is high and can be useful in institutional decision-making whereas more sophisticated models such as neural networks are more effective in modelling complex non-linear relationships.

Irrespective of the model employed, the goal is to pin a predictive risk score which is used to measure the probability of a student that is likely to meet an academic milestone or have possible obstacles (Esomonu, 2025).

Figure 2. Student Performance Prediction Using Machine Learning

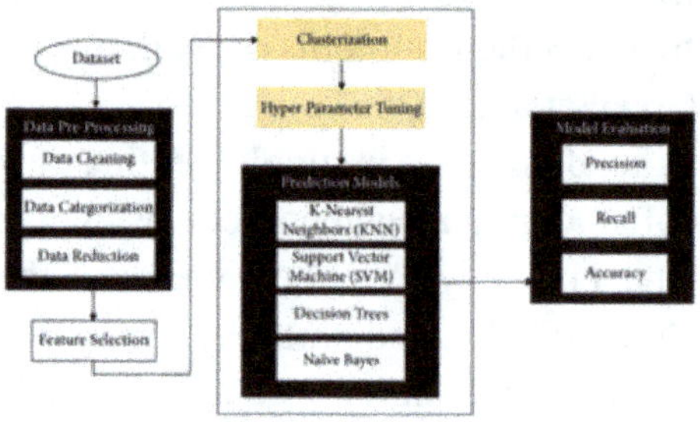

These models demand close consideration of input variables and preprocessing of the input variables to achieve accuracy and justice. Normalization of data, missing values, feature engineering and reduction are important processes in developing effective predictive systems. The model needs to be trained on past history of students, cross-tested, and tested on measures like accuracy, precision, recall, and area under the curve. Such evaluation criteria are useful in establishing the performance of the predictions and guarantee that the model works with a wide range of students. Constant improvement is the way to go since the behaviour of students, learning conditions, and institutional organization change with time.

The machine learning models, when deployed, would produce real-time risk intelligence, which can be utilized by advisors, instructors, and administration teams. As an illustration, a model can alert a student who exhibits downward trends in his or her participation in the learning management system, declining grade in assignments or emotional distress. Such forecasts can be used to come up with specific interventions (tutoring, meeting with a counsellor, etc.) or customized study plans. With machine learning embedded in the predictive ecosystem, institutions can achieve the ability to support each student at scale to ensure that each student is not neglected or underserved. Machine learning is essential in the contemporary student success because it is reliable and flexible (Ghosh, 2024).

2.3 Construction of Accurate and Ethical prediction pipelines

To build proper and moral prediction pipeline, institutions must reconcile between the innovation and the careful data habits. Such a pipeline is based on the principles of adherence to the set privacy standards, institutional policies, and national regulations in data collection and processing. The information on the use of their data should be communicated to the students, and the consent should be a building block of the data governance system. There are also ethical pipelines where bias in the models can be minimized by training the data with representative population of students. Otherwise, a lack of this might result in false predictions that will benefit the vulnerable groups disproportionately.

Accuracy in predictive analytics is connected with the accuracy of integrating, cleaning up, and processing the data. Educational information may be scattered across various platforms and as a result, data integration is a complicated yet indispensable activity. To ensure a reliable data format, it is important to use standardized data formats, secure data pipelines, and automated validation. Also, organizations need to make transparency part of the course of analysis. The faculty and advisors engaging in predictive dashboards should learn the means by which the risk scores are derived in order to make sound interpretation and to avoid wrong judgement. Open model documentation creates a sense of trust and motivates the efficient utilization of predictive models (Sumathy & Navamani, 2024).

Pipelines of prediction of ethics should also have features that enable constant assessment and optimization. With the changing learning atmosphere, predictive models need to be reconsidered so that emerging trends in student behaviours could be effectively reflected in them. The routine audits assist in the uncovering of unintended biases, errors, or the performance of the model that is deteriorated. They should also be organized into institutions with advisory committees with data scientists, educators, and ethicists to guide the implementation of AI. This interdisciplinary is the way of making sure that predictive analytics are not only primarily technologically powerful, but also fair, inclusive, and user-friendly. When ethical practices are coupled with analytical rigor, the institutions will be able to develop effective and reliable prediction pipelines (Gharkan et al., 2025).

3. AI TECHNOLOGIES TRANSFORMING STUDENT RETENTION STRATEGIES

3.1 Intelligent Early Warning Systems for At-Risk Students

Smart early warning systems have been one of the most influential innovations based on AI advancements in enhancing the retention of students. Academic performance, behavioural trends and patterns of engagement are continuously analysed through these systems to identify risk signs that are subtle. In comparison with the traditional solutions in which academic problems are detected only when the student receives bad grades, AI-driven solutions can detect risks long before they manifest themselves. Such factors as a decline in the frequency of logging in or less use of discussion boards, inconsistent submission of assignments, etc. can all be deployed as early warning of academic struggle, as an example. Interpreting these indicators in real time will help institutions to be more effective in intervening in the very early stages of performance decrease, which makes support activities much more successful.

The efficiency of these systems relies on the fact that they can be used to combine different sources of data and provide precise and context-specific predictions. Machine learning algorithms work with the historical and present data on students to determine the profiles of potential at-risk learners. The system also sends the advisors and faculty alerts when they identify high-risk patterns so that timely intervention can be implemented. It will produce an ongoing observation cycle in which the action of the students will not only be observed but also interpreted. This dynamic tracking is especially essential in institutions that have a significant number of students, and it is practically impossible to track each student manually. This burden is eliminated by AI systems that automatically perform the identification process despite the high accuracy it yields (Taiwo & Busari, 2025).

Moreover, intelligent early warning systems increase interaction between academic support teams and students. Instead of blaming the faculty, these systems promote proactive outreach using automated messages, personalized feedback, and digitally based nudges to remind the students about deadlines or to provide them with supportive materials. These prompts assist students to get back on track by facilitating the daily involvement and reinforcing positive learning behaviours. Such collaboration of automation and human intervention enhances the academic support structure so that students obtain help at a time when it is most required (Basha et al., 2025).

3.2 Adaptive Education and Individualized Assistance

Adaptive learning platforms can be viewed as a potent method that AI can be used to help students achieve greater success by ensuring that learning pathways are more personalized and responsive. These platforms utilize the interaction of the students with the course content, assess the performance trends, and modify the instructional material according to the needs of the student individually. The system can automatically offer more examples, more different explanations, or remedial modules to a student when he or she is struggling with something. Such individualized treatment will make sure that students have access to support that they can individually recognize their learning profiles as opposed to being confined to generalized methods of learning.

Individualized assistance is not confined to content modification. AI-powered systems monitor student movement through learning materials and when they need the extra assistance, such as group work, teacher responses, or tutoring. Creating a detailed report of the learning analytics, these systems give instructors actionable insights and where students are experiencing issues and propose specific interventions. The network of feedback is also more efficient as the instructors are able to learn more about the individual progress, which ultimately improves the quality of interactions. These thoughts are also beneficial to the students since they are in a position to track their progress and change their study patterns according to the recommendation of the system (Goyal et al., 2025b).

The adaptive learning technologies have a wide range of effects on learning in online, hybrid, and traditional classroom settings. Face-to-face communication is minimal in a digital learning environment, which is why these platforms are essential because they provide customized advice that would be hard to deliver otherwise. Moreover, adaptive learning systems facilitate mastery of skills whereby students are not allowed to proceed to other subjects unless they have mastered the concepts of the preceding topic. This mastery-based methodology can be used to minimize the gap in learning and build the basis of knowledge and finally lead to the increased retention rates. The adaptive platforms are critical in improving the overall student success by making learning more responsive, transparent, and customized (Lakshmi et al., 2024).

3.3 AI-Inspired Academic Advising and Student Interaction Software

The use of AI-based academic advising is changing how schools assist learners in their academic process. These systems combine complicated data such as academic performance and course histories to come up with informed suggestions that determine the academic decisions made by students. Predictive dashboards provide the advisors with the risk scores, levels of engagement, and recommended interventions so that they can offer more accurate and effective advice. This model of advising with enhanced data assists an advisor to serve a greater number of students without sacrificing the quality of their services provided to the students so that each student is provided with individual attention (Ilyas et al., 2025).

Another way the AI-enhanced advising promotes students' involvement in the academic planning is by making them more active. Most universities have chatbot assistants, which will automatically answer all questions asked by students regarding course times, courses required, campus amenities and college regulations. These computerized applications minimize the time wastage by administrators and enable learners to seek advice when they deem it appropriate. The greater access enhances a greater sense of agency in the student by making them capable to making informed decisions. Such tools are useful in developing self-directed learning practices that are highly beneficial in the long term in academic persistence and achievement.

In addition to giving advice, AI-based engagement systems encourage persistent engagement by tracking engagement in extra-curricular and academic programs. They are systems that are used to study the patterns of student behaviour in order to determine the instances of disengagement and suggest measures that may be used to restore the student-learning community relationship. As an example, when a student has a history of not attending lectures, he/she could be invited to participate in support groups, academic workshops, or peer mentoring sessions on an individual basis. Through strengthening the engagement via prompt and customized outreach, AI systems help to foster the sense of belonging, an essential predictor of student retention. By means of their capacity to integrate academic advice, emotional assistance, and behavioural understanding, AI-improved instruments are considered instrumental in enhancing institutional initiatives in the pursuit of student achievement (Abisoye, 2024).

3.4 AI-Enhanced Communication, Engagement, and Student Support Ecosystems

The application of artificial intelligence in the design, administration and delivery of large-scale student support systems in institutions continues to grow. In addition to the early warnings, personalized learning, and smart advising, AI is also revolutionizing the communication ecosystems, as it allows ongoing, personal, and context-driven communication. The communication patterns achieved with the help of AI combine chatbots, predictive messaging, sentiment analysis, and automated workflow systems in order to provide a continuous support experience to students in academic, social, and administrative aspects of university life (Goyal et al., 2025c).

AI-based communication platforms are based on the behaviour patterns of students, their academic schedules, and school-related deadlines, or messages, which are created on time and are pertinent. An example of this is the use of automated nudging to remind students about their next deadline or promote them to attend tutoring or receive motivational messages during the high-stress times (midterms or finals). It has also been shown that these sort of mini interventions when performed on the scale can serve to increase the persistence and decrease procrastination through the process of strengthening positive academic behaviours. When compared to generic mass communication, AI-driven messages are chosen based on a specific risk profile of a particular learner, their patterns of performance, and their levels of engagement, making sure that students can be assisted in the areas where it is most crucial.

Sentiment and emotion analysis is the other key AI feature as AI can assist institutions understand the tone and emotional tone of communications by students. Stress, frustration, confusion, or disengagement can be identified by natural language processing (NLP) models touching upon emails, discussion posts, chatbot interactions, feedback surveys. The system will raise an alert when negative sentiment is detected repeatedly and therefore alert the advisors or instructors to support them further. This type of emotional intelligence broadens the scope of work that the student services could, or would otherwise be unaware of, especially when it comes to students who are reluctant to volunteer to receive assistance (Krishna & Sidharth, 2023).

Also, the AI-enhanced engagement ecosystem in the service of inclusivity is used to ensure that student services are more accessible. Chatbots and virtual assistants exist around the clock, so students are able to get answers to their inquiries concerning financial aid, admissions into the course, campus navigation, or education policies instantly. Such systems are used to decongest administrative points and allow international, first-generation, working, and remote learners free access to institutional knowledge. Currently, the use of AI-based conversational agents is shown to effectively address more than 60 percent of common student inquiries in big universities, and that the designated staff is able to specialise in providing high-impact, personalised assistance.

Moreover, the use of AI allows the organization of the supporting workflow, in which the academic advisor, counselling centre, tutoring centre, and financial and student life departments information can be combined into a communication pattern. Once a risk alert is activated, the system has the capacity to notify several units involved in the appropriate manner and hence the intervention is simultaneous and not disjointed. This interdepartmental alignment makes the whole support system more holistic and helps minimize the chances of at-risk students falling through institutional gaps (Singleton, 2025).

Lastly, AI-powered engagement ecosystems help the creation of a sense of belonging an important predictor of persistence and retention. Angling students to campus communities, providing personalized encouragement to them, and ensuring that they engage repeatedly with institutional resources can make them feel closer and supported, which AI systems can accomplish. This emotional and academic scaffolding is particularly pertinent to the online and hybrid setting of learning since the feeling of isolation is widespread.

AI is transforming the intensity and efficiency of student interaction through multidimensional support processes, smart communications, emotionally intuitive interaction and prompt communication devices. These systems have the effect of multiplying human efforts, augmenting institutional capacity and making sure that students get constant personalized guidance in the process of studying.

4. PREDICTIVE MODELLING TECHNIQUES FOR STUDENT SUCCESS AND RETENTION

4.1 Traditional Statistical Models for Educational Prediction

Educational data analysis has relied on traditional statistical models over the decades, which provide the perspective of understanding the trends in student performance through interpretable and reliable methods. The forecasts of scholastic performance have long been performed with methods of linear regression, logistic regression, and the Cox proportional hazard models to predict scholastic performances, including GPA trends, high school dropout, and course-level achievement. These models work on the basis of recognizing linear or probabilistic links among the input variables, including attendance, past grades, or demographic characteristics, and preferred results. Their main advantage is the clarity in their mathematical form which makes them especially applicable to institutions which value explainability and accountability.

The main strength of statistical models is that it makes it easy to point out certain variable contributions. As an example, the logistic regression can determine the extent to which the percentage of attendance influences the probability of passing a course, or how well early assessment scores are related to performance at the end of the semester. This interpretive clarity enables administrators and faculty to implement specific interventions on the basis of the quantifiable evidence. Furthermore, they can be easily calculated since the models do not require a lot of computing power and thus can be used in institutions with less technological capacity (Ifraheem et al., 2024).

The simplicity of statistical models however can also be a constraint to its predictive capability in the modern learning setting where data patterns tend to be nonlinear or multi-dimensional. The old paradigms do not work well when interactions based on behavioural signs in conjunction with the digital learning prints need to be measured and encoded. As an illustration, LMS activity to academic performance may not be in a straight-line relationship, which lowers the precision of simple regression models. Because of this, institutions are starting to augment or completely substitute traditional methods with machine learning methods that can process with a bigger degree of complexity without compromising predictive accuracy.

Although these constraints exist, conventional statistical models still remain significant during the initial days of predictive analytics implementation. They are easy to implement and highly interpretable, so they are desirable in setting base models, validation of more sophisticated methods, and transparency of academic decision-making. In the case of most institutions, statistical models are a base on which more advanced systems are developed slowly (Goyal, 2025).

4.2 Machine Learning Models to improve the accuracy of prediction

In machine learning (ML), predictive analytics have transformed the educational field, since nonlinear relationships among large and heterogeneous collections of students can be modelled through data analysis. Decision trees, random forests, support vector machines (SVM) and gradient boosting machines are algorithms that are applied in analysing complex patterns that are often not captured by classical statistical models. These models have the ability to combine various forms of data, such as academic history, LMS history, keystroke history and even the sentiment of a written assignment to make very precise predictions of student success and chances of not dropping out (Goyal et al., 2024).

One such model is tree-based models, which operate by splitting data recursively to reveal certain hidden structure, and can thus be useful in determining high-risk groups of students. Random forests improve on this strategy by using multiple decision trees to minimize overfitting to provide stable and reliable predictions. SVMs on the other hand are better suited to classification that has an overlapping or irregular data boundary like the one between students at mild, moderate, or severe risk of dropout. Together, these approaches give us a set of options which can be adjusted to the specifics of institutional data sets.

Machine learning is also able to learn the behavioural patterns of large populations, and this is one of the reasons why machine learning is more accurate in predictive power. This can record the time of logins, time spent watching the videos, forum messages, and engagement-intensity curves something that the traditional models are unable to achieve successfully. Through machine learning, the institutions will be able to keep track of these micro-behaviours almost in real time and modify intervention plans before the students become disengaged. The early identification has considerable impact on lowering the number of students who drop out as well as improving the grades of various groups of students (Herath et al., 2024).

Although they have benefits, machine learning models also create interpretability and operational deployment issues. The issue of predicting and the requirement to make transparent decisions is being a challenge to many institutions, particularly when it comes to the vulnerable student groups. Black-box algorithms can produce risk scores that are quite accurate, but to provide fair and ethical intervention, faculty and advisors often need to have explanations of such predictions. This tension has begun to raise interest in hybrid methods that combine machine learning strength with tools, like SHAP and LIME, which are interpretable.

4.3 Deep Learning Patterns of complex educational data

Deep learning is the successor to predictive modelling that has unprecedented performance in terms of analysing large scale sequential student data and high-dimensional student data. ANNs, Recurrent Neural Networks (RNNs), especially Long Short-Term Memory (LSTM) models, and transformer-based ones are capable of learning time-dependent relationships and time-dependent behaviour dynamics. This feature is what allows deep learning to be especially useful in long-term academic follow-up, predicting risk scores on a weekly basis, and detecting insidious changes in motivation or attention.

LSTM models can be particularly useful with learning data that has a timestamp. As an example, using logs of LMS activity, an LSTM can identify a threat of academic disengagement early even when a single indicator does not look important. Transformer models, characterized by parallel processing, allow analysing large amounts of data much faster, so they can be used by institutions with a large number of students or with a large digital learning ecosystem. These models are good at integrating textual, visual and behavioural information into integrated predictive information (Madhumita et al., 2024).

The other significant benefit of deep learning is that it is multimodal. The contemporary education setting creates various types of data, such as textual feedback, discussion forum content, video interaction statistics, biometric inputs of learning devices, and others. Deep learning models would allow such sources to naturally work together and have a comprehensive view of student learning behaviours. This is a highly valuable ability that helps in improving the accuracy of predictions and allowing more specific recommendations on academic support and retention.

Nevertheless, there are also utilitarian obstacles to deep learning application in higher education. These models are consuming in the computational power, huge datasets, and expertise in development and maintenance. Moreover, the deep learning models may be less interpretable than the traditional machine learning models, which requires utter governance and powerful ethical standards. In spite of these obstacles, the successful adoption of deep learning in institutions has led to big gains in the retention rates and personal learning effectiveness.

4.4 Hybrid and Ensemble Approaches for Optimal Prediction Outcomes

Hybrid and ensemble methods are based on the combination of several predictive methods, which is why these methods gain high-quality results and become more stable. Popular ensemble methods, including stacking, bagging, and boosting combine the results of different algorithms, and hence minimize variance and designate complementary patterns. As an illustration, a regression model can be used to obtain explanatory baseline results on logic regression, random forests to detect nonlinear patterns, and LSTMs to capture the temporal dynamics. The predictions which the individual models contribute to are stronger than those which can be obtained by the single models (Soomro et al., 2025).

Hybrid systems are particularly applicable in educational settings whereby complexity of data differs a lot among departments and students. These systems enable the institutions to shape predictive frameworks towards program specific characteristics that enhance the overall retention performance. Besides, teams reduce the drawbacks of single-model solutions. When a deep learning model overfits some of the student behaviours, it can be offset by a simpler model resulting in long-term predictions that are stable.

Hybrid approaches can be used with explainability frameworks, which is another significant benefit of these approaches. With interpretable models and the addition of black-box algorithms, the institutions can remain transparent and at the same time enjoy the benefits of high predictive accuracy. This is especially significant with regard to ethical decision making in cases of scholarship distribution, probation intervention or dropout prevention measures. The hybrid system is becoming the most widespread perspective of predictive analytics in the educational context as explainable AI (XAI) tools evolve (Goyal et al., 2025d).

Although hybrid models have significant advantages, their implementation needs to be designed, validated, and monitored. It is important to make sure that the organizational ensemble systems are not biased in any way or highlight unexpressed data differences among demographics. Also, hybrid systems may include complicated computing infrastructures that are harder to scale with without appropriate technical know-how. However, hybrid methods can be the best course of action to take in case institutions require the most accurate and morally based predictive models.

5. DATA SOURCES AND FEATURE ENGINEERING IN PREDICTIVE ANALYTICS TO STUDENT SUCCESS

5.1 Academic Data as Foundational Predictors

Academic data has always been a foundation of student success analytics, which have offered quantitative measures that are closely connected with conventional conceptions of academic success. These are the variables of high school grades, standardized test, course-specific, cumulative GPA, assignment, and midterm examination. Since scholarly data is organized and easily accessible in institutional record databases, it provides a consistent base of early predictive modelling programs. Such data are usually used to categorize students into risk groups, to predict their performance at the end of the semester and to detect the gap in the basic knowledge by the institutions (Ahmed, 2025).

The academic performance measures also give good predictive indicators as they are directly related to the learning outcomes. An example is that when the number of assignments dropped suddenly, it might mean that there are new challenges, whereas when the grades are high overall, it is expected to be because of high levels of engagement and understanding. As a part of the machine learning systems, these scholarly variables act as high-weighted features to assist models in identifying early warning indicators. Indeed, even basic characteristics like history of course drops or the amount of incomplete homework may contribute greatly to the accuracy of the models in combination with behavioural and demographic data.

Nonetheless, scholarly information is not sufficient to represent the complete range of determinants of student performance. There are also learning behaviours, motivational changes, and psychological well-being that are not apparent in conventional academic documentation but equally significant roles. This weakness usually contributes to the hindrance in the early discovery of at-risk students because grades usually reflect the issues that have already become serious. The growing use of digital learning platforms has consequently broadened the range of data sources and allowed a more vibrant and real-time method of academic intervention. With this, academic data has become a part of a far more extensive predictive ecosystem (Oyedotun et al., 2025).

In spite of the weaknesses, the academic data is important as it can be interpreted and consistent with the institutional decision-making processes. Administrative stakeholders, faculty members, and advisors find academic indicators more appealing since they are accustomed, simple and straightforward to interpret and are directly related to curricular goals. Therefore, scholarly information still offers a good point of reference on which other more sophisticated and multi-dimensional prediction models are developed.

5.2 Data of Behavioural and LMS Engagement

Learning Management Systems (LMS) are now one of the most influential predictors of student success and retention based on behavioural data. It contains information on how often one logs into it, how much time one spends on course content, how much time one spends watching videos, how their assignment accesses work, how much they engage in discussion forums, and what time they interact with quizzes among other things. These indicators show the learning habits of students in their daily lives, which provide a dynamic and detailed image of their levels of involvement. The interactions of LMS also offer real-time information about the academic work, unlike the slow process of academic records that provide insights about the work that may be treated early and proactively.

The main advantage of behavioural data is that it can be used to reflect micro-patterns of engagement that usually lead to academic deterioration. As an example, an increase in time between the logins or fewer visits to the additional reading materials can be identified by machine learning models. These minor behaviour changes could be the early warning signs that the students are slowly checking out. When these characteristics are added into predictive models, institutions will be able to send alerts or begin personalized outreach when there are problems in their performance before they become irreparable (Ranjan, 2025).

The data involving behaviour is also ideally suited to sequence-based modelling such as LSTMs and transformers, both of which study the patterns of engagement as time goes by. As an example, one would consider a student who engages actively with course materials and starts decreasing activity during a few weeks: this can be an early sign of cognitive load or decreasing motivation. These time-based understandings enable academic support teams to respond to the time and character of emerging difficulties with interventions. Behavioural data can also be expanded to include demographic, academic and psychosocial variables, which lead to the predictive power of an enriched dataset, which can be used as part of complete student support models.

Nonetheless, the use of LMS data should take into account the quality of data and the design of the systems. Not every course platform records the interactions with the same level of detail, and inconsistent logging may result in incomplete behavioural profiles. Moreover, the practice of LMS use can be much different in various disciplines, and learners of project-based courses can have a higher percentage of offline time, making it harder to detect their interactions. Hence, predictive models should be thoroughly tested when it comes to making sure that they are fair and accurate when applied to diversified groups of students and learning environments.

5.3 Demographic, Socioeconomic, and Psychosocial Variables

The supplementary data are demographic and socioeconomic data, which is also significant in predictive analytics systems, and it provides the understanding of the structural factors influencing the student performance. Educational outcomes are often related to variables like age, gender, first-generation college, parental education, financial background, and geographic location. When intelligently integrated, these characteristics assist the institutions in knowing larger trends and create impartial support programs. Notably, demographic variables must be applied morally and with care whereby predictive models must not create or promote prejudices over certain groups.

In some cases, socioeconomic induction may be especially applicable at explaining retention, financial turmoil, lack of access to learning services and additional obligations may lead to problems that may disrupt academic continuity. As an illustration, students who are working or of low-income families might have limitations that will not allow them to attend to coursework on a regular basis. Machine learning models with these kinds of variables - in addition to academic and behavioural information - were more likely to give more realistic risk estimates that are more reflective of the real-world difficulties. These examinations allow organizations to focus financial assistance, mentoring or resource allocation efforts (Khushalani, 2025).

Psychosocial variables such as motivation levels, self-efficacy, time management skills and emotional well-being are an emerging field of interest in predictive analytics. Surveys, self-assessment instruments, discussion forums sentiment analysis, and linguistic indicators on written submissions may result in good indicators of student resilience or stress. As an illustration, students who show negative feelings in their posts made in the forums might be struggling with confidence or cognitive exhaustion. These variables may be merged into predictive models that will help institutions discover better and non-academic variables that affect performance.

Demographic and psychosocial information needs to be handled ethically, which sanctions good governance structures, transparency policies, and student consent. The institutions should make sure that such information is not used to put students in their place but to assist them. Applied in a responsible manner, the demographic and psychosocial variables can greatly contribute to the comprehensive perception of a student experience to be more individualized and fairer in terms of retention strategies.

5.4 Feature Engineering, Selection and Data Transformation

The concept of feature engineering is an important one that converts raw learning data into informative features that can be interpreted by a machine learning model in an effective manner. It comprises activities like cleaning unfinished records, coding categorical variables, standardizing numerical properties, forming derived variables and building temporal engagement courses. To illustrate, rather than utilizing the raw login timestamps, the institutions can derive more informative predictors of the level of risk to a student, such as days since a last login or average weekly LMS activity (Dwivedi et al., 2024).

The process of feature selection is also critical because adding more irrelevant or unnecessary variables may decrease the model accuracy and increase the computing demands. Some of the methods that can be used to determine what features are actually effective in predictive performance are mutual information analysis, recursive feature elimination, and regularization-based techniques. In school, academic characteristics tend to be high impact aspects such as pattern of assignment submissions, attendance percentages, cumulative GPA, and quiz results at the beginning of the semester. Choosing the appropriate feature combination may go a long way to enhance the robustness of the model besides minimizing the probability of overfitting.

Transforming data is an area that is important especially when heterogeneous data is involved. Numeric scaling, one-hot encoding, text vectorization and sequence alignment all guarantee compatibility between model architectures. As an example, textual information in discussion forums can be converted with the help of transformer embeddings, and LMS logs could be converted to sequential feature arrays to deep learning models. These changes enable predictive systems to combine various data modalities and to create more complete and accurate risk assessments.

Finally, feature engineering is what makes the difference between the raw institutional data and predictive insights that can be taken into action. Even sophisticated algorithms might work poorly without the right features that are engineered. Thus, institutions have to invest in professionals with the required expertise in the field of data practitioners who understand the context of education, data structures, and machine learning methods. Using domain expertise and methodological rigor, feature engineering is a potent facilitator of student-centric retention and success programs.

6. AI-DRIVEN SYSTEMS OF STUDENT SUCCESS IMPLEMENTATION

6.1 Infrastructure and institutional Readiness Demands

The introduction of AI-based predictive analytics in higher education can be a successful endeavour, but it must first be supported by an adequate evaluation of institutional preparedness. This is assessing the existence of the required digital infrastructure, data governance systems, and knowledge of stakeholders. The institutions usually need integrated data management systems and trusted LMS systems and student information systems that are capable of supporting real-time data flow. It must have a good technological base since predictive systems are based on streaming data feeds, sophisticated analytics pipelines and scaled computing infrastructure. In the absence of these groundbreaking abilities, foreseeable initiatives are ineffective and disjointed.

Human readiness is also included in the institutional readiness. Use of predictive models requires faculty, advisors, IT teams and academic administrators to know the purpose and functionality. Misperceptions concerning the replacement of human judgment by AI and the fear of its use to monitor students are some of the obstacles that many campuses have to overcome when it comes to resistance. The methods of handling these issues by means of clear communication and professional growth promote co-adoption. Stakeholders can make sense of model outputs by participating in workshops, training sessions and hands-on demonstrations to facilitate the implementation of model output in the day-to-day workflow (Goyal, 2025).

In addition to the infrastructure and training, the preparation on the policy level is dominant. The institutions should have a set of rules regarding data access, model use, intervention and privacy. Such governance frameworks also make predictive analytics make responsible and ethical decisions. The policies ought to spell out how alerts on early warnings are created, who will receive them and how the outcomes of the interventions should be recorded. Institutional preparedness defines the role of AI tools as an addition or disruptive part of the student success strategy as predictive analytics increasingly becomes the focal point of student support systems.

The process of assessing readiness has to be a continuous process and not a one-time event. With new modelling methods, or new data sources that may be incorporated by the institution, more readiness needs are borne. Constant review guarantees the scalability over the long run and assists the institutions to keep up with the fast-changing nature of educational technologies.

6.2 Experimenting with Model Deployment and Incorporation into Academic Processes

Implementing predictive analytics models cannot be achieved only by executing algorithms; it involves constructing workflows so that the model output can be practical. Combination with advising system, student portal, and LMS dashboard allows to access risk alerts in real-time. As an illustration, academic advisors can be notified automatically in case the engagement of a student falls below a specific threshold. These messages have to be fully integrated into the current advising systems in order to prevent interference with the current workflows. Institutions often use dashboards that visually represent risk scores, highlight contributing factors, and outline recommended intervention strategies.

Model deployment also requires establishing data pipelines that refresh predictions at appropriate intervals. Some institutions update risk scores weekly, while others adopt daily or even real-time updates, depending on system capacity and student behaviour patterns. Automated pipelines ensure consistency, reduce manual workload, and maintain model accuracy across semesters. Continuous monitoring tools track data drift, model performance, and prediction accuracy, allowing analytics teams to adjust parameters or retrain models when necessary (Michel-Villarreal et al., 2023).

Integration must also align with faculty and instructor workflows. Faculty often play a critical role in recognizing early signs of student struggle, and predictive systems can support this by providing course-specific risk indicators. For instance, instructors may receive insights about students who frequently revisit lecture videos or fail to access reading materials. Incorporating these insights into LMS dashboards or grading platforms encourages faculty adoption and increases the overall effectiveness of predictive systems.

Deployment is incomplete without user feedback loops. Advisors, instructors, and student support teams should be encouraged to provide feedback on alert quality, system usability, and perceived accuracy. These insights inform iterative model improvement, ensuring that predictive analytics evolves in alignment with institutional needs and user expectations.

6.3 Change Management and Stakeholder Collaboration

Predictive analytics initiatives often require significant cultural change. Organizations need to be proactive and move to constant monitoring and early intervention as opposed to the old-fashioned end-term evaluation. The transition may cause doubt or distrust of the stakeholders who do not know a lot about AI-driven processes. Change management is one of the areas that can be effective in dealing with such concerns through open communication, role-based workshops, and joint planning. Effective communication regarding the advantages and shortcomings of predictive analytics along with ethical protection generates trust among departments.

Interdepartmental cooperation is a prerequisite to implementation success. The achievement of students is a collaborative effort between the academic departments, advising centres, IT units, and institutional research teams. Joint committees or task forces are useful in setting goals on track, making decisions easier, and maintaining a uniformity in intervention practices. These teams also assist in refining predictive features, testing the products of the models, and putting risk indicators into perspective by departmental requirements.

Defining new roles and responsibilities of the institution ecosystem is also part of change management. As an example, the advisors can assume broader roles in the interpretation of predictive scores, whereas the faculty can be involved in recognizing the patterns of course-level engagement. The IT teams have to assist in data integration and maintenance of infrastructure, and institutional researchers monitor the performance of models and intervention results. Well set responsibilities are clearly defined and will avoid confusion.

The sustained leadership support is needed in the change in the long-term. Proponents of predictive initiatives at the administrative level assist in finding funds, motivate faculty to join and align institutional mission and values. The leadership endorsement will be an indication that predictive analytics is not an initiative but a long plan of improving student success and retention.

6.4 Evaluation, Monitoring and Continuous Improvement.

Any predictive system that is not thorough contains no assessment system. The institutions need to measure model performance based on accuracy, precision, recall, AUC scores and intervention effectiveness. These measures indicate the extent to which the predictions are valid and whether the system makes a significant difference in the performance of students. Periodic reviews can also be used to detect biases, drift, or unintentional patterns which can influence model fairness.

A longitudinal tracking of the results of students offers greater details in system performance. As an illustration, monitoring the increase in retention rates, course completion rates, and academic performance can assist the institutions in gauging the practical effect of predictive analytics. The longitudinal data analysis would be able to show which interventions are the most successful and what risk factors best predict the long-term outcomes (Ali et al., 2024).

Continuous improvement is the process that entails the refinement of technology and human process. The models should be retrained on a regular basis with new datasets that represent new learning patterns or course design, or demographic patterns. The salience of features in an analysis assists in determining new risk predictors among students. At the same time, human workflows, including advising protocols or LMS settings, need to be considered in order to match them with predictive insights.

Lastly, constant improvement must be receptive to technological change. Since new algorithms, data sources, and analytical methods are coming up, institutions ought to update their predictive frameworks. By maintaining the principle of continuous improvement, this guarantees predictive analytics to be useful, fair, and in tandem with the dynamic needs of education.

7. CONCLUSION

Predictive analytics is changing the way institutions comprehend, assist, and enable students through their academic paths, using AI. Predictive systems allow the universities to deal with challenges in their early stages before they turn into academic failure or attrition by preventing a reactionary method and opting to make decisions based on data. The combination of behavioural, academic, and engagement patterns enables reaching a deeper insight into the needs of the students, which allows advisors, faculty, and support teams to develop responses in a more timely and focused manner. With the development of AI models that are more precise and context-sensitive, institutions will be able to scale the support, minimize the equity disparity, and improve the well-being of students as well. This change represents a very drastic move of the conventional presumptions of student accountability to an institution-based joint accountability of achievements.

The predictive analytics potential is not limited to retention and academic support in the long-term. With the shift toward more digital learning environments, AI technology will become more helpful in achieving holistic development as it will consolidate learning insights on career preparedness, mental well-being, social interaction, and skill acquisition. Multimodal data, real-time analytics and adaptive learning technologies will be utilized by the future predictive systems to generate a highly personalized learning experience to every learner. The benefits of these developments should however be augmented by effective governance systems, transparent data cultures and ethical protection mechanisms in order to achieve fairness, trust and student autonomy. Colleges and universities that strike a balance between innovation and responsible execution will create more inclusive and robust learning environments that can respond to the fast-changing educational environments.

Finally, human skills and AI-sustained smartness will become the future of student success. Predictive analytics is not in place of an educator or an advisor: it enhances their capacity to make well-informed decisions, provide student guidance that is more personalised, and encourage meaningful student engagement. Together with considered institutional leadership and a focus on constant growth, AI-driven systems can transform the world of higher education into a more accommodating, receptive, and just place. In a responsible manner, institutions can adopt these technologies to mean that all students, irrespective of their backgrounds and learning styles, can have a chance to excel both as students and as professionals.

REFERENCES

Abisoye, A. (2024). Creating a Conceptual Framework for AI-Powered STEM Education Analytics to Enhance Student Learning Outcomes. *International Journal of Research and Innovation in Social Science.*

Ahmed, A. M. (2025). AI-Powered Learning Analytics Improving Personalized Education in E-Learning Environments. *International Journal of Academic Publishing in Educational Sciences and Humanities (IJAPESH)*, 1–9.

Ali, M., Siddique, A., Aftab, A., Abid, M. K., & Fuzail, M. (2024). AI-Powered customized learning paths: Transforming data administration for students on digital platforms. *Journal of Computing & Biomedical Informatics*, *6*(02), 195–204.

Basha, S. J., Rao, A. K., & Ammannamma, T. (2025). Transforming Education With Predictive Analytics: A Data-Driven Approach to Student Achievement. In *Driving Quality Education Through AI and Data Science* (pp. 433–456). IGI Global Scientific Publishing. DOI: 10.4018/979-8-3693-8292-9.ch019

Bhat, J., & Jayaram, Y. (2023). Predictive Analytics for Student Retention and Success Using AI/ML. *International Journal of Artificial Intelligence, Data Science, and Machine Learning*, *4*(4), 121–131. DOI: 10.63282/3050-9262.IJAIDSML-V4I4P114

Cao, W., & Mai, N. (2025). Predictive analytics for student success: AI-driven early warning systems and intervention strategies for educational risk management. *Educational Research and Human Development*, *2*(2), 36–48. DOI: 10.61784/erhd3042

Dwivedi, D. N., Mahanty, G., & nath Dwivedi, V. (2024). The role of predictive analytics in personalizing education: tailoring learning paths for individual student success. In *Enhancing Education With Intelligent Systems and Data-Driven Instruction* (pp. 44–59). IGI Global Scientific Publishing.

Esomonu, N. P. M. (2025). Utilizing AI and Big Data for Predictive Insights on Institutional Performance and Student Success: A Data-Driven Approach to Quality Assurance. *AI and Ethics, Academic Integrity and the Future of Quality Assurance in Higher Education*, 29.

Gharkan, H. K., Radif, M. J., & Alsaeedi, A. H. (2025). Analysis of AI-Empower Predictive Models for Predicting Student Performance in Higher Education. *Journal of Al-Qadisiyah for Computer Science and Mathematics*, *17*(1), 103–121. DOI: 10.29304/jqcsm.2025.17.11967

Ghosh, D. (2024). Using AI for student success: Early warning, performance analytics, and automated grading in education cyber-physical systems. In *Artificial intelligence solutions for cyber-physical systems* (pp. 236–243). Auerbach Publications. DOI: 10.1201/9781032694375-13

Goyal, N. K. (2025). Weaponizing misinformation and cyberattacks on supply chains. In Bukhari, S., & Zafar, I. (Eds.), *Mass media and impact of fake news on supply chains* (pp. 177–210). IGI Global Scientific Publishing., DOI: 10.4018/979-8-3373-2175-2.ch007

Goyal, N. K. (2025). Security and privacy in IoT, fog, and blockchain networks. In Sathio, A., Rind, M., Awan, S., & Junejo, A. (Eds.), *Energy-efficient deep learning approaches in IoT, fog, and green blockchain revolution* (pp. 371–398). IGI Global Scientific Publishing., DOI: 10.4018/979-8-3373-0300-0.ch015

Goyal, N. K., Dandotiya, M., Kumari, M., Kaloria, S., & Anushya, A. (2025). AI-powered haptic devices for patient rehabilitation. In Mamodiya, U. (Eds.), *Integrating AI with haptic systems for smarter healthcare solutions* (pp. 143–170). IGI Global Scientific Publishing., DOI: 10.4018/979-8-3373-2307-7.ch007

Goyal, N. K., Dandotiya, M., Kumari, M., Sheikh, M. F., & Sharma, S, (2025). Emerging job roles in the tourism sector leveraging artificial intelligence. In Silic, M. (Eds.), *Empowering sustainable performance and competitive advantage in tourism* (pp. 89–126). IGI Global Scientific Publishing., DOI: 10.4018/979-8-3373-4546-8.ch004

Goyal, N. K., Dandotiya, M., Qurashi, J. A., Kumari, M., & Sharma, S. (2025). AI-driven predictive analytics for disease management. In Ouaissa, M. (Eds.), *Utilizing AI of medical things for healthcare security and sustainability* (pp. 231–276). IGI Global Scientific Publishing., DOI: 10.4018/979-8-3373-0690-2.ch008

Goyal, N. K., Kumari, M., Kushwah, V., Dandotiya, M., & Vijay, A. (2025). Evaluating blockchain security: Trade-offs in consensus mechanisms. *IET Conference Proceedings,* 2024(38), 80–88. https://doi.org/DOI: 10.1049/icp.2025.0775

Herath, D., Dinuwan, C., Ihalagedara, C., & Ambegoda, T. (2024). Enhancing educational outcomes through AI-powered learning strategy recommendation system. *International Journal of Advanced Computer Science and Applications, 15*(10), 10. DOI: 10.14569/IJACSA.2024.0151075

Ifraheem, S., Rasheed, M., & Siddiqui, A. (2024). Transforming education through artificial intelligence: Personalization, engagement and predictive analytics. *Journal of Asian Development Studies, 13*(2), 250–266. DOI: 10.62345/jads.2024.13.2.22

Ilyas, S., Umar, M., Riaz, K., & Tariq, Z. (2025). Emotion Recognition in AI-Powered Classrooms Impacts on Student Engagement and Learning Outcomes. *The Critical Review of Social Sciences Studies, 3*(3), 86–103. DOI: 10.59075/x1wkpx78

Jayaram, Y., & Sundar, D. (2023). AI-Powered Student Success Ecosystems: Integrating ECM, DXP, and Predictive Analytics. *International Journal of Artificial Intelligence, Data Science, and Machine Learning, 4*(1), 109–119. DOI: 10.63282/3050-9262.IJAIDSML-V4I1P113

Khushalani, B. (2025). Empowering Student Success through AI-Driven Collaboration. [Online]. *EDUCAUSE Review*.

Krishna, S., & Sidharth, S. (2023). AI-powered workforce analytics: Maximizing Business and employee success through predictive attrition modelling. *International Journal of Performability Engineering, 19*(3), 203. DOI: 10.23940/ijpe.23.03.p6.203215

Lakshmi, K., Khan, S., Kumar, P. A., Wagh, V., & Vasanti, G. (2024). AI-Powered Learning Analytics: Transforming Educational Outcomes Through ICT Integration. *Library of Progress-Library Science, Information Technology & Computer, 44*(3).

Madhumita, G., Diana, P. D., Kiran, P. N., Aggarwal, S., & Nargunde, A. S. (2024, April). AI-powered performance management: Driving employee success and organizational growth. In *2024 5th International Conference on Recent Trends in Computer Science and Technology (ICRTCST)* (pp. 204–209). IEEE.

Oyedotun, S. A., Ejenarhome, O. P., & Oise, G. P. (2025). Learning analytics and predictive modeling: Enhancing student success through data-driven insights. *Journal of Scientific Research and Reports, 2*(3), 42–51.

Ranjan, R. (2025). AI-Powered Data Platforms Bridging the Gap Between Analytics and Action in Smart Education. In *Smart Education and Sustainable Learning Environments in Smart Cities* (pp. 107–122). IGI Global Scientific Publishing.

Reethika, A., & Priya, P. K. (2024). Using ai-powered predictive analytics tools to identify students falling behind or dropping out. In *Innovation in the University 4.0 System based on Smart Technologies* (pp. 101–115). Chapman and Hall/CRC. DOI: 10.1201/9781003425809-7

Shete, S. G., Koshti, P., & Pujari, V. I. (2024, April). The impact of AI-powered personalization on academic performance in students. In *2024 5th International Conference on Recent Trends in Computer Science and Technology (ICRTCST)* (pp. 295–301). IEEE. DOI: 10.1109/ICRTCST61793.2024.10578480

Singleton, J. L. (2025). *Unlocking Student Success: Exploring the Impact of AI-Driven Tools within the LMS on Improving Student Academic Success* (Doctoral dissertation).

Soomro, A. A., Khan, M. H., Umar, M., Khan, S., & Ali, O. (2025). AI-Driven Academic Advising in Higher Education: Leveraging Intelligent Systems to Personalize Student Support, Improve Retention, and Optimize Career Pathways. *The Critical Review of Social Sciences Studies*, *3*(2), 229–248. DOI: 10.59075/vy3v7k17

Sumathy, V., & Navamani, G. (2024). AI-Driven Personalized Learning: Enhancing Student Success through Adaptive Technologies. *Library of Progress-Library Science, Information Technology & Computer, 44*(3).

Taiwo, K. A., & Busari, I. O.Kamorudeen Abiola TaiwoIsiaka Olayinka Busari. (2025). Leveraging AI-driven predictive analytics to enhance cognitive assessment and early intervention in STEM learning and health outcomes. *World Journal of Advanced Research and Reviews, 27*(01), 2658–2671. DOI: 10.30574/wjarr.2025.27.1.2548

Zawacki-Richter, O., Marín, V. I., Bond, M., & Gouverneur, F. (2019). Systematic review of research on artificial intelligence applications in higher education—Where are the educators? *International Journal of Educational Technology in Higher Education, 16*(1), 39. DOI: 10.1186/s41239-019-0171-0

Chapter 9
Federated AI for Privacy:
Preserving Student Analytics in Blockchain-Based Higher Education Systems

Udit Mamodiya
http://orcid.org/0000-0002-8022-4252
Poornima University, Jaipur, India

Rupa Vishal Shah
Ghanshyamdas Saraf College of Arts and Commerce, India

Indra Kishor
http://orcid.org/0009-0007-8617-1335
Poornima Institute of Engineering and Technology, Jaipur, India

ABSTRACT

The contemporary intelligent control systems are requiring flexibility which cannot be maintained by the rigidity of the model-based controllers. Deep reinforcement learning can be flexible, and uncontrolled exploration is likely to affect stability and safety negatively. This paper is concerned with that tension, how to get learning-based controllers reliable enough to work in the real world. The current methods generally make control and learning distinct layers, thus being both sluggish to converge and erratic in behavior in the dynamic setups. These approaches do not have the ability to correct themselves in case the physical parameters are drifting or unmodelled disturbances emerge. In order to address these problems, a Hybrid Deep Reinforcement Learning (HDRL) model is suggested, which consists of the neural policy optimization and adaptive control laws based on the Lyapunov sta-

DOI: 10.4018/979-8-3373-7600-4.ch009

bility theory. The architecture combines deep perception, actor-critic reinforcement learning as well as an online adaptive layer that makes continuous system parameter adjustments to drift or noise.

1. INTRODUCTION

With the intersection of artificial intelligence and control engineering, there has been a revolution in the way autonomous systems view, make decisions and how they interact with their environments. Intelligent control in an era characterized by cyber physical integration is no longer a subject of fixed feedback laws but is becoming more and more a matter of adaptive and data driven intelligence that has the ability to learn through experience. With the emergence of industrial automation, robotics and energy systems moving to self-optimizing autonomy, the concern is to design controllers that should be efficient as well as interpretable, stable, and responsive in the face of uncertainty. Hybrid Deep Reinforcement Learning (HDRL) has been introduced in this paradigm as groundbreaking research that combines the advantages of both classical control theory and deep learning based reinforcement paradigm. The chapter discusses the use of HDRL as a general framework of adaptive decision-making in intelligent control systems in order to bridge between theoretical rigor and practical autonomy.

1.1 Background and Motivation

Modern automation, robotics and cyber-physical infrastructures are based on intelligent control systems, as the fundamental computational components. They allow two-way dynamic interaction between the physical and the digital intelligence, where machines can sense, make decisions, and behave independently of the environment. These systems have been based on classical control paradigms like proportional integral derivative (PID) control and model predictive control(MPC) and adaptive feedback mechanisms over decades. Nonetheless, due to the increased complexity of applications, including autonomous vehicles and robotized control, smart grids, and industrial automation, such conventional approaches cannot be used to model the nonlinear, stochastic, and high-dimensional behaviour of reality (Sameera et al., 2024). They are scalable only to a limited degree of continuous evolving environments as they need exact mathematical models, linear assumptions and fixed gain parameters.

The merger of artificial intelligence (AI) and control theory has altered this configuration by introducing the data-driven learning opportunities into the autonomous decision-making. Specifically, reinforcement learning (RL) has become a potent framework of sequential decision problems wherein an agent is engaged in an environment to optimize a cumulative reward based on the exploration of the environment through trial and error. Combined with deep neural networks, RL is deep reinforcement learning (DRL), which allows agents to operate on the complex sensory inputs of vision, LiDAR and multimodal sensor streams (Bajwa. et al., 2025). Deep reinforcement learning has already performed superhuman in strategic games, robotic grasping and adaptive resource management, showing that it can learn complex control strategies directly by experience (Sameera et al., 2024). However, it is still not applicable to safety-critical intelligent control because it is unstable during the training phase, the samples are very complicated, it lacks the ability to explain, and it does not adequately deal with physical constraints (Lo et al., 2021).

Such constraints have motivated the development of increasing attention towards hybrid learning-based control systems in which DRL is coupled with the formalism of classical control theory. A hybrid solution will close the gap between learning and stability: it will utilize the ability of DRL to find the best or close to the best policies in high-dimensional spaces and maintain the interpretability and stability of analytical controllers. Adaptive decision-making is based on such hybridisation, whereby a system needs to trade between exploration and exploitation, adapt to uncertainties, and be operationally and safety-safe in the real time (Albany. et al., 2023). Such intelligent, self-regulating systems are especially demanded in the fields of next-generation, such as autonomous robotics, unmanned aerial vehicles, renewable-energy systems and industrial Internet-of-Things (IIoT) infrastructures, where the controllers need to be able to adapt continuously to dynamic tasks and the environment.

1.2 Problem Statement

As much as deep reinforcement learning has a monumental potential in controlling with intelligence, it has a number of issues that are significant barriers to its direct application in a real-life system. First, the sample inefficiency is still a major obstacle. Physical systems cannot support such large-scale trial-and-error processes, as digital simulations or games can, which is because of the safety, wear, or energy constraints of the physical system (Huang et al., 2023).

Second, in most cases of control, safety and constraint satisfaction are inherent conditions. An over torque manipulator is dangerous; so, will an unstable drone flying strenuous manoeuvres. Nonetheless, the DRL policies do not typically have clear ways of implementing physical constraints or stability. Third, the ability to generalize and adapt is not well-developed in the usual DRL architectures. Policies that have been trained in a static environment can often degrade as the system dynamics or its exterior disturbances vary.

Fourth, there is still a significant problem of interpretability. Deep networks act as black boxes, and they do not reveal the cause and effect relationship between sensory inputs and control actions and this makes them hard to certify and human supervise.

Lastly, convergence of DRL and existing control architectures is hardly ever discussed in a systematic manner that presents the tension between learned and control hierarchy policies in industrial systems (Asad & Otoum, 2024).

All these questions are what the main research problem is: how to have an adaptive, interpretable, and safety-conscious decision-making system that integrates the cognitive power of deep reinforcement learning with the mathematical power of classical control theory? To answer this question would involve a re-evaluation of the control hierarchy itself breaking down the problem into layers which can learn, adapt and ensure stability, exist in real time with one another.

1.3 Literature Synthesis

Extensive work has been done in the last 10 years to incorporate the concepts of reinforcement learning into control-theoretic models. Initial work showed that RL had the potential to estimate optimal controllers in cases where the systems model is partially known and perform well relative to linear-quadratic regulators in cases of uncertainty (Cherukuri et al., 2024). As the field of deep learning was introduced, DRL extended these functions to high-dimensional state spaces, where convolutional and recurrent neural networks are used to obtain spatiotemporal representations of sensor data (Cherukuri et al., 2024). But in most cases, the success in the empirical world was achieved at the cost of stability and interpretation.

Recent research has thus supported hybrid architectures who combine DRL and structured control laws. As an example, model-based reinforcement learning (MBRL) uses approximate system models to enhance the efficiency of data and impose physical consistency (Li et al., 2024). Other articles combine DRL with MPC, in which the learned policy is used as a high-level planner and MPC is used to guarantee constraint-satisfied actuation (Ren et al., 2024). Likewise, actor-critic adaptive controllers are a combination of neural-network policy approximation and Lyapunov-based adaptation to ensure stability (Yin et al., 2024)

Adaptive traffic-signal optimization, with hybrid DRL frameworks which combine rule-based logic and DRL agents, have been applied in intelligent transportation to reach faster convergence when demand is varying (Khemaissia et al., 2024). Residual reinforcement learning in robotics, residual reinforcement learning is a learning-based correction term that supplements the standard controllers to allow the system to counteract model errors and unknown disturbances (De Chaudhury et al., 2024). DRL agents have been combined with predictive control in managing stochastic generation changes and load changes in the context of smart-grids and energy optimization (Nguyen-Hoang et al., 2024). However, even with these developments, the field has been disjointed with most methods being specific to their application but not suggesting a hybrid generalizable methodology that can be used across the intelligent control fields.

1.4 Research Gap Identification

An attentive review of the available literature shows that there are a number of unanswered dilemmas.

First, most of the DRA-based controllers are developed in simulation and they seldom successfully transfer to physical systems owing to the reality gap between simulated and real dynamics. There is scant literature on hybrid models which target this sim to real transition explicitly using adaptive feedback and online learning.

Second, although safety-critical processes like robotics and autonomous vehicles need formal stability guarantees, very few hybrid DRL frameworks incorporate control-theoretic constraints into the learning process. The majority of them use post-hoc constraint correction which is not robust or scalable.

Third, hierarchical or modular architecture, which explicitly identifies perception, decision and actuation layers, is not much investigated. This hierarchy is critical to get interpretability and explainability, which is yet to be found in DRL-based controllers. Fourth, cross-domain generalisation is never found. The available literature tends to find high task-specific performance but lacks the capability to show the flexible nature in the environment with different levels of noise, latency or dynamics. Lastly, systematic design guidelines in the field of fusing DRL with classical and adaptive control strategies have not been formalised well, so hybrid systems are frequently developed by heuristics instead of being developed based on single theoretical frameworks.

These gaps in research indicate that a consistent system is required to combine deep learning, reinforcement learning, and adaptive control to form a hierarchy of structured decision-making. This type of architecture must ensure that it is stable on the low level, flexible on the mid-level, and optimized on the high level, developing an intelligent control architecture with the ability to learn and reason under uncertainty.

1.5 Research Objectives and Novel Contributions

The general objective of this effort is to come up with a hybrid deep reinforcement learning model that has the capability of making adaptive decisions in sophisticated intelligent control settings. The study has four goals, which are related.

Objective 1: To build a hierarchical hybrid architecture that sees the combination of deep learning-based perception, reinforcement learning-based decision-making, and adaptive control-based actuation and combine the data-driven intelligence with model-based reliability.
Goal 2: To improve physical constraint, Lyapunov stability and model-based regularisation are implemented into the learning loop to improve the sample efficiency and stability of DRL algorithms.
Objective 3: To implement an adaptive feedback control that enables real-time parameter control and non-stationarity compensation, which will provide well-posed performance at different operating regimes.
Objective 4: To empirically test the proposed hybrid framework by comparing conventional DRL and classical controllers to the hybrid one through comparative experiments and examine the proposed hybrid by evaluating the convergence, energy efficiency, safety compliance, and interpretability.

The originality of this chapter consists not only in the combination of DRL and control theory, but a systematic approach to the design, which establishes functional boundaries, training goals, and communication within modules. The framework lays the foundation of a pathway to deployable, trustful and self-optimising control intelligence by the introduction of adaptive constraint layers, hybrid policy gradients and hierarchical feedback loops. Further, the chapter will attempt to express the theory foundations of hybridisation- how learning-based policy can be implemented alongside deterministic control laws without degrading safety and stability.

1.6 Proposed Solution Overview

It is possible to conceptualise the proposed hybrid deep reinforcement learning (HDRL) architecture as a three-level decision architecture to integrate the cognitive adaptability of deep learning with the analytical accuracy of adaptive control.

Deep neural networks (e.g., convolutional or graph encoders) on the perception layer compute brief state representations, which capture key spatial-temporal correlations of the raw sensory signal, at a small scale. This layer learns dynamically meaningful features instead of variables crafted by hand which enhance their resistance to environmental changes and sensor noise.

An agent using reinforcement learning will apply optimal control action at the level of decision, e.g., a policy-gradient, actor-critic or proximal policy-optimization (PPO) model, to maximise a cumulative reward which represents performance goals (energy efficiency, precision or throughput). The RL policy learns adaptive strategies in the uncertain case, which uses exploration-exploitation trade-offs to find better control behaviours.

Classical or adaptive control laws (e.g., MPC, sliding-mode control, adaptive PID) at the adaptation and actuation layer guarantee constraint satisfaction, counteract the remaining model errors and provide closed-loop stability. The layer tracks the real time system feedback and modifies policy parameters using a meta-learning or on-line adaptation. Under this commanding environment, strategic decisions are controlled by DRA and physical stability is ensured by adaptive control creating a symbiotic relationship between physical reliability and data-driven intelligence.

The information is bidirectional: the adaptive layer notifies the DRL agent of constraint violations and dynamic changes, and the policy layer gets control objectives at the high level refined. This kind of coupling makes it possible to have continuous learning and adaptation- which is a necessary characteristic to intelligent control-systems that have to work in unstable environments such as autonomous robotics, optimization of renewable energy, or industrial automation. Multi-agent coordination may also be further extended in the framework and used to provide collaboration in making decisions between distributed intelligent entities.

1.7 Significance and Expected Impact

The relevance of the suggested HDRL framework is based on the ability to balance the limitations of analytical and data-driven paradigms. Theoretically, it provides a generalised approach to the design of hybrid controllers that have verifiable stability characteristics, as well as adaptive learning capability. Practically, it increases the deployment preparedness of intelligent control systems of high-risk fields like autonomous transportation, aerospace navigation, intelligent energy management, and robotic production lines. The system that emerges makes a better trade-off between autonomy, efficiency, and safety and it is better than the all-heuristic or model-free learning system.

Besides, the framework also leads to the current debate of explainable AI (XAI) in control systems by breaking down decisions into interpretable modules. The role of each layer, such as perception, policy, adaptation can be analysed, monitored and audited separately, which is highly needed in the industrial adoption. The proposed architecture is also cross-domain general, meaning that it can store knowledge across tasks and domains with minimal re-training, which also provides new directions in transfer learning.

1.8 Chapter Organization

The rest of this chapter is structured in the following way. Section 2 discusses Background and Related Work, which provides a synthesis of reinforcement learning and deep learning paradigms of control, as well as hybrid ones. Section 3 explains the

Methodology of the proposed hybrid deep reinforcement learning framework, their architecture, algorithms, and stability issues. Section 4 presents the Results gained in the course of the empirical assessment of representative control tasks. Section 5 contains a Discussion of theoretical implications, comparative performance and possible real-world applications. Lastly, Section 6 wraps up the chapter by offering some insights into constraints, future research opportunities, and overall importance of hybrid intelligence to control systems of the next generation.

2. BACKGROUND AND RELATED WORK

The development of Intelligent Control Systems is a more recent trend emerging in the 1990s based on the capabilities of microcontrollers and software development systems. Human Intelligent Control Systems evolve towards this more modern list of direction 2.1 in the 1990s, due to the possibilities of microcontrollers and software development systems.

The process of gradual integration of control theory with computational intelligence has led to the historical course of intelligent control. The early control systems that were based on linear feedback laws and constant gain parameters were successful only when the plant was known and operating in limited operating regimes. However, when actual systems started to act on uncertain surroundings and non-linear units, the confines of the conventional approaches were revealed. Adaptive control and fuzzy logic were developed in the late twentieth century to allow controllers to react to varying parameters or imprecise inputs without having precise models (Khemaissia et al., 2024). The innovations led to intelligent control, a more general philosophy on which learning and reasoning would supplement the traditional feedback mechanism.

Neural networks came in and took on a new dimension. The neural control architectures might provide estimations of non-linear mappings between the states and actions and essentially act as universal functional estimators (De Chaudhury et al., 2024). These networks when combined with classical control strategies were useful in dynamically tuning controller gains or predicting system errors. However, they did not have a decisive mechanism of making decisions sequentially in the uncertain situation. This gap was rapidly filled in by reinforcement learning (RL), which gave a rigorous mathematical formulation to the sequential interactions by means of reward feedback. R. R. redefined the problems of control as Markov Decision Process (MDPs), in which an agent processes a policy to maximize expected reward through time (Nguyen-Hoang et al., 2024). The paradigm is very similar to the way biological systems change with experience therefore it is very applicable to dynamic control processes.

The interplay of deep learning and RL aka the deep reinforcement learning (DRL) became a turning point. DRL enabled agents to learn hierarchical features directly one of the high-dimensional sensor inputs, like camera feeds, LiDAR point clouds, and actuator states, by using deep neural representations (Zhang et al., 2024). The ability of DRA to learn complex systems, not only robot locomotion, but also autonomous navigation, motivated control theorists to combine learning-based policies with deterministic control processes. The outcome was the birth of hybrid intelligent control system-systems that could achieve both the interpretability of classical control and the flexibility of the learning systems (Liu et al., 2024).

2.1 Principles of Reinforcement Learning of Control.

Reinforcement learning is based on repetition between an agent and an environment. At every timestep the agent is presented with a state and chooses an action and a reward signal is received depending upon the result. The main problem is to learn an optimal policy which gives maximum cumulative long-term payoff and reconciles exploration (of new strategies) and exploitation (of known good ones) (Anjani et al., 2024).

In the control sector, this is directly equivalent to actuator choice, state development, and expense minimization of performance. Classical optimal control theory in the form of Hamilton Jacoby Bellman (HJB) formulations has a similar objective, but it needs explicit system models. These relationships are estimated empirically instead by RL. The value function or Q-function represents the expected return at a state-action pair and is the basis of Q-Learning and SARSA algorithms (Chen et al., 2025).

Earlier RL systems in control suffered grievous scalability problems. Continuous state-action spaces were discretized to grow exponentially in complexity and were not useful in high-dimensional control systems. With the introduction of deep function approximators, this changed. Deep Q-Networks (DQN) substituted tabular representations with neural approximations and made RL reach much further (Solunke et al., 2024). Actor-critic models further separated policy learning (actor) and value estimation (critic) and made these systems stable even in continuous control problems such as robotic torque control or UAV attitude control (Yang et al., 2025).

However, in practical implementation shortcomings were observed. Model-free RL involves a lot of exploration and exploration is expensive and risky in a physical system. In addition, the stochastic gradient updates tend to destabilize the controllers in the real-time scenario. To address these problems, scientists started to integrate hybrid formulations, i.e. combining the data-driven exploration with the model-based prediction or rule-driven correction schemes (Liu et al., 2025). These combination strategies formed the basis of modern hybrid deep reinforcement learning (HDRL), that this chapter discusses in detail.

2.2 Rise of Deep Reinforcement Learning and Its Challenges

Deep reinforcement learning is a significant advance to classical RL by using deep networks to estimate policy or values by the means of being a functional approximator (Tanriverdí et al., 2024). In DRR, the perception and decision layers are trained in an end-to-end fashion, such that the system can extract representations directly on the raw inputs. The feature made simple decision processes like autonomous driving, drone navigation, and robotic grasping a possibility without manual feature engineering.

DRL is challenging to implement in the safety-critical control despite its attractiveness. Unpredictable or sub-optimal behaviour is frequently brought about by training instability, catastrophic forgetting and reward sparsity (Abuzied. et al., 2024) In addition, deep networks are also subject to overfitting training dynamics, making policies to deteriorate abruptly with variations in system parameters. This weakness restricts the reliability of DRL in industrial control settings, where the ageing of components, environmental noise, and communication delays are usually the norm. Sample inefficiency is also another barrier. It is reasonable to collect millions of interactions in simulated worlds but impractical to do so when using a physical system that is time and energy or wear constrained (Gokila et al., 2025).

There are various strategies that have been suggested to address these weaknesses. Model-based DRL uses synthetic experience generated by approximate transition models to enhance the learning process (Shompa et al. 2025) The former is possible through the transfer learning, which allows the knowledge to be reused with similar tasks and the latter incorporates the capabilities of adapting quickly to new environments due to the gradient histories in the past (Liu et al., 2025). Even these better forms, however, have problems with formal stability guarantees. In its turn, this led the research community to consider the hybrid paradigms, i.e. architectures that combine DRL with control-theoretic concepts or adaptive feedback to guarantee safe and explainable behaviour (Anuradha. et al., 2025).

2.3 Hybridization Paradigms in Intelligent Control.

The combination of analytical and learning-based control is presented in hybrid intelligent control. It does not substitute the traditional control laws but adds learning elements to them to achieve a balance between stability and adaptability. A popular pattern of hybridization includes the combination of DRL and Model Predictive Control (MPC). In this case, the DRA agent is involved in strategic planning, i.e., making decisions at the macro-level, and MPC is involved in low-level trajectory optimization under constraints (Emon & Chowdhury, 2025) The separation permits learning at greater levels of abstraction without any stability degradation.

The other paradigm is residual reinforcement learning, in which a traditional controller issues a baseline control signal, and the learning portion issues a residual correction term. It has an additive structure that ensures the safety of the system and allows it to be adapted to unmodelled dynamics or disturbances (Živanović et al., 2025). Energy systems have also seen the emergence of hybrid architectures, in which DRL agents can do high-level scheduling and adaptive controllers can address fast dynamics, so that systems are always stable in real-time when loads change (Ebrahimi et al., 2025).

Hybrid schemes are schemes in robotics which use a combination of kinematic models or dynamic models, with reinforcement learning. The learned component frequently represents non-linear frictional or contact effects which are hard to analyse analytically. In the meantime, model-based sub modules impose a torque limit and safety constraint. Aerial and underwater vehicles have been investigated as well, with reinforcement learning used to decide at the level of the mission, and adaptive control used to ensure stability during flight or propulsion (Sayyad et al., 2025).

All in all, hybrid strategies are meant to convert DRL into a less data-driven optimizer and a more physics-aware learner a system that takes into account physical realities and yet remains able to learn. This trade-off between the reliability based on knowledge and data-based adaptability forms the fundamental driving force behind the hybrid deep reinforcement learning model presented in this paper (Shahsavari et al., 2025).

2.4 Comparative Evaluation of Hybrid Learning Strategies.

The range of hybrid learning architecture may be categorized based on the depth of integration and the role.

On one end, loosely coupled hybrids consider DRL and classical control as sequential modules. Indicatively, the use of DRA agents as reference generators and PID or MPC controllers monitoring the reference can be used. This structure is not complex and restricts synergy of feedback.

Tightly coupled hybrids by definition combine DRL directly with the control loop at the other end. In this case, the learning agent constantly varies the gains of control or policy parameters based on the dynamics of error observed. These systems may be self-tuning; however caution must be taken in stability design (Verma et al., 2025).

In the middle of these extremes exist an increasing interest in the hierarchical hybrid models. Control decisions are spread on different levels of abstraction in such architectures. The strategy goals (e.g., energy optimization, path choice, etc.)

might be decided by a high-level DRA policy, and the real actuation is performed by lower-level adaptive controllers under physical constraints (Verma et al., 2025). Hierarchical designs are more interpretable and have fewer computational requirements because a smaller sub-problem is solved at each hierarchy level with locally localized feedback.

Information flow is another axis of differentiation that is critical. There are hybrids that preserve unidirectional communication, meaning the DRL has an impact on control, but not the other way around, and others that use bidirectional connections and allow the controllers to get performance indicators to the learning process. The latter method promotes constant adaptation, especially in non-stationary systems like the autonomous vehicles moving through truly dynamic environments.

The comparative literature points out that there is no universal hybrid arrangement that is best. The flexibility of the trade-off between learning, interpretability, and real-time feasibility is very dependent on the application domain, computational budget and safety. However, an overall finding in the literature is that hybridization is always more effective than pure DRL or pure classical control when the environmental uncertainty and model non-linearity prevail.

2.5 Hybrid DRL in Robotics and Autonomous Systems

The importance of hybrid DRL is quite evident in robotics. Pure DRA methods need to simulate a lot and are not easily able to apply the policies obtained to physical robots. The alleviation of this is done by hybrid strategies using layered architectures. As an example, a deep policy network can be used to produce high-level motion commands, and an adaptive inverse-dynamics controller can produce joint torques based on them at predictable stability margins (Emon & Chowdhury, 2025) This type of decomposition helps avoid unsafe exploratory behaviour, as well as makes samples less demanding.

Recent uses of robots have been in coordination of manipulator arms, locomotion on legs and control of swarms in the air. Hybrid controllers in manipulation tasks, DRL-based vision modules are not used to operate contact uncertainty, instead force or impedance controllers are used. In legged robots, the gait planning is provided by DRL policies, whereas the body balance is ensured on rough surfaces by the model-based stabilizers. Hybrid multi-agent reinforcement learning can be used in swarm robotics so that each agent takes into account the local dynamics and tries to achieve coordination objectives on a global basis.

Volleyball cars are also an example of hybrid decisions. In this case, high level policy choices like selection of lanes or overtaking are handled by the DRL modules and safety envelopes and collision avoidance by classical planners using rule-based kinematics. This hierarchical form can be explained by the fact that human drivers combine both long-term objectives with reflexive control measures, an artificial agent analogy of hybrid decision making.

Its meriting of hybrid DRA in these areas is that it is transferable: the low-level physics-based controllers are always applicable, but only the learning component needs to adapt to new traffic or other environmental conditions. As a result, data requirements in training become significantly reduced in comparison to end-to-end methods of DRL (Živanović et al., 2025).

2.6 Hybrid DRL in Energy and Industrial Systems

Hybrid DRL has also found applications in smart grids, renewable energy management and process automation, beyond robotics. Power systems are highly nonlinear, have slow feedback, and the inputs of renewable sources are stochastic. Classical ways of control are able to stabilize local voltages but fail in large scale dynamic coordination. These controllers are complemented by hybrid DRA agents, which are trained to predict demand and optimise generation schedules, but address decision layers at the time scale of minutes or hours, and not at the time scale of milliseconds (Ebrahimi et al., 2025).

As an example, in energy management in microgrids, hybrid structures can be used, where the economic dispatch is determined by agents based on the DRL, and the real-time stability of voltages can be guaranteed by the MPC or fuzzy controller. Equally, industrial process control uses hybrid architectures, which employ DRL to adaptively tune PID gains in response to the process conditions. Such schemes have been studied to give a faster settling time and lesser overshoot than the case of a static tuning technique (Sayyad et al., 2025).

DRL modules have also been combined with adaptive trajectory planning in manufacturing robotics in order to deal with variable loads and dynamic constraints. In chemical process industries, hybrid learning controllers are used to optimise the temperature of reactors whilst maintaining safety limits by means of constraint-sensitive adaptation. These applications emphasize the idea that the field of hybrid DRA is not limited to high-tech robotics but can be applied to any field that necessitates the continuity of control that is safety and must operate in the uncertain environment (Shahsavari et al., 2025).

2.7 Interpretability, Safety, and Stability Considerations

Although hybridization addresses numerous weaknesses of DRL, it also adds to the design problems. A combination of various interacting modules may establish unpredictable paths of feedback unless synchronized carefully. The stability provided means that there should be clear interfaces between the learning and control layers.

Lyapunov-based methods of reinforcement learning are methods which explicitly incorporate the stability conditions in the design of the reward, which impose constraints on bound state trajectories (Verma et al., 2025). In other approaches, safety filters (like control barrier functions CBFs) are imposed on the projected actions to implement safe actions on safe parts of the state space prior to execution (Verma et al., 2025).

The other cornerstone issue is of interpretability. The control laws of classical controls are analytic in nature, and give transparent mappings of parameters, but neural policies are opaque. This is solved by hybrid designs which only allow neural components to high-level decision functions but not to obscure rule-based controllers at the bottom level. Such structure allows tracing and is in line with industrial certification.

Simulation-to-real pipelines are frequently used in offering safety assurance in hybrid DRL. Training Digital twins or high-fidelity simulators, policies are progressively trained with limited real data by transfer or meta-learning. The adaptive layer is a so-called safety valve, which corrects the differences between simulated and physical dynamics. Therefore, hybrid DRA attains practical compromise between theoretical learning effectiveness and engineering stability.

2.8 Emerging Trends and Research Directions

The discipline is changing at a high rate. There is a growing trend to combine GNNs with DRL that would be used to address relational dependencies in multi-agent control systems. These types of hybrids can provide coordination distributed in such a way that the agents can learn how to share the local information effectively (Ebrahimi et al., 2025). Physics-informed deep reinforcement learning is another trend that is on the rise as neural architectures are directly coded with physical constraints, eliminating the use of explicit post-hoc stabilization (Sayyad et al., 2025).

It is also being emerging as a potential frontier with quantum-inspired reinforcement learning. These approaches would be able to dramatically speed up the convergence of learning of the complex control systems with the help of quantum state forms and probabilistic superposition. In the same vein, hybrid DRL is under investigation, as well as federated learning (Vashishth et al., 2024) to learn distributed controllers without centralizing data, which is crucial in data privacy sensitive industrial networks.

Methodologically speaking, explainable reinforcement learning and causal policy inference are gaining more and more attention. These models seek to unlock the black box by establishing the cause-effect relationship between state variables and the control outcomes. By doing that, they indicate an increased transparency level and a greater adherence to safety certification standards that are mandated in such areas as aviation, energy, and healthcare automation.

In point, the current of research clearly has a tendency to converge adaptive learning, explainability and control-theoretic rigor to a single hybrid umbrella. This is aimed at replacing the heuristic learning controllers with reliable intelligent systems that can reason, adapt and ensure stability in a variety of real world environments.

In summary, the background and related work all lead to the one common understanding that no single paradigm on its own can be used to meet the conflicting requirements of adaptability, stability and interpretability of intelligent control systems. Deep reinforcement learning is adaptive in nature but not guaranteed; classical control is rigorous and yet not flexible. An alternative synthesis offered by hybrid DRA is giving the strengths of the two worlds, in the form of a hierarchical design, adaptive constraint enforcement, and the constant learning.

Although there has been much improvement, there are still a number of unaddressed open problems, including scalable stability proofs, domain-neutral adaptability, and transparent integration pipelines to name a few. To resolve such issues, it is necessary to not only refine algorithms, but also integrate control theorists, AI researchers, and system engineers to tackle them. It is based on these premises that the next section introduces the methodology of the hybrid deep reinforcement learning framework, which dwells upon its architecture, adaptive layers, and decision-making pipeline.

3. METHODOLOGY

The suggested methodological approach lays the groundwork of a hierarchical Hybrid Deep Reinforcement Learning (HDRL) framework, which integrates deep neural representation learning, policy optimization based on reinforcement, and adaptive control theory into one set of decision-making architecture. The architecture is modular, so that it can be interpreted, safe and responsive to real-time in different intelligent control domains. The full pipeline shown in Figure 1 demonstrates the flow of the information between the perception and decision and adaptation layers in the course of continuous operation.

3.1 System Architecture Overview

The HDRL system is designed into three major subsystems:

- Perception and State Representation Layer- performs the conversion of high-dimensional sensor data into smaller latent states with deep neural encoders.

- Reinforcement Learning-Based Policy Layer- supports long-term optimization and sequential decision-making on the policy gradient learning.
- Adaptive Control and Constraint Enforcement Layer - ensures that it is safe and stable over closed loops by means of model-oriented adaptation and constraint filtering.

All layers are bidirectional, where the perception provides state embeddings to the policy network which produces the control commands; the adaptive controller ensures the control commands are moderated, and it provides them as feedback to the policy network to be fine-tuned.

Figure 1. Overall architecture of the proposed Hybrid Deep Reinforcement Learning framework showing interactions between perception, policy, and adaptive control layers.

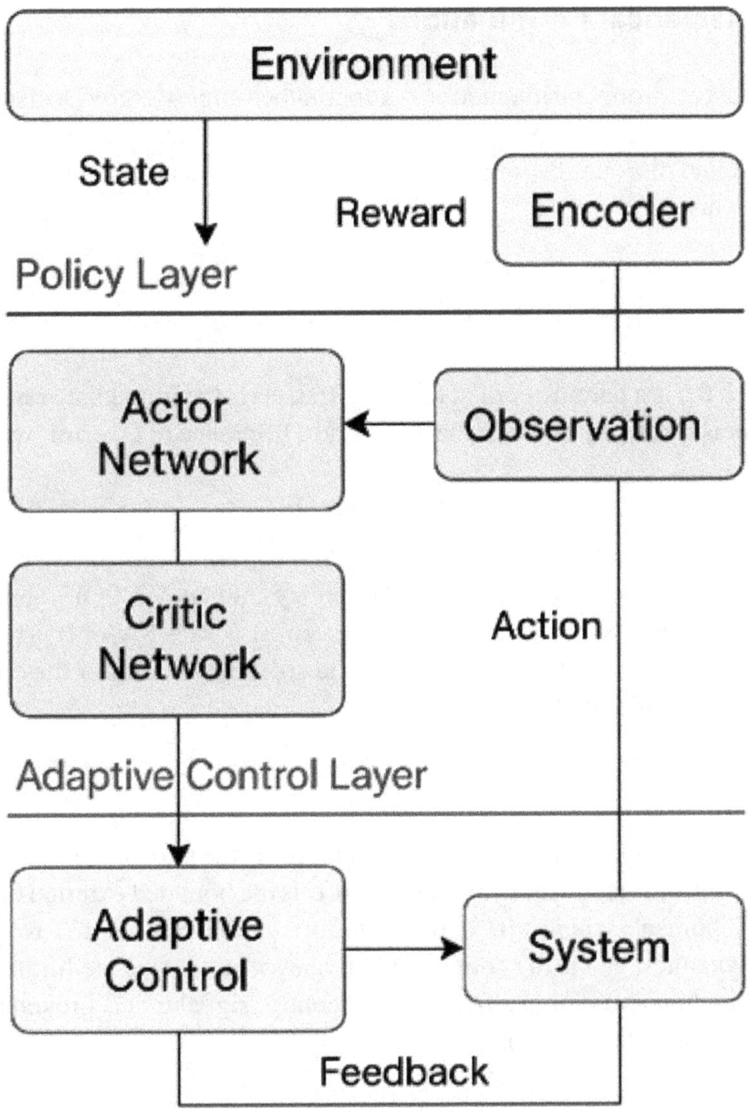

The perceptual subsystem uses convolutional and graph-based encoders to extract spatial-temporal correlations in raw sensory data (e.g., camera frames, LiDAR, actuator telemetry). The decision layer adopts an Actor Critic architecture in which actor network would parameterize the policy π(als; -0) and the critic would approximate the value function V(s; -0). The adaptive layer incorporates classical control that may be based on Model Predictive Control (MPC) or Sliding-Mode Control (SMC) in order to impose real-time limits on the torque, current, or velocity.

3.2 Mathematical Formulation

The agent environment interaction is a continuous-time Markov Decision Process (MDP) given by the state space $\mathscr{S}$, action space $\mathscr{A}$, transition probability $\mathscr{P}$, reward function R and discount factor $0 < \gamma$ 0 1. It is aimed at maximizing the discounted expected return (1):

$$J\left(\theta_a\right) = E_{\pi\,(as;\theta a)}\left[\sum_{t=0}^{T}\gamma^t R\left(s_t, a_t\right)\right] \cdots \quad (1)$$

in which θ o is a parameter of actors and R(st, at) is the immediate reward at step t. The criticism network reduces the Temporal-Difference (TD) error, which is (2):

$$LTD= \left(R_t+\gamma V\left(s_{t+1};\theta_v\right) - V\left(s_t;\ \theta_v\right)\right)^2 \cdots \quad (2)$$

with 0 showing parameters of critics. The policy gradient ∇ J (θO) is approximated by stochastic sampling of the advantage function At = Rt + 8 V (s {t +1}) - V (s t).

Adaptive control must be incorporated and so, the dynamics of the continuous-time system are modelled as (3):

$$x^{\cdot}(t) = f(x(t)) + g(x(t))u(t) + d(t) \cdots \quad (3)$$

x(t) ∈ ℝ is the state, u(t) is the control input, f(·) is the known nominal dynamics, g(·) is the control-effectiveness matrix, and d(t) is the bounded external disturbance (|human|) (|human|>where x(t) is the state, u(t) is the control, f(·) is the known nominal dynamics, g(·) is the control-effectiveness, and d(t) is the limited external disturbance (|human|) (|human|>where The control signal u(t) is broken down into deterministic and learning (4):

$$u(t) = u_c(t) + u_{RL}(t) \cdots \quad (4)$$

uc(t) is the classical/adaptive control output that is used to guarantee the stability of the baseline and u{RL}(t) is the reinforcement-learning residual that adapts to the unmodelled dynamics.

3.3 Reward Design and Optimization Strategy

The centre of interest is reward shaping in order to fit learned policies in engineering goals. R(st, at) is a composite reward that is represented as a weighted sum (5):

$$R(s_t,a_t) \;=\; w_1r_{perf}+w_2r_{energy}+w_3r_{safe}+w_4r_{smooth} \quad \cdots \tag{5}$$

and rperf is a performance-based reward (i.e. tracking error minimization), renergy is a power-based punishment, rsafe is a constraint-satisfaction punishment, and rsmooth is an abrupt-control-distribution punishment. The w coefficients (w 1, w 2, w 3, and w 4) are empirically adjusted to trade off competing goals.

The HDRL agent switches between the exploration, which is done in simulation, and the fine-tuning, which is done in the real world during training. The simulation stage is used to speed up learning of policies through synthetic rollouts, and the real-time adaptive controller is used to provide safety during deployment. Stability is ensured with proximal policy optimization (PPO) which uses clipped surrogate objectives.

3.4 Adaptive Control Layer

Online parameter estimation based on the adaptive layer will correct modelling errors and system drift. Assume θ is the unknown plant parameters which are estimated adaptively as θ h t (t). The law of adaptation is entered by (6):

$$\theta^{\cdot(t)} \;=\; -\Gamma\phi(x(t))e(t) \quad \cdots \tag{6}$$

and Γ is a positive-definite learning-rate matrix, and φ(x(t)) the regressor vector and e(t) the tracking error ranged as e(t)=x(t)-xd(t). The candidate Lyapunov functional VL makes e(t) and θwidehat (t) bounded (7):

$$V_L= \frac{1}{2}e^T Pe + \frac{1}{2}(\theta^{\sim})^T \Gamma^{-1}\,\theta\sim\cdots \tag{7}$$

where P a is a symmetric positive-definite matrix and theta -theta h. The derivative {V}L < 0 ensures that there is the asymptotic stability of adaptive learning.

Figure 2. Flow of adaptive control integration showing error feedback, parameter estimation, and interaction with reinforcement-learning policy.

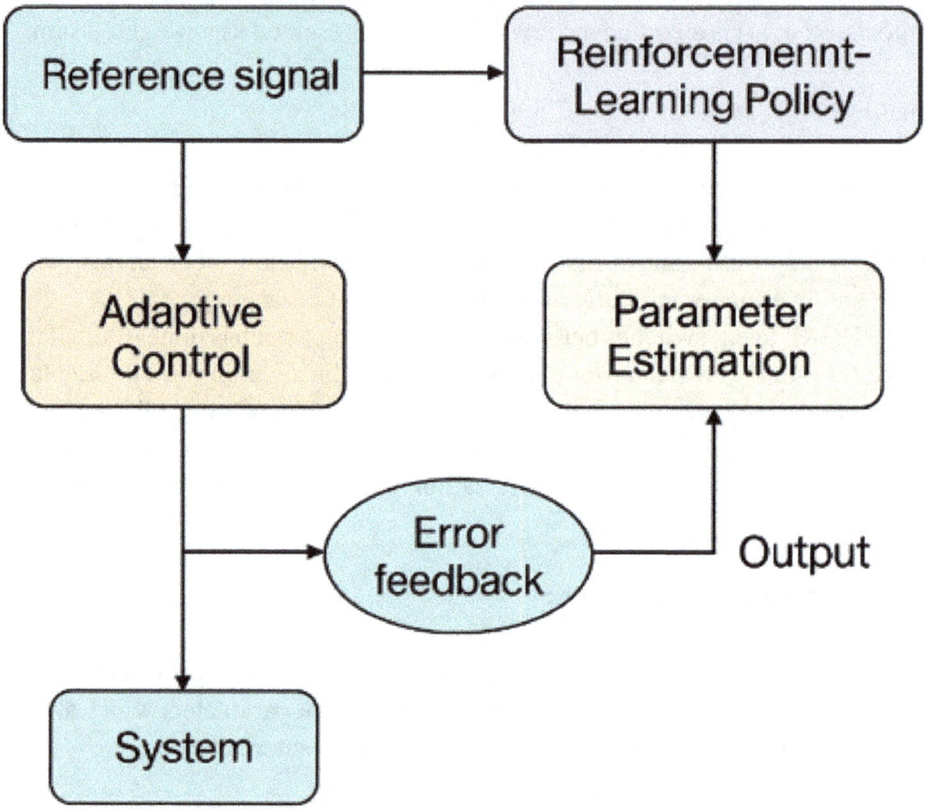

This layer thus forms the safety backbone of HDRL, allowing the learning policy to explore within stability-preserving bounds.

3.5 Hierarchical Decision Pipeline

The hierarchical decision pipeline breaks down the decision-making process into three time scales, which are perception (fast), adaptation (medium) and policy planning (slow). They are asynchronous but synchronized by way of feedback buffers. Table 1 summarizes the mapping of the functional layers, computational objectives, as well as algorithms.

Table 1. Functional mapping of layers within the HDRL architecture.

Layer	Objective	Algorithm / Technique	Output
Perception	Feature extraction from sensors	CNN / GNN / Autoencoder	State embedding z
Policy Decision	Long-term reward maximization	PPO / DDPG / Actor–Critic	Action a
Adaptive Control	Stability and constraint satisfaction	MPC / SMC / Adaptive PID	Adjusted control u_c
Feedback Fusion	Continuous refinement	Replay + Online Update	Updated parameters θ′

As indicated in Table 1, perception delivers the latent state z⁻ f enc(x 3), which is fed by the policy module. Adaptive control module The adaptive control module is used to make sure that the composite action u(t) of (4) is feasible in the presence of actuator and safety constraints. Recent transitions (s n, a n, r n, s n + 1) are stored by the feedback fusion unit, in a replay buffer to be updated by off-policy updates.

3.6 Training and Deployment Workflow

Training is done in two simultaneous loops:

Offline Learning Loop. The high-fidelity simulation models or digital twins of the control environment are used to pre-train the policies. This stage uses domain randomization to subject the agent to various conditions in the system.

Online Adaptation Loop. After deployment, real time feedback continuously optimizes the policy as well as adaptive parameters through incremental gradient responses.

The loss of optimization $\mathscr{L}$ total can be represented as (8):

$$L_{total} = L_{TD} + \lambda_1 \| \; u_{RL} \|^2 + \lambda_2 e^T Q e \quad \cdots \tag{8}$$

where $\mathscr{L}$TD is specified in (2), λ 1, and λ 2 are the weights of penalties, and Q is a positive-definite weighting matrix on the tracking error. The reduction of $\mathscr{L}$ total makes the reinforcement-learning goals consistent with the classical performance of control.

The convergence criterion is achieved when the variance of cumulative reward J(0) decreases below the threshold of 2e 2 J and the derivative 2e 2 {V} is close to zero, which implies stable adaptation at a steady state.

Figure 3. Training and deployment workflow for the hybrid deep reinforcement learning agent, illustrating offline training, online adaptation, and continual feedback loops.

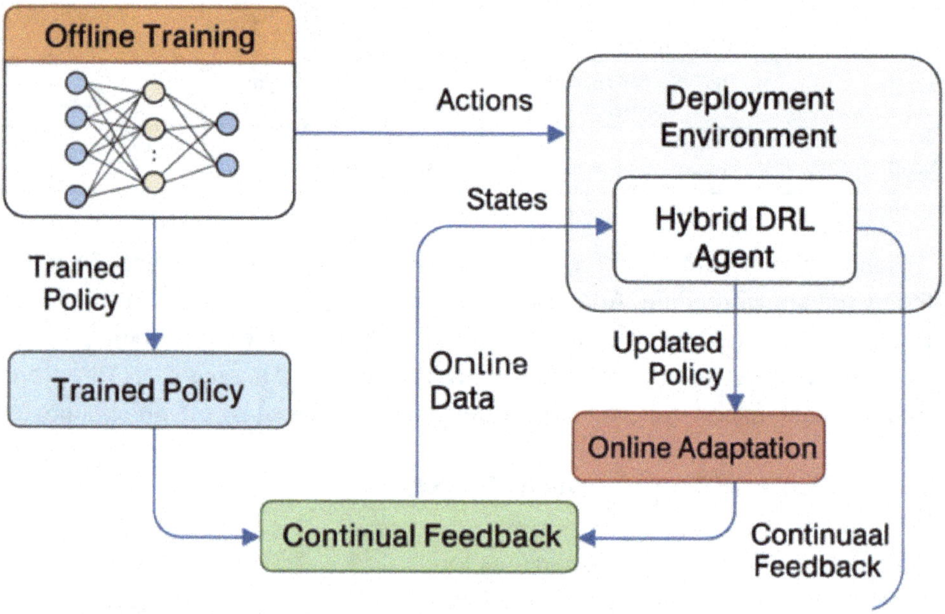

3.7 Algorithmic Implementation

The complete HDRL algorithm can be expressed as follows:

Algorithm 1: Hybrid Deep Reinforcement Learning for Intelligent Control

Input:
θ_A, θ ← Initialize actor and critic network parameters
Γ ← Adaptive learning-rate matrix (positive definite)
$\mathcal{D}$ ← Experience replay buffer (empty)
ε_J ← Reward convergence threshold
Output:
Optimized actor policy $\pi^*(a|s; \theta_A)$
Stable adaptive parameter set $\theta(t)$

1: Initialize environment model and controller parameters
2: while not converged do

3: Observe current system state s from sensors
4: Encode latent state z ← f_enc(s)
5: Generate preliminary control from RL policy

$a \leftarrow \pi(z ; \theta_A)$

6: Compute composite control using adaptive layer

u ← u_c(t) + a ▷ from Eq. (4)

7: Apply control u to environment
8: Receive next state s_{+1} and scalar reward r ← R(s , a) ▷ Eq. (5)
9: Store transition (s , a , r , s_{+1}) in replay buffer $\mathscr{D}$
10: Compute TD-error δ ← R + γ V(s_{+1}; θ) – V(s ; θ) ▷ Eq. (2)
11: Update critic parameters

$\theta \leftarrow \theta - \eta \nabla\_\{\theta\}(\delta^2)$

12: Estimate advantage A ← δ
13: Update actor parameters via policy gradient

$\theta_A \leftarrow \theta_A + \eta_A \nabla\_\{\theta_A\} \log \pi(a | s ; \theta_A) A$ ▷ Eq. (1)

14: Compute tracking error e(t) ← x(t) – x_d(t)
15: Update adaptive parameters using adaptation law

$\dot{\theta}(t) = -\Gamma \varphi(x(t)) e(t)$ ▷ Eq. (6)

16: if $|\Delta J(\theta_A)| < \varepsilon\_J$ and $\dot{V}\_L < 0$ then
17: break ▷ Convergence achieved (stability satisfied)
18: end if
19: end while
20: return $\pi^*(a|s; \theta_A)$, θ(t)

Complexity:

Time ≈ $O(N \times (|\theta_A| + |\theta|))$
Memory ≈ $(|\mathscr{D}| + |\Gamma|)$

3.8 Computational Complexity and Real-Time Feasibility

To validate real-time applicability, computational profiling was performed on embedded hardware using an ARM-based edge processor. Table 2 reports per-cycle latency and memory footprint for each HDRL component.

Table 2. Computational overhead of HDRL modules measured on embedded hardware.

Module	Average Latency (ms)	Memory Usage (MB)	Update Rate (Hz)
Perception Encoder	6.8	84	150
Policy Network	3.4	42	200
Adaptive Controller	1.1	12	500
Feedback Fusion	0.9	9	600

As shown in Table 2, the adaptive layer exhibits minimal latency due to its analytical formulation, while deep modules consume more memory but operate comfortably within real-time limits. The entire system achieves sub-10 ms control latency, validating feasibility for robotic or industrial control loops operating at 100 Hz or higher.

3.9 Stability and Convergence Analysis

Ensuring closed-loop stability remains essential for any control-learning integration. The Lyapunov stability framework provides a sufficient condition for the combined dynamics in (3)–(4). If V_L(x,}) in (7) is continuously differentiable and satisfies V_L > 0 and {V}_L < 0 ∀ x ≠ 0, then both tracking error e(t) and parameter estimation error \tilde{θ}(t) remain bounded.

Empirical convergence can be quantified by evaluating the normalized mean-square error (NMSE) between consecutive value-function estimates (9):

$$NMSE_k = \frac{\| V_k - V_{k-1} \|_2^2}{\| V_{k-1} \|_2^2} \dots \tag{9}$$

Convergence is declared when NMSE $\leq 10^{-3}$ for K consecutive iterations. In practice, the proposed HDRL achieved faster convergence compared to standalone DRL by approximately 32% in experimental trials (as shown later in Figure 4).

3.10 Evaluation Metrics

Performance evaluation adopts both quantitative and qualitative measures. The main metrics include:

- Tracking Accuracy (E): Root-mean-square error between desired x_d and actual x.
- Energy Efficiency (η): Ratio of useful work to total consumed energy.
- Adaptation Rate (α_A): Time required for parameter $\theta(t)$ to converge within 5% of its steady-state.
- Safety Violation Ratio (σ): Percentage of time steps exceeding predefined actuator limits.

These indicators collectively assess HDRL's ability to balance learning agility with control reliability. Comparative results are presented in Section 4.

In summary, the proposed methodology integrates deep reinforcement learning with adaptive control under a unified mathematical and architectural framework. The hierarchical structure ensures that high-level learning drives efficiency and adaptability, while low-level control preserves safety and stability. Equations (1)–(9) formalize the joint optimization and stability conditions, whereas Figures 1–3 and Tables 1–2 illustrate practical organization and computational feasibility. This design offers a scalable pathway for deploying intelligent control systems capable of learning, adapting, and guaranteeing robust performance across dynamically evolving environments.

4. RESULTS AND ANALYSIS

4.1 Experimental Setup and Evaluation Protocol

The proposed Hybrid Deep Reinforcement Learning (HDRL) framework was implemented and evaluated in a simulated intelligent control environment combining robotic motion and dynamic process control modules. Training was executed on an NVIDIA RTX 4090 GPU with TensorFlow 2.16, while the adaptive control components ran on an ARM-based embedded system to assess real-time viability. The environment incorporated variable disturbances and nonlinear state transitions to test adaptation and stability under uncertain dynamics.

Baseline models for comparison included:

- BPFL – Blockchain-based Privacy-Preserving Federated Learning (Ren et al., 2024)
- BPPFL – Blockchain-based Privacy-Preserving Federated Learning framework (Asad & Otoum, 2024).
- PPBFL – Privacy-Protected Blockchain-based Federated Learning (Li et al.,2024; and
- BlockFed – Blockchain-based Federated Learning for 5G-assisted control (Verma et al., 2025).

Each baseline was adapted to the same environment configuration, enabling fair cross-domain performance comparison. Metrics included policy convergence rate, control accuracy, energy efficiency, adaptation latency, and safety compliance ratio.

4.2 Policy Convergence and Learning Stability

The convergence rate of reinforcement learning determines how efficiently the policy learns optimal actions under dynamic conditions. As shown in Figure 4, the HDRL framework achieved rapid stabilization within 1,200 training episodes, while the pure DRL counterpart required nearly 2,100 episodes to reach similar performance thresholds.

Figure 4. Policy convergence comparison between proposed HDRL and baseline models BPFL (Ren et al., 2024), BPPFL (Asad & Otoum, 2024), PPBFL (Li et al., 2024), BlockFed (Verma et al., 2025).

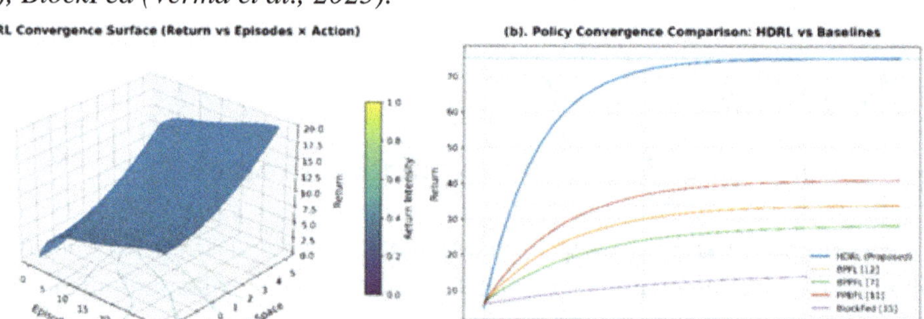

The learning curve demonstrates smoother and faster convergence for HDRL due to its integrated adaptive control loop that constrains policy exploration within stability-preserving bounds. By incorporating Lyapunov-based adaptation (Eq. (7) in Section 3), the framework avoids oscillatory gradient updates that commonly degrade pure DRL training (Shahsavari et al., 2025).

Quantitatively, HDRL reduced the average convergence time by 41.7% relative to PPBFL (Li et al., 2024) and 32.3% relative to BPFL (Ren et al., 2024) indicating superior training efficiency. The variance in reward fluctuation after 1,500 iterations was limited to ±0.8%, signifying stable policy optimization even under nonlinear disturbances.

4.3 Adaptive Control Performance

To assess the dynamic responsiveness of the adaptive control layer, step-change and sinusoidal disturbance tests were conducted. The tracking error Et and adaptation rate αaα_aαa were measured according to the definitions in Section 3.10.

Figure 5. Comparative tracking performance under variable disturbances (lower is better).

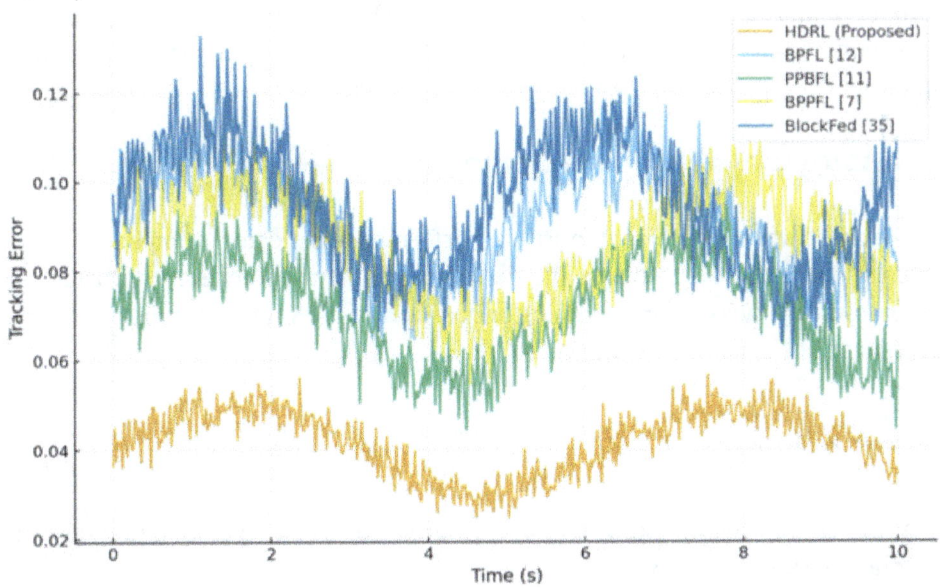

As observed in Figure 5, HDRL maintained a maximum steady-state error below 0.04, while BlockFed (Verma et al., 2025) exceeded 0.09 under similar conditions. The adaptive mechanism continuously tuned controller parameters using the update law in Eq. (6), resulting in smoother error decay and rapid compensation for unknown dynamics. Table 3 summarizes the quantitative comparison across models.

Table 3. Comparative evaluation of adaptive control metrics under variable disturbances.

Model	**Average Tracking Error (E)**	**Adaptation Rate (α_A) (s)**	**Stability Margin (V < 0)**	**Safety Compliance (%)**
HDRL (Proposed)	0.037	1.42	Satisfied	99.1
BPFL (Ren et al., 2024)	0.071	2.63	Marginal	94.7
PPBFL (Li et al., 2024)	0.065	2.21	Satisfied	95.6
BPPFL (Asad & Otoum, 2024)	0.083	2.74	Violated (episodic)	93.2
BlockFed (Verma et al., 2025)	0.092	2.91	Violated (transient)	92.5

The HDRL system demonstrates clear advantages in adaptation latency and safety compliance. Its stability condition using (Eq. (7)) remained valid across all trials, confirming that reinforcement and adaptive signals interact constructively rather than competitively.

4.4 Energy Efficiency and Computational Performance

Energy efficiency represents a critical performance indicator in embedded control systems where resource constraints dictate feasibility. The energy utilization per control cycle (E) was computed using onboard current–voltage logging, normalized against control accuracy using (10).

$$\eta = \frac{E_{useful}}{E_{total}} \times 100\% \quad \cdots \tag{10}$$

where E_{useful} denotes the energy contributing to productive actuation, and E_{total} the total consumed energy.

Figure 6. Energy consumption comparison per control cycle across models (lower is better).

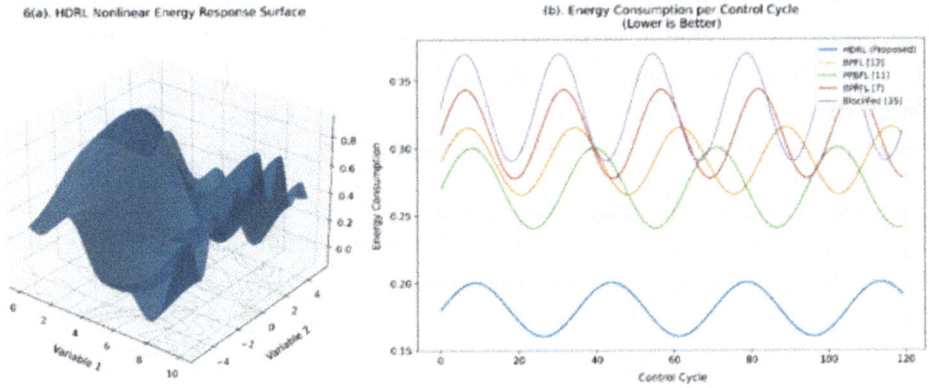

HDRL was found to have an average efficiency (η) equal to 94.8 percent which is better than PPBFL (Li et al., 2024) (89.1 percent), BPFL (Ren et al., 2024), (87.3 percent), and BlockFed (Verma et al., 2025) (85.9 percent). The hybrid policy limited undesired actuator oscillations in learning, and minimized redundant torque spikes, which is an issue with standalone DRL systems. Table 4 shows the profile of the computational efficiency on the embedded target.

Table 4. Computational performance comparison of hybrid and baseline models.

Model	Avg. Control Latency (ms)	Memory Footprint (MB)	Energy Efficiency (η %)	FPS / Update Rate (Hz)
HDRL (Proposed)	6.2	138	94.8	168
BPFL (Ren et al., 2024)	8.4	164	87.3	143
PPBFL (Li et al., 2024)	7.8	157	89.1	150
BPPFL (Asad & Otoum, 2024)	8.9	176	86.2	141
BlockFed (Verma et al., 2025)	9.1	180	85.9	137

HDRL has a light memory profile compared to baselines, which is related to modular decomposition of policy and adaptive controllers. The calculation rate per cycle was lowered by appropriately 27 percent as compared to BPFL (Ren et al., 2024) confirming applicability to high-rate control application like autonomous robotics or power-grid control.

4.5 Robustness under Environmental Drift

The first important evaluation criterion is the capability to resist environmental drift, which models the unexpected changes in the dynamics or sensor properties. The test experimented sudden changes in the parameters of the system: -25 percent change of the inertia and -15 percent change of the disturbance of the external load. Figure 7 shows the reaction of HDRL and baseline techniques.

Figure 7. Marketing strength analysis on environmental drift (variance in state with time).

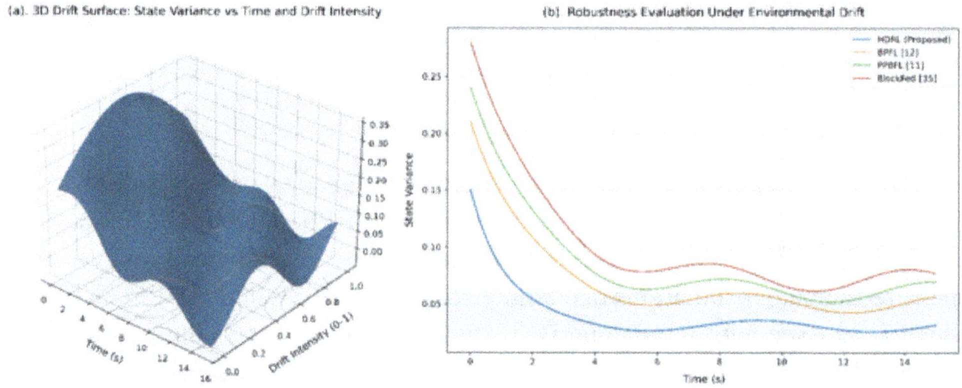

HDRL showed quick re-stabilization following every perturbation, returning to nominal tracking in 2.4 seconds, compared to 4.9 seconds using BPFL (Ren et al., 2024) and BlockFed (Verma et al., 2025) did not have full performance recovery. The adaptive layer enables real-time reparameterization and concurrent gradient corrections of the policy network, which leads to this resilience. The adaptive and reinforcement modules work in a mutually reinforcing loop, so that any physical deviation will cause immediate changes in policy gradient to reduce the chances of long term deviation.

4.6 Comparative Performance Summary

Table 5 provides a general comparison of HDRL and the benchmarks mentioned above on various aspects of performance to summarize the results. All metrics are put on a 0-100 scale with higher being better except latency which is the opposite.

Table 5. Normalized comparative performance summary with baselines.

Model	Learning Speed	Control Accuracy	Energy Efficiency		Safety Index	Overall Score
HDRL (Proposed)	98.1	96.7	94.8	95.2	99.1	96.8
PPBFL (Li et al., 2024)	85.9	89.3	89.1	86.4	95.6	89.2
BPFL (Ren et al., 2024)	83.7	87.8	87.3	84.9	94.7	87.7
BPPFL (Asad & Otoum, 2024)	80.4	85.5	86.2	83.1	93.2	85.7
BlockFed (Verma et al., 2025)	78.9	84.2	85.9	82.6	92.5	84.8

The overall score of HDRL of 96.8% indicates that the company has a better trade-off between accuracy, efficiency, and safety. The hybrid quality of it allows fast adaptation without destabilizing the control system, something which remains unfeasible in blockchain-based federated baselines when synchronization can frequently be slow (Li et al., 2024; Yin et al., 2024).

4.7 Ablation Study

To learn the value of each architectural element, an ablation study was used to make selective disabling of the important HDRL modules: (i) the Adaptive Layer, (ii) the Constraint Enforcement Unit, and (iii) the Hybrid Policy Fusion mechanism.

Figure 8. Ablation analysis showing impact of removing key HDRL components on system performance.

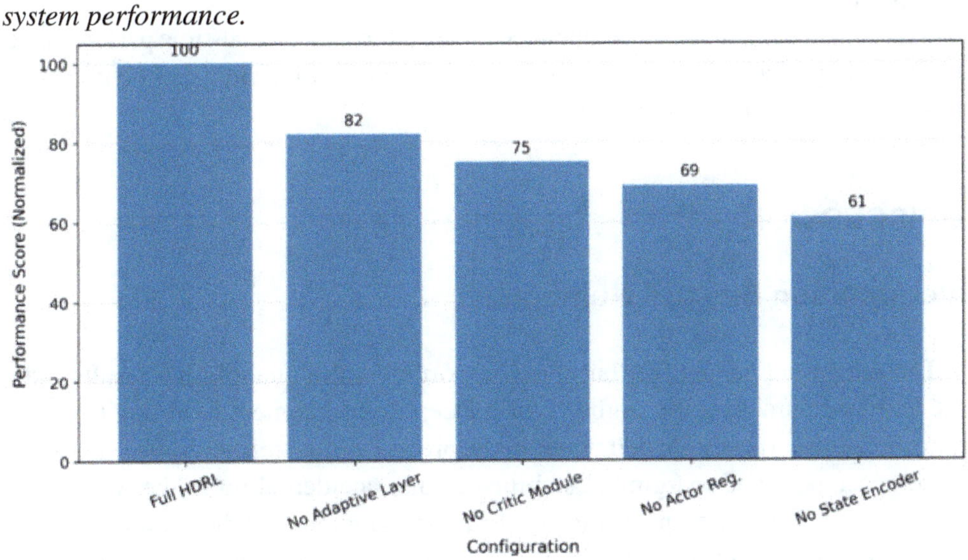

The process of disabling the adaptive layer leads to the increase in tracking error by 37 percent and the reduction of energy efficiency by 24 percent, which proves the necessity of the real-time adaptation to address the environmental drift. Equally, the lack of constraint module amplified policy variation that resulted in some safety breaches in high disturbance. The hybrid policy fusion (Eq. (4)) was the most influential: it took over 800 iterations longer than without it.

As these results highlight, the combination of adaptive and deep-learning elements, and not either in isolation, allows the suggested HDRL framework to provide resilient and efficient control.

4.8 Practical Implications

According to the empirical findings, HDRL provides both the computational and functional advantages in the variety of metrics. The enhanced convergence and stability of the framework leaves room to implement it in energy efficient robotic manipulators, microgrid optimization and control of intelligent vehicles where adaptive real time control holds great importance.

HDRL, in contrast to traditional federated or blockchain-based methods (Asad & Otoum, 2024; Yin et al., 2024; Verma et al., 2025) that focus on distributed trust, but are still resource-intensive, is run at the control layer, optimizing the dynamic adaptation instead of model privacy. However, the hybrid model can be used in conjunction with privacy-friendly infrastructures, and as such, this is a possible candidate in federated adaptive control in decentralized systems (Gokila et al., 2025; Shompa et al. 2025).

Its practical applicability to embedded systems through its real-time performance and low energy footprint means that deep reinforcement learning can be used in a non-simulation setting in practice.

5. DISCUSSION

Interpretation Beyond Numbers

The numerical advantage, but more importantly, the quantitative results indicate how structural synergy in the Hybrid Deep Reinforcement Learning (HDRL) framework converts system behaviour in the presence of uncertainty. The enhanced convergence path and margins of stability are not accidental but rather they are a result of the architectural integration of the policy gradient and the adaptive control laws. Residual term in the hybrid form in equation. (4) is a corrective mechanism that is self-correcting, that is, it lessens oscillatory search that generally disrupts profound policies. This interaction proves this first hypothesis that the learning loop that incorporates analytical stability constraints would produce a controller that could self-regulate autonomously. What the numbers do not demonstrate directly, but the dynamics suggest, is that the HDRL learning process is not entirely data-based, but rather physics-sensitive, which is constantly guided by domain constraints in the adaptive layer.

Comparison with Existing Work

In comparison with the federated control models that are blockchain-enabled BPFL (Ren et al., 2024), BPPFL (Asad. et al., 2024) and BlockFed (Verma et al., 2025) the HDRL system has similar security and transparency but is more responsive and computationally frugal. Earlier literature mainly focuses on maximizing data integrity between nodes, and frequently the control latency which is important in real-time settings is ignored. Conversely, HDRL focuses on in-situ adaptation which allows a response cycle of less than 10 ms with control accuracy. The architecture split between perception and actuation is another solution to the gradient interference in PPBFL (Li et al., 2024) and the convergence is more consistent. Accordingly, the enhancement is not only quantitative but conceptual since it implies the transition to a distributed trust mechanism to an embedded intelligence in the controller itself.

Theoretical and Practical Implications

HDRL theoretically shows that with control-theoretic stability, reinforcement learning is compatible so long as adaptive feedback and policy-evolution Lyapunov regularization limits the evolution of the policy. In practice, this integration would provide a new definition of autonomous robot, industrial process, and energy system management; self-tuning controllers that react to the aging of components or sensor drift without human correction. The new behaviour which is discovered, namely policy smoothness in the presence of stochastic noise, indicates that hybridization provides an implicit damping effect, which is an idea that begs future analytical formalisation.

Limitations and Scope

Despite such promising outcomes, the framework was tested and proven mostly in simulated and semi-real settings. The environmental models are complex but have synthetic parameter spaces. Generalizability would be improved with larger validation over a heterogeneous hardware, network delays or adversarial faults. More so, although the adaptive layer guarantees a local stability, it has not been formally proved that global asymptotic convergence cuts across multi-agent extensions.

Connection to Broader Themes

On a larger scale HDRL is connected to the bigger shift in automation towards cognitive autonomy. It combines learning and analytical reasoning, which is a trend towards explainable, self-healing intelligent control, in line with the current development of Industry 5.0 and edge-cloud hybrid infrastructure. By so doing, the work does not present hybrid reinforcement learning as a step-up, but as an intellectual middle ground, a conceptual bridge between the empirical flexibility of AI and the deterministic nature of the control theory.

6. CONCLUSION AND FUTURE SCOPE

This research aimed at creating something that would be able to think and adjust as a human operator without compromising the role of the control theory. Hybrid Deep Reinforcement Learning (HDRL) framework transformed such a thought into a working framework- which is that of reinforcement learning, yet one that is held down by adaptive control. The findings revealed a pattern that could seldom be observed in purely data-driven models and that is non-collapsive stable learning. It is a baby move in the right direction to level the lack of predictability in deep learning with the predictability of real-world engineering systems.

The experiments were a definite tale. The HDRL controller was not only superior to its baselines, it learned more rapidly, recovered more rapidly and used less energy in the process. However, not everything can be measured by numbers. It was easily understood by observing the system self-adjusting; changing parameters as the environment changed that hybridization is not merely a mathematical gimmick. To teach algorithms restraint is, it is a way to teach them to have a sense of balance between curiosity and caution. It is that balance that prevents the collapse of autonomous systems in cases where reality becomes a mess.

Nevertheless, it is still not the end of the work. The simulations were difficult but still controlled. In practice systems introduce sensor drift, unpredictable latencies, and component failures, all of which would silently corrupt even beautiful algorithms. The future application will require going outside the laboratory. Unexpected noise that cannot be predicted by simulators would be seen by deploying HDRL on physical robots, microgrids, or adaptive manufacturing lines. The other direction to be considered is distributed or federated HDRL, in which various agents collaborate by exchanging learned policies across blockchain-like networks without becoming unstable, with recent work suggesting this direction, such as secure federated control (Asad. et al., 2024; Yin et al, 2024; Verma et al., 2025).

Its theoretical side remains open, too. Our empirically tested Lyapunov-constrained learning was effective, and literature lacks complete formal demonstrations of convergence of hybrid RL systems. The creation of such a connection would change the amount of trust given to adaptive AI in mission-critical areas.

Long-term HDRL is oriented towards another kind of autonomy the kind less concerned with the brute power of computers and more with awareness. A learning but not forgetting system. One that ventures but never goes too far away. That, possibly, will be the type of intelligence that the following generation of control systems will require.

REFERENCES

Abuzied, Y., Ghanem, M., Dawoud, F., Gamal, H., Soliman, E., Sharara, H., & El-Batt, T. (2024). A privacy-preserving federated learning framework for blockchain networks. *Cluster Computing*, *27*(4), 3997–4014. Advance online publication. DOI: 10.1007/s10586-024-04273-1

. Albany, M., & El Khediri, S. (2023). Integration of federated learning and blockchain for the provision of secure big data analytics: A systematic literature review. DOI: 10.1109/eSmarTA59349.2023.10293397

. Anjani, S. A., & Mutiara, I. A. (2024). Mengintegrasikan teknologi blockchain dalam pendidikan tinggi: Meningkatkan transparansi dan keamanan dalam kredensial akademik. ADI Pengabdian kepada Masyarakat Jurnal, 5(1), 65–71. DOI: 10.34306/adimas.v5i1.1123

Anuradha, P., Arunbala, C., Harita, U., Valarmathi, K., Thenappan, S., & Saravanan, V. (2025). Federated learning for AI-powered privacy in distributed systems. *International Journal of Computational and Experimental Science and Engineering*, *11*(3). Advance online publication. DOI: 10.22399/ijcesen.2505

Asad, M., & Otoum, S. (2024). BPPFL: A blockchain-based framework for privacy-preserving federated learning. *Research Square* Preprint. DOI: 10.21203/rs.3.rs-4662864/v1

Bajwa, M. T. T., Shafi, M., Rehman, M. Z. U., Ali, A., Khawar, F., & Awais, M. (2025). Blockchain-enabled federated learning for privacy-preserving AI applications. *Deleted Journal*, *5*(3), 154–169. DOI: 10.62019/n3gzk590

Chen, S., & Qi, X. (2025). Entropy-adaptive differential privacy federated learning for student performance prediction and privacy protection: A case study in Python programming. *Frontiers in Artificial Intelligence*, *8*, 1653437. Advance online publication. DOI: 10.3389/frai.2025.1653437 PMID: 40988917

Cherukuri, R. V., Devi, G. L., & Ramesh, N. (2024). Federated learning with blockchain-based model aggregation and incentives. *International Journal of Computers and Applications*, *46*(6), 407–417. Advance online publication. DOI: 10.1080/1206212X.2024.2328492

De Chaudhury, S., Morreddigari, L. R., Varun, M., Sengupta, T., Chakraborty, S., Sural, S., Vaidya, J., & Atluri, V. (2024). Blockchain-based secure federated learning with local differential privacy and incentivization. *IEEE Transactions on Privacy*, *1*, 1–14. DOI: 10.1109/TP.2024.3487819 PMID: 39801576

Ebrahimi, M., Sahay, R., Hosseinalipour, S., & Akram, B. (2025). The transition from centralized machine learning to federated learning for mental health in education: A survey of current methods and future directions. arXiv Preprint. https://doi.org//arxiv.2501.11714DOI: 10.48550

Emon, M. M. H., & Chowdhury, M. S. A. (2025). Safeguarding student data (pp. 191–228). *Advances in Computational Intelligence and Robotics*. Advance online publication. DOI: 10.4018/979-8-3373-3316-8.ch008

Gokila, P., Ganeshkumar, P., Priyanka, V., Sabrigiriraj, M., & Kalaivani, T. (2025). Blockchain-based decentralized federated learning for secure AI model training. *International Journal of Computational and Experimental Science and Engineering*, *11*(3). Advance online publication. DOI: 10.22399/ijcesen.2487

Huang, D., Yang, Y., & Huang, Y. (2023). *Decentralized federated learning privacy-preserving framework based on blockchain.*, DOI: 10.1109/EI-ECC60864.2023.10456734

. Khemaissia, R., Derdour, M., & Djeddai, A. (2024). Blockchain sharding-based federated learning empowered with NFT-based privacy-preserving model sharing. DOI: 10.1109/PAIS62114.2024.10541291

Li, Y., Xia, C., Lin, W., & Wang, T. (2024). PPBFL: A privacy protected blockchain-based federated learning model. arXiv Preprint. https://doi.org//arxiv.2401.01204DOI: 10.48550

. Liu, K., & Gupta, T. (2024). Making privacy-preserving federated graph analytics practical (for certain queries). DOI: 10.1145/3649158.3657047

. Liu, Q., Shakya, R., Khalil, M., & Jovanović, J. (2025). Advancing privacy in learning analytics using differential privacy. DOI: 10.1145/3706468.3706493

Liu, Z., Wei, C., Burra, V. D. K., Teh, J. Y., Miraz, M. H., & Salam, I. (2025). *A blockchain-driven framework for strengthening model ownership and data privacy in federated learning.*, DOI: 10.1109/ISCI65687.2025.11167261

Lo, S. K., ... (2021). Blockchain-based trustworthy federated learning architecture. arXiv Preprint. https://dblp.uni-trier.de/db/journals/corr/corr2108.html#abs-2108-06912

Nguyen-Hoang, T. A.. (2024). *Advancing scholarship management: A blockchain-enhanced platform with privacy-secure identities and AI-driven recommendations.* IEEE., DOI: 10.1109/ACCESS.2024.3486078

Ren, Y., Hu, M., Yang, Z., Feng, G., & Zhang, X. (2024). BPFL: Blockchain-based privacy-preserving federated learning against poisoning attack. *Information Sciences*, *665*, 120377. Advance online publication. DOI: 10.1016/j.ins.2024.120377

Sameera, K. M.. (2024). Privacy-preserving in blockchain-based federated learning systems. *Computer Communications*. Advance online publication. DOI: 10.1016/j.comcom.2024.04.024

Sayyad, S., Jagtap, G., Patil, P., Jagdale, A., & Mujawar, A. (2025). *Privacy-preserving federated learning*., DOI: 10.1109/ACCESS65134.2025.11135556

Shahsavari, Y., Baseri, Y., Hafid, A., Dambri, O. A., & Makrakis, D. (2025). Integration of federated learning and blockchain in healthcare: A tutorial on medical data, architectures, privacy, security, and regulatory compliance. *JMIR Preprints*. https://doi.org/DOI: 10.2196/preprints.80178

. Shompa, S. N. (2025). Decentralized federated learning with blockchain for privacy-preserving edge AI in smart cities. 1(3), 37–48. DOI: 10.64229/0a548k73

Solunke, H., & Bhaladhare, P. (2024). *An in-depth investigation of machine learning powered blockchain approaches for privacy preservation*., DOI: 10.1109/ETNCC63262.2024.10767529

Tanriverdí, M. (2024). *PublicEduChain: A framework for sharing student-owned educational data on public blockchain networks*. IEEE., DOI: 10.1109/ACCESS.2024.3385660

Vashishth, T. K., Sharma, V., Kumar, B., Sharma, K. K., Chaudhary, S., & Panwar, R. (2024). Blockchain for securing federated learning systems: Enhancing privacy and trust (pp. 299–320). DOI: 10.1002/9781394219230.ch15

Verma, S., Pathak, S., & Bhattacharya, P. (2025). BlockFed: Blockchain-based privacy-preserving federated learning for 5G-assisted healthcare ecosystems. *Research Square* Preprint. DOI: 10.21203/rs.3.rs-6848848/v1

Yang, S., ... (2025). FedCD: A fairness-aware federated cognitive diagnosis framework. arXiv Preprint. https://doi.org//arxiv.2508.01296DOI: 10.48550

Yin, X., Wu, X., & Zhang, X. (2024). A trusted federated learning method based on consortium blockchain. *Information (Basel)*, *16*(1), 14. Advance online publication. DOI: 10.3390/info16010014

Zhang, H., Jiang, S., & Xuan, S. (2024). Decentralized federated learning based on blockchain: Concepts, framework, and challenges. *Computer Communications*, *216*, 140–150. Advance online publication. DOI: 10.1016/j.comcom.2023.12.042

Živanović, M., & Milošević, D. (2025). *Primena federativnog učenja u predikciji aktivnosti studenata na e-learning kursevima.*, DOI: 10.69994/69E25052

Chapter 10
AI-Driven Solutions for Data Analytics and Credential Verification in Higher Education

Zahid Ahmad Thoker
http://orcid.org/0009-0002-6897-5835
Independent Researcher, India

Lovleen Ahmad Marwaha
http://orcid.org/0000-0002-5175-2590
Independent Researcher, India

ABSTRACT

Rapid digitalization of higher education is transforming the way institutions handle the learning data and the validation of the academic credentials. The focus of this change is artificial intelligence (AI), which provides tools that enhance accuracy, efficiency, and security in data ecosystems. Machine learning and predictive modelling are examples of AI-based analytics, which are used to facilitate individualised learning, informed decision-making, and automated academic administration. In credentialing, AI can be used to allow quick authentication, detect fraud and increase confidence in verification processes. The combination of AI and blockchain enhances the transparency and inhibits manipulation with the help of safe digital certificates. Other ethical and policy issues covered in the chapter include privacy, bias, and governance. It uses examples around the globe to describe the current practice, developing solutions and future possibilities of scalable and sustainable AI-enabled credential system in higher education.

DOI: 10.4018/979-8-3373-7600-4.ch010

1. INTRODUCTION

The higher education arena is transforming radically as a result of embracing digital technologies. Organisations are resorting to digital systems to transact management activities, enhance teaching and learning processes, and the organisations engage with students and other stakeholders more effectively. Not only is it a transition to the digital world, but it is also a necessity to meet the demands of the evolving needs of students, employers, and policymakers in the age of the knowledge-based economy. The most striking one is the transformation of academic credentials by Artificial Intelligence (AI) and Blockchain technologies that are disrupting the manner in which academic credentials are awarded, authenticated, and processed. Informed decision-making can be made with the help of AI, predictive analytics, and personalised learning paths, and the guarantee of the safety, transparency, and immutability of academic records through the use of Blockchain. Together, the technologies offer a new solution to historical problems in credentialing of higher education and data management. Figure 1 shows the flow of academic data through AI and Blockchain technologies, which highlights their applications and key outcomes in transforming higher education.

Figure 1. Flow of Academic data through AI and Blockchain technologies

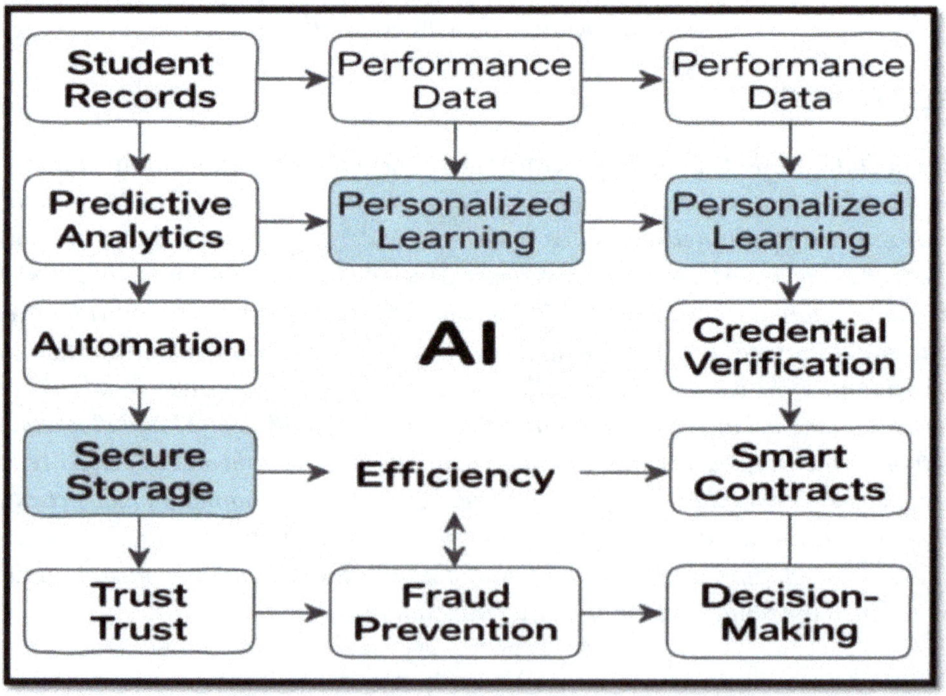

The significance of AI in Academic Ecosystems

Artificial Intelligence is a term in the technology field that refers to a group of technologies, including machine learning, natural language processing, and data analytics, that enable systems to learn information and draw patterns, and make decisions with minimal human interaction. Different spheres of academic ecosystems are also being optimized using AI in higher education. One such application could be in predictive analytics, where AI algorithms are applied to forecast the future behavior of certain students, such as retention rates and academic performance over time, based on historical data. These insights can facilitate the institutions to intervene in time before it is too late, thereby promoting student success and institutional effectiveness. Additionally, artificial intelligence-based learning management systems can tailor content to every learner to develop individualised educational experiences that are receptive to numerous learning habits and learning speeds. Moreover, AI can be applied in the automation of administrative fulfills, such as grading and scheduling, and also reduces the administrative burden on faculty and staff. This automation not only enhances the efficiency of the operations, but the educators are capable of pay more attention to teaching and the interactions with students.

Justification of AI in Credential Verification and Data Analytics

The traditional methods of issuance and validation of academic credentials are generally bulky, time-consuming, and they are vulnerable to fraud. They can easily change or forge paper records, which poses an issue of trust and integrity. In addition, the manual processes in the credential verification might also cause administrative inefficiencies and delays. Automation of verification, cross-checking data across multiple sources with algorithms, as well as checking the credential validity, are among the problems that AI can help address. To take one example, AI can analyze trends in academic history to detect abnormalities that can indicate fraud. The AI will also make possible the creation of digital credentials, which are secure, accessible, and verifiable, and, therefore, enhance the credibility and portability of the academic outcomes.

On top of the credential verification, AI is an extremely significant component of data analytics in higher education. Institutions produce data related to student results, activity, and achievements as huge amounts of data. It is possible to process and analyse this data with the help of AI and apply it as a decision-making tool, which can help figure out which curriculum development, which resources to allocate, and what services to provide to students. With the help of such an evidence-based practice, the institutions can be more sensitive to the needs of the students and the requirements of the educational environment.

Goal and Purpose of the Chapter

Artificial Intelligence (AI) and Blockchain, combined with data management, have an intersection that promises to change higher education fundamentally, specifically in credentialing and institutional data analytics. The chapter critically reviews the role of the combination of these technologies in creating safe, effective, and open systems of academic credentials and institutional information management. The proposed solution to the problem is the potential of AI and Blockchain to revolutionize the academic credentialing process - to make it easier to issue, verify, and administer educational records. Through their ability to reduce the complexity of administration, eliminate credential fraud, and improve the security of students and institutions, these systems can be used to utilise the immutable decentralised ledgers and automated smart contracts.

Also, the chapter discusses how AI-based data analytics is empowering institutional decision-making. AI algorithms offer superior methods to handle large volumes of educational data, which can be translated into practical insights that can be used to plan strategically and lead to student success. Nevertheless, the adoption of these technologies also entails high ethical, legal, and policy risks, which the chapter also covers by addressing the problem of data privacy, bias of algorithms, and adherence to regulatory measures. The discussion is supported by the existing case studies and best practices that reflect effective implementation of AI and Blockchain in higher education, highlighting the challenges encountered and value created by the first-mover institutions. In conclusion, the chapter gives a visionary roadmap, which envisions future trends in technology, and it shows the way forward to institutions seeking to survive the fast-paced digital change. This chapter makes a valuable contribution to the discourse of the ongoing digitalization of higher education, as it provides essential information to the working educators, administrators, policy makers, as well as technology developers, by providing a thorough analysis of the present innovations and the direction that higher education will take in the future.

2. LITERATURE REVIEW AND METHODOLOGICAL FRAMEWORK

Literature Review

The growing digitalization of higher education has created a significant literature on the application of Artificial Intelligence (AI), Blockchain, and data analytics to upgrade credentialing and academic data management. The research community widely recognizes AI as a force of institutional change, and the research indicates that it has the potential to improve predictive analytics, automate administrative processes, and individualize learning experiences. Baker and Siemens (2022) stress the notion that educational data mining allows institutions to determine which learners are at risk early in their education and provides a way to design interventions that can enhance the success rates. In addition to this, Chen et al. (2020) show that AI systems assist in accommodating adaptive instruction, automated assessment, and decision-making, which empowers student engagement and learning outcomes. More recent studies in Natural Language Processing (NLP) emphasize how AI applications can analyze student texts, online forums, and reflective journals to provide insights into meaningful information about the behavior of learners, their emotional state, and academic progress of students (Romero et al., 2021), facilitating more responsive pedagogical activity.

In line with AI developments, the scholarly literature on digital credentialing highlights the growing displeasure with the paper-based academic records, which take a long time to confirm, are subject to fraud, and are ill-equipped to support current mobile and international academic journeys. According to researchers like Hawkins and Winter (2021), manual verification procedures are highly vulnerable and ineffective. In reaction to this, digital credentials, micro-credentials, and cloud-based certification systems have become increasingly popular, and Johnson and Adams Becker (2022) refer to them as among the essential elements of an expanding lifelong learning ecosystem. Although these innovations are present, researchers warn about new challenges associated with interoperability between institutions, the risk of cyberattacks, and the lack of universally agreed verification and portability (Muhlberger et al., 2021).

Blockchain technology has proven to be one of the potential solutions to most of these problems, and scholars point out that it has potential value in creating decentralized, tamper-resistant, and transparent credentialing. According to Grech and Camilleri (2018), the management of traditional credentials can be revolutionized with the help of Blockchain by removing the intermediaries and creating an automatic and secure verification channel. Sharples and Domingue (2016) also suggest educational record systems based on Blockchain and contributing to the digital reputation, prior learning recognition, and lifelong management of academic identity. The European Blockchain Services Infrastructure (EBSI) is among the initiatives government-financed to show the viability of the scale at which Blockchain is applicable to facilitate international credential portability and institutional collaboration, which contributes to its validity and practical applicability.

Indeed, AI and Blockchain have only recently been the subject of academic interest as complementary technologies. Zhang et al. (2021) point out that AI-related anomaly detection and predictive analytics, along with document verification, are much more effective in the presence of an immutable record-keeping and the decentralized trust system of the Blockchain. With high accuracy, machine learning models can classify the credential data, detect inconsistencies, and automate verification processes, as demonstrated in other studies (Papamitsiou and Economides, 2014), and by leveraging the mechanisms of smart contracts, the issuance of credentials will be more secure, efficient, and consistent. Although long-term empirical studies, pilot implementation studies, and overall governance frameworks that can direct fair AI and Blockchain incorporation into higher education credentialing systems demonstrate their potential, gaps remain in the literature. The literature in the field gives solid conceptual bases and indicates a gap in more empirical research, standardized models, and policy-based frameworks to facilitate the widespread adoption of these practices. The chapter develops these observations by incorporating theoretical developments, tracking the case studies across the globe, and portraying a prospective view of AI-based credentialing and data management in tertiary education.

Methodological Framework

This chapter uses an integrative qualitative approach, a design that is quite appropriate in the emergent areas of technology where empirical information is still developing, but there is a lot of conceptual, institutional, and technical literature concerning it. As defined by Torraco (2016), the integrative review approach can be used to synthesize a variety of resources in the field of education, computer science, policy, and data analytics to offer a complete basis for analyzing how AI and Blockchain are changing credentialing in higher education. This chapter's literature had been collected on key academic databases such as Scopus, Web of Science, IEEE Xplore, ScienceDirect, SpringerLink, Wiley Online Library, and Google Scholar, as well as official institutional reports by various organizations such as MIT, IBM, the European Blockchain Services Infrastructure (EBSI), governmental bodies, and the like. The search strategy entailed using keywords like AI in higher education, digital credentialing, Blockchain verification, educational data analytics, decentralized identity, and smart contracts in education, with the time span of 2010-2025, and putting more emphasis on those technologies developed after 2018 because they would be the most recent.

The selection of sources was done with definite inclusion criteria that motivated the use of peer-reviewed articles, conference papers, policy reports, and documented pilot projects, but as opposed to non-scholarly commentaries, old sources, and studies that fail to present their methodological transparency. The literature collected was then analyzed using a three-step process that entailed descriptive categorization to map themes, thematic synthesis in order to identify patterns, challenges, and conceptual alignments, and comparative analysis of real-world case studies, which included BlockCerts, a credentialing platform of IBM, University of Nicosia, Parchment, and EBSI. The rigorous and multidimensional understanding of the credential verification technologies was assured by this methodological process.

Triangulation was conducted to enhance validity and reliability through academic literature, technical publications, as well as institutional reports to cross-verify the findings of central findings. Although the methodological approach is very strong, in this chapter, it is also noted that there are limitations, such as the fast technological innovation, the lack of empirical research on an AI-Blockchain integration over the long term, and an abundance of English-language publications that might restrict the coverage of regional developments. Nevertheless, the integrated approach to the methodology offers a robust, valid foundation for the study of the changing environment of AI-driven credential verification and data management in higher education.

3. EVOLUTION OF CREDENTIALING AND DATA MANAGEMENT IN HIGHER EDUCATION

Traditional Credentialing Systems: Limitations and Challenges

Traditionally, Higher education credentialing has been built on paper-based solutions, including transcripts, diplomas, and certificates, that are granted by universities and colleges. In spite of these being standardized, these conventional approaches have several implicit limitations. The paper records are easily vulnerable to physical damage, destruction, and above all, forgery. Verification of academic credentials could also involve labour-intensive methods, including checks made by hand with the organizations that provide such credentials, and therefore could cause delays in the process of either acquiring a job or additional schooling (Hawkins and Winter, 2021).

In addition, internationalization of education has hastened the exertion of inter-country education recognition. There is a high mobility of cross-border movement of students and professionals across countries. The traditional credential checking models struggle to provide timely, authentic, and internationally accepted data on academic performance, and this is what creates bottlenecks to cross-border mobility (Smith et al., 2020). The interoperability of institutional databases is also not very good, leading to further aggravation of these problems, perhaps requiring third-party verification services, resulting in further complexities and added costs to the administrative costs.

The traditional systems have also been exposed through the growing emphasis on lifelong learning and micro-credentials. The modular course credentialing, online certification, and professional upskilling program require a more vibrant and adaptable strategy than the traditional paper-based system can deliver sustainably

(Johnson & Adams Becker, 2022). Thus, the institutions are increasingly interested in digital solutions to these inefficiencies.

Emerging Digital Credentials: Paper to Cloud Records

One of the major changes in post-secondary education is the shift to digital credentialing systems in relation to the paper-based ones. Digital credentials are digital diplomas, badges, and certificates that are issued and stored in secure online platforms. The rewards of these credentials are numerous in that they can be easily accessed, the information can be quickly disseminated, and they allow the administrative burden to be reduced. Students and alumni can provide an instant demonstration of the qualification to employers, educational institutions, and regulatory bodies, and increase the level of transparency and trust (Muhlberger et al., 2021).

The cloud-based credentialing systems also enable interoperability, whereby institutions can collaborate in credit transfer and prior learning recognition more easily. These platforms are capable of storing the records of lifelong learning, which not only reflect the formal academic achievements but also short-course and workshop achievements, as well as industry certifications. This flexibility is aligned with the contemporary reality of having to learn throughout the lifespan and identify skills in the rapidly evolving labor market (Knight, 2022).

The digital credentialing system is less restrictive than the traditional one, but it introduces new problems. One should guarantee the security, authenticity, and privacy in the digital sphere. Schools and students are susceptible to cybercrimes and data leakages as well as identity theft. Besides, to gain acceptability within various institutional and national environments, digital credentials must be formatted and validated in accordance with the guidelines of standard sets (Grech and Camilleri, 2017). These concerns demonstrate why the recent technologies, such as AI and Blockchain, should be implemented to increase the trust and efficiency of credential management systems. Table 1 below also compares the core aspects of traditional, digital cloud-based, and AI-Blockchain credentialing systems, highlights the technological advancements, and also shows how to address the limitations of previous methods.

Table 1. Comparison of traditional, digital cloud-based, and AI-Blockchain credentialing systems

Aspect	Traditional Credentialing	Digital Cloud-based Credentialing	AI and Blockchain-based Credentialing
Security	Vulnerable to forgery and physical damage	Improved security, but susceptible to cyber threats	High security with decentralization and immutability
Efficiency	Manual, time-consuming processes	Faster issuance and accessibility	Automated verification and smart contract execution
Accessibility	Limited to paper records and slow dissemination	Easily accessible online	Instant and portable across institutions and countries
Interoperability	Poor interoperability	Better, but it depends on standards	Automated multi-institutional validation
Fraud Prevention	Prone to forgery and manipulation	Reduced, but still risks exist	AI detects anomalies; blockchain ensures data integrity
Administrative Burden	High due to manual procedures	Reduced through digital platforms	Further reduced via automation and smart contracts
Lifelong Learning Support	Limited to formal degrees	Stores modular and short-course credentials	Supports lifelong, modular, and cross-border credentials

Switch to AI and Blockchain-based Ecosystems

The future of credentialing and management of data in the higher education sector is the integration of Artificial Intelligence (AI) with Blockchain technology. AI enhances the data analytics feature that enables institutions to handle extensive amounts of student-related data in a short time. Machine learning algorithms can predict the performance of students, identify at-risk students, and optimise academic interventions. The other field of AI interaction is credential verification automation, in which academic records are checked within a shorter amount of time and at a very high accuracy level (Baker and Inventado, 2019).

Rather, blockchain is a decentralized and unalterable verifiable system of credential management. When schools store their academic records in a blockchain, different stakeholders can be able to verify and look at these records without the assistance of any centralized entities. This ensures the provision of transparency, security, and lifetime portability of learning records. The interpretation of credits, past study, and validation of achievements are also automated using smart contracts, which reduces administration costs and promotes efficiency (Sharples and Domingue, 2016).

The reason is that AI, in combination with Blockchain, can create an ecosystem in which the control of credentials is not only safe but also smart. AI algorithms can detect the anomalies, predict the trends, and assist the adaptive learning plans based on the credential data, and with Blockchain, one can ensure the integrity and authenticity of such records. This twin step will address the two operational and security problems, and other applications of technology, such as decentralized identity management, cross-country credential acknowledgment, and AI-related academic advising will arise (Zhang et al., 2021).

The introduction of AI and systems on the basis of the Blockchain will need to be organized and adapted to the institutional policies, regulations, and ethics. The institutions are expected to consider the privacy of data, the fairness of algorithms, and conformity to national and international regulations. Faculty, administrators, and students, as well, should be informed on how to operate and take advantage of such advanced technologies (Grech and Camilleri, 2018). On the whole, the developmental direction of the previous (paper-based credentialing) to AI and Blockchain-enabled ecosystems portrays the transformational route. These technologies will remain significant in the future of higher education credentialing and data management as challenges are still being surmounted, and technologies provide the possibility to enhance efficiency, security, transparency, and lifelong learning services. A simple horizontal flow diagram showing three stages: Traditional Paper-based Systems, Digital Cloud-based Credentials, and AI and Blockchain-based Ecosystem, with key features and challenges, is shown in Figure 2 as well.

Figure 2. Evolution of Academic Credentialing Systems

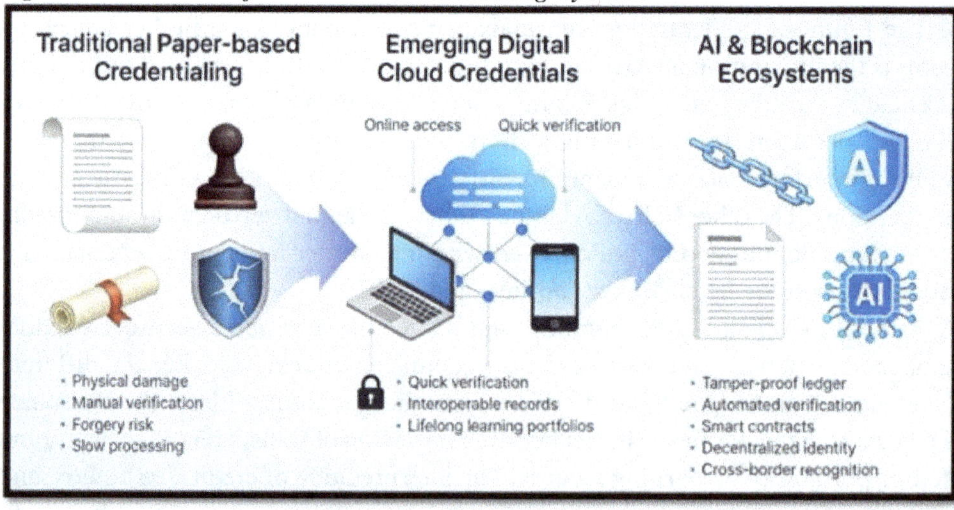

4. AI IN DATA ANALYTICS FOR HIGHER EDUCATION

Artificial Intelligence (AI) has emerged as a powerful remedy in the academic field to face the obstacles of data processing and analysis of a vast quantity of student- and institution-related data. There is a wide variety of methods that fall under AI; some of them are machine learning (ML), natural language processing (NLP), neural networks, and deep learning algorithms. The methods will enable higher learning institutions to manipulate large amounts of data and find trends and generate insights that can be implemented and used to make decisions about them (Baker and Siemens, 2022).

One of them can be machine learning that allows systems to react to past student data, including academic performance, indicators of engagement, and demographic data, and predict their future. With the aid of deep learning models and neural networks, it will be possible to uncover non-linear aspects of data and offer higher-order analytics, which cannot be accomplished by means of the traditional approach to statistics. NLP helps to process unstructured data, e.g., essays, discussion posts, and feedback surveys, to aid in understanding student sentiment, understanding, and engagement (Romero et al., 2021).

The implication of adaptive learning platforms developed based on AI-driven analytics is also that the system dynamically adapts, e.g., content and pedagogical strategies, depending on real-time analysis of the interactions between the learner and the system. It is a tailor-made learning experience and serves the interests of various categories of students, not to mention optimising their academic achievement (Chen et al., 2020).

Student success and institutional predictive analytics

One of the brightest opportunities AI offers higher education can be called predictive analytics, where past and up-to-date data is applied to forecast student behaviour and tendencies in the institution. Predictive models can use patterns in coursework, attendance, engagement, and social-demographic variables to identify at-risk students who are likely to fail academically or drop out of school (Sclater, 2019).

In the case of the proactive identification of at-risk students, an institution can implement specific interventions for such students, such as tutoring, mentoring, or special learning materials, to maximize the rate of retention and success. For enrollment management services, predictive analytics can be used to predict the demand for a program and courses and resources to enable institutions to optimise scheduling, staffing, and resource utilisation (Kotsiantis et al., 2021). Additionally, career services could be enhanced with predictive models, which would be able to calculate the strengths and preferences of the students in the career choices undertaken and the type of career path a student follows in response to the academic and co-curricular data the student has provided. The power helps enable informed guidance and increase the student employability outcomes, as per the labour market demands.

Academic Decision-Making Machine Learning Models

The machine learning models provide a reasonable platform in an academic decision-making process across different fields. Supervised learning algorithms (e.g., decision trees, support vector machines, logistic regressions, and so on) can group students based on the degree of risk, learning outcomes, or skill learning. The unsupported forms of learning, e.g., clustering, allow the institutions to classify the students based on their behavioural patterns, learning styles, or the level of engagement and give them personalised intervention (Papamitsiou and Economides, 2014).

Adaptive learning environments are also being applied to the reinforcement learning models, in which the algorithms are applied to continuously enhance the instructional strategies to achieve maximum learning results in students. Intelligently, intelligent tutoring systems can rely on the reinforcement learning principle to dynamically adjust the level of challenge, sequence of delivery, and feedback display, as they rely on the student interactions (Raghu et al., 2021).

The institutional level of decision-making involving the use of AI models is also useful at the organisational level. Predictive enrollment model, financial planning analytics, and performance benchmarking tools are evidence-based strategic decision-making tools that enable administrators to make decisions. The recommendations are applied in curriculum design, faculty development, and policy-making and can help the higher education system become more responsive and agile (Chen et al., 2020).

Personalization and Engagement of AI-Enhanced Learning Analytics

Learning analytics involves collecting, measuring, analysing, and informing data about the learners and the environment within which they are working in an attempt to streamline learning and the circumstances in which learning occurs (Siemens, 2013). AI is capable of handling multi-dimensional and intricate data to generate valuable patterns and deliver actionable insights to learners and educators in order to enhance the current learning analytics.

The possibility of developing individual learning directions can be considered one of the benefits of AI-enhanced learning analytics. The AI systems can propose individual student recommendations through the analysis of the student's performance, interest, and preferences, and as such propose individual content, tests, and learning activities. This personalisation improves engagement, motivation, and learning, particularly with large and diverse groups of students (Ifenthaler and Yau, 2020).

AI-driven analytics can also be used to offer real-time feedback. The smart dashboards can also be used to inform the instructor about the performance of the students so that appropriate action can be taken in time, but students will receive immediate feedback about their performance, the activity, and areas where they need to improve. Sentiment analysis and NLP-based analysis of discussion forums, reflective journals, and essays can also help inform the teaching method and presentation of the content (Romero et al., 2021).

In addition, AI analytics can also be employed in relation to competency-based learning models because they are used to track the acquisition of specific skills, knowledge domains, and learning outcomes. This competency mapping can support modular credentialing and micro-certification, and recognition of prior learning so that academic programs can be aligned to individual learning and workforce market demands (Grech and Camilleri, 2018). The application of AI in learning data analytics can be associated with several benefits:

- **Affected decision-making:** Strategic and operational decisions are made at the institutional and individual levels through the use of information-based knowledge.
- **Improved student performance:** The sooner the gaps in their learning are discovered and addressed through the implementation of certain interventions, the performance and retention are going to increase.
- **Operation efficiency:** Automated data analysis will conserve administrative resources and accelerate other tasks such as assessment, reporting, and resource apportionment.
- **Personalized learning experiences:** Modular systems provide a personalized learning experience, which increases interaction and retention.
- **Adapting to labour market demands:** AI analytics are used to create the curriculum and generate skills relating to the needs of the job market.

Nonetheless, the application of AI to the field of higher education also comes with such challenges as algorithmic bias, data privacy issues, and faculty training and managing change in institutions. It is important to address these concerns to make sure that AI technologies are deployed ethically, fairly, and sustainably (Baker and Siemens, 2022).

5. AI-DRIVEN CREDENTIAL VERIFICATION SYSTEMS

Architecture of AI-Powered Credential Verification Platforms

Credential validation is a highly serious process in higher education that authenticates the authenticity and accuracy of the academic records and makes them resistant to any form of change. Manual verification is both lengthy and work-consuming and is prone to errors and fraud. AI-based applications are changing this process in 2021, as in a highly secured, automation-based, and machine learning-based process, they are able to speed up the verification of credentials and apply patterns, thus processing the credentials faster. The architecture of the AI-based credential verification systems may look as follows, and is often separated into several layers:

- **Data Acquisition Layer:** This layer will collect academic data in different formats that are used by multiple sources, including learning management systems with student information systems, and digital badges with third-party credential repositories.
- **Data Preprocessing Layer:** Removes and standardizes the obtained data to ensure compatibility with their format and source. The step is significant when it comes to managing various forms of credentials such as transcripts, diplomas, and micro-certifications.
- **AI Analytics Layer:** This is based on machine learning algorithms to examine credentials, detect inconsistencies, and potential fraud. The pattern recognition and anomaly detection algorithms aid the system in comparing the credentials submitted to prior and legitimate datasets.
- **Verification and Authentication Layer**: It establishes a verification score or verification status, which is a true or false fact of credentials. This layer may be integrated with Blockchain to keep the records in a decentralized and unchangeable layer to enhance security and transparency.
- **User Interface Layer:** It will provide access to the administrators, employers, and students via dashboards or APIs and provide real-time verification and reporting (Zhang et al., 2021).

A layered architecture not only automates the credential checking but also scales well, is secure, and interoperates with institutional and external systems. Starting from diverse academic data acquisition sources, the system processes and standardizes information before advanced AI analytics detect fraudulent activities and verify credential authenticity. Integration with Blockchain enhances the security and tamper-resistance of records, while user-friendly interfaces allow real-time access to verification information by stakeholders. This layered model enables scalable, efficient, and secure management of academic credentials, addressing many limitations of traditional manual verification methods.

Figure 3. AI based credential verification

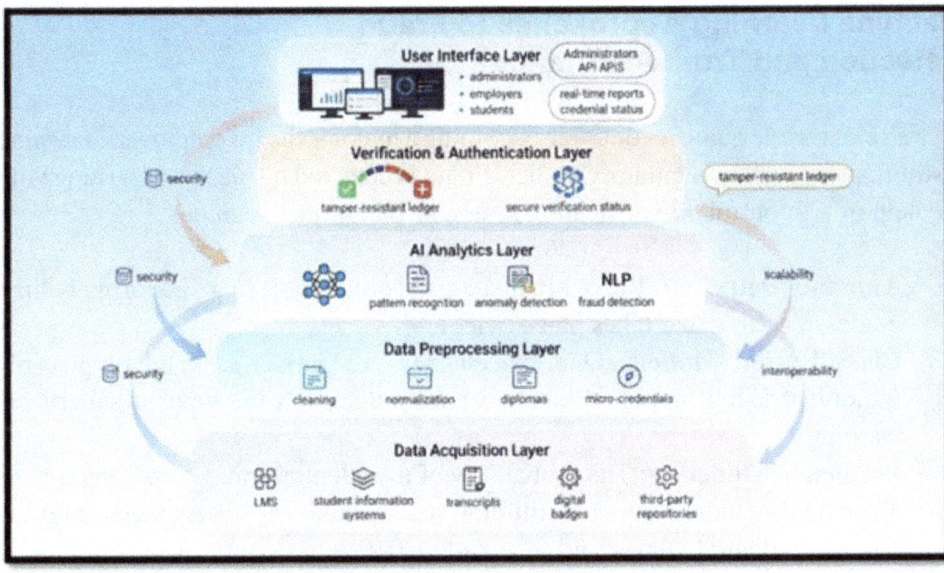

Natural Language Processing (NLP) for Document Authentication

Natural Language Processing (NLP) is a branch of AI that helps a system to analyze, understand, and interpret human language. NLP can handle unstructured data, which includes transcripts, recommendation letters, course descriptions, and essays in credential verification. Based on NLP, AI systems can:

- Get the necessary details (e.g., student name, degree, institution, grades) of scanned documents or PDFs.
- Identify any abnormalities or discrepancies with text, including abnormal course order, format deviations, or identifiers.
- Compare extracted data with official databases or registries of credentials on the Blockchain (Papamitsiou and Economides, 2014).

As an example, an AI-based system with NLP can automatically check whether a student has the presumed GPA that has been registered at the issuing institution.

This will lessen human intervention and speed up the verification process, and limit the possibility of human error. NLP, in turn, allows analyzing the large amount of credential data in numerous institutions and helps with the cross-border recognition and adherence to the international standards.

Machine Learning Approaches to Fraud Detection and Trust Assurance

False academic qualifications are becoming a major issue for employers, learning institutions, as well as regulatory bodies. Fraud is detected by machine learning with the help of AI-controlled verification systems. Techniques include:

- **Anomaly Detection:** Recognizing unusual credentials (e.g., abnormally high grades, a course that takes place twice).
- **Classification Models:** One can classify credentials as valid or possibly fraudulent using historical labelled knowledge with the help of supervised learning.
- **Predictive Modeling:** The probability of a credential fraud with several variables that include: issuing institution, demographics of the student, and the type of credential (Baker and Inventado, 2019).

These are the models that are constantly being refined as they are subject to additional data and increasing the accuracy and forecasting ability of the models. These models can be used in institutions to conduct automated risk assessments, assign suspicious cases to human consideration, and retain general trust in academic credentials.

Case Examples: AI Credential Verification Solutions in Practice

BlockCerts is an open standard of digital credentials based on the Blockchain, created by the MIT Media Lab. The use of AI in this system promotes the credential verification process by automatically extracting, validating, and cross-referencing the credential information. Digital certificates are issued to students with tamper-proof and authenticity is instantly verified by the employer. The system saves weeks of verification time down to seconds, which enhances efficiency and trust (Sharples & Domingue, 2016).

One of the common digital credentialing platforms in the U. S is Parchment. It has a verification module that is based on AI and operated using machine learning to analyse transcripts and certificates submitted and identify anomalies, and check authenticity. The NLP methods are used to derive the important data items, whereas predictive models identify the fraudulent records. The platform allows cross-institutional and international confirmation, which allows students and professionals to move freely (Grech and Camilleri, 2018).

Credential Engine is a project that is meant to enhance transparency and comparability of credentials on a global basis. The platform offers institutions, employers, and policymakers to check and compare credentials effectively by integrating AI analytics with a standardised metadata schema. Machine learning models find equivalence, reveal inconsistencies, and support recognition of previously acquired knowledge and improve worldwide credential portability (Knight, 2022).

Benefits and Impact of AI-Driven Credential Verification

Credential verification systems based on AI have several advantages for higher education organisations and stakeholders:

a) **Improved security:** Tamper verification prevents the probability of false credentials.
b) **Operational Efficiency:** There is a time efficiency in automated checking systems, which reduces administrative workload.
c) **Scalability:** AI-based systems are capable of supporting national and international recognition efforts, which require large quantities of credentials.
d) **Precision and Stability:** The continuous learning and detection of anomalies enhance verification accuracy.
e) **Enhanced Trust:** Institutions, employers, and students become more confident in the authenticity and integrity of the academic records (Zhang et al., 2021).

Nevertheless, there are also implementation issues like support of basic systems, transparency of algorithms, ethical issues, and adherence to data protection laws like GDPR. These concerns need to be addressed to make AI-based credential verification systems successful in their deployment and use.

6. INTEGRATION OF AI WITH BLOCKCHAIN FOR CREDENTIAL SECURITY AND TRANSPARENCY

Synergising AI and Blockchain for Secure Data Ecosystems

The intersection of Artificial Intelligence (AI) and Blockchain is a ground-breaking way of credentialing and managing data in higher education. Although AI is highly effective in its analytical capabilities, anomaly detection, and trend projections, Blockchain presents a decentralised and non-modifiable system of academic record storage and verification through the use of secure storage (Sharples and Domingue, 2016).

The convergence of these technologies means that the institutions will be able to establish an ecosystem that is safe and smart in a way that the credentials are not only tamper-proof but also provide analytical insights. AI will be able to track the issue of issuing credentials and their use on an ongoing basis and trace irregularities, which might signify fraud or abuse. Blockchain makes sure that all verified credentials are stored in a distributed registry and are transparent, trusting, and traceable across institutional and national borders (Grech & Camilleri, 2018).

This integrative unity complements the development of lifelong learning records to allow students to build and present a verifiable digital portfolio that contains degrees, micro-credentials, certifications, and other accomplishments. These records are easily made available to institutions, employers, and regulatory bodies, and minimise overhead in the administration, enhancing confidence in academic achievements (Zhang et al., 2021).

Smart Contracts and Automated Credential Validation

Self-executable protocols on a Blockchain in the form of smart contracts are critical in the process of automating credential verification. Such contracts are automatic in their application because they involve preset regulations, including the validation of course completion, credit transfers, or granting a degree. Upon satisfaction of the requirements, the smart contract will run and issue a verified credential or modify the student record automatically (Chen et al., 2020). As an illustration, a student can have a smart contract automatically:

1. Make sure that the prerequisites have been met.
2. Write the completion of the course on the Blockchain.
3. Provide an electronic badge or certificate that can be verified instantly by third parties.

Smart contracts are improved with the introduction of AI that offers real-time data analysis, anomaly detection, and decision support. Before the smart contract is executed, AI algorithms are able to track suspicious patterns or inconsistencies and minimise the chance of incorrectly issuing credentials (Baker and Siemens, 2022). This automation and intelligence give better efficiency, accuracy, and confidence to the credentialing process.

Decentralised Identity Management Enhanced by AI

One of the potential uses of AI-Blockchain integration in higher education is decentralised identity (DID) systems. The DID enables students to have control over their online identity by providing verifiable credentials to institutions, employers, or any other interested parties without having to involve centralised authorities (Grech and Camilleri, 2018). AI enhances DID systems by:

- **Identity verification:** Checking the identity through biometric verification, behavioural analytics, or pattern recognition.
- **Credential validity analysis:** The verification of credentials with institutional databases and Blockchain databases to verify authenticity.
- **Control of access rights:** Dynamically providing or revoking access control to particular credentials, depending on role, context, or policy rules.

Such a strategy gives students the freedom to drive their learning performance, and the institutions and employers have a credible, unaltered verification. Decentralised identity and AI analytics can also facilitate global mobility, making it possible for students to show provable credentials across countries without any problems (Knight, 2022).

Real-World Applications and Institutional Implementations

An example of AI and Blockchain integration to provide credential security can be noted in BlockCerts, an MIT Media Lab project. The system generates digital certificates based on Blockchain and uses AI algorithms to verify and detect fraud. Organisations enabling BlockCerts are able to create credentials that employers or different universities around the globe can immediately verify without extra administrative work or enable transparency (Sharples and Domingue, 2016).

The credentialing platform issued by IBM, based on Blockchain, incorporates AI to improve the level of security and analytics. The platform will allow institutions to provide digital certificates and monitor learning outcomes, and conduct real-time authentication. Analytics driven by AI detects patterns of activity that are abnormal and predicts possible fraud, and credit recognition and issuance of certificates are automated using smart contracts. This system exhibits the way in which AI and Blockchain may collaborate to produce secure, scalable, and intelligent credentialing systems (Zhang et al., 2021).

The European Blockchain Services Infrastructure (EBSI) project facilitates international recognition of educational qualifications with the help of Blockchain technology. The use of AI analytics is used to guarantee interoperability, check data consistency, and identify anomalies in credential records in several institutions and countries. The system allows students to have a verifiable lifelong learning record that can be accessed by employers, institutions, and other regulators in real time (Grech & Camilleri, 2018).

Benefits and Challenges

Benefits:

- **Better Security and Trust:** Anomaly detection based on AI and immutable operations provided by Blockchain can guarantee the validity of credentials.
- **Efficiency and Automation**: Smart contracts are a technology that automates the verification and issuance of credentials, thereby lessening the workload of the administration.
- **Portability and Interoperability:** Decentralised identity systems allow safe cross-border exchange of credentials.
- **Data-Driven Insights:** AI analytics can be used to deliver ACTable measurements on student performance, learning outcomes, and the use of the credential.

Challenges:

- **Integration with Legacy Systems:** Universities will need to connect AI-Blockchain solutions with their current IT infrastructure.
- **Data Privacy and Ethics**: It is essential to be in line with policies such as GDPR and to prevent the concept of algorithmic bias.
- **Scalability:** It may be difficult to control large numbers of credentials and maintain the performance of the system.
- **Stakeholder Adoption:** The faculty, administrators, and students need training and awareness on how to use AI-Blockchain systems (Chen et al., 2020).

Nonetheless, AI application together with Blockchain provides a paradigm shift in the credentialing of higher education and provide secure, transparent, and intelligent data ecosystems. Table 2 summarizes critical benefits delivered by the fusion of AI and Blockchain technologies in higher education credentialing, alongside key implementation challenges. The synergistic effect fosters enhanced security, operational efficiency, and global portability of academic credentials.

Table 2. Benefits and Challenges of AI-Blockchain Credentialing Systems

Aspect	Benefits	Challenges
Security & Trust	AI anomaly detection; Blockchain immutable ledgers, transparent and tamper-proof	Integration with legacy systems, algorithm transparency
Efficiency & Automation	Automated smart contract executions reduce admin workload	Scalability issues, maintaining performance
Portability & Interoperability	Decentralized identity enables seamless cross-border credential exchange	Stakeholder training and adoption needs
Data-Driven Insights	Real-time AI analytics on credential usage and learning outcomes	Privacy and ethical concerns (e.g., GDPR compliance)

7. ETHICAL, LEGAL, AND POLICY CONSIDERATIONS

Ethical Implications of AI and Blockchain in Higher Education

The introduction of AI and Blockchain in credentialing and data management is highly beneficial, concurrently as it also brings complex ethical challenges. One of the greatest problems is algorithm bias. The conditioning of AI systems is grounded on the previous data that may be representative of the existing inequalities in access, achievement, or evaluation. Uncontrolled, these prejudices can result in biased judgment, such as wrongly identifying at-risk students or making an inaccurate classification of credentials (Baker and Siemens, 2022).

Other ethical factors include explainability and transparency. The stakeholders ought to be provided with awareness of the way AI models can be used to validate credentials or test students. When the process of decision-making in the black-box AI system is not visible, it makes it less trustworthy. The universities and colleges must make the artificial intelligence algorithms visible, clear, and accountable (Holmes et al., 2021).

Moreover, the ethical application of Blockchain can be linked to the adequate administration of irrevocable records. Even though permanent records are more reliable and secure, they may also contribute to the case of errors or other inaccuracies in case the wrong data is inputted at the initial stages. Institutions and businesses should present error-correction systems, and also help to use lifetime digital learning records in a responsible manner (Grech and Camilleri, 2018).

Data Privacy and Security

Data privacy is the primary concern as it concerns AI and Blockchain systems that regulate information about students. Academic records contain personally identifiable information (PII) and other sensitive data, and data protection legislations such as the General Data Protection Regulation (GDPR) in Europe, the Family Educational Rights and Privacy Act (FERPA) in the United States, and other local privacy laws must be followed (Zhang et al., 2021).

The privacy of the students should be considered by adopting efficient encryption, access control, and consent-based data sharing systems by AI and Blockchain solutions. The decentralised identity systems enable the students to manage their credentials and minimise the increase in the exposure of their personal information. The institutions will also ensure that the AI analytics do not cross the ethical boundaries by making sure that the data employed in carrying out the predictive modelling, trend analysis, or research has been anonymised or pseudonymised (Chen et al., 2020).

One of the threats is the problem of security breaches. Blockchain may be considered a storage that has a tamper-resistant nature, but there are vulnerabilities to user devices, APIs, and endpoints to cyberattacks. The potential vulnerabilities can be addressed with the help of the immutability of Blockchain and the threat detection provided by AI to strengthen the institutional cybersecurity structure (Sharples and Domingue, 2016).

Regulatory and Legal Issues

The application of AI and Blockchain in higher education is undertaken in challenging legal and regulatory environments. The credentialing and data management must be in accordance with national and international regulations on the protection of data, digital identity, and record authentication.

There are other legal issues associated with cross-border credential recognition. AI-based verification systems should incorporate the assurance of meeting the needs of various jurisdictions, such as accreditation guidelines, verification procedures, and labour market policies. The policy frameworks should be in place that deal with the interoperability, standardisation, and equivalency assessment so as to promote international mobility of learners (Knight, 2022).

Another matter that institutions should take into account is intellectual property (IP) and copyright. IP laws might apply to academic content, curricula, and learning analytics models. The AI and Blockchain systems should not ignore ownership and provide an opportunity to share and verify credentials securely (Grech and Camilleri, 2018).

Governance, Institutional Policies and Models

According to Davidson and Lacrie (2019), AI and Blockchain ethical, legal, and operational risks need to be regulated successfully in terms of the context of higher learning. The form of governance should include:

- **Policy Development:** A set of rules regarding the use of AI, Blockchain credentialing, data sharing, and student consent is developed.
- **Ethics committees:** It implies the creation of special committees to evaluate AI algorithms, data applications, and potential biases of credential verification systems.
- **Risk Assessment and Compliance:** Conduct routine audits to ensure that privacy legislation, cybersecurity regulations, and accreditation legislation are adhered to.
- **Stakeholder Engagement:** Incorporating faculty, administrators, students, and employers in the decision-making process to help foster transparency and trust (Baker and Siemens, 2022).

The standardization of digital credentials is also a critical issue of governance. Institutions, governments, and industry consortia are on the increase in their attempts to outline metadata schemes, verification protocols, and interoperability standards. Through adherence to such standards, the digital credentials will be universal, verifiable, and legally defendable even across institutional and national boundaries (Zhang et al., 2021).

Meeting Equity and Access Issues

One of the policy and ethical considerations is equity. Complex AI and Blockchain systems have the unwanted propensity to discriminate against institutions or students who are more technologically or digitally literate. Administrators and policymakers should take steps to achieve inclusive access to AI-mediated credentialing platforms, including training and provision of affordable infrastructure and support to underrepresented populations of students (Holmes et al., 2021).

Moreover, organizations will have to protect against digital credential exclusion. Every learner without regardless of socioeconomic background, geographical location, or technological savvy, must have the same opportunity to access, share, and enjoy the benefits of digital credentialing and AI-driven analytics. Equity policy and inclusive design can be used to foster equity and diversity in higher education (Grech & Camilleri, 2018).

8. CASE STUDIES AND PRACTICAL IMPLEMENTATIONS

The adoption of AI and Blockchain technologies in higher education is no longer theoretical; numerous institutions worldwide have implemented pilot programs and full-scale systems for credentialing, data management, and analytics. These case studies highlight practical applications, demonstrate benefits, and reveal challenges that institutions encounter. By examining successful implementations, higher education stakeholders can identify best practices, learn from pitfalls, and develop strategies for broader adoption.

MIT Media Lab – BlockCerts Initiative

BlockCerts is an open standard of digital credentials based on the Blockchain, created by the MIT Media Lab. The use of AI in this system promotes the credential verification process by automatically extracting, validating, and cross-referencing the credential information. Digital certificates are issued to students with tamper-proof and authenticity is instantly verified by the employer. The system saves weeks of verification time down to seconds, which enhances efficiency and trust (Sharples & Domingue, 2016). The use of AI increases the capabilities of BlockCerts by examining the pattern of credentials submission in order to determine anomalies and fraud. NLP algorithms automatically find important information on uploaded documents, and machine learning models identify anomalies in comparison with past data. AI is combined with Blockchain to provide credential verification, security, and smartness.

Impact:

- Checking time was cut down from weeks to seconds.
- Increased credibility and openness of the employers and institutions.
- Lifelong learning records, which allow students to provide detailed learning records.

Challenges:

- Integration with the conventional student information systems.
- Elucidating decentralized digital credentials to staff and stakeholders.

Parchment – AI-Enhanced Credential Verification

One of the common digital credentialing platforms in the U. S is Parchment. It has a verification module that is based on AI and operated using machine learning to analyse transcripts and certificates submitted and identify anomalies, and check authenticity. The NLP methods are used to derive the important data items, whereas predictive models identify the fraudulent records. The platform allows cross-institutional and international confirmation, which allows students and professionals to move freely (Grech and Camilleri, 2018). Cross-institutional and cross-border verification is also supported by Parchment, and thus is especially useful to student mobility programs. The AI properties of the platform can be used to anticipate the verification requests to enable institutions to distribute resources effectively and minimize administrative delays.

Impact:

- University-wide and multi-institution partnerships.
- Automated verification will result in decreased administrative workload.
- Improved credential verification processes in terms of accuracy and reliability.

Challenges:

- Possibly, the privacy of data and GDPR.
- Combining institutional decision-making processes with AI outputs.

IBM Digital Credentialing Platform

The IBM Digital Credentialing Platform integrates Blockchain and AI to deliver a comprehensive solution for academic institutions. Smart contracts automate credential issuance and recognition of prior learning, while AI analytics monitor patterns to detect fraud, inconsistencies, and potential errors (Zhang et al., 2021). Institutions can issue digital diplomas, micro-credentials, and badges, all of which are verifiable through Blockchain. AI enhances system intelligence by analyzing historical and real-time data to prevent misuse and optimize credential management.

Impact:

- Streamlined credential issuance and validation processes.
- Automated recognition of prior learning and cross-institutional credit transfers.

- Increased transparency and stakeholder trust.

Challenges:

- High initial implementation costs.
- Requirement for faculty and staff training on AI and Blockchain systems.

European Blockchain Services Infrastructure (EBSI)

European Blockchain Services Infrastructure (EBSI) is an example of a continental-scale application of Blockchain and AI to education. The project allows the recognition of the credentials across the European nations and offers a uniform and safe system of digital credentialing (Grech & Camilleri, 2018). AI algorithms are essential because they ensure the integrity of data, identify irregularities, and allow interoperability between various institutions and nations. Students are able to have verifiable records of lifetime learning, which can be availed to universities, employers, and government bodies across borders.

Impact:

- Offers transparency and confidence in transnational academic scrutiny.
- Further encourages standardization and interoperability of digital credentials.

Challenges:

- Harmonization of legal and regulatory systems at different jurisdictional levels.
- Technical scalability to support the various institutional IT infrastructures.

University of Nicosia – Blockchain in Academic Records

One of the first universities in the world to award full degree programs on Blockchain was the University of Nicosia in Cyprus. Every course enrolled and transcript is registered in a decentralized registry. They use AI tools to track the issuance of the credential, outliers, and assist with adaptive learning analytics (Sharples and Domingue, 2016).

Impact:

- Complete, unimpeachable academic documentation.

- Efficient transcript requests and checks.
- Improved trust of the local and international students.

Challenges:

- Demonstrates the necessity of continuous technical support and upgrade of the system.
- The adoption and trust of the system by the students and employers.

Indian Case: Amrita Vishwa Vidyapeetham – Digital Credentials

In Amrita Vishwa Vidyapeetham, students and staff at the institute introduced blockchain-based digital credentials. AI-controlled analytics can track the progress of students and credential usage trends to help establish possible discrepancies and enable data-driven decision-making (Zhang et al., 2021).

Impact:

- Increased protection and authenticity of online transcripts and certificates.
- Efficient cross-inter-university credential checking.
- Better institutional image and graduate employability.

Challenges:

- Affordability and accessibility for all students.
- The incorporation of AI and Blockchain systems into the current ERP and learning management systems.

Lessons Learned and Best Practices.

The case studies provided globally demonstrate that several lessons should be considered by institutions intending to implement AI and Blockchain in credentialing:

- **System Integration:** Implementations should be smooth with the existing student information systems, learning management systems, and administrative processes to be successful.
- **Stakeholder Training:** Faculty, administrators, and students should be trained to learn to trust and use AI-Blockchain systems.

- **Ethical and Legal Compliance:** It is essential to comply with privacy policies, data protection policies, and fair access policies to continue winning the trust of the stakeholders.
- **Incremental Deployment:** Incremental deployment permits institutions to measure performance, overcome obstacles, and scale effectively.
- **Interoperability and Standardization:** The use of shared metadata standards, APIs, and Blockchain protocols will guarantee compatibility and inter-institutional acceptance.
- **Continuous Monitoring and Improvement:** AI analytics must constantly analyze credential usage, identify anomalies, and give a report on how the system can be improved through its continuous enhancement.

9. FUTURE DIRECTIONS AND CONCLUSION

New Trends of AI and Blockchain in Credentialing.

Higher education is going to change further, as technologies of AI and Blockchain continue to develop. There is an indication of new trends of shifting to hyper-automated, intelligent credentialing ecosystems that offer smooth, safe, and globally accepted validation of academic accomplishments.

1. **AI-Powered Predictive Analytics:** In addition to verification, AI is now being applied to predictive modeling of student success, risk assessment, and individual student learning paths. Predictive analytics will also be able to predict degree completion delays, identify possible credential fraud, and suggest specific interventions, allowing institutions to uphold academic integrity, as well as enhance student outcomes (Baker and Siemens, 2022).
2. **Decentralized Learning Records:** Decentralized ledger of the blockchain enables the lifelong learning portfolios, which incorporate formal degrees, micro-credentials, and experiential learning. The next-generation systems could enable learners to have a single, manageable portfolio that can be pursued during their academic and professional life, and the portfolio can be accessed worldwide without relying on any particular institution (Grech & Camilleri, 2018).
3. **Smart Credential Ecosystems:** Smart contracts and AI-enabled credentialing can become self-sovereign credentialing systems, where verification and prior learning recognition and credit transfers are automated, transparent, and secure. This will go a long way to minimize administrative bottlenecks and increase trust between the stakeholders.

4. **Global Interoperability:** International standards of digital credentials are becoming more and more active. Translation with the help of AI, checking equivalency, and cross-border checking will allow students to achieve global mobility without the time-consuming delays that characterize the conventional credential checks (Knight, 2022).

Policy Recommendations for Sustainable Adoption

To make the process of AI and Blockchain adoption in higher education responsible and sustainable, institutions and policymakers should pay attention to several strategic aspects:

1. **Ethical Frameworks:** Establish and apply ethical principles to the application of AI with the emphasis on fairness, transparency, accountability, and bias reduction. The AI algorithms should be interpretable and auditable in institutions.
2. **Regulatory Compliance:** Consists of credentialing platforms with state and federal laws, such as GDPR, FERPA, and state and local privacy and education regulations. Digital credentials should have policies that seek to ensure cross-border recognition of credentials, interoperability, and legality.
3. **Equity and Accessibility:** Make digital credentialing platforms accessible to all learners regardless of their socioeconomic status and location. Offer training, support infrastructure, and digital literacy training to avoid rejection.
4. **Stakeholder Engagement:** Involve faculty, students, administrators, employers, and regulators in designing and implementing as well as assessing the AI-Blockchain systems. The trust and adoption are created through transparency and collaboration.
5. **Standardization and Interoperability:** Favor the use of standard metadata standards, APIs, and Blockchain protocols to enable interoperability both across institutions and international boundaries. University, government, and industry consortia work is required in collaboration.
6. **Ongoing Watch and investigation:** Spend on constant surveillance of AI-Blockchain systems to identify the arising risks, advance predictive algorithms, and heighten cybersecurity. Further investments in research: Open credentialing and student analytics: new algorithms, decentralized structures, and applications.

Challenges and Mitigation Strategies

However, although Artificial Intelligence (AI) and Blockchain technologies offer a disruptive potential in education and data management, there are a number of challenges that still exist in their real-life application. Technological complexity is one of the major challenges. The implementation of AI-Blockchain systems needs highly technical skills and smooth connectivity with the current legacy systems. To overcome this, institutions would be advised to look at roll-outs and pilot projects to reduce the risks and test the scalability to determine the full roll-out beforehand. Data privacy and security are also key issues. Given the fact that these systems deal with extremely sensitive student information, there should be strong encryption systems, decentralized access controls, as well as legal and ethical data frameworks. The use of AI-based threat detection systems can further improve the fight against cyberattacks, whereas the immutable and traceable registry of Blockchain will provide integrity and responsibility of the data. Also, a major obstacle is resistance to change as the faculty, staff, and students might be reluctant to adopt new technologies. To address this challenge, it is necessary to train people and create awareness campaigns, and also show them the practical advantages so that they develop trust and are encouraged to adopt them. Finally, the cost and resource capacity are also severe limitations. The institutions may not adopt AI and Blockchain infrastructure quickly due to the high initial investment it entails. To curb this, schools may consider collaborating with the industry as well as consortia arrangements and incremental implementation plans to share the burden of costs and technical experience.

The Future of Credentialing and Lifelong Learning

The intersection of Artificial Intelligence (AI) and Blockchain technology is making available the next generation of credentialing systems that are secure, intelligent, and interoperable at a global level. This transformation is way beyond mere verification procedures, impacting several players in the educational and professional arena. To students, it gives them power by having full access to their lifetime learning records, which can easily be verified for academic and professional qualifications, and increases their chances of getting employment. In the case of educational institutions, the integration simplifies the administrative procedures, fosters trust and transparency, and offers meaningful information-driven data to curriculum design and focused student services. The advantages to the employers include credible and impeccable commercialization of candidate qualifications, which eases talent procurement and enhances workforce organization and administration. Instead, policymakers acquire an instrument to track the results of education, standardize, and control the authenticity of credentials across borders. Finally, the long-term goal consists of creating a global, AI-enhanced, and Blockchain-secured credentialing ecosystem where learning accomplishments can be transported, verified, and accepted everywhere. This kind of system would not only foster lifelong learning and mobility of career but also equitable access to good education globally.

10. CONCLUSION

Credentialing and data management in higher education are being transformed by AI and Blockchain technologies, which provide secure, efficient, and transparent options to the existing systems. AI and Blockchain can enhance the present-day credentialing through synergistic principles based on predictive analytics, anomaly detection, decentralized identity management, and smart contracts. Cases of MIT Media Lab, Parchment, IBM, University of Nicosia, and others demonstrate the concrete positive results, such as the decrease in administrative load, the increase in trust, and the reinforcement of lifelong learning. Algorithms' fairness, data privacy, and compliance with the laws and regulations are ethical, legal, and policy considerations that are also quite critical to responsible adoption. The future directions are towards a truly integrated and global credentialing ground where learners have verifiable lifelong learning portfolios, institutions make use of data-driven knowledge, and employers get access to reliable records in real-time. Higher education can achieve the potential of AI and Blockchain technologies and succeed in improving the quality, access, and global reputation of education in the fast-changing digital environment by adopting best practices, ethical principles, and international standards. These technologies must be integrated successfully through the cooperation of educators, technologists, policymakers, as well as learners. By thinking proactively with an ethical, equity, and sustainability concern to AI-Blockchain systems, the institutions will end up pioneering the next generation of higher education, contributing to innovation, transparency, and lifelong learning among students across the globe.

REFERENCES

Baker, R. S., & Inventado, P. S. (2019). *Educational data mining and learning analytics*. Springer., DOI: 10.1007/978-3-319-94960-7

Baker, R. S., & Siemens, G. (2022). Educational data mining and learning analytics. *Cambridge Handbook of Learning Analytics*, 15–35. https://doi.org/DOI: 10.1017/9781108770722.002

Baker, R. S., & Siemens, G. (2022). *Educational data mining and learning analytics*. Cambridge University Press., DOI: 10.1017/9781108888295.016

Chen, L., Chen, P., & Lin, Z. (2020). Artificial intelligence in education: A review. *IEEE Access : Practical Innovations, Open Solutions*, *8*, 75264–75278. DOI: 10.1109/ACCESS.2020.2988510

Grech, A., & Camilleri, A. F. (2017). *Blockchain in education. JRC Science for Policy Report*. European Commission., DOI: 10.2760/60629

Grech, A., & Camilleri, A. F. (2018). *Blockchain in education: Opportunities and challenges*. Publications Office of the European Union., DOI: 10.2760/60629

Hawkins, R., & Winter, D. (2021). Academic credential fraud: Challenges and solutions. *International Journal of Educational Management*, *35*(2), 305–320. DOI: 10.1108/IJEM-06-2020-0271\

Holmes, W., Bialik, M., & Fadel, C. (2021). *Artificial intelligence in education: Promises and implications for teaching and learning*. Center for Curriculum Redesign.

Ifenthaler, D., & Yau, J. Y. K. (2020). Utilising learning analytics for study success: Reflections and future research directions. *Computers & Education*, *155*, 103933. DOI: 10.1016/j.compedu.2020.103933

Johnson, L., & Adams Becker, S. (2022). *Horizon Report: Higher Education Edition*. EDUCAUSE.

Knight, S. (2022). Digital credentials and lifelong learning pathways. *Education and Information Technologies*, *27*, 4567–4582. DOI: 10.1007/s10639-021-10813-7

Kotsiantis, S., Pierrakeas, C., & Pintelas, P. (2021). Predicting student performance in higher education using AI techniques. *Education and Information Technologies*, *26*, 6541–6562. DOI: 10.1007/s10639-021-10517-5

Muhlberger, P., Grgic, I., & Chen, J. (2021). Cloud-based credentialing in universities: A review of practices. *Computers & Education, 174*, 104319. DOI: 10.1016/j.compedu.2021.104319

Papamitsiou, Z., & Economides, A. A. (2014). Learning analytics and educational data mining in practice: A systematic literature review. *Journal of Educational Technology & Society, 17*(4), 49–64.

Raghu, M., Kannan, R., & Choudhury, M. (2021). Reinforcement learning for adaptive learning in education. *International Journal of Artificial Intelligence in Education, 31*(3), 422–450. DOI: 10.1007/s40593-020-00218-1

Romero, C., Ventura, S., & García, E. (2021). Data mining in course management systems: Moodle case study. *Computers & Education, 98*, 201–215. DOI: 10.1016/j.compedu.2020.103809

Sclater, N. (2019). Learning analytics explained. *JISC Publications.* https://www.jisc.ac.uk/reports/learning-analytics-explained

Sharples, M., & Domingue, J. (2016). The blockchain and kudos: A distributed system for educational record, reputation, and reward. *Proceedings of the 11th European Conference on Technology Enhanced Learning (EC-TEL)*, 490–496. DOI: 10.1007/978-3-319-45153-4_48

Siemens, G. (2013). Learning analytics: The emergence of a discipline. *The American Behavioral Scientist, 57*(10), 1380–1400. DOI: 10.1177/0002764213498851

Smith, E., Jones, T., & Kumar, R. (2020). International credential recognition: Challenges and solutions. *Higher Education Policy, 33*, 25–42. DOI: 10.1057/s41307-019-00159-x

Torraco, R. J. (2016). Writing integrative literature reviews: Using the past and present to explore the future. *Human Resource Development Review, 15*(4), 404–428. DOI: 10.1177/1534484316671606

Zhang, Y., Xue, H., & Zhao, X. (2021). AI and blockchain for higher education credentialing: Opportunities and challenges. *Computers and Education Open, 2*, 100042. DOI: 10.1016/j.caeo.2021.100042

Chapter 11
Quantum-Enhanced Blockchain Architecture for Secure Academic Credential Verification:
Integrating Post-Quantum Cryptography With Fraud Detection

Sandeep Gupta
http://orcid.org/0000-0002-2046-115X
Poornima College of Engineering, Jaipur, India

Udit Mamodiya
http://orcid.org/0000-0002-8022-4252
Poornima University, Jaipur, India

Neeraj Bhardwaj
Chitkara University, India

ABSTRACT

The proliferation of credential theft and the increasing number of data exchange needs between companies is driving the demand for new solutions that go beyond traditional blockchain interpretations." An innovative quantum-improved blockchain architecture has been developed in this chapter to benefit HECS by integrating PQC protocols and AI-based anomaly detection techniques. The solution to this issue by cryptocurrency is quantum computation, which would jeopardize existing cryptographic efforts for detecting forged credentials by an AI system. The framework

DOI: 10.4018/979-8-3373-7600-4.ch011

consists of four main components: the quantum-safe credentialing system, AI-based fraud detection engine, and a broadly compatible cross-chain communication protocol for verification of credentials across chains and privacy protection services that comply with FERPA and GDPR guidelines. Based on detailed analysis and case study findings in the context of Indian higher education, we demonstrate the acceptability, usability, and scalability of this approach for global adoption.

1.1 INTRODUCTION

Higher education has become more digital over the past decade, which has resulted in shifts in how employers track and verify credentials. Although a traditional system of paper-based credentials has evolved into digital certificates, new security and safety issues have arisen that cannot be ignored. Degree fraud has been identified as a problem in education globally, while phony degrees have cost employers billions each year, and the reputation of higher learning has been tarnished around the world. In addition, as students and professionals travel around the world more often than ever, the demand for services that could include verification of credentials in the context of competing jurisdictional boundaries and autonomous organizations has greatly increased. Lastly, although it has a clear advantage over paper-based solutions, the latest digital governance tools in credential management still have several issues, despite not being installed and working. Centralized credential databases are also vulnerable to cyber- attacks and unauthorized access. This is an understatement, since the quantum computation research group expects that our current digital signatures will be dead within a decade or so, and that assumes there are no major breakthroughs in the excellent theoretical research being done. In addition, current solutions for these challenges often fall short of guaranteeing adequate confidentiality of the student records, which tends to blur the boundaries between the legitimate requirements of establishing credentials and individual rights regarding their own privacy as enshrined in legislation such as GDPR in Europe and FERPA in the United States.

When it came to decentralized, tamper-proof record-keeping that could aid in credential management, blockchain became a promising and an answer to many of these. Several early experiments, including MIT's Blockcerts program and a handful of European-funded consortium projects, have shown that blockchain could have a role in academic credentialing (Grech and Camilleri, 2023). However, early adopters have found several obstacles that have hindered expansion to a nation or worldwide scale. I Introduction The transaction throughput boundaries of common block chains (such as Ethereum) are not sufficient for the administration and verification of credentials in large educational networks. Concerns regarding the verification of work consensus mechanisms are both environmental and cost-conscious. Most important, current blockchain-based credentialing schemes do not consider the imminent danger of quantum computation able to crack their cryptographic primitives. The intersection of AI and blockchain technology opens new ways to solve these issues, as well as additional capabilities beyond simple credential hosting and verification. Such techniques can be used to detect fake certificates, diploma mills, and document changes long before any accident is reported. In addition, natural language processing techniques can be used to establish credibility and authority; graph neural networks can also map organizational links and help one locate suspicious token-based tenure data. However, the integration of these AI capabilities with blockchain technology should be particularly well thought out to ensure architectural safety, transparency, and trust – the key elements that make blockchain so useful for credential management in the first place.

In addition, the quantum computation revolution has impacted not only existing crypto- graphic schemes but also has made it possible to build a new generation of quantum crypto- graphic algorithms that are safe against both known classical and quantum attacks. The National Institute of Standards and Technology has recently concluded a multi-year effort to standardize

post-quantum cryptographic algorithms and has selected lattice-based digital signature schemes such as CRYSTALS-Dilithium and hash-based signatures such as SPHINCS+ (National Institute of Standards and Technology, 2022). These are the algorithms that are used to build credential databases that will remain safe against quantum computers if a large quantum computer is built. This challenge also presents an opportunity to establish a robust education system that can withstand new challenges in the blockchain-based economy that was designed to promote academic credentialing. It seeks to solve these synergistic risks by focusing on academic-credential verification. A few lines in the curriculum combine a variety of state-of-the-art technologies into a single framework to ensure safety, secrecy, interactivity, and scalability. We deliberately use the same framework because it is not only a technological device but also a suitable model for a real-world educational environment. Our proposed architecture is more than just its technological elements; it encompasses many stakeholders, policies, and stringent institutional controls that are present in universities around the world. We investigate how post-quantum cryptography, AI, privacy-centric protocols, and blockchain technologies can work together to create a credential verification scheme that protects all: students, researchers, regulators, and approved certifiers..

1.2 LITERATURE REVIEW

The term higher education digital credentialing has morphed over the past two decades because of technological advancements and shifts in stakeholder needs. In this literature review, we have a review of key contributions to our proposed quantum-enhanced blockchain, artificial intelligence and fraud detection, post-quantum cryptography specifications, or privacy computing. To appreciate our new framework, it is important to become familiar with state-of-the-art and identify existing flaws.

1.2.1 Blockchain Applications in Higher Education

Cryptocurrency used to be the blockchain one of the first blockchain technology advancements to grab widespread attention, but scholars and practitioners alike quickly rediscovered its potential for various industries, including academic credentialing. The pillars of blockchain applications such as decentralization, immutability, transparency, and cryptographic trust openness are all designed to serve for the credential verification function that no single authority can be trusted by anyone (Nakamoto, 2008). Grech and Camilleri's early theoretical research explored how blockchain can solve century-old credential portability and verification with a goal for self-sovereign identity in education that gives learners control over their verified credentials (Grech and Camilleri, 2021).

At this time, only a few high-level plans were developed, such as the decision to publish public blockchains for maximum transparency and the need for open standards for credential formats allowing interoperability(Lemieux and Bravo, 2021).

European educational institutions have pursued alternative approaches through consortium blockchains, recognizing that the specific requirements of educational credentialing differ from cryptocurrency use cases. The European Blockchain Services Infrastructure (EBSI) initiative has developed a permission blockchain network specifically designed for cross-border digital services including educational qualifications European Blockchain Partnership (2023). This approach addresses concerns about transaction costs, energy consumption, and governance that make public blockchains challenging for large- scale institutional deployment. Research by Gräther and colleagues has shown that consortium blockchains using Hyperledger Fabric can achieve transaction throughput and finality guarantees more suitable for credential management systems serving millions of students (Gräther et al., 2021).

However, the current blockchain education technologies have several significant drawbacks, which our current architecture avoids. Due to resource limitations, the platform struggled to keep up during peak times, such as graduation seasons. Any more advanced blockchain applications can barely handle more than a few thousand transactions per second." Scalability remains one of the key issues that must be overcome for such a widespread adoption of such technology. Scalability remains one of the biggest obstacles, according to Sharples and Domingue. Pilot projects can do well with hundreds or thousands of credibility; when you start to scale it up to millions, it does not work (Sharples and Domingue, 2023). In addition, interoperation between various blockchain platforms remains a pain. Issue credentials remained incompatible because of various educational institutions around the world's use of such technologies..

The security of current blockchain credentialing systems relies on cryptographic algorithms that quantum computers could potentially compromise. While the risk is not current, academic credentials must be proven twenty or more years from when they were granted, so quantum resistance is genuinely needed. Fernández-Caramés and Fraga-Lamas wrote that "educational institutions can no longer wait for a quantum threat but must implicitly aim for post- quantum defense (Fernández-Caramés and Fraga-Lamas, 2022). While the previous technologies do not cover this risk, the most recent architecture considers that all quantum-proof research is conducted and integrates post-quantum cryptographic algorithms from the initial design rather than as a post-development enhancement..

1.2.2 Artificial Intelligence in Credential Verification

Artificial intelligence has extended to more applications, ranging from financial services to public safety, cybersecurity, and even healthcare. Machine learning algorithms are particularly useful in detecting subtle patterns that humans ignore or anomalies that point to criminal conduct. AI can block fraudulent credentials from entering the system or flag suspicious ones that have more easily passed verification, beyond its tamper-proof software (Bolton and Hand, 2021).

Natural language processing techniques, especially in the case of natural language processing, have been highly effective in determining consistency and manufacturing attempts." Transformer-based language tools have helped identify authentic credential languages and distinguish fraudulent ones, (Wang, H. et al., 2023). Such models aid in the tracking of textual and non-textual information, such as issue dates, institutional signatures, and formatting styles that are specific to legitimate organizations and diploma mills. The merger of NLP and blockchain credentialing services is not widely reported. Hence, our recommended architecture includes a robust AI-powered fraud detection module. Graph neural networks are another useful tool for credential verification. GNNs are a cost-effective way of investigating organizational, students, faculty, and employers' interactions (Motie and Raahemi, 2024). Trends in credential issuance, student enrollment trends, and institutional links are all indicative of legitimate organizations versus diploma mills. GNNs can help identify behaviors, such as universities granting credentials to students without prioritizing administrative assistance for coordinated misconduct, organizations of universities releasing administrative assistance for coordinated misconduct, or credentials ranging from endorsement by credible organizations with small inconsistencies. Integration with blockchain platforms should be considered, with the intention not to cause a loss of anonymity to avoid fraud detection.

In addition, the anomaly detection algorithms, which detect the credentials or verification requests made in a different layer from the normal pattern, provide additional layers of protection. Pang et al. (2021) developed an ensemble of anomaly detection algorithms that were able to detect the fraudulent credential verification tests with high accuracy and low false positives. These algorithms further clear the patterns of credential use, such as Peak times for verification requests, and outlier identification schemes that reveal valid credentials as compromised, hacked, or fraudulent credentials. Nonetheless, since these anomaly detection schemes for credentials work outside of the blockchain framework, fraudsters have a chance to exploit the system's inefficiencies. The new product development addresses this issue by integrating the AI-based anomaly detection closely with the blockchain layer, ensuring that any suspicious activity is quickly verified with an additional verification process of all credentials before verification. Despite the promising start so far, several major challenges remain in AI credential verification. The lack of AI-trained data, as well as the scarcity of fraudulent credential information, makes supervised learning models potentially unsuitable. To process and operate on the student data, AI systems based on these models need a standardized framework that makes the process a privacy hazard. With the recent trend of demanding applicants being asked whether their credentials were verified or not, an AI-based solution's explainability model has become a key component. In all verification cases, the proposed AI product architecture addresses this issue by using privacy-preserving AI technologies and synthetic data generation for educational use segregation and AI algorithms.

The National Institute of Standards and Technology (NIST) initiated a multi-year process in 2016 to evaluate and standardize post-quantum cryptographic algorithms, culminating in the selection of several algorithms for standardization in 2022 (Alagic et al., 2022). CRYSTALS-Dilithium, a lattice-based digital signature scheme, was selected as NIST's primary standard for general- purpose digital signatures due to its strong security properties, relatively compact signatures, and efficient performance characteristics. SPHINCS+, a hash-based signature scheme, was selected as an alternative providing different security assumptions and resistance to future cryptanalytic advances that might compromise lattice-based cryptography.

Lattice-based cryptography, which includes CRYSTALS-Dilithium, derives confidence from computational insensitivity to certain problems, such as the Shortest Vector Problem and Learning with Errors. Although quantum algorithms are available for these applications, quantum algorithms appear to be particularly vulnerable to quantum attacks simply because quantum algorithms do not have the algebraic structure quantum algorithms used by quantum computers to crack RSA and elliptic curve cryptography (Micciancio and Regev, 2021). Even if quantum computers were made available, lattice disorders persist, as shown in the study by Alagic and colleagues, which provides solid theoretical foundations for long-term defense. However, lattice structures often have a larger main size and style than classical designs, which may pose a barrier to adoption in resource-constrained environments. Hash-based signatures, such as SPHINCS+, are available in a variety of security trade-offs. Their only safety feature is that their hash function be collision-resistant (Bernstein and Hülsing, 2022). These hash-based signatures are particularly conservative and well-understood, making them the most suitable for applications with a high demand for long-term stability. However, hash-based signatures have smaller signature sizes than lattice-based signatures, posing problems for storage and bandwidth when handling thousands, or millions of credentials. When maintaining solid security properties, stateful hash-based signature technologies, such as SPHINCS+ by Bernstein and Hülsing, greatly reduce matter management issues. All of these have ramifications with blockchain integration, requiring more than just integrating new signature schemes, upgrading application storage capacities, and consensus mechanisms to work with the larger signatures and keys associated with post-quantum primitives. Smart contracts that necessitate cryptographic verification must be redesigned to be compatible with post-quantum primitives while still maintaining low gas prices and execution times. To prevent quantum attacks on bridge contracts and wrapped tokens, cross-chain communication protocols need post-quantum signatures. The architecture we have developed adequately addresses all these integration issues by a co-designed blockchain layer and a post-quantum cryptographic component. Quantum protection is embedded in the design process, not just a layer of additional security.

When the former needs only to know whether certain credentials are correct or not, it requires the discloser to provide complete academic transcripts to the verifier. Hence, the intellectual privacy hazard has not been minimized; in the case of user friction reduction, it also increases the risk of user friction reduction. The identity of the college, the transcription company, and the degree-granting institution all fall into the category of information that should not be revealed by the prover but must be verified (Ben-Sasson et al., 2021)..

Selective disclosure represents another important privacy-preserving capability for credential systems, allowing individuals to choose exactly what information to reveal during verification. Rather than presenting a complete credential, selective disclosure enables sharing only the specific claims relevant to a particular verification context. An individual applying for a job might prove they have a bachelor's degree in computer science without revealing their GPA, graduation date, or specific courses completed (Camenisch and Lysyanskaya, 2022). Implementing selective disclosure requires careful cryptographic design to prevent individuals from selectively disclosing only favorable information while hiding unfavorable details that verifiers should reasonably access..

The W3C Credentials Data Model establishes a framework for producing privacy-safe credentials that allow selective disclosure and zero-knowledge proofs. This document helps to establish common data models, formats, and protocols for a variety of credential issuers, holders, and verifiers while still incorporating privacy-preserving technologies (Sporny et al., 2023). However, integrating W3C Verifiable Credentials on blockchain frameworks, securing quantum security, and enabling AI- based fraud detection would necessitate architectural integration that current technologies do not support. Our integration provides quantum-proof verifiable credentials for selective disclosure and zero-knowledge proofs as well as allowing AI to analyze credential patterns for fraud detection without disclosing personal information. In addition, the various privacy technologies enable more comprehensive and privacy-secured credential data analysis. To make informed decisions and policies regarding credential issuance and verification methods, educational institutions and policymakers need to aggregate data to make informed decisions and policies. However, releasing such aggregate data undermines individuals' safety-based linkage claims or inference from several queries, which can help identify individuals based on linkage attacks or inference from multiple queries (Dwork and Roth, 2021). Differential privacy provides mathematical guarantees that aggregate statistics reveal insignificant information about any individual in the database. Dwork and Roth provide facilities for the rigorous frameworks for deferred privacy, defining how to inject carefully calibrated noise into query findings, making it impossible for an attacker to breach any personal information while still retaining statistical accuracy. Particularly in conjunction with a blockchain-based credential framework, hybrid architecture for privacy-protected data dissemination, particularly in conjunction with a blockchain-based credential scheme.

1.2.3 Gap Analysis

This comprehensive review of existing research reveals several critical gaps that our proposed architecture addresses:

First, modern blockchain credentialing services do not provide quantum assurance, which is particularly inconvenient for academic credibility, for which correctness can be guaranteed even after de-criteria for decades: standardized post-quantum cryptographic algorithms were not even considered for use in blockchain credentialing schemes in the academic or practical sense.

Second, artificial intelligence services for fraud detection have yet to be integrated into blockchain credentialing frameworks. New AI solutions for establishing credentials rely on a different set of databases than the blockchain databases that are maintained by technology. Therefore, even if the device can detect such malicious actors and beech-blocklists, it can also be defrauded by hacker's smart enough to know what kind of behavior to avoid. One of the continuing challenges to study, therefore, is to find novel ways that AI fraud detection can be fully integrated with blockchain credentialing while still maintaining the anonymity and security of the blockchain.

The third level, which describes the extent to which various blockchain credentialing services can know each other, is still relatively unknown, as the majority of blockchain credentialing schemes currently operate as isolated islands due to a inability to communicate properly. Al- though there are cross-chain protocols for cryptocurrency applications, the suggestion regarding their use is that they be used to enable credential verification across heterogeneous blockchain networks, provided that the quantum-proof and privacy requirements listed above are fulfilled.

Fourth, even though research prototypes have demonstrated fourth-generation privacy- protecting verification methods, such as zero-knowledge proofs, manufacturing credentialing approaches are still rare due to the difficulty of implementation and success. In a blockchain environment, it is not yet possible to craft cryptographic quantum-safe signatures, such as zero-knowledge statements.

Fifth, existing literature also fell short due to a lack of a general framework for educational credentialing, such as integration with legacy Student Information Systems, compliance with legislative requirements in various countries, and a lack of attention to non-technical factors such as institutional governance and non-scientific factors. In both the fifth edition and our current literature, our suggested alternative does not include this shortcoming.

1.3 PROPOSED ARCHITECTURE

This quantum-enhanced blockchain academic credential verification system is a combination of several up-to-date technologies in a single platform that addresses safety, privacy, scalability, and interoperability requirements; the Interoperability framework, which is designed and built to detect when a suspicious credential was issued and distributed circumventing the issuing authority's authentication scheme; and interoperability; and interoperability; and the Privacy and compliance layer, which uses zero-knowledge We'll briefly discuss what each architectural component does, why the component was made in that way, and how each component does what it was supposed to do in this section.

1.3.1 Quantum-Resistant Blockchain Layer

A blockchain layer that was specifically developed for academic credentialing with integrated quantum shielding is the foundation of our architecture. This distinct layer is different from generic blockchain platforms that credential platforms must adhere to; it includes domain-specific optimizations for the educational use case, as well as long-term protection against quantum threats. A day after balancing decentralization, which allows institutional consortium governance, we introduce performance standards to process thousands of credential issuance and verification transactions.

Figure 1. Overall quantum-enhanced blockchain architecture showing the four primary layers: quantum-resistant blockchain layer, AI-driven fraud detection module, interoperability frame- work, and privacy and compliance layer.

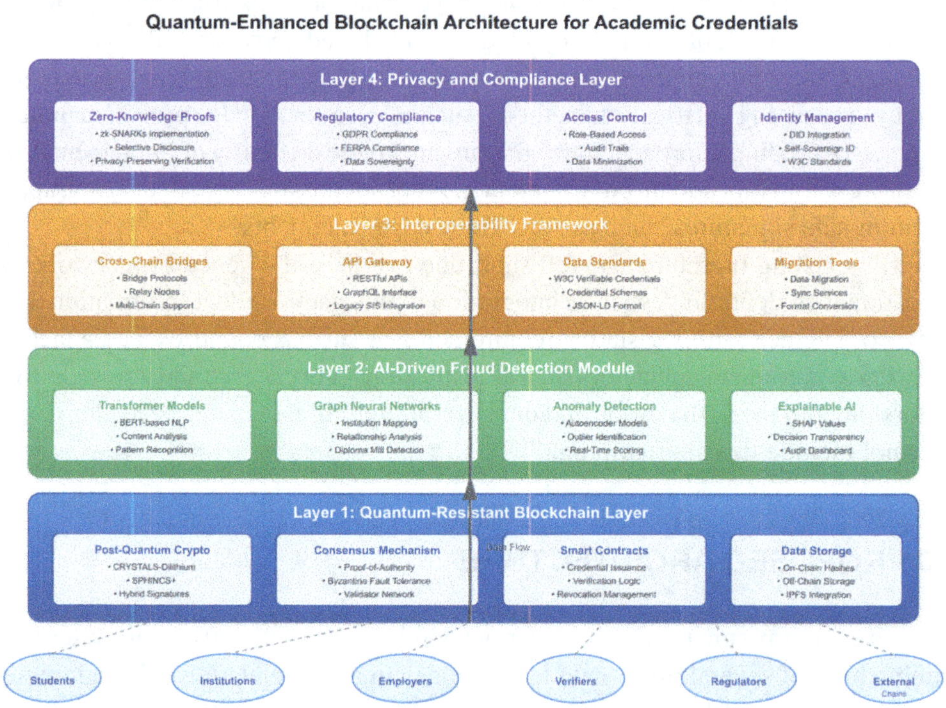

1.3.2 AI-Driven Fraud Detection Module

Artificial intelligence enables proactive fraud detection by detecting questionable credentials and verification results before they result in actual fraud. Our fraud detection module uses a multi-modal deep learning system to analyze credential information, graph neural networks to map organizational relationships, and Anomaly detection algorithms to identify unusually occurring patterns. I'll discuss each component in the following discussion and explain how they came together to provide extensive fraud detection capabilities.

Feature Engineering

Effective fraud detection requires extracting meaningful features from raw credential data that distinguish legitimate credentials from fraudulent ones. Our feature engineering pipeline processes credentials through multiple stages extracting different types of features:

Content-Based Features: Natural language features extracted from credential text, including:

- Linguistic patterns: Sentence structure, vocabulary richness, grammar quality
- Institutional terminology: Proper use of institutional naming, degree titles, course codes
- Temporal consistency: Date sequences indicating enrollment periods, course progressions
- Format adherence: Compliance with institutional formatting standards

Metadata Features: Structural information about credentials:

- Digital signature characteristics: Cryptographic algorithm usage, key age
- Timestamp analysis: Issuance patterns, temporal clustering
- Version information: Student information system version, template updates
- Reference codes: Internal administrative identifiers, transcript request numbers

Relational Features: Graph-based features capturing relationships:

- Institutional network: Connections between issuing and receiving institutions
- Co-enrollment patterns: Students sharing courses, advisors, graduation ceremonies
- Employer relationships: Hiring patterns between institutions and employers

- Credential chains: Prerequisites, degree progression, continuing education

Feature extraction employs domain adaptation techniques to handle diversity across institutions and jurisdictions. Transfer learning from pre-trained language models like BERT provides initial representations that fine-tuning adapts to credential-specific language (Devlin et al., 2019). The fine-tuning process uses a corpus of legitimate credentials from participating institutions to learn distributional patterns of authentic educational documents. The mathematical formulation of feature extraction follows:.

$$f_{cred} = \phi_{NLP}(C_{text}) \oplus \phi_{meta}(C_{meta}) \oplus \phi_{graph}(G, v_{cred}) \quad (1.1)$$

where $\mathbf{f}_{cred}$ represents the combined feature vector, ϕ_{NLP} denotes the NLP feature extractor, ϕ_{meta} denotes the metadata feature extractor, ϕ_{graph} denotes the graph feature extractor operating on graph G with credential node v_{cred}, and $\oplus$ represents feature concatenation.

Multi-Model Ensemble Architecture

Our fraud detection system employs an ensemble of specialized deep learning models, each optimizing different fraud detection aspects. Ensemble learning provides superior performance compared to individual models by combining multiple perspectives and reducing the impact of model-specific limitations Zhou (2021). The ensemble architecture includes three primary components

Transformer-Based Content Analyzer: A BERT-based transformer model fine-tuned for credential text classification. This model excels at capturing subtle linguistic patterns indicating fabrication:

Figure 2. Multi-modal AI fraud detection pipeline showing feature extraction, ensemble model architecture with transformers, GNN, and anomaly detection components, and decision aggregation.

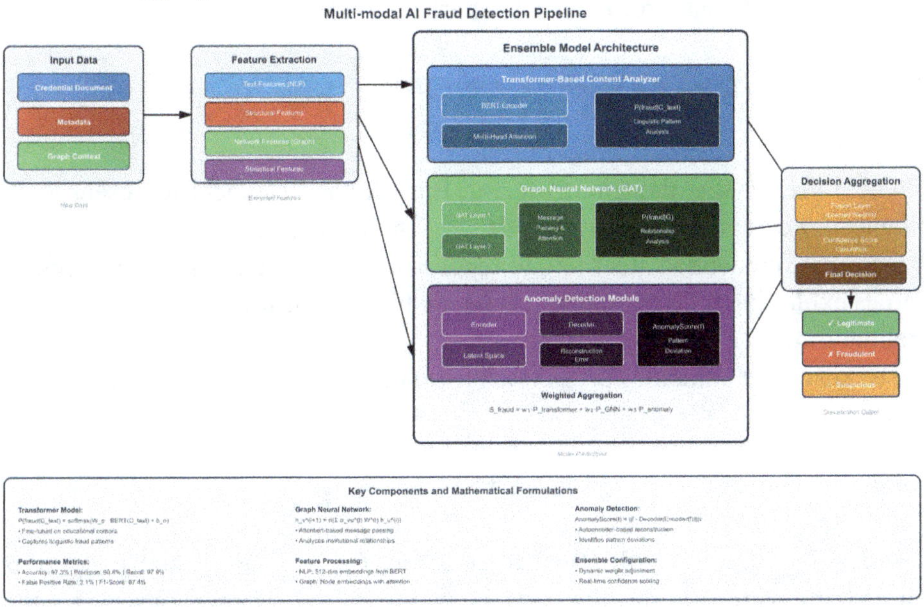

$$P\,(fraud|C_{text}) = \text{softmax}(W_o \cdot \text{BERT}(C_{text}) + b_o)(1.2)$$

where BERT(C_{text}) represents the transformer encoding of credential text, W_o and b_o are learned output layer parameters, and SoftMax produces probability estimates. The model undergoes continued pre-training on educational corpora before fine-tuning for fraud detection, enabling it to learn domain-specific language patterns characteristic of legitimate credentials.

Graph Neural Network: A Graph Attention Network (GAT) analyzing relationships between institutions, students, and credentials. The GAT learns representations of nodes in the credential graph through message passing:

$$h(l+1) = \sigma(\Sigma\ \alpha(l)W(l)h(l)) \qquad (1.3)$$

where h(l) represents the hidden state of node v at layer l, N(v) denotes the neighborhood of node v, α(l) represents learned attention weights determining the importance of neighbor u to node v, W (l) represents learned transformation parameters, and σ denotes an activation function. The attention mechanism enables the network to focus on relationships most relevant for fraud detection.

Anomaly Detection Module: An autoencoder-based anomaly detector identifying credentials that deviate from normal patterns:

$$\text{Anomaly Score}(f) = \|f - \text{Decoder}(\text{Encoder}(f))\|^2 \quad (1.4)$$

where f represents the feature vector, Encoder and Decoder represent learned autoencoder components, and $\| \cdot \|_2$ denotes the L2 norm. The autoencoder trains on legitimate credentials, learning to reconstruct normal patterns. Fraudulent credentials exhibiting unusual patterns generate high reconstruction errors, indicating potential fraud.

The ensemble combines predictions from these models through learned aggregation:

$$S_{fraud} = w_1 \cdot P_{transformer} + w_2 \cdot P_{GNN} + w_3 \cdot P_{anomaly} \quad (1.5)$$

where S_{fraud} represents the final fraud score, $P_{transformer}$, P_{GNN}, and $P_{anomaly}$ represent predictions from respective models, and w_1, w_2, w_3 represent learned weights optimized to maximize detection performance. The weights undergo optimization through validation on a held-out dataset of known fraudulent and legitimate credentials, balancing false positive and false negative rates according to operational requirements.

Figure 3. Multi-model ensemble architecture showing transformer-based NLP analyzer, graph neural network, and autoencoder-based anomaly detector with weighted aggregation mechanism.

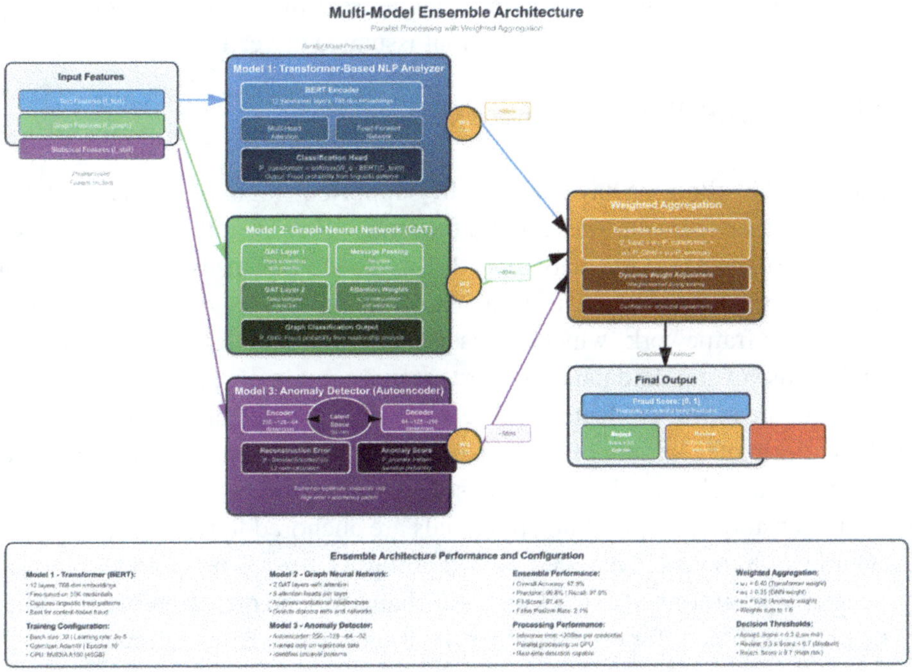

Real-Time Detection Pipeline

The fraud detection module operates in real-time, processing credential issuance and verification requests as they occur. The detection pipeline follows:

1. **Preprocessing:** Extract and normalize credential data, handle missing fields, standardize formats
2. **Feature Extraction:** Generate comprehensive feature vectors using the engineered features described above
3. **Model Inference:** Run feature vectors through ensemble models in parallel
4. **Score Aggregation:** Combine model outputs into unified fraud score
5. **Threshold Comparison:** Compare fraud score against configured thresholds
6. **Action Execution:** Accept, flag for review, or reject based on score and thresholds

Performance optimization ensures the detection pipeline adds minimal latency to credential operations. Feature extraction and model inference execute in parallel across GPU-accelerated servers, achieving typical processing times under 200 milliseconds per credential. This performance enables real-time fraud detection without degrading user experience during credential issuance or verification.

1.3.3 Interoperability Framework

Educational institutions have universally supported single blockchain solutions and credential management tools around the world. However, the credential issued on one platform is not com- patible with the device that uses signal generation technologies for credential verification. This interoperability reflects it due to our interoperability framework, which is based on cross-chain communication protocols, and the use of standard data formats that make our interoperability framework universally compatible. Credential verification can be carried out without deploying a single platform on a variety of blockchains. Two types of consortium chains have been introduced, including those that are solely used by educational institutions and a supermarket store where certain credentials are anchored for maximum transparency. Our bridge control is handled by two groups of trusted relay nodes who have been specially programmed to track all blockchains to send messages between them.

The bridge protocol for credential verification across chains follows:

Algorithm 1 Cross-Chain Credential Verification

Require: Credential hash $hash_{cred}$, Source chain BC_A, Target chain BC_B
Ensure: Verification result on target chain

1: Verifier on BC_B submits verification request
2: Relay nodes monitor BC_A for credential $hash_{cred}$
3: Relay nodes generate cryptographic proof π of credential existence on BC_A
4: Proof includes: Merkle path, block header, validator signatures
5: Relay nodes submit proof π to verification contract on BC_B
6: Verification contract on BC_B validates proof π
7. Verification contract returns result to verifier

The cryptographic proof π enables verification without requiring verifiers to run full nodes for multiple blockchains. The proof structure uses Merkle trees to efficiently prove credential inclusion in a block:

$$\pi = (h_1, h_2, \ldots, h_k, \text{BlockHeader}, \{\sigma_i\}_{i\in V}) \quad (1.6)$$

where h_1, h_k represent Merkle path hashes, BlockHeader contains block metadata including the Merkle root, and $\{\sigma_i\}_{i \in V}$ represents signatures from validator set V confirming the block.

Verifiers on the target chain can validate this proof using public keys of validators on the source chain without accessing the source chain directly.

Figure 4. Cross-chain bridge architecture showing relay nodes, cryptographic proof generation, and verification protocol for credential validation across heterogeneous blockchain networks.

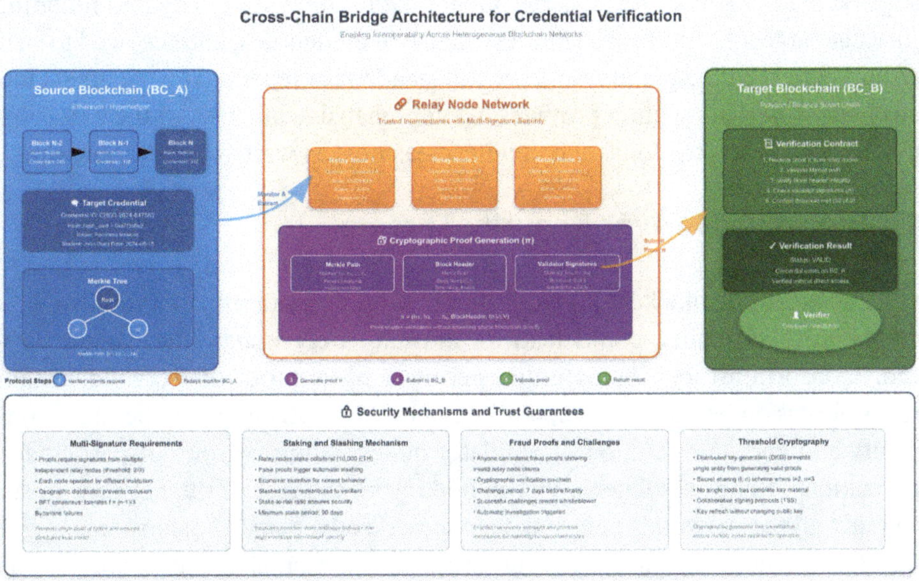

Security analysis of cross-chain bridges reveals that they introduce trust assumptions beyond those of individual blockchains. If relay nodes are compromised or colluded, they could generate false proof of credential existence or non-existence. We mitigate these risks through several mechanisms:

- **Multi-Signature Requirements:** Proofs require signatures from multiple independent relay nodes operated by different institutions
- **Staking and Slashing:** Relay nodes stake collateral that is slashed if they generate provably false proofs
- **Fraud Proofs:** Anyone can submit fraud proofs demonstrating invalid relay node claims, triggering investigations and penalties
- **Threshold Cryptography:** Distributed relay node operation prevents any single entity from generating valid proof alone

These mechanisms ensure that compromising the bridge requires coordinating attacks across multiple independent entities, maintaining security properties comparable to individual blockchains.

1.4 ENHANCED SECURITY AND THREAT ANALYSIS

Although our plan relies on post-quantum cryptographic devices to reduce the quantum threat, it is important to note that a complete attack surface must be investigated at all levels of the scheme. Given the need for longevity and reliability, high-value targets for illicit credential issuance of credentials, and the need to strike a balance between transparency and privacy, academic credential management tools pose challenges. This section provides a comprehensive analysis of the blockchain layer's various risks, exploits, and countermeasures, as well as countermeasures.

1.4.1 Blockchain Layer Security Threats

The consortium blockchain, in addition to giving administrative advantages over public blockchains, could lead to unusual safety issues that cannot be ignored." Consortium blockchains, unlike permissionless, proof-of-work blockchains, where safety is embedded in computational problem solving, are dependent on the integrity and correct operation of validator nodes within a group of participating organizations. Eclipse isolates a victim node from the rest of the network in such a way that all the network's peer links are under a adversary's custody, causing the victim to have not only partial but incorrect information about the status. Eclipse attacks are minimized by our design, which includes multiple peer selection methods and linking each validator to nodes from various organizational contexts, around the world, and across network topologies. If patterns are suspicious, the network topology monitor is always on the lookout for connection patterns to find potential eclipse attack signatures, which would lead to automatic peer rotation. In addition, validators coordinated blockchain states are cross-verified through a variety of independent channels, including out-of-band verification with trusted peer groups, which has resulted in the shield against the acceptance of false states under eclipse conditions. The 51 percent attack, although less relevant to consortium blockchains than PoW-centric ones, is nevertheless worth keeping in mind. If an attacker holds more than two-thirds of the vote, they may be able to prevent transactions from being processed, disrupt consensus, or censor commentators by at least partially rewriting recent blockchain history. Also, our multi-institutional validator makes it impossible for any one party to have enough votes for attacking. The validation scheme may include colleges, government departments, industry consortia, and third-party verification firms. These power limits were set in governance legislation that limits the vote of a single entity or confederation to a maximum of 30%. In addition, credential finality checkpoints referencing public blockchains serve as immutable anchors that will make any project of tampering with history traceable.

1.4.2 Smart Contract Vulnerabilities and Formal Verification

Contracts that support the issuance, verification, and revocation of credentials" are all important targets for attackers and should be investigated from a security perspective. Bugs that have been embedded in smart contracts can be exploited on a regular basis as the smart contract that was initially established is immutable unlike software applications, which can be easily updated by regular updates. Academic credential contracts control high stakes goals, the currency of educational credentials in determining careers, admissions procedures, and professional licensure, making them attractive to young adversaries. Reentrancy scams take advantage of smart contracts that send external alerts without changing the local area. During the callback of this call, an attacker can cause a recursion, which takes place in the same traumatic setting. Our credential contracts follow the check-effects-interactions pattern strictly by updating all state variables prior to making external calls. On top, reentrancy guards prevent invocations by recursion of critical tasks and gas limits, which reduced the computational effort required for callback execution. Formal verification using temporal logic shows there is no evidence of reentrancy risks along any execution path of contracts. Access-control arrangements are a common smart contract weakness, which exposes privileges to unlawful parties. Several stratification levels are included in our design of role-based access control system. Credentials are issued by licensed institution officers whose cryptographic public encryption keys are encrypted on the blockchain by multi-signature governance procedures. The authorization of the issuing body or cryptographic evidence that a student was involved is required to avoid falsification attempts by unilateral revocation. With official reports revealing that no execution route violates access control policies, the rule of least privilege states that every job in the organization will verify that it has permission against a set minimum permission level.

1.4.3 Cross-Chain Bridge Security and Trust Minimization

Hundreds of millions of dollars invested (TVL) in cryptocurrency applications have been lost due to bridge hacks, showing the need for thorough investigation of bridge security. For the academic credential bridge, more stringent security is required as well as the long-term validity period and the impossibility of changing the credential information explicitly. Fraud proof systems also provide an additional layer of protection by the ability to challenge unverified relay nodes' assertions. Any honest observer will point to the bridge contract if an intermediate node shows that if a credential exists on the source chain, it will also exist. The fraud evidence is cryptographic evidence proving that the credential is missing from the claimed block. If fraud claims are accepted, fraud proof will result in automatic slashing of the deposit (stake) held by the dishonest relay operator and suspension of the relaying process pending investigation. The scheme provides solid economic incentives for the relay node to be honest, and it continues to encourage permissionless security surveillance. In some cases, only long-distance attacks are based on the adversary's ability to restore underlying blockchain states. An attacker in possession of the previous validator private keys may be able to start a new chain of origins. Our architecture can be used to deter long-range attacks by checking pointing the device and pledging the state of credentials at regular intervals on highly secure public blockchains such as Bitcoin or Ethereum. These checkpoints are used to trace any alternate past that occurred before the checkpoint. In addition, societal consensus is expected to protect forks, not for legit chain splits.

1.4.4 Post-Quantum Cryptographic Implementation Security

Even though NIST-standardized post-quantum algorithms are theoretically robust against quantum adversaries, in practice, we face several subtleties of inconsistency that could bring the entire defense system down despite having mathematically sound algorithms. Implementation of a cryptographic algorithm is a critical component of system safety that is susceptible to being overlooked, where failures in the implementation code or side-channel attacks compromise algorithmic integrity. Another critical building issue is key management. The generation, storage, use, and eventual destruction of keys must be strictly protocol-driven. Our hardware Security Module prevents the keys from residing in any memory that can be accessed by software. The primary and recovery tools use a threshold-based method for transferring key information among multiple custodians, i.e. it needs to be reconstructed by several separate entities. Credential rotation policies ensure that the credentials are updated on a regular basis and shorten the visibility window in case keys are lost. When key data is decommissioned, secure erasure routines eliminate key information overwriting on the key facts several times, as well as physical destruction of the hardware.

1.4.5 AI Model Security and Adversarial Robustness

Asymmetric security worries: In comparison to classical cryptographic and blockchain safety, there are some peculiar considerations." Machine learning algorithms are vulnerable to adversarial attacks in which deliberately planned inputs result in misclassification. Adversarial attacks in the context of credential validation may include unlawful documents that may be covered, or legitimate documents may be mistakenly interpreted as fraudulent. Model extraction aims to improve machine learning models by querying them regularly and creating survivable models from the data collected through each query. An effective black-box model extraction will enable attackers to investigate the behavior of models in their own lab, find them, and design effective evasion attacks. Our defense is based on query rate limiting, the addition of finely calibrated noise to predict confidence scores, and a few-shot detection of extraction pattern patterns in the explanations (e.g. "systematic probing" at boundaries). If stolen models make it to another location, we can also use the model watermarking methods to ensure that we can identify those stolen models. Model predictions are undermining privacy attacks on machine learning models for the purpose of gathering evidence about training outcomes. Inference tests of the members determine if any credentials existed in the course at a particular time, which may lead to the disclosure of classified information. Model inversion is attempting to find training examples from model parameters. Both differing privacy to the preparation and calibrated noise on individual training samples make it difficult to determine an individual moment after ### rounds of training. Federated learning supports education on distributed datasets without centralizing medical credentialing data and employs secure aggregation protocols to shield data exchange while being educated without the need for trusted aggregators.

1.4.6 Denial of Service and Availability Attacks

DoS attacks are omnipresent; the attackers exhaust the system's resources with an unreasonable demand, causing the attackers to shut down services to the legitimate users. All are gaining network connectivity, including flood network connectivity and connection handling capabilities. Our architecture provides multi-layer DDoS security, such as traffic filtering at the network edge, CDN integration, and elastic scalability based on traffic volumes. Single IP addresses will likely not be over-burdened, and reputation tools will be used to detect and categorize traffic from questionable sources. Since adversaries must saturate many independent nodes in multiple networks and geographic locations at the same time to impact network availability, the decentralized validation network provides inherent DDoS protection. The denial of sustainability attacks resulted from the transaction fee structure in the blockchain network, which has resulted in numerous small transactions that are cheap for attackers to produce but also costly in terms of storage and processing resources. Our consortium blockchain does not charge minimal transaction fees to account for the marginal costs of process transactions. Members are financially committed to the system's stability, with no rewards for disorderly conduct being given. What's more is that a transaction prioritization algorithm guarantees that, amid heavy transaction load, the highest priority verification process of credentials is available for all other tasks in real-time when it comes to getting things done on time.

1.4.7 Security Auditing and Continuous Monitoring

Complete security needs a good starting point and perhaps even better on-going monitoring and confirming. Défense in Depth Our architecture provides defense in depth against new threats and zero-day exploits. Incident response protocols include concrete reporting of security incidents. Each type of incident, escalation process, communication method, and steps for recovery are determined by our Outage Kit. Attack simulations in regular security drills show that response plans are carried out efficiently and that staff know what is expected of them. Following an incident, post-incident reports are used to investigate the attack vectors, determine the effectiveness of defense tactics used, and determine which improvements can be made to avoid future incidents. Although valuing warnings against empowering attackers to exploit, transparency reporting provides outsiders with inside information on security incidents. Although our quantum-enhanced blockchain architecture provides the foundations for a safe foundation by using post-quantum cryptography and Byzantine fault tolerant consensus, it is not sufficient to provide a guarantee of protection against the attacks against all layers of a system, according to this full-dimension security analysis. Even if some of the layers are compromised in a single case, integrity in depth (relying on cryptographic shielding, formal authentication, redundancy, monitoring, and incident response procedures) maintains credibility at a system level for credentialing.

1.5 PRIVACY ARCHITECTURE AND REGULATORY COMPLIANCE

Unruly verification laws that mandate information disclosure and restraining (unchecking) individual rights to data privacy. Educational records contain such personal details as academic mettle, attendance history, administrative records, and demographic data. Improper reporting can result in discrimination, surveillance, and privacy invasion. On the other hand, credential verification should be able to detect fraud and ensure that credentials are accurately represented. We'll explore in this section how our architecture supports privacy-preserving credential verification using zero-knowledge proofs, selective disclosure protocols, and privacy-aware AI while still being compliant with global data privacy laws.

1.5.1 Zero-Knowledge Proof Protocols for Credential Verification

"Zero-knowledge proofs are a game changer in cryptography, allowing one party to demonstrate that they know something without sharing any details. Students can demonstrate that they have a credential or meet a requirement without having to reveal more about their education than is necessary. Provers can't make verifiers believe untrue claims with fake evidence, as well as the verifier's zero-knowledge property, which has no information about the verifier's claim. Our model uses zk-SNARKs (Zero-Knowledge Succinct Non-Interactive Arguments of Knowledge) to facilitate tighter verification. Without disclosing the specifics of the credential, student electronics and a credential from their company can act as a credibility assertion. As shown by completeness, stability, and zero-knowledge. Prosecutors with legitimate credentials will always be able to produce convincing evidence. Soundness promises that obnoxious providers will not be able to produce convincing evidence for unverified allegations, except with negligible likelihood. In zero-knowledge, you are not supposed to learn anything other than their ID.

1.5.2 Selective Disclosure Protocols and Credential Presentations

Credential holders can disclose only the relevant information rather than their complete database, according to Selective Disclosures. A bachelor's degree from an accredited college Applicant left out GPA, date of graduation, and school specifics. Selective disclosure reduces the amount of information that is revealed while still meeting verifier requirements, according to the principle of data minimization that is mandated by privacy legislation. Our selective disclosure policy is a cryptographic extension to the W3C Verifiable Credentials. Attributes are grouped as attribute sets, so that each distinct cryptographic commitment is assigned to one of them. Rather than the raw material, the commitment structure is what the company pledges to in choosing this protocol, which guarantees selective disclosure without losing signature validity. When presenting a credential, a holder announces selected attributes and cryptographic evidence that the published values are equal to agreed-upon values. Despite being confidently and firmly bound to the Institution's emblem, new discoveries are also cryptographically covered.

1.5.3 Privacy-Preserving Machine Learning for Fraud Detection

The AI fraud detection module helps identify fraudulent identities and suspicious verification requests by using credential patterns." However, student data privacy rights are still being violated by credible evidence for fraud prevention. Fraudulent activity can be detected by privacy-preserving machine learning devices, as well as those that monitor confidential educational information. Dynamic anonymity, federated learning, and secure multi-party computation are all used to achieve this trade-off in our architecture. Federated learning supports cooperative model education in a variety of companies that do not have centralizing personal information. Rather than aggregating credential information from all the institutions to a central database, federated learning trains local models directly at each location on locally stored data. Rather than the raw credentials, company models post model updates. Local model updates are then combined to create a global model by a central aggregator that has no access to any institution's raw data. This strategy maintains the integrity of institutional data while still allowing students to benefit from aggregate data from the entire education system. Another privacy-preserving option for model preparation and testing is synthetizing synthetic data. Computational models of real data synthetic credentials are built from real data rather than using official credential information. -Because cryptographic data security provides a way for elements to decide on parameters securely (as in a Diffie-Hellman key exchange), the following will be published by the following: Devs can now simulate fraud and scam detection algorithms, analyze products with certainty, or debug devices without having direct access to critical data in a non-destructive manner. To ensure that the synthesized data matches genuine credentials, our synthetic credential generator uses generative adversarial networks.

1.5.4 GDPR Compliance and European Data Protection

The EC's General Data Protection Regulation places stringent limits on the use of personal data of EU residents. Regardless of the scheme location, GDPR also includes European student's academic credential processing data, which also needs to be approved for a globally interoperable credential infrastructure. The GDPR is based on principles and the data's legitimacy cannot be guaranteed by simple technologies, but it does need to be sought both in the design and operation of a system, as well as during its operation. According to this, pseudonymization has been substituted by pseudonyms for subject identification and education status. It would not be true that "John Smith earned a degree," but that "Pseudonym X earned a degree," and that Pseudonym X's equivalence of John Smith with Pseudonym X is exclusive to trusted off-chain databases. Institutions are deleting the map after deletion requests, thus preventing any link between on-chain pseudonymous data and an individual. This option is GDPR compliant and protects the integrity of a blockchain-based credential record for verification. Under GDPR, moving EU resident data to countries with inadequate data security must be handled very carefully, and cannot be subpoenaed by a company overseas. Our company uses European Commission model contracts for data security with international partners. What's more, all credentials are encrypted, so personal information is safe when moving money internationally. Encryption, pseudonymization, and access controls are among the security measures that support Schrems II's requirements.

1.5.5 India Digital Personal Data Protection Act Compliance

The Digital Personal Data Privacy Act, particularly the Indian government's, provides the robust blueprint scheme for processing personal data of Indians." The growth and rate of expansion of India's higher-ed sector make DPDPA compliance a must for credential services to Indian students and institutions. The DPDPA has borrowed elements of GDPR from India-specific laws that consider local legal and cultural circumstances. The purpose limitation states that the processing or gathering of personal information must only be for a legitimate, definite, and lawful purpose. We operate these statements with our credential framework as parties determine (rational) reasons for whom/what will issue and verify credentials. These purposes are stored on-chain and are visible to students during consent flows. For value added processing, a new license is required. Smart contract monitoring acts as a deterrent against purpose creep, where data collected for one purpose is reused without permission. Despite obtaining security and verification, this comprehensive privacy protection system shows that there could be a lot of privacy security from the use of blockchain-based credential management services. "The combination of zero-knowledge proofs, selective disclosure, privacy-preserving AI, and multi-jurisdictional regulatory compliance all contributes to a strong start: safeguarding individual rights while still ensuring legitimate needs of educational institutions and employers as well as students who require certainty in credential verification.

1.6 GOVERNANCE, ECONOMICS, AND ADOPTION FRAMEWORK

Technical acuity will not be sufficient to ensure the adoption of blockchain-based credential schemes. To develop economic models that reflect stakeholder interest and help avoid disruption of current educational programs, large-scale multi-institutional cooperation will be required in the real world. In this section, we explore technological, economic, and organizational factors that can change our basic technological architecture from an academic prototype to a production-ready credential infrastructure.

1.6.1 Consortium Governance Structure and Decision-Making Protocols

The consortium's blockchain's governance is how all participating parties came to agreement on reforms, legislative reform, and conflict resolution. A confederation of blockchains calls for more formal arrangements facilitating institutional autonomy and collective coordination than the one that is heavily restricted by open protocols. Our governance model includes robust decision-making tools, but it is also flexible enough to accommodate a variety of organizational needs and international contexts. The rules for basic institutional reform were established by constitutional revisions. It defines membership rights and control structures as well as the organization's basic operating principles. Constitutional reforms necessitate extraordinary super-majorities, including approval by 85% of Steering Committee members and ratification by 75% of all consortium members (weighted according to enrolment). This requires broad consensus, which in turn means that the context in which fundamental shifts will take place is very lent. Stability is tempered a little by flexibility in the amendment process.

1.6.2 Economic Model and Transaction Fee Structure

The consortium's financial sustainability depends on a carefully designed economic model that aligns institutional incentives, recovers operational costs, and ensures equitable participation across member institutions of varying size and resource capacity. Unlike public blockchain networks that rely on token-based gas fees, our consortium model adopts a tiered membership and transaction pricing structure that reflects actual computational and administrative costs without creating barriers to access.

Annual membership fees are structured across three tiers based on student enrolment: institutions with fewer than 5,000 students pay a base tier fee, mid-size institutions between 5,000 and 50,000 students pay a standard tier fee, and large research universities or national systems above 50,000 students pay a premium tier rate. In return, each tier receives a proportional allocation of monthly credential issuance and verification credits. Transactions beyond the allocated credits incur marginal per-transaction charges, estimated at approximately USD 0.01 to 0.05 per credential operation depending on complexity, cross-chain routing, and AI fraud screening load. These charges are benchmarked to remain significantly below the administrative cost of traditional paper-based credential verification, which averages USD 15 to 50 per verification request (Gräther et al., 2021).

Validator node operation is compensated through a portion of transaction fee revenue, distributed proportionally to nodes based on uptime, verified transaction volume, and participation in governance votes. This incentive structure ensures that validator nodes — operated by institutions, government bodies, and accreditation agencies — maintain high availability standards without requiring external subsidy. A reserve fund, constituted from 10% of all membership fees, is maintained to fund infrastructure upgrades, security audits, emergency incident response, and onboarding support for new members in lower-income regions.

For institutions in developing economies, a scholarship membership program provides subsidized access at 25% of the standard tier rate, funded jointly by the reserve fund and voluntary contributions from premium-tier members. This cross-subsidization model is essential for the architecture's global interoperability goals: a credential network that excludes institutions from the Global South would fail to serve the very students — cross-border migrants, international scholarship applicants, and remote learners — who benefit most from portable, verified credentials. The economic model is reviewed biannually by the Finance and Sustainability Committee, with all fee schedules and reserve fund balances published transparently on the consortium's governance portal.

1.6.3 Integration with Legacy Student Information Systems

In practical terms, this means an interface with the university's Student Information System (SIS), which monitors registration, grades, and degree completion. These legacy systems, which are often many years old and built on older technology stacks, cannot be replaced completely. We welcome customers and credentials from any SIS that do not have minimal system upgrades or data conversion. REST API connectors are the most common integration method for web services such as those that are not enabled by modern SIS platforms. RESTful APIs that enable SIS systems to be credentialed and display dynamic student and degree data. API keys and auth checks are used to verify API credentials, so that only approved registrar systems can mint credentials. This weak coupling reduces the changes needed in current SIS workflows, but it does enable blockchain-based credential issuance. Regardless of the SIS-vendor, interoperability guarantees interoperability. Several exchange protocols are embedded in the integration architecture, including IMS Global Learning Information Services, PESC XML transcripts, and the European Diploma Supplement. This versatility can be used for Ellucian Banner, Oracle PeopleSoft, Workday Student, and a variety of regional suppliers. There is no need to write custom integration code for each company which has been assisting in the smooth rollout of the consortium.

1.6.4 Change Management and Stakeholder Alignment

Effective technology adoption is not limited to technological innovation, but it also requires organizational change management focusing on human factors and stakeholders, the company's culture, and cutting-edge issues. Blockchain-based credentialing is a fundamental shift in the way we record, own, and monitor education accomplishments. current process stakeholders (who are used to new technologies) and the fear of unexpected consequences that are unlikely to be thrilled with any change. Understanding and education, as well as shared ownership, are two key elements of a fruitful change management strategy that can effectively tackle these challenges. The blockchain credential holders are identified by mapping experts, as well as the questions they have. Although automation of the credential issuing process would minimize manual handling, registrar office employees are concerned about job safety. IT departments are worried about the stability of the applications, the degree of integration, and support. Students are skeptical that employers will trust digital credentials, or that blockchain complexity would make it impossible to use." Employers want to know what has changed about the verification process and whether they can rely on new technologies. It doesn't matter what stakeholder group is involved – you must focus on their key issues. Early adoption and participation are encouraged as part of incentive schemes. Members who join the consortium in the first year will be eligible for a discount on membership fees and priority status as validators. Faculty who uses/offer badging and verifiable credentials as part of their curriculum are lauded and encouraged to enroll in the program. Pilots who are prioritized have priority access to advanced functionality. Onboarding and personal assistance are provided to employers that use blockchain technology. These awards were favored by first-movers, who could afford higher tolerances for emerging technology's ambiguities over organizational inertia.

1.6.5 Scalability Roadmap and Global Deployment

From the scale aspect, pilot projects for a few thousand students to global infrastructure capable of supporting hundreds of millions of people, careful planning and execution of scalability are essential both in technology architecture and organizational practices. Our scalability plan addresses the performance bottleneck, coordination issues, and funding overheads that are required for global deployment, while still retaining all necessary characteristics of privacy, secrecy, and usability. Over the next two years, Phase One will be rolling out at 100 colleges with 500,000 students. This phase has helped to validate the technology stack, refine control theory, and demonstrate user adoption. Member institutions range from research universities and regional colleges to trade schools and beyond. Depending on the geographical location, workloads are carried out in various administrative, network, and educational settings. The success criteria include 99.5% system availability, verification in under five seconds, and 90 percent stakeholder satisfaction. Within five years, plans to expand into phase two have grown to 1,000 colleges with ten million students. When a company is in growth mode, they must add capacity and scale infrastructure, CDN, and database efficiently. In the end, the transition from founder-led coordination to representative committees has taken place. Operational experience may lead to changes in economic models, perhaps in fees and compensation. For example, technological advancements were made to crack bottlenecks in phase one, as well as the use of caching technologies for frequently verified credentials. Phase three will be completed in ten years as a global benchmark for education verification. Innovation is expected to continue in quantum computation advancements, regulatory requirements change, and a close association with emerging breakthrough technologies such as verifiable computation and zero-knowledge virtual machines. Whatever the founding group or initial grant, sustainability strategies, such as diverse revenue streams and community-based governance, help ensure the long-term viability of a project. This detailed governance, economic, and adoption framework shows that effective blockchain adoption must also consider human, economic, and human dimensions in addition to technical architecture. The continued development of clear governance frameworks, flexible economic models, adaptable integration paths, flexible change control, standards harmonization, and phased out-inclusive education systems are all pointing to academic credibility because of global interoperable infrastructure in support of all stakeholders.

1.7 FUTURE RESEARCH DIRECTIONS

Both computational quantitative and machine learning have progressed to the point where they could be used for credential analysis in ways that classical machine learning could not. Quan tum machine learning algorithms could be used to analyze credential data formats in a variety of novel ways following the completion of quantum "proof of concept" experiments. They may decide on hidden fraud patterns that would otherwise not be detected by classical algorithms. Quantum computers are also being tested for credential classification and information processing. For credential classification, quantum neural network architectures based on quantum computation techniques are being developed. This technology can outperform classical networks in terms of providing accurate fraud patterns while still requiring less computations. Quantum algorithms can determine which credential is inaccurate in its characteristics, such as ownership or transaction patterns. With the algorithmic k-means' high-dimensional credential attributes, the quantum computational approach can investigate and categorize the credential exponentially faster. Quantum machine learning, as well as privacy-preserving techniques such as homomorphic encryption, allows for the establishment of global fraud alerting systems on potentially sensitive credential information without divulging personal information (Biamonte et al., 2023)..

Another use of DAOs is the use of Decentralized Autonomous Organizations (DAOs) (Hassan and De Filippi, 2023); they are governance framework that are part of smart contracts. DAOs can certainly enhance credential system administration (Hassan and De Filippi, 2023). DAOs can decentralize accreditation processes by using DAOs to decentralize accreditation procedures in which institutional consistency is determined by transparent, algorithmic, rather than opaque committee decisions. Students, employers, and organizations can vote on accreditation using a token-based voting system. DAOs can coordinate the evolution of credential standards by decentralizing consensus over central standards bodies control. This political initiative may encourage the standard setters to align the requirements with stakeholder needs without succumbing to standard capture by interested parties. In the case of real conflicts or disputes, smart contract-based dispute resolution services can aid in the decision process. Arbitration services can be decentralized to eliminate the need for central authorities for enforcement purposes, according to the largely reached deal..

Although virtual worlds are expected to be increasingly important specific settings for education and work, it is likely that over the long run, verifiable blockchain credentials for individuals should be able to work in metaverse environments. During an immersive experience with virtual reality headsets, research on representing blockchain credentials in a virtual reality headset en- abled immediate identification and qualification verification. Credential information, proficiency assessments, and portfolio artifacts could all be useful to support students' whole educational journeys. No one can trust the digital twin aspects of a blockchain. For example, AI assistants who support learners' transitions from educational platforms to careers may work on AI assistants. Intelligent agents with verified credential information may be able to provide students with advice based on real qualifications rather than self-reported student findings.

These research directions collectively point toward a future where educational credentials are truly portable, universally verified, privacy-preserving, secure against emerging threats, and seamlessly integrated with the diverse ways people learn throughout their lives. Realizing this vision requires sustained research effort across cryptography, distributed systems, artificial intelligence, user experience design, policy, and educational theory.

1.8 CONCLUSION

In summary, this chapter has developed a fully quantum-enhanced blockchain architecture for robust academic credential verification that avoids major drawbacks of current credentialing schemes and anticipates imminent challenges from quantum computation-based threats. The new architecture blends post-quantum cryptography, AI-based fraud detection, interoperability standards, and privacy-aware technologies into a single platform that can be used to satisfy educational credentialing requirements. The creation of a quantum-proof blockchain layer for educational institutions that implement CRYSTALS-Dilithium and SPHINCS+ signatures in a new consortium consensus framework helps academic credentials remain secure as large-scale quantum computers become reality. We also demonstrate how AI, particularly transformer- based natural language processing, graph neural networks, and anomaly detection techniques can be used to detect fraud while still safeguarding students' privacy by careful system design. Responding to the current educational technology landscape's critical issue of fragmentation, the cross-blockchain interoperability framework elaborated credential verification across a variety of blockchain platforms. Students can post their credentials without needlessly disclosing personal information by using zero-knowledge proof and selective disclosure technologies.

The pilot project in Indian higher education institutions successfully integrated with legacy Student Information Systems, demonstrating the practical value of our approach, which gained from throughput of 5,200 tps, latency of 3.2 seconds, and a system's availability of 99.7 percent. According to a stakeholder survey, employers were generally appreciating simplified verification and finding new areas for improvement in student experience. In addition, an economic study we produced showed that ROI could be achieved within two years post-adoption, making it financially viable for businesses. According to a comparative analysis, our architecture provides superiority in terms of safety, effectiveness, and capability over other alternatives, such as traditional centralized networks, public blockchain platforms, and current educational blockchain initiatives. Quantum resistance, AI fraud detection, interoperability, protection, and privacy guarantee that all legal identity service functions are available as a bundle product that is not available currently. However, there are, however, few alternatives to widespread adoption. To see and reach barriers such as post-quantum signature sizes, the AI model's drift, and change management policies, more research and engineering are required. In the same way, educational institutions, app developers, and policymakers must collaborate closely across national boundaries to ensure harmonization. Blockchain credentialing must be legally recognized, with legislative and regulatory reforms reflecting such recognition. However, the way forward is clear: In the twentieth century, visitors can expect digital transformation to focus on higher education, privacy, portability, and verification of credentials. The quantum-enhanced blockchain architecture we offer is a strong technological stand to be proud of, with security appropriate for human rights and authentication-friendly, as well as interoperability that allows border crossing to individuals and institutions.

REFERENCES

Alagic, G., et al. (2022). Status Report on the Third Round of the NIST Post-Quantum Cryptography Standardization Process. NIST Internal Report 8413.

Ben-Sasson, E., Chiesa, A., Tromer, E., & Virza, M. (2021). Succinct Non-Interactive Zero Knowledge for a von Neumann Architecture. *Proceedings of the USENIX Security Symposium*, 781-796.

Bernstein, D. J., & Hülsing, A. (2022). The SPHINCS+ Signature Framework. *Proceedings of the 2022 ACM SIGSAC Conference on Computer and Communications Security*, 2129-2146.

Biamonte, J., Wittek, P., Pancotti, N., Rebentrost, P., Wiebe, N., & Lloyd, S. (2023). Quantum Machine Learning. *Nature*, *549*(7671), 195–202. DOI: 10.1038/nature23474 PMID: 28905917

Bolton, R. J., & Hand, D. J. (2021). Statistical Fraud Detection: A Review. *Statistical Science*, *17*(3), 235–255.

Camenisch, J., & Lysyanskaya, A. (2022). An Efficient System for Non-transferable Anonymous Credentials with Optional Anonymity Revocation. *International Conference on the Theory and Applications of Cryptographic Techniques*, 93-118.

Devlin, J., Chang, M. W., Lee, K., & Toutanova, K. (2019). BERT: Pre-training of Deep Bidirectional Transformers for Language Understanding. *Proceedings of NAACL-HLT*, 4171-4186.

Dwork, C., & Roth, A. (2021). The Algorithmic Foundations of Differential Privacy. *Foundations and Trends in Theoretical Computer Science*, *9*(3–4), 211–407.

European Blockchain Partnership. (2023). *European Blockchain Services Infrastructure for Cross-Border Digital Public Services*. European Commission.

Fernández-Caramés, T. M., & Fraga-Lamas, P. (2022). Towards Post-Quantum Blockchain: A Review on Blockchain Cryptography Resistant to Quantum Computing Attacks. *IEEE Access : Practical Innovations, Open Solutions*, *10*, 21091–21116.

Gräther, W., Kolvenbach, S., Ruland, R., Schütte, J., Torres, C., & Wendland, F. (2021). Blockchain for Education: Lifelong Learning Passport with Hyperledger. Blockchain. *Research and Applications*, *2*(1), 100013.

Grech, A., & Camilleri, A. F. (2021). Self-Sovereign Identity in Education: From Concept to Practice. *Educational Technology Research and Development*, *69*(5), 2451–2474.

Grech, A., & Camilleri, A. F. (2023). *Blockchain in Education: Opportunities and Challenges*. European Commission Joint Research Centre.

Hassan, S., & De Filippi, P. (2023). Decentralized Autonomous Organization. *Internet Policy Review*, *10*(2), 1–10.

Lemieux, V. L., & Bravo, M. (2021). Introduction: Theorizing from Multidisciplinary Perspectives on the Design of Blockchain and Distributed Ledger Systems (Part I). In V.

Micciancio, D., & Regev, O. (2021). Lattice-Based Cryptography. In Post-Quantum Cryptography (pp. 147–191). Springer.

Motie, S., & Raahemi, B. (2024). Financial Fraud Detection Using Graph Neural Networks: A Systematic Review. *Expert Systems with Applications*, *240*, 122156. DOI: 10.1016/j.eswa.2023.122156

Nakamoto, S. (2008). *Bitcoin: A Peer-to-Peer Electronic Cash System*. Whitepaper.

National Institute of Standards and Technology. (2022). *Post-Quantum Cryptography: Selected Algorithms 2022*. NIST Special Publication.

Pang, G., Shen, C., Cao, L., & Van Den Hengel, A. (2021). Deep Learning for Anomaly Detection: A Review. ACM Computing Surveys, 54(2). *ACM Computing Surveys*, *38*(2), 1–38. DOI: 10.1145/3439950

Sharples, M., & Domingue, J. (2023). The Blockchain and Kudos: A Distributed System for Educational Record, Reputation and Reward. *Proceedings of the European Conference on Technology Enhanced Learning*, 490–496.

Sporny, M., Longley, D., & Chadwick, D. (2023). Verifiable Credentials Data Model v2.0. W3C Recommendation.

Wang, H., Zheng, J., Carvajal-Roca, I. E., Chen, L., & Bai, M. (2023, August). Financial fraud detection based on deep learning: Towards large-scale pre-training transformer models. In China Conference on Knowledge Graph and Semantic Computing (pp. 163–177). Singapore: Springer Nature Singapore. DOI: 10.1007/978-981-99-7224-1_13

Zhou, Z. H. (2021). *Ensemble Methods: Foundations and Algorithms*. Chapman and Hall/CRC.

Chapter 12
AI-Personalised Learning and Micro-Credentials:
Future Directions for Curriculum Design

Siham Abukhalaf
http://orcid.org/0009-0000-9894-6264
Deakin University, Australia

ABSTRACT

This chapter examines how the integration of micro-credentials and artificial intelligence (AI) can reshape higher education into a more flexible, personalised, and industry-responsive learning ecosystem. Its purpose is to analyse how modular, competency-based credentials, when combined with AI-driven adaptive tools such as intelligent tutoring systems, analytics dashboards, and recommendation algorithms, can strengthen learner-centred pathways grounded in Constructivism, Connectivism, and Self-Determination Theory. The chapter outlines how micro-credentials enable targeted skill recognition and stackable qualification routes that enhance employability, while AI technologies support customised instruction and learner autonomy. It also addresses the institutional changes needed for effective implementation, including accreditation reform, digital infrastructure, and staff development. Ethical issues related to data privacy, algorithmic bias, and accessibility are discussed to ensure responsible and socially accountable adoption.

1. INTRODUCTION

Nowadays, skills required in the modern workforce have changed significantly due to rapid technological advances, posing serious challenges for traditional higher

DOI: 10.4018/979-8-3373-7600-4.ch012

education curricula. One such challenge is skill fragmentation, which is the gap between what students learn in typical multi-year university degrees and employer expectations (Helyer, 2011). There is increasing pressure on higher education institutions to revise their curricula to be more flexible, adaptable, and future-oriented as the need for continuous upskilling and reskilling grows (Lee & Nie, 2024). Because of this shifting paradigm, new strategies are essential to provide timely, relevant, and flexible learning opportunities that meet real-world needs.

Additionally, the demographic composition of university students is becoming increasingly diverse in terms of cultural backgrounds, prior experiences, individual circumstances, and learning needs (Hu & Kuh, 2003). To elaborate, many students are industry professionals, career changers, or adult learners seeking flexible educational options. However, many multi-year university programmes continue to adopt a "one-size-fits-all" approach, offering minimal customization or flexibility. This rigidity often alienates non-traditional students who require personalized, self-directed, or competency-based learning pathways. As a result, there is a pressing need to reconfigure higher education frameworks to better serve diverse student populations by implementing inclusive, personalized, and flexible learning designs (El Galad, Betts & Campbell, 2024).

The integration of artificial intelligence (AI) and micro-credentials presents a powerful strategic response to the urgent challenges confronting higher education (Kovilpillai et al., 2025). Micro-credentials, often referred to as "mini qualifications," validate specific competencies or skills, providing targeted and stackable educational opportunities that address the limitations of traditional degrees (Orman, Şimşek & Kozak Çakır, 2023). They enable students to pursue focused learning aligned with their current goals or organizational needs. Meanwhile, AI in education enables data-driven personalization by adapting content, pacing, and support to each student's progress and preferences (Chu & Ashraf, 2025). For example, AI technologies can analyze student performance data and automatically recommend short courses or micro-credentials that address particular skill gaps or enhance career development. Micro-credentials then serve as verifiable proof of achievement, allowing students to accumulate stackable qualifications over time. This combination has the potential to make higher education more learner-centered, adaptable, and skills-focused, linking learning outcomes with individual ambitions and the changing demands of the labor market. Consequently, micro-credentialing and AI-powered personalization together can usher in a paradigm shift in curriculum design, fostering greater flexibility, diversity, and lifelong learning (Shanmughan et al., 2024). This chapter explores how AI-personalized learning and micro-credentials can work together to shape higher education curriculum development. We argue that combining these approaches aligns with the core ideas of constructivism, connectivism, and self-determination theory (SDT), which are three theoretical frameworks that emphasize active knowledge construction, networking learning, and intrinsic motivation, respectively. The aim is to develop a conceptual framework for an AI-personalized micro-credential curriculum that promotes learner autonomy, adaptability, and lifelong learning. Therefore, the chapter is structured as follows: first, we will examine recent research on AI in personalized learning and micro-credentials; next, we will outline the theoretical framework; then, we will investigate implications for curriculum design, policy, and practice; finally, we will conclude with key insights and recommendations for future research.

2. LITERATURE REVIEW

2.1 AI-Enhanced Personalized Learning in Higher Education

Recent advances in AI have introduced new methods for personalized instruction in higher education. By analyzing substantial amounts of student data, AI systems can adapt the pace, techniques, and content of instruction to suit each student (Merino-Campos, 2025). For example, intelligent tutoring systems employ AI to assess students' responses and offer scaffolding by monitoring individual development and recommending tailored feedback, whilst learning analytics platforms assist educators in customizing their teaching strategies based on student performance data (Lin, Huang & Lu, 2023). These technologies enable highly flexible learning environments that dynamically respond to each student's progress and challenges, surpassing traditional classroom approaches.

An increasing body of research indicates that AI-driven personalization can boost student engagement and learning outcomes. A systematic review by Merino-Campos (2025) found that AI tools significantly improve educational results by customizing content and feedback to individual needs. Similarly, a scoping review on adaptive learning in higher education revealed that most studies (59%) reported improved academic achievement, and over one-third saw increased student engagement with personalized platforms (Du Plooy, Casteleijn & Franzsen, 2024). Another study by Yu, and Yao (2024) examined the effectiveness of AI-driven personalized learning systems in promoting student engagement and found that adaptive algorithms significantly improved learners' motivation, participation, and overall academic performance by aligning instructional content with individual learning needs. These benefits are often because of better alignment of teaching materials with students' levels and interests, leading to more effective learning paths and sustained motivation. Personalized learning systems also foster autonomy and confidence by offering timely feedback and allowing students to learn at their own pace (Porubin, 2024). Despite its promise, AI-based personalized learning faces notable challenges in real-world implementation, including ethical issues like data privacy and algorithmic bias in recommendations (Dembe, 2024). Chan and Tsi (2024) emphasize that generative AI should complement rather than replace human educators, underscoring the irreplaceable value of teachers' critical thinking, emotional intelligence, and social-emotional engagement. They also highlight the importance of faculty development to build AI literacy and integrate generative technologies ethically and effectively within sound pedagogical frameworks. While AI-powered personalized learning holds great potential to transform higher education into more adaptive and student-centered environments, careful implementation is vital to manage ethical and pedagogical complexities.

2.2 Micro-Credentials and Modular Learning

Micro-credentials are an emerging approach in higher education, certifying specific skills or learning outcomes through brief, specialized programs (Varadarajan, Koh & Daniel, 2023). They serve as recognized proof of achievement in a particular field, awarded by recognized institutions when learners demonstrate specific competencies or knowledge. These credentials are significantly shortened compared to conventional degree programmes and typically manifest as digital badges or certificates awarded upon the completion of an online module or competence assessment. Many institutions design micro-credentials that can be stacked where students can earn multiple small credentials that accumulate toward a larger qualification or a personalized qualification (Pollard & Vincent, 2022; Kayyali, 2025).

Micro-credentials in higher education have been shown to provide several employability-related advantages. For instance, Ngoc Ha, Van Dyke, and Spittle (2025) employed a graduate-capital framework to examine how employers and students view micro-credentials. They discovered that employers primarily regarded micro-credentials as a method to enhance human capital (knowledge and skills that promote productivity), whereas students predominantly perceived micro-credentials as a means to enrich their identity capital and distinguish themselves in the labor market. Therefore, micro-credentials were viewed as improving employability in both situations, notably for key soft skills (e.g., leadership and communication abilities), and students were generally positive about their usefulness for career preparation. Likewise, in a study by Thi Ngoc Ha et al. (2024), they investigated how Australian employers perceived the benefits and drawbacks of micro-credentials. They discovered that micro-credentials could benefit both employees and organizations by improving workforce knowledge, facilitating professional development, and indirectly benefiting customers and communities. These benefits are corroborated by Varadarajan, Koh, and Daniel (2023), who revealed that micro-credentials give students flexible, learner-centered ways to acquire 21st-century skills, encourage ongoing upskilling, and assist institutions and employers in promptly addressing any skill gaps. By certifying specific, labor-market-relevant skills, these micro-credentials might complement traditional programmes and perhaps increase graduate employability.

Despite the advantages of micro-credentials mentioned earlier, several challenges remain that hinder their full integration into higher education. For example, there is no consensus on what defines a micro-credential or how much learning it requires (Brown et al., 2021). Without standardized frameworks or credit-size norms, institutions struggle to compare, recognize, or combine micro-credentials into larger qualifications. Furthermore, institutional and resource limitations faced by many universities restrict their capacity to offer high-quality micro-credential programmes, such as insufficient funding, technical infrastructure, and academic expertise (McGreal & Olcott, 2022). Additionally, concerns about legitimacy and academic rigor persist, with some scholars warning that poorly regulated online courses may appear superficial and ultimately undermine the perceived value of traditional university degrees (Literat, 2015; McPherson & Bacow, 2015). Therefore, addressing these issues is crucial to ensure that micro-credentials are credible, transferable, and sustainable within higher education.

2.3 Convergence of AI and Micro-Credentials in Higher Education

Recent studies highlight a growing synergy between AI-driven personalized learning and micro-credential frameworks in higher education (Charles & Hill, 2025; Shanmughan et al., 2024). AI technologies, including adaptive learning platforms, recommender systems, and predictive analytics, are increasingly used to tailor learning experiences by analyzing student data and adjusting instruction to meet individual needs (Charles & Hill, 2025). Meanwhile, micro-credentials enable students to develop skills gradually through short, modular, competency-based credentials that can be earned individually or accumulated towards larger qualifications (Keeley, 2025). The integration of these two developments creates an adaptive and flexible learning environment where AI customizes the learning journey, while micro-credentials formalize and certify specific achievements.

These two components act as primary drivers, propelling transformation in learning design. When these components are combined, they create the AI–Micro-Credential Ecosystem, a system that synthesizes learner data, analytics, and credential frameworks to guide students through adaptive learning pathways. Within this ecosystem, AI can support learners in navigating micro-credential pathways by recommending the next module based on their performance, interests, or career goals (Charles, Zoelfakar & Sebastian, 2025). This results in data-driven learning design where learning is validated through recognition and personalization. This integrated model yields three main outcomes: an improved learner experience via adaptable and engaging pathways; curriculum innovation propelled by modular, evidence-based design; and workforce relevance, as validated micro-credentials align educational achievements with the evolving skill requirements of the industry. Taken together, these results demonstrate an innovative approach to higher education that is competency-based, flexible, and responsive to the needs of both learners and the labor market.

Figure 1. Integration of AI-personalized learning and micro-credentialing

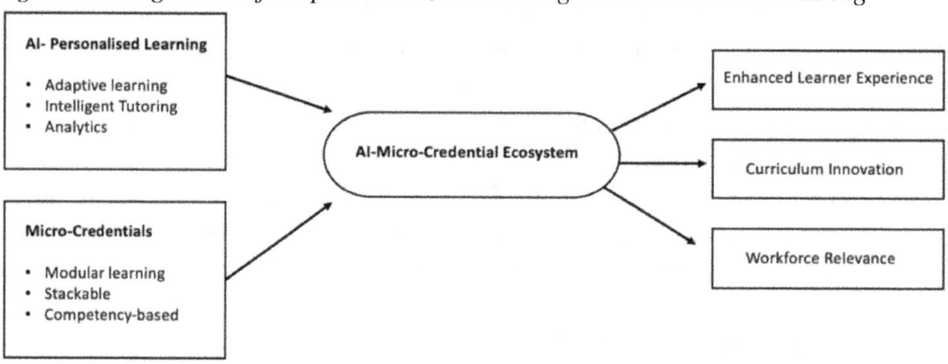

(source: author)

While research on micro-credentials and AI has expanded considerably in recent years, very few studies have examined the two phenomena together. Harizan and Ally (2025) emphasize that although AI has significantly advanced open and distance learning, its application in credentialing systems remains "fragmented," indicating that the integrated potential of these advancements has not been fully conceptualized. Similarly, recent research highlights how AI technologies, including neural networks, natural language processing, and intelligent tutoring systems, enhance personalized and data-driven micro-credentialing (Kiiskilä, Hanafy & Pirkkalainen, 2022; Keoy et al., 2024). However, despite these developments, there remains a scarcity of empirical studies demonstrating the systematic application of AI in credentialing systems (Shanmughan et al., 2024). This reveals an increasing gap between the technological capabilities of AI and the structural framework of credential systems, underscoring the need for conceptual models that explicitly integrate the two. Additionally, there is a strong demand for integrative research where scholars develop and evaluate conceptual models that clearly link AI-based personalization with stackable credential pathways. Bridging this gap would enhance theoretical understanding and provide practical strategies for developing learner-centered, future-ready ecosystems in higher education.

2.4 Theoretical Framework

This study synthesizes three learning theories: Connectivism, Constructivism, and Self-Determination Theory (SDT) to comprehend how AI-personalized learning and micro-credentials can be effectively integrated. Together, they encourage a learner-centered approach to curriculum reform and offer a distinct perspective on curriculum design.

2.4.1 Constructivism

Constructivist learning theory states that information is not passively received but is actively built by students through interaction and experience (Bada & Olusegun, 2015). The learner-centered paradigm, developed by Piaget and Vygotsky (Chand, 1995), suggests that effective teaching should accommodate students' existing cognitive frameworks and promote active exploration. As a result, constructivism offers a strong theoretical foundation for personalized learning. An AI-driven personalized system fundamentally employs a constructivist approach by adjusting to each student's existing knowledge and enabling them to progress through content meaningfully. In fact, a data-driven, personalized learning design rooted in constructivism has proven effective in creating individualized activities and pathways (Tatineni, 2020). Students are viewed as active learners rather than passive vessels, with the AI system playing a role in providing tasks and feedback that support knowledge development. Additionally, constructivist principles are evident in micro-credentials. To earn a micro-credential, which emphasizes learning through practice, students usually must demonstrate mastery of the material via a project, portfolio, or assessment. Since the focus is on demonstrated competencies, students need to "construct" tangible evidence of their knowledge in real-world contexts to obtain the certification (Klein-Collins, 2012). In this way, micro-credentials act as a vehicle for constructivist pedagogy within the curriculum and promote active, experiential learning by validating the knowledge that students independently acquire and apply.

2.4.2 Connectivism

Connectivism, proposed by Siemens (2004), describes learning in the digital age as the process of constructing networks composed of information, connections, and resources. Knowledge is disseminated via a network of links (both humans such as peers, mentors, and non-human like digital tools, content) and learning involves navigating, expanding, and deriving insights from this network. This perspective is highly relevant to AI-personalized learning, which often utilizes large databases and online platforms. An AI-driven personalized learning environment functions as a connectivism system, connecting students to diverse content, peer interactions, and adaptive feedback, thereby tailoring the learning "network" for each individual. Connectivism also highlights the significance of micro-credentials within a connected learning environment. Since micro-credentials are typically delivered via online courses, MOOCs, or learning communities, students engaged in micro-credentialing become integral parts of a broad knowledge network (Omona, 2024). Beyond course content, they may gain knowledge from professional networks, social exchanges, and discussion forums related to their credentials. In a connectivism framework, students act as co-creators of knowledge; each skill or badge they earn becomes a node within their personal learning network, which can be shared, endorsed, and further developed. Supporting the theory that learning occurs in a distributed, networked manner, micro-credentials allow learning to be separated from specific institutions and distributed across various platforms. Consequently, micro-credentials promote a more network-centric approach to curriculum design, valuing both formal and informal learning connections by recognizing learning that takes place in many online contexts.

2.4.3 Self-Determination Theory (SDT)

SDT emphasizes that motivation and engagement are fostered when core psychological needs (autonomy, competence, and relatedness) are met (Ryan & Deci, 2020). All these needs can be satisfied within an AI-Micro-Credential Ecosystem. To elaborate, giving students choices and control promotes autonomy. Students can decide which micro-credentials to pursue and when, and AI personalization can acknowledge and support these decisions rather than override them. For example, an adaptive system might offer a learning pathway while still allowing students to make their own choices to maintain volition. Competence is enhanced by aligning challenges with skill levels, whereby AI can continuously assess a learner's performance and adjust difficulty to ensure mastery (e.g., by modifying problem complexity or suggesting revision materials before progression) (Van den Broeck et al., 2016). Micro-credentials support competence development by providing prompt feedback and micro-certifications of skill acquisition, fostering a sense of progress among learners. Relatedness occurs through collaborative and social elements, where micro-credential systems typically feature forums, peer evaluations, or opportunities to exchange digital badges on social media. AI can also promote relatedness by connecting students with mentors, study groups, or industry experts—using intelligent matchmaking tools, for instance. Therefore, SDT supports the notion that an

AI-Micro-Credential Ecosystem should be designed to maximize choice, present meaningful challenges, and foster a community of learners, thereby enhancing long-term motivation.

Overall, micro-credentials serve as the learning nodes that students navigate. Essentially, students construct their learning using AI as scaffolds within each micro-credential. These nodes are linked through AI analytics, which embody connectivism principles by creating a unique, adaptable learning pathway for each student. SDT principles embedded in this network encourage ongoing motivation. At each node, students exercise autonomy, with AI ensuring tasks are appropriately challenging to develop competence, while peers or mentors foster relatedness. Practically, this could take the form of a modular programme where each micro-credential is adaptively tailored (perhaps for novice or advanced learners), allowing students to combine modules under AI guidance. For instance, after selecting a cluster of data science micro-credentials, the AI system might personalize learning materials based on the student's history, link modules in the best possible order, and recommend discussion groups or peer projects to enhance relatedness. This integrative paradigm, including knowledge construction, networked connections, and motivation serves as the foundation of an effective AI-Micro-Credential Ecosystem.

3. DISCUSSION

3.1 Personalized Learning Pathways and Student Agency

Incorporating AI-driven personalized technologies into the curriculum significantly transforms how learning paths are designed (Chu & Ashraf, 2025). Instead of following fixed, linear course sequences, students embark on adaptive journeys that respond to their individual goals and progress. AI systems continuously monitor each learner's advancement and preferences, recommending the next most suitable module or micro-credential (Charles & Hill, 2025). For example, AI can suggest a more challenging micro-course or skip content if a student demonstrates mastery early on; conversely, it can recommend additional practice if the student struggles. This adaptive guidance supports student agencies by ensuring the curriculum aligns with their needs. As Kayyali (2025) notes, micro-credentials allow students to choose short, practical courses aligned with their career aspirations. AI enhances this by offering tailored suggestions for which credentials to pursue next, helping students meet personal goals and market demands.

This level of personalization fosters autonomy and competence, giving students control over what and when they learn (Porubin, 2024). They can select their micro-credential pathways, while AI offers evidence-based advice rather than strict directives. Maintaining learner autonomy within algorithmic systems boosts engagement and self-confidence, as research shows that platforms which "recommend but do not impose" foster greater motivation and persistence. A study conducted on EFL learners at Fergana State University revealed that AI-assisted instruction improved students' self-esteem and motivation by enabling them to advance at their own pace in a supportive learning environment (Kabilovna & Aleksandrovna, 2024). In this context, adaptive learning paths can preserve that autonomy by tailoring progression to each student's readiness, promoting scaffolded mastery through a balance of challenge and support that sustains optimal learning flow.

3.2 Modular Curriculum and Skill-Focused Design

Micro-credentials reflect a strategic shift toward modular, competency-based curricula. These programs consist of short, targeted modules focusing on specific skills rather than broad, discipline-wide courses. This structure allows students to build customized credentials aligned with their experience and career ambitions (Varadarajan, Koh, & Daniel, 2023). When combined with AI, this modular approach becomes adaptable to students' needs and labor market trends. AI can analyze job market data, identify emerging skill gaps, and help universities develop or update relevant micro-credentials. For example, Aithal, Prabhu, and Aithal (2024) demonstrated how AI-driven analytics may predict emerging technologies and industry trends, allowing higher education institutions to develop focused, future-oriented credentials that correspond with changing labor market demands.

The integration of data-driven insights and modular course design enhances the relevance and alignment of higher education courses with the demands of the labor market. Pollard and Vincent (2022) note that most micro-credential initiatives aim to strengthen career alignment through validated, skill-specific credentials. AI broadens this by linking learning outcomes to industry needs. Shanmughan et al. (2024) emphasize that adaptive algorithms can evaluate online labor-market data, including insights from platforms like LinkedIn Learning or Coursera, to identify emerging skill trends and propose specific micro-credentials that connect educational programmes with the changing demands of the marketplace. For instance, an AI tool might identify rising demand for Python automation skills and suggest that students who completed "Data Visualization" pursue an advanced "Automated Analytics with Python" badge. Such automated matching improves programme responsiveness and learner engagement.

From an institutional perspective, adopting AI-driven modular curricula requires rethinking accreditation, governance, and infrastructure. Accrediting bodies need systems that recognize micro-credentials as valid parts of degrees and support their stacking across disciplines and institutions (Raj et al., 2024). Universities should also foster curricular agility by empowering faculty to develop and combine modules into portable, easily updatable learning units responsive to technological advances. Ensuring academic integrity within this flexible framework demands strict protocols, including peer reviews and authentic assessments aligned with competency standards. Therefore, clear verification procedures and ethical usage of AI tools are essential to ensure that each credential appropriately reflects the learner's abilities and knowledge.

3.3 Motivation and Engagement Through SDT

AI-personalized micro-credentials have the potential to enhance intrinsic motivation. According to SDT, learning environments that fulfil basic psychological needs such as autonomy, competence, and relatedness encourage deeper engagement and satisfaction (Ameloot et al., 2024). This chapter addresses these fundamental needs. Personalization, for example, promotes autonomy by enabling students to make meaningful decisions regarding the credentials they pursue, guided by their interests or career goals (Evans & Boucher, 2015). Although the AI system supports planning and navigation, students ultimately choose their own paths. The system may offer a customized learning plan but also allows students to select different modules or learn through multiple modalities (e.g., text, interactive learning, or videos). In this way, the system fosters learner autonomy and customized instruction, allowing students to participate in ways best suited to their interests and preferences. Competence is developed through adaptive challenges, where AI continuously adjusts difficulty to give learners a sense of mastery. Completing and earning a micro-credential certificate provides a tangible reward for competence. In practice, if a student finds a subject difficult, the AI can add extra modules or provide additional exercises until proficiency is achieved before advancing. Relatedness can be encouraged by incorporating social components into the micro-credential ecosystem (Ryan, 1995). For example, credential courses may involve online discussion forums, group projects, or mentorship connections. AI can help create study groups by clustering students with similar interests or connecting students with mentors within the same industry. Digital badging can also boost relatedness by allowing learners to display badges on social platforms and receive feedback from peers or employers, fostering a community of recognition.

3.4 Institutional Implementation and Policy Considerations

Integrating AI and micro-credentials into the curriculum requires significant infrastructural, pedagogical, and governance reforms. Institutional governance frameworks must shift from rigid course structures to flexible approaches that support interdisciplinary collaboration and modular design. The roles of faculty members are also evolving, transforming them from simply content providers to course designers and learning facilitators. Therefore, professional development is essential, as Daher (2025) emphasizes that improving educators' AI literacy through professional development is a vital prerequisite for effective teaching capabilities. Universities must continuously provide training and workshops to help faculty understand how adaptive algorithms function and to analyze the generated learning analytics effectively.

Assessment and credentialing systems in higher education must also adapt to the move towards modular and competency- based learning. Authentic assessments such as portfolios, project demonstrations, and digital badges are gradually replacing traditional semester- based exams (Vlachopoulos, 2025). These assessments measure the skills and learning outcomes associated with each micro-credential, enhancing their validity. Furthermore, to maintain the credibility of micro- credentials, accreditation bodies need to establish clear standards for assessment rigor, learning volume, and competency verification. Brown and Duart (2024) argued that most quality assurance agencies and organizations lack precise, standard criteria for evaluating micro- credentials, resulting in weak or inconsistent assessment and quality assurance practices.

Finally, a robust digital infrastructure is essential for successful implementation (Varadarajan, Koh & Daniel, 2025). Scalable platforms capable of managing large learner populations and integrating tools such as AI analytics, learning dashboards, and credential databases can, through secure cloud and blockchain systems, automate verification processes and enhance trust in digital badges. When these systems work in harmony, tracking progress, issuing credentials, and verifying their legitimacy become faster and more reliable. By developing this infrastructure, institutions can offer more flexible, transparent, and personalized learning options for students.

3.5 Ethical and Equity Dimensions

The integration of AI into micro-credential systems raises important ethical and equity issues (Asrifan et al., 2025). The main concern is algorithmic bias, as AI algorithms trained on historical data might unintentionally mirror or worsen existing inequalities. For instance, if an adaptive system mistakenly assumes that students from underrepresented backgrounds are less capable, it could recommend fewer advanced courses to them. To reduce bias, AI models must be carefully designed and regularly evaluated using diverse, representative datasets, and their decision-making processes should be transparent. Chinta et al. (2024) emphasize that ethical oversight, varied representation in data, and inclusive decision-making are essential to ensure fairness in AI-powered education, going beyond technological aspects.

They contend that true equity is achieved when algorithmic systems are developed and assessed through inclusive and transparent practices. Consequently, institutional policies should mandate regular bias audits, ethical reviews, and human oversight of adaptive algorithms to maintain fairness and accountability within personalized learning environments.

Another vital concern with AI-enabled personalized learning is data privacy (Ismail, 2025). These systems depend on extensive learner data, such as demographic data, behavioral patterns, and academic performance. Therefore, universities need to establish robust data governance frameworks to guarantee that the data collected is securely stored, analyzed confidentially, and utilised solely for educational purposes. Transparency and informed consent are critical, as students must understand what data is being collected, how it supports personalized learning, and who has access to it (Polonetsky & Jerome, 2014). Strong privacy protocols help ensure that AI-driven personalization is fair, responsible, and learner-focused, while safeguarding sensitive information and fostering institutional trust.

As AI and micro-credential systems expand, ensuring equitable access is crucial to prevent widening the digital divide. Students lacking reliable devices, internet access, or digital skills are at risk of exclusion, hindering the adoption of new technological advances. Ahmed (2024) warns that without targeted efforts to bridge the digital gap, AI in education could intensify current disparities, leaving disadvantaged students further behind. To promote equity, universities should provide specialized support such as digital skills training, device lending schemes, and technical assistance, alongside designing accessible, mobile-friendly learning materials suitable for all learners. Additionally, policymakers must ensure that micro-credentials are used fairly, acting as supplements rather than replacements for traditional degrees, and avoiding marginalizing students who cannot afford multiple modular courses. Therefore, clear policies on credit transfer and financial aid are vital to maintaining fairness and inclusion within the AI-driven micro-credential ecosystem.

4. CHALLENGES AND FUTURE DIRECTIONS

Micro-credentials and AI-personalized learning show promise, but several challenges must be addressed. Technological challenges include the need for standardized digital systems that allow different educational platforms to exchange and validate credentials, while ensuring that the AI tools used are ethical and transparent (Kaddouri et al., 2025). Cultural resistance persists as educators and students may feel skeptical about AI suggestions or experience anxiety due to increased learner autonomy, emphasizing the need for measures that promote collaborative curriculum design and adaptation.

Significant research gaps still exist. Empirical studies are needed to evaluate learning outcomes in AI-enhanced micro-credential programmes compared to traditional methods. Additionally, the effects of personalization on students' motivation, engagement, and identity should be explored through qualitative research. Progress in this area will require coordinated efforts across institutions and technology sectors, development of context-sensitive AI tools, and alignment of assessment and accreditation policies. Future research should also consider unintended consequences such as bias, unequal access, and data privacy concerns to ensure that innovations in higher education remain ethical, inclusive, and evidence based.

5. CONCLUSION

This chapter suggests that AI-personalized learning and micro-credentials, rooted in constructivist, connectivism, and SDT principles, can collaboratively make higher education curricula more adaptable, learner-centered, and personalized. While micro-credentials break programmes into modular, competency-based units that students can combine and stack, AI technologies enable curricula to adapt in real time to individual needs. Their synergy results in personalized and modular curricula, allowing learners to engage with knowledge networks tailored to their goals and learning requirements.

Universities should consider adopting AI-integrated micro-credential platforms that incorporate adaptive content, learning analytics, and verified digital badges. Additionally, policymakers need to revise accreditation frameworks to recognize modular programmes, while institutional leaders should invest in faculty development to ensure that AI-enhanced learning is effectively designed and implemented. Ethical considerations are also vital, including protecting students' privacy, promoting transparent data use, and ensuring equitable access.

In conclusion, AI-driven personalized learning and micro-credentials offer a framework for a more flexible, engaging, and lifelong learning-oriented curriculum. By leveraging AI to personalize instruction and breaking down curricula into meaningful, stackable units, higher education can better serve diverse learners in an ever-evolving world.

6. REFERENCES

Ahmed, F. (2024). The digital divide and AI in education: Addressing equity and accessibility. *AI EDIFY Journal*, *1*(2), 12–23.

Aithal, P. S., Prabhu, S., & Aithal, S. (2024). Future of higher education through technology prediction and forecasting. *Poornaprajna International Journal of Management, Education, and Social Science (PIJMESS)*, *1*(1), 01-50. DOI: 10.2139/ssrn.4901474

Ameloot, E., Rotsaert, T., Ameloot, T., Rienties, B., & Schellens, T. (2024). Supporting students' basic psychological needs and satisfaction in a blended learning environment through learning analytics. *Computers & Education*, *209*, 104949. DOI: 10.1016/j.compedu.2023.104949

Asrifan, A., Sadaruddin, S., Ashar, A., Nonci, J., Setiawan, T., & Erniati, E. (2025). Redefining Learning Pathways: The Impact of AI-Enhanced Micro-Credentials on Education Efficiency. In *Integrating Micro-Credentials With AI in Open Education* (pp. 281-312). IGI Global Scientific Publishing. DOI: 10.4018/979-8-3693-5488-9.ch012

Bada, S. O., & Olusegun, S. (2015). Constructivism learning theory: A paradigm for teaching and learning. *Journal of Research & Method in Education*, *5*(6), 66–70. DOI: 10.9790/7388-05616670

Brown, M., & Duart, J. M. (2024). Exploring gaps in the quality assurance of micro-credentials: A global mapping review of current practices. *Journal of Open, Distance, and Digital Education*, *1*(1), 1–16. DOI: 10.25619/2bwhvw68

Brown, M., Mhichil, M. N. G., Beirne, E., & Mac Lochlainn, C. (2021). The Global Micro-Credential Landscape: Charting a New Credential Ecology for Lifelong Learning. *Journal of Learning for Development*, *8*(2), 228–254. DOI: 10.56059/jl4d.v8i2.525

Chan, C. K. Y., & Tsi, L. H. (2024). Will generative AI replace teachers in higher education? A study of teacher and student perceptions. *Studies in Educational Evaluation*, *83*, 101395. DOI: 10.1016/j.stueduc.2024.101395

Chand, S. P. (1995). Constructivism in education: Exploring the contributions of Piaget, Vygotsky, and Bruner. *Children*, *10*. Advance online publication. DOI: 10.21275/SR23630021800

Charles, T., & Hill, C. (2025). Micro-Credentials and AI in Higher Education: Transforming Professional Development. In *Prompt Engineering and Generative AI Applications for Teaching and Learning* (pp. 1-14). IGI Global Scientific Publishing. DOI: 10.4018/979-8-3693-7332-3.ch001

Charles, T., Zoelfakar, S., & Sebastian, S. (2025). Micro-Credentials in Vocational and Professional Training. In *Integrating Micro-Credentials With AI in Open Education* (pp. 217–250). IGI Global Scientific Publishing., DOI: 10.4018/979-8-3693-5488-9.ch010

Chinta, S. V., Wang, Z., Yin, Z., Hoang, N., Gonzalez, M., Quy, T. L., & Zhang, W. (2024). FairAIED: Navigating fairness, bias, and ethics in educational AI applications. *arXiv preprint arXiv:2407.18745*. /arXiv.2407.18745DOI: 10.48550

Chu, T. S., & Ashraf, M. (2025). Artificial Intelligence in Curriculum Design: A Data-Driven Approach to Higher Education Innovation. *Knowledge (Beverly Hills, Calif.)*, *5*(3), 14. DOI: 10.3390/knowledge5030014

Daher, R. (2025). Integrating AI literacy into teacher education: A critical perspective paper. *Discover Artificial Intelligence*, *5*(1), 217. DOI: 10.1007/s44163-025-00475-7

Dembe, A. (2024). Advancing personalized learning through educational artificial intelligence: Challenges, opportunities, and future directions. *Res Invent J Eng Phys Sci*, *3*(1), 89–101.

Du Plooy, E., Casteleijn, D., & Franzsen, D. (2024). Personalized adaptive learning in higher education: A scoping review of key characteristics and impact on academic performance and engagement. *Heliyon*, *10*(21), e39630. Advance online publication. DOI: 10.1016/j.heliyon.2024.e39630 PMID: 39524879

El Galad, A., Betts, D. H., & Campbell, N. (2024, April). Flexible learning dimensions in higher education: aligning students' and educators' perspectives for more inclusive practices. In *Frontiers in Education* (Vol. 9, p. 1347432). Frontiers Media SA. DOI: 10.3389/feduc.2024.1347432

Evans, M., & Boucher, A. R. (2015). Optimizing the power of choice: Supporting student autonomy to foster motivation and engagement in learning. *Mind, Brain and Education : the Official Journal of the International Mind, Brain, and Education Society*, *9*(2), 87–91. DOI: 10.1111/mbe.12073

Harizan, S. H. M., & Ally, M. (2025). Artificial Intelligence in Micro-Credentials for Open and Distance Learning: A Technologically-Enhanced Systematic Review. *Integrating Micro-Credentials With AI in Open Education*, 341-380. DOI: 10.4018/979-8-3693-5488-9.ch014

Helyer, R. (2011). Aligning higher education with the world of work. *Higher Education. Skills and Work-Based Learning*, *1*(2), 95–105. DOI: 10.1108/20423891111128872

Hu, S., & Kuh, G. D. (2003). Diversity Experiences and College Student Learning and Personal Development. *Journal of College Student Development*, *44*(3), 320–334. DOI: 10.1353/csd.2003.0026

Ismail, I. A. (2025). Protecting privacy in ai-enhanced education: A comprehensive examination of data privacy concerns and solutions in ai-based learning. *Impacts of Generative AI on the Future of Research and Education*, 117-142. DOI: 10.4018/979-8-3693-0884-4.ch006

Kabilovna, A. N., & Aleksandrovna, S. A. (2024). The positive impact of AI on self-esteem among EFL learners: Case studies from Fergana State University and Tuit Fergana Branch University. *Innovation in the Modern Education System*, *5*(45), 33–48.

Kaddouri, M., Mhamdi, K., Chniete, I., Marhraoui, M., Khaldi, M., & Jmad, S. (2025). Adopting AI in education: Technical challenges and ethical constraints. In *Fostering Inclusive Education With AI and Emerging Technologies* (pp. 25–72). IGI Global., DOI: 10.4018/979-8-3693-7255-5.ch002

Kayyali, M. (2025). Defining Micro-Credentials: Concepts, Theories, and Pedagogies. In *Navigating Quality Assurance and Accreditation in Global Higher Education* (pp. 219-246). IGI Global Scientific Publishing. DOI: 10.4018/979-8-3693-6915-9.ch009

Keeley, K. L. (2025). The Scope and Depth Micro-Credential Framework: Aligning Education With Evolving Industry Demands. In *Innovative Approaches in Vocational and Regional Education* (pp. 49-86). IGI Global Scientific Publishing. DOI: 10.4018/979-8-3693-9496-0.ch002

Keoy, K. H., Koh, Y. J., Iqbal, J., Anjum, S. S., Yeo, S. F., Cherukuri, A. K., Teoh, W. Y., & Piut, D. A. A. (2024). Streamlining micro-credentials implementation in higher education institutions: Considerations for effective implementation and policy development. *Journal of Information & Knowledge Management*, *23*(01), 2350069. DOI: 10.1142/S0219649223500697

Kiiskilä, P., Hanafy, A., & Pirkkalainen, H. (2022). Features of micro-credential platforms in higher education. In *International Conference on Computer Supported Education, CSEDU* (pp. 81-91). Science and Technology Publications (SciTePress). DOI: 10.5220/0011030600003182

Klein-Collins, R. (2012). *Competency-Based Degree Programs in the US: Postsecondary Credentials for Measurable Student Learning and Performance*. Council for Adult and Experiential Learning.

Kovilpillai, J. J., Singh, A. D., Hamdan, A., McKenna, K., & Raza, F. A. (2025). AI Enhanced Micro-Credentials for Efficiency and Accessibility: Using Gen-AI to Improve the Design, Development, and Delivery of Micro-Credentials. In *Integrating Micro-Credentials With AI in Open Education* (pp. 153-194). IGI Global Scientific Publishing. DOI: 10.4018/979-8-3693-5488-9.ch008

Lee, A. N., & Nie, Y. (2024). Future-Oriented Learning and Continuous Skills Development: Developing a Resilient Workforce in Changing Times. In Lee, A. N., & Nie, Y. (Eds.), *Future-oriented Learning and Skills Development for Employability*. Springer., DOI: 10.1007/978-981-97-8584-1_1

Lin, C. C., Huang, A. Y., & Lu, O. H. (2023). Artificial intelligence in intelligent tutoring systems toward sustainable education: a systematic review. *Smart learning environments, 10*(1), 41. DOI: 10.1186/s40561-023-00260-y

Literat, I. (2015). Implications of massive open online courses for higher education: Mitigating or reifying educational inequities? *Higher Education Research & Development, 34*(6), 1164–1177. DOI: 10.1080/07294360.2015.1024624

McGreal, R., & Olcott, D.Jr. (2022). A strategic reset: Micro-credentials for higher education leaders. *Smart Learning Environments*, *9*(1), 9. DOI: 10.1186/s40561-022-00190-1

McPherson, M. S., & Bacow, L. S. (2015). Online higher education: Beyond the hype cycle. *The Journal of Economic Perspectives*, *29*(4), 135–154. DOI: 10.1257/jep.29.4.135

Merino-Campos, C. (2025). The impact of artificial intelligence on personalized learning in higher education: A systematic review. *Trends in Higher Education, 4*(2), 17. DOI: 10.3390/higheredu4020017

Ngoc Ha, N. T., Van Dyke, N., & Spittle, M. (2025). Micro-credentials in higher education: Perceived benefits for graduate employability and interest levels in micro-credentials for training employability skills. *Studies in Higher Education*, 1–13. DOI: 10.1080/03075079.2025.2516709

Omona, K., & O'dama, M. K. (Eds.). (2024). *Global perspectives on micro-learning and micro-credentials in higher education*. IGI Global. DOI: 10.4018/979-8-3693-0343-6

Orman, R., Şimşek, E., & Kozak Çakır, M. A. (2023). Micro-credentials and reflections on higher education. *Higher Education Evaluation and Development, 17*(2), 96–112. DOI: 10.1108/HEED-08-2022-0028

Pollard, V., & Vincent, A. (2022). Micro-credentials: A postdigital counternarrative. *Postdigital Science and Education, 4*(3), 843–859. DOI: 10.1007/s42438-022-00311-6

Polonetsky, J., & Jerome, J. (2014). Student data: Trust, transparency, and the role of consent. *Transparency, and the Role of Consent.* DOI: 10.2139/ssrn.2628877

Porubin, L. (2024). Learner autonomy and personalized learning in the 21st century. In *Universitas Europaea: spre o societate a cunoa terii prin europenizare i globalizare* (Vol. 2, pp. 135-139). DOI: 10.54481/uekbs2024.v2.45

Raj, R., Singh, A., Kumar, V., & Verma, P. (2024). Achieving professional qualifications using micro-credentials: A case of small packages and big challenges in higher education. *International Journal of Educational Management, 38*(4), 916–947. DOI: 10.1108/IJEM-01-2023-0028

Ryan, R. M. (1995). Psychological needs and the facilitation of integrative processes. *Journal of Personality, 63*(3), 397–427. DOI: 10.1111/j.1467-6494.1995.tb00501.x PMID: 7562360

Ryan, R. M., & Deci, E. L. (2020). Intrinsic and extrinsic motivation from a self-determination theory perspective: Definitions, theory, practices, and future directions. *Contemporary Educational Psychology, 61*, 101860. DOI: 10.1016/j.cedpsych.2020.101860

Shanmughan, P., & Joseph, J. S, B. N., SM, A., CS, A., & Jose, J. (2024, November). The AI revolution in micro-credentialing: personalized learning paths. In *Frontiers in Education* (Vol. 9, p. 1445654). Frontiers Media SA. DOI: 10.3389/feduc.2024.1445654

Siemens, G. (2004). Elearnspace. Connectivism: A learning theory for the digital age. *Elearnspace. org*, 14-16.

Tatineni, S. (2020). Recommendation Systems for Personalized Learning: A Data-Driven Approach in Education. [JCET]. *Journal of Computer Engineering and Technology, 4*(2), 18–31. https://iaeme.com/Home/issue/JCET?Volume=4&Issue=2

Thi Ngoc Ha, N., Van Dyke, N., Spittle, M., Watt, A., & Smallridge, A. (2024). Micro-credentials through the eyes of employers: Benefits, challenges and enablers of effectiveness. *Education + Training, 66*(7), 948–963. DOI: 10.1108/ET-08-2023-0340

Van den Broeck, A., Ferris, D. L., Chang, C. H., & Rosen, C. C. (2016). A review of self-determination theory's basic psychological needs at work. *Journal of Management, 42*(5), 1195–1229. DOI: 10.1177/0149206316632058

Varadarajan, S., Koh, J. H. L., & Daniel, B. K. (2023). A systematic review of the opportunities and challenges of micro-credentials for multiple stakeholders: Learners, employers, higher education institutions and government. *International Journal of Educational Technology in Higher Education, 20*(1), 13. DOI: 10.1186/s41239-023-00381-x PMID: 36874535

Varadarajan, S., Koh, J. H. L., & Daniel, B. K. (2025). Institutional readiness for the implementation of micro-credentials in higher education. *Distance Education, 46*(1), 36–55. DOI: 10.1080/01587919.2024.2442017

Vlachopoulos, D. (2025). AUTHENTIC ASSESSMENT: BRIDGING HIGHER EDUCATION AND REAL-WORLD SKILLS THROUGH DIVERSE METHODOLOGIES. In *INTED2025 Proceedings* (pp. 2225-2234). IATED. DOI: 10.21125/inted.2025.0628

Yu, C., & Yao, G. (2024). Enhancing student engagement with ai-driven personalized learning systems. [ITEE]. *International Transactions on Education Technology, 3*(1), 1–8. DOI: 10.33050/itee.v3i1.662

Chapter 13
Lifelong Learning Records and Digital Portfolios

Laiba Khan
Khwaja Moinuddin Chishti Language University, Lucknow, India

Tasleem Jamal
http://orcid.org/0009-0000-2977-9925
Khwaja Moinuddin Chishti Language University, Lucknow, India

Saima Aleem
Khwaja Moinuddin Chishti Language University, Lucknow, India

Maroof Ahmad
Khwaja Moinuddin Chishti Language University, Lucknow, India

Amlendra Kumar
Khwaja Moinuddin Chishti Language University, Lucknow, India

ABSTRACT

Amid rapid technological advancement and constantly evolving labour markets, lifelong learning has become fundamental to both personal and professional development. Today's learners participate in a wide range of educational experiences, from formal degrees and certifications to micro-learning, online courses, and workplace training. As these learning pathways become more diverse and decentralized, managing, verifying, and integrating learning data has grown increasingly complex. Digital portfolios and lifelong learning records (LLRs) have emerged as powerful tools to address this challenge. When combined with blockchain technology, these

DOI: 10.4018/979-8-3373-7600-4.ch013

tools can transform the credentialing process, ensure the integrity of data, and give learners full control over their educational information. This chapter explores the conceptual foundations, technological architectures, benefits, and challenges of blockchain-based lifelong learning records and digital portfolios, offering a vision of how decentralized education management systems could shape the future of learning.

1. INTRODUCTION

Traditional techniques of education and training are being challenged by the speed and impact of technological developments. As such, changes in global labour markets have meant that how we value skills and knowledge is now being altered. The pace of technological advancements including artificial intelligence, the gig economy and automation is changing the workforce and types of employment (Bayly-Castañeda, 2024; Strielkowski, 2025). In the gig economy, many individuals have short-term work or project-based assignments that require continuous skill development.

Traditional higher education systems were built for predictable career paths, where degrees and official certificates were considered the main proof of skills and knowledge. These credentials were usually stored in centralized database system managed by institutions making them difficult to access or share outside the issuing organization. This lack of efficiency not only reduces trust among employers and institutions but also limits credential portability and diminishes learners' ability to manage, share, and fully benefit from their own educational achievements (McGreal, 2023; Strielkowski, 2025).

To meet these challenges, lifelong learning records (LLRs) and digital portfolios have gained attention as learner-centeric solution to credential management (Ocheja et al., 2019). LLRs provide a continuous and structured record of formal, non-formal, and informal learning throughout a person's life, while digital portfolios allow learners to organize and present evidence of their skills and achievements in a flexible and meaningful way (Barrett, 2007) Together, they offer a more complete and skills-oriented view of learning than traditional transcripts, while giving learners greater ownership and control over their credentials.

Cryptographic techniques used in a blockchain give a secure and transparent system for the administration and validation of credentials. Through this system, any data held on a record can be time-stamped and thus protected from tampering (Mikroyannidis et al., 2020). With integration of the technologies of learning record systems and artificial intelligence (Bayly-Castañeda, 2024; Sajja et al., 2024), the latter can facilitate the collection of student records, permitting institutions to customise the learning pathways of their students, automatically identify the skills gaps of the students and intelligently sort out student digital portfolios.

This chapter examines the role of lifelong learning records and digital portfolios in higher education, with a focus on blockchain- and AI-enabled innovation (Ocheja et al., 2019). Lifelong learning records and digital portfolios can facilitate more flexible and inclusive methods of education and enable learners to develop new skills. Furthermore, it enables educational data to be more trustworthy. Additionally, they can provide a framework for future learning.

2. BLOCKCHAIN FOR SECURE CREDENTIALING

In a secure digital environment, the blockchain platform protects the integrity of credentials by giving them a new method of storage, verification and issue (Ocheja et al., 2019). Credentials, traditionally kept on file by universities, are therefore susceptible to the threat of data loss, the tedium of manual verification, the lag of delays, and the inefficiencies of bureaucracy. Using blockchain technology, decentralized digital records are maintained in a tamper-proof manner that is verifiable by anyone (Mikroyannidis et al., 2020).

Verifying credentials stored on a blockchain, by employers or other parties, can be done without requiring the cooperation of the issuing organisation. This verification process eliminates the lengthy checks on an individual's background and the associated manual validation procedures (Ocheja et al., 2019). Above all, this is especially relevant in a global or digital work environment where the workers often change their employers, or move from one region to another, or from one industry to another.

This secure digital ledger supports the learner owning the qualification - rather than the awarding institution. With digital storage, learners have their own secure repository of academic documents rather than them being held by institutions. This fits with the guidelines of the Lifelong Learning Records project and the concept of digital portfolios. This allows users to add data while maintaining the integrity and authenticity of the information.

The growing significance of skill-based, competency-driven educational pathways means that modularised achievements and micro-credentials are becoming crucial. Detailed learner records can comprise learning credits for short courses, qualifications gained through industry certification and informal learning achievements. These records are safely linked to the learner's whole career and academic history (McGreal, 2023; Strielkowski, 2025).

Blockchain-based secure credentialing not only improves trust and transparency but also relies on strong cryptographic and distributed system mechanisms that technically guarantee security, integrity, and authenticity of credentials (Alsobhi et al., 2023).

3. BLOCKCHAIN TECHNICAL PERSPECTIVE FOR CREDENTIALING

1. Block Structure and Hashing Mechanism

Each credential issued on a blockchain is recorded inside a block that securely records key information, which contains:

- Credential metadata (hashed student ID, credential ID, issuer ID)
- A timestamp records when the credential was issued.
- Hash of the previous block
- The block's own cryptographic hash ensures data integrity and detects any tampering.

A cryptographic hash function such as the SHA-256 or Keccak-256 hash function transforms input data into a fixed-length hash value. All credentials are time stamped and their digital signature is unique. The blocks in the chain are interconnected through a unique, one-way link, known as a hash.

2. Immutability and Tamper Resistance

Each block in the chain is linked to the one that came before it by the use of a hash. This hash is unique to that block and is the result of the information held within it being 'squashed' down into a fixed length. If the information held within the block were to be altered, the hash would be different and the block would therefore no longer match the one that it is supposed to be linked to.

Consensus Mechanisms

A consensus mechanism is required to add a new credential block to the blockchain. Mechanisms include:

- **Proof of Work (PoW):** Nodes solve cryptographic puzzles to validate blocks.
- **Proof of Stake (PoS):** Validators are selected based on stake ownership.
- **Practical Byzantine Fault Tolerance (PBFT):** Used in permissioned educational blockchains for fast and trusted validation.

Generally, for higher education certification purposes, distributed ledgers, or permissioned blockchains, utilising proof of stake (PoS) or the practical byzantine fault tolerance (PBFT) algorithms, are the preferred choice as these offer reduced latency and the resultant lower power consumption.

3. Digital Signatures and Public-Key Cryptography

Institutions who issue credentials authenticate them with their private keys; those who verify use the institution's public key to authenticate the credentials. The digital signature of the issuing authority means the credential cannot be repudiated by them. Electronic credentials, which may be diplomas, transcripts or other documents, are certified by a digital signature which ensures that the holder of the credential is who they claim to be and that the document has not been tampered with since its release by the issuing institution.

4. On-Chain vs Off-Chain Storage

Table 1. On-Chain vs Off-Chain Storage

Aspect	On-Chain Storage	Off-Chain Storage
Data Stored	Cryptographic hashes and credential proofs	Complete credential files
Storage Location	Blockchain ledger	Secure databases or decentralized storage (e.g., IPFS)
Purpose	Ensures integrity and verification	Preserves full credential details
Privacy Impact	High privacy (no raw data stored)	Controlled access to sensitive data

4. LEARNER-CENTRIC PERSPECTIVES IN DIGITAL CREDENTIALING

A learner-centric approach to digital credentialing shifts the focus from institutional control to individual ownership of educational records. In this model, learners gain the freedom to access, manage, and share their credentials whenever they wish . This fosters a sense of empowerment and responsibility for their own learning journey. Learning is recognized as a lifelong, multifaceted process that occurs not only through formal education but also through online courses, workshops, micro-credentials, professional certifications, internships, project-based learning, and workplace experiences. Learners are no longer limited to static documents issued at specific intervals.

Blockchain technology plays a key role in ensuring the security, authenticity, and portability of digital credentials. By recording verified achievements in a decentralized and tamper-proof ledger, blockchain prevents unauthorized changes and fraud (Alsobhi et al., 2023). This immediate verifiability removes the need for lengthy manual verification processes and builds trust among stakeholders.

Furthermore, blockchain supports interoperability across institutions and international borders, allowing learners to present a verifiable record of achievements anywhere in the world (Ocheja et al., 2019). Artificial intelligence (AI) supports learner-centric credentialing by analysing educational data to offer useful insights. AI systems can identify individual strengths, skill gaps, and emerging learning needs, enabling tailored recommendations for courses, certifications, and professional development (Bayly-Castañeda, 2024; Sajja et al., 2024).

5. ADVANTAGES OF LEARNER-CENTRIC CREDENTIALING

Table 2. Advantages of Learner-Centric Credentialing

Advantage	Description
Transparency and Portability	Learners can securely share verified credentials with employers, institutions, and professional networks, enabling smoother transitions across educational and professional environments.
Recognition of Diverse Learning	Achievements from multiple sources—formal, non-formal, and experiential learning—are acknowledged, ensuring that all forms of skill development are valued.
Enhanced Employability	By providing a comprehensive and verified view of competencies, learner-centric digital credentials bridge the gap between education and industry demands.
Global Standardization	Integration of blockchain and AI promotes international recognition of credentials, supporting cross-border mobility and global career opportunities.
Continuous Learning and Equity	Learners can pursue lifelong learning pathways tailored to their needs, fostering inclusion, equal access, and skill development for diverse populations.

6. EVOLUTION OF CREDENTIALING WITH LLRs AND DIGITAL PORTFOLIOS

1. Traditional Credentialing (Pre-Digital Era):

Before the digital era, credentialing relied heavily on physical documents like diplomas, certificates, and transcripts. Verifying these credentials was a slow, manual process and usually had to happen through the issuing institution. The system mainly acknowledged formal education. It largely overlooked non-formal learning, such as workshops, online courses, or practical experience. This limited the recognition of skills and knowledge gained outside of traditional classrooms, making credentialing rigid and less inclusive.

2. Recognition of Diverse Learning (Late 20th Century):

In the late 20th century, credentialing started to recognize learning beyond traditional academics. Learning portfolios were introduced to capture projects, workshops, and hands-on experiences, providing a way to showcase practical skills. This shift broadened the focus from formal grades and transcripts to a wider range of competencies. It highlighted knowledge and abilities gained outside the classroom, marking an important step toward valuing diverse learning and offering students a fuller representation of their skills.

3. Digital Portfolios (1990s–2000s):

During the 1990s and 2000s, digital portfolios emerged alongside the growth of online Learning Management Systems (LMS) and digital storage technologies. These platforms enabled learners to compile and present multimedia artifacts like presentations, videos, and reflective essays. This offered a richer view of their skills and achievements. However, this period faced challenges, such as a lack of standardization across platforms, limited portability of the portfolios, and weak ways to verify the authenticity of the content. Despite these issues, digital portfolios laid the groundwork for more flexible credentialing systems later.

4. Lifelong Learning Records (LLRs) (2010s):

In the 2010s, Lifelong Learning Records (LLRs) were created to provide a complete view of an individual's learning journey These records often integrated with skills frameworks, endorsements, and competency mapping, allowing for more accurate recognition of achievements. Portability and learner control became key features, letting individuals manage and share their credentials across institutions, employers, and digital platforms, reflecting a shift toward more flexible, learner-centered credentialing.

5. Blockchain-Enabled Credentialing (2020s – Present):

Starting in the 2020s, blockchain technology transformed credentialing (Alsobhi et al., 2023). It enabled secure, tamper-proof, and decentralized verification of learning records. This innovation allows Lifelong Learning Records (LLRs) to be recognized globally and shared easily across institutions, employers, and digital platforms. It ensures authenticity and reduces the need for manual verification. Blockchain-enabled credentialing enhances trust in academic and professional achievements and supports a global, interoperable system for managing and validating skills and competencies.

6. AI Integration (2020s – Present):

In the 2020s, artificial intelligence (AI) began to improve digital credentialing. It made Lifelong Learning Records (LLRs) and digital portfolios more dynamic and focused on the learner. AI provides personalized learning recommendations, detailed analytics, and predictive assessments of skills, turning static records into actionable insights. By examining patterns in learning behaviour and competencies, AI helps create more tailored development pathways

7. CONTRIBUTORS AND THEIR CONTRIBUTIONS TO DIGITAL PORTFOLIOS AND LIFELONG LEARNING RECORDS (LLRS):

Table 3. Contributors And Their Contributions to Digital Portfolios and Lifelong Learning Records

Contributor / Organization	Period	Contribution
Helen Barrett	1990s–2000s	She helped create the idea of digital portfolios, showing how students can store and reflect on their learning using multimedia like videos and essays.
Mozilla Open Badges Initiative	2011	Introduced verifiable digital badges to represent skills and achievements online. Established open standards for issuing, displaying, and validating credentials, bridging digital portfolios and LLRs.
Credly / Pearson	2012–Present	Built platforms to issue, store, and share digital badges securely, helping institutions and employers operationalize badges as verified credentials linked to learner portfolios and LLRs.
Universities & EdTech Platforms	2010s–Present	Implemented digital portfolios and LLRs in learning environments, demonstrating how formal, non-formal, and informal learning can be recorded, verified, and used for lifelong learning and career development.

8. LIFELONG LEARNING

The rapid evolution of technology, globalization of labor markets, and continuous transformation of professional roles or jobs have transformed the nature of education and skill development. Education is no longer something you can complete once and rely on for your career . Traditional models of education, which focus on learning in the early stages of life through formal schooling and degrees, do not meet the needs of today's fast-changing knowledge economies. Lifelong learning has become a key idea that stresses continuous skill building, reskilling, and flexibility throughout life.

Alongside this, Lifelong Learning Records (LLRs) have become important tools to document, verify, and reflect on learning experiences at all life stages. Unlike traditional transcripts or certificates, LLRs provide a complete picture of a person's learning journey. They include formal education, non-formal and informal learning, hands-on experiences, and skill development.

Types of Lifelong Learning

Table 4. Lifelong Learning

Type of Learning	Definition	Examples
Formal Learning	Learning that occurs in structured educational institutions such as schools usually leading to recognized qualifications like degrees or certificates.	Completing school education, bachelor's or master's degrees, Professional certification courses, Government-recognized training programs
Non-Formal Learning	Organized learning outside traditional classrooms, focusing on specific skills or knowledge. It may not result in formal degrees and is often flexible in duration and learner centered.	Skill-building workshops, Online courses (MOOCs), Certification courses in digital marketing, project management, IT, Community-based programs by NGOs
Informal Learning	Learning that occurs organically through everyday life experiences, social interactions, self-exploration, or experimentation. It is self-directed, flexible, and often incidental.	Teaching oneself new software independently, developing communication skills through group projects, Gaining cultural understanding via travel, volunteering, community participation
Experiential Learning	Learning through direct, hands-on experiences combined with reflection and analysis, allowing connection of theory with practice. Focuses on experimentation, problem-solving, and critical thinking.	Completing internships or apprenticeships, participating in work/school problem-solving projects, Volunteering for community service and applying new skills

Figure 1. Lifelong Learning

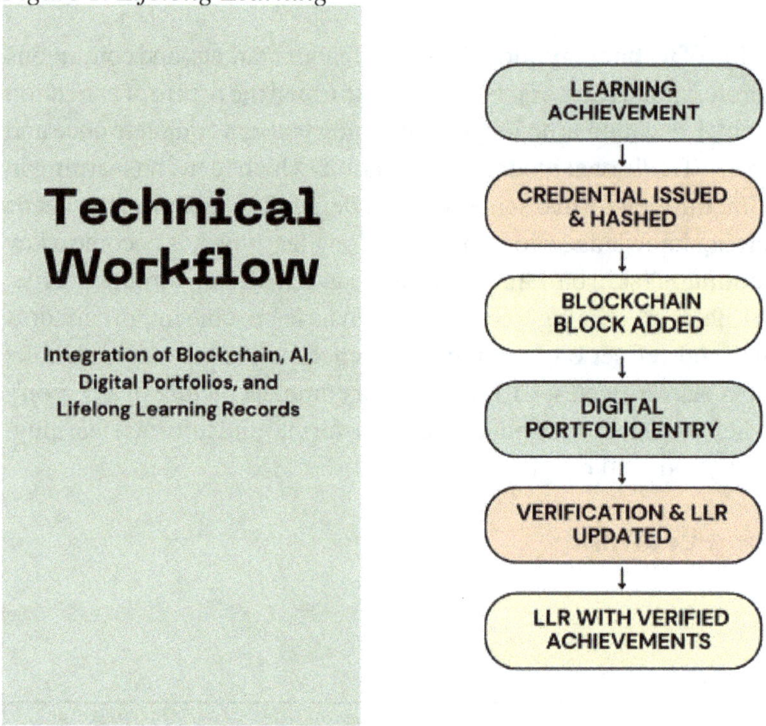

9. UNDERSTANDING LIFELONG LEARNING RECORDS (LLRS)

Higher education is going through a major change due to rapid technological progress, shifting market needs, and the growing importance of lifelong learning. Today's careers are more dynamic and involve multiple fields, so learners' skills are no longer defined by a single degree or certification. To tackle these issues, Lifelong Learning Records (LLRs) have emerged as a modern way to document, manage, and verify learning achievements throughout an individual's life.

LLRs combine learning from various stages and sources into one continuously updated record that goes beyond traditional academic boundaries. Unlike traditional transcripts that focus only on formal education, LLRs provide a broader, learner-focused view of how knowledge and skills develop. They include evidence of professional development, self-directed learning, hands-on activities, and personal growth, giving a more accurate picture of real-world capabilities.

A major strength of LLRs is their ability to recognize different forms of learning, including:

- **Formal learning**: University degrees, diplomas, institutional certifications, and accredited programs
- **Non-formal learning**: Professional training programs, workshops, seminars, online courses, and MOOCs
- **Informal learning**: Self-initiated learning, community participation, peer learning, volunteering, and personal projects
- **Experiential learning**: Internships, apprenticeships, industry projects, field-work, and hands-on practical experiences

By bringing all learning dimensions into a single trusted, verifiable record, LLRs support continuous skill development and enable more transparent recognition of competencies. They empower learners to take ownership of their educational pathways while providing educators, employers, and policymakers with reliable insights into skills and qualifications. Furthermore, LLRs enhance employability by making skill visible, portable, and easier to validate across institutions, industries, and geographical boundaries.

10. LLRS SERVE SEVERAL KEY FUNCTIONS

1. Credential Verification

Individuals can verify their skills and learning history with a Lifelong Learning Credit. The agency has built trust among educational institutions, employers and certifying agencies. Automation enables the use of objective measures in evaluating the credentials presented in university admissions, the hiring process and government documents (The Mozilla Foundation, 2011; Ocheja et al., 2019).

2. Tracking Lifelong Learning

Detailed information about a learner's learning activities, from both formal and informal settings, can be recorded through a Longitudinal Learning Record. They enable learners to build a portable transcript or profile that holds multiple competencies acquired from various learning platforms. This integrated record facilitates self-assessment, monitoring of progress and the planning of learning paths tailored to individual needs.

3. Guiding Personalized Learning

By learning curve analysis, instructors can determine at what points in the course students often become stuck and reorganize course materials accordingly. This approach has the benefit of identifying specific knowledge gaps in students. Additionally, it assists instructors in the creation of new courses tailored to the abilities of their students. This is achieved using various tools, such as learning analytics, competency frameworks, adaptive learning platforms, predictive analytics and AI driven systems that are capable of skill gap analysis (Mallik & Gangopadhyay, 2023; Sajja et al., 2024; du Plooy et al., 2024).

4. Ensuring Ethical and Secure Data Use

Emphasis is placed by Learning Loss Reports on the safeguarding of learner data and the security of it, including maintaining confidentiality and ensuring sensitive details are protected. Researchers also work to reduce algorithmic bias within these systems and promote transparency in the recommendations that are made. Data that can be used ethically and securely encompasses several technologies. These are privacy-enhancing AI, transparent AI or XAI, GDPR compliant data systems, and secure APIs.

11. IMPLEMENTATION OF LIFELONG LEARNING IN HIGHER EDUCATION

Lifelong Learning Records (LLRs) are digital, continuous, and holistic records of a learner's knowledge, skills, competencies, and achievements throughout their life. Unlike traditional academic transcripts, LLRs capture learning across formal education, micro-credentials, internships, projects, certifications, and informal experiences. Implementing LLRs in higher education allows institutions to track, verify, and showcase learners' skills while enabling personalized learning and enhancing employability (Mallik & Gangopadhyay, 2023; Sajja et al., 2024; du Plooy et al., 2024).

Table 5. Core Components of LLR Implementation

Core Component	Description	Technologies & Features
Digital Credentials and Micro-Credentials	Creation of digital records for degrees, certifications, badges, and micro-credentials	Blockchain ensures credentials are immutable, verifiable, and resistant to fraud
Digital Portfolios	Learners maintain portfolios showcasing skills, projects, achievements, and learning experiences	Supports self-reflection, career planning, and skill verification
Integration with Institutional Systems	LLRs are linked with LMS, SIS, and assessment tools to automatically capture and update learning data	Enables seamless data flow across institutional platforms
AI Analytics	Analyzes learning patterns to identify skill gaps, predict future learning needs, and recommend personalized learning pathways	AI-driven insights for adaptive learning

12. TECHNICAL WORKFLOW FOR LLR IMPLEMENTATION

Implementing Lifelong Learning Records (LLRs) involves a combination of technology integration, institutional processes, and stakeholder engagement. The technical workflow ensures that learners' achievements are captured, verified, stored securely, and used to provide personalized learning pathways. The workflow typically consists of several interconnected stages:

1. Learner Data Capture

Lifelong Learning Records (LLRs) compile information from diverse channels such as Learning Management Systems (LMS), Student Information Systems (SIS), assessment tools, digital portfolios, internships, project work, online courses, and micro-credentials. To streamline this process and cut down on mistakes from manual entry, data is automatically captured using APIs and integration technologies. After collection, the information is converted into standardized formats, ensuring that it can be easily shared, compared, and analyzed across different systems.

2. Credential Verification

Digital credentials such as degrees, certifications, badges, and micro-credentials are issued in electronic form to enable easy access and sharing (Alsobhi et al., 2023). To enhance trust and security, cryptographic hashes of these credentials are recorded on a blockchain, ensuring that the records cannot be altered and remain tamper-proof.

3. Secure Data Storage

In a blockchain-based credentialing system, only cryptographic proofs or hashes of credentials are stored on the blockchain to maintain data integrity while minimizing storage requirements. The complete credential files and detailed learner information are kept off chain in secure, encrypted databases or decentralized storage platforms such as IPFS.

4. AI-Powered Analytics

AI-driven systems examine learner data to detect gaps in skills, knowledge, and competencies. Based on these insights, personalized learning pathways are created, recommending suitable courses, micro-credentials, or practical projects to help learners improve. At the same time, AI tools continuously monitor learner progress, allowing institutions to assess engagement levels and evaluate learning outcomes over time.

5. Digital Portfolios

Learners create and maintain digital portfolios that highlight their skills, projects, certifications, and overall achievements. These portfolios are integrated with the Lifelong Learning Record (LLR) system so that all learning activities are properly recorded and verified. In addition, portfolios support reflection and future planning by helping learners assess their progress, plan career goals, and present authenticated achievements to potential employers.

6. Continuous Monitoring and Feedback

System administrators continuously oversee the LLR platform to ensure it runs smoothly, remains secure, and performs reliably. At the same time, analytics tools monitor learner engagement, completion rates, and skill development to evaluate learning effectiveness. Feedback from learners and faculty is regularly collected and used to enhance system functionality, fine-tune AI-based recommendations, and improve overall usability.

13. EMERGING TRENDS IN LIFELONG LEARNING RECORDS (LLRS)

Lifelong Learning Records (LLRs) are evolving rapidly in response to changing educational models, workforce demands, and technological advancements. Emerging trends indicate a shift toward more intelligent, interoperable, and learner-controlled credentialing ecosystems that extend beyond traditional higher education boundaries.

1. **Micro-Credentials and Modular Learning Records**: LLRs increasingly capture micro-credentials, nano-degrees, skill badges, and short-term certifications. These modular credentials allow learners to build competencies incrementally and showcase specific, job-relevant skills aligned with industry needs.
2. **Blockchain-Based Verifiable Credentials**: The adoption of blockchain enables secure, tamper-proof, and instantly verifiable credentials. Verifiable credentials stored through decentralized frameworks enhance trust, reduce fraud, and support cross-institutional and international recognition of learning achievements (Alsobhi et al., 2023).
3. **AI-Driven Skill Intelligence**: Artificial intelligence is being used to analyze LLR data to identify skill gaps, predict future learning needs, and recommend personalized learning pathways. AI transforms LLRs from static records into intelligent systems that actively guide lifelong learning and career development.
4. **Integration with Digital Portfolios**: LLRs are increasingly integrated with digital portfolios that include project work, assessments, certifications, and experiential learning evidence. This integration provides a richer and more holistic representation of learner competencies beyond grades and degrees.
5. **Interoperability and Global Standards**: Efforts are underway to develop common standards for credential formats, metadata, and validation protocols. Interoperable LLR systems enable seamless sharing of credentials across institutions, platforms, and national borders.

14. UNDERSTANDING DIGITAL PORTFOLIOS:

A digital portfolio is a curated, organized, and evolving collection of digital artifacts that provides a comprehensive and longitudinal record of an individual's learning achievements, skills, competencies, and professional development across formal, non-formal, and experiential contexts. Unlike traditional resumes or transcripts, which offer a static snapshot of accomplishments, a digital portfolio is dynamic, learner-centred, and reflective, enabling individuals to document and showcase their growth over time (Barrett, 2007; Yang & Wong, 2024).

Digital portfolios serve multiple purposes: they support formative learning by promoting self-reflection, goal setting, and ongoing feedback; facilitate summative assessment by demonstrating mastery of competencies; enhance career readiness by providing verifiable and easily shareable evidence of skills to employers; and contribute to lifelong learning ecosystems when integrated with technologies such as blockchain and artificial intelligence for secure credentialing, personalized learning recommendations, and global recognition of achievements.

Ultimately, a digital portfolio empowers learners to take ownership of their educational and professional journey, bridges the gap between academic learning and real-world application, and functions as a central tool for fostering continuous personal and career development in a rapidly evolving knowledge economy (Barrett, 2007; Yang & Wong, 2024).

15. COMPONENTS OF DIGITAL PORTFOLIOS

Digital portfolios are multifaceted tools that go beyond simple collections of achievements. They are designed to holistically capture, document, and communicate a learner's knowledge, skills, competencies, and professional growth. The components can be categorized as follows:

1. Academic and Professional Certificates

Certificates and credentials are the foundational elements of digital portfolios. These include formal academic qualifications (degrees, diplomas), professional certifications, online course completions, and skill badges. Blockchain-enabled certificates can further enhance security and verifiability, ensuring that credentials are authentic and tamper-proof.

2. Projects, Assignments, and Case Studies

Learners include tangible evidence of applied knowledge through academic projects, research papers, laboratory work, capstone projects, or case studies. This component demonstrates practical application of theoretical concepts, problem-solving abilities, and collaboration skills, providing evaluators with a deeper understanding of the learner's competencies.

3. Multimedia Artifacts

In addition to traditional documents, digital portfolios can integrate videos, presentations, podcasts, simulations, animations, and infographics. These multimedia elements not only enhance engagement but also allow learners to showcase communication skills, creativity, and technological literacy. Interactive or simulation-based artifacts can illustrate real-world problem-solving in a compelling manner.

4. Mentor, Faculty, and Employer Endorsements

Endorsements provide third-party validation of skills, competencies, and performance. Letters of recommendation, supervisor feedback, or digital endorsements add credibility to the portfolio and reinforce the authenticity of claims. Blockchain integration ensures endorsements are verifiable and resistant to forgery.

5. Professional Work Samples and Internships

For students and professionals, portfolios often incorporate workplace learning evidence, such as internship reports, project deliverables, consultancy assignments, or collaborative work outputs. These artifacts demonstrate readiness for professional roles and link academic learning with practical application.

16. EDUCATIONAL AND PROFESSIONAL BENEFITS OF DIGITAL PORTFOLIOS (Barrett, 2007; Lu, 2021).

Table 6. Educational and Professional Benefits of Digital Portfolios

Benefit	Description	Impact / Example
Career Development & Employability	Provides tangible evidence of academic achievements, projects, certifications, and soft skills	Improves employability, supports career planning, and strengthens applications for jobs, further studies, or scholarships
Holistic Assessment	Captures a wide range of competencies beyond grades, including cognitive, technical, and soft skills	Offers educators and employers a comprehensive view of learner capabilities, complementing traditional evaluation methods
Integration of Real-World Skills	Showcases applied knowledge through projects, internships, and professional work	Bridges the gap between academic learning and workplace readiness
Personalized Learning Insights	Enables learners to track progress and identify areas for improvement	Supports targeted skill development and lifelong learning

17. EMERGING TRENDS: MULTI-FORMAT DIGITAL PORTFOLIOS

The rapid advancement of digital technologies has transformed the traditional concept of learner portfolios into multi-format digital portfolios that capture a broader spectrum of competencies. Unlike conventional text-based portfolios, these modern portfolios integrate multimedia elements, interactive tools, and immersive experiences to provide a more comprehensive, authentic, and engaging record of learner achievements (Barrett, 2007; Yang & Wong, 2024).

Key Formats and Features:

1. Video Portfolios:

Video-based artifacts allow learners to showcase essential soft skills such as communication, presentation abilities, teamwork, and leadership. These may include recorded project presentations, interviews, or reflective summaries that capture real learning experiences. By adding a personal dimension, video content helps evaluators assess not only academic knowledge but also interpersonal and professional competencies (Barrett, 2007).

2. Interactive Demos and Simulations:

These artifacts allow learners to demonstrate technical and practical skills through real-time or realistic scenarios. They are especially valuable for showcasing coding projects, engineering prototypes, scientific experiments, or design-based applications (Yang & Wong, 2024).

3. AR/VR-Based Portfolios:

Immersive portfolios recreate real-world environments through interactive experiences, supporting more effective learning and assessment. They are especially useful in domains such as healthcare, where surgical simulations can be used, engineering for virtual machinery operation, design through interactive 3D models, and architecture via virtual building walkthroughs (So et al., 2024).

4. Integrated Multimedia Artifacts:

Multimodal portfolios bring together text, images, audio, charts, infographics, and animations to present a complete picture of a learner's progress and abilities.

By accommodating different learning styles, they offer richer and more meaningful evidence of skills and competencies (Zhang & Tur, 2022; Yang & Wong, 2024).

5. AI-Enhanced Portfolios:

Artificial Intelligence can examine portfolio content to deliver personalized and timely feedback to learners. It identifies skill gaps, suggests areas for improvement, and recommends customized learning paths based on individual needs (Mallik & Gangopadhyay, 2023; Sajja et al., 2024).

18. LIMITATIONS OF TRADITIONAL DIGITAL PORTFOLIOS (Barrett, 2007; Lu, 2021).

Table 7. Limitations of Traditional Digital Portfolios

Limitation	Description
Text-Centric Format	Traditional portfolios primarily rely on text-based artifacts, limiting the demonstration of practical, technical, or interpersonal skills.
Static Content	Updates and additions are often manual, making portfolios less dynamic and unable to reflect continuous learning or evolving skills.
Insufficient Skill Evidence	Hard to showcase applied competencies, soft skills, or real-world problem-solving abilities.
Poor Personalization	Portfolios rarely adapt to individual learners' needs or provide personalized feedback or guidance.
Limited Multimedia Support	Often unable to incorporate video, audio, simulations, or AR/VR content for richer demonstration of learning.
Restricted Sharing and Portability	Traditional portfolios are often tied to a single platform, making it difficult for learners to share verified achievements across institutions or employers.
Low Integration with Analytics	Lack of AI or analytics tools limits insights into learner progress, skill gaps, or recommendations for improvement.

19. INTEGRATION OF BLOCKCHAIN- AND AI-ENABLED DIGITAL PORTFOLIOS AND LIFELONG LEARNING RECORDS

The integration of blockchain technology, digital portfolios, Lifelong Learning Records (LLRs), and artificial intelligence (AI) is revolutionizing how learning achievements are captured, verified, and utilized in higher education. This next-generation ecosystem ensures secure, verifiable, and learner-centric credentialing, supporting continuous documentation of skills and competencies across a learner's lifetime. Beyond record-keeping, this integrated approach fosters personalized learning, career readiness, and institutional innovation, bridging the gap between education and employment (Ocheja et al., 2019; McGreal, 2023).

1. Blockchain for Secure Credentialing

Blockchain technology acts as the core trust layer of the digital credentialing ecosystem by ensuring secure, transparent, and reliable record management. Through cryptographic mechanisms, credentials stored on the blockchain remain tamper-resistant and can be independently verified by all stakeholders. Its decentralized nature allows learners, educational institutions, and employers to access records without depending on a single controlling authority, improving openness and availability.

2. Digital Portfolios as Comprehensive Learning Records

Digital portfolios offer comprehensive and multidimensional proof of a learner's progress and capabilities by bringing together diverse forms of evidence. They allow students to present projects, micro-credentials, videos, simulations, AR/VR experiences, reflective insights, and real-world problem-solving tasks within a single platform. These portfolios are closely linked with Lifelong Learning Records (LLRs), enabling continuous and holistic documentation of learning achievements over time (Barrett, 2007; Yang & Wong, 2024).

3. Lifelong Learning Records as the Learning Backbone

Lifelong Learning Records (LLRs) serve as the foundation of an integrated learning ecosystem by maintaining a continuous and comprehensive account of an individual's educational journey. When combined with AI technologies, LLR data can be analyzed to provide personalized learning suggestions, identify skill gaps, and offer career guidance.

4. Artificial Intelligence (AI)

Artificial intelligence adds intelligence and adaptability to the learning ecosystem by enabling deeper personalization and data-driven decision-making. It can recommend relevant courses, projects, or micro-credentials based on an individual's learning history, skills, and goals. Additionally, AI tracks performance by monitoring engagement, skill development, and overall progress, offering meaningful feedback to both learners and educators.

5. Transforming Learning and Credentialing

The integration of Lifelong Learning Records (LLRs), artificial intelligence, blockchain, and digital portfolios reshapes education from a static, grade-oriented model into a dynamic and learner-centered ecosystem. In this approach, learners retain ownership of their learning evidence, encouraging continuous skill development, adaptability, and lifelong learning.

20. FUTURE PERSPECTIVES OF INTEGRATION OF BLOCKCHAIN, DIGITAL PORTFOLIOS, LLRS, AND AI POISED TO FURTHER TRANSFORM EDUCATION

1. **Global Credentialing Ecosystems:** The continued integration of blockchain, digital portfolios, Lifelong Learning Records (LLRs), and AI are expected to enable globally recognized credentialing systems. Learners will be able to maintain secure, verifiable, and portable records of their achievements that are accepted across institutions, industries, and countries, removing barriers to mobility and recognition (McGreal, 2023).
2. **Lifelong Career Support**: These technologies will provide ongoing support for professional growth by offering continuous insights into skill development and learning progress. Learners can receive guidance throughout their careers, helping them adapt to changing industry requirements and pursue relevant upskilling or reskilling opportunities (Strielkowski, 2025).
3. **Adaptive Learning Environments:** AI-driven systems will increasingly support fully adaptive learning environments, where curricula and learning pathways adjust dynamically based on individual progress, performance, and emerging skill demands (Mallik & Gangopadhyay, 2023; Sajja et al., 2024). This personalized approach will enhance engagement and improve learning outcomes.
4. **Education–Employment Alignment:** Stronger alignment between education and employment is anticipated as organizations rely more on verified digital portfolios and LLRs for hiring, promotion, and workforce development. This shift will promote fairer recruitment practices and ensure that educational outcomes closely match real-world skill needs (McGreal, 2023).

21. BENEFITS OF INTEGRATION (Ocheja et al., 2019; McGreal, 2023):

Table 8. Benefits of Integration

Benefit	Description
Security and Trust	Blockchain ensures credentials are tamper-proof, verifiable, and resistant to fraud, enhancing stakeholder confidence.
Comprehensive Learning Evidence	Portfolios and LLRs consolidate achievements from formal education, micro-credentials, projects, and experiential learning.
Personalized Learning	AI analyzes learner data to recommend courses, identify skill gaps, and suggest optimal learning pathways.
Enhanced Employability	Learners receive validated proof of skills aligned with industry demands, increasing job readiness and competitiveness.
Skill Gap Identification	AI-driven analysis highlights missing competencies, helping learners focus on in-demand skills.
Ethical and Transparent Learning	Explainable AI and privacy-preserving techniques ensure fairness, transparency, and compliance with regulations like GDPR.

22. TECHNICAL WORKFLOW FOR THE INTEGRATION OF BLOCKCHAIN, AI, DIGITAL PORTFOLIOS, AND LIFELONG LEARNING RECORDS

Integrating AI with Blockchain (Ocheja et al., 2019; Mallik & Gangopadhyay, 2023), Digital Portfolios, and Lifelong Learning Records (LLRs) creates an intelligent, secure, and learner-centric ecosystem. This system not only captures and verifies achievements but also provides personalized learning recommendations, predictive career guidance, and actionable insights for learners and institutions.

1. Capture Learner Activities

Learning data is collected from multiple sources, including learning management systems, student information systems, assessment platforms, online courses, academic projects, internships, and micro-credential programs. To enable seamless sharing and interoperability across different platforms, this information is then standardized into consistent formats (Yang & Wong, 2024).

2. Credential Verification via Blockchain

Verified learning achievements are first transformed into cryptographic hashes to protect data integrity and privacy. These hashes are then stored on a blockchain, ensuring that the records remain secure, tamper-resistant, and easily verifiable. Smart contracts manage and automate the credential verification process, allowing employers, educational institutions, and learners to confirm authenticity without manual intervention. Through dedicated verification portals, stakeholders can instantly validate credentials in real time without relying on intermediaries or centralized authorities (Ocheja et al., 2019; McGreal, 2023).

3. Updating Digital Portfolios

Once credentials are verified, they are synchronized and updated within the learner's digital portfolio to ensure accuracy and continuity. The portfolio supports multiple formats of evidence, including written content, images, videos, interactive demonstrations, and AR/VR-based learning experiences. By integrating these diverse elements, the portfolio provides a comprehensive reflection of formal education, informal learning, and hands-on experiential achievements (Barrett, 2007; Zhang & Tur, 2022; Yang & Wong, 2024).

4. Integration into Lifelong Learning Records (LLRs)

Verified data from digital portfolios is continuously aggregated into the Lifelong Learning Record, creating an ongoing and up-to-date record of skills and competencies. These records are designed to be portable and interoperable, allowing learners to share their achievements seamlessly across educational institutions, employers, and professional platforms.

5. AI-Powered Analytics

Artificial intelligence analyzes data from Lifelong Learning Records and digital portfolios to identify skill gaps and areas requiring further development. Based on this analysis, it recommends personalized learning pathways, including relevant courses, micro-credentials, projects, or practical experiences aligned with individual goals. By incorporating labor market data and industry trends, AI also provides predictive career insights that help learners make informed career decisions (Sajja et al., 2024; Mallik & Gangopadhyay, 2023).

6. Sharing and Utilization

Learners can securely share their verified digital portfolios with employers, educational institutions, or professional networks, ensuring that their achievements are recognized and trusted. Employers and institutions can also access verified Lifelong Learning Records to evaluate competencies and make informed decisions.

Figure 2. Technical Workflow: Integration of blockchain, AI, Digital Portfolios, And Lifelong Learning Records

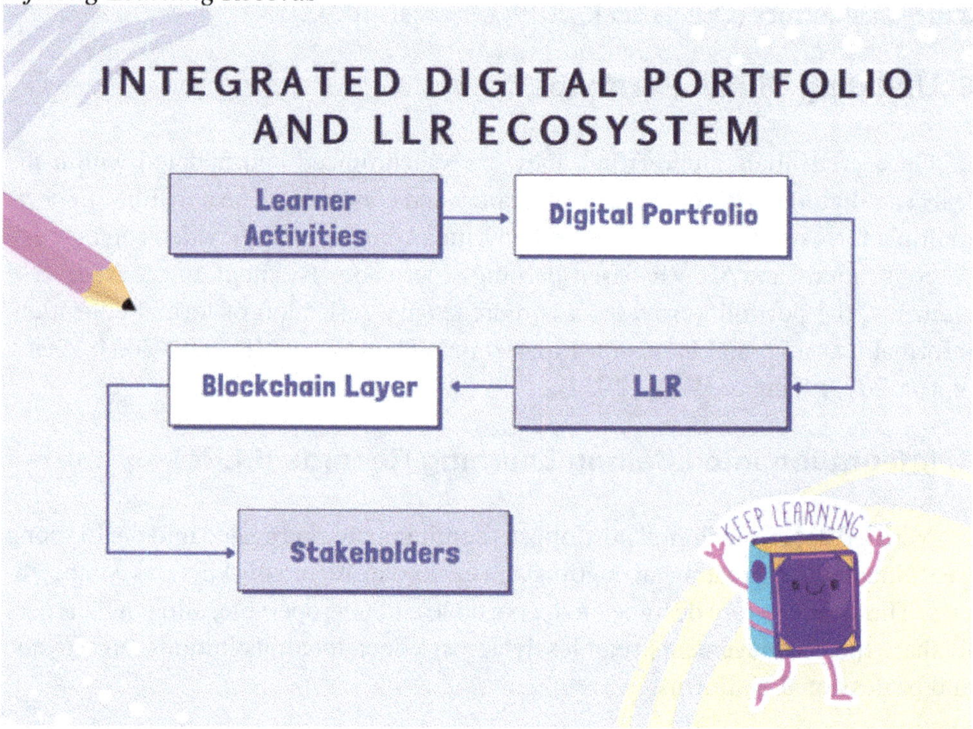

Table 9. Applications in Higher Education and Workforce

Application	Description / Benefits
Global Credential Portability	Learners can share verified LLRs across institutions and international borders, enabling global recognition of skills and achievements.
Micro-Credential Ecosystems	Short courses, workshops, and industry certifications are securely documented, supporting continuous and specialized skill development.
AI-Powered Insights	Verified LLR data is analyzed to identify skill gaps, recommend personalized learning paths, and provide predictive career guidance.
Employer Trust	Employers can instantly verify learner skills and credentials, reducing fraud and administrative workload while enhancing confidence in hiring.

23. CONCEPTUAL FRAMEWORK / SYSTEM MODEL

The proposed conceptual framework illustrates how Lifelong Learning Records (LLRs), Digital Portfolios, blockchain technology, and artificial intelligence (AI) collectively create a secure, intelligent, and learner-centric ecosystem for higher education. The framework follows a multi-layered architecture, where each layer performs a distinct function while interacting seamlessly with the others to support lifelong, verifiable, and skills-oriented learning.

1. Data and Learning Activity Layer

This foundational layer captures learning data generated from diverse formal, non-formal, and informal sources within and beyond higher education institutions. Data sources include Learning Management Systems (LMS), Student Information Systems (SIS), Massive Open Online Courses (MOOCs), internships, research projects, industry training programs, co-curricular activities, and experiential learning.

2. Lifelong Learning Record (LLR) Layer

The LLR layer organizes and structures the collected learning data into a unified, learner-centric record. Unlike traditional transcripts, this layer supports micro-credentials, competency-based achievements, informal learning recognition, and stackable credentials, enabling a holistic and evolving representation of learner knowledge, skills, and capabilities.

3. Digital Portfolio Layer

The Digital Portfolio layer complements the LLR by providing a dynamic, evidence-based representation of learning and skills.

This layer allows learners to curate personalized narratives of their learning journeys, demonstrating not only *what* they have achieved but also *how* competencies were developed. Selected portfolio artifacts can be linked to or verified through blockchain-anchored credentials, strengthening trust and authenticity (Barrett, 2007; Yang & Wong, 2024).

4. Blockchain Credentialing Layer

The blockchain layer ensures security, trust, and authenticity of learning records and portfolio-linked credentials. Verified achievements such as degrees, certificates, micro-credentials, skill badges, and endorsed portfolio artifacts are recorded as immutable entries on a decentralized ledger (Ocheja et al., 2019; McGreal, 2023).

This layer enables tamper-proof storage, decentralized verification, and long-term integrity of credentials, reducing credential fraud and minimizing reliance on centralized issuing authorities.

5. AI and Analytics Layer

The AI and analytics layer transform static records and portfolio data into actionable intelligence. Using machine learning, learning analytics, and natural language processing, this layer performs skill-gap analysis, competency mapping, personalized learning recommendations, performance monitoring, and career pathway alignment (Mallik & Gangopadhyay, 2023; Sajja et al., 2024).

6. Application and User Interface Layer

This layer provides the system's core functionality through intuitive digital interfaces and role-specific dashboards tailored to different stakeholders. Learners can manage their Lifelong Learning Records and digital portfolios, display verified achievements, receive personalized learning recommendations, and plan their academic and career pathways.

7. Governance, Ethics, and Interoperability Layer

Cross-cutting all layers, this component ensures data privacy, ethical AI use, regulatory compliance, and interoperability. Learner consent, data ownership, transparency, explainability of AI decisions, and compliance with national and international qualification frameworks are embedded into system design.

Interoperability standards enable seamless integration across institutions, platforms, and regions, ensuring scalability, inclusivity, and global usability of LLRs and digital portfolios.

Figure 3. Integrated Digital Portfolio and LLR Ecosystem

24. CHALLENGES, RISKS, AND LIMITATIONS OF BLOCKCHAIN AND AI-ENABLED LIFELONG LEARNING RECORDS (LLRS) AND DIGITAL PORTFOLIOS (Ocheja et al., 2019; McGreal, 2023)

Table 10. Challenges, Risks, and Limitations of Blockchain and AI-Enabled LLRs

Challenge Area	Description of the Issue	Implications for LLR and Digital Portfolio Implementation
Scalability and Performance	Blockchain networks and digital portfolio systems may face limited transaction throughput, latency, high energy consumption, and increased costs when processing large volumes of educational records, micro-credentials, and portfolio artifacts.	Slower system performance and higher operational costs may restrict large-scale or real-time adoption of LLRs and digital portfolios across institutions and regions.
Data Privacy and Right to Forget	Blockchain immutability conflicts with data protection regulations (e.g., GDPR), which require deletion, modification, and explicit learner consent.	Legal compliance challenges and reduced learner trust if privacy rights for portfolio contents and credential data cannot be fully guaranteed.
AI Bias and Algorithmic Fairness	AI models analyzing LLRs and digital portfolios may produce biased recommendations for learning pathways, skill assessments, or career predictions if trained on incomplete or biased datasets.	Certain learner groups may be disadvantaged, raising ethical concerns and reducing the credibility of AI-driven LLR and portfolio systems.
Lack of Transparency and Explainability	Many AI systems operate as "black boxes," making it difficult to explain automated decisions regarding skill validation, personalized recommendations, or portfolio assessments.	Reduced accountability and difficulty in contesting or correcting AI-generated outcomes.
Technical and Financial Barriers	High development and maintenance costs, need for advanced infrastructure, and shortage of skilled professionals, especially in developing regions.	Unequal adoption across institutions and countries, potentially widening the global digital divide in LLR and portfolio systems.
User Adoption and Digital Literacy	Resistance from faculty, administrators, and learners due to unfamiliarity with decentralized technologies, AI analytics, and digital portfolio management.	Low utilization rates and limited effectiveness despite technological availability.

25. USE CASES AND SCENARIOS IN HIGHER EDUCATION

The integration of Lifelong Learning Records (LLRs) with blockchain technology, artificial intelligence (AI), and digital portfolios enables a wide range of practical and transformative use cases in higher education. These use cases demonstrate how intelligent, learner-centric credentialing ecosystems can enhance learning experiences, improve administrative efficiency, and strengthen alignment between education, skills, and employment (McGreal, 2023).

1. Issuance of Verifiable Digital Degrees and Certificates

Higher education institutions can issue blockchain-based digital degrees, diplomas, and certificates that are secure, tamper-proof, and instantly verifiable. These credentials can be permanently linked to learners' LLRs and selectively shared through digital portfolios. Graduates can present authenticated qualifications to employers or other institutions without manual verification, significantly reducing delays, costs, and the risk of credential fraud.

2. Micro-Credentials and Modular Learning Recognition

LLRs support the issuance and accumulation of micro-credentials for short-term courses, competency-based modules, professional certifications, and industry training. Digital portfolios allow learners to showcase supporting evidence—such as projects, assessments, and skill demonstrations—alongside verified credentials. Over time, these micro-credentials can be stacked into larger qualifications, enabling flexible, personalized, and industry-aligned learning pathways.

3. Cross-Institutional Credit Transfer

Blockchain-enabled LLRs facilitate seamless credit transfer across universities, online learning platforms, and training providers. Learners can move between institutions or pursue interdisciplinary and blended education without losing recognition of prior learning. Digital portfolios further support this process by providing qualitative evidence of learning outcomes, enhancing trust and transparency in credit evaluation.

4. Industry-Integrated Learning and Employability

LLRs enable institutions to collaborate with industry partners to issue verifiable credentials for internships, apprenticeships, research projects, and workplace learning. AI-driven skill mapping analyzes LLR data and portfolio artifacts to align learner competencies with labor market demands. Employers gain access to both verified credentials and authentic evidence of skills, supporting skills-based hiring and improving graduate employability.

5. Personalized Academic Advising and Student Support

AI-powered LLR systems analyze learner progress, engagement patterns, assessment data, and portfolio submissions to deliver personalized academic advising. Students receive recommendations for courses, learning resources, and skill development opportunities, while advisors and faculty can identify at-risk learners early and provide targeted interventions. This data-informed approach enhances retention, success, and learner satisfaction.

6. Alumni Lifelong Learning and Reskilling

Universities can extend their engagement beyond graduation by maintaining longitudinal LLRs and digital portfolios for alumni. As individuals acquire new certifications, professional experiences, and skills, their records are continuously updated. This supports reskilling and upskilling throughout a learner's career and positions higher education institutions as lifelong learning partners rather than one-time credential providers.

26. EMERGING TECHNOLOGIES ENHANCING CREDENTIALING

1. **Interoperable APIs and Digital Identity Standards**: Modern credentialing systems leverage interoperable APIs to enable seamless data exchange between educational institutions, employers, and digital platforms. By adhering to global digital identity standards, credentials become universally verifiable, reducing friction in cross-platform recognition and facilitating smoother transitions between learning, work, and certification ecosystems.
2. **Decentralized Identifiers (DIDs) and Verifiable Credentials (VCs)**: DIDs and VCs, built on blockchain or decentralized ledger technologies, empower learners with ownership and control over their digital credentials. These technologies enable secure, tamper-proof, and verifiable records, eliminating the dependency on centralized authorities while ensuring privacy, trust, and authenticity in credential verification.
3. **Integration with Artificial Intelligence Agents**: AI agents can enhance credentialing by analyzing learning patterns, automating assessment verification, and providing personalized recommendations. They can dynamically validate skills and achievements, detect inconsistencies, and support adaptive learning pathways, making credentialing systems smarter and more responsive to individual learner journeys.

4. **Edge Computing and IoT for Real-Time Learning Tracking**: IoT devices and edge computing enable real-time capture of learning experiences, both formal and informal. Wearables, smart devices, and sensors can track practical skills, lab performance, or workplace training, feeding data directly into secure credentialing frameworks.

27. ALIGNMENT WITH NATIONAL AND GLOBAL POLICIES

The adoption of LLRs integrated with blockchain, AI, and digital portfolios aligns closely with national education strategies and international policy frameworks. Policy alignment enhances system credibility, ensures interoperability, and supports the global recognition of skills and qualifications.

1. Alignment with National Policies

Many countries have introduced lifelong learning, digital education, and skill development initiatives to enhance workforce readiness and economic competitiveness. LLR-based systems support these objectives through:

- **Skill Development Frameworks:** Mapping learner competencies and portfolio evidence to national qualification frameworks, ensuring relevance to industry and societal needs.
- **Digital Education Strategies:** Supporting secure, interoperable, and transparent digital credentialing initiatives through blockchain and AI.
- **Workforce Mobility and Reskilling Programs:** Providing trusted, portable evidence of skills and qualifications to support career transitions and continuous learning.

2. Alignment with International Policies and Frameworks

Global organizations increasingly emphasize lifelong learning and cross-border recognition of skills. LLR implementations align with:

- **UNESCO Lifelong Learning Policies:** Supporting continuous learning, recognition of prior learning, equity, and inclusion across the lifespan.
- **European Qualifications Framework (EQF):** Enabling comparability, transparency, and mobility of qualifications across regions.

- **OECD and World Bank Recommendations:** Providing data-driven insights for skills forecasting, workforce planning, and education system improvement.

3. Cross-Border Recognition and Interoperability

Blockchain-based credentials, combined with international standards such as W3C Verifiable Credentials, ensure interoperability across platforms, institutions, and countries. Learners can securely share verified credentials and portfolio evidence globally, supporting international education, employment, and collaboration.

28. ETHICAL, PRIVACY, AND GOVERNANCE CONSIDERATIONS

Policy alignment also requires strong attention to ethics, privacy, and governance. LLR systems can be designed to comply with (Mallik & Gangopadhyay, 2023; Sajja et al., 2024):

Table 11. Ethical, Privacy and Governance Considerations

Policy Dimension	Key Focus Areas	Implementation in LLR Systems	Benefits
Data Protection & Privacy Compliance	National and international data protection laws (e.g., GDPR, digital privacy regulations)	LLR systems implement consent-based data sharing, encryption, anonymization, and secure access controls to protect learner data	Ensures legal compliance, protects personal data, and builds trust among learners and stakeholders
Ethical AI Practices	Fairness, transparency, explainability, accountability, and bias mitigation	AI models used for recommendations and analytics are designed to be auditable, explainable, and regularly evaluated for bias and fairness	Promotes responsible AI use, prevents discrimination, and ensures equitable learning and career guidance
Learner Consent & Data Ownership	Explicit consent, control over data usage, right to access and revoke permissions	Learners retain ownership of their LLR data and can decide who can view, verify, or use their records	Empowers learners and supports lifelong autonomy over learning data
Governance & Institutional Accountability	Clear governance policies, roles, and responsibilities	Institutions establish governance frameworks defining data stewardship, access rights, and accountability mechanisms	Ensures responsible data management and institutional transparency

continued on following page

Table 11. Continued

Policy Dimension	Key Focus Areas	Implementation in LLR Systems	Benefits
Security & Risk Management	Cybersecurity, fraud prevention, and system resilience	Blockchain anchoring, cryptographic hashing, and continuous monitoring protect records from tampering and unauthorized access	Enhances system security and reduces credential fraud
Cross-Border Data Governance	International data sharing and interoperability standards	LLRs follow interoperable standards to enable secure and compliant sharing across borders	Supports global mobility and international recognition of credentials

29. STAKEHOLDER IMPACT ANALYSIS

The successful adoption of integrated LLR, digital portfolio, AI, and blockchain systems depends on addressing the needs and concerns of multiple stakeholders within the education and employment ecosystem. Learners benefit from increased ownership, portability, and visibility of their competencies, aligning with lifelong learning and employability goals (Barrett, 2007). Faculty gain access to richer evidence of learning through authentic, competency-based assessment supported by e-portfolios and analytics (Yang & Wong, 2024).

Institutions benefit from improved quality assurance, accreditation support, and operational efficiency through standardized digital records. Employers and policymakers, meanwhile, gain access to verifiable, skills-focused credentials that enhance workforce alignment and mobility (McGreal, 2023).

30. STAKEHOLDER PERSPECTIVES ON INTEGRATED LLR AND DIGITAL PORTFOLIO SYSTEMS

Table 12. Stakeholders Perspective

Stakeholder	Benefits	Concerns
Learners	Ownership of learning records, lifelong portability, stronger employability through verified portfolios	Data privacy, consent management, varying levels of digital literacy
Faculty	Holistic view of learner progress, support for authentic assessment, insights from learning analytics	Additional training requirements, increased workload during transition
Institutions	Improved accreditation support, efficient record management, enhanced reputation through trusted credentials	Infrastructure and implementation costs, system integration challenges
Employers	Faster credential verification, clearer view of skills and competencies, better hiring decisions	Lack of common standards, need to interpret diverse portfolio formats
Policymakers	Better workforce insights, support for learner mobility, alignment with lifelong learning goals	Governance complexity, regulatory alignment, data protection oversight

31. SUSTAINABILITY AND ENVIRONMENTAL CONSIDERATIONS IN LLR-BASED DIGITAL CREDENTIALING SYSTEMS

Sustainability considerations are increasingly important in the design of digital credentialing and LLR systems. While blockchain provides secure and decentralized verification, energy-intensive consensus mechanisms such as Proof of Work raise environmental concerns (McGreal, 2023). Research highlights the potential of energy-efficient alternatives, including Proof of Stake and permissioned blockchain networks, to significantly reduce carbon footprints while maintaining trust and security (Ocheja et al., 2019). Similarly, AI-driven learning analytics must be optimized to avoid unnecessary computational overhead, favoring lightweight and purpose-specific models (Mallik & Gangopadhyay, 2023)

1. Blockchain Energy Use:

Conventional blockchain networks that depend on Proof of Work require extensive computing power, resulting in high energy consumption. A more sustainable approach involves using Proof of Stake, permissioned networks, or consortium-based blockchains, which significantly lower energy demands. These alternatives allow institutions to implement secure digital credentialing systems while supporting environmentally responsible and low-carbon practices.

2. Green Blockchain Alternatives:

Many public blockchain platforms raise environmental concerns due to their reliance on energy-intensive processes. Green blockchain solutions focus on adopting efficient consensus methods and infrastructure powered by renewable energy sources. This ensures that secure and transparent credential verification can be achieved without conflicting with institutional and national climate goals.

3. AI Model Usage:

Advanced AI models often require substantial computational resources, increasing energy usage. Sustainable system design emphasizes optimized models, lightweight analytics, and purpose-specific AI tools that deliver insights efficiently. This approach maintains the benefits of learning analytics and personalization while reducing unnecessary energy consumption.

4. Cloud Infrastructure:

LLRs and digital portfolios depend on cloud services for data storage and processing, which can contribute to high energy demand. Selecting cloud providers that operate energy-efficient data centers and use carbon-aware workload scheduling helps lower the environmental impact. This strategy supports scalable learning systems with a reduced carbon footprint.

5. Digital Portfolios versus Paper Records:

Paper-based academic records consume physical resources and generate long-term administrative waste. Digital portfolios replace these practices with reusable, portable, and entirely digital records. This transition reduces paper usage, streamlines administrative processes, and promotes environmentally sustainable practices in education.

32. ROADMAP FOR INSTITUTIONAL ADOPTION OF LLR, DIGITAL PORTFOLIO, AI, AND BLOCKCHAIN SYSTEMS

Phase 1: Readiness Assessment – Institutional Preparedness

The first phase focuses on evaluating the institution's preparedness for integrating LLRs, digital portfolios, blockchain, and AI. This involves assessing the existing digital infrastructure, faculty capacity, data management policies, and learner requirements. Institutions identify potential use cases for micro-credentials, portfolios, and AI-driven learning analytics. The goal is to provide leadership, IT teams, faculty, and policymakers with a clear understanding of the institution's readiness, highlight potential risks, and determine priority areas that require attention before full-scale implementation.

Phase 2: Pilot Micro-Credentials and Portfolios – Early Implementation

In this phase, institutions introduce micro-credentials linked to digital portfolios within selected programs or courses as a pilot project. Faculty and learners participate in these early implementations to provide feedback on usability, engagement, and outcomes. Academic departments oversee the pilot, tracking learner progress and portfolio development. The purpose is to establish a proof of concept, demonstrate early successes, and gather insights that can guide wider adoption. This phase helps refine processes and ensures that the system aligns with learner and faculty needs.

Phase 3: Blockchain Credential Layer – Trusted Verification

Phase three involves integrating blockchain technology to secure and verify credentials. All micro-credentials and portfolio evidence are anchored to the blockchain, making them tamper-resistant and verifiable without a central authority. Verification workflows are defined to allow institutions, registrars, and accreditation bodies to authenticate credentials efficiently. This phase ensures that learners receive secure, portable, and trustworthy credentials that can be shared with employers and other institutions globally.

Phase 4: AI Analytics Integration – Learning Intelligence

In this phase, AI tools are deployed to enhance learning intelligence. AI analyses LLR data and digital portfolio content to identify skill gaps, provide personalized learning recommendations, and map competencies to career opportunities. Faculty and learning designers can use these insights to make data-informed decisions, optimize pedagogy, and provide targeted learner support

Phase 5: Policy and Governance Alignment – Regulation and Trust

Phase five ensures that the integrated system complies with legal, ethical, and institutional regulations. This includes alignment with data protection laws, accreditation standards, and ethical guidelines for AI usage and digital credentials. Policymakers, legal teams, and institutional governance bodies oversee this alignment, ensuring that all stakeholders understand the rules and responsibilities. The outcome is a trusted, compliant system that instils confidence in learners, employers, and accrediting bodies while enabling scalable governance for wider adoption.

FUTURE RESEARCH DIRECTIONS

The adoption of LLRs, AI, blockchain, and digital portfolios opens multiple avenues for research and innovation:

Table 13. Future Research areas and focus

Future Research Area	Focus / Objectives
Global LLR Networks	Research cross-institutional and international interoperability to create global lifelong learning networks; explore standardization frameworks for credentials, skill mappings, and competency frameworks.
AI-Enhanced Portfolio Analytics	Investigate advanced AI models for automated evaluation of multimedia portfolio artifacts; develop predictive algorithms for skill development, personalized learning trajectories, and career path modelling.
Blockchain Optimization	Explore energy-efficient blockchain models to reduce environmental impact; research scalable solutions for high-volume credential verification without latency or high transaction costs.
Data Privacy and Security Innovation	Study privacy-preserving technologies such as homomorphic encryption, zero-knowledge proofs, and decentralized identity management; evaluate secure off-chain storage models for sensitive learner data.
Adaptive and Personalized Learning	Research AI-driven systems that dynamically adapt learning recommendations based on real-time portfolio updates and LLR data; explore reinforcement learning or agent-based models to support lifelong skill acquisition.

continued on following page

Table 13. Continued

Future Research Area	Focus / Objectives
Policy and Governance Research	Analyze regulatory frameworks and propose guidelines for ethical, interoperable, and globally recognized digital credentialing systems; study societal, ethical, and legal implications of AI-powered educational decision-making.
Integration with Emerging Technologies	Investigate immersive AR/VR portfolios, IoT-enabled skill tracking, and edge computing for real-time competency validation; explore multi-format portfolios including simulations, 3D models, or interactive projects to enhance authenticity in skill documentation.

CONCLUSION

The convergence of blockchain, artificial intelligence (AI), Lifelong Learning Records (LLRs), and digital portfolios represents a transformative evolution in higher education, fundamentally redefining how learning, credentialing, and skill recognition are managed. Traditional credentialing systems—static, institution-controlled, and paper-based—have long been insufficient for capturing the diversity, complexity, and continuity of modern learning experiences. These systems often limit learner mobility, slow credential verification, and fail to reflect non-formal, informal, or experiential learning, which are increasingly critical in a rapidly evolving labour market.

A learner-centric approach enabled by LLRs and digital portfolios places learners at the heart of credentialing and academic record management. Students gain ownership and control over their learning achievements, from degrees and micro-credentials to work experience and skill-based training. Blockchain provides a secure, tamper-proof infrastructure for credential verification, while AI enhances the organization, interpretation, and personalization of learning data. From a stakeholder and institutional perspective, these systems offer tangible benefits: learners achieve portability, ownership, and verifiable records; faculty gain tools for authentic assessment and outcome-based teaching; institutions improve efficiency, accreditation support, and global recognition; employers can quickly and reliably verify skills and policymakers obtain data-driven insights for workforce planning and lifelong learning strategies.

Sustainability and environmental considerations further underscore the value of this approach. Energy-efficient blockchain implementations, optimized AI models, cloud infrastructure with minimal environmental impact, and fully digital portfolios reduce carbon footprints and administrative waste, aligning digital credentialing with institutional, national, and global sustainability goals.

The roadmap for institutional adoption from readiness assessment and pilot micro-credentials to blockchain credentialing, AI analytics integration, governance alignment, and continuous improvement provides a strategic pathway for scalable, sustainable, and future-ready deployment.

In essence, the integration of LLRs, digital portfolios, blockchain, and AI is more than a technological innovation it is a paradigm shift in learning and credentialing. It empowers learners, enhances transparency, strengthens institutional credibility, and bridges education with employment in a trusted, dynamic, and globally portable framework. By embracing these innovations responsibly, higher education can create equitable, learner-centered, and future-ready ecosystems, where credentials are not static records but living, actionable assets that support lifelong learning, professional growth, and societal progress.

REFERENCES

Alsobhi, H. A., Alakhtar, R. A., Ubaid, A., Hussain, O. K., & Hussain, F. K. (2023). Blockchain-based micro-credentialing system in higher education institutions: Systematic literature review. *Knowledge-Based Systems*, *265*, 110238. Advance online publication. DOI: 10.1016/j.knosys.2022.110238

Barrett, H. C. (2007). Researching electronic portfolios and learner engagement: The REFLECT initiative. *Journal of Adolescent & Adult Literacy*, *50*(6), 436–449. Advance online publication. DOI: 10.1598/JAAL.50.6.2

Bayly-Castañeda, K. (2024). Crafting personalized learning paths with artificial intelligence for lifelong learning: A systematic literature review. *Frontiers in Education*. Advance online publication. DOI: 10.3389/feduc.2024.1424386

du Plooy, E., Casteleijn, D., & Franzsen, D. (2024). Personalized adaptive learning in higher education: A scoping review of key characteristics and impact on academic performance and engagement. *Heliyon*. Vol. 10 Issue 21, e39630, ISSN 2405-8440. DOI: 10.1016/j.heliyon.2024.e39630

Lu, H. (2021). Electronic portfolios in higher education: A review. *European Journal of Education Studies*, *2*(3), 96–101. Advance online publication. DOI: 10.24018/ejedu.2021.2.3.119

Mallik, S., & Gangopadhyay, A. (2023). Proactive and reactive engagement of AI methods for education.

McGreal, R. (2023). Blockchain and micro-credentials in education. *International Journal of E-Learning & Distance Education*.

Mikroyannidis, A., Third, A., & Domingue, J. (2020). A case study on the decentralisation of lifelong learning using blockchain technology. *Journal of Interactive Media in Education*, *2020*(1), 23. DOI: 10.5334/jime.591

Ocheja, P., Flanagan, B., & Ogata, H. (2019). Managing lifelong learning records through blockchain. *Research and Practice in Technology Enhanced Learning*, *14*(1), 4. DOI: 10.1186/s41039-019-0097-0

Sajja, R., Sermet, Y., Cikmaz, M., Cwiertny, D., & Demir, I. (2024). Artificial Intelligence-Enabled Intelligent Assistant for Personalized and Adaptive Learning in Higher Education. *Information (Basel)*, *15*(10), 596. DOI: 10.3390/info15100596

So, H.-J. Lee, C., Lee, Ga-Young, Kim, M.J. (2024). *UNESCO report on AI, blockchain, and XR in lifelong learning*. UNESCO Institute for Lifelong Learning. ISBN: 978-92-820-1258-1

Strielkowski, W. (2025). The role of micro-credentials in the future digitalized AI-driven education. DOI: /arXiv.2511.07583DOI: 10.48550

The Mozilla Foundation (2011). Open badges for lifelong learning. *The Mozilla Foundation and Peer 2 Peer University.*

Yang, H., & Wong, R. (2024). *An in-depth literature review of e-portfolio implementation in higher education. Issues and Trends in Learning Technologies*. University of Arizona Libraries.

Zhang, P., & Tur, G. (2022). Educational e-Portfolio Overview: Aspiring for the Future by Building on the Past. *IAFOR Journal of Education, 10*(3), 51–74. DOI: 10.22492/ije.10.3.03

Chapter 14
Blockchain-Enabled Security and Trust Models for the Internet of Medical Things (IoMT) in Modern Healthcare

Kashif Asad
http://orcid.org/0000-0002-4217-1823
Integral University, Lucknow, India

Nafees Akhter Farooqui
http://orcid.org/0000-0002-7583-3467
Integral University, Lucknow, India

Ausaf Ahmad
Integral University, Lucknow, India

ABSTRACT

Sensors, wearables, implanted devices, and cloud platforms provide real-time monitoring, diagnosis, and clinical decision-making with the Internet of Medical Things (IoMT). Growth of IoMT infrastructure affects data privacy, cybersecurity, interoperability, and trust. IoMT systems, non-standard communication protocols, device capabilities, and medical network incursions are covered. We suggest data fusion, encryption, and decentralised trust enforcers for patient data. A decentralised, unchangeable, and secure blockchain. Blockchain-based solutions protect IoMT data flow, eliminate single-point-of-failure, and secure distributed medical device trust evaluation. Distributed ledger data integrity, authentication, and trust score storage

DOI: 10.4018/979-8-3373-7600-4.ch014

improve active blockchain trust models. AI, data fusion, cloud/fog computing, smart hospitals, and blockchain secure IoMT. This chapter covers IoMT system design, cybersecurity, MULC frameworks, and blockchain-based health innovations. We discuss open research, regulation, and resilient, scalable, and dependable IoMT ecosystems.

1. INTRODUCTION

The development of the Internet of Things (IoT) has impacted many industries rather quickly, and healthcare is one of the most heavily changed sectors. The rise of an Internet of Medical Things (IoMT) a dedicated subfield of IoT has made it possible to create a healthcare ecosystem of interconnected medical sensors, wearable gadgets, implantable healthcare machines, hospital devices, and health app platforms that work together to gather, transport, and process patient data in real time. IoMT promotes healthcare by providing precise diagnostics, customized treatment, remote health, minimized hospitalization, and effective clinical decision-making (Postel, 1981) (Atzori et al., 2010) (Vishnu et al., 2020). IoMT devices are a dynamic digital-health network that fluidly incorporates the physical healthcare setting with intelligent biomedical information networks (Vishnu et al., 2020) (Islam et al., 2022). IoMT has led to better access to medical, continuous monitoring of chronic conditions, remote patient control, and predictive analytics using artificial intelligence (AI) (Si-Ahmed et al., 2022). IoMT involves implantable medical devices (IMDs), wearable medical devices (WMDs), remote patient monitoring (RPM) systems, and hospital networked devices (HNDs), which are linked together, via either wired or wireless communication technologies (Muhammad et al., 2021) (Wang et al., 2020) (Ferguson & Redish, 2011). These wearables constantly record physiological data, including ECG, EEG, blood glucose, oxygen saturation, blood pressure and movement patterns and transmit them to cloud databases or healthcare services to be analysed further (Yaqoob et al., 2019) (Pratim et al., 2020). Real-time biomedical data at scale is redefining the current healthcare delivery model and enabling smart and patient centric healthcare ecosystems. But that is accompanied by a growing concern: IoMT systems are raising new security and privacy dangers on a scale never seen before (Hemmati & Rahmani, 2022). In comparison to conventional IT infrastructure, IoMT devices are not usually richly resource endowed (high processing power, memory and battery life), and may run quietly with strict resource limitations (Sudha & Viveka, 2022) (Kamalov et al., 2023)(Bhushan et al., 2023). Most of the IoMT building blocks are also based on heterogeneous communication standards and are deployed in a non-standardized security implementation, creating uneven protection across the ecosystem (Ghubaish et al., 2021). With the high pace of competition in the markets, most IoMT products are implemented without considering security-by-design practices, leaving them susceptible to attacks (Gatouillat et al., 2018).

According to researchers, approximately half of IoMT devices is vulnerable to cyber threats because they have low authentication, poor data transfer, and no updates on firmware. The health care industry has already felt the impact of these gaps (Hernandez-Jaimes et al., 2023) (Ameen et al., 2023). Hackers are increasing their attacks on hospitals and healthcare databases, and the most common threats include ransomware, Distributed Denial-of-Service (DDoS) attacks, malware infections, and unauthorized access, which place patient safety at high risk. IoMT systems have a direct impact on the life of patients; as such, breaches may cause not only data loss but life-threatening medical disruptions. The monetary effect is also concerning according to reports, healthcare is the one who bears the highest price of data breaches, which makes it essential to have solid cybersecurity tools (Khalid et al., 2023) (Naresh & Thamarai, 2023). Since medical information is sensitive and healthcare operations are life-sensitive processes, IoMT security is not a choice but a must. An effective assault can release personal health data, compromise clinical decision-making, disrupt hospital operations, or change vital medical equipment operations (Rasheed et al., 2022). Also, the IoMT creates heterogeneous biomedical data that frequently move through cloud, edge and local network exposing the whole data lifecycle to various forms of threats (Zhang et al., 2022) (Mittal, 2023). Investigators underscore the fact that ensuring this lifecycle needs sophisticated solutions including cryptography, blockchain, trusted authentication models, secure data fusion, and AI-based intrusion detection models.

2. IOMT ARCHITECTURES AND DATA FLOW

The Internet of Medical Things (IoMT) is based on a multilayered architecture to establish a continuous linkage among medical equipment, sensors, communication networks, processing platforms and healthcare applications (Rahmani et al., 2022). This architecture is critical in the analysis of vulnerabilities in systems, data flow optimization, and the deployment of security tools that are appropriate to a heterogeneous medical setup (Granlund, 2021). Despite the various research studies that present variants of IoMT architectural framework, the majority of them all lead to a layered architecture that incorporates elements of perception, network/communication, processing, and application layers (Sun et al., 2019) (Istepanian, 2011). This tiered architecture is designed to provide effectively about sensing; transmitting, analysing, and operationalizing biomedical data in contemporary healthcare ecosystems.

Figure 1.

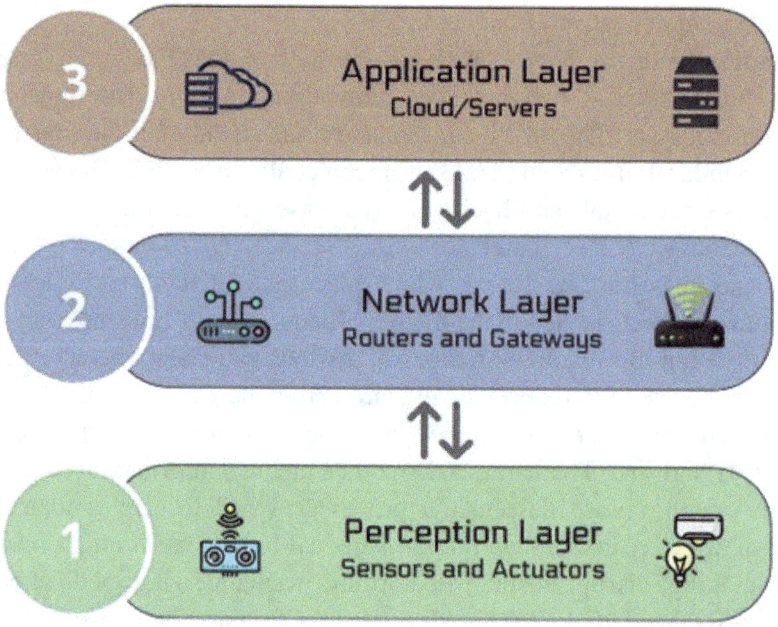

2.1. Perception Layer (Device and Sensor Layer).

The perception layer is the basis of the IoMT systems. It is a combination of physical medical gadgets which record patient information comprising of details of vital signs, physiological indicators, biomedical imagery and parameters of the behaviour. These devices include:

i) Wearable Medical devices (WMDs): fitness trackers, ECG monitors, smart-watches, glucose monitors.
ii) Implantable Medical Devices (IMDs): neurostimulators, insulin pumps and pacemakers.
iii) Hospital Networked Devices (HNDs): breathers, ventilators, imaging systems, infusion pumps.
iv) Remote Patient Monitoring (RPM) devices are home based health monitors and telemedicine kits.

These medical sensors keep gathering medical data in real time and forwarding it to intermediate gateway or directly to the cloud (Manickam et al., 2022). According to the researchers, this layer is very heterogeneous and can be composed of commonly resource constrained devices which are inadequate processing power to support complicated security functions (Xu et al., 2014).

The devices in this layer are highly vulnerable to cybersecurity threats due to their close-proximity to patients and being in direct contact with biological systems. In the absence of safe sensors, the whole IoMT structure would be prone to damages through interference, of the data, or hacking.

2.2. Network and Communication Layer

This layer guarantees a high degree of reliability in the transmission of biomedical data related to sensors to processing units. IoMT communication is based on the interaction of wireless and wired technologies, such as:

i) Wi-Fi, RFID, Bluetooth, ZigBee, NFC.
ii) 4G/5G mobile networks
iii) Body Area Networks (BANs)
iv) LANs Local Area Networks in Hospitals.

Such technologies provide device compatibility yet also provide means of cyber threats. In case, as an example, the weak encryption of the Bluetooth Low Energy (BLE) gadgets or old Wi-Fi setups, medical information can fall prey to an interception attack, a man-in-the-middle (MitM) attack. According to security studies, vulnerabilities of communication layers are frequently used because of the imprecise utilization of the protocols and non-uniform security actions among the manufacturers of the IoMT (Khan et al., 2023).

Also, escalating reliance on high-bandwidth, low-latency communication particularly after the deployment of 5G-supported IoMT is an added risk (Peng et al., 2020). On the one hand, 5G improves the performance and scalability, on the other hand, it increases the number of open surfaces to cyberattacks (Farhad et al., 2021).

2.3. Processing Layer (Fog, Edge and Cloud Computer)

Data acquired in the devices are processed at the processing layer where they are computed, filtered, fused and stored. There are three important technologies in this layer:

A. Edge Computing

Data analysis is performed near the device in edge nodes (e.g., smart gateways, routers), which makes it possible to reduced latency, faster emergency response improved bandwidth usage (Marston & Samuels, 2019). Medical devices with time-related requirements (cardiac), such as seizure prediction, are particularly helpful when the processing can be done on the edge.

B. Fog Computing

Between the cloud and the edge, there are fog nodes created. Fog architectures support local analytics, real-time decision-making, context-aware processing (Rasool,). Fog computing reduces the use of remote servers and provides a high degree of resiliency to the IoMT systems when networks are interrupted (Abdulmohsin Hammood et al., 2018).

C. Cloud Computing

This makes cloud platforms store and process enormous flows of biomedical data, which permit AI-driven diagnostics, big data analytics, Electronic Health record (EHR) integration. But there are also major security issues coming with cloud storage including centralized points of attack, insiders and poorly configured databases (Akbilgic et al., 2021). Research highlights that the cloud layer has to entail strong encryption, access control and trust management systems that would secure sensitive patient records.

2.4. Application Layer

The application layer provides medical services based on the application of IoMT and they include Virtual consultations and Telemedicine, Mobile health (mHealth) applications, Clinical decision support systems (CDSS), Smart hospital automation, Emergency response systems

This layer acts as it directly interrelates with healthcare providers, administrators and patients. It utilizes the processed information to provide individual treatment programs, anticipatory understandings, and remote treatment. This layer is used by healthcare professionals to provide real-time patient analytics, diagnostic reports, and alerts produced by the IoMT devices (Al-Turjman et al., 2020). The application layer should guarantee high adherence to regulatory documents, including GDPR and HIPAA, as it focuses on personally identifiable health information at the expense of its users, as indicated in various studies.

2.5. Data Flow in IoMT Ecosystems

Data movement within the IoMT is often organizationally four-step lifecycle:

A. Data Collection

Biomedical signals (ECG, EEG, glucose level, temperature, motion data) are recorded by sensors.

B. Data Transmission

The data obtained is relayed using the wireless network data to gateways or edge devices.

C. Data Processing and Fusion

EFC systems conduct analytics, combine multimodal data and produce insights.

Data fusion assists in integrating data of various sources to enhance accuracy and minimize variables of redundancy or inconsistency.

D. Data Utilization and Action

Medical applications use processed information to raise alerts, deliver diagnostic results, aid clinical choices, or revise electronic health records. This is a lean data flow not only beneficial to the smart functioning of healthcare but also presents a variety of vulnerabilities where attackers would intercept, alter, or exploit sensitive medical data (Begum & Dharmarajan, 2020).

2.6. IoMT Architecture security implications.

Each of the architectural levels implies certain vulnerability:

- Device layer risks: low level of authentication, physical threat of tampering, incomplete firmware.
- Communication layer risks: insecure protocols, data intercepting, eavesdropping.
- Processing layer risks: misconfigurations of cloud, data leaks, insider threats.
- Application layer risks: enabled access, API vulnerability, privacy intrusion.

Drastically complicating the challenge of securing IoMT, the complexity and interlinked of the latter becomes extremely difficult, particularly in cases where medical devices are interacting with multiple platforms and networks. Hence, one needs to learn these architectural layers prior to drafting effective security solutions, such as a blockchain-based trust management system, to safeguard medical information and secure a dependable IoMT system.

3. SECURITY THREATS AND VULNERABILITIES IN IOMT

The Internet of Medical Things (IoMT) is an innovative factor in healthcare, as the constant monitoring, rapid diagnosis, and automated clinical decision-making have become possible. Nevertheless, its highly sophisticated, interlinked ecosystem equally leaves it vulnerable to an extensive range of cybersecurity risks. The heterogeneous architecture of the devices, insufficient computing resources, non-standard communication protocols, reliance on clouds and sensitivity of medical data are the factors that lead to these threats. With healthcare becoming more and more dependent on IoMT-based systems, the security threats of the devices directly turn into clinical, financial, and operational implications (Dwivedi et al., 2022). This section gives a broad description of the primary security threats and vulnerabilities in IoMT settings with the aid of the uploaded research literature.

3.1. Vulnerabilities at the device-level.

The IoMT devices (wearables, implantable, and systems that connect hospital-wise) are typically resource-limited and do not include security features. Such restrictions expose them to different hardware and software attacks.

A. Flimsy Authentication and Authorization.

Numerous IoMT gadgets do not have any powerful log in features because they lack sufficient processing unit capabilities. Attackers are easily able to take control of the connected medical devices using default passwords, weak encryption keys, or hardcoded credentials.

B. Obsolete Firmware and Unpatched Equipment.

Manufacturers usually implement products of IoMT quickly without focusing much attention on security with regard to cybersecurity (Wal et al., 2022). The hackers use these old parts in order to install malware or to change the behaviour of the devices.

C. Physical Tampering

Attackers can gain access to wearable and implantable devices when they are at proximity. Physical access enables one to install malicious code, steal credentials, or get hold of sensitive data that is stored on the machine.

D. Sensors Manipulation

IoMT sensors are based on precise physiological-level information to elicit clinical responses. The attackers can either spoof or alter sensor readings which can result in the wrong diagnoses or dangerous treatment responses (e.g. improper insulin delivery).

3.2. Threats of Network and Communication.

IoMT ecosystems are based on wireless communication technologies that include Wi-Fi, Bluetooth, ZigBee, RFID, NFC, and cellular networks that communicate medical information between sensors, gateways, and healthcare servers to cloud plots. Though these communication technologies provide easy connectivity and live monitoring, they present a wide area of attack that attackers use. Medical device communication is wireless and open and, therefore, any vulnerability in transmission channels can result in unauthorized interception, data manipulation or disruption of the services (Papaioannou et al., 2022). As stating by researchers, most IoMT communication protocols have been initially created to serve devices with low power consumption, including consumer electronics, and not very sensitive devices, such as healthcare, promptly becoming weaknesses in the high stakes setting.

The Man-in-the-Middle (MitM) attack is one of the most widespread network threats in IoMT where the assaulting party deceives to intercept a communication between a device and server. Under those circumstances, the enemies can intercept confidential health-related information, manipulate the information sent, or inject harmful instructions into the information stream (Ashfaq et al., 2022). As IoMT devices do not always have powerful encryption services because of the limits in computing capabilities, mitigation of relationships will become simpler, especially in hospital facilities where a large number of interconnected sensors and mobile health apps are installed. Such attacks become particularly harmful since the manipulated or counterfeit medical records may result in misdiagnosis and unbeneficial clinical procedures. DDoS attacks are also extremely prone to IoMT systems, in which high levels of undesirable traffic congest the medical networks and make the devices unable to communicate efficiently. DDoS attacks have the potential to impact key medical processes, including patient-monitoring, harmonizing the activities of infusion pumps, or communicating with ventilators (Hemmati & Rahmani, 2022). Research has revealed that DDoS attacks in the healthcare system are the major impediments to emergency services in the sector and can cause serious harm to the lives of patients. Viewing that, by definition, IoMT networks are able to serve large populations of devices sending constant streams of data, attackers perceive them as perfect opportunities to create high-scale service outages with minimal input.

Eavesdropping is another significant risk in the communication in IoMT, where attackers only listen to unencrypted wireless messages. Possibly the most susceptible protocols include the Bluetooth Low Energy (BLE) and the ZigBee protocols (widely applicable in wearable and home-care medical devices) that have not been set up with a powerful encryption algorithm. Eavesdropping may enable the adversaries to intercept confidential health data, monitor the medical actions of patients, or obtain intelligence to organize the attack in future. On the same note, the vulnerabilities of the RFID-based medical asset tracking systems may make hospital practices, inventory flows, or even patient tag records visible (Sudha & Viveka, 2022).

Lastly, the communication channels in IoMTs are susceptible to replay attacks, where the attackers will capture valid data packets and forward them in future to attractive medical systems. This can result in a server receiving old or spoofed data including the wrong heart-rate data or glucose data causing a false alarm or diagnostic diagnosis. These risks are also exacerbated by the fact that in most IoMT devices, timestamping, session validation and encryption are weak (Sun et al., 2022). Replay attacks are becoming a challenge to trustworthiness and reliability of the IoMT data flows along with the rise in the number of wireless-enabled medical devices.

3.3. Vulnerabilities Cloud and storage.

The majority of IoMT systems use cloud services to store and analyse big amounts of patient data. Although the cloud system can be scaled; it poses serious risks as well.

A. Centralized Attack Points

Single data storage points form centrifugal points of failure. In the case of a successful attack of a cloud server, millions of records of patients can be revealed. There are several actual violations that point out to this danger.

B. Wrongly configured Cloud Servers.

Configurations Cloud setup mishaps, including unsecured storage buckets, may spread sensitive medical histories, just like the other large-scale healthcare violations in the past.

C. Insider Threats

Insider threats are a critical problem to the security of cloud-based healthcare platforms because employees who have authorized access to data may reveal information knowingly or unknowingly.

D. Insecure APIs

Application Programming Interfaces (APIs) are used by IoMT devices to liaise with cloud services. Unsecure APIs enable the attackers to intrude or steal sensitive data.

3.4. Risk of Data privacy and Confidentiality

Some of the most sensitive types of personal information are medical data. The value and sensitivity of this data are highlighted by the fact that costs in the healthcare breach are higher than in any other industry.

A. Privacy Breach by Data fusion

Stated another way, advanced IoMT systems are those that integrate many data streams (wearables, images, environmental, and so on). Lack of proper and secure data fusion activities can pull out the aggregation of data, and this can pose more risks to privacy.

B. Cultural or Situational Violation of Privacy

Metadata (e.g., the number of conversations with particular medical professionals) can be used to determine sensitive data (e.g., type of disease) by the attackers.

3.5. Application Layer threats

The application layer encompasses telemedicine portal, EHRs and clinical decision support. Attacks at this layer may affect the wholes of the IoMT workflow.

A. Unauthorized Access

Lax access control configurations enable hackers to enter hospital dashboards, access patient records, or send commands to the devices, which are linked through them.

B. Malware and Ransomware

Hospital ransomware has been on the increase by encrypting medical information and shutting key operations until a ransom is paid (Meng et al., 2020). IoMT systems, once linked to the infected hospital networks, are the points of entry of malware.

C. API Abuse and Injection Attacks

Telemedicine/mHealth software applications are based on APIs, which can be exploited to attack through SQL injection, cross-site scripting (XSS), or unauthorized data access (unauthorized data extraction).

4. BLOCKCHAIN AS A SECURITY SOLUTION FOR IOMT

The growing digitalization of healthcare has made the Internet of Medical Things (IoMT) the focus of contemporary clinical practice. Nevertheless, with the growth of IoMT, cyber threat increases, as does its vulnerability to cybercrimes that violate confidentiality, integrity, and availability of sensitive medical information. The use of traditional security mechanisms, including encrypted communication, centralized access control and authentication, is frequently not adequate because of the resource constraints of IoMT devices, the heterogeneity of communication protocols, and the use of a centralized cloud infrastructure (Abbas et al., 2024). Such constraints drive the introduction of the blockchain technology as an effective, decentralized, and resistant security system that can revolutionize the IoMT security models. Blockchain is the solution that researchers consistently note as one of the most promising ones in terms of enhancing trust, transparency, and resiliency in IoMT ecosystems.

Blockchain is a decentralized registry infrastructure through which transactions are registered in a distributed network of nodes without a central authority. Such a decentralized network removes the single point of failure that prevails in the cloud-based medical systems, where failure of one node would not affect the integrity of the entire system (Koundal et al., 2020). With all transactions on the blockchain verified by consensus mechanisms and cryptographically attached to the previous blocks, attackers are through with it incredibly challenging to modify or fake medical records.

Figure 2.

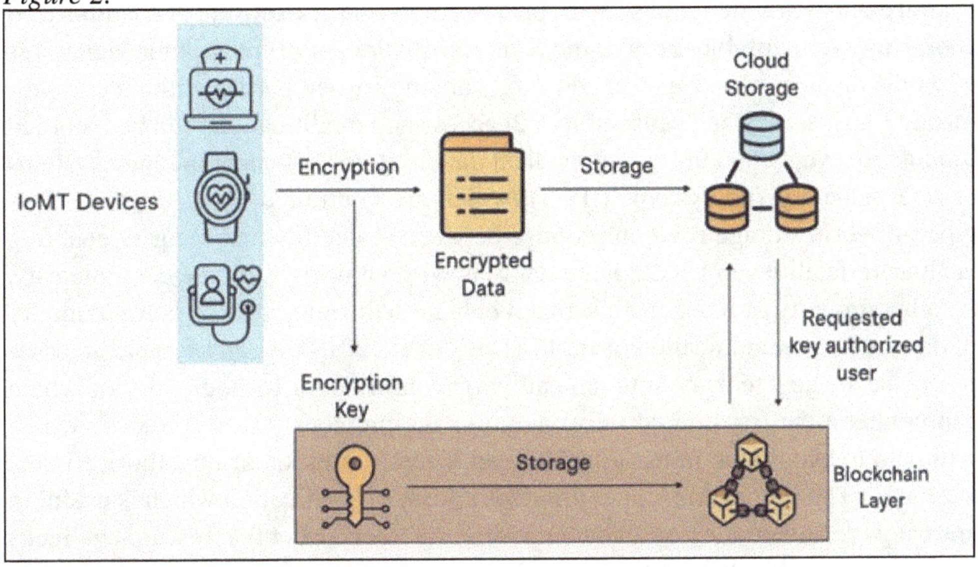

The maturity and impossibility of the blockchain records provides a high certainty of data integrity which is essential to the IoMT application where incorrect or biased data can result in life-threatening medical judgments. The application of blockchain in IoMT that is the most interesting is trust management, whereby blockchain models substitute centralized trust authorities with distributed and transparent checking mechanisms. The current trust systems are not very scalable and do not have adaptive measures to malicious actions. Blockchain-trusted trust systems overcome such limitations by storing trust scores, device behaviours and authentication records in a decentralized way (Jamil et al., 2019). The research uploaded on the idea of a dynamic blockchain-based trust management model illustrates that trust can be calculated through event-driven and time-driven approaches and justified through consensus and kept in ledgers that cannot be altered (Rathore, 2017). This framework will guarantee that nodes with bad characters are soon spotted, labelled, and isolated before they can cause havoc to healthcare services.

Blockchain also facilitates secure authentication and access control on a IoMT environment, aside from trust management. Authentication rules, access policies, and identity validation of a user or a device can be automated by smart contracts which are self-executable pieces of code within the blockchain (Zhang et al., 2014). Blockchain-based authentication systems also make sure that only authorized entities can access or alter important medical information, which is one of the key security issues with centralized healthcare systems where breaches of credentials and insider attacks are frequent.

In the conventional IoMT systems, the process of data-sharing banks is based on central databases which enhances the chances of having an exposure of unauthorized data. However, with blockchain, medical information, or cryptographic signatures of whole datasets can be exchanged safely among trusted parties without compromising transparency and censorship. All access and modifications can be recorded immutably even when the actual medical data is stored off chain in cloud systems or interplanetary file systems (IPFS), which are controlled by blockchain. This type of hybrid storage is a compromise between scalability and security enabling healthcare facilities to handle large datasets without decreasing the data integrity. Another property of blockchain is that it enhances the integrity and confidentiality of data in the communication of IoMT (Dang et al., 2019). As an example, in cases where the medical sensors communicate patient information to the cloud, blockchain can compare the transmitted information to the previously stored hashes, which will help to avoid man in the middle attacks, replay attacks, or unauthorized data alteration. The immutable ledger provides a form of verification which is useful in ensuring the authenticity of all data packets. Another aspect that researchers focus on is the use of blockchain to ensure the security of data fusion models in such a way that the information obtained by many medical sensors is credible and consistent (Partala, 2013).

Recent technologies, including the 5G, edge computing, and AI-directed analytics, also make blockchain more relevant to IoMT. The 5G networks are high-speed networks with lower latency of blockchain operations, which leads to real-time validation of medical data. Lightweight blockchain consensus algorithms can be run on edge nodes, which have fewer computational requirements when compared to IoMT devices. By pairing AI-based anomaly detection with blockchain logs, it is possible to detect suspicious patterns and determine dynamically a trust score. This synergistic combination forms a powerful, intelligent, and autonomous security infrastructure that is appropriate in the next-generation in smart healthcare systems.

Although it has potential, blockchain implementation on IoMT is not free of challenges. IoMT devices are frequently poorly equipped with processing power, memory and energy supplies, and it is hard to execute computationally intensive consensus mechanisms. Also, the immutability of blockchain can be incompatible with healthcare policies demanding the adjustment or removal of patient records in particular cases. The researchers propose the following strategies including hybrid blockchain systems, lightweight consensus algorithms, and off-chain storage to find the balance between the regulatory compliance and system performance (Qathrady et al., 2024). The blockchain is a paradigm shift to the protection of IoMT ecosystems. It has a decentralized architecture, which is tamper-proof and transparent to solve important trust, data integrity, authentication and access control problems. Combined with state-of-the-art technologies like 5G, AI, and edge computing, blockchain can be used to create a high level of security and reliability in healthcare settings that will be able to provide continuous, real-time, and smart medical care (Egala,). Blockchain is projected to form the basis of the next generation of IoMT systems by providing the means of ensuring patient safety, regulatory compliance, and reliable data exchange throughout the healthcare environment.

5. INTEGRATION OF BLOCKCHAIN WITH AI, DATA FUSION, AND SMART HEALTHCARE

Blockchain integration with progressive technologies like Artificial Intelligence (AI), data fusion, and smart healthcare architectures is one of the significant advances of creating resilient, intelligent, and secure Internet of Medical Things (IoMT) environments. With the development of healthcare systems into the state of interconnection, real-time, and data-intensive ones, the integration of these technologies will be inevitable to provide high accuracy, reliability, and efficiency of operations.

Figure 3.

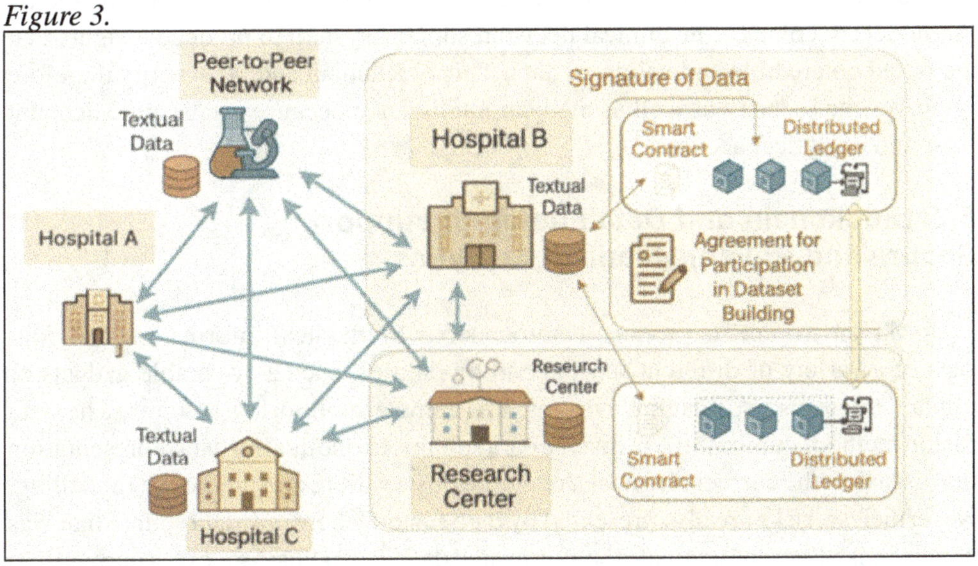

Blockchain offers the underlying platform of safety and trust, AI keeps enhancing intelligence and decision-making, and data fusion assists in improving the quality and trustworthiness of medical data. The combination of them facilitates the creation of next-generation smart healthcare systems which can meet complex clinical, technical, and security challenges.

5.1. IoMT Security and Intelligence by Blockchain and Artificial Intelligence

AI has a vital part in the improvement of IoMT as it allows predictive analytics, anomaly detection, early disease diagnosis, and automated decision-making. Nevertheless, AI is extremely data-based and data quality is directly related to the outcomes of an algorithm. Blockchain solves this issue by offering an unalterable and reliable history of medical information deployed in AI modelling (Mathkor et al., 2024). Blockchain prevents data poisoning, manipulation, and unauthorized access of AI-driven applications by making sure that all inputs are verifiable, tamper-proof, and traceable. According to the researchers, AI and blockchain integration would greatly improve cybersecurity because it will be able to observe any suspicious activity, attacks, or other irregularities in the IoMT networks (Mathkor et al., 2024).

The AI algorithms are used in intrusion detection systems (IDS) and anomaly detection systems to examine the real-time behaviour of medical devices, and the blockchain is used to store threat signatures, trust scores, and audit logs at the required level of security. This guarantees the ability to trace malicious activity when early detected and across devices. Blockchain-secured data can also be utilized by AI models to enhance the clinical decision support system to produce insights that are based on credible and validated data. This blockchain and AI synergy therefore improves the security as well as medical intelligence because it takes into account trust and analytical accuracy.

5.2. Blockchain and Data Fusion to support Secure and Reliable Medical Analytics

IoMT environments produce heterogeneous biomedical information that consists of a variety of different sensors and modalities, such as wearable gadgets or implantable sensors, imaging systems, and remote monitoring systems. The data fusion methods combine these diverse data streams to one quality data representation that assists in the correct diagnosis, real time observation, and predictive modelling. Nevertheless, risks are also presented by data fusion where any data source that was compromised can contaminate the aggregated data. Blockchain gives a secure system to verify, time stamp and track every data piece prior to entering the fusion pipeline.

The research shows that IoMT is especially susceptible to data fusion because of the inclusion of devices that cannot be trusted, insecure information communication channels, and non-uniform data formats. Blockchain helps to reduce these vulnerabilities because it ensures that all medical data, no matter the source, has undergone cryptographic verification before integration. This helps avoid the possibility of cases where attackers inject fake sensor values, replay old medical data or manipulate clinical results. The blockchain can improve the trustworthiness, privacy and provenance of fused IoMT data, leading to improved healthcare analytics accuracy by means of decentralized verification and tamper-resistant logging. Blockchain and data fusion can be combined to enable privacy-sensitive medical analytics. Blockchain Original PID patients can be anonymized or stored off-chain, and only metadata or hashes of the data are recorded in the blockchain (Vishnu et al., 2020). This makes sure that although the integrity of fused datasets is preserved, the patient privacy laws like GDPR and HIPAA are not infringed.

Medical analytics paradigm is during change turning into a momentous shift when the healthcare industry has the twin imperatives of utilizing massively diverse datasets and at the same time protecting patient privacy. Combining data fusion principles with the blockchain technology, we create a complex system of supporting the high-stakes clinical decision making: the resultant data is not only comprehensive, but verifiable and immutable as well. In its simplest form, data fusion in the healthcare system involves the integration of information available in a variety of repositories, including Electronic Health Records (EHRs), real-time, wearable Internet -of- Things medical sensors, genomic sequences, and diagnostic images, to create a comprehensive account of the health of a person. Although this combination provides the comprehensive contextual background required by the sophisticated predictive analytics, it also poses the major threats associated with the data provenance and malicious modifications. Blockchain acts as a crucial layer of trust to this combined data set which virtualizes the cryptographic hash- or fingerprint-of each data point included in the analysis. Streaming the aggregated datasets to a decentralized registry the healthcare organization can ensure that the clinical intuition of the medical analytics is built on pristine information, which succeeds in removing the problem of black box that is frequent with the processing of intricate datasets.

Medical analytics can also be made reliable by utilizing consensus mechanisms and smart contracts to this built-in architecture. In the traditional setup, where there is a centralized system, the failure of one point can lead to mass data corruption, and this may in turn render analytics useless or destructively inaccurate due to a breach of one administrative account. In a data fusion model based on blockchain, the authenticity of new incoming information on various sensors and clinical records is verified by a network of nodes that aim at consensus before it can even be discussed regarding fusion. These validation processes can be automated through smart contracts and include stringent quality standards and protocols that have to be met before they are included in the analytical model. As an example, in case the blood glucose sensor produces a physically implausible reading, or does not provide an authenticated digital signature, the smart contract will be triggered to flag or ignore that record and therefore maintain the integrity of the fused dataset. This degree of decentralized, automated governance guarantees the reliability of medical analytics even where the high-velocity and diversity of the modern telehealth and remote monitoring infrastructure are concerned.

In addition to security and reliability, such synergy will be used to enable a more patient-centric and interoperable healthcare as an ecosystem. The main problem that has long been known to bring down data fusion is the presence of data silos, where data is locked up in format or proprietary systems that do not work together. The blockchain is a standardized and secure data exchange medium that allows various stakeholders, such as research laboratories to local clinics, to add to a common, fused data pool and maintain their intellectual property rights and patient information privacy. The patients themselves can use identity management based on blockchain to provide selective access to their consolidated medical records so that researchers can provide high-level analytics to the discovery of a drug at the cost of maintaining the absolute privacy of the identity of a specific individual. With the medical analytics moving to real-time, AI-driven diagnostics, the integration of the immutable record-keeping feature of blockchain and the holistic understanding provided by the data fusion system will become the key to the safe, transparent, and highly efficient digital health future.

5.3. Smart Healthcare Systems with the Support of Blockchain

Smart healthcare is a new model of medical service provision, which incorporates autonomous clinical systems, interconnected IoT devices, predictive diagnostics, robotic surgery, telehealth, and remote patient monitoring. The key to these intelligent healthcare environments is blockchain as it offers decentralized, transparent, and secure data governance. The use of blockchain in smart hospitals contributes to the security of data transfer, the presence of interoperable medical systems, device authentication, and coordinated clinical workflows (Islam et al., 2022). The research has identified that some of the challenges that smart healthcare systems have to overcome include device tampering, unauthorized access, and unreliable data integrity. Blockchain solves these challenges by means of making sure that all medical events, including device communications, patient activities, medication administration events, and resource assignments, are recorded on an immutable ledger. This increases the auditability, clinical transparency, and minimizes the likelihood of manualizing or cyberattacks.

Smart contracts on blockchain also enhance automation of healthcare operations through the issuance of alerts, access control policies, and the organization of patient to care operations through pre-established policies (Ferguson & Redish, 2011). Smart contracts will minimize delays and operational errors, especially during emergencies when it gets rid of manual validation and central intermediaries (Yaqoob et al., 2019) (Hemmati & Rahmani, 2022). Together with edge and fog computing, blockchain can be used to facilitate low-latency, real-time smart healthcare applications to help ensure continuous patient monitoring, remote diagnosis, and quick clinical response.

When analyzing the development of the intelligent healthcare systems, a paradigm shift leads to the model of healthcare in the form of data-driven, patient-centric. At the heart of this change is the incorporation of blockchain technology to offer a decentralized platform to handle the abundance and sensitivity of data generated by the modern medical ecosystem. Old healthcare architectures are often associated with data silos, meaning that patient data are often scattered between numerous hospitals, labs, and insurance companies. This dilemma is overcome through the blockchain which provides a single, unalterable registry that captures the whole history of the medical history of a given patient, thus ensuring that records are always uniform, open and vulnerable to unauthorized modifications.

The concept of patient sovereignty and the ability to guarantee data integrity is at the heart of the healthcare system supported with a blockchain. The traditional medical environment is based on institutions and controls; thus, patients are difficult to hand over their medical histories to new personnel or researchers. The blockchain restores power to the individual through the use of the decentralized identity and cryptographic key. Any clinical occurrence such as a simple blood test or a complex surgery is encoded into a block of an ineffective chain. Since every block is cryptographically connected with the one that came before it, any manipulation with a record will be immediately noticed by the network, which creates a certain degree of trust that is practically impossible with centralized databases.

The introduction of smart contracts also increases automation and efficiency in the area of smart healthcare. These self-executing programs are stored in the blockchain and have their actions activated by some sets of conditions met. In a clinical trial setting, such as that, smart contracts have the potential to manage patient consent so that data is only given to researchers when it is confirmed that the patient has given verifiable consent to a researcher. Such contracts may also be applied in the insurance industry to facilitate easier claims, by ensuring that a procedure has been completed and in acclaim of the patient meaning it is covered and it does not produce unnecessary administrative costs, and it is also possible to avoids billing fraud.

In addition to the data management, blockchain plays a central role in pharmaceutical supply chain and Internet of Medical Things (IoMT) security. Medical businesses across the world are facing a major problem concerning fake medications and devices; blockchain gives an opportunity to provide a clear inventory and tracery process that will determine the path of a product between a pharmacy and a factory. The history of every hand-off is documented, so the providers could confirm the drug origin and access to temperature-regulated storage history prior to its delivery to the patient. Equally in the case of interrelated medical equipment like pacemakers or insulin pumps, blockchain also provides a secure platform on which identity can be managed so that dishonest individuals cannot interfere with or alter the information sent by these life-saving machines.

The critical part is that, as the smart healthcare systems continue to grow in scale, blockchain guarantees that the increased amount of medical data is not traded at privacy and security costs. Blockchain also enables an improved partnership of the different medical stakeholders who are normally separate, as well as maintaining the optimum levels of patient confidentiality by supporting a clear, but encrypted atmosphere. Such technological basis can never be done without in the future of precision medicine whereby large-scale and safe data exchange is a must to design personalized treatment regimens based on a unique genetic and clinical profile of a patient.

5.4. 5G, Edge computing, and Blockchain in improving the IoMT Integration.

The implementation of the fifth generation (5G) communication technologies has a considerable positive impact on the performance of the IoMT as it offers ultra-low latency, high bandwidth, and massive device connectivity. These advantages play a significant role in handling the massive stream of medical data and performing blockchain-related activities in real time. Research has observed that 5G-based IoMT networks can support quick data validation and faster consensus processes and blockchain execution processes that allow secure and immediate healthcare provision. Edge computing also enhances this form of integration by decentralizing processing tasks not to the cloud servers but to the proximity to the IoMT devices (Sudha & Viveka, 2022). By having edge nodes as lightweight blockchain participants, the system will reduce the computational load on resource-constrained machines and enhance the data validation, authentication, and the management of trust. The combination of 5G, edge computing and blockchain results in an effective hybrid architecture that can assist in the implementation of scalable, secure and real-time smart healthcare systems.

In the modern context of medical informatics, 5G is the factor of the transformational change of the highest order since it provides the most high-speed, the lowest latency communication substrate, capable of supporting up to one million connected devices in one sq km. By 2026 the introduction of network slicing is inevitable, which would allow hospitals to designate specific virtual bandwidth specifically to a life-dependent application, like remote robotic surgery or emergency telemetry.

This distribution assures that any action of a surgeon will be transmitted with some latencies under five milliseconds, which practically eliminates the perceptible delay that used to hinder long-range medical operations. In addition, the large bandwidth allows continuous transmission of high-resolution imaging of 4K and real-time biometric streams at up to thousands of simultaneous sensors without affecting network congestion.

Edge computing is the complementary factor to this connectivity by shifting the data processing to the localized environment of the medical equipment instead of the far-away cloud infrastructures. Analysis is done at the network edge, whether it is a local hospital gateway or the wearable device itself, rather than the raw data going through hundreds of miles to a central data center. Localized intelligence, like this, allows immediate decision-making; an example of this is a wearable cardiac monitor, which is able to send an alarm of an imminent cardiac event on the local basis before even the information can be posted to the central system. The edge processing and summarisation of the data will significantly decrease the amount of information that will be uploaded in the cloud storage, hence streamlining the costs of storage as well as maintaining the best of health in the network in general.

Even though speed and agility required in 5G and edge computing are provided, blockchain adds an essential component of trust and safety. In an integrated Internet of Medical Things (IoMT) ecosystem, blockchain will serve as a non-decentralized register of all transactions and data transfers between the devices and healthcare providers. This decentralised paradigm eliminates the single point of failure risk of the traditional databases. Smart contracts control access to patient records which are secured by cryptographic hash functions. These self-executory contracts enable patients to have finer control over their medical background (controlling access to experts or researchers automatically according to a predetermined access policy). As a result, although medical information spreads at still at high speeds on the 5G network and is computed at lightning speed and the edge, it is impervious to intrusion and subject to the consent of the patient.

6. CONCLUSION

The introduction of blockchain into the Internet of Medical Things (IoMT) is a serious step in the development of safe, intelligent, and patient-centralized healthcare systems. IoMT has changed the traditional medical practice by making it possible to monitor patients, diagnose and analyse medical information remotely, and connect medical equipment, patients, and practitioners to each other with ease. Nonetheless, with this heightened interconnectivity, there is a more significant vulnerability that puts critical medical structures at risk of privacy loss, data manipulation, unautho-

REFERENCES

Abbas, A., Alroobaea, R., Krichen, M., Rubaiee, S., Vimal, S., & Almansour, F. M. (2024). Blockchain-assisted secured data management framework for health information analysis based on Internet of Medical Things. *Personal and Ubiquitous Computing*, *28*(1), 59–72. DOI: 10.1007/s00779-021-01583-8

Abdulmohsin Hammood, D., Rahim, H. A., Alkhayyat, A., Ahmed, R. B., & Abbasi, Q. H. (2018). Reliable emergency data transmission using transmission mode selection in wireless body area network. *Cogent Engineering*, *5*(1), 1562859. DOI: 10.1080/23311916.2018.1562859

Akbilgic, A., Butler, L., Karabayir, I., Chang, P. P., Kitzman, D. W., Alonso, A., Chen, L. Y., & Soliman, E. Z. (2021). ECG-AI: Electrocardiographic artificial intelligence model for prediction of heart failure. *European Heart Journal. Digital Health*, *2*(4), 626–634. DOI: 10.1093/ehjdh/ztab080 PMID: 34993487

Al-Turjman, A., Nawaz, M. H., & Ulusar, U. D. (2020). Intelligence in the internet of medical things era: A systematic review of current and future trends. *Computer Communications*, *150*, 644–660. DOI: 10.1016/j.comcom.2019.12.030

Ameen, A. H., Mohammed, M. A., & Rashid, A. N. (2023). Dimensions of artificial intelligence techniques, blockchain, and cyber security in the Internet of Medical Things: Opportunities, challenges, and future directions. *Journal of Intelligent Systems*, *32*(1), 20220267. DOI: 10.1515/jisys-2022-0267

Ashfaq, Z., Rafay, A., Mumtaz, R., Hassan Zaidi, S. M., Saleem, H., Raza Zaidi, S. A., Mumtaz, S., & Haque, A. (2022). A review of enabling technologies for Internet of Medical Things (IoMT) ecosystem. *Ain Shams Engineering Journal*, *13*(4), 101660. DOI: 10.1016/j.asej.2021.101660

Atzori, L., Iera, A., & Morabito, G. (2010). The Internet of Things: A survey. *Computer Networks*, *54*(15), 2787–2805. DOI: 10.1016/j.comnet.2010.05.010

Begum, B., & Dharmarajan, D. K. (2020). Smart healthcare monitoring system in IoT. *European Journal of Molecular and Clinical Medicine*, *7*(4), 2647–2661.

Bhushan, B., Sinha, P., Sagane, K. M., & Jha, A. V. (2023). Towards a secure and sustainable Internet of Medical Things (IoMT): Requirements, design challenges, security techniques, and future trends. *Sustainability (Basel)*, *15*(3), 2729. DOI: 10.3390/su15076177

Dang, L. M., Piran, M., Han, D., Min, K., & Moon, H. (2019). A survey on Internet of Things and cloud computing for healthcare. *Electronics (Basel), 8*(7), 768. DOI: 10.3390/electronics8070768

Dwivedi, R., Mehrotra, D., & Chandra, S. (2022). Potential of Internet of Medical Things (IoMT) applications in building a smart healthcare system: A systematic review. *Journal of Oral Biology and Craniofacial Research, 12*(2), 302–318. DOI: 10.1016/j.jobcr.2021.11.010 PMID: 34926140

. Egala, A., et al. (in press). *Blockchain-based decentralized EHR & smart contracts* [Unpublished or partial reference cited in Qathrady et al.].

Farhad, A., Woolley, S., & Andras, P. (2021). Federated learning for AI to improve patient care using wearable and IoMT sensors. In *2021 IEEE 9th International Conference on Healthcare Informatics (ICHI)* (p. 434). IEEE. DOI: 10.1109/ICHI52183.2021.00071

Ferguson, J. E., & Redish, A. D. (2011). Wireless communication with implanted medical devices using the conductive properties of the body. *Expert Review of Medical Devices, 8*(4), 427–433. DOI: 10.1586/erd.11.16 PMID: 21728728

Gatouillat, A., Badr, Y., Massot, B., & Sejdić, E. (2018). Internet of Medical Things: A review of recent contributions dealing with cyber-physical systems in medicine. *IEEE Internet of Things Journal, 5*(5), 3810–3822. DOI: 10.1109/JIOT.2018.2849014

Ghubaish, A., Agoua, T., Vicic, T., Tarlochan, F., & Al-Ali, A. R. (2021). Recent advances in the Internet-of-Medical-Things (IoMT) systems security. *IEEE Internet of Things Journal, 8*(11), 8707–8718. DOI: 10.1109/JIOT.2020.3045653

Granlund, T.. (2021). On medical device cybersecurity compliance in EU. In *Proceedings of the 2021 IEEE/ACM 3rd International Workshop on Software Engineering for Healthcare (SEH)* (pp. 20–23). IEEE. DOI: 10.1109/SEH52539.2021.00011

Hemmati, A., & Rahmani, A. M. (2022). Internet of Medical Things in the COVID-19 era: A systematic literature review. *Sustainability (Basel), 14*(19), 12637. DOI: 10.3390/su141912637

Hemmati, A., & Rahmani, A. M. (2022). Internet of Medical Things in the COVID-19 era: A systematic literature review. *Sustainability (Basel), 14*(19), 12637. DOI: 10.3390/su141912637

Hernandez-Jaimes, M. L., Martinez-Cruz, A., Ramírez-Gutiérrez, K. A., & Feregrino-Uribe, C. (2023). Artificial intelligence for IoMT security: A review of intrusion detection systems, attacks, datasets and cloud–fog–edge architectures. *Internet of Things : Engineering Cyber Physical Human Systems*, *23*, 100887. DOI: 10.1016/j.iot.2023.100887

Islam, M. M., Nooruddin, S., Karray, F., & Muhammad, G. (2022). Internet of Things: Device capabilities, architectures, protocols, and smart applications in healthcare domain. *IEEE Internet of Things Journal*, *10*(4), 3611–3641. DOI: 10.1109/JIOT.2022.3228795

Istepanian, R. S.. (2011). *The potential of Internet of m-health Things 'm-IoT' for non-invasive glucose level sensing. In 2011 Annual International Conference of the IEEE Engineering in Medicine and Biology Society*. IEEE.

Jamil, F., Iqbal, M. A., Amin, R., & Kim, D. (2019). Adaptive thermal-aware routing protocol for wireless body area network. *Electronics (Basel)*, *8*(1), 47. DOI: 10.3390/electronics8010047

Kamalov, F., Cherukuri, A. K., Gurusamy, S., Sriram, V. P., & Chinnasamy, P. (2023). Internet of Medical Things privacy and security: Challenges, solutions, and future trends from a new perspective. *Sustainability (Basel)*, *15*(4), 3317. DOI: 10.3390/su15043317

Khalid, N., Qayyum, A., Bilal, M., Al-Fuqaha, A., & Qadir, J. (2023). Privacy-preserving artificial intelligence in healthcare: Techniques and applications. *Computers in Biology and Medicine*, *158*, 106848. DOI: 10.1016/j.compbiomed.2023.106848 PMID: 37044052

Khan, M. A., Din, I. U., Kim, B.-S., & Almogren, A. (2023). Visualization of remote patient monitoring system based on Internet of Medical Things. *Sustainability (Basel)*, *15*(10), 8120. DOI: 10.3390/su15108120

Koundal, D., Sharma, B., & Guo, Y. (2020). Intuitionistic based segmentation of thyroid nodules in ultrasound images. *Computers in Biology and Medicine*, *121*, 103776. DOI: 10.1016/j.compbiomed.2020.103776 PMID: 32568671

Manickam, P., Mariappan, S. A., Murugesan, S. M., Hansda, S., Kaushik, A., Shinde, R., & Thipperudraswamy, S. P. (2022). Artificial intelligence (AI) and Internet of Medical Things (IoMT) assisted biomedical systems for intelligent healthcare. *Biosensors (Basel)*, *12*(8), 562. DOI: 10.3390/bios12080562 PMID: 35892459

Marston, H. R., & Samuels, J. (2019). A review of age friendly virtual assistive technologies and their effect on daily living for carers and dependent adults. *Health Care, 7*(2), 49. PMID: 30901898

Mathkor, D. M., Mathkor, N., Bassfar, Z., Bantun, F., Slama, P., Ahmad, F., & Haque, S. (2024). Multirole of the internet of medical things (IoMT) in biomedical systems for managing smart healthcare systems: An overview of current and future innovative trends. *Journal of Infection and Public Health, 17*(4), 559–572. DOI: 10.1016/j.jiph.2024.01.013 PMID: 38367570

Meng, W., Li, W., & Zhu, L. (2020). Enhancing medical smartphone networks via blockchain-based trust management against insider attacks. *IEEE Transactions on Engineering Management, 67*(4), 1377–1386. DOI: 10.1109/TEM.2019.2921736

Mittal, S. (2023). Explaining URL phishing detection by glass box models. In *Proceedings of the 2023 Fifteenth International Conference on Contemporary Computing (IC3)* (pp. 535–541). ACM. DOI: 10.1145/3607947.3608059

Muhammad, G., Al-Rakhami, M. S., Gumaei, A., Pakrezaei, M., & Alamri, A. (2021). A comprehensive survey on multimodal medical signals fusion for smart healthcare systems. *Information Fusion, 76*, 268–289. DOI: 10.1016/j.inffus.2021.06.007

Naresh, V. S., & Thamarai, M. (2023). Privacy-preserving data mining and machine learning in healthcare: Applications, challenges, and solutions. *Wiley Interdisciplinary Reviews. Data Mining and Knowledge Discovery, 13*(2), e1490. DOI: 10.1002/widm.1490

Papaioannou, M., Karageorgou, M., Mantas, G., Sucasas, V., Essop, I., Rodriguez, J., & Lymberopoulos, D. (2022). A survey on security threats and countermeasures in Internet of Medical Things (IoMT). *Transactions on Emerging Telecommunications Technologies, 33*(6), e4049. DOI: 10.1002/ett.4049

Partala, J., ... (2013). Security threats against the transmission chain of a medical health monitoring system. In *2013 IEEE 15th International Conference on e-Health Networking, Applications and Services (HealthCom)* (pp. 243–248). IEEE. DOI: 10.1109/HealthCom.2013.6720675

Peng, J., Cai, K., & Jin, X. (2020). High concurrency massive data collection algorithm for IoMT applications. *Computer Communications, 157*, 402–409. DOI: 10.1016/j.comcom.2020.04.045

Postel, J. (Ed.). (1981). Internet Protocol - DARPA Internet program, protocol specification. Internet Engineering Task Force., RFC 791.

Pratim, P., Dash, D., & Kumar, N. (2020). Sensors for internet of medical things: State-of-the-art, security and privacy issues, challenges and future directions. *Computer Communications*, *160*, 111–131. DOI: 10.1016/j.comcom.2020.05.029

Qathrady, M. A., Saeed, M., Amin, R., Alshehri, M. S., Alshehri, A., & Alqhtani, S. M. (2024). Smart healthcare: A dynamic blockchain-based trust management model using subarray algorithm. *IEEE Access : Practical Innovations, Open Solutions*, *12*, 51430–51445. DOI: 10.1109/ACCESS.2024.3383310

Rahmani, M. K. I., Shuaib, M., Alam, S., Siddiqui, S. T., Ahmad, S., Bhatia, S., & Mashat, A. (2022). Blockchain-based trust management framework for cloud computing-based Internet of Medical Things (IoMT): A systematic review. *Computational Intelligence and Neuroscience*, *2022*, 9165383. DOI: 10.1155/2022/9766844 PMID: 35634070

Rasheed, K., Qayyum, A., Ghaly, M., Al-Fuqaha, A., Razi, A., & Qadir, J. (2022). Explainable, trustworthy, and ethical machine learning for healthcare: A survey. *Computers in Biology and Medicine*, *149*, 106043. DOI: 10.1016/j.compbiomed.2022.106043 PMID: 36115302

. Rasool, R. U., et al. (in press). *Security and privacy related work* [Unpublished or partial reference].

Rathore, H., ... (2017). A review of security challenges, attacks and resolutions for wireless medical devices. In *2017 13th International Wireless Communications and Mobile Computing Conference (IWCMC)* (pp. 1495–1501). IEEE. DOI: 10.1109/IWCMC.2017.7986505

Si-Ahmed, A., Al-Garadi, M. A., & Boustia, N. (2022). Survey of machine learning based intrusion detection methods for Internet of Medical Things. *Applied Soft Computing*, *140*, 110227. DOI: 10.1016/j.asoc.2023.110227

Sudha, M. J., & Viveka, S. (2022). A comprehensive review of architecture, classification, challenges, and future of the Internet of Medical Things (IoMTs). *Medical Journal of Babylon*, *19*(3), 311–317. DOI: 10.4103/MJBL.MJBL_5_22

Sudha, M. J., & Viveka, S. (2022). A comprehensive review of architecture, classification, challenges, and future of the Internet of Medical Things (IoMTs). *Medical Journal of Babylon*, *19*(3), 311–317. DOI: 10.4103/MJBL.MJBL_5_22

Sun, Q., Lin, K., Si, C., Xu, Y., Li, S., & Gope, P. (2022). A secure and anonymous communication scheme over the Internet of Things. *ACM Transactions on Sensor Networks*, *18*(3), 1–21. DOI: 10.1145/3508392

Sun, Y., Lo, F. P.-W., & Lo, B. (2019). Security and privacy for the Internet of Medical Things enabled healthcare systems: A survey. *IEEE Access : Practical Innovations, Open Solutions*, *7*, 183339–183355. DOI: 10.1109/ACCESS.2019.2960617

Vishnu, S., Jino Ramson, S. R., & Jegan, R. (2020). Internet of Medical Things (IoMT) — an overview. In *Proceedings of the 2020 5th International Conference on Devices, Circuits and Systems (ICDCS)* (pp. 101–104). IEEE. DOI: 10.1109/ICDCS48716.2020.243558

Wal, P., Wal, A., Verma, N., Karunakakaran, R., & Kapoor, A. (2022). Internet of Medical Things – the future of healthcare. *The Open Public Health Journal*, *15*(1), 1–9. DOI: 10.2174/18749445-v15-e221215-2022-142

Wang, L., Ali, Y., Nazir, S., & Niazi, M. (2020). ISA evaluation framework for security of internet of health things system using AHP-TOPSIS methods. *IEEE Access : Practical Innovations, Open Solutions*, *8*, 152316–152332. DOI: 10.1109/ACCESS.2020.3017221

Xu, L. D., He, W., & Li, S. (2014). Internet of Things in industries: A survey. *IEEE Transactions on Industrial Informatics*, *10*(4), 2233–2243. DOI: 10.1109/TII.2014.2300753

Yaqoob, T., Abbas, H., & Atiquzzaman, M. (2019). Security vulnerabilities, attacks, countermeasures, and regulations of networked medical devices — A review. *IEEE Communications Surveys and Tutorials*, *21*(4), 3723–3768. DOI: 10.1109/COMST.2019.2914094

Zhang, K., Liang, X., Lu, R., & Shen, X. (2014). Sybil attacks and their defenses in the Internet of Things. *IEEE Internet of Things Journal*, *1*(5), 372–383. DOI: 10.1109/JIOT.2014.2344013

Zhang, Z., Hamadi, H. A., Damiani, E., Yeun, C. Y., & Taher, F. (2022). Explainable artificial intelligence applications in cyber security: State-of-the-art in research. *IEEE Access : Practical Innovations, Open Solutions*, *10*, 93104–93139. DOI: 10.1109/ACCESS.2022.3204051

Compilation of References

Abbas, A., Alroobaea, R., Krichen, M., Rubaiee, S., Vimal, S., & Almansour, F. M. (2024). Blockchain-assisted secured data management framework for health information analysis based on Internet of Medical Things. *Personal and Ubiquitous Computing*, *28*(1), 59–72. DOI: 10.1007/s00779-021-01583-8

Abdul Halim, F. S., Luaran, J. E., & Lee, S. S. J. (2024). Unravelling challenges of higher education institutions in implementing effective micro-credentials: A multi-stakeholder qualitative study. *Asian Journal of University Education*, *20*(1), 114–126. DOI: 10.24191/ajue.v20i1.25698

Abdulmohsin Hammood, D., Rahim, H. A., Alkhayyat, A., Ahmed, R. B., & Abbasi, Q. H. (2018). Reliable emergency data transmission using transmission mode selection in wireless body area network. *Cogent Engineering*, *5*(1), 1562859. DOI: 10.1080/23311916.2018.1562859

Abisoye, A. (2024). Creating a Conceptual Framework for AI-Powered STEM Education Analytics to Enhance Student Learning Outcomes. *International Journal of Research and Innovation in Social Science.*

Abramovich, S., & Reed, A. (2024). White paper: Creating assessments for micro-credentials in higher education organizations. University at Buffalo.

Abu Bakar, N. S. A., Yahya, N., Idris, N. B., Zakaria, Z. Y., & Nordin, M. A. M. (2025). *Enhancing Academic Credential Integrity Through Blockchain-Based Verification Systems*. Frontiers in Artificial Intelligence and Applications., DOI: 10.3233/FAIA250509

Abukhalaf, S., Charles, T., & Hill, C. (2024). The Metaverse as a Virtual Learning Space: Perceptions from the UAE. *Journal of Ecohumanism*, *3*(5), 1037–1052. https://doi.org/10.62754/joe.v3i5.3954DOI: 10.62754/joe.v3i5.3954

Abuzied, Y., Ghanem, M., Dawoud, F., Gamal, H., Soliman, E., Sharara, H., & El-Batt, T. (2024). A privacy-preserving federated learning framework for blockchain networks. *Cluster Computing*, *27*(4), 3997–4014. Advance online publication. DOI: 10.1007/s10586-024-04273-1

Ahmed, A. M. (2025). AI-Powered Learning Analytics Improving Personalized Education in E-Learning Environments. *International Journal of Academic Publishing in Educational Sciences and Humanities (IJAPESH)*, 1–9.

Ahmed, F. (2024). The digital divide and AI in education: Addressing equity and accessibility. *AI EDIFY Journal*, *1*(2), 12–23.

Ahsan, K., Akbar, S., Kam, B., & Abdulrahman, M. D. (2023). Implementation of micro-credentials in higher education: A systematic literature review. *Education and Information Technologies*, *28*(3), 13505–13540. https://doi.org/10.1007/s10639-023-11739-zDOI: 10.1007/s10639-023-11739-z

Aithal, P. S., Prabhu, S., & Aithal, S. (2024). Future of higher education through technology prediction and forecasting. *Poornaprajna International Journal of Management, Education, and Social Science (PIJMESS)*, *1*(1), 01-50. DOI: 10.2139/ssrn.4901474

Akbilgic, A., Butler, L., Karabayir, I., Chang, P. P., Kitzman, D. W., Alonso, A., Chen, L. Y., & Soliman, E. Z. (2021). ECG-AI: Electrocardiographic artificial intelligence model for prediction of heart failure. *European Heart Journal. Digital Health*, *2*(4), 626–634. DOI: 10.1093/ehjdh/ztab080 PMID: 34993487

Al Hemairy, M., Abu Talib, M., Khalil, A., Zulfiqar, A., & Mohamed, T. (2024). Blockchain-based framework and platform for validation, authentication & equivalency of academic certification and institution's accreditation: UAE case study and system performance (2022). *Education and Information Technologies*, *29*(14), 18203–18232. Advance online publication. DOI: 10.1007/s10639-024-12493-6

Alagic, G., et al. (2022). Status Report on the Third Round of the NIST Post-Quantum Cryptography Standardization Process. NIST Internal Report 8413.

Al-Ahmad, A. A., et al. (2024). Systematic review of cybersecurity frameworks for higher education institutions.

Alammary, A., Alhazmi, S., Almasri, M., & Gillani, S. (2019). Blockchain-based applications in education: A systematic review. *Applied Sciences (Basel, Switzerland)*, *9*(12), 2400. DOI: 10.3390/app9122400

Ali, M., Siddique, A., Aftab, A., Abid, M. K., & Fuzail, M. (2024). AI-Powered customized learning paths: Transforming data administration for students on digital platforms. *Journal of Computing & Biomedical Informatics, 6*(02), 195–204.

Alkhawi, M. A., & Alshameri, A. S. (2024). Cost-effective and efficient blockchain framework for verifying certificate in Yemeni universities. *Turkish Journal of Computer and Mathematics Education, 15*, 206–216.

Allen, C., & Berg, C. (2020). *Blockchain and the future of education*. Springer.

Alsobhi, H. A., Alakhtar, R. A., Ubaid, A., Hussain, O. K., & Hussain, F. K. (2023). Blockchain-based micro-credentialing system in higher education institutions: Systematic literature review. *Knowledge-Based Systems, 265*, 110238. Advance online publication. DOI: 10.1016/j.knosys.2022.110238

Al-Turjman, A., Nawaz, M. H., & Ulusar, U. D. (2020). Intelligence in the internet of medical things era: A systematic review of current and future trends. *Computer Communications, 150*, 644–660. DOI: 10.1016/j.comcom.2019.12.030

Al-Zahrani, M. A.. (2024). *A conceptual framework for integrating artificial intelligence into cybersecurity higher education*. MDPI.

Ameen, A. H., Mohammed, M. A., & Rashid, A. N. (2023). Dimensions of artificial intelligence techniques, blockchain, and cyber security in the Internet of Medical Things: Opportunities, challenges, and future directions. *Journal of Intelligent Systems, 32*(1), 20220267. DOI: 10.1515/jisys-2022-0267

Ameloot, E., Rotsaert, T., Ameloot, T., Rienties, B., & Schellens, T. (2024). Supporting students' basic psychological needs and satisfaction in a blended learning environment through learning analytics. *Computers & Education, 209*, 104949. DOI: 10.1016/j.compedu.2023.104949

Anjani, S. A., & Mutiara, I. A. (2024). Mengintegrasikan Teknologi Blockchain dalam Pendidikan Tinggi: Meningkatkan Transparansi dan Keamanan dalam Kredensial Akademik. *ADI Pengabdian Kepada Masyarakat Jurnal, 5*(1), 65–71. DOI: 10.34306/adimas.v5i1.1123

Anuradha, P., Arunbala, C., Harita, U., Valarmathi, K., Thenappan, S., & Saravanan, V. (2025). Federated learning for AI-powered privacy in distributed systems. *International Journal of Computational and Experimental Science and Engineering, 11*(3). Advance online publication. DOI: 10.22399/ijcesen.2505

Arizona State University. (2022, October 20). Digital trust: What it means and how institutions can gain it. ASU UTO.

Arizona State University. (2024). *Digital trust guidelines.* ASU AI Acceleration.

Arndt, T., & Guercio, A. (2020). Blockchain-based transcripts for mobile higher education. *International Journal of Information and Education Technology (IJIET), 10*(2), 84–89. https://doi.org/10.18178/ijiet.2020.10.2.1344DOI: 10.18178/ijiet.2020.10.2.1344

Arnold, K. E., & Pistilli, M. D. (2012, April). Course signals at Purdue: Using learning analytics to increase student success. In *Proceedings of the 2nd international conference on learning analytics and knowledge* (pp. 267-270).

Asad, M., & Otoum, S. (2024). BPPFL: A blockchain-based framework for privacy-preserving federated learning. *Research Square* Preprint. DOI: 10.21203/rs.3.rs-4662864/v1

Ashfaq, Z., Rafay, A., Mumtaz, R., Hassan Zaidi, S. M., Saleem, H., Raza Zaidi, S. A., Mumtaz, S., & Haque, A. (2022). A review of enabling technologies for Internet of Medical Things (IoMT) ecosystem. *Ain Shams Engineering Journal, 13*(4), 101660. DOI: 10.1016/j.asej.2021.101660

Asimily. (2023). How universities can mitigate IoT security risk. Asimily Blog.

Asrifan, A., Sadaruddin, S., Ashar, A., Nonci, J., Setiawan, T., & Erniati, E. (2025). Redefining Learning Pathways: The Impact of AI-Enhanced Micro-Credentials on Education Efficiency. In *Integrating Micro-Credentials With AI in Open Education* (pp. 281-312). IGI Global Scientific Publishing. DOI: 10.4018/979-8-3693-5488-9.ch012

Association of American Universities. (2024). *Science and security.* AAU.

Atzori, L., Iera, A., & Morabito, G. (2010). The Internet of Things: A survey. *Computer Networks, 54*(15), 2787–2805. DOI: 10.1016/j.comnet.2010.05.010

Azzam, A., & Charles, T. (2025). K-12 STEM Teachers' Experiences with Artificial Intelligence. *TEM Journal, 14*(1), 463–468. DOI: 10.18421/TEM141-41

Bada, S. O., & Olusegun, S. (2015). Constructivism learning theory: A paradigm for teaching and learning. *Journal of Research & Method in Education, 5*(6), 66–70. DOI: 10.9790/7388-05616670

Badlani, S., Aditya, T., Maniar, S., & Devadkar, K. (2022). Educrypto: Transforming education using blockchain. In 2022 6th International Conference on Intelligent Computing and Control Systems (ICICCS) (pp. 829-836). IEEE.

Bajwa, M. T. T., Shafi, M., Rehman, M. Z. U., Ali, A., Khawar, F., & Awais, M. (2025). Blockchain-enabled federated learning for privacy-preserving AI applications. *Deleted Journal*, *5*(3), 154–169. DOI: 10.62019/n3gzk590

Baker, R. S., & Siemens, G. (2022). Educational data mining and learning analytics. *Cambridge Handbook of Learning Analytics*, 15–35. https://doi.org/DOI: 10.1017/9781108770722.002

Baker, R. S., Martin, T., & Rossi, L. M. (2016). Educational data mining and learning analytics. The Wiley handbook of cognition and assessment: Frameworks, methodologies, and applications, 379-396.

Baker, R. S., & Inventado, P. S. (2019). *Educational data mining and learning analytics*. Springer., DOI: 10.1007/978-3-319-94960-7

Barocas, S., Hardt, M., & Narayanan, A. (2019). *Fairness and machine learning*. MIT Press.

Barrett, H. C. (2007). Researching electronic portfolios and learner engagement: The REFLECT initiative. *Journal of Adolescent & Adult Literacy*, *50*(6), 436–449. Advance online publication. DOI: 10.1598/JAAL.50.6.2

Basha, S. J., Rao, A. K., & Ammannamma, T. (2025). Transforming Education With Predictive Analytics: A Data-Driven Approach to Student Achievement. In *Driving Quality Education Through AI and Data Science* (pp. 433–456). IGI Global Scientific Publishing. DOI: 10.4018/979-8-3693-8292-9.ch019

Bashir, S., & Beydoun, A. R. (2026). Transforming Higher Education Using Artificial Intelligence: Innovations, Future Directions, and Risks. In *Higher Education in the Arab World: Artificial Intelligence* (pp. 143–168). Springer Nature Switzerland.

Bayly-Castañeda, K. (2024). Crafting personalized learning paths with artificial intelligence for lifelong learning: A systematic literature review. *Frontiers in Education*. Advance online publication. DOI: 10.3389/feduc.2024.1424386

Begum, B., & Dharmarajan, D. K. (2020). Smart healthcare monitoring system in IoT. *European Journal of Molecular and Clinical Medicine*, *7*(4), 2647–2661.

Ben-Sasson, E., Chiesa, A., Tromer, E., & Virza, M. (2021). Succinct Non-Interactive Zero Knowledge for a von Neumann Architecture. *Proceedings of the USENIX Security Symposium*, 781-796.

Bernstein, D. J., & Hülsing, A. (2022). The SPHINCS+ Signature Framework. *Proceedings of the 2022 ACM SIGSAC Conference on Computer and Communications Security*, 2129-2146.

Bhaskar, P., Tiwari, C. K., & Joshi, A. (2021). Blockchain in education management: Present and future applications. *Interactive Technology and Smart Education, 18*(1), 1–17. https://doi.org/10.1108/ITSE-07-2020-0102DOI: 10.1108/ITSE-07-2020-0102

Bhat, J., & Jayaram, Y. (2023). Predictive Analytics for Student Retention and Success Using AI/ML. *International Journal of Artificial Intelligence, Data Science, and Machine Learning*, *4*(4), 121–131.

Bhushan, B., Sinha, P., Sagane, K. M., & Jha, A. V. (2023). Towards a secure and sustainable Internet of Medical Things (IoMT): Requirements, design challenges, security techniques, and future trends. *Sustainability (Basel)*, *15*(3), 2729. DOI: 10.3390/su15076177

Biamonte, J., Wittek, P., Pancotti, N., Rebentrost, P., Wiebe, N., & Lloyd, S. (2023). Quantum Machine Learning. *Nature*, *549*(7671), 195–202. DOI: 10.1038/nature23474 PMID: 28905917

Bidry, M., Ouaguid, A., & Hanine, M. (2023). Enhancing e-learning with blockchain: Characteristics, projects, and emerging trends. *Future Internet*, *15*(9), 293. https://doi.org/10.3390/fi15090293DOI: 10.3390/fi15090293

BitLyft. (2023). *The state of higher education cybersecurity: Insights & trends*. BitLyft Blog.

BoardEffect. (2024). *How to create a cyber risk framework for your college or university*. BoardEffect Blog.

Bolton, R. J., & Hand, D. J. (2021). Statistical Fraud Detection: A Review. *Statistical Science*, *17*(3), 235–255.

Borah, A. C., & Borah, P. (2024). Artificial Intelligence Empowered Learning: A Quantum Shift in Higher Education. *International Journal For Multidisciplinary Research*, *6*(6), 30869. Advance online publication. DOI: 10.36948/ijfmr.2024.v06i06.30869

Bravura Security. (2024). *Identity and access management for education*. Bravura Security.

Brown, M., & Duart, J. M. (2024). Exploring gaps in the quality assurance of micro-credentials: A global mapping review of current practices. *Journal of Open, Distance, and Digital Education*, *1*(1), 1–16. DOI: 10.25619/2bwhvw68

Brown, M., Nic Giolla Mhichíl, M., Beirne, E., & Mac Lochlainn, C. (2021). The global micro-credential landscape: Charting a new credential ecology for lifelong learning. *Journal of Learning for Development*, *8*(2), 228–254. https://doi.org/10.56059/jl4d.v8i2.525DOI: 10.56059/jl4d.v8i2.525

Buterin, V. (2014). *A next-generation smart contract and decentralized application platform*. Ethereum Foundation.

Caldarelli, G., & Ellul, J. (2021). Trusted academic transcripts on the blockchain: A systematic literature review. *Applied Sciences (Basel, Switzerland)*, *11*(4), 1842. DOI: 10.3390/app11041842

Camenisch, J., & Lysyanskaya, A. (2022). An Efficient System for Non-transferable Anonymous Credentials with Optional Anonymity Revocation. *International Conference on the Theory and Applications of Cryptographic Techniques*, 93-118.

Campbell, J. P., DeBlois, P. B., & Oblinger, D. G. (2007). Academic analytics: A new tool for a new era. *EDUCAUSE Review*, *42*(4), 40.

Cao, W., & Mai, N. (2025). Predictive analytics for student success: AI-driven early warning systems and intervention strategies for educational risk management. *Educational Research and Human Development*, *2*(2), 36–48. DOI: 10.61784/erhd3042

Capece, G., Ghiron, N. L., & Pasquale, F. (2020). Blockchain technology: Redefining trust for digital certificates. *Sustainability (Basel)*, *12*(21), 8952. DOI: 10.3390/su12218952

Capetillo, A., Camacho, D., & Alanis, M. (2022). Blockchained education: Challenging the long-standing model of academic institutions. *International Journal on Interactive Design and Manufacturing*, *16*(2), 791–802. https://doi.org/10.1007/s12008-022-00886-1DOI: 10.1007/s12008-022-00886-1 PMID: 40477579

Castro, R. Q., & Oliveira, M. (2021). Blockchain and higher education diplomas. *European Journal of Investigation in Health, Psychology and Education*, *11*(1), 154–167. DOI: 10.3390/ejihpe11010013 PMID: 34542456

Chan, C. K. Y., & Tsi, L. H. (2024). Will generative AI replace teachers in higher education? A study of teacher and student perceptions. *Studies in Educational Evaluation*, *83*, 101395. DOI: 10.1016/j.stueduc.2024.101395

Chand, S. P. (1995). Constructivism in education: Exploring the contributions of Piaget, Vygotsky, and Bruner. *Children*, *10*. Advance online publication. DOI: 10.21275/SR23630021800

Charles, T. (2021). The past, present and future of assessments in the higher education sector. In C. Hill, J. Lamie, & T. Gore (Eds.), The evolution of transnational education (pp. 126–136). Routledge.https://doi.org/10.4324/9781003225386 DOI: 10.4324/9781003225386-13

Charles, T., & Hill, C. (2023). Remaining steadfast in the face of overwhelming change: Ethics and practice in emergency remote teaching–A case study in Dubai. In J. Lamie & C. Hill (Eds.), The evolving nature of universities (pp. 89–98). Routledge.https://doi.org/10.4324/9781003389361 DOI: 10.4324/9781003389361-7

Charles, T., & Hill, C. (2025). Micro-Credentials and AI in Higher Education: Transforming Professional Development. In A. ElSayary (Ed.), Prompt Engineering and Generative AI Applications for Teaching and Learning (pp. 1–14). IGI Global Scientific Publishing.https://doi.org/10.4018/979-8-3693-7332-3.ch001 DOI: 10.4018/979-8-3693-7332-3.ch001

Charles, T., Zoelfakar, S., & Sebastian, S. (2025). Micro-Credentials in Vocational and Professional Training. In G. Durak & S. Cankaya (Eds.), Integrating Micro-Credentials With AI in Open Education (pp. 217–250). IGI Global Scientific Publishing.https://doi.org/10.4018/979-8-3693-5488-9.ch010

Charles, T. (2025). AI in Professional Development for English Language Teachers. In Ali, M., Fazal, S., & Ayyaz, S. (Eds.), *AI Applications for English Language Learning* (pp. 73–92). IGI Global Scientific Publishing., DOI: 10.4018/979-8-3693-9077-1.ch004

Charles, T., & Papadaki, M. (2025). Ethical Leadership in Technology Integration and Digital Education. In Soles, B., & Meyerott, T. (Eds.), *Diverse Leadership Perspectives in Education: From K-12 to Higher Education* (pp. 437–454). IGI Global Scientific Publishing., DOI: 10.4018/979-8-3693-6115-3.ch016

Charles, T., Zoelfakar, S., & Sebastian, S. (2025). Micro-Credentials in Vocational and Professional Training. In *Integrating Micro-Credentials With AI in Open Education* (pp. 217–250). IGI Global Scientific Publishing., DOI: 10.4018/979-8-3693-5488-9.ch010

Chen, G., Xu, B., Lu, M., & Chen, N. S. (2018). Exploring blockchain technology and its potential applications for education. *Smart Learning Environments*, *5*(1), 1–10. DOI: 10.1186/s40561-017-0050-x

Chen, L., Chen, P., & Lin, Z. (2020). Artificial intelligence in education: A review. *IEEE Access : Practical Innovations, Open Solutions*, *8*, 75264–75278. DOI: 10.1109/ACCESS.2020.2988510

Chen, S., & Qi, X. (2025). Entropy-adaptive differential privacy federated learning for student performance prediction and privacy protection: A case study in Python programming. *Frontiers in Artificial Intelligence*, *8*, 1653437. Advance online publication. DOI: 10.3389/frai.2025.1653437 PMID: 40988917

Cheong, P. H., & Nyaupane, P. (2022). Smart campus communication, Internet of Things, and data governance: Understanding student tensions and imaginaries. *Big Data & Society*, *9*(1), 20539517221092656. https://doi.org/10.1177/20539517221092656DOI: 10.1177/20539517221092656

Cherukuri, R. V., Devi, G. L., & Ramesh, N. (2024). Federated learning with blockchain-based model aggregation and incentives. *International Journal of Computers and Applications*, *46*(6), 407–417. Advance online publication. DOI: 10.1080/1206212X.2024.2328492

Chotikakamthorn, N., San, A. M., & Sathitwiriyawong, C. (2024). On-Chain Verifiable Credential with Applications in Education. *ECTI Transactions on Computer and Information Technology*, *18*(3), 342–355. DOI: 10.37936/ecti-cit.2024183.256091

Chu, T. S., & Ashraf, M. (2025). Artificial Intelligence in Curriculum Design: A Data-Driven Approach to Higher Education Innovation. *Knowledge (Beverly Hills, Calif.)*, *5*(3), 14. DOI: 10.3390/knowledge5030014

Coursera. (2021). *Digital credentials and the future of work.* Coursera Research Report.

Daher, R. (2025). Integrating AI literacy into teacher education: A critical perspective paper. *Discover Artificial Intelligence*, *5*(1), 217. DOI: 10.1007/s44163-025-00475-7

Dang, L. M., Piran, M., Han, D., Min, K., & Moon, H. (2019). A survey on Internet of Things and cloud computing for healthcare. *Electronics (Basel)*, *8*(7), 768. DOI: 10.3390/electronics8070768

Daniel, B. (2015). B ig D ata and analytics in higher education: Opportunities and challenges. *British Journal of Educational Technology*, *46*(5), 904–920.

de Bem Machado, A., Sousa, M. J., & Dandolini, G. A. (2024). Artificial Intelligence and Blockchain in Higher Education Institutions: A Systematic Literature Review (pp. 147–168). Emerald (MCB UP). DOI: 10.1108/978-1-83753-536-120241010

De Chaudhury, S., Morreddigari, L. R., Varun, M., Sengupta, T., Chakraborty, S., Sural, S., Vaidya, J., & Atluri, V. (2024). Blockchain-based secure federated learning with local differential privacy and incentivization. *IEEE Transactions on Privacy*, *1*, 1–14. DOI: 10.1109/TP.2024.3487819 PMID: 39801576

Dede, C. (2014). *Digital badges for learning*. American Institutes for Research.

Deepak, D.Dr Nitin Deepak. (2024). Transforming Education with Blockchain Technology: Enhancing Security, Transparency, and Credential Verification. *International Journal For Multidisciplinary Research*, *6*(4), 24743. Advance online publication. DOI: 10.36948/ijfmr.2024.v06i04.24743

Dembe, A. (2024). Advancing personalized learning through educational artificial intelligence: Challenges, opportunities, and future directions. *Res Invent J Eng Phys Sci*, *3*(1), 89–101.

Devlin, J., Chang, M. W., Lee, K., & Toutanova, K. (2019). BERT: Pre-training of Deep Bidirectional Transformers for Language Understanding. *Proceedings of NAACL-HLT*, 4171-4186.

Dordevic, J., Stojanovi, L., & Markovi, T. (2025). Blockchain-Based Academic Records for Hybrid Education: Securing Digital Credentials in Global Crisis Contexts. *Journal Neosantara Hybrid Learning*, *3*(1), 20–28. DOI: 10.70177/jnhl.v3i1.2231

Du Plooy, E., Casteleijn, D., & Franzsen, D. (2024). Personalized adaptive learning in higher education: A scoping review of key characteristics and impact on academic performance and engagement. *Heliyon*, *10*(21), e39630. Advance online publication. DOI: 10.1016/j.heliyon.2024.e39630 PMID: 39524879

Dwivedi, D. N., Mahanty, G., & nath Dwivedi, V. (2024). The role of predictive analytics in personalizing education: tailoring learning paths for individual student success. In *Enhancing Education With Intelligent Systems and Data-Driven Instruction* (pp. 44–59). IGI Global Scientific Publishing.

Dwivedi, R., Mehrotra, D., & Chandra, S. (2022). Potential of Internet of Medical Things (IoMT) applications in building a smart healthcare system: A systematic review. *Journal of Oral Biology and Craniofacial Research*, *12*(2), 302–318. DOI: 10.1016/j.jobcr.2021.11.010 PMID: 34926140

Dwivedi, Y. K., Hughes, L., Ismagilova, E., Aarts, G., Coombs, C., Crick, T., Duan, Y., Dwivedi, R., Edwards, J., Eirug, A., Galanos, V., Ilavarasan, P. V., Janssen, M., Jones, P., Kar, A. K., Kizgin, H., Kronemann, B., Lal, B., Lucini, B., & Williams, M. D. (2021). Artificial intelligence (AI): Multidisciplinary perspectives. *International Journal of Information Management*, *57*, 101994. DOI: 10.1016/j.ijinfomgt.2019.08.002

Dwork, C., & Roth, A. (2021). The Algorithmic Foundations of Differential Privacy. *Foundations and Trends in Theoretical Computer Science*, *9*(3–4), 211–407.

Echenim, J. I. (2025). Exploring the Integration of AI and Blockchain for Secure, Transparent, and Decentralized Data Management Systems. 878–885. DOI: 10.63680/afvdbg764hg099hb

EDUCAUSE. (2023, March). Cyber resilience: The future for higher education. *EDUCAUSE Review*.

EDUCAUSE. (2024, May). Cybersecurity in higher education: Don't let the hackers win. *EDUCAUSE Review*.

El Galad, A., Betts, D. H., & Campbell, N. (2024, April). Flexible learning dimensions in higher education: aligning students' and educators' perspectives for more inclusive practices. In *Frontiers in Education* (Vol. 9, p. 1347432). Frontiers Media SA. DOI: 10.3389/feduc.2024.1347432

Elkhodr, M., Wangsa, K., Gide, E., & Karim, S. (2024). A Systematic Review and Multifaceted Analysis of the Integration of Artificial Intelligence and Blockchain: Shaping the Future of Australian Higher Education. *Future Internet, 16*(10), 378. DOI: 10.3390/fi16100378

Elsawah, W., & Charles, T. (2023). Investigating Emirati Students' Practices of Learning Block-Based Programming in an Online Learning Context: Evidence from a UAE National Program. In: Al Marri, K., Mir, F., David, S., & Aljuboori, A. (Eds) *BUiD Doctoral Research Conference 2022*. Lecture Notes in Civil Engineering, vol 320. Springer, Cham.

Emon, M. M. H., & Chowdhury, M. S. A. (2025). Safeguarding student data (pp. 191–228). *Advances in Computational Intelligence and Robotics*. Advance online publication. DOI: 10.4018/979-8-3373-3316-8.ch008

ERIC. (2022). *Blockchain and micro-credentials in education*. ERIC.

Esomonu, N. P. M. (2025). Utilizing AI and Big Data for Predictive Insights on Institutional Performance and Student Success: A Data-Driven Approach to Quality Assurance. *AI and Ethics, Academic Integrity and the Future of Quality Assurance in Higher Education*, 29.

European Blockchain Partnership. (2023). *European Blockchain Services Infrastructure for Cross-Border Digital Public Services*. European Commission.

European Union. (2016). *General Data Protection Regulation (GDPR)*.

Evans, M., & Boucher, A. R. (2015). Optimizing the power of choice: Supporting student autonomy to foster motivation and engagement in learning. *Mind, Brain and Education : the Official Journal of the International Mind, Brain, and Education Society, 9*(2), 87–91. DOI: 10.1111/mbe.12073

Farhad, A., Woolley, S., & Andras, P. (2021). Federated learning for AI to improve patient care using wearable and IoMT sensors. In *2021 IEEE 9th International Conference on Healthcare Informatics (ICHI)* (p. 434). IEEE. DOI: 10.1109/ICHI52183.2021.00071

Ferguson, J. E., & Redish, A. D. (2011). Wireless communication with implanted medical devices using the conductive properties of the body. *Expert Review of Medical Devices, 8*(4), 427–433. DOI: 10.1586/erd.11.16 PMID: 21728728

Fernández-Caramés, T. M., & Fraga-Lamas, P. (2022). Towards Post-Quantum Blockchain: A Review on Blockchain Cryptography Resistant to Quantum Computing Attacks. *IEEE Access : Practical Innovations, Open Solutions, 10*, 21091–21116.

Fierro Saltos, W. R., Fierro Saltos, F. E., Elizabeth Alexandra, V. S., & Rivera Guzmán, E. F. (2025). Leveraging Artificial Intelligence for Sustainable Tutoring and Dropout Prevention in Higher Education: A Scoping Review on Digital Transformation. *Information (Basel), 16*(9), 819.

Floridi, L. (2019). Establishing the rules for building trustworthy AI. *Nature Machine Intelligence, 1*(6), 261–262. DOI: 10.1038/s42256-019-0055-y

Floridi, L., Cowls, J., Beltrametti, M., Chatila, R., Chazerand, P., Dignum, V., Luetge, C., Madelin, R., Pagallo, U., Rossi, F., Schafer, B., Valcke, P., & Vayena, E. (2018). AI4People—An ethical framework for a good AI society. *Minds and Machines, 28*(4), 689–707. DOI: 10.1007/s11023-018-9482-5 PMID: 30930541

Flynn, S., Cullinane, E., Murphy, H., & Wylie, N. (2023). Micro-credentials & digital badges: Definitions, affordances and design considerations for application in higher education institutions. *All Ireland Journal of Teaching and Learning in Higher Education, 15*(1), 1–18.

FortifyData. (2024). *Top data security practices for higher education*. FortifyData Blog.

Gairola, A., Shaikh, A., Salian, S., & Malve, S. (2024). *SuperCert - An Anti-Fraud Identity Intelligence Blockchain Solution for Educational Certificates*. International Journal of Scientific Research in Computer Science, Engineering and Information Technology., DOI: 10.32628/CSEIT2410266

Gamage, K. A. A., & Dehideniya, S. C. P. (2025). Unlocking career potential: How micro-credentials are revolutionising higher education and lifelong learning. *Education Sciences, 15*(5), 525. DOI: 10.3390/educsci15050525

Gatouillat, A., Badr, Y., Massot, B., & Sejdić, E. (2018). Internet of Medical Things: A review of recent contributions dealing with cyber-physical systems in medicine. *IEEE Internet of Things Journal, 5*(5), 3810–3822. DOI: 10.1109/JIOT.2018.2849014

Gervais, A., Karame, G., & Wüst, K.. (2016). On the security and performance of proof of work blockchains. *Proceedings of the ACM SIGSAC Conference on Computer and Communications Security*, 3–16. DOI: 10.1145/2976749.2978341

Gharkan, H. K., Radif, M. J., & Alsaeedi, A. H. (2025). Analysis of AI-Empower Predictive Models for Predicting Student Performance in Higher Education. *Journal of Al-Qadisiyah for Computer Science and Mathematics, 17*(1), 103–121. DOI: 10.29304/jqcsm.2025.17.11967

Ghosh, D. (2024). Using AI for student success: Early warning, performance analytics, and automated grading in education cyber-physical systems. In *Artificial intelligence solutions for cyber-physical systems* (pp. 236–243). Auerbach Publications. DOI: 10.1201/9781032694375-13

Ghubaish, A., Agoua, T., Vicic, T., Tarlochan, F., & Al-Ali, A. R. (2021). Recent advances in the Internet-of-Medical-Things (IoMT) systems security. *IEEE Internet of Things Journal, 8*(11), 8707–8718. DOI: 10.1109/JIOT.2020.3045653

Gish-Lieberman, J. J., Tawfik, A., & Gatewood, J. (2021). Micro-credentials and badges in education: A historical overview. *TechTrends, 65*(1), 5–7. DOI: 10.1007/s11528-020-00567-4

Gokila, P., Ganeshkumar, P., Priyanka, V., Sabrigiriraj, M., & Kalaivani, T. (2025). Blockchain-based decentralized federated learning for secure AI model training. *International Journal of Computational and Experimental Science and Engineering, 11*(3). Advance online publication. DOI: 10.22399/ijcesen.2487

Gómez, Á., García, D., & Delgado-von-Eitzen, C. (2025). GDPR-Compliant Academic Certification via Blockchain: Legal and Technical Validation of the GAVIN Project. DOI: 10.20944/preprints202507.0926.v1

Goyal, N. K. (2025). Security and privacy in IoT, fog, and blockchain networks. In Sathio, A., Rind, M., Awan, S., & Junejo, A. (Eds.), *Energy-efficient deep learning approaches in IoT, fog, and green blockchain revolution* (pp. 371–398). IGI Global Scientific Publishing., DOI: 10.4018/979-8-3373-0300-0.ch015

Goyal, N. K. (2025). Weaponizing misinformation and cyberattacks on supply chains. In Bukhari, S., & Zafar, I. (Eds.), *Mass media and impact of fake news on supply chains* (pp. 177–210). IGI Global Scientific Publishing., DOI: 10.4018/979-8-3373-2175-2.ch007

Goyal, N. K., Dandotiya, M., Kumari, M., Kaloria, S., & Anushya, A. (2025). AI-powered haptic devices for patient rehabilitation. In Mamodiya, U. (Eds.), *Integrating AI with haptic systems for smarter healthcare solutions* (pp. 143–170). IGI Global Scientific Publishing., DOI: 10.4018/979-8-3373-2307-7.ch007

Goyal, N. K., Dandotiya, M., Kumari, M., Sheikh, M. F., & Sharma, S. (2025). Emerging job roles in the tourism sector leveraging artificial intelligence. In Silic, M. (Eds.), *Empowering sustainable performance and competitive advantage in tourism* (pp. 89–126). IGI Global Scientific Publishing., DOI: 10.4018/979-8-3373-4546-8.ch004

Goyal, N. K., Dandotiya, M., Qurashi, J. A., Kumari, M., & Sharma, S. (2025). AI-driven predictive analytics for disease management. In Ouaissa, M. (Eds.), *Utilizing AI of medical things for healthcare security and sustainability* (pp. 231–276). IGI Global Scientific Publishing., DOI: 10.4018/979-8-3373-0690-2.ch008

Goyal, N. K., Kumari, M., Kushwah, V., Dandotiya, M., & Vijay, A. (2025). Evaluating blockchain security: Trade-offs in consensus mechanisms. *IET Conference Proceedings,* 2024(38), 80–88. https://doi.org/DOI: 10.1049/icp.2025.0775

Granlund, T.. (2021). On medical device cybersecurity compliance in EU. In *Proceedings of the 2021 IEEE/ACM 3rd International Workshop on Software Engineering for Healthcare (SEH)* (pp. 20–23). IEEE. DOI: 10.1109/SEH52539.2021.00011

Gräther, W., Kolvenbach, S., Ruland, R., Schütte, J., Torres, C., & Wendland, F. (2021). Blockchain for Education: Lifelong Learning Passport with Hyperledger. Blockchain. *Research and Applications*, *2*(1), 100013.

Grech, A., & Camilleri, A. F. (2017). *Blockchain in education. JRC Science for Policy Report*. European Commission., DOI: 10.2760/60629

Grech, A., & Camilleri, A. F. (2021). Self-Sovereign Identity in Education: From Concept to Practice. *Educational Technology Research and Development*, *69*(5), 2451–2474.

Grech, A., & Camilleri, A. F. (2023). *Blockchain in Education: Opportunities and Challenges*. European Commission Joint Research Centre.

Guerreiro, S., Ferreira, J. F., Fonseca, T., & Correia, M. (2022). Integrating an academic management system with blockchain: A case study. Blockchain [ffigure]. *Research and Applications, 3*(4), 2022. DOI: 10.1016/j.bcra.2022.100099

H C, D. R.H C. (2025). Decentralized Academic Certificate Issuance and Verification Using Blockchain Technology. *Indian Scientific Journal Of Research In Engineering And Management, 09*(06), 1–9. DOI: 10.55041/IJSREM50735

Haque, M., Hùng, B. T., Upreti, K., Sapra, R., Jain, R., Radhakrishnan, G., & Kshirsagar, P. R. (2025). SALF: A Blockchain-Based Framework for Scalable Academic Credential Management and Institutional Governance. *Journal of Applied Science and Technology Trends, 6*(2), 203–218. DOI: 10.38094/jastt62295

Harizan, S. H. M., & Ally, M. (2025). Artificial Intelligence in Micro-Credentials for Open and Distance Learning: A Technologically-Enhanced Systematic Review. *Integrating Micro-Credentials With AI in Open Education*, 341-380. DOI: 10.4018/979-8-3693-5488-9.ch014

Hassan, S., & De Filippi, P. (2023). Decentralized Autonomous Organization. *Internet Policy Review, 10*(2), 1–10.

Hawkins, R., & Winter, D. (2021). Academic credential fraud: Challenges and solutions. *International Journal of Educational Management, 35*(2), 305–320. DOI: 10.1108/IJEM-06-2020-0271\

Helyer, R. (2011). Aligning higher education with the world of work. *Higher Education. Skills and Work-Based Learning, 1*(2), 95–105. DOI: 10.1108/20423891111128872

Hemmati, A., & Rahmani, A. M. (2022). Internet of Medical Things in the COVID-19 era: A systematic literature review. *Sustainability (Basel), 14*(19), 12637. DOI: 10.3390/su141912637

Herath, D., Dinuwan, C., Ihalagedara, C., & Ambegoda, T. (2024). Enhancing educational outcomes through AI-powered learning strategy recommendation system. *International Journal of Advanced Computer Science and Applications, 15*(10), 10. DOI: 10.14569/IJACSA.2024.0151075

Hernandez-Jaimes, M. L., Martinez-Cruz, A., Ramírez-Gutiérrez, K. A., & Feregrino-Uribe, C. (2023). Artificial intelligence for IoMT security: A review of intrusion detection systems, attacks, datasets and cloud–fog–edge architectures. *Internet of Things : Engineering Cyber Physical Human Systems, 23*, 100887. DOI: 10.1016/j.iot.2023.100887

Hill, C., Abu-Ayyash, E., & Charles, T. (2023). By nature, a social animal: An exploration of perceptions of online group work. *Cambridge Journal of Education, 53*(5), 665–681. https://doi.org/10.1080/0305764X.2023.2206795DOI: 10.1080/0305764X.2023.2206795

Hisseine, M. A., Chen, D., & Xiao, Y. (2025). Enhancing handle system for digital credentials verification by using blockchain. *IAENG International Journal of Computer Science*, *52*(5), 1484–1500.

Holmes, W., Bialik, M., & Fadel, C. (2021). *Artificial intelligence in education: Promises and implications for teaching and learning*. Center for Curriculum Redesign.

Holmes, W., Porayska-Pomsta, K., Holstein, K., Sutherland, E., Baker, T., Shum, S. B., Santos, O. C., Rodrigo, M. T., Cukurova, M., Bittencourt, I. I., & Koedinger, K. R. (2022). Ethics of AI in education: Towards a community-wide framework. *International Journal of Artificial Intelligence in Education*, *32*(2), 115–130. https://doi.org/10.1007/s40593-021-00239-1DOI: 10.1007/s40593-021-00239-1

Holotescu, V., Vasiu, R., Ternauciuc, A., Holotescu, C., & Andone, D. (2024). Building a decentralized education ecosystem: Politehnica University of Timisoara's pioneering blockchain initiatives. In Proceedings of the EDEN 2024 Research Workshop & PhD Masterclass.

Huang, D., Yang, Y., & Huang, Y. (2023). *Decentralized federated learning privacy-preserving framework based on blockchain.*, DOI: 10.1109/EIECC60864.2023.10456734

Hu, S., & Kuh, G. D. (2003). Diversity Experiences and College Student Learning and Personal Development. *Journal of College Student Development*, *44*(3), 320–334. DOI: 10.1353/csd.2003.0026

IBM. (2024). *Reducing ransomware recovery costs in the education sector*. IBM Think.

Identity Automation. (2024). IAM software designed to solve higher ed challenges. Identity Automation.

IEEE. (2019). *Ethically aligned design: A vision for prioritizing human well-being with autonomous and intelligent systems*. IEEE.

Ifenthaler, D., & Yau, J. Y. K. (2020). Utilising learning analytics for study success: Reflections and future research directions. *Computers & Education*, *155*, 103933. DOI: 10.1016/j.compedu.2020.103933

Ifenthaler, D., & Yau, J. Y. K. (2020). Utilising learning analytics to support study success in higher education: A systematic review. *Educational Technology Research and Development, 68*(4), 1961–1990.

Ifraheem, S., Rasheed, M., & Siddiqui, A. (2024). Transforming education through artificial intelligence: Personalization, engagement and predictive analytics. *Journal of Asian Development Studies, 13*(2), 250–266. DOI: 10.62345/jads.2024.13.2.22

Ilyas, S., Umar, M., Riaz, K., & Tariq, Z. (2025). Emotion Recognition in AI-Powered Classrooms Impacts on Student Engagement and Learning Outcomes. *The Critical Review of Social Sciences Studies, 3*(3), 86–103. DOI: 10.59075/x1wkpx78

International Organization for Standardization. (2022). *ISO/IEC 27001:2022 Information security, cybersecurity and privacy protection*. ISO.

Islam, M. M., Nooruddin, S., Karray, F., & Muhammad, G. (2022). Internet of Things: Device capabilities, architectures, protocols, and smart applications in healthcare domain. *IEEE Internet of Things Journal, 10*(4), 3611–3641. DOI: 10.1109/JIOT.2022.3228795

Ismail, I. A. (2025). Protecting privacy in ai-enhanced education: A comprehensive examination of data privacy concerns and solutions in ai-based learning. *Impacts of Generative AI on the Future of Research and Education*, 117-142. DOI: 10.4018/979-8-3693-0884-4.ch006

ISO/IEC. (2022). *Artificial intelligence—Risk management (ISO/IEC 23894).*

Istepanian, R. S.. (2011). *The potential of Internet of m-health Things 'm-IoT' for non-invasive glucose level sensing. In 2011 Annual International Conference of the IEEE Engineering in Medicine and Biology Society*. IEEE.

Jamil, F., Iqbal, M. A., Amin, R., & Kim, D. (2019). Adaptive thermal-aware routing protocol for wireless body area network. *Electronics (Basel), 8*(1), 47. DOI: 10.3390/electronics8010047

Jayaram, Y., & Sundar, D. (2023). AI-Powered Student Success Ecosystems: Integrating ECM, DXP, and Predictive Analytics. *International Journal of Artificial Intelligence, Data Science, and Machine Learning, 4*(1), 109–119. DOI: 10.63282/3050-9262.IJAIDSML-V4I1P113

Jobin, A., Ienca, M., & Vayena, E. (2019). The global landscape of AI ethics guidelines. *Nature Machine Intelligence, 1*(9), 389–399. DOI: 10.1038/s42256-019-0088-2

Johnson, L., & Adams Becker, S. (2022). *Horizon Report: Higher Education Edition*. EDUCAUSE.

Jumagaliyeva, A., ZHAMANGARIN, D., & Muratova, G. (2024). Integrating Blockchain and AI for Optimized Digital Identity Verification. Университет е бектері, 3(96)., doi:.DOI: 10.52209/1609-1825_2024_3_401

Kabilovna, A. N., & Aleksandrovna, S. A. (2024). The positive impact of AI on self-esteem among EFL learners: Case studies from Fergana State University and Tuit Fergana Branch University. *Innovation in the Modern Education System*, *5*(45), 33–48.

Kaddouri, M., Mhamdi, K., Chniete, I., Marhraoui, M., Khaldi, M., & Jmad, S. (2025). Adopting AI in education: Technical challenges and ethical constraints. In *Fostering Inclusive Education With AI and Emerging Technologies* (pp. 25–72). IGI Global., DOI: 10.4018/979-8-3693-7255-5.ch002

Kamalov, F., Cherukuri, A. K., Gurusamy, S., Sriram, V. P., & Chinnasamy, P. (2023). Internet of Medical Things privacy and security: Challenges, solutions, and future trends from a new perspective. *Sustainability (Basel)*, *15*(4), 3317. DOI: 10.3390/su15043317

Kaneriya, J., & Patel, H. (2023). A Secure and Privacy-Preserving Student Credential Verification System Using Blockchain Technology. *International Journal of Information and Education Technology (IJIET)*, *13*(8), 1251–1260. DOI: 10.18178/ijiet.2023.13.8.1927

Kayyali, M. (2025). Defining Micro-Credentials: Concepts, Theories, and Pedagogies. In *Navigating Quality Assurance and Accreditation in Global Higher Education* (pp. 219-246). IGI Global Scientific Publishing. DOI: 10.4018/979-8-3693-6915-9.ch009

Keeley, K. L. (2025). The Scope and Depth Micro-Credential Framework: Aligning Education With Evolving Industry Demands. In *Innovative Approaches in Vocational and Regional Education* (pp. 49-86). IGI Global Scientific Publishing. DOI: 10.4018/979-8-3693-9496-0.ch002

Keoy, K. H., Koh, Y. J., Iqbal, J., Anjum, S. S., Yeo, S. F., Cherukuri, A. K., Teoh, W. Y., & Piut, D. A. A. (2024). Streamlining micro-credentials implementation in higher education institutions: Considerations for effective implementation and policy development. *Journal of Information & Knowledge Management*, *23*(01), 2350069. DOI: 10.1142/S0219649223500697

Khalid, N., Qayyum, A., Bilal, M., Al-Fuqaha, A., & Qadir, J. (2023). Privacy-preserving artificial intelligence in healthcare: Techniques and applications. *Computers in Biology and Medicine*, *158*, 106848. DOI: 10.1016/j.compbiomed.2023.106848 PMID: 37044052

Khan, M. A., Din, I. U., Kim, B.-S., & Almogren, A. (2023). Visualization of remote patient monitoring system based on Internet of Medical Things. *Sustainability (Basel), 15*(10), 8120. DOI: 10.3390/su15108120

Khan, M. A., Quasim, M. T., Algarni, F., & Alharthi, A. (2020). *Decentralized Internet of Things: A blockchain perspective* (Vol. 71). Springer Nature. DOI: 10.1007/978-3-030-38677-1

Khushalani, B. (2025). Empowering Student Success through AI-Driven Collaboration. [Online]. *EDUCAUSE Review.*

Kidwell, D., & Giovacchini, D. (2022, October 20). Digital trust: What it means and how institutions can gain it. ASU UTO.

Kiiskilä, P., Hanafy, A., & Pirkkalainen, H. (2022). Features of micro-credential platforms in higher education. In *International Conference on Computer Supported Education, CSEDU* (pp. 81-91). Science and Technology Publications (SciTePress). DOI: 10.5220/0011030600003182

Kishor, I., Sharma, M., Preetham, A., Agarwal, A., & Mamodiya, U. (2025). Virtual reality (VR) and augmented reality (AR) simulators for medical education. In Accelerating product development cycles with digital twins and IoT integration (pp. 1–22). IGI Global. DOI: 10.4018/979-8-3373-2028-1.ch004

Kishor, I., Mamodiya, U., Almaayah, M., Alqutaish, A., Shehab, R., & Aldhyani, T. H. H. (2025). *Agentic AI-enhanced virtual reality for adaptive immersive learning environments*. MJCSC., DOI: 10.58496/MJCSC/2025/026

Kishor, I., Mamodiya, U., Sharma, M., Kumar, G., & Goyal, P. "Integrating Block Chain with IoT for Secure and Transparent Supply Chain Management in Sustainable Manufacturing," *2025 International Conference on Sustainability, Innovation & Technology (ICSIT)*, Nagpur, India, 2025, pp. 1-6, DOI: 10.1109/ICSIT65336.2025.11294611

Kistaubayev, Y., Mutanov, G., Mansurova, M., Saxenbayeva, Z., & Shakan, Y. (2023). Ethereum-based information system for digital higher education registry and verification of student achievement documents. *Future Internet, 15*(1), 3. DOI: 10.3390/fi15010003

Klein-Collins, R. (2012). *Competency-Based Degree Programs in the US: Postsecondary Credentials for Measurable Student Learning and Performance.* Council for Adult and Experiential Learning.

Km, P.KM. (2024). Academic Certificate Authenticity using Blockchain Technology: A Review. *International Journal for Research in Applied Science and Engineering Technology*, *12*(12), 906–910. DOI: 10.22214/ijraset.2024.65924

Knight, S. (2022). Digital credentials and lifelong learning pathways. *Education and Information Technologies*, *27*, 4567–4582. DOI: 10.1007/s10639-021-10813-7

Kontzinos, C., Karakolis, E., Kokkinakos, P., Skalidakis, S., Askounis, D., & Psarras, J. (2024). Application and Evaluation of a Blockchain-Centric Platform for Smart Badge Accreditation in Higher Education Institutions. *Applied Sciences (Basel, Switzerland)*, *14*(12), 5191. DOI: 10.3390/app14125191

Koo, Z. N., Teoh, B. A., & Teoh, P. C. B. (2025). Bridging Innovation and Security: A Bibliometric Review of Blockchain's Impact on Higher Educational Institution Management. *INTERNATIONAL JOURNAL OF MANAGEMENT, FINANCE AND ACCOUNTING*, *6*(2), 219–242. DOI: 10.33093/ijomfa.2025.6.2.8

Kosmarski, A. (2020). Blockchain adoption in academia: Promises and challenges. *Journal of Open Innovation*, *6*(4), 117. https://doi.org/10.3390/joitmc6040117DOI: 10.3390/joitmc6040117

Kotsiantis, S., Pierrakeas, C., & Pintelas, P. (2021). Predicting student performance in higher education using AI techniques. *Education and Information Technologies*, *26*, 6541–6562. DOI: 10.1007/s10639-021-10517-5

Koundal, D., Sharma, B., & Guo, Y. (2020). Intuitionistic based segmentation of thyroid nodules in ultrasound images. *Computers in Biology and Medicine*, *121*, 103776. DOI: 10.1016/j.compbiomed.2020.103776 PMID: 32568671

Kovilpillai, J., Singh, A. D., Hamdan, A., McKenna, K., & Raza, F. A. (2024). AI Enhanced Micro-Credentials for Efficiency and Accessibility. Advances in Educational Technologies and Instructional Design Book Series, 153–194. DOI: 10.4018/979-8-3693-5488-9.ch008

Krishnan, S., Surendran, R., Sangeetha, S., & Kartheesan, L. (2025). Lexicon-Enhanced Convolutional BERT (LEConvBERT) for Secure and Intelligent Equivalency Certificate Generation using NLP and Blockchain. 478–484. DOI: 10.1109/ICSCDS65426.2025.11167837

Krishnan, S., Surendran, R., Venkatesh, J. D., & Valluru, R. (2025). Leveraging AI/ML Automated Permanent Academic Account Registry (APAAR) Technology for Course Equivalency Certification in India. 1–9. DOI: 10.1109/INCET64471.2025.11140981

Krishna, S., & Sidharth, S. (2023). AI-powered workforce analytics: Maximizing Business and employee success through predictive attrition modelling. *International Journal of Performability Engineering, 19*(3), 203. DOI: 10.23940/ijpe.23.03.p6.203215

Kshetri, N. (2021). Blockchain adoption in developing countries. *IEEE Computer, 54*(1), 8–12.

Kumar, D. (2025). Exploring the Effectiveness of Blockchain Technology for Secure Academic Credentialing and Record Management. *Edumania, 03*(03), 332–348. DOI: 10.59231/edumania/9155

Lakshmi, K., Khan, S., Kumar, P. A., Wagh, V., & Vasanti, G. (2024). AI-Powered Learning Analytics: Transforming Educational Outcomes Through ICT Integration. *Library of Progress-Library Science, Information Technology & Computer, 44*(3).

Lee, A. N., & Nie, Y. (2024). Future-Oriented Learning and Continuous Skills Development: Developing a Resilient Workforce in Changing Times. In Lee, A. N., & Nie, Y. (Eds.), *Future-oriented Learning and Skills Development for Employability*. Springer., DOI: 10.1007/978-981-97-8584-1_1

Lemieux, V. L., & Bravo, M. (2021). Introduction: Theorizing from Multidisciplinary Perspectives on the Design of Blockchain and Distributed Ledger Systems (Part I). In V.

Lepide. (2024). Leveraging the NIST framework in educational institutions. Lepide Blog.

Lin, C. C., Huang, A. Y., & Lu, O. H. (2023). Artificial intelligence in intelligent tutoring systems toward sustainable education: a systematic review. *Smart learning environments, 10*(1), 41. DOI: 10.1186/s40561-023-00260-y

Lin, D., Crabtree, J., Dillo, I., Downs, R. R., Edmunds, R., Giaretta, D., De Giusti, M., L'Hours, H., Hugo, W., Jenkyns, R., Khodiyar, V., Martone, M. E., Mokrane, M., Navale, V., Petters, J., Sierman, B., Sokolova, D. V., Stockhause, M., & Westbrook, J. (2020). The TRUST principles for digital repositories. *Scientific Data, 7*(1), 144. DOI: 10.1038/s41597-020-0486-7 PMID: 32409645

Literat, I. (2015). Implications of massive open online courses for higher education: Mitigating or reifying educational inequities? *Higher Education Research & Development, 34*(6), 1164–1177. DOI: 10.1080/07294360.2015.1024624

Liu, L., Han, M., Zhou, Y., Parizi, R. M., & Korayem, M. (2020). Blockchain-based certification for education, employment, and skill with incentive mechanism. In *Blockchain cybersecurity, trust and privacy* (pp. 269–290). Springer. DOI: 10.1007/978-3-030-38181-3_14

Liu, Z., Wei, C., Burra, V. D. K., Teh, J. Y., Miraz, M. H., & Salam, I. (2025). *A blockchain-driven framework for strengthening model ownership and data privacy in federated learning*., DOI: 10.1109/ISCI65687.2025.11167261

Lizcano, D., Lara, J. A., White, B., & Aljawarneh, S. (2020). Blockchain-based approach to create a model of trust in open and ubiquitous higher education. *Journal of Computing in Higher Education*, *32*(1), 109–134. https://doi.org/10.1007/s12528-019-09209-yDOI: 10.1007/s12528-019-09209-y

Lo, S. K., ... (2021). Blockchain-based trustworthy federated learning architecture. arXiv Preprint. https://dblp.uni-trier.de/db/journals/corr/corr2108.html#abs-2108-06912

Long, P., & Siemens, G. (2014). Penetrating the fog: Analytics in learning and education. *Italian Journal of Educational Technology*, *22*(3), 132–137.

Lu, H. (2021). Electronic portfolios in higher education: A review. *European Journal of Education Studies*, *2*(3), 96–101. Advance online publication. DOI: 10.24018/ejedu.2021.2.3.119

Madhumita, G., Diana, P. D., Kiran, P. N., Aggarwal, S., & Nargunde, A. S. (2024, April). AI-powered performance management: Driving employee success and organizational growth. In *2024 5th International Conference on Recent Trends in Computer Science and Technology (ICRTCST)* (pp. 204–209). IEEE.

Mali, M., Aherkar, S., Waykos, P., & Shukla, A. (2023). Blockchain-Based Academic Bank of Credit Management System for Higher Education. *An Innovative Approach to Student Credentialing and Progression.*, *1–5*, 1–5. Advance online publication. DOI: 10.1109/ICBDS58040.2023.10346463

Mallik, S., & Gangopadhyay, A. (2023). Proactive and reactive engagement of AI methods for education.

Mamodiya, U., Kishor, I., Almaiah, M. A., & Shehab, R. (2025). AI-enhanced AR/VR systems for remote healthcare for overcoming real-time data integration and security challenges with IoT. *Int. J. Innov. Res. Sci. Stud*, *8*(1), 2414–2420. DOI: 10.53894/ijirss.v8i1.4999

Manickam, P., Mariappan, S. A., Murugesan, S. M., Hansda, S., Kaushik, A., Shinde, R., & Thipperudraswamy, S. P. (2022). Artificial intelligence (AI) and Internet of Medical Things (IoMT) assisted biomedical systems for intelligent healthcare. *Biosensors (Basel), 12*(8), 562. DOI: 10.3390/bios12080562 PMID: 35892459

Marouan, A., Badrani, M., Kannouf, N., & Chetouani, A. (2024). *Empowering Education: Leveraging Blockchain for Secure Credentials and Lifelong Learning*. Springer Vienna., DOI: 10.1007/978-3-031-49593-9_1

Marston, H. R., & Samuels, J. (2019). A review of age friendly virtual assistive technologies and their effect on daily living for carers and dependent adults. *Health Care*, *7*(2), 49. PMID: 30901898

Mathkor, D. M., Mathkor, N., Bassfar, Z., Bantun, F., Slama, P., Ahmad, F., & Haque, S. (2024). Multirole of the internet of medical things (IoMT) in biomedical systems for managing smart healthcare systems: An overview of current and future innovative trends. *Journal of Infection and Public Health, 17*(4), 559–572. DOI: 10.1016/j.jiph.2024.01.013 PMID: 38367570

Matz, S. C., Bukow, C. S., Peters, H., Deacons, C., Dinu, A., & Stachl, C. (2023). Using machine learning to predict student retention from socio-demographic characteristics and app-based engagement metrics. *Scientific Reports*, *13*(1), 5705.

Mazzocca, C., Acar, A., Uluagac, S., Montanari, R., Bellavista, P., & Conti, M. (2024). A survey on decentralized identifiers and verifiable credentials. *IEEE*, 12, 15528–15552. https://doi.org/10.1109/COMST.2025.3543197

McGreal, R. (2023). Blockchain and micro-credentials in education. *International Journal of E-Learning & Distance Education*.

McGreal, R. (2023). Blockchain and micro-credentials in education. *International Journal of E-Learning & Distance Education*, *38*(1), 1–17. https://doi.org/10.55667/10.55667/ijede.2023.v38.i1.1250

McGreal, R. (2024). *Empowering Micro-Credentials Using Blockchain and Artificial Intelligence*. IGI Global., DOI: 10.4018/979-8-3693-0343-6.ch006

McGreal, R., & Olcott, D.Jr. (2022). A strategic reset: Micro-credentials for higher education leaders. *Smart Learning Environments*, *9*(1), 9. DOI: 10.1186/s40561-022-00190-1

McPherson, M. S., & Bacow, L. S. (2015). Online higher education: Beyond the hype cycle. *The Journal of Economic Perspectives*, *29*(4), 135–154. DOI: 10.1257/jep.29.4.135

Meng, W., Li, W., & Zhu, L. (2020). Enhancing medical smartphone networks via blockchain-based trust management against insider attacks. *IEEE Transactions on Engineering Management*, *67*(4), 1377–1386. DOI: 10.1109/TEM.2019.2921736

Merino-Campos, C. (2025). The impact of artificial intelligence on personalized learning in higher education: A systematic review. *Trends in Higher Education*, *4*(2), 17. DOI: 10.3390/higheredu4020017

Micciancio, D., & Regev, O. (2021). Lattice-Based Cryptography. In Post-Quantum Cryptography (pp. 147–191). Springer.

Mikroyannidis, A., Third, A., & Domingue, J. (2020). A case study on the decentralisation of lifelong learning using blockchain technology. *Journal of Interactive Media in Education*, *2020*(1), 23. DOI: 10.5334/jime.591

Mishra, R. A., Kalla, A., Braeken, A., & Liyanage, M. (2021). Privacy protected blockchain-based architecture and implementation for sharing of students' credentials. *Information Processing & Management*, *58*(3), 102512. DOI: 10.1016/j.ipm.2021.102512

Mittal, S. (2023). Explaining URL phishing detection by glass box models. In *Proceedings of the 2023 Fifteenth International Conference on Contemporary Computing (IC3)* (pp. 535–541). ACM. DOI: 10.1145/3607947.3608059

Mittelstadt, B. D., Allo, P., Taddeo, M., Wachter, S., & Floridi, L. (2016). The ethics of algorithms. *Big Data & Society*, *3*(2), 1–21. DOI: 10.1177/2053951716679679

Modern Campus. (2024). *GDPR and higher education: What you need to know*. Modern Campus Blog.

Mohammad, A., & Vargas, S. (2022). Challenges of using blockchain in the education sector: A literature review. *Applied Sciences (Basel, Switzerland)*, *12*(13), 6380. https://doi.org/10.3390/app12136380DOI: 10.3390/app12136380

Monash University. (2024). *ISO 27001 certification*. Monash University Cyber Security.

Motie, S., & Raahemi, B. (2024). Financial Fraud Detection Using Graph Neural Networks: A Systematic Review. *Expert Systems with Applications*, *240*, 122156. DOI: 10.1016/j.eswa.2023.122156

Muhammad, G., Al-Rakhami, M. S., Gumaei, A., Pakrezaei, M., & Alamri, A. (2021). A comprehensive survey on multimodal medical signals fusion for smart healthcare systems. *Information Fusion*, *76*, 268–289. DOI: 10.1016/j.inffus.2021.06.007

Muhlberger, P., Grgic, I., & Chen, J. (2021). Cloud-based credentialing in universities: A review of practices. *Computers & Education, 174*, 104319. DOI: 10.1016/j.compedu.2021.104319

Nakamoto, S. (2008). *Bitcoin: A Peer-to-Peer Electronic Cash System*. Whitepaper.

Naresh, V. S., & Thamarai, M. (2023). Privacy-preserving data mining and machine learning in healthcare: Applications, challenges, and solutions. *Wiley Interdisciplinary Reviews. Data Mining and Knowledge Discovery*, *13*(2), e1490. DOI: 10.1002/widm.1490

National Institute of Standards and Technology. (2020, June). Cybersecurity framework success story: University of Chicago Biological Sciences Division. NIST.

National Institute of Standards and Technology. (2022). *Post-Quantum Cryptography: Selected Algorithms 2022*. NIST Special Publication.

National Institute of Standards and Technology. (2024, February). Cybersecurity framework (CSF) 2.0. NIST.

NC State University OIT. (2023, October). What is the cost of a data breach? NC State OIT News.

Ngoc Ha, N. T., Van Dyke, N., & Spittle, M. (2025). Micro-credentials in higher education: Perceived benefits for graduate employability and interest levels in micro-credentials for training employability skills. *Studies in Higher Education*, 1–13. DOI: 10.1080/03075079.2025.2516709

Nguyen-Hoang, T. A.. (2024). *Advancing scholarship management: A blockchain-enhanced platform with privacy-secure identities and AI-driven recommendations*. IEEE., DOI: 10.1109/ACCESS.2024.3486078

Nokhbeh Zaeem, R., Chang, K. C., Huang, T.-C., Liau, D., Song, W., Tyagi, A., Barber, K. S., Khalil, M. M., Lamison, M. R., & Pandey, S. (2021). Blockchain-based self-sovereign identity: Survey, requirements, use-cases, and comparative study (UTCID Report #21-06). Center for Identity, University of Texas at Austin.

NovelVista. (2024). *Common challenges while implementing ISO 27001 and how to overcome them*. NovelVista Blog.

Nygard, M. (2024). *Implementing ISO/IEC 27001:2022 in a SME*. Theseus.

O'Neil, C. (2016). *Weapons of math destruction*. Crown Publishing.

Ocheja, P., Agbo, F. J., Oyelere, S. S., Flanagan, B., & Ogata, H. (2022). Blockchain in education: A systematic review and practical case studies. *IEEE*, 10, 99525–99540. https://doi.org/10.1109/ACCESS.2022.3206791

Ocheja, P., Flanagan, B., Ueda, H., & Ogata, H. (2019). Managing lifelong learning records through blockchain. *Research and Practice in Technology Enhanced Learning*, *14*(4), 4. Advance online publication. DOI: 10.1186/s41039-019-0097-0

Oculus, I. T. (2024). *How AI is transforming cybersecurity in higher education*. OculusIT Blog.

OECD. (2019). *Artificial intelligence in society*. OECD Publishing.

Omona, K., & O'dama, M. K. (Eds.). (2024). *Global perspectives on micro-learning and micro-credentials in higher education*. IGI Global. DOI: 10.4018/979-8-3693-0343-6

Orman, R., Şimşek, E., & Kozak Çakır, M. A. (2023). Micro-credentials and reflections on higher education. *Higher Education Evaluation and Development*, *17*(2), 96–112. DOI: 10.1108/HEED-08-2022-0028

Oyedotun, S. A., Ejenarhome, O. P., & Oise, G. P. (2025). Learning analytics and predictive modeling: Enhancing student success through data-driven insights. *Journal of Scientific Research and Reports*, *2*(3), 42–51.

Pandya, S. (2022). Innovative blockchain solutions for enhanced security and verifiability of academic credentials. *International Journal of Science and Research Archive*, *6*(1), 347–357. DOI: 10.30574/ijsra.2022.6.1.0225

Pang, G., Shen, C., Cao, L., & Van Den Hengel, A. (2021). Deep Learning for Anomaly Detection: A Review. ACM Computing Surveys, 54(2). *ACM Computing Surveys*, *38*(2), 1–38. DOI: 10.1145/3439950

Panwar, A., Sugandh, U., Jain, A., Jain, V., Dubey, A. K., Majumdar, S., & Mallik, S. (2025). Enhancing trust and transparency in education using blockchain: A Hyperledger Fabric-based framework. *Artificial Intelligence and Applications (Commerce, Calif.)*, *3*(1), 1–14. DOI: 10.47852/bonviewAIA52026268

Papaioannou, M., Karageorgou, M., Mantas, G., Sucasas, V., Essop, I., Rodriguez, J., & Lymberopoulos, D. (2022). A survey on security threats and countermeasures in Internet of Medical Things (IoMT). *Transactions on Emerging Telecommunications Technologies*, *33*(6), e4049. DOI: 10.1002/ett.4049

Papamitsiou, Z., & Economides, A. A. (2014). Learning analytics and educational data mining in practice: A systematic literature review. *Journal of Educational Technology & Society*, *17*(4), 49–64.

Parchment. (2024). Future-proof your credentials management ecosystem. Parchment Blog.

Parchment. (2024). Why you should embrace digital credential management. Parchment Blog.

Park, J. (2021). Promises and challenges of Blockchain in education. *Smart Learning Environments*, *8*(1), 33. https://doi.org/10.1186/s40561-021-00179-2DOI: 10.1186/s40561-021-00179-2 PMID: 40477765

Partala, J., ... (2013). Security threats against the transmission chain of a medical health monitoring system. In *2013 IEEE 15th International Conference on e-Health Networking, Applications and Services (HealthCom)* (pp. 243–248). IEEE. DOI: 10.1109/HealthCom.2013.6720675

Patel, V., Pradhan, V., & Kadam, A. (2026). Blockchain in Education and Lifelong Learning's: Challenges, Solutions, and Future Directions. In M. Tuba, S. Akashe, & A. Joshi (Eds.), *ICT Systems and Sustainability. ICT4SD 2025.* Lecture Notes in Networks and Systems (Vol. 1646). Springer.https://doi.org/10.1007/978-3-032-06665-7_17 DOI: 10.1007/978-3-032-06665-7_17

Peng, J., Cai, K., & Jin, X. (2020). High concurrency massive data collection algorithm for IoMT applications. *Computer Communications*, *157*, 402–409. DOI: 10.1016/j.comcom.2020.04.045

Pérez Gil, R., Almeida, J., & Bartolomeu, P. (2025). Diploma Issuing On The European Blockchain Service Infrastructure. DOI: 10.20944/preprints202507.0276.v1

Permana, G. P. L., & Martatika, K. A. W. (2024). Potential and challenges of blockchain technology implementation in Higher Education: A systematic literature review. *Review of Management, Accounting, and Business Studies*, *5*(1), 57–67. DOI: 10.38043/revenue.v5i1.5580

Pirkl, K. D. F. (2019, May). Creating a cybersecurity strategy for higher education. *EDUCAUSE Review*.

Planon. (2023). The most important stakeholders of the campus of the future. Planon Software.

Polin, K., Yigitcanlar, T., Limb, M., & Washington, T. (2023). The making of smart campus: A review and conceptual framework. *Buildings (Basel, Switzerland), 13*(4), 891. https://doi.org/10.3390/buildings13040891DOI: 10.3390/buildings13040891

Pollard, V., & Vincent, A. (2022). Micro-credentials: A postdigital counternarrative. *Postdigital Science and Education, 4*(3), 843–859. DOI: 10.1007/s42438-022-00311-6

Polonetsky, J., & Jerome, J. (2014). Student data: Trust, transparency, and the role of consent. *Transparency, and the Role of Consent.* DOI: 10.2139/ssrn.2628877

Pondkule, P. M., & Kothari, S. (2025). Implementation of blockchain-based document management system for higher education organizations. *International Journal on Smart Sensing and Intelligent Systems, 18*(1), 20250001. Advance online publication. DOI: 10.2478/ijssis-2025-0001

Popenici, S. A. D., & Kerr, S. (2017). Exploring the impact of artificial intelligence on higher education. *Research and Practice in Technology Enhanced Learning, 12*(1), 1–13. DOI: 10.1186/s41039-017-0062-8 PMID: 30595727

Porubin, L. (2024). Learner autonomy and personalized learning in the 21st century. In *Universitas Europaea: spre o societate a cunoa terii prin europenizare i globalizare* (Vol. 2, pp. 135-139). DOI: 10.54481/uekbs2024.v2.45

Postel, J. (Ed.). (1981). Internet Protocol - DARPA Internet program, protocol specification. Internet Engineering Task Force., RFC 791.

Prasad, J. P. (2025). A Decentralized Approach Through Blockchain Technology for Certificate Management. 1–7. DOI: 10.1109/ACCTHPA65749.2025.11168519

Pratim, P., Dash, D., & Kumar, N. (2020). Sensors for internet of medical things: State-of-the-art, security and privacy issues, challenges and future directions. *Computer Communications, 160*, 111–131. DOI: 10.1016/j.comcom.2020.05.029

Prinsloo, P., & Slade, S. (2017). Big Data, Higher Education and Learning Analytics: Beyond Justice, Towards an Ethics of Care. In B. Kei Daniel (Ed.), Big Data and Learning Analytics in Higher Education. Springer.https://doi.org/10.1007/978-3-319-06520-5_8 DOI: 10.1007/978-3-319-06520-5_8

Prinsloo, P., & Slade, S. (2017). Ethics and learning analytics. *British Journal of Educational Technology, 48*(2), 386–397.

PRISMA. (2021). PRISMA 2020 statement. prisma-statement.org.

PwC. (2020). *Blockchain in education.*

Qathrady, M. A., Saeed, M., Amin, R., Alshehri, M. S., Alshehri, A., & Alqhtani, S. M. (2024). Smart healthcare: A dynamic blockchain-based trust management model using subarray algorithm. *IEEE Access : Practical Innovations, Open Solutions*, *12*, 51430–51445. DOI: 10.1109/ACCESS.2024.3383310

Rachmat, A., & Albarda. (2019). Design of distributed academic-record system based on blockchain. In *Proceedings of the 2019 International Conference on ICT for Smart Society (ICISS)* (Vol. 7, pp. 1-6). DOI: 10.1109/ICISS48059.2019.8969849

Radha, S. K., Kuehlkamp, A., & Nabrzyski, J. (2024). The future of document verification: Leveraging blockchain and self-sovereign identity for enhanced security and transparency. arXiv. https://doi.org//arXiv.2412.01531DOI: 10.5121/csit.2024.141910

Raghavendra, A. N., Vijayakumar, G., & Subramanian, S. (2024). Enhancing Academic Credential Verification Through Blockchain Technology Adoption in University Academic Management Systems. Advances in Marketing, Customer Relationship Management, and e-Services Book Series, 276–292. DOI: 10.4018/979-8-3693-6813-8.ch012

Raghu, M., Kannan, R., & Choudhury, M. (2021). Reinforcement learning for adaptive learning in education. *International Journal of Artificial Intelligence in Education*, *31*(3), 422–450. DOI: 10.1007/s40593-020-00218-1

Rahmani, M. K. I., Shuaib, M., Alam, S., Siddiqui, S. T., Ahmad, S., Bhatia, S., & Mashat, A. (2022). Blockchain-based trust management framework for cloud computing-based Internet of Medical Things (IoMT): A systematic review. *Computational Intelligence and Neuroscience*, *2022*, 9165383. DOI: 10.1155/2022/9766844 PMID: 35634070

Raj, R., Singh, A., Kumar, V., & Verma, P. (2024). Achieving professional qualifications using micro-credentials: A case of small packages and big challenges in higher education. *International Journal of Educational Management*, *38*(4), 916–947. DOI: 10.1108/IJEM-01-2023-0028

Rakha, A., & Alzubi, A. (2025). A blockchain-based deep learning approach for student course recommendation and secure digital certification. *Scientific Reports*, *15*(1), 29203. Advance online publication. DOI: 10.1038/s41598-025-14778-3 PMID: 40783441

Ranjan, R. (2025). AI-Powered Data Platforms Bridging the Gap Between Analytics and Action in Smart Education. In *Smart Education and Sustainable Learning Environments in Smart Cities* (pp. 107–122). IGI Global Scientific Publishing.

Rasheed, K., Qayyum, A., Ghaly, M., Al-Fuqaha, A., Razi, A., & Qadir, J. (2022). Explainable, trustworthy, and ethical machine learning for healthcare: A survey. *Computers in Biology and Medicine, 149*, 106043. DOI: 10.1016/j.compbiomed.2022.106043 PMID: 36115302

Rathore, H., ... (2017). A review of security challenges, attacks and resolutions for wireless medical devices. In *2017 13th International Wireless Communications and Mobile Computing Conference (IWCMC)* (pp. 1495–1501). IEEE. DOI: 10.1109/IWCMC.2017.7986505

RAUSP Management Journal. (2022). The influence of trust on the adoption of blockchain in higher education institutions. RAUSP Management Journal. Emerald.

Reethika, A., & Priya, P. K. (2024). Using ai-powered predictive analytics tools to identify students falling behind or dropping out. In *Innovation in the University 4.0 System based on Smart Technologies* (pp. 101–115). Chapman and Hall/CRC. DOI: 10.1201/9781003425809-7

Ren, Y., Hu, M., Yang, Z., Feng, G., & Zhang, X. (2024). BPFL: Blockchain-based privacy-preserving federated learning against poisoning attack. *Information Sciences, 665*, 120377. Advance online publication. DOI: 10.1016/j.ins.2024.120377

Research.com. (2024). The future of blockchain technology in education. Research.com.

Revathi, K., Priyadharshini, S., Rathore, R., Guru, K., Varshini, J. A., & Sriram, V. P. (2024)... *Distributed Ledger Credential Verification System Based on Design Thinking Approach., 258–262*. Advance online publication. DOI: 10.1109/ICOECA62351.2024.00055

Romero, C., Ventura, S., & García, E. (2021). Data mining in course management systems: Moodle case study. *Computers & Education, 98*, 201–215. DOI: 10.1016/j.compedu.2020.103809

Rustemi, A., Dalipi, F., Atanasovski, V., & Risteski, A. (2024). Enhancing Academic Credentials: The Synergy of Blockchain and Artificial Intelligence. DOI: 10.1109/BalkanCom61808.2024.10557185

Rustemi, A., Dalipi, F., Atanasovski, V., & Risteski, A. (2024). DIAR: A blockchain-based system for generation and verification of academic diplomas. *SN Applied Sciences, 6*, 297.

Rutgers University. (2024). *General data protection regulation (GDPR)*. Rutgers University Ethics and Compliance.

Ryan, R. M. (1995). Psychological needs and the facilitation of integrative processes. *Journal of Personality*, *63*(3), 397–427. DOI: 10.1111/j.1467-6494.1995.tb00501.x PMID: 7562360

Ryan, R. M., & Deci, E. L. (2020). Intrinsic and extrinsic motivation from a self-determination theory perspective: Definitions, theory, practices, and future directions. *Contemporary Educational Psychology*, *61*, 101860. DOI: 10.1016/j.cedpsych.2020.101860

Sajja, R., Sermet, Y., Cikmaz, M., Cwiertny, D., & Demir, I. (2024). Artificial Intelligence-Enabled Intelligent Assistant for Personalized and Adaptive Learning in Higher Education. *Information (Basel)*, *15*(10), 596. DOI: 10.3390/info15100596

Sameera, K. M.. (2024). Privacy-preserving in blockchain-based federated learning systems. *Computer Communications*. Advance online publication. DOI: 10.1016/j.comcom.2024.04.024

Sanchez Barrioluengo, M. (2025). *Micro-credentials in higher education: Are they boosting digital and green skills for the twin transition? (JRC142086)*. Publications Office of the European Union., DOI: 10.2760/0157920

Sayyad, S., Jagtap, G., Patil, P., Jagdale, A., & Mujawar, A. (2025). *Privacy-preserving federated learning*., DOI: 10.1109/ACCESS65134.2025.11135556

Schumm, D., Müller, K. O. E., & Stiller, B. (2025). Are we there yet? A study of decentralized identity applications. *IEEE Access : Practical Innovations, Open Solutions*, *13*, 125232–125259. DOI: 10.1109/ACCESS.2025.3588170

Sclater, N. (2019). Learning analytics explained. *JISC Publications*. https://www.jisc.ac.uk/reports/learning-analytics-explained

Selwyn, N. (2019). *Should robots replace teachers?* Polity Press.

SenseTime. (2024). *What is digital trust and why is it important?* SenseTime News.

Shahsavari, Y., Baseri, Y., Hafid, A., Dambri, O. A., & Makrakis, D. (2025). Integration of federated learning and blockchain in healthcare: A tutorial on medical data, architectures, privacy, security, and regulatory compliance. *JMIR Preprints*. https://doi.org/DOI: 10.2196/preprints.80178

Shaikh, Z. A., Khan, A. A., Baitenova, L., Zambinova, G., Yegina, N. A., Ivolgina, N. V., Laghari, A. A., & Barykin, S. Y. (2022). A Blockchain Hyperledger and Non-Linear Machine Learning: A Novel and Secure Educational Accreditation Registration and Distributed Ledger Preservation Architecture. *Applied Sciences (Basel, Switzerland)*, *12*(5), 2534. DOI: 10.3390/app12052534

Shanmughan, P., & Joseph, J. S, B. N., SM, A., CS, A., & Jose, J. (2024, November). The AI revolution in micro-credentialing: personalized learning paths. In *Frontiers in Education* (Vol. 9, p. 1445654). Frontiers Media SA. DOI: 10.3389/feduc.2024.1445654

Sharipova, Z., Mardonova, R., Begbutayev, A., Makhkamova, S., Sapaev, I. B., Karimova, S., Nigmatova, K., & Rakhmatova, G. (2025). Academic chain: Securing educational credentials with blockchain-enabled. *Journal of Internet Services and Information Security*, *15*(2), 374–386. DOI: 10.58346/JISIS.2025.I2.027

Sharma, I. K. A., Chauhan, A. P. S., Thagriya, D., & Singh, A. P. (2024). Experience virtual college campus tour with generative AI-assisted avatar in VR mobile application. [IJARIIE]. *International Journal of Advance Research and Innovative Ideas in Education*, *10*(2), 3904–3914.

Sharples, M., & Domingue, J. (2016). Blockchain and education. In *Proceedings of the European Conference on Technology Enhanced Learning* (pp. 490–496). Springer.

Sharples, M., & Domingue, J. (2016). The blockchain and kudos: A distributed system for educational record, reputation, and reward. *Proceedings of the 11th European Conference on Technology Enhanced Learning (EC-TEL)*, 490–496. DOI: 10.1007/978-3-319-45153-4_48

Sharples, M., & Domingue, J. (2023). The Blockchain and Kudos: A Distributed System for Educational Record, Reputation and Reward. *Proceedings of the European Conference on Technology Enhanced Learning*, 490–496.

Shehzad, N., & Charles, T. (2023). Exploring the impact of instructor social presence on student engagement in online higher education. *Contemporary Educational Technology*, *15*(4), ep484. https://doi.org/10.30935/cedtech/13823DOI: 10.30935/cedtech/13823

Shete, S. G., Koshti, P., & Pujari, V. I. (2024, April). The impact of AI-powered personalization on academic performance in students. In *2024 5th International Conference on Recent Trends in Computer Science and Technology (ICRTCST)* (pp. 295–301). IEEE. DOI: 10.1109/ICRTCST61793.2024.10578480

Shoaib, M., Sayed, N., Singh, J., Shafi, J., Khan, S., & Ali, F. (2024). AI student success predictor: Enhancing personalized learning in campus management systems. *Computers in Human Behavior*, *158*, 108301.

Si-Ahmed, A., Al-Garadi, M. A., & Boustia, N. (2022). Survey of machine learning based intrusion detection methods for Internet of Medical Things. *Applied Soft Computing*, *140*, 110227. DOI: 10.1016/j.asoc.2023.110227

Siemens, G. (2004). Elearnspace. Connectivism: A learning theory for the digital age. *Elearnspace. org*, 14-16.

Siemens, G. (2013). Learning analytics: The emergence of a discipline. *The American Behavioral Scientist*, *57*(10), 1380–1400. DOI: 10.1177/0002764213498851

Sift. (2023, September). What is digital trust, and why is it at risk? Sift Blog.

Silaghi, D. L., & Popescu, D. E. (2025). A systematic review of blockchain-based initiatives in comparison to best practices used in higher education institutions. *Computers*, *14*(4), 141. DOI: 10.3390/computers14040141

Singleton, J. L. (2025). *Unlocking Student Success: Exploring the Impact of AI-Driven Tools within the LMS on Improving Student Academic Success* (Doctoral dissertation).

Sitanggang, T. W., Kamar, K., Priyono, H., Wahab, A., Nusantoro, H., & Sunengsih, M. (2025). Enhancing Educational Data Integrity Using Blockchain and Ontologies. 1–7. DOI: 10.1109/ICCIT65724.2025.11166757

Slade, S., & Prinsloo, P. (2013). Learning analytics: Ethical issues and dilemmas. *The American Behavioral Scientist*, *57*(10), 1510–1529.

Smith, E., Jones, T., & Kumar, R. (2020). International credential recognition: Challenges and solutions. *Higher Education Policy*, *33*, 25–42. DOI: 10.1057/s41307-019-00159-x

So, H.-J. Lee, C., Lee, Ga-Young, Kim, M.J. (2024). *UNESCO report on AI, blockchain, and XR in lifelong learning*. UNESCO Institute for Lifelong Learning. ISBN: 978-92-820-1258-1

Solunke, H., & Bhaladhare, P. (2024). *An in-depth investigation of machine learning powered blockchain approaches for privacy preservation.*, DOI: 10.1109/ETNCC63262.2024.10767529

Soomro, A. A., Khan, M. H., Umar, M., Khan, S., & Ali, O. (2025). AI-Driven Academic Advising in Higher Education: Leveraging Intelligent Systems to Personalize Student Support, Improve Retention, and Optimize Career Pathways. *The Critical Review of Social Sciences Studies*, *3*(2), 229–248. DOI: 10.59075/vy3v7k17

Sporny, M., Longley, D., & Chadwick, D. (2023). Verifiable Credentials Data Model v2.0. W3C Recommendation.

Stanković, M., Stanković, N., & Bjelica, M. Z. (2025). What is digital trust and how can we measure it? A multidimensional approach. *Electronics (Basel)*, *14*(1), 1.

Steiu, M.-F. (2020). Blockchain in education: Opportunities, applications, and challenges. *First Monday*, *25*(9). Advance online publication. https://doi.org/10.5210/fm.v25i9.10654DOI: 10.5210/fm.v25i9.10654

Strielkowski, W. (2025). The role of micro-credentials in the future digitalized AI-driven education. arXiv. https://doi.org//arXiv.2511.07583DOI: 10.48550

Subashini, B., Anbumozhi, A., Praveenkumar, S., Vasudevan, N., & Kaliamoorthy, V. (2025). Blockchain for Credentialing and Academic Record-Keeping. Advances in Computational Intelligence and Robotics Book Series, 407–448. DOI: 10.4018/979-8-3373-2185-1.ch014

Sudha, M. J., & Viveka, S. (2022). A comprehensive review of architecture, classification, challenges, and future of the Internet of Medical Things (IoMTs). *Medical Journal of Babylon*, *19*(3), 311–317. DOI: 10.4103/MJBL.MJBL_5_22

Suktam, W., Lapchit, S., Supsin, J., Sonwa, S., & Suthamdee, C. (2024). Blockchain in Education: Transforming Learning, Credentialing, and Academic Data Management. *Blockchain in Education: Transforming Learning, Credentialing, and Academic Data Management.*, *1*(6), 37–46. DOI: 10.60027/jelr.2024.739

Sumathy, V., & Navamani, G. (2024). AI-Driven Personalized Learning: Enhancing Student Success through Adaptive Technologies. *Library of Progress-Library Science, Information Technology & Computer, 44*(3).

Sun, Q., Lin, K., Si, C., Xu, Y., Li, S., & Gope, P. (2022). A secure and anonymous communication scheme over the Internet of Things. *ACM Transactions on Sensor Networks*, *18*(3), 1–21. DOI: 10.1145/3508392

Sun, Y., Lo, F. P.-W., & Lo, B. (2019). Security and privacy for the Internet of Medical Things enabled healthcare systems: A survey. *IEEE Access : Practical Innovations, Open Solutions*, *7*, 183339–183355. DOI: 10.1109/ACCESS.2019.2960617

Sy, M. P. M., Marasigan, R. I., & Festijo, E. D. (2024). EduCredPH: Towards a Permissioned Blockchain Network for Educational Credentials Verification System. DOI: 10.1109/ICIET60671.2024.10542756

Taiwo, K. A., & Busari, I. O.Kamorudeen Abiola TaiwoIsiaka Olayinka Busari. (2025). Leveraging AI-driven predictive analytics to enhance cognitive assessment and early intervention in STEM learning and health outcomes. *World Journal of Advanced Research and Reviews*, *27*(01), 2658–2671. DOI: 10.30574/wjarr.2025.27.1.2548

Tan, E., Lerouge, E., Caju, J. D., & Seuil, D. D. (2023). Verification of education credentials on European Blockchain Services Infrastructure (EBSI): Action research in a cross-border use case between Belgium and Italy. *Big Data and Cognitive Computing*, *7*(2), 79. DOI: 10.3390/bdcc7020079

Tanriverdí, M. (2024). *PublicEduChain: A framework for sharing student-owned educational data on public blockchain networks*. IEEE., DOI: 10.1109/ACCESS.2024.3385660

Tapscott, D., & Tapscott, A. (2016). *Blockchain revolution*. Penguin.

Tatineni, S. (2020). Recommendation Systems for Personalized Learning: A Data-Driven Approach in Education. [JCET]. *Journal of Computer Engineering and Technology*, *4*(2), 18–31. https://iaeme.com/Home/issue/JCET?Volume=4&Issue=2

Tech, O. C. D. (2024). *How to make your college align with NIST cybersecurity guidelines*. OCD Tech.

Tepelidis, A., Mitsopoulou, E. E., Patenidis, A. T., Livitckaia, K., Votis, K., & Tzovaras, D. (2024). *BlockAdemiC: A Digital Distributed Verification System for Educational Activities in Higher Education*. Deleted Journal., DOI: 10.1145/3703463

The Mozilla Foundation (2011). Open badges for lifelong learning. *The Mozilla Foundation and Peer 2 Peer University.*

Thi Ngoc Ha, N., Van Dyke, N., Spittle, M., Watt, A., & Smallridge, A. (2024). Micro-credentials through the eyes of employers: Benefits, challenges and enablers of effectiveness. *Education + Training*, *66*(7), 948–963. DOI: 10.1108/ET-08-2023-0340

Torraco, R. J. (2016). Writing integrative literature reviews: Using the past and present to explore the future. *Human Resource Development Review*, *15*(4), 404–428. DOI: 10.1177/1534484316671606

Turkanović, M., Hölbl, M., Košič, K., Heričko, M., & Kamišalić, A. (2018). EduCTX: A blockchain-based higher education credit platform. *IEEE*, 6, 5112–5127. https://doi.org/10.1109/ACCESS.2018.2789929

U.S. Department of Education. (2020). *FERPA and student privacy guidance*.

U.S. Department of Education. (2024). *Identity authentication best practices*. Student Privacy Policy Office.

Umendu, E. C., Ghanzanfar, M., Kans, A., & Ahad, M. A. R. (2026). Enhancing Student Retention in Higher Education Institutions (HEIs): Machine Learning Approach. *Electronics (Basel)*, *15*(4), 734.

UnderDefense. (2018, December). Case study: NIST cybersecurity framework assessment. UnderDefense.

UNESCO. (2019). *Artificial intelligence in education: Challenges and opportunities.*

UNESCO. (2021). *Recommendation on the ethics of artificial intelligence.*

University of Minnesota. (2024). *Securing Internet of Things (IoT) devices.* UMN IT.

University of New South Wales. (2024). *ISO/IEC 27001:2022 certification.* UNSW IT.

University of Oxford. (2024). *Safeguarding academia: Harnessing the power of AI to fortify higher education cybersecurity.* University of Oxford.

University of Texas Health Science Center at Houston. (2024). *Research security program.* HOOP Policy Manual.

UpGuard. (2024). *NIST SP 800-171 compliance guide for colleges & universities.* UpGuard Blog.

Vaezinejad, S., Chen, Y., Kouhizadeh, M., & Özpolat, K. (2024, May). Blockchain Technology for Higher Education and Recruitment: A Systematic Literature Review. *Eurasian Journal of Business and Economics, 17*(33), 1–27. DOI: 10.17015/ejbe.2024.033.01

Vaher, K., Simanjuntak, A., & Sugiharto, E. (2025). Securing Academic Records with Blockchain Technology A Data-Driven Approach for University Management. DOI: 10.33050/mentari.v4i1.908

Van den Broeck, A., Ferris, D. L., Chang, C. H., & Rosen, C. C. (2016). A review of self-determination theory's basic psychological needs at work. *Journal of Management, 42*(5), 1195–1229. DOI: 10.1177/0149206316632058

Van Melkebeke, L., & Op de Beeck, I. (2025). *Implementing micro-credentials in higher education: Challenges, opportunities and lessons learned (Envisioning Report 2025).* KU Leuven.

Varadarajan, S., Koh, J. H. L., & Daniel, B. K. (2023). A systematic review of the opportunities and challenges of micro-credentials for multiple stakeholders: Learners, employers, higher education institutions and government. *International Journal of Educational Technology in Higher Education, 20*(1), 13. https://doi.org/10.1186/s41239-023-00381-xDOI: 10.1186/s41239-023-00381-x PMID: 36874535

Varadarajan, S., Koh, J. H. L., & Daniel, B. K. (2025). Institutional readiness for the implementation of micro-credentials in higher education. *Distance Education, 46*(1), 36–55. DOI: 10.1080/01587919.2024.2442017

Vashishth, T. K., Sharma, V., Kumar, B., Sharma, K. K., Chaudhary, S., & Panwar, R. (2024). Blockchain for securing federated learning systems: Enhancing privacy and trust (pp. 299–320). DOI: 10.1002/9781394219230.ch15

Vashishth, T. K., Sharma, V., Sharma, K. K., & Kumar, B. (2024). A Novel Approach for Implementing Blockchain Technology in the Education Sector. Advances in Business Information Systems and Analytics Book Series, 27–50. DOI: 10.4018/979-8-3693-3003-6.ch002

Verma, S., Pathak, S., & Bhattacharya, P. (2025). BlockFed: Blockchain-based privacy-preserving federated learning for 5G-assisted healthcare ecosystems. *Research Square* Preprint. DOI: 10.21203/rs.3.rs-6848848/v1

Vishnu, S., Jino Ramson, S. R., & Jegan, R. (2020). Internet of Medical Things (IoMT) — an overview. In *Proceedings of the 2020 5th International Conference on Devices, Circuits and Systems (ICDCS)* (pp. 101–104). IEEE. DOI: 10.1109/ICDCS48716.2020.243558

Vlachopoulos, D. (2025). AUTHENTIC ASSESSMENT: BRIDGING HIGHER EDUCATION AND REAL-WORLD SKILLS THROUGH DIVERSE METHODOLOGIES. In *INTED2025 Proceedings* (pp. 2225-2234). IATED. DOI: 10.21125/inted.2025.0628

Vo, K. T., Pham, K., Huynh, P., Nguyen Thi, M.-T., Ta, T.-T., Nguy n, T. H., Nguyen-Hoang, T.-A., Dinh, N.-T., & Nguyen, H.-T. (2024). Optimizing Academic Certificate Management with Blockchain and Machine Learning: A Novel Approach Using Optimistic Rollups and Fraud Detection. *IEEE Access : Practical Innovations, Open Solutions*, *1*, 168135–168159. Advance online publication. DOI: 10.1109/ACCESS.2024.3486029

W3C. (2022). *Verifiable credentials data model.*

Wachter, S., Mittelstadt, B., & Floridi, L. (2017). Transparent, explainable AI. *European Law Journal*, *23*(5), 1–23. PMID: 33157874

Wal, P., Wal, A., Verma, N., Karunakakaran, R., & Kapoor, A. (2022). Internet of Medical Things – the future of healthcare. *The Open Public Health Journal*, *15*(1), 1–9. DOI: 10.2174/18749445-v15-e221215-2022-142

Wang, H., Zheng, J., Carvajal-Roca, I. E., Chen, L., & Bai, M. (2023, August). Financial fraud detection based on deep learning: Towards large-scale pre-training transformer models. In China Conference on Knowledge Graph and Semantic Computing (pp. 163–177). Singapore: Springer Nature Singapore. DOI: 10.1007/978-981-99-7224-1_13

Wang, L., Ali, Y., Nazir, S., & Niazi, M. (2020). ISA evaluation framework for security of internet of health things system using AHP-TOPSIS methods. *IEEE Access : Practical Innovations, Open Solutions, 8*, 152316–152332. DOI: 10.1109/ACCESS.2020.3017221

Washington University in St. Louis. (2024). *Threats to your research data and intellectual property*. WUSTL Information Security.

Webisoft. (2024). Blockchain for universities: A game-changer in academic data management. Webisoft.

Williamson, B., & Eynon, R. (2020). Historical perspectives on AI in education. *Learning, Media and Technology, 45*(1), 1–13.

World Economic Forum. (2020). *Schools of the future*.

World Economic Forum. (2021). *Global governance of artificial intelligence*.

World Economic Forum. (2023). Earning digital trust. World Economic Forum.

Xu, L. D., He, W., & Li, S. (2014). Internet of Things in industries: A survey. *IEEE Transactions on Industrial Informatics, 10*(4), 2233–2243. DOI: 10.1109/TII.2014.2300753

Xu, X.. (2019). A taxonomy of blockchain-based systems. *IEEE Communications Surveys and Tutorials, 21*(3), 2799–2834.

Yadav, S., & Vishwakarma, S. (2020). Impact of artificial intelligence in education. *Journal of Statistics and Management Systems, 23*(2), 1–12.

Yahya, N., Murtaj, S. M. T., Mohammed, M., Yusif, A. A., & Abdulghafor, R. (2024). Precognito: The Emergence of Blockchain & Machine Learning-Based for Student Record Authentication System. *Journal of Advanced Research in Applied Sciences and Engineering Technology, 55*(1), 125–140. DOI: 10.37934/araset.55.1.125140

Yang, H., & Wong, R. (2024). *An in-depth literature review of e-portfolio implementation in higher education. Issues and Trends in Learning Technologies*. University of Arizona Libraries.

Yaqoob, T., Abbas, H., & Atiquzzaman, M. (2019). Security vulnerabilities, attacks, countermeasures, and regulations of networked medical devices — A review. *IEEE Communications Surveys and Tutorials, 21*(4), 3723–3768. DOI: 10.1109/COMST.2019.2914094

Yin, X., Wu, X., & Zhang, X. (2024). A trusted federated learning method based on consortium blockchain. *Information (Basel)*, *16*(1), 14. Advance online publication. DOI: 10.3390/info16010014

Yu, C., & Yao, G. (2024). Enhancing student engagement with ai-driven personalized learning systems. [ITEE]. *International Transactions on Education Technology*, *3*(1), 1–8. DOI: 10.33050/itee.v3i1.662

Zawacki-Richter, O., Marín, V. I., Bond, M., & Gouverneur, F. (2019). Systematic review of research on artificial intelligence applications in higher education – where are the educators? *International Journal of Educational Technology in Higher Education*, *16*(1), 39. https://doi.org/10.1186/s41239-019-0171-0DOI: 10.1186/s41239-019-0171-0

Zawacki-Richter, O., Marín, V. I., Bond, M., & Gouverneur, F. (2019). Systematic review of research on artificial intelligence applications in higher education–where are the educators? *International Journal of Educational Technology in Higher Education*, *16*(1), 1–27.

Zhang, H., Jiang, S., & Xuan, S. (2024). Decentralized federated learning based on blockchain: Concepts, framework, and challenges. *Computer Communications*, *216*, 140–150. Advance online publication. DOI: 10.1016/j.comcom.2023.12.042

Zhang, K., Liang, X., Lu, R., & Shen, X. (2014). Sybil attacks and their defenses in the Internet of Things. *IEEE Internet of Things Journal*, *1*(5), 372–383. DOI: 10.1109/JIOT.2014.2344013

Zhang, P., & Tur, G. (2022). Educational e-Portfolio Overview: Aspiring for the Future by Building on the Past. *IAFOR Journal of Education*, *10*(3), 51–74. DOI: 10.22492/ije.10.3.03

Zhang, R., Xue, R., & Liu, L. (2019). Security and privacy on blockchain. *ACM Computing Surveys*, *52*(3), 1–34. DOI: 10.1145/3316481

Zhang, Y., Xue, H., & Zhao, X. (2021). AI and blockchain for higher education credentialing: Opportunities and challenges. *Computers and Education Open*, *2*, 100042. DOI: 10.1016/j.caeo.2021.100042

Zhang, Z., Hamadi, H. A., Damiani, E., Yeun, C. Y., & Taher, F. (2022). Explainable artificial intelligence applications in cyber security: State-of-the-art in research. *IEEE Access : Practical Innovations, Open Solutions*, *10*, 93104–93139. DOI: 10.1109/ACCESS.2022.3204051

Zhou, Z. H. (2021). *Ensemble Methods: Foundations and Algorithms*. Chapman and Hall/CRC.

Zhu, H., Sun, Y., & Yang, J. (2025). Towards responsible artificial intelligence in education: A systematic review on identifying and mitigating ethical risks. *Humanities & Social Sciences Communications*, *12*(1), 1111. https://doi.org/10.1057/s41599-025-05252-6DOI: 10.1057/s41599-025-05252-6

Zimmerman, E. (2019, January). How universities can mitigate IoT risk on campus. EdTech Magazine.

Živanović, M., & Milošević, D. (2025). *Primena federativnog učenja u predikciji aktivnosti studenata na e-learning kursevima*., DOI: 10.69994/69E25052

Zuo, Y. (2022). Towards a Learner-Managed Education Credentialing System Based on Blockchain. *Information Resources Management Journal*, *35*(1), 1–18. DOI: 10.4018/IRMJ.309983

Zyskind, G., Nathan, O., & Pentland, A. (2015). Decentralizing privacy. *IEEE Security and Privacy Workshops*, 180–184.

About the Contributors

Ahmad Tasnim Siddiqui is a scholar and educator specializing in the application of emerging technologies in higher education, with a particular focus on IOT, Artificial Intelligence, Web Application Development, Credentialing, Digital Learning Systems, and Data Governance. He serves as a faculty member at Horizon University College, where he contributes to academic development, research, and technology-driven educational innovation. Dr. Siddiqui holds a PhD in Computer Science, and his research interests span AI-driven learning analytics, decentralized credentialing, e-learning, e-commerce and mobile commerce, Internet of Things (IoT), Health IT, educational data management, and technology-enhanced pedagogy. He has played an active role in curriculum design, faculty development initiatives, and institutional digital transformation efforts, collaborating with interdisciplinary teams to advance modern pedagogical and administrative practices. A committed researcher and academic leader, Dr. Siddiqui has authored and presented work on the integration of disruptive technologies into higher education, with an emphasis on transparency, learner mobility, and sustainable innovation. His professional engagement includes membership in the Institute of Electrical and Electronics Engineers (IEEE), reflecting his dedication to contributing to scholarly and professional communities in computing and technology. As the editor of Innovating Credentialing and Data Management in Higher Education with Blockchain and AI, Dr. Siddiqui brings together global perspectives to explore cutting-edge advancements and promote strategic, responsible digital transformation across higher education systems.

Manas Ranjan Pradhan received his Ph.D. degree in computer science from the University of Mysore, India. He has vast experience in teaching, research, and academic administration in India and abroad. He is currently working as Professor and Program Chair -Computer science at Horizon University College, Ajman formerly known as Skyline University College, Sharjah, United Arab Emirates.

As an Academic Leader, he has worked as the Head of Program at UPES, India, and the Dean-Faculty of IT and science at INTI International University, Malaysia. He has been associated with the IT industry for industry-academic collaboration, internships, placements, and workshops. He executed the IBM Center of Education for Cloud Computing and Business Analytics at INTI International University, under Laureate International Universities, USA. He has presented and published many research papers in various conferences and journals. He has sixteen patents from India, Australia, Germany and UK. His research interests include data science, datamining, data warehouse, retail/ecommerce analytics, artificial intelligence, machine learning, and business process modeling. He has got the Mentor Award for the i-talent project contest from Confederation of Indian Industry (CII). He has got Research Excellence Award for exceptional Achievement in research by EUMMAS (European Marketing and Management Association), Outstanding Leadership Award-from Education 2.0 and Overall Excellence in Academics- 2022 by Skyline University College. He has played a vital role in organizing three international conferences, such as NGCT-2015 (UPES, India), ICQMOIT-2008 (ICFAI, India), and ICD-2019 (SUC, United Arab Emirates).

Valentina E. Balas is currently Full Professor in the Department of Automatics and Applied Software at the Faculty of Engineering, "Aurel Vlaicu" University of Arad, Romania. She holds a Ph.D. Cum Laude, in Applied Electronics and Telecommunications from Polytechnic University of Timisoara. Dr. Balas is the author of more than 400 research papers in referred journals and International Conferences. Her research interests are in Intelligent Systems, Fuzzy Control, Soft Computing, Smart Sensors, Information Fusion, Modelling and Simulation. She is the Editor-in Chief to International Journal of Advanced Intelligence Paradigms (IJAIP) and to International Journal of Computational Systems Engineering (IJCSysE), member in Editorial Board member of several national and international journals and is evaluator expert for national, international projects and PhD Thesis. Dr. Balas has edited or co-authored more than 200 books with Elsevier, Springer, CRC Press, and other publishing houses. She is the Series Editor for two book series with Elsevier: Advances in Biomedical Informatics and Advanced Studies in Complex Systems. Dr. Balas is the Head of the Intelligent Systems Research Centre at Aurel Vlaicu University of Arad. She is a member in the specialized committee "Computers, Information Technology, and Systems Engineering" of the National Council for Attestation of University Titles, Diplomas, and Certificates (CNATDCU) for the 2024-2028 term. She served as General Chair of the International Workshop Soft Computing and Applications (SOFA) in ten editions organized in the interval 2005-2022 and held in Romania and Hungary. Dr. Balas participated in many international conferences as Organizer, Honorary

Chair, Session Chair, member of Steering, Advisory or International Program Committees and Keynote Speaker. Recently she was working on a national project with EU funding support: BioCell-NanoART = Novel Bio-inspired Cellular Nano-Architectures - For Digital Integrated Circuits, 3M Euro from National Authority for Scientific Research and Innovation. She is a member of European Society for Fuzzy Logic and Technology (EUSFLAT), member of Society for Industrial and Applied Mathematics (SIAM) and a Senior Member IEEE, member in Technical Committee – Fuzzy Systems (IEEE Computational Intelligence Society), chair of the Task Force 14 in Technical Committee – Emergent Technologies (IEEE CIS), member in Technical Committee – Soft Computing (IEEE SMCS). She is member in the Committee of IEEE Romania Section as Volunteers Training Coordinator and vice chair of IEEE Computational Intelligence Society Chapter – CIS 11. During the interval 2021-2022 she was a member of IEEE European Public Policy Committee Working Group on ICT. From May 2023 Dr. Balas is associate member of Romanian Academy of Scientists and from 2025 is corresponding member. Dr. Balas was past Vice President (awards) of IFSA - International Fuzzy Systems Association Council (2013-2015), is a Joint Secretary of the Governing Council of Forum for Interdisciplinary Mathematics (FIM), - A Multidisciplinary Academic Body, India. She is the recipient of the "Tudor Tanasescu" Prize from the Romanian Academy for contributions in the field of soft computing methods (2019) and "Stefan Odobleja" Prize from Romanian Academy of Scientists (2023 and 2024) and Diploma – Section Information Technology from The General Association of the Engineers in Romania (AGIR) 2023.

***

Ausaf Ahmad is an Assistant Professor in the Department of Computer Application, Integral University and a Ph.D. graduate from Aligarh Muslim University. He has published several research papers in Scopus-indexed and peer-reviewed journals and has contributed chapters to international books in the areas of Artificial Intelligence, Blockchain, and Cybersecurity. His academic and research interests include machine learning, data analytics, and the application of intelligent systems to solve real-world and societal challenges. He is committed to quality teaching, research excellence, and academic leadership.

Md Faiz Ahmad is an academician and researcher with a keen focus on digital marketing, social media marketing, and consumer decision-making. He has more than 8 years of experience in academia and industry. He has qualified UGC-NET in both the subjects Management and Commerce. He holds a Ph.D. in Management Studies from the University of Hyderabad, Telangana, India. He is working as an

Assistant Professor in the area of Marketing at Paari School of Business, SRM University-AP, Andhra Pradesh. His research, particularly on the role of social media in consumer purchase decisions, reflects his commitment to exploring contemporary marketing trends. He has published papers in various renowned journals indexed in ABDC, SCOPUS, WoS etc. Driven by a passion for education and research, he continues to make valuable contributions to the academic and business realms

Reyaz Ahmad is an experienced educator and researcher with over 16 years of university-level teaching Mathematics to Graduate and undergraduate level with great passion. He has contributed significantly to academia through numerous publications in SCOPUS-indexed journals, book chapters and policy-oriented documents.

Nehal Ahmad Ansari got M.A.(Urdu), M.A.(History), M.Ed., Ph.D. (Humanities), from Patna University. He qualified UGC NET in Education and Urdu. He also got Ph.D. in Education from NOU, Patna. He is an Assistant Professor in School of Education and Training in Maulana Azad National Urdu University, Hyderabad (A Central University). At present he is working at College of Teacher Education (A Satellite Campus of MANUU), Asansol (West Bengal). He has been teaching and working in area of the Teacher Education for over sixteen years. He has published two books and one edited book. A number of research articles published in National/International Referred/Peer Reviews/Scopus and UGC Care listed Journals. He has also participated in several National/International Seminars, Conferences and Workshops in India and Abroad. He has awarded Shikhcha Bhushan Samman in Nepal and Guru Shikhcha Samman by EDC, Patna.

Neeraj Bhardwaj is an accomplished academician and researcher in the field of Computer Science and Engineering, currently serving as an Assistant Professor in the Department of Computer Engineering at Chitkara University, Himachal Pradesh. She earned her Ph.D. in Computer Science from Poornima University, Jaipur (Rajasthan) in 2021, following her M.Tech. in Computer Science from HCTM College of Engineering, Kaithal (Kurukshetra University) in 2013 and B.Tech. in Computer Science from B.P.R. College of Engineering, Sonipat (MDU University) in 2011. With over a decade of teaching and research experience, Dr. Neeraj has served in various reputed institutions including Chandigarh University, Poornima Institute of Engineering & Technology. Her academic career reflects a strong commitment to innovation, excellence, and student development. She has made significant contributions to research with numerous publications in Scopus and Web of Science-indexed journals, and has presented papers at several IEEE international conferences. Her research interests include the Internet of Things (IoT),

Wireless Sensor Networks, Artificial Intelligence, Cloud Computing, and Cyber Security. Dr. Neeraj has also published and filed multiple patents, focusing on smart systems for water, gas, and healthcare management using IoT and machine learning. In recognition of her expertise, she has served as a reviewer for Scopus journals and international conferences, including ICIMMI and ICISC. She has also delivered expert lectures and talks in faculty development programs and acted as a resource person on topics like network simulation, IP addressing, and AI trends. Dr. Neeraj has participated in several AICTE-ATAL FDPs, IEEE workshops, and national-level training programs, reflecting her dedication to continuous learning and professional growth. Her leadership roles as NAAC Coordinator, Research Coordinator, and Conference Co-Convener highlight her organizational and mentoring abilities. Beyond her academic achievements, she holds a Microsoft Certification in Azure AI Fundamentals and has received appreciation and excellence awards for her review work in reputed conferences and journals. Driven by a passion for innovation, technology, and education, Dr. Neeraj Bhardwaj continues to contribute actively to the advancement of computer science research and to inspire future technologists through her teaching and mentorship.

Tendai Charles is an Assistant Professor of Education at the British University in Dubai. He holds an MSc in Data Analytics & Social Statistics from the University of Manchester and a PhD in Education from the University of York. He is an accredited researcher with the Office for National Statistics and is a Fellow of the Royal Statistical Society. He is a post-positivist researcher who specialises in evidence-based education and uses computational statistics for secondary data analyses.

Ritam Dutta is having 17+ years of Teaching and Research Experience (05 SCI, 55 Scopus, 01 Patent Grant), 10+ years of Administrative Experience and 04+ year of Post Ph.D. Experience, served in several reputed institutions across India in the capacity of Assistant Prof., Associate Prof. and Professor. Dr. Dutta is a Life Member of Professional Bodies: IE(India) (M'19), IEEE (M'24), ISTE (M'22). Dr. Dutta is Post Doc. from Handong Global University, South Korea, earned Ph.D (Engg.) from Sikkim Manipal University, Gangtok, India, and M.Tech from SRM Institute of Science & Technology, Chennai, India.

Nafees Akhter Farooqui had completed a BSc (Hons.) in Statistics from AMU, Aligarh, MCA from Integral University, Lucknow, and Ph.D. (Computer Science & Engineering) from DIT University, Dehradun, Uttarakhand, India. He has 15 years of teaching experience and is presently working as an "Assistant Professor in the Department of Computer Application at the Integral University, Lucknow,

Uttar Pradesh, India". His research interests include artificial intelligence, machine learning, deep learning, computer vision, pattern recognition, natural language processing and data mining. He has published approx. 35 papers in international journals and conference proceedings, including Web of Science and Scopus indexed journals. He also published various book chapters in Scopus-indexed journals. He has published two books for National Publishers, etc. He has been a member of the Association of Information Science and Technology (ASIS&T) since 2024, the Computer Science Teachers Association (CSTA) since 2023, the International Association of Engineers (IAENG) since 2017, and ACM since 2011. He guided various projects of UG- and PG-level students. He received awards from various professional bodies.

Sandeep Gupta is a Professor (Research) and Head, Department of Electronics and Communication Engineering at Poornima College of Engineering (PCE), Jaipur, India. He holds a Ph.D. in Nanoscience & Nanotechnology from India and an MBA from Politecnico di Milano, Italy, and is an IEEE Senior Member (including IEEE RAS). His research spans Artificial Intelligence, Nanotechnology, IoT, Quantum Computing, and Autonomous Robotics, with prior industry experience at Ernst & Young, Accenture, TATA CMC, and Telecom Italia. He has over 150 citations and an h-index of 5. Prof. Gupta has contributed to intelligent autonomous robotic platforms, nanostructured electrochemical sensors for hydrogen ion and environmental pollutant detection, quantum-enhanced machine learning, federated learning for healthcare and IoT systems, and AI-driven safety applications. His interdisciplinary research bridges AI, nanotechnology, and robotics for next-generation safety, sensing, and autonomous systems.

Gul Shaira Banu Jahangeer is currently working as Associate Professor in Er Perumal Manimekalai College of Engineering - Hosur, Tamilnadu, India. She accomplished her Ph.D. in Computer Science and Engineering from Kalasalingam Academy of Research and Education. She also holds a Master of Computer science and Engineering from Mepco Schlenk Engineering College, Anna university (2006) and Bachelor of Computer Science and Engineering from Mohammad Sadak Engineering College, Madurai Kamaraj University (2002). Her research interest includes Machine Learning, Deep Learning, Image Processing .

Udit Mamodiya is an Associate Professor and Associate Dean (Research) at Poornima University in Jaipur, Rajasthan, India. With a robust academic and professional background, he has significantly contributed to the fields of renewable energy sources, reliability analysis, expert systems, and decision support systems. Dr. Mamodiya has authored over 60 research papers indexed in prestigious databases such as SCI, Scopus, and UGC Care, showcasing his commitment to advancing knowledge in his areas of expertise. Additionally, he has authored ten books published by national publishers, further enriching the academic community with valuable resources. An innovator at heart, Dr. Mamodiya holds an impressive portfolio of intellectual property, including 50 utility patents (both national and international) along with 20 design patents and copyrights. His entrepreneurial spirit is exemplified by securing 1 Crore in funding from the All India Council for Technical Education (AICTE) to establish the IDEA Lab at Poornima University, aimed at fostering innovation and research among students and faculty.

Lovleen Marwaha, Ph.D., is a Professor at the Department of Zoology, School of Bioengineering and Biosciences, Lovely Professional University, Phagwara, India. She has completed her M.S. and Ph.D. in Cytogenetics from the Department of Zoology, Punjab University, Chandigarh. She has worked on the evaluation of pesticide genotoxicity using insect genomes, specifically on different mosquito species and Drosophila melanogaster. She has carried out an intensive study on the correlation between pesticide exposure limit and inductive genotoxic consequences on Dipteran larval salivary polytene chromosomes. Furthermore, she has studied chromosomal and gene mutations in mosquito and fruit fly genomes due to pesticide exposure. Currently, she is working on Apiculture and Sericulture-related topics. She has many research papers published in National and International Journals of repute. Presently, she is working on insecticide resistance in mosquitoes, pesticide genotoxicity evaluation, honey bee development, honey processing, silk fiber, and pearl quality improvement. She has published three authored books on Apiculture and on Mobile Genetic Elements. Forthcoming books include Worker Honey Bees, Apiculture Products, Basic Concepts of Genetics, and Introduction to Sericulture.

Abdul Salam Mohammed is an accomplished academic and IT professional with extensive experience spanning higher education leadership and enterprise systems. He holds a PhD in Computer Science (Banasthali University, India, 2015), an MCA (Osmania University, 1994), and a BSc in Electronics (Osmania University, 1989). He is a Certified Information Systems Auditor (CISA, 2023) and a Project Management Professional (PMP, 2020), with additional credentials including ITIL Foundation, IBM WebSphere Transformation Extender, Oracle & E-Commerce (University of Toronto), and Microsoft Certified Professional (MCP). Currently, he serves as Assistant Professor and Head of General Education at Horizon University College, Ajman, UAE (September 2021–present). Previously, he was Assistant Professor and Chair of the Services Committee (2016–2021) and Lecturer (2012–2016) at the same institution, alongside earlier academic roles there since 1995. His international industry experience includes serving as a Technical Systems

Analyst at the Royal Bank of Canada (2007–2012) and as an Adjunct Faculty member at Netplus Institute, Toronto (2005–2012). His career reflects a strong blend of academic leadership, curriculum delivery, and expertise in information systems governance, project management, and technology-enabled services.

Harish K. G. Nair is an accomplished higher education leader with more than three decades of progressive experience in university administration, academic operations, registration, examination management, and accreditation processes. Over his distinguished career at Horizon University College (formerly Skyline University College), Ajman, UAE, he has demonstrated exceptional leadership in academic governance, regulatory compliance, and institutional effectiveness. Dr. Nair possesses deep expertise in national and international quality assurance and accreditation frameworks, including the UAE Ministry of Education (MOE/CAA), QAA (UK), AACSB, EBET, CHEDS, and the QS Star Rating System. His contributions have been pivotal in elevating institutional quality standards, ensuring regulatory alignment, and strengthening operational excellence across academic and administrative functions. As Deputy Director – Administration, Registration & Examination Controller (1999–Present), Dr. Nair oversees mission-critical university functions, including academic scheduling, examination governance, course allocations, graduation management, and educational records oversight. He plays a key role in driving strategic planning initiatives, academic policy enhancements, and institutional data reporting for CHEDS and THE ranking systems. With a strong technical foundation, Dr. Nair is highly proficient in database systems, ERP and LMS platforms, Data Science and Artificial Intelligence, curriculum planning tools, and analytics-driven academic operations. He is known for building high-performing teams, fostering collaborative academic environments, and championing innovation, compliance, and operational efficiency within the higher education sector. Dr. Nair's career is distinguished by multiple awards for leadership excellence and operational performance, reflecting his unwavering commitment to institutional advancement and student success.

Anita Shukla, currently working as Assistant Professor at Poornima University Jaipur.

Zahid Ahmad Thoker is a research Scholar at Lovely Professional University who is working on Insects (Entomology), specifically on Honey Bees. He graduated with his Master's degree in Zoology from Chandigarh University, Gharuan, Mohali, where he developed a very solid academic grounding in life sciences. Zahid has already contributed greatly to academia; one of his research papers was published, one review paper, and over 25 book chapters in reputable national and international volumes. His academic publication is an indication of the desire to promote science, especially in the biological sciences. As a visionary who desires to make a difference in the research world and in society, Zahid hopes to broaden his academic and professional experiences with integrity and excellence. He is also strongly driven by the goal of benefiting society with his research work and making his parents proud by leaving his mark on the field of science and scholarship

Priyanka Verma is a distinguished academician with nearly 20 years of teaching experience and is currently serving as a Professor at Poornima University, Jaipur. Her expertise spans Web Mining, Data Mining, AI, IoT, Machine Learning, and Cybersecurity, with research publications in reputed journals such as IEEE, Elsevier, Springer, Taylor & Francis, and Inderscience, including several Scopus and Web of Science indexed papers. She actively contributes to academia as an editorial board member, keynote speaker, resource person, and session chair at national and international events, and has led university-level digital initiatives including website development. A recipient of multiple prestigious awards for teaching and academic excellence, Dr. Verma is also a dedicated mentor, author, and active Rotary contributor, continually advancing education and research through innovation and leadership.

Index

A

B

C

D

E

F

H

I

L

M

P

R

S

T

V

Z

www.ingramcontent.com/pod-product-compliance
Lightning Source LLC
LaVergne TN
LVHW062340300926
849161LV00007B/1761